Here and Now

CURRENT READINGS FOR WRITERS

Here and Now

CURRENT READINGS FOR WRITERS

Gilbert H. Muller
The City University of New York
LaGuardia

Boston, Massachusetts Burr Ridge, Illinois Dubuque, Iowa
Madison, Wisconsin New York, New York San Francisco, California
St. Louis, Missouri

McGraw-Hill

A Division of The **McGraw-Hill** *Companies*

HERE AND NOW: CURRENT READINGS FOR WRITERS

This book is printed on acid-free paper.

1 2 3 4 5 6 7 8 9 DOC/DOC 9 0 9 8 7

ISBN 0-07-021022-5

Editorial director: *Phillip A. Butcher*
Sponsoring editor: *Tim Julet*
Marketing manager: *Lesley Denton*
Project manager: *Karen J. Nelson*
Production supervisor: *Charlene R. Perez*
Designer: *Matthew Baldwin*
Compositor: *Shepherd Incorporated*
Typeface: *10/12 Aster*
Printer: *R.R. Donnelley & Sons Company*

Library of Congress Cataloging-in-Publication Data

Muller, Gilbert H (date)
Here and now : current readings for writers/Gilbert H. Muller.
p. cm.
Includes index.
ISBN 0–07–044372–6
1. College readers. 2. English language—Rhetoric. 3. Report writing. I. Title.
PE1417.M795 1998
808'.0427—dc21 97–15994

http://www.mhhe. com

For My Family
Laleh
Parisa
Darius

ABOUT THE AUTHOR

Gilbert H. Muller, who received a Ph.D. in English and American Literature from Stanford University, is currently professor of English and Special Assistant to the President at LaGuardia campus of the City University of New York. He has also taught at Stanford, Vassar, and several universities overseas. Dr. Muller is the author of the award-winning study *Nightmares and Visions: Flannery O'Connor and the Catholic Grotesque,* and books on Chester Himes and John A. Williams. His essays and reviews have appeared in *The New York Times, The New Republic, The Nation, The Sewanee Review, The Georgia Review,* and elsewhere. He is also a noted author and editor of textbooks in English and composition, including *The McGraw-Hill Reader, The Short Prose Reader* with Harvey S. Wiener and, with John A. Williams, *The McGraw-Hill Introduction to Literature.* Among Dr. Muller's awards are National Endowment for the Humanities Fellowships, a Fulbright Fellowship, and a Mellon Fellowship.

CONTENTS

5
College Sports 181

6
Common Addictions 230

7
Popular Entertainment 263

10
Armed and Dangerous 381

11
New Americans 420

PREFACE FOR INSTRUCTORS

Here and Now, a thematic anthology consisting of 55 very recent selections from periodicals, offers a full range of topics that are of immediate interest to students in college composition courses. Rooted in reader response pedagogy, the text encourages students to read, discuss, and write critically about topics and issues that intimately inform their lives and their place in contemporary society. With all selections taken from some 50 different magazines, journals, and newspapers published since 1993, this text addresses the needs and expectations of a diverse generation of students preparing for life in the 21st century. The essays in *Here and Now* explore the brave new world of reconstituted families, generational differences, career options, ethnic and gender identity, political correctness, sports and popular entertainment, and other issues that serve to define campus life, American culture, and emerging global realities for college students today.

Organized in 11 chapters, each containing a brief preface and five essays, the text builds on reader response theory by presenting topics and themes that are of greatest concern to today's college students. Susan Miller points out in *Textual Carnivals* that academicians often think erroneously that the beginning composition student is a "presexual, preeconomic, prepolitical person" for whom writing "is divorced from participation in active cultural roles." By engaging and motivating students to read, think, and write about issues that are important to them, *Here and Now* appeals to a contemporary community of informed, curious, pragmatic individuals prepared to deal critically with contemporary social realities. Applying Wolfgang Iser's terminology in *The Act of Reading: A Theory of Aesthetic Response,* I would suggest that today's college students—a generation that has experienced everything from single-parent families, to corporate downsizing, to "virtual reality" on the Net, to trips to Kathmandu—can bring a diverse collection of "past feelings, views, and values" to bear on the "new experience" of academic life. They do not have to be taught the conflicts because they contend with them on a daily basis. With its fresh, provocative, well-written selections, *Here and Now* permits students to examine competing responses to essays, defend personal positions, create interpretive communities, and establish consensus within the increasingly diverse composition classroom.

Here and Now has been designed expressly for the general composition classroom that typically contains students of mixed ages and abilities, including students emerging from basic writing sequences. Some essays are very short, and others relatively long. Most are of middle length, and many have been written by well-known essayists: Joyce Carol Oates, Susan Cheever, Barbara Ehrenreich, Shelby Steele, Richard Rodriguez, and William J. Bennett among them. Some contain citations and documentation, tables, and graphs—the sort of professional formats that composition students need to know and practice. Some essays are experiential. Many more are analytical and argumentative, carving out positions on the "right," "left," and "center" of the ideological spectrum. However, rather than advocating personal writing or analytical writing (one typical cleavage between basic writing and basic composition courses as well as a contested point among composition theorists), *Here and Now* provides an intersubjective approach to reading and writing whereby students can identify immediately with issues, take positions on them, and harness personal experiences in order to make intellectual connections with an informed audience. Already immersed in and knowledgeable about the culture of this text, and attracted by the timeliness of its recent readings, students using *Here and Now* can measure their lives against the dynamic and controversial picture of American civilization that emerges from the organically structured and connected units of the book.

Here and Now offers an introduction to reader response theory followed by units dealing with topics that enable beginning composition students to express and define themselves. The text capitalizes on the relevance and immediacy of such topics as peer pressure, generational conflicts, sexuality and gender, family life, and affirmative action, as well as such social issues as gun violence and immigration, thereby establishing a foundation enabling students to examine the contours, institutions, and artifacts of contemporary culture from a critical and analytical perspective based on personal experience, a growing body of objective knowledge, and gradual exposure to a variety of disciplines professional writers touch on in their essays. The 11 chapters in *Here and Now* reflect those topics that will enable teachers to establish an ongoing dialogue with their students about the nature of contemporary American culture. The text's apparatus supports this interactive process. Each selection in *Here and Now* is prefaced by headnotes offering biographical and bibliographical information as well as prereading guidelines entitled *Previewing the Essay.* Apparatus following each essay reflects a tripartite format—*Thinking about the Essay, Responding in Discussion,* and *Responding in Writing*—that nurtures reader response processes and encourages integrated literacy skills to evolve in a classroom committed to collaborative learning. The exercise material stresses the need to blend one's personal voice with those forms of analytical and argumentative writing expected of students in academic situations. A *Connections: For Writing and Research* section at the end of each chapter encourages students to synthesize knowledge within and among units. Finally, an instructor's edition offers teaching tips and pedagogical insights into every essay in the text.

Here and Now is a highly relevant text for a generation of students anxious to think, talk, and write about the contours of their world at the end of one century and the start of the next.

ACKNOWLEDGMENTS

I am deeply indebted to Tim Julet, the sponsoring editor at McGraw-Hill, who proposed this project and was supportive and generous of his time as the textbook evolved. To Phil Butcher, McGraw-Hill's Editorial director and Lesley Denton, its marketing director, I owe thanks for encouragement and advice. Christopher Fitzpatrick, assitant to Tim Julet, was an avid fan of the textbook and a contributor to its Web exercises. Dr. Alan Gerstle of Philadelphia College of Textiles and Science provided valuable assistance, and prepared the instructor's manual for *Here and Now.* Sharon Geremia and Michelle Smalls prepared manuscripts with diligence. Karen Nelson guided the book skillfully through production. A special thank you goes to the copyeditor, Bruce Sylvester. Special appreciation goes to a fine group of reviewers who helped to mold the text: Victoria Gaydosik, East Central State University; Randol Popkin, Tarleton State University; Jim Murphy, Southern Illinois University; Ltc. Verner Mitchell, U.S. Air Force Academy; Laurel Smith, Vincennes University; Margaret Racin, West Virginia University; David Steinhart, Community College of Allegheny County, Allegheny Campus; Marty Graham, Iowa State University; Sherrie Graden, Portland State University; Sylvia Martin, Blackhawke College; Jane Rose, Georgia College; R. J. Willey, Oakland Community College; Richard Pepp, Massasoit Community College.

INTRODUCTION: READING, DISCUSSING, AND WRITING ESSAYS

It is ironic that in the Information Age, where mastery of computer literacy and visual literacy is so significant in managing our lives and planning our careers, that college students often have trouble dealing with written texts. Some critics say that people have trouble with written texts because our culture privileges new forms of technology over the older forms such as books, newspapers, and magazines. But a visit to your nearest bookstore or magazine stand will easily demonstrate that more people are writing and reading about more subjects than ever before. Others say that students do not consider the act of reading as essential to their lives given the many new ways to acquire information through the electronic media. While there is some truth in this latter statement, you should not assume that technology will ultimately replace the art of reading. Comprehending what you read, responding in discussion to what you read, and writing about what you read remain critical to your education.

Despite the proliferation of new forms of knowledge, there is no other way to transmit the complexities of our daily lives, the essential issues of our day, or the depth and breadth of our experience than through reading and writing. How else can you transmit the intricacies of your opinions concerning such issues as the family, society, politics, work, or issues of gender and class? You can talk about them, but speech does not provide the tools necessary to offer lengthy, orderly presentations of ideas. Additionally, the speaker must rely on the ability of the listener to process and remember all that is said. There is no way to review a speaker's words once they have been uttered, and the longer the speech, the more difficult it will be to recall of all of its details. Thus, our most respected thinkers—whatever their field—still use the written word when they want to address complex subjects, particularly when they want their views to be considered and remembered.

As students, therefore, you have the obligation to approach written material, particularly "professional" writing, in a way that will allow you to extract the most meaning from it, compare it to your own views, and respond to it in an informed and coherent manner. You need a method that will facilitate a mastery of the entire reading process.

This textbook has been designed so that you will become an *active* and *critical* reader of the essays you encounter. This means that you will be encouraged to become engaged in the study of the selections in this text by learning skills that will help you derive the greatest benefit from reading and responding to what you read. For "active" reading (as opposed to casual reading) is in many ways analogous to a two-way silent conversation. True, the author has presented you with her or his ideas or opinions or experiences. That is her or his obligation. But *your* obligation is to bring an alert, critical, and responsive perspective to your encounter with the written word. The result of this encounter will be a rich experience that can lead to cognitive growth, a finely honed skill in comprehending the various types and styles of writing, and a means to respond intelligently and critically to what you read.

To develop your reading abilities, this text encourages you to consider the encounter with its variety of essays as a three-part process: learning various means of reading critically; learning to respond in class, either independently or in small groups; and responding through your own writing. Rather than considering these activities as individual, linear acts, it is perhaps better to consider them as the three points of a triangle in order to emphasize their holistic nature.

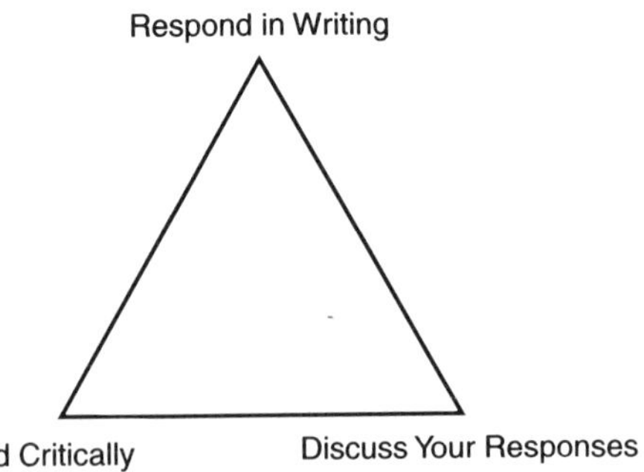

WAYS OF READING: READING AND RESPONDING TO TEXTS

Over the past 50 years, experts in the field of reading have grappled with understanding the reading comprehension process. Some have stressed the primacy of the written text; others have stressed the personality of the reader as the most significant aspect of the act of reading and responding. Still others have stressed the influence of the social and cultural background of the reader in her or his interpretation of texts. There are many theories of reading and responding to what you read. And of late, many of these theories have been loosely defined as "reader response theory." What follows in this section is a brief overview of a number of variations on this theory. Listing and explaining them is not meant to be mere academic exercise, but rather a means of helping you understand the sources of your responses and the types of responses you may have to what you read. Such an understanding will help you discern the hidden influences behind how you respond to the essays in this text; it also will help you to develop self-knowledge that will result in cultivating strategies that can make you a more effective and confident reader.

Textual Theories of Response

A reaction to 19th- and early-20th-century theories that stressed impressionistic, subjective, and moralistic criticism to what one read, the "New Criticism" as it came to be called, significantly influenced the philosophy of reading beginning in the 1940s. The trademark of this group of theorists was a focus on the text as the be-all and end-all of understanding. The meaning of what was written was contained within the poem, story, or essay, and it was up to the reader—serving as a sort of literary detective—to decode the message. The closer the reader got to the "true" meaning of the work, the better she or he was to be praised. One problem with this approach, however, was to find an objective truth against which one's own interpretation could be measured. Who were the "keepers of the truth"? Usually the implied answer was people who shared the same educational and interpretative perspective of the New Critics themselves. Thus, students were encouraged to emulate their teachers by finding symbols, hidden meanings, and deep resonances in the text. Students were told to be attentive to developing objective powers of analysis, parking their personal experiences and social influences at the door of the text.

While "pure" objectivity is impossible, more recent critics have suggested that not all New Criticism should be dismissed out of hand. Certain items in a text are obviously significant. Thus, if a writer repeats a phrase or word, one can be fairly certain that she or he considered the term to be a key one to the meaning of the written document. From this recognition, a new field of study arose called semiotics (the study of codes and signs). Semioticians argue that there are certain rules and conventions embedded in texts that we must "decode" in order to derive meaning. If you were to analyze a church sermon, you would have to be familiar with the rhetoric of sermons, biblical study, and religious symbols to understand the "world" of the sermon. Similarly, if you were to read science fiction (or, for that matter, any fiction) intelligently, you would have to be familiar with the concept that what was written was not fact but imaginative literature. This may seem obvious at first, but consider how easy it would be to create a story and pass it off as fact. Orson Welles, the famous film director, actually inadvertently created mass hysteria on Halloween night of 1939 by broadcasting an adaptation of H. G. Wells's *War of the Worlds* on the radio, causing thousands of people to flee their homes in fear of an alien invasion.

Experiential Theories of Response

Experiential theories of reader response shift the focus of the reading encounter from the text to the effects of the unique patterns of experience each reader brings to what she or he reads. Emphasizing the social context of reading, experiential theories consider the singular events of each person's life and their imprints on the individual as profoundly salient in understanding the reading encounter. For example, one person might feel pain or sadness when reading an essay about abortion, while another might feel anger and moral indignation, depending on the tenor of personal events brought to the reading experience. Or, imagine an essay about the baby boomer generation. Different people's various experiences with members of that generation may generate different mental images. One reader might envision a burnt-out hippy. Another might envision a self-involved hedonistic member of the me generation.

Identification and empathy also figure heavily in the experiential theory equation. The degree to which a reader's consciousness seems to merge with the writer's or an element in the writer's work can profoundly influence how he or she judges, interprets, and responds to it. For example, in your text there is an essay entitled "Stillborn" by Maribeth Fischer that describes the feelings of a daughter whose mother has abandoned the family for an old flame. Whether one feels resentment toward the mother and sympathy toward the daughter may be—at least—a result of experiences of abandonment in the reader's own life. There may be a distinct difference in response if the reader perceives herself or himself as an abandoner or the one who has been abandoned. By considering how one's personal experience is interwoven with the printed word in order to generate meaning, you have an excellent opportunity to reflect on the fact that mere denotative "comprehension" of a text is really the first step in encountering it. Many students read essays with the intention of remembering those details that the teacher will be looking for in class or asking for on an exam. By appreciating the vast undercurrent of experience you bring to any reading event, your responses can become more meaningful to you and even do justice to the intent of the writer who is not seeking a mere mechanical "decoding" of her or his text, but a full engagement on the part of the reader.

Psychological Theories of Response

With the contemporary interest in cognitive development, moral reasoning, and theories of the way the mind processes and interprets information, it was only a matter of time before studies in the field of psychology penetrated the field of reader response theory. The basic tenet of psychological theories of response holds that to understand how we read requires an understanding of how we think. If you recall vivid responses to fairy tales and fantasy as a child, you probably understand now that part of your powerful response to imaginary creatures and worlds was the result of your young mind "experimenting" with what was real and what was make-believe. Today, you might look back on that time in your life and catch fleeting moments of the way you felt then. But because of your psychological maturation, you can now distinguish reality from fantasy.

Proponents of psychological theories of response even make distinctions between the cognitive processes of young teenagers (age 13 to 15) and older teenagers (age 16 to 19). The former group, according to these theorists, are in a mode where they think about the one "true" meaning of a text. Older students, on the other hand, are at the "interpretation" stage, a time when their minds can now consider a variety of "correct" interpretations of a single piece of writing. Thus, in reading June Jordan's "The Street Where I Live" (an essay in "The Diversity Debate" section of your text), a college student may discern several goals of the writer: to praise diversity, to celebrate the day-to-day experience of living, and to reprove abstract pronouncements on the contours of racial conflict. Other psychological theorists consider moral development of the mind to be as significant as cognitive development. Therefore, young readers may respond to essays that describe injustice or unfairness with fantasies of revenge and punishment; older readers may respond with more mature readings that broaden the context of a tale of inequity to include considerations of both the victim and the perpetrator. Reading, for example, Suneel Ratan's "Generational Tension in the Office" in the "Pay Scales" section of your text from an impartial perspective may help you understand that both supervisors and their subordinates have gripes that are equally valid.

While a complete inventory of psychological theories is beyond the scope of this introduction, it will be helpful for you to know about the "cognitive-processing model of response" both for what it posits as well as for what it lacks in explanatory power. According to this model, our minds have mental "schemata" which, when fully developed, provide us with powerful tools such as reasoning, categorizing, hypothesizing, defining, and predicting. Thus, minds with well-developed cognitive tools will allow us to engage a text with a variety of strategies so that we can participate fully in understanding, considering, and even challenging the author because of our own highly developed thinking skills. For example, consider the confusion of the term *Generation X.* Is it an actual phenomenon? Are there truly individuals who belong to this group? If so, who are they? Or, is it a convenient media invention, or a way to "cubby-hole" young people by older ones who are seeking a means of understanding a significant social group without really making the mental effort to formulate their own opinions? Cognitive-processing proponents would probably contend that the more evolved your mind through experience and education, the better you will be able to consider these issues.

Social Theories of Response

Many psychological theories of response treat the individual as an enclosed "self-generator of meaning." Conversely, theorists who hold to social theories of response are much more concerned with the self within her or his community—whether that community be one of class, education, geographic region, religion, politics, or gender. For these thinkers, to consider the individual as an independent thinker—free from all social influence—would be like thinking of a person living in a cognitive "isolation tank." Rather than focusing on the individual as the primary unit in responding to texts, the American Stanley Fish and the Russian Michael Bakhtin, among others, envision the basic unit of participation in textual response as the group. After all, what would be the point of reading, interpreting, and responding to what one read if one had no one else with which to share one's insights? As social beings, our purpose in life is to communicate, and who better to communicate with than those who share our concerns and goals? Whether it is students in a college classroom discussing an essay, a group of scientists meeting to exchange and discuss research findings, or a poetry group to share its latest creations, people derive satisfaction and meaning by contributing toward the common purpose of mutual understanding, or at least mutual respect for each other's ideas. Fish has called this notion the "interpretive community." By this he means groups of individuals who have had their reading skills formed through the learning of conventions and strategies that make written communication possible.

Dialogical theory as advanced by Bakhtin and others takes this idea of an interpretive community a bit further. This theory focuses on the fact that we do not learn merely one set of conventions and strategies, but (owing to our social roles, historical backgrounds, and diverse experiences) have several sets of strategies to rely on in the reading process. Thus, the more we are open to the possibilities of life, the greater will be our chance to read fully from a multiperspective viewpoint. For example, in reading William Tucker's "Three Strikes and You're Dead" in the "Armed and Dangerous" section of your text, you will encounter an author who has been a street-smart kid, a respected sociologist, and a keen observer of contemporary at-risk youth. While any one of these attributes could serve the author well to write on current ideas about crime and punishment, a combination of all three allows him to speak from a vantage point of multiple authorities.

Perhaps the easiest place to observe social theories of reader response is in your own classroom. Consider what role you play within the group. What role does the teacher play? Does her or his role as a competent teacher confer status? Or is it merely her or his status that confers the attribute of competent teacher? You may find that as you progress through the term that those students who have had a rich and varied experience are more able to draw from it for class discussion and writing assignments than others. There is nothing wrong with this, and there is nothing wrong if you perceive yourself as one of those who lacks life experience. You will have plenty of time to explore, read, interpret, make new connections, and transcend old ones as you develop into an informed and active reader.

Cultural Theories of Response

Cultural theorists of reader response do not so much oppose the views of social theorists, as lament the fact that they examine a stratum of social life without exploring the depths of the *substratum* that serves as the compost that gives rise to social existence. Cultural theorists view groups as determined more by deep-rooted ideological worldviews than mere self-selected members who have common interests. Such worldviews may be determined by gender, deep-rooted cultural conventions, power structures, and "fields of discourse" such as medicine, law, religion, and even education. Thus, while a social theorist may be interested in understanding the "language of psychiatry," a cultural theorist may be concerned with how psychiatry was formed as an institution, how its language arose to such prominence and privilege over, say, commonsense responses to mental health. Social theorists place much greater stock in the influence *over* the individual by these "deterministic" controls. After all—they would claim—the individual is born into an institution that already has its rules and conventions, and it is the rare person who can transcend such authority. For this reason, much of cultural theory can sound pessimistic and frustrating to the inquiring student. After all, who wants to think of oneself as being merely manipulated by linguistic forces beyond one's control that determine how we respond and interpret what we read.

However, the "upside" of this equation is that by understanding the constraints under which we live—whether they are gender roles, cognitive manipulation by the media that prevents us from understanding what we "honestly" think, or the cultural legacy of our parents—we can determine whether they fit within our worldview. Awareness of these constraints gives us the opportunity to confront them and come to terms with them. For example, as you read the articles in the section "New Americans," you will find that several authors view immigration as a positive economic and social phenomenon in our country. If your initial response is that "all immigrants cause trouble" or "all immigrants take jobs from Americans," a moment's reflection will make you aware that you may be responding out of cultural biases rather than from reasoned thought. "Checking your biases at the door" when you read these essays may help you to consider their arguments, compare them to your own, and perhaps negotiate the views of the authors with your own. But a *failure* to understand your cultural biases can only serve to keep your cognitive doors closed, and to keep your responses to what you read uninspired and unconsidered.

THE READING EXPERIENCE

The following selection is a reproduction of one of the shorter essays in your text. It is followed by an annotation/discussion section that includes notes and reflections on reading that correspond to some of the theories described above.

The D-Day Generation

Peggy Noonan

I keep wondering about who we are these days, all of us. I keep wondering if we're way ahead of our parents—more learned, more tolerant, and engaged in the world—or way behind them. They touch my soul, that generation. They are an impenetrable inspiration. They got through the Depression and the war—they got drafted for five years and said Okay, Uncle Sam! and left, and went home. They expected so little, their assumptions were so modest. A lot of them, anyway. The women shared the common trauma of a childhood in hard times and the men had the common integrator of the barracks, and I feel that they understood each other. They knew what they shared. When Communism fell we should have had a parade for them, for it meant their war was finally over. We should have one for them anyway, before they leave.

They weren't farmers, or the ones I knew weren't farmers, but they were somehow—closer to the soil, closer to the ground. The ones in Brooklyn, Rochester, wherever, they were closer to the ground.

Affluence detaches. It removes you from the old and eternal, it gets you out of the rain. Affluence and technology detach absolutely. Among other things, they get you playing with thin plastic things like Super Nintendo and not solid things like—I don't know—wood, and water. Anyway, the guy who said "Plastics" to Benjamin 25 years ago in "The Graduate" was speaking more truth than we knew.

Also, our parents were ethnic in a way I understood. Back in that old world the Irish knew they were better than the Italians and the Italians knew they were better than the Irish and we all knew we were better than the Jews and they knew they were better than us. Everyone knew they were superior, so everyone got along. I think the prevailing feeling was, everyone's human. Actually, that used to be a saying in America: "Everyone's human."

They all knew they were Americans and they all knew they weren't, and their kids knew it too, and understood it was their job to become the Americans. Which we certainly have. A while ago a reporter told me how an old Boston pol summed up Mario Cuomo. The pol said, "He's not a real ethnic. He's never been ashamed of his father." The reporter—45, New York, Jewish—laughed with a delighted grunt. The ordeal of ethnicity. I Remember Papa.

There were ethnic, religious, and racial resentments, but you didn't hear about them all the time. It was a more reticent country. Imagine chatty America being reticent. But it was.

I often want to say to them, to my parents and the parents of my friends, "Share your wisdom, tell me what you've learned, tell me what we're doing wrong and right." But, you know, they're still reticent. Loose lips sink ships. Also, they tend not to have big abstract things to say about life because they were actually busy living it, and forgot to take notes. They didn't have time, or take time, to reflect. They were not so inclined.

They're like an old guy I met a few years ago when I was looking for a house in Washington. He had gray hair and was stooped in a crouched, still-muscular way and had just one good eye; the other was scarred and blind. He had an old brick house off George Washington Parkway and I had walked through it; it was perfect but too near the highway for a woman with a two-year-old. When I was in the basement I saw his World War II memorabilia—he still had framed citations on the wall, and I could see he'd seen action island-hopping in the South Pacific. And one of the old framed papers said Guadalcanal, and this was exciting, so I said to him, for the most interesting things you hear in life come by accident, "Did you know Richard Tregaskis?" And his good eye squinted. I thought he might not recognize the reference, so I said to him, "He was the one who wrote *Guadalcanal Diary.*" And the squint gets deeper and he says, "Yeah, well, I was a grunt. We'd already done the work and left by the time the writers came." I sort of smiled and asked if I could use the bathroom, where I plucked a piece of shrapnel from my heart.

Now they're all retired, and most of the ones I know are in pretty good shape. My friend Susan's parents go to Atlantic City and catch a few shows, play the slots. They own their house. My father—army infantry, Italy under Blood 'n' Guts—has a small apartment in Santo Domingo and swims and says he can feel the sun to his bones. My mother lives here in town and flies off when one of her children is having a baby, to be a continuity, to say by her presence, "We did this too, years ago, so don't worry." Lisa's parents just got back from Europe. George's father, who for 25 years worked in a Newark welfare office, married a woman with a farm in Pennsylvania. Now he walks in the mud in big rubber boots, holding a piece of corn. He's happy. There was more divorce than I think we've noted in our parents' generation, and a lot of them did it in a funny way, not after a year or 10 years but after 25, 35 years. After a life. There are always serious and individual reasons for such things, but I would include the seventies, the decade when American went crazy, the decade when, as John Updike said, the sixties had finally percolated down to everybody.

Annotations: Lines 21–22, 30, 38, 56, and 64 provide examples of how *textual knowledge* is required to fully understand references. The author takes for granted the reader's knowledge of the film *The Graduate,* Mario Cuomo (former governor of New York), the popular World War II term "Loose lips sink ships" (which indicated the need for discretion in discussing personal knowledge of military activities), *Guadalcanal Diary* (a famous memoir from World War II), and "Blood 'n' Guts" (a reference to General George Patton).

Lines 1–13, 23–29, and 47–63 provide examples of *personal or experiential elements* in the writer's world that can probably be only fully appreciated if the reader is acquainted with members of the D-Day generation as well as their values, worldview, and "reticence." The reader might be able to imagine or picture the people whom the author presents, but unless he or she has had direct experience with them, such images are probably impressionistic and inaccurate. An interview with men and women of that generation or research into photo archives of life during World War II might help connect the experience of the writer to that of the younger reader.

The title and lines 1–4 provide examples of how *cognitive processing* can either help or hinder readers to understand the implications of "paying tribute" to a generation. This will probably be determined by their ability to generalize the concept of "sacrifice" for a cause. Some students may just not have had such experiences; for them, the concept may be psychologically distant. The reader, while not sharing the specifics of having D-Day–generation parents, may interpret the need for the author to come to terms with her parents as a universal need among all generations. The more sophisticated the reader's ability to draw inferences and hypothesize in the absence of such a sense, the easier it should be to comprehend the larger implication of the author's gratitude.

Lines 4–13, 14–18, 23–39, and 40–46 provide the reader with a window into the *social milieu* within which the author is reflecting—basically, a hard-working blue collar ethnic class who were not particularly verbal or literary. The degree to which the reader can appreciate this world will be partially dependent on her or his knowledge of that social class, either first hand or through observation. It is important, however, for students who feel distant from this knowledge to admit it to their peers and teachers. There is really no point in pretending to fit in within an "interpretative community" if you are having trouble doing so. Discussion with other students who feel closer to the material can help those who feel less at home with it.

Lines 9–11 and 21–26 are pertinent to examining the *cultural theories of response*. For example, the word *communism* can evoke a range of emotions in a reader from outright indignation and hate (for example, if the reader were a Vietnamese boat person) to that of a quaint, outmoded economic system that a young American student whose formative years have been since the fall of the Berlin wall may view as fairly benign. Understanding the sensitivities of others to this potentially controversial word can help transcend barriers of cultural background and belief. Also, today's student, particularly if she or he holds to a strong racial or ethnic identity, may find it difficult to accept the levity with which Noonan discusses the way the various "hyphenated Americans" were able to negotiate their differences. Students whose cultural readings of ethnic conflict make other students feel uncomfortable can have the opportunity of venting their views in the public forum of the classroom, where class discussion can reveal that talking about difference can reduce it.

STEPS TO READING CRITICALLY

To paraphrase a famous quotation about writing, it may be said that critical reading is re-reading. One cannot hope to gain sufficient information from a text of any seriousness or depth by reading it only once. That is why developing a "system" for reading can be helpful in extracting salient details, considering the author's argument, methods of support, stylistic techniques, and style, and developing an ability to respond to all these factors intelligently and succinctly. Here is a brief list to help you extract the most benefit from what you read:

1. Find a spot that can serve as your reading nook. Try to make it free of distractions. Make it conducive to thought by placing attractive objects of personal meaning in close proximity.
2. Read through your material with pencil or paper in hand, annotating in the margins those elements you find particularly significant or underlining others you may wish to review upon a second reading.
3. Pause to reflect on what you read. What was the author's main thesis or point of view? What was her or his method (or rhetorical approach) in articulating that view? What tone or voice did the author use in communicating that view? What types of support—for example, statistics, direct quotations, citations from other sources, or personal experience—did the author use in developing her or his argument?
4. Re-read the essay, now focusing on those aspects of the writing that struck you as particularly salient. Consider whether the author is making a coherent statement about her or his thesis. Challenge the writer and interrogate the text, using your own powers of analysis. Consider some or all of the reader-response theories discussed earlier in the introduction as they pertain to the text and to your study of it. Consider whether there are any inconsistencies in the author's argument. If so, what are they, and how are they manifested?
5. Consider the implied audience for whom the text was written. To what degree are you a part of this audience? If you find yourself

excluded from it, what in your own experience or the experience of the author caused you to feel as though you were not a direct member of this "reading universe"? Consider how you might more closely tie your own background, knowledge, and experience with those of the authors.

6. Summarize either mentally or on paper the major argument of the text. This "shorthand" method will help you articulate your response to the work later as you enter into class discussion and develop themes for writing.
7. Prior to formal classroom discussion, you may wish to discuss informally with a classmate your responses to the work. To what degree does your understanding of it resemble that of your peer? Where do you differ in your psychological, experiential, social, and cultural responses?

By going through these preliminary steps, you should be ready to enter the individual or group discussion process in the classroom, and the subsequent process of responding in writing with a more informed eye and ear to the material you have encountered.

RESPONDING IN CLASS

Often students believe that the more vocal members of a class have the most to say. But there are many other variables that may enter into the equation of whether a student actively participates in group discussion and response to the teacher's inquiries. Some students may simply enjoy the attention they receive from being the focus of attention. Others may participate selectively, generously offering their views on topics they find particularly interesting or relevant to their lives. Still others may feel restrained to participate based on hidden social or cultural habits, based on implicit gender rules, cultural background, or simple shyness. Regardless, you should not feel that the degree of participation in class discussion determines how intelligent or enthusiastic you are in your views.

If you have read your text with care, there is no reason to feel reluctant in voicing your views on it. Active listening to the teacher's remarks as well as those of your fellow students should make it clear that their concerns, insights, observations, and disclaimers are very much like your own. In addition, hearing what others have to say may encourage you to respond to their remarks, whether it is to voice agreement with them or challenge them. Note the style of your teacher's leadership in discussion. Does she or he anticipate the "right" answer to questions? Most good teachers attempt to elicit spontaneous yet considered responses from their students. It is a good idea not to fall into a pattern of attempting to answer the way your teacher implies you should. Remember that in our exploration of the various theories of reader-response, we found many variables that went into interpretation and reaction to texts. Your teacher will probably be aware of these factors as well. Don't be shy if your view does not follow that of the majority. Here are some basic conventions to follow to help you make the most of your classroom discussion experience.

1. Understand that students and teachers really want to know what you think. You are in an environment that focuses its concern on informed ideas, responses, and opinions. This should not give you free reign to say whatever you like, however. There are may correct ways of interpreting a text, but there are also certain "incorrect" ways. For example, if you were to conclude that Noonan's essay "The D-Day Generation" was about the joys of aging, there is probably something you have failed to recognize in your encounter with the text.
2. Respect the responses of other students as you would have them respect yours. Sometimes, we are so keen on presenting our own ideas that once we have finished talking, we "shut off" responses or critiques of others toward our own views. Classroom discussion should be a democratic process. No student (or the teacher) is the center of the discursive universe in the classroom. Listening attentively can help us understand how others respond to our ideas, and help us modify or hone them if we find another student presenting a valid alternative to what we have to say. In addition, by actively listening to the responses of others, we are better able to critique their views in a fair and equitable manner. No student wants to be shortchanged because a classmate responds to her or his views without truly absorbing and understanding them. This undermines individual learning as well as group dynamics that are essential to the pedagogic process. A class session is ideally a coherent unit of listening, speaking, and responding. It requires each student to take an active role in the process to make this enterprise a success.
3. Respect the diversity of views among your peers. As you should understand by now, each of us brings a unique conglomeration of beliefs, experience, cultural and social values, and cognitive styles to the act of reading. For example, students who are particularly close to their grandparents may be moved by Noonan's tribute to the D-Day generation. While these feelings may not be within the purview of your own lived experience, listening to students who are particularly affected by this essay may help

you comprehend the import of personal experience on one's reading experience. Disrespecting a student for not sharing your worldview flies in the face of everything healthy discussion is all about. Being open-minded regarding the opinions and ideas of others who do not share our cultural or social milieu makes us more well-rounded and tolerant individuals, leaves us better able to negotiate diverse viewpoints in the classroom, and, perhaps more importantly, assists us in tolerating the views and values of the growing number of diverse cultures in our society.

4. Defer immediate positive or negative responses for the sake of fairly considering the arguments of others. Many of us like to take sides and are all too willing to reject out-of-hand opinions we disagree with and side with those students whom we believe mirror our own views. However, classroom discussion is not meant solely as a soap box for one's responses. The quality and thought that go into these responses are significant. Deferring your judgment concerning a student's viewpoint will enable you to determine the thought and consideration a student has given to her or his response. You may, in fact, discover that the student whose views you disagree with has the better-articulated argument. To cite one example from the text, in his essay "How Liberals Lost Their Virtue over Race" Shelby Steele presents an articulate condemnation of affirmative action. Wherever you stand on the issue, however, an emotional response to his views may blind you to the method and nature of his argument. If this should occur, chance are you will read his considered argument with an attitude that will prevent you from objectively considering his personal perspective. Remember, it is not necessarily the intensity of a person's remarks that makes them valid, but rather their coherence and elegance.
5. Respect the classroom encounter as you would any other serious endeavor. You are not in class merely to "get by." You have the unique opportunity to develop a number of cognitive, reasoning, and communicative skills that can serve you well throughout your college career and beyond. For example, at first glance Noonan's essay may appear to be solely a reminiscence. But a more careful reading and discussion of what you read with others may bring out the layers of significance that imbue the essay including those on experiential, philosophical, and perhaps spiritual levels. If you take all classroom discussion seriously, you will find yourself developing skills that allow you to "decode" many of the messages around us, whether they exist in the media, casual conversation, or political speech.

RESPONDING IN WRITING

No informed essay erupts full-blown from the writer's head. The idea of the divinely inspired scribe who sets words to paper without the need for revision is a myth that has been disproved nearly every time a professional writer has sat down to tackle an issue of importance so that it can be conveyed from thought to paper. As a college student, you are in the early stages of your writing career, and may not have developed some of the methods that more experienced writers use when they compose. Although it would not be fair to say that all writers use the same methods of composition, it is fairly safe to say that all experienced writers have developed their own unique methods. So, what you read in a published essay is the result of planning, forethought, revision, editing, and a host of writing strategies that are invisible to the eye.

1. Prewriting

Prewriting begins with the text, your responses to the text, and reflections of classroom discussions made concerning the text. If you have annotated or underlined or marked in any other way the essays you've read, you should review them to extract those salient ideas and details you believe are most relevant to your written response.

Another prewriting activity is known as brainstorming. This method can be performed in a number of ways. You may wish to just list all the significant points you've extracted from what you've read, and then explore that list for potential topics for your paper. You may wish to rank order the points in their order of importance. A brainstorming session preceding a written assignment on Noonan's essay, for example, might be a listing of the abstract concepts of veneration, tribute, and admiration, followed by details such as her memories of growing up, followed by more contemporary anecdotes of the present lives of the aging D-Day generation. From this session, you might find a means of ordering your thoughts on the subject, and then planning an essay in which you relate how the author equates qualities such as quiet endurance and determination with lost values and a diminishment of the American character. Brainstorming is a means of assembling ideas, and (just as the psychological theorists of reader response suggest), there is no correct way to do this. We all have different methods of mapping our responses and ideas.

2. Considering Your Audience

All serious writers have an implied audience, whether that audience is their peers in age, ethnicity, education, interests, or whatever.

Classroom discussion is useful because it helps you to define a sense of your audience. From your classmates' responses, you will learn about their level of discourse and their expectations when it comes to providing supports for your arguments. Perhaps most importantly, discussion helps you understand that most writers do not write in a vacuum, but rather write as an opportunity to communicate those ideas and opinions that are too elaborate or lengthy to be discussed in conversation. Understanding the concept of audience takes time, but it is time well spent. Many students write with the implicit assumption that the audience is their teacher and their goal is to get a good grade. This narrows the imaginative range of their writing immensely. Most teachers welcome writing that takes chances, that is geared for an audience that goes beyond their own administrative office, and that demonstrates the student is not afraid of voicing her or his views in response to other writing, classroom discussion, and outside reading, or demonstrates a concern with writing that takes it beyond the confines of the textbook into the world at large. A well-known British playwright once said he writes plays to present arguments in the form of dramatic presentations to his friends. As you read the broad selection of essays in this text, you will find that each writer has a strong view of his or her subject, and a strong sense of whom she or he is writing for. With practice, the skills you learn in critical reading and discussion will help articulate not only what you say but to whom you are addressing what you say.

3. Composing

Once you have a broad idea of your main point and the means you wish to support it, it is time for the composing process. Some students find the standard outline form helpful when structuring their essays. Others feel this is too restricted and prefer to "write as they go." The main elements to consider are whether your introduction sufficiently sets up your main thesis, whether your support is varied, accurate, and coherent, and whether your conclusion adds something to your essay rather than merely summing up what has been previously said. You should particularly incorporate transitions to ensure that sentences flow smoothly into one another, and that paragraphs join seamlessly to make the reading experience a logical one. With your understanding of your implied audience, a handy way to discover if your writing flows logically is to ask yourself, If I were reading this text as an informed reader, would I feel that the author has provided me with the authority, conviction, and form required for me to consider this an adequate piece of writing?

4. Rewriting

Writing the first draft of your essay—regardless of how much time, thought, and consideration you have devoted to presenting your ideas, considering your audience, and culling and selecting what should be included and what is unnecessary—is not the end of the writing process. The final step is writing for presentation. Like any other product you may wish to present to the world, whether it is a bookcase, a wardrobe, a science project, or a formal dinner, you want your product to be a reflection of the best work you are capable of. Once you have completed your draft, you should review it carefully, seeking out grammatical problems, problems with coherence and unity, and unnecessary repetition. Regardless of the degree to which you are influenced by your culture, society, or experience, people only have the final draft with which to evaluate what you have presented them in written form. When you reach this point in the writing process, you must shift from a "macro-mode" of ideas to the "micro-level" of the sentence. Consider your essays to be well-wrought constructions. Consider the selections in your text as models to help you understand the rules of coherence, unity, and style. You should not expect to write professional-level work immediately. You can be sure that the writers represented in your text did not develop their skills overnight either. But the process in which they did develop their abilities probably matches to a great degree the suggestions incorporated here.

Through the study of texts, the understanding of the nature of informed discussion and argument, and the practice of oral response, you should find writing a task that becomes more meaningful and purposeful. By incorporating the various skills of reading, responding, and thinking critically, the act of writing will seem like a natural extension of these cognitive skills. Rather than fearing or disliking writing, you should consider writing as a means of communication that can serve as a tool to guide, inform, and persuade others. If you write with a purpose, the act of writing becomes more than just an uncomfortable exercise to fulfill school requirements. Nearly all professions require some form of writing. Writing for purpose in the classroom can be transferred to writing for purpose in the workplace. And the workplace has more similarities to the classroom than many people acknowledge: the implied audience, the critical examination of what is written, the discussion of the merits and demerits of ideas and plans, and the like. The reading and writing you encounter in composition will serve you well in college, career, and private life.

STRATEGIES FOR USING THE INTERNET IN THIS COURSE

Books on using the Internet occupy ample areas of just about every college bookstore in the United States, so this brief introduction focuses primarily on how to use the Internet in conjunction with your textbook. It is also meant to encourage you to keep tuned to those strategies that will keep you focused on your assignment, for the temptation to go cyber-navigating is great, and you could easily spend every moment of your waking life during this semester checking out stuff that's fun to explore rather than using your computer judiciously to assist you with your classroom assignments. (In fact, you could spend the rest of your life in cyberspace—but that's another story.)

As a student, you may have the luck of attending a college or university that provides free dial-up accounts or dedicated connections for the entire student body, either at a centralized location like a computer lab or at stand-alone PCs in your college dorm or home. If your school does have this service, find out who's in charge of setting up an account and get one! When you're out in the real world, chances are you'll have to pay for one, and access will not be as efficient, since you don't have the kind of money for the sophisticated wizardry of your school's master server, the host machine that is "the mother of all your school's Internet access." Get yourself an account number and a user ID, think of a password no one is liable to guess (your first name is probably a poor choice), and, since systems vary from school to school, get a little training from the Internet Czar (or one of his or her assistants) on how to access information on the particular configuration your school has chosen to use, and you're pretty much all set.

Since the objective of this course is for you to be able to think about, discuss, and write about the essays in your textbook, we will limit ourselves to examples on how to use the Internet specifically for these purposes. If you want information on how to turn yourself into a virtual fish, and take a cyber-swim through a program that makes your computer screen look like outer space, you won't find it here.

What follows are the basic resources available to enhancing your learning experience in this class by accessing the Internet. This information, however, is provisional. Things change so rapidly on the information superhighway that by the time you read this, there may be new tools to use and easier and faster ways to access them. Just how fast do things change in the computer world? To give one example, there is a weekly radio show about computers wherein the host ends each program with the statement, "Everything you have learned tonight will be null and void by the next show." This is a bit of an overstatement, but you get the message. Nevertheless, new forms of obtaining data are usually built on previous ones, so that using the Internet for research will become more a matter of fine-tuning than retooling.

The four primary domains we will examine here—and those that are most likely to be helpful to you in this course are the following: a) e-mail; b) Gophers; c) the World Wide Web; d) Newsgroups. A brief description of each and how they may assist you with assignments in general, and a hypothetical assignment follow.

A) e-mail

You may use e-mail or electronic mail several ways to enhance your goal of mastering the objectives of your course. For one, you may send and receive messages from your classmates, and perhaps your instructor, if he or she encourages it, to clarify specific references in a reading selection. Let's take a hypothetical example. Many obscure references from history, for example, "Loose lips sink ships" or "Blood 'n' Guts" (from Noonan's essay "The D-Day Generation") may be foreign to you, and if you wish to get a head start with your reading, and do not have an opportunity to discuss the references in class, it would be very difficult to ascertain their meanings. It would be nearly impossible to track down these terms through reference books such as dictionaries or encyclopedias. An e-mail inquiry to members of your class may result in a "hit" or a knowledgeable response to your question from one of your classmates. Some campuses have volunteers to whom you can send questions, and you can often get a turnaround in a couple of minutes. You may also use e-mail to set up a "chat room" composed solely of members of your class. You can create a name for your room that is only shared by class members, and select "meeting times" when you will "meet" and discuss the week's class work. Even a one-hour time slot reserved once per week can enhance your learning experience owing to the opportunity of discussing your assigned essays. A third way to use e-mail is by making it act as a "search engine," in other words, a device to seek out individuals who may have expertise in the area of focus of a particular essay. So, for example, a student who has been assigned the essay by Fisher and Greenberg, "Prescriptions for Happiness?" (who criticize the way antidepressant medications are tested), may wonder whether the methodology of the authors themselves is wanting. Feeling a bit intimidated by medical research—and wanting to learn more about how, where, under what conditions, and under whose sponsorship medications are tested—the student may start a "listserv search" through his or her e-mail. A "listserv" is basically a directory of interest groups concerned about particular social, personal, political, economic and other issues. So the student might consider what might be the names of some lists by inserting in his or her e-mail "send" box the generic message to access lists: "listserv@listserv.net." The student then puts in the message box the following: list global/antidepressant research list global/psychiatry research.

Since it takes a while to get back a search, the student can re-read the article or discuss it with a classmate via e-mail to see if he or she has some insights into the article's argument. Getting back to the listserv search, the student may now find some lists that appear pertinent to his quest. For example, he or she might find in his "in-box" references such as the following:

AARON AARON@COLUNIVJ1.BITNET
APA/Antidepressant Drug Studies

ESP ESP@UNIVARIZPSY.BITNET
Ethical Studies in Psychiatry Research

The entries all in capital letters simply refer to the list supervisor and his or her e-mail address. The name of the list should clue the student to what type of people subscribe to the list and what the nature of their interests are. The student may then wish to call up the list and check out some of the messages between and among members to see if he would feel comfortable leaving an e-mail message with them. Finally, deciding a message to the members of the list might yield some results to help the student better master the essay's topic, he sends the following "global" message to the lists' members.

> Hi,
>
> My name is Robert, and I am a college sophomore. I am writing a research paper on the ethics and methods of psychiatric drug testing. I am wondering whether anyone is familiar with the article entitled "Prescriptions for Happiness?" by Fischer and Greenberg, originally published in the September/October 1995 issue of *Psychology Today*. I am concerned about the following:
>
> 1. Do you believe the methods used by the authors to challenge some of the research on antidepressants were valid?
> 2. Do you believe their conclusions are accurate?
>
> Also, do you know of any secondary source material I might look at to help me with my research? I promise to give full credit in my Works Cited page for any information you provide me.
>
> Sincerely,
>
> Robert

B) Gophers

If you are familiar with the World Wide Web (with its incredible graphic and sound capabilities), you probably are wondering why someone would use the Gopher system, the first research tool developed for the general population to access Internet information (way back in 1992). The Gopher system is a "text-only" system, meaning the only information you will get on it is in the form of words on your monitor. In other words, "Gopherspace" looks merely like an electronic form of the printed page. However, if you think about it, such information in most cases should suit you just fine. True, you could find a site on the World Wide Web that could simulate a crowd of Elizabethans entering the Globe Theatre if you were doing research on a Shakespearean play, but there probably isn't much need to see such an electronic construct. In fact, such flourishes could easily take your attention and focus away from your learning. Once you log onto the Gopher system, the easiest means to use it for research and study is to access its "Veronica" search engine. Once accessed, you will be met with a series of options, for example, search by topic, title words, menus, and so forth. Nearly every topic from A to Z is available via Gopher, and as you access one area, say, Education, you can narrow your choices to such areas as Secondary Education, Science Education, Literature, then streamline your choice even finer until you reach an area closest to what you wish to study. To give you an idea of the breadth of topics, a search using the word Shakespeare using "Veronica" returns about 1,500 references.

To give an example of how you might use the Gopher system for your studies, let's turn to the article "Violent Reaction" by Richard Lacayo in the "Popular Entertainment" section of your text. This article describes the politics and policies behind society's response to violent rap lyrics and violent movies. Suppose a student wishes to write an argumentative essay in which he claims that politicians take stands against such material simply to garner votes. One way to buttress his argument is to see what "experts" say about the correlation between media violence and crime. He can then jump to the "Education and Social Sciences" section of Gopher, and then, through a procedure of defining and narrowing his search through the use of key words, he can locate articles, statistics, and essays on the relationship between the variables he is seeking. He may—in the end—find dozens of references that pertain to his topic, and just so he doesn't have to reach each one individually, the Gopher system gives him a one-line summary of each entry. So, for example, if the student finds an entry entitled "Stop Blaming the Media: It's the Parents Who Influence Violent Behavior in Their Children" he will know that there's the potential for a lot of information he can use to support his argument.

Another reason using Gopher has its advantages over the World Wide Web is that since all information is in text format, Gopher moves much faster from screen to screen since there aren't tons of graphical information that must be downloaded. If you have a computer system that is not all that powerful, you will certainly appreciate this feature.

C) World Wide Web

The "Mother" of all Internet services, the World Wide Web has become very simple to operate thanks to the ever-increasing efficiency of "search engines" that are now available. You can browse through the Web much like you would through the stacks of a library or go directly to a website (the specific place an item of information is stored) if you know its URL or Uniform Resource Locator (all of which start with the prefix http://). An easy way of conceptualizing a website's URL is that it is the equivalent to the call number of a library book. Your strategy, however, will probably be to seek out websites that meet your research needs unless you care to purchase an unwieldy Web Yellow Pages which goes out of date the day it's published. Browsing through the Web is similar to Gopher. Through the imaginative use of keywords, you will be able to sort through the hundreds of thousands of websites available to find what you're looking for. One word of warning, however: Be sure to consider the repercussion of typing in a keyword that may be too general or too narrow. For example, if a student is seeking information on "Generation X," and she types in the keywords "Generation" or "X," she might be surprised to find dozens or hundreds of references to X-rays because the preposition "or" means she is seeking sites with either the word "Generation" *or* "X." The proper way to seek information on the topic would be "Generation X." If that is not helpful, she may try "twentysomethings" or "baby busters." If the student simply requests information with sites that possess "Generation" in the title, she may get a list that includes information about genealogies, genetics, animal research, and the like.

D) Newsgroups

Newsgroups are sites where people with similar interests share information, dialogue, questions, announcements, debates, and so on. Newsgroups are usually located with the USENET research tool if you are computing in a college environment. Others can have access to them through commercial on-line services like Prodigy and America On-Line or through local bulletin boards. Newsgroups themselves are grouped under categories like education, social studies, sociology, psychology, current events, and so on, and their names make it pretty easy to determine just what subject matter interests their members. So, if you were to find a newsgroup in the literature section entitled "rec.arts.poems," you would interpret it as a newsgroup that has been set up for the purpose of casually exchanging and discussing members' own poetry or responses to poetry. If you were doing a high-powered research paper on T.S. Eliot, for example, this probably would *not* be the place to make your inquiries. But let's say a female student wants to explore how men feel about attending consciousness raising groups as background for an expository paper responding to the essay in the "Gender Issues" section of your text written by Ellen Frankel Paul and entitled "Silly Men, Banal Men." Perhaps the student thinks that getting a first-hand male perspective on the issue will help her get a better grasp on why men attend such groups and what they feel they get out of them. Searching through the sociology news groups, she finds two that seem promising. One is entitled soc.cult.men; another is entitled soc.cult.gender. She may then "enter" these groups and read what sorts of messages are contained within them. For example, if the soc.cult.men newsgroup contains messages with titles such as "Robert Bly" or "Men's Consciousness Group—May 17th" or "Has anyone read *Fire in the Belly*?" (all references to men's consciousness raising concerns), she may read the messages to see more specifically the sorts of information the newsgroup members are sharing. If it seems appropriate, she may then place a message of her own. It might read as follows.

> Dear Group Members:
>
> I am a college sophomore writing a research paper whose goal is to explore the reasons why men attend consciousness-raising groups, and their post-group responses. If you could provide me with a 150 to 200 word summary of your experience, I would be very appreciative. You need not mention your name, but I would like you to mention where and when the meeting occurred, and any other salient information you think of. Please e-mail me your response or post it to this newsgroup inquiry.
>
> Sincerely,
>
> Atrax (a pseudonym)

Depending on how active the group is and how many members it has, the student should receive a number of interesting responses. Note that it might be appropriate to use a pseudonym with your inquiry simply because it's a good idea not to reveal too much about yourself to a group of strangers (on the Internet or otherwise!). Within a few days, the student can check her e-mail or "attached" responses to her inquiry via the newsgroup. If the student receives just five or six useful responses, she should be on her way to having sufficient research to start her expository essay.

With this brief survey of accessing the Internet as a tool for your class work, you are on your way to mastering a tool which no doubt will become essential in your college years and after you graduate. Like any skill, gaining facility with researching the Internet increases through use. Active use of the various features enumerated here will make you proficient fairly soon. One good way to get comfortable with the Internet is to "browse" through it, testing its features, and locating information that is of interest to you—whether it be for your class or leisure. However, be forewarned that "cybersurfing" becomes addictive to many people. The intention of the information provided here is not to encourage you to become distracted from your studies. Rather it's to use the Internet to help you focus on thinking about, discussing, and writing about the essays in your text. You most likely already have a major "distractor" in your room: Television.

1

GENERATIONS AT THE CROSSROADS

Heraclitus, the Greek philosopher, stated that we can never step into the same river twice. If we consider time as a river, and the changing generations those who enter and define that river, it is obvious that values, issues, and "defining moments" change as the years go by. Each essay in this chapter deals with one or more of three generations: "twentysomethings," "baby boomers," and the "D-Day generation." In terms of generational order, one might say they range from the children to the parents to the grandparents. Admittedly, the definition of *generation* is no easy task. Does it refer to age only, the time in which one was born, a summary of specific traits, a style, outlook, ideology, or what? The following essays address this complex and provocative issue. All of the writers in this chapter agree that the age in which one grows up determines a number of significant personal outlooks and values, ranging from cynicism about national politics (as Zill and Robinson point out) to a breaking away from strong traditional family and cultural values (as do the Hispanic youth whom Aguilar interviews). Some authors use such methods as polls, others use observation, others employ interviews, still others like Barbara Kingsolver utilize personal experience to support their analysis or argument. All have clearly defined perspectives and positions on their subjects. Before becoming swayed by the opinions of others, it may be best to examine yourself and your peers. What elements do you share regarding your beliefs about institutions, about the concept of a future, about the generation that preceded you? To what degree do you feel a sense of solidarity with people your own age? To what degree do you feel like a separate entity? After such reflection, you will have a better understanding of other generations as they are described in the following essays.

The Generation X Difference

Nicholas Zill and John Robinson

As suggested by the title of the periodical—*American Demographics*—where this essay first appeared in April 1995, "The Generation X Difference" provides a cross-section of numerical indicators comparing the "newer generation" with its predecessor in several areas including family life, work, behavior, and outlook. The word *demographics,* after all, is a term signifying the "counting of people." However, individuals of most groups—whether they are identified by gender, race, age or political persuasion—would balk at being classified as merely "a number." Zill (who is vice president of Estat, Inc., in Rockville, Maryland) and Robinson (a professor of sociology at the University of Maryland and contributing editor of *American Demographics*) do, in the end, make some conclusions about "busters" that you will want to evaluate after you have read this essay.

PREVIEWING THE ESSAY

We have a penchant for classifying, dividing, and defining our reality. Professionals from many fields including philosophers, anthropologists, and, today, neuroscientists would say that such pursuits are some of the distinguishing activities that make us human. What purpose do such cognitive tasks suggest about us as beings? What, specifically, is the value of these faculties in analyzing generational differences?

Some of them wear their baseball caps backwards. Some put safety pins through their nipples and rings through their noses. But are today's young people really all that different from the young adults of 10 or 20 years ago? Do they merit labels like "Grunge Kids," "Slackers," or "Generation X"? 1

A few years ago, American newspapers and magazines were filled with stories about a peculiar new generation that faced terrible employment prospects, exhibited perverse tastes and behavior patterns, and was even more politically apathetic than its predecessors. Then researchers found that some of the characteristics the media attributed to Xers contradicted each other. Other Xer labels were not supported by trend data, and still others applied to a minority of young adults. The media began running articles like *Newsweek*'s cover story, "The Myth of Generation X: Seven Great Lies About Twentysomethings." That story concluded, "There are only two generalizations we can make about them with any degree of certainty: they are Americans, and they are in their 20s." 2

Sweeping generalizations about any generation are bound to be incorrect. But so too is the notion that there is nothing different or 3 noteworthy about today's young adults. In fact, trend data from national surveys such as the Current Population Survey and the National Endowment for the Arts' Survey of Public Participation in the Arts demonstrate that the current crop of 18-to-29-year-olds differs from it predecessors in several important regards. Their economic situations and prospects are different, as are their educational enrollment and attainment patterns. Their media and recreation habits are different, too. Even their relationships with their parents are different than were those of baby boomers. Taking a close look at these facts is the best way to separate the truth about today's young adults from the media-fueled hype.

EARNINGS AND EDUCATION

When young adults complain about their dim financial prospects, many older adults accuse them of being whiners. A *Washington Post* headline proclaimed: "Grow Up, Crybabies. You're America's Luckiest Generation." The critics seem not to have noticed the slide in young workers' wage rates. Between 1983 and 1992, the median weekly earnings of young men aged 16 to 24 who were full-time workers fell 9 percent, from $314 per week to $285 per week in constant 1992 dollars. Over the same period, inflation-adjusted earnings of young women in the same age group slipped 4 percent, from $277 to $267 per week. The earnings of men aged 25 and older also declined during this period, but only by 6 percent. Wage rates for women aged 25 and older increased by 6 percent. 4

The reasons behind wage declines are familiar, but that doesn't make them any easier for young workers to live with. They include a loss of high-paying manufacturing jobs due to automation, foreign competition, and shifting of jobs to countries with lower labor costs. In contrast, service industries are creating masses of low-paying jobs that offer meager benefits. In addition, technological changes have put a premium on workers possessing the high-level skills needed to read and understand abstract prose, operate computers and complex machinery, and easily adapt to rapidly changing work environments. That is good news for the twenty-somethings who have grown up computer-literate. But it is bad news for the large number of young people whose reading and math skills never advanced beyond the eighth-grade level and whose only familiarity with microprocessors comes from hanging out in video arcades. 5

Given the need for technical skills and education credentials to earn decent wages, it is hardly surprising that today's young adults are flocking to two- and four-year colleges at record rates. The percentage 6

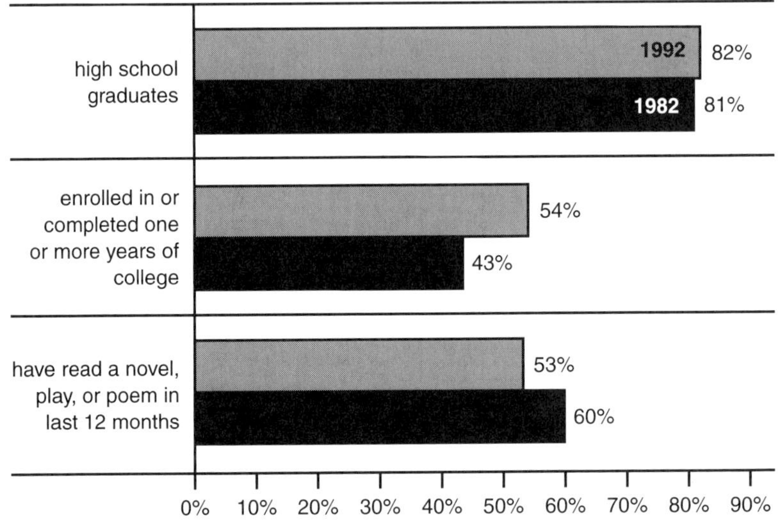

Source: Current Population Survey, Census Bureau; and Survey of Public Participation in the Arts, National Endowment for the Arts.

of 18-to-24–year-olds currently enrolled in college or having completed one or more years of college was 54 percent in October 1992, up from 43 percent a decade earlier, according to the Current Population Survey.

Baby busters may be the most college-bound generation ever, but 7
they aren't necessarily the best-educated. As of March 1993, 24 percent of adults aged 25 to 29 had bachelor's degrees, not much different from the 22 percent with such degrees in 1982. So while today's young adults may be eager for college credentials, many have not attained these passports to higher earnings. Furthermore, the proportion of young adults who attain college degrees is only half as large among blacks as it is among whites.

THE VISUAL ARTS

Perhaps it's natural that young people of the post-television era seem 8
moved more by the visual image than by the written word. The percentage of 18-to-24-year-olds who read any novels, short stories, poetry, or plays in the previous 12 months fell from 60 percent in 1982 to 53 percent in 1992, according to the arts survey. Over the same period, literature reading declined 2 percentage points among middle-aged

Good Visuals

Young adults are increasingly interested in the visual arts.
(percent of adults aged 18 to 24 who have participated in selected arts activities, 1982 and 1992)

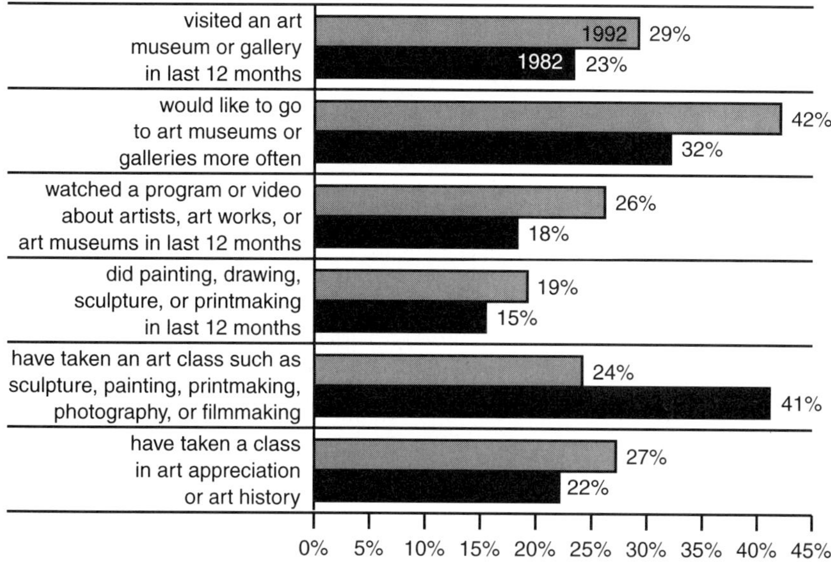

Source: Survey of Public Participation in the Arts, National Endowment for the Arts.

adults and held its own among adults aged 50 and older. The survey also found that 41 percent of today's young adults did not read a single book not required for school or work in the last 12 months, and 60 percent had read fewer than four.

9 While the proportion of young adults who read literature regularly has been on the decline, the proportion who go to art museums or galleries has been rising. Twenty-nine percent of 18-to-24-year-olds in 1992 reported attendance at an art museum or gallery during the previous 12 months, compared with 23 percent in 1982. The percentage of young adults who say they would like to go to art museums or galleries more often showed an even larger increase, from 32 percent in 1982 to 42 percent in 1992. The proportion who watched a television program or video about artists, art works, or art museums in the last 12 months also increased, from 18 percent to 26 percent.

10 Some of the increase in fine arts attendance may reflect the greater availability of art in traveling shows, videos, and cable, as well as the more effective packaging and promotion of art by museum officials. But it also seems likely that the pervasive media environment in which today's young adults have grown up has helped to nurture their awareness of and interest in the graphic arts.

Young adults' increased interest in the visual arts has occurred despite the decline of formal art education in childhood. The proportion of 18-to-24-year-olds who have ever taken lessons or classes in visual arts such as sculpture, painting, printmaking, photography, or film dropped from 41 percent in 1982 to 24 percent in 1992. The decline is probably attributable to a downgrading of arts instruction in the nation's public schools, a deemphasis now apparently in the process of being reversed in many school systems. On the other hand, the proportion of young adults who had taken a class in art appreciation or art history did not decline during the 1980s: it was 22 percent in 1982 and 27 percent in 1992, and the apparent increase is not statistically significant. 11

Young adults spend much of their time with the omnipresent visual form of the late 20th century. Eighteen-to-24-year-olds report watching three hours of television on an average day, according to the arts survey. This makes them no different from young adults of the previous decade. Stereotypes portray baby busters transfixed by MTV, but the reality is that, like their elders, young adults are far more likely to be watching top-rated shows on network television. In spring 1994, the most popular TV programs among 18-to-29-year-olds were "Seinfeld," "Roseanne," "Home Improvement," and "Coach," also among the top-drawing programs for viewers of all ages. 12

The big differences in television viewing patterns are found not between busters and boomers, but between adults under age 50 and those aged 50 and older. The latter are far more likely to be tuned in to shows such as "60 Minutes" and "Murder, She Wrote." It remains to be seen whether this age gap will shift when boomers enter their 50s in the next decade. 13

SPORTS AND SEX

When young adults do get off the couch and out of the house for entertainment, they're probably going to the movies. Eighty-two percent of 18-to-24-year-olds reported attending a movie in the last 12 months, according to the 1992 SPPA. This was down slightly from the 87 percent of the same age group who reported film attendance a decade earlier, but was still considerably higher than the 59 percent movie attendance rate among adults of all ages. 14

The proportion of young adults who attended films in 1992 surpassed the proportions who attended amusement or theme parks (68 percent), amateur or professional sports events (51 percent), arts or crafts fairs or festivals (37 percent), or historic parks or monuments (33 percent). And it greatly exceeded the proportions who went to 15

Youth at Play

Today's young adults are more likely to go to art festivals and less likely to go to jazz concerts.

(percent of adults aged 18 to 24 who attended selected places or events in previous 12 months, 1982 to 1992)

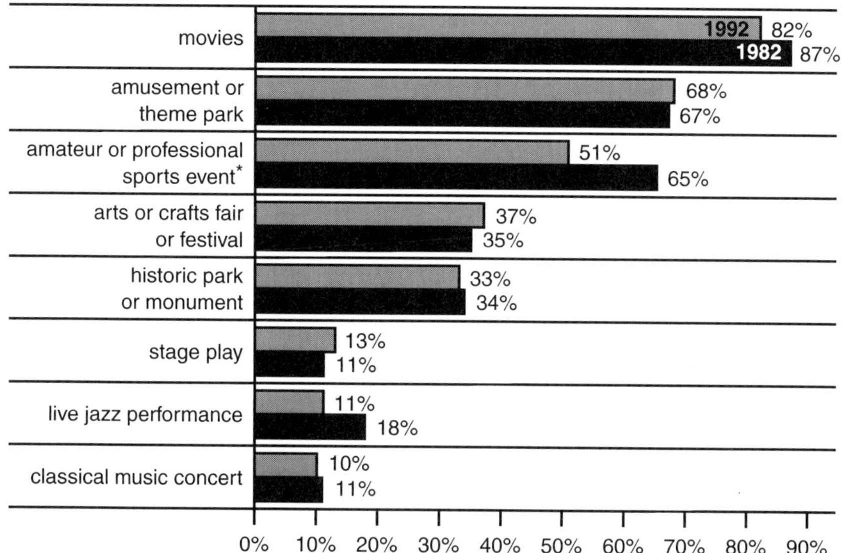

* *Question worded differently in the two surveys.*

Source: Survey of Public Participation in the Arts, National Endowment for the Arts.

stage plays (13 percent) or live performances of jazz (11 percent) or classical music (10 percent). 16

Young adults like to exercise their eyeballs with art, TV, and movies, but they are less fond of exercise for the rest of their bodies. Perhaps the most perplexing trend involving young adults is the decline in their levels of physical activity. Medical science continues to find evidence of the benefits of an active, vigorous lifestyle over a sedentary one. Yet compared with their counterparts of a decade ago, baby busters are less likely to engage in sports and outdoor activities. 17

According to the arts survey, the proportion of 18-to-24-year-olds who engaged in sports such as softball, basketball, golf, bowling, skiing, or tennis in the last 12 months declined from 66 percent in 1982 to 59 percent in 1992. The proportion who went camping, hiking, canoeing, or took part in other outdoor activities fell from 51 percent to 43 percent over the same period. The share who reported jogging, lifting weights, walking, or engaging in other regular exercise did not change significantly, from 70 percent in 1982 to 67 percent in 1992. But the overall proportion of adults who exercised regularly increased during this time period from 51 percent to 60 percent.

18 The decline in physical activities among young adults is documented even more dramatically in a detailed survey of 22 fitness activities conducted by the National Center for Health Statistics. Based on samples of more than 30,000 adult respondents nationwide, the 15 percent decline in fitness activities between 1985 and 1990 for those under age 30 was almost twice as large as the decline for older Americans.

19 The drop has been particularly pronounced for young women. Women under age 30 took part in fitness activities at 61 percent the rate of young men in 1990—compared with a 75 percent gender ratio for older women and men. This suggests that women may fall further behind men in fitness in the years ahead.

20 Today's young adults are also less involved in sexual activity. The authors of *Sex in America* (1994) found that the youngest adults report levels of sexual intercourse that are closer to people aged 50 to 59 than to those in their 30s. While that may be due in large part to their being single rather than married, young adults also report lower rates of masturbation.

DIVORCE AND PARENTS

21 Both the divorce rate and the percentage of children born outside of marriage in the U.S. doubled between 1965 and 1977, the years in which today's young adults were born. As busters grew up, the divorce rate leveled off and even declined slightly, but it remains much higher than it had been before the mid-1960s. The percentage of children born to unmarried parents also continued to rise, reaching 30 percent in 1992. As a result, more than 40 percent of today's young adults spent at least some time in a single-parent family by age 16.

22 These events left their marks on young-adult psyches. The National Survey of Children, a longitudinal study of people born in the late 1960s, found that 26 percent of these busters had received psychological treatment for emotional, learning, or behavior problems by the time they reached adulthood. The share who had been in therapy was twice as high among those whose parents had divorced as it was among those whose parents had not, 41 percent versus 22 percent.

23 Young adults whose parents divorced are twice as likely as others to have poor relationships with their parents, especially their fathers. Two-thirds of young adults whose parents divorced report poor relationships with their fathers, and one-third with their mothers. By comparison, among busters whose parents did not divorce, 29 percent have poor relationships with their fathers and 13 percent with their mothers.

24 In some respects, however, relations between busters and their parents are more harmonious than were those between baby boomers

and their parents. In particular, there seems to be less of a generation gap with respect to tastes in music. Large majorities of busters and their parents like oldies rock and roll. Three-fourths of 18-to-29-year-olds and 40-to-59-year-olds say they like oldies, according to the 1993 General Social Survey from the National Opinion Research Center in Chicago.

There is more generational discord regarding heavy metal and 25
rap, although it is not absolute. Five percent of 40-to-59-year-olds say they like heavy metal, while 81 percent dislike or hate it; the remainder have mixed feelings. The pattern is similar for rap; 8 percent like it, and 71 percent don't. However, these music forms also have minority followings among the baby-bust generation itself. One in four 18-to-29-year-olds likes heavy metal, while half dislike or hate it. Thirty percent like rap, but 45 percent don't.

It is a good thing that busters and their parents agree on some 26
musical matters, because young adults are spending more of their lives bunking with Mom and Dad. The proportion of women in their 20s living in their parents' homes rose from 17 percent in 1977 to 24 percent in 1993, according to the Current Population Survey. Young men the same age are even more likely to remain in or return to the parental nest (35 percent in 1993, up from 30 percent in 1977).

One reason why many busters have not left home is because they 27
are marrying later. The share of women aged 25 to 29 who had never married tripled from 11 percent in 1970 to 33 percent in 1993. The share of men in their late 20s who have never married climbed from 19 percent to 48 percent during the same period. Another factor underlying the "long goodbye" phenomenon is the high cost of housing. Coupled with busters' diminished earning power, living rent-free may be the only feasible way of saving enough for an eventual down payment on a house or condo.

When young adults do leave home, they are likely to wind up in a 28
legal marriage. But the chances are greater that they will live with a partner before marrying that person or someone else. The number of unmarried-couple households rose from 500,000 in 1970 to 3.5 million in 1993. At the same time, the ratio of unmarried couples to married couples rose from 1 per 100 to 6 per 100. About half of these nontraditional households involve one or both partners under age 30.

A NEW DEFINITION

Young adults are almost twice as likely as older adults to have tried 29
microbrewed beer in the last year, according to a recent national survey. This could eventually turn out to be one of the hallmark activities that identifies Generation Xers in the years ahead—not because it

involves beer, but because it may signify a trend toward seeking out local, specialized products with a distinctive flavor. Busters may favor beer over wine because they prefer its informality. Many of them may find the specialized vocabulary of wine appreciation intimidating and potentially embarrassing.

Besides preferring visual to physical exercise, twentysomethings 30 of the 1990s are clearly not the same as young adults of the past. In many ways, they are more diverse and complex, yet they exhibit a few unifying traits. The first is insecurity. Today's young adults are less confident than their predecessors about the stability of jobs, earnings, and relationships. This may be good news for companies that want to hire twentysomethings for modest wages and minimal benefits. It also means that busters may be looking beyond salaries for jobs that offer meaningful opportunities for skill building and advancement.

A second unifying theme is the critical importance of education 31 in shaping the life chances of today's young adults. Busters appreciate the value of education, but many are frustrated about their inability to achieve the schooling they would like. As they move through the work world, they will be an eager market for adult education and job-related training. Although their focus will be practical for some years, they may later seek the arts, humanities, and even spiritual instruction lacking in their earlier schooling. They will probably prefer to learn about these subjects through multimedia avenues rather than traditional books.

The third theme that distinguishes busters from previous genera- 32 tions is how long it is taking them to fully enter the adult world. In the book *Childhood and Society,* Erik Erikson described adolescence as a psychological stage between childhood and adulthood. Now it seems that a new pre-adult life stage has emerged. This isn't to say that people in their 20s are merely overgrown children. It's more that they are understandably hesitant to take on some of the tasks at which they have seen their elders fail. Busters will undoubtedly make their own mistakes in life, but they don't want to repeat ours.

THINKING ABOUT THE ESSAY

1. Were any of the authors' findings of particular significance to your own life experience? If so, which ones? Did the explanations behind their findings ring true? If they did, how did it make you feel to realize that "objective" observers could peer inside you and understand your feelings and thoughts?
2. Where do the authors conclude that Generation X is a troubled generation? Do you feel this is an unfair representation? How do their conclusions about the inner life of 18-to-29-year-olds reflect

your own feelings or the feelings of those you know in this age bracket?

3. The authors make observations about their subject through a number of rhetorical (methodological) strategies, including comparison and contrast, definition, and illustration. What are the strengths and weaknesses of each strategy? Cite examples of each method. What other methods are available for observers to draw conclusions about groups?
4. Demographics are often used by advertisers to develop marketing strategies to sell their products. Politicians employ them to plan campaigns. To what purpose have the authors of this particular essay used the methods of demographics? To inform? To advise? To warn? Or something else? What effect has the method had on you? For example, do you view demographics as a mere intellectual exercise or a lesson from which you can derive benefits?

RESPONDING IN DISCUSSION

1. The knowledge, biases, experience, and culture the reader brings to a text are as important as what the authors have written down for its comprehension. Men may respond differently than women; students who have grown up in single-parent households may respond differently than those whose environment more closely approximated the conventional nuclear family. Persons born and raised in the United States may have different perspectives than immigrants or students visiting from other countries. Select any one of these distinguishing features and discuss how it affects responses to the essay.
2. Nowhere in the essay is there a discussion of "individuality" or "difference." But often those who live outside the mainstream have the most to offer in understanding its dynamics. If your life experience varies from those that are generalized in the essay, harness your background so that you can make a special contribution to understanding the generation in question.
3. The essay has a section entitled "A New Definition" in which the authors present three unifying themes among Generation Xers. Divide into groups of three or four, and provide expanded examples of each theme. Or, if you disagree with any of these themes, provide examples that challenge the authors' conclusions.
4. At the end of the first section, the authors state, "Taking a close look at these facts is the biggest way to separate the truth about today's young adults from the media-fueled hype." This statement implies that authors are separating the "truth" from "fiction." However, *truth* is a difficult term to nail down. Have the

authors indeed addressed the important issues surrounding their subject or are they off-base? Discuss in class.

RESPONDING IN WRITING

1. Write a letter to your local newspaper explaining why you wish to write a new weekly column "From the X Point of View" or "From the Buster Point of View."
2. Select a TV program that appeals to you owing to its viewpoint, characterization, issue-orientation, and so on, and write a persuasive essay of approximately 500 words on why it is particularly appealing to 18-to-24-year-olds.
3. Argue for or against the proposition that a person—by the time he or she reaches age 21—is more savvy about politics, society, and consumerism than his or her counterpart 20 years ago.
4. Many social commentators argue that a group can become defined by the media through repetition of messages, so that even the targeted individuals are brainwashed into believing they are part of a group with particular distinguishing features. Argue for or against the idea that today's young person is too sophisticated to be seduced by media ploys.
5. Visit Web sites such as MTV (http://mtv.com) and Comedy Central (http://www.comcentral.com). How are these sites tailored to appeal to you and your generation? Find another site that conspicuously targets Generation X. What is your reaction to this targeting? Write a 500-to-1,000-word analysis of your findings.

The Making of a Generation

Arthur Levine

How acute are differences between and among generations? Are generational identities so profoundly changed that intergenerational conflict is inevitable; or are the changes slighter, so that there is a basic agreement in beliefs and outlook concerning society and the self from one group to the next? Arthur Levine, former chair of the Institute for Educational Management and senior faculty member of the Harvard Graduate School of Education, and currently the president of Teachers College at Columbia University, has seen much generational change in his career. This essay, which appeared in the September–October 1993 issue of *Change,* is a result of two surveys that asked similar questions about the social events of their time; one survey targeted those who were undergraduates in 1979 and the other, those in 1992. Although each group gleaned different meanings from the significant moments in their lives, has there been significant change in outlook among the two? Levine describes the differences he discerned. But for the reader, perhaps the ultimate issue is the significance of these differences.

PREVIEWING THE ESSAY

Levine seems to have faith in the sophistication and knowledge of college undergraduates, for if he didn't, there would have been little reason to conduct his research. The fact that the students interviewed for this study had strong opinions on many current affairs issues seems to indicate that today's students read more, know more, and think more about the world outside their "personal experience" than previous generations of students. Would you agree that today's students are well informed about their world? Why?

Every college generation is defined by the social events of its age. The 1
momentous occurrences of an era—from wars and economics to politics and inventions—give meaning to the lives of the individuals who live through them. They also serve to knit those individuals together by creating a collective memory and a common historic or generational identity. In 1979, I went to 26 college and university campuses, selected to represent the diversity of American higher education, and asked students what social or political events most influenced their generation. I told them that the children who came of age in the decade after World War I might have answered the Great Depression. The bombing of Pearl Harbor, World War II, or perhaps the death of Franklin Roosevelt might have stood out for those born a few years later. For my generation, born after World War II, the key event was the assassination of John F. Kennedy. We remember where we were when we heard the news. The whole world seemingly changed in its aftermath.

THE ME GENERATION

I asked what stood out for that generation of undergraduates on the 2
eve of the 1980s. They said Vietnam and Watergate. These events had defined their world. Few could remember a time in their lives when there had been no war, and Watergate seemed a confirmation about the way the world worked in business, government, and all sectors of society. On Watergate, students' comments echoed one another:

> "Government doesn't give a damn."
>
> "All politicians are crooks."

"Nixon was like all of us, only he got caught."

"It happens all the time."

"I don't trust government as far as I can throw the Capitol building."

"Nixon was a victim, that's all."

"The whole thing was out of proportion."

For three out of four students, the effects of Watergate and Vietnam had been distinctly negative, causing undergraduates to turn away from politics, politicians, and government. Most said they had no heroes. 3

Trust in all social institutions had declined among college students. A plurality of undergraduates described the major social institutions of society—Congress, corporations, labor unions, and the rest—as dishonest and immoral. They expressed a belief that there was nothing left to hold onto: "Everything is bad." 4

In response, the students had turned inward, and the refuge they had chosen was "me." They described the mood on campus this way: 5

"People only care about me, me, me."

"We're just interested in staying alive."

"We're part of the me generation."

"Concerns today are not about social issues, but about me."

"People are looking out for number one."

"The me generation is not concerned with the good of society, but with what's good for themselves."

Ninety-one percent of the undergraduates interviewed were optimistic about their personal futures, but only 41 percent expressed hope about our collective future together. Student interests focused increasingly on being well-off financially. At the same time they had become more and more vocationally oriented, seeking careers in the platinum professions—law, medicine, and business. They had adopted what might be called a Titanic ethic: a sense that they were riding on a doomed ship called the United States or the world, and as long as it remained afloat, they would go first class. 6

THE CURRENT GENERATION

The findings of the 1979 study were so telling that I decided to repeat it this academic year. Once again I, along with several colleagues, visited a diverse selection of colleges and universities across the country. 7

We followed the same approach as the original study, meeting with intentionally heterogeneous groups consisting of 8 to 10 students on each campus. The number of institutions was raised to 28 to reflect the changing character of higher education since 1979. (This was part of a larger study including a survey of 10,000 undergraduates, a survey of 300 chief student affairs officers, and interviews with undergraduate student body presidents, newspaper editors, vice presidents and deans of students, and others.) Again we asked the undergraduate groups what social and political events had most influenced their generation. They gave five common answers.

8 *Challenger.* The most frequent answer was the *Challenger* explosion. Once a student mentioned it, members of the group commonly nodded in affirmation or said "yes." It was the equivalent of the Kennedy assassination for this generation. The students all knew where they had been when they heard the news. Many had watched it on television in school. Those who had not, saw it "on the news over and over and over again." Some had been scheduled to have teacher-astronaut Christa McAuliffe teach them from space. For a number it was the first time they had ever seen an adult, their own teacher, break down and cry. It was a first brush with death for quite a few.

9 That students answered the *Challenger* explosion surprised me. When I thought about the responses students might give to my question, the Shuttle disaster was not on the list. My generation had witnessed other fatalities in the space program, and while the *Challenger* explosion was a very sad occurrence, it did not seem to me to be a defining moment for the nation.

10 I asked them why they had selected the *Challenger?* Beyond the fact that it was the first shared generational tragedy, students talked of a shattering of both their idealism and their sense of safety:

"I always thought NASA was perfect."

"There were smashed dreams because of it."

"My hopes were in it. There was an Asian, a black, and a woman."

"Thought America invincible."

"Burst my bubble."

"It was something good and then it blew up."

"NASA fell off its pedestal."

11 Students also said the *Challenger* explosion had marked a "wake-up call" or "reality check" for them and the nation. For some it was "a sign of a lot of things wrong" with the United States, such as in manufacturing, and for others it highlighted the decline of America due to its inability to compete economically and technologically. As one

student put it, until then "I thought we were the best; we're really only second class."

End of the Cold War. The fall of communism was a second event students cited. They spoke in terms of "pride," "hope," "drama," "energy," and "a closer world." The symbol that stood out for them was the razing of the Berlin Wall. 12

Today's undergraduates are the last Cold War generation. They had studied Russia in school as an evil power to be feared. Although none of the 18-to-24-year-old undergraduates had seen Khrushchev bang his shoe at the U.N. or lived through the Cuban Missile Crisis, and only a small minority had engaged in duck-and-cover exercises in school, most had seen films like *The Day After,* which warned of the danger of a nuclear war. As a group, the students interviewed had been scared of the Soviet Union and afraid of the prospect of nuclear holocaust. In this sense the fall of communism was an extremely positive event. 13

However, the students were quite somber about the results. They regularly talked of the instability of Central and Eastern Europe, but in recent months, their focus shifted to U.S. involvement in a potential Vietnam-like ground war in Bosnia. They noted almost as frequently the danger of a now uncontrolled Soviet nuclear arsenal. They often worried whether the world was, in retrospect, a better place because of the demise of communism. One student put it this way: "For my generation, every silver lining brings a cloud." 14

Persian Gulf War. The third event students mentioned was the 1991 Gulf War, which they described as "our first war"—"Every generation has a war; this was ours." Like the Challenger explosion, they had watched it on television. TVs in student lounges, which were usually tuned to soap operas, had stayed fixed on the war. With the rise of CNN, students joked that friends would drop by and say, "You want to watch the war for a while?" and off they would go. 15

Despite fear of a draft and another potential Vietnam, students said the Gulf War had pulled them together. Many knew people who had been called up to serve in the Gulf. On their campuses, demonstrations against war had tended to be tiny or absent in comparison to those in favor. The initial student reaction was pride: "We're still number one"; and "We can get things done." This seemed to be generally true among both liberal and conservative undergraduates. Students talked of flags and yellow ribbons appearing in profusion on many campuses. 16

By the 1992–93 academic year, undergraduate reactions had changed, with students becoming much more critical: 17

"It's still a mess."

"We didn't finish the job."

"We botched another one."

"No reason to be there."

"Only a political show."

"Bush just wanted to be a hero."

"People were risking their lives and then had to return and not get jobs."

"We were in there to keep our oil prices down."

"Did it for economic interest only."

Few students were willing to speak out in favor of the Gulf War in spring of 1993 or to offer non-economic rationales for it. In conversation after conversation, students disavowed the U.S. role as world peace officer. They rejected the notion that when "anything goes wrong, we have to straighten it out." 18

AIDS. A fourth event the students cited was the AIDS epidemic. AIDS has been a fact of life for this generation as long as sexuality has been a possibility for them. Many reported lectures, pamphlets, films, and condom demonstrations in school. They commonly lamented, "I hear about it all the time"; "I'm tired of it." 19

But more than being tired, the students were often angry. They frequently compared their situation with that of the baby boomers, complaining, "When the boomers had sex, they got laid. When we have sex, we get AIDS." One student said it this way: "Free love is more expensive [now]." 20

Nonetheless, even though undergraduates resented a sword dangling over their heads, they acted as if it were not there. Though most said they knew what constituted safe sex, only a minority said they practiced it consistently. Students interviewed felt AIDS could not happen to them. They felt immortal. Very few knew anyone who had been diagnosed as HIV positive. Women undergraduates regularly expressed a greater fear of rape and pregnancy than AIDS. 21

Rodney King. The final event students mentioned was the verdict in the Rodney King beating trial and the riots that followed. 22

Minorities—African-Americans, Hispanics, and Asian-Americans—cited it most frequently, but by no means exclusively. Students expressed polar opinions; some had been appalled by the verdict, and others repulsed by the subsequent violence. The commonality was the strong negative reaction: "I lost faith in the judicial system." " I lost faith in the police." "I lost confidence in people." "It was a lesson in how to buy off a jury." "Everything is politics." "I used to believe the civil rights movement made a difference." "Racism lives." "Laws were created, but minds were not changed." "Another shock to the system." "Rioting inexcusable." "Lawless." "Verdict really disturbed me." 23

"I was glad. It's the only way to get people to see." "It reminded me that society treats me differently." "Police jobs are stressful."

WHAT DO THESE EVENTS MEAN?

What stands out about the five events the students cited is first how recent they were. Most of today's freshmen were born in 1975—after John F. Kennedy's death, the end of the Great Society, the assassinations of Martin Luther King, Jr., and Robert Kennedy, the moon landing, the Watergate break-in and Richard Nixon's resignation, and the end of the war in Vietnam. They were a year old when Jimmy Carter was elected president, four when the hostages were taken in Iran, five when Ronald Reagan entered the White House, 10 when Gorbachev came to power, and 13 when George Bush became president. More than 40 percent have never heard of Hubert Humphrey, Ralph Nader, and Barry Goldwater. 24

As a consequence, the events that stand out to their parents and faculty have little meaning to current undergraduates. Those events do not stir the same anger, elation, frustration, or vivid emotions in students that they do in older adults. They are at best history to contemporary undergraduates. 25

Today's students really know only two presidents of the United States, Ronald Reagan and George Bush. They have lived through three wars, Granada, Panama, and Iraq. The longest war in their lives lasted six weeks. They are living through a period of profound demographic, economic, global, and technological change. 26

In addition to being recent, the five events the students cited were at least in part negative. They described three—the *Challenger* explosion, AIDS, and the Rodney King affair—in wholly negative terms, and their initial optimism about the fall of communism and the Gulf War has faded significantly. In general, students thought they were living in a deeply troubled nation in which intractable problems were multiplying and solutions were growing more distant: 27

> "Our experience is of flaws, problems, decline. We're not number one in anything. Our generation grew up with that."
>
> "The world seems to be falling apart."
>
> "We don't have anything that stable to hold onto."

The students interviewed shared a sense that their "generation would be called on to fix everything." As a group, they rejected the likelihood of broadscale solutions. For them the five events they cited 28 showed that such solutions are unlikely to occur and unlikely to work. They also dismissed the possibility that answers would come from government. They saw Congress as bankrupt, but held out hope for the Clinton presidency in its earliest days.

AN INCREASED, IF GUARDED, OPTIMISM

Yet the students I interviewed expressed some optimism about the future. Again, more than nine out of 10 were optimistic about their personal fates, but the level of optimism about our collective future shot up to 55 percent. This is in large measure because students have shifted their focus. While they were rather negative about the future of the country, they were remarkably optimistic about the future of their communities. Today's students emphasize the local in their thinking and their action. 29

Heroes are back too. More than three out of four students had heroes, but those heroes were local—Mom and Dad, my teacher, my neighbor, the person leading the community clean-up campaign. 30

Participation in service activities increased dramatically as well. Prior to coming to college about half of all current undergraduates had been engaged in some form of community service. Such programs are booming on college campuses today as well, particularly in the area of environmentalism, a common interest among today's undergraduates. Even on some campuses in which political action was low or absent, recycling bins have appeared at the behest of students. 31

Nonetheless, fear and anger were a part of the conversation with every student group I interviewed. Current undergraduates were afraid of being unable to find jobs, of living in an economy in which they will do less well than their parents, of facing a mounting national debt, of having to contend with environmental disasters, and much, much more. They felt put upon, cheated, and robbed of the opportunity that had been given to previous generations. They especially resented the baby boomers for their advantages. They criticized the students of the 1980s for their "me-ism." 32

For most of the students interviewed, the real struggle was choosing between making money and performing good deeds. Six out of eight undergraduates said it was essential or very important to be very well-off financially, but five out of eight said it was essential or very important to have a career that would make a meaningful social contribution. The big issue facing students I interviewed was how to choose. Most didn't want to be Donald Trump, but the prospect of Mother Theresa was not all that appealing either. Above all, this is a generation torn between doing good and doing well. 33

THINKING ABOUT THE ESSAY

1. Why has Levine selected college students as his target population for his surveys? As a college student yourself, do you believe you have a special responsibility to stay abreast of events and trends in the news? If so, why?
2. Discuss the methodology that Levine employed in eliciting his responses. How appropriate and effective do you believe the methodology is? If you had been assigned to conduct a survey concerning the opinions of college students, how might you have revised or refined the method? Also, how would your role as a peer of the target population possibly affect the outcome of the responses? Finally, how does Levine structure the essay around his findings? Specifically, how effective is his use of comparison and contrast and his presentation of evidence to support his thesis? Explain.
3. There's an old expression in journalism, "If it bleeds, it leads," meaning sensationalism is always given prominence in news reporting for it attracts readers/viewers/listeners. It seems the author addressed mainly events with a negative valence such as the Rodney King beating and the *Challenger* disaster. Could the type of questions posed to the respondents have biased the results of the survey, or is it a fact that there is very little to trust in the institutions that Americans once basically trusted? Do you feel as though you are personally manipulated by the onslaught of negative reporting, or do you feel—as do many—that it holds your attention? Explain.
4. One major issue that comes up in polling is how to know whether the respondent is telling the truth. In the conclusion, Levine states that five out of eight students "said it was essential or very important to have a career that would make a meaningful social contribution." Did they provide that answer because they were sincere or because they thought it was the right thing to say? What might motivate them to do the latter? If you were asked the question, how influenced would you be to "say the right thing"?

RESPONDING IN DISCUSSION

1. Levine's research seems to suggest that young Americans have gradually lost their trust in the political and social institutions of the nation. Discuss in class whether there really has been a change in the integrity of these institutions or whether it has been merely the perception of them that has changed. If you agree with the latter, discuss why you believe perceptions have changed.

2. Levine discusses events of national interest that have swayed public opinion. But personal encounters with institutions can influences one's views about society as well. Discuss with your classmates a personal encounter with an institution—whether governmental, school, church, or corporate—that belied your trust.
3. While the author posed many questions that addressed responses to public events, these events often led to personal responses—in other words, not just how events would affect the nation and the world, but how they would affect the individual who was being asked. In our electronic age—where information is conveyed instantaneously—is it safe to say there is no longer a difference between the "private" self and the "public" self? Or, has the very concept of selfhood itself changed, so that our minds do not solely consider our immediate surroundings like home, family, and neighborhood, but instead also consider currents and trends worldwide? Discuss in groups of three or four students, and then report your collective viewpoint to the class.
4. By responding to questions concerning corruption in government, response to the AIDS crisis, and to the grim outlook for economic success in life, American students demonstrate they are, at least, comfortable with responding to questions that go to the very core of our values and beliefs. What does this imply about our culture? What traditions about our culture encourage frank discussion? For students who may be visiting from other countries or recent immigrants, what differences, if any, would there be in both the nature of the questions that were posed and the responses, or, for that matter, the entire concept of conducting a poll of college students?

RESPONDING IN WRITING

1. Select a "defining historical moment" in your life—for example, seeing and hearing the results of the O. J. Simpson trial or the Rodney King beating or the beating of Mexicans by U.S. law enforcement officers or another media event. In diary form, write a one-page description of your intellectual, emotional, and behavioral response to the incident.
2. Write a letter to a local, state, or national political leader imploring him or her to enact a piece of legislation (either real or devised by yourself) that would reduce government corruption. Be sure to provide a rationale for the legislation and a discussion of its benefits.

3. Argue for or against the proposition that current 18-to-24-year-olds are more sophisticated regarding political and social matters than past generations at that age. Support your view through personal experience and observation.
4. For a research assignment, do a bibliographic search of four editorials responding to one of the events cited in the essay. Select two pairs: one pair that defended the event, another that condemned it. Compare and contrast the editorials, discussing both the arguments presented as well as the assumptions behind the arguments.
5. Research the Gulf War, the *Challenger* disaster, or the Rodney King case on the World Wide Web. Considering it as a media event, characterize its coverage that you encounter on the Internet. Is it neutral or biased, factual or emotional? Are there perspectives on the event that are underrepresented? Write a report on your findings.

The D-Day Generation

Peggy Noonan

The specific historical event from which this essay borrows its title was D-Day, June 4, 1944, when thousands of Allied (Americans, Canadians, and British) troops landed in Normandy, France, directly facing German machine gun fire and artillery, many dying within seconds of their disembarking from their vessels. The author is a former speechwriter for President Reagan. She recounts her experience in *What I Saw at the Revolution* (1990), using this date in 1944 as a metaphor for her parents' generation, those who were in their twenties during World War II. This was a generation who complained little, worked hard, and accepted its fate. One might say they viewed life as a battle to be won. There is historical significance for the publication of this essay, for it was published in June 1994, exactly 50 years after the event. This anniversary may have been in the author's mind when she selected it as a theme for writing. Originally published in 1994 in *Washington Monthly* (a magazine whose readers tend to be affluent, sophisticated, and political-minded, having a more than superficial knowledge of politics), this essay nonetheless appeals more to the heart than to the head.

PREVIEWING THE ESSAY

The following essay describes a generation that is now well into its seventies and beyond. It identifies a number of traits and behaviors about this generation that you will probably find are different from your own. Do you have a close relationship with someone from that generation—for example, a grandparent, great-uncle or great-aunt, or perhaps a family friend or neighbor? Consider that person's values and attitudes. Do they differ from your own solely because of the difference between your ages, or is there something more, something at the core of their view of life? Perhaps you have seen members of that generation interviewed on television—for example, during documentaries, news programs, or talk shows. In what ways do they seem to have a unique attitude toward duty, authority, and responsibility? Why does this essay's description of this generation seem accurate based on your own experience with its representative members? Or does it?

I keep wondering about who we are these days, all of us. I keep wondering if we're way ahead of our parents—more learned, more tolerant, and engaged in the world—or way behind them. They touch my soul, that generation. They are an impenetrable inspiration. They got through the Depression and the war—they got drafted for five years and said Okay, Uncle Sam! and left, and wrote home. They expected so little, their assumptions were so modest. A lot of them, anyway. The women shared the common trauma of a childhood in hard times and the men had the common integrator of the barracks, and I feel that they understood each other. They knew what they shared. When Communism fell we should have had a parade for them, for it meant their war was finally over. We should have one for them anyway, before they leave. 1

They weren't farmers, or the ones I knew weren't farmers, but they were somehow—closer to the soil, closer to the ground. The ones in Brooklyn, Rochester, wherever, they were closer to the ground. 2

Affluence detaches. It removes you from the old and eternal, it gets you out of the rain. Affluence and technology detach absolutely. Among other things, they get you playing with thin plastic things like Super Nintendo and not solid things like—I don't know—wood, and water. Anyway, the guy who said "Plastics" to Benjamin 25 years ago in "The Graduate" was speaking more truth than we knew. 3

Also, our parents were ethnic in a way I understood. Back in that old world the Irish knew they were better than the Italians and the Italians knew they were better than the Irish and we all knew we were better than the Jews and they knew they were better than us. Everyone knew they were superior, so everyone got along. I think the prevailing feeling was, everyone's human. Actually, that used to be a saying in America: Everyone's human. 4

They all knew they were Americans and they all knew they weren't, and their kids knew it too, and understood it was their job to become the Americans. Which we certainly have. A while ago a reporter told me how an old Boston pol summed up Mario Cuomo. The 5 pol said, "He's not a real ethnic. He's never been ashamed of his father." The reporter—45, New York, Jewish—laughed with a delighted grunt. The ordeal of ethnicity. I Remember Papa.

There were ethnic, religious, and racial resentments, but you didn't hear about them all the time. It was a more reticent country. Imagine chatty America being reticent. But it was. 6

I often want to say to them, to my parents and the parents of my friends, "Share your wisdom, tell me what you've learned, tell me what we're doing wrong and right." But, you know, they're still reticent. Loose lips sink ships. Also, they tend not to have big abstract things to say about life because they were actually busy living it, and forgot to take notes. They didn't have time, or take time, to reflect. They were not so inclined. 7

They're like an old guy I met a few years ago when I was looking for a house in Washington. He had gray hair and was stooped in a crouched, still-muscular way and had just one good eye, the other was scarred and blind. He had an old brick house off George Washington Parkway and I had walked through it; it was perfect but too near the highway for a woman with a two-year-old. When I was in the basement I saw his World War II memorabilia—he still had framed citations on the wall, and I could see he'd seen action island-hopping in the South Pacific. And one of the old framed papers said Guadalcanal, and this was exciting, so I said to him, for the most interesting things you hear in life come by accident, "Did you know Richard Tregaskis?" And his good eye squinted. I thought he might not recognize the reference, so I said to him, "He was the one who wrote *Guadalcanal Diary*." And the squint gets deeper and he says, "Yeah, well, I was a grunt. We'd already done the work and left by the time the writers came." I sort of smiled and asked if I could use the bathroom, where I plucked a piece of shrapnel from my heart. 8

Now they're all retired, and most of the ones I know are in pretty good shape. My friend Susan's parents go to Atlantic City and catch a few shows, play the slots. They own their house. My father—army infantry, Italy under Blood 'n' Guts—has a small apartment in Santo Domingo and swims and says he can feel the sun to his bones. My mother lives here in town and flies off when one of her children is having a baby, to be a continuity, to say by her presence, "We did this too, years ago, so don't worry." Lisa's parents just got back from Europe. George's father, who for 25 years worked in a Newark welfare office, married a woman with a farm in Pennsylvania. Now he walks in the mud in big rubber boots, holding a piece of corn. He's happy. There was more divorce than I think we've noted in our parents' generation, and a lot of them did it in a funny way, not after a year or 10 years but after 25, 35 years. After a life. There are always serious and individual reasons for such things, but I would include the seventies, 9 the decade when America went crazy, the decade when, as John Updike said, the sixties had finally percolated down to everybody.

THINKING ABOUT THE ESSAY

1. Most careful readers would agree that writing is a form of communication and that an author has an implied or target audience in mind when writing. Considering solely the first paragraph, who do you believe is this audience? Is there more than one audience implied? Explain.
2. What is the tone of the essay or the emotional stake the writer has invested in communicating her thoughts? How does the use of the "first-person-singular" or "I" point of view affect the tone? What other elements of style influence the tone? Does the tone involve you on an emotional level, or is the subject matter too remote for you to identify with? What group of readers is most likely to respond on an emotional level?
3. The subtitle of this essay reveals the author to be a baby boomer. She speaks with veneration and admiration for her parents' generation. For a member of the current young generation, however, it is the baby boomers who are the parents. How would you compare and contrast your reflections on your parents' generation to those that Noonan expresses?
4. How does the author use anecdotes to enliven her essay? Do they create a "mind picture" for you as you read? Would they have the same impact upon you as they might upon a boomer? Explain.

RESPONDING IN DISCUSSION

1. As a mobile society, intergenerational attitudes may vary more widely in America than in other countries. In addition, attitudes may vary between generations more or less deeply depending upon one's social class, ethnicity, and geographic region. Select several of these variables and discuss how each affects the generation gap. Use your own experiences and background as a source for your observations and reflections.
2. Is the author placing a value judgment on her observations? Does she imply that the values and attitudes of her parents' generation were better than her own generation's or just different? In small groups, compare your peers' values and attitudes with those of your parents. Are yours better, worse, or just different?
3. Noonan demonstrates a significant value of her parents' generation when she discusses "an old guy" whom she met in Washington.

She demonstrates her generation's values concerning education, scholarship, and fame by asking the former soldier if he knew of a particular author. The old soldier reminds her that he did the work, the author did the reporting. How was the clash of generations demonstrated in this brief exchange? How does it relate to your own sense of what's important and your sense of hero worship? For example, do you place an actor who portrays a hero in higher regard than a real-life hero?

RESPONDING IN WRITING

1. Imagine that you are a soldier on the eve of D-Day. Write a fictional letter to your family discussing your mission, duty, fears, and hopes. Consider the values of the day as discussed by the author in the essay you have read.
2. Have two members of the D-Day generation read the essay, if possible. Try to find one male and one female. Discuss their responses and summarize them in note form. Write a 500-word essay exploring their responses.
3. Argue for or against the proposition that there is nothing admirable about the values of the D-Day generation that "expected so little" and whose "assumptions were so modest."
4. Using a search engine, input the word *D-Day* and, by skimming the most promising citation, write a brief history of this formative event in the lives of the generation currently in its seventies. Explain how the event would have had a lasting effect on values, outlook, rituals, and beliefs of that generation.

Boom or Bust?

Dahlia Aguilar

Once thought of as a monolithic group with a strong ethnic identity that set them apart from the mainstream, Hispanics—at least the 18-to-29-year-olds—now venture into the society at large as much as any other group. This assertion is made by the author, a twentysomething freelance writer in Washington, D.C. Aguilar claims you can be aware of your cultural roots while at the same time placing your roots in another culture that is inevitably going to be the one that determines the nation's destiny. You can appreciate your parents' values while forging your own. The fact that this essay was published in a 1993 issue of the magazine *Hispanic* underlies the change in this ethnic group's status. The magazine is a commercial, mainstream publication published in English in the United States; its readership is made up of a population that is adapting to and synthesizing the entire cultural world around them, not merely the one of the family and neighborhood.

PREVIEWING THE ESSAY

Are such well-known figures as Martin Sheen, Edward James Olmos, and Gloria Estafan Hispanic-Americans or just plain Americans? Do we think of Al Pacino or Robert DeNiro as Italian or even Italian-Americans? Aguilar suggests that young Hispanics are closer in spirit and outlook to their non-Hispanic peers than to their parents. To quote the author, "Hispanic twentysomethings are not waiting for a green light or a pat on the back from their elders." Does this go against your image or stereotype of Hispanics? If so, from where do you suppose your concepts arose?

Baby busters, twentysomethings, Generation X—call them what you 1 will. These terms have been used to describe the generation of people ages 18–29 who now trail the baby boomers, those born between the end of World War II and the start of the Korean War. Baby boomers' lives were changed forever by the Civil Rights Movement, the Vietnam War, the sexual revolution, and the start of the Space Age. These movements united a group of young people excited about their struggles, committed to their future, and inspired by the prospect of a new and improved America.

Hispanic twentysomethings have grown up in a country that re- 2 neged on its liberalism, with the election of conservative leadership that lasted over a decade. Their futures have been marked by threats of AIDS, increased racial tension, "Just Say No," and little prospect of the luxuries the baby boomers have come to realize: cars, homes, and comfortable standards of living.

The lives of twentysomethings are marked by conservation, cau- 3 tion, adaptiveness, and uncertainty. They know this because of the massive amounts of information the tube provides, from sources as different as CNN and MTV. Furthermore, the sons and daughters of this country, who make up the largest group of 20 year olds ever in U.S. history, are on the receiving end of a backlash.

Baby boomers describe twentysomethings as lazy, hostile, unedu- 4 cated, anti-authority, apathetic couch potatoes with the attention of—well, a spud. Boomers see twentysomethings shunning the importance of appearance, convention, respect, and deviating from a work ethic that boomers deem necessary to keep this country moving.

"They don't know how to work hard because so many of them 5 had two parents working, and they had more things," says Jessica

Mercado, a 38-year-old sales support manager for Pacific Bell. "They expect things to fall into their laps. They have no objectives, and they're spoiled. When they get into the real world, they're going to have a rude awakening. If not, this country's in serious trouble."

Such comments surprise twentysomethings, who see themselves as the generation that poses the greatest risk to boomers' success and the greatest promise to heal America's wounds. 6

Boomers suggest that anger is one of the major characteristics of busters, and explain that they understand the forces that inspire the nasty attitudes of the twentysomething generation. As children, twentysomethings were stuck between divorced parents, waited at home in the dark for working parents to return, and rotted in front of the television. Their beginnings as adults haven't been much more rosy. They're sustaining economic hardship, finding themselves ill-prepared for college, crashing with mom and dad because they can't find work, and searching to identify heroes or phenomenal events that have shaped them. No wonder they're so screwed up! 7

Twentysomethings agree that those influences shaped them, but they define themselves as a generation far less screwed up than prepared, far less hostile than realistic, and more true to America than America dares admit. Hispanic twentysomethings identify much more strongly with their generation than that of their parents. If Hispanic busters find themselves closer to their non-Hispanic peers than to Hispanic boomers, what does this mean for the Hispanic community in the years to come? 8

For years, Hispanics in the United States have tried to escape being assimilated and fragmented with equal fervor. The parents of twentysomethings wanted their children to live free of the ethnic discrimination and prejudice that hindered their own happiness and success. At the same time, they wanted their children to maintain appreciation and respect for their Hispanic roots. For the most part, Hispanic youth have tried to live up to these expectations. The legislation and activism of the Civil Rights Movement made it possible for collegiate twentysomething Hispanics to experience little or no overt prejudice and discrimination in their lifetimes. Surprisingly, many say most of the discrimination they have experienced has come from older Hispanics and peers. Although some would guess that such experiences desensitize them to the state of Hispanics in this country, twentysomething Hispanics haven't lost their vision of the struggles Hispanics face. 9

A 24-year-old graduate of Notre Dame, Marisa Fernandez is a temporary worker for Arthur Andersen in Chicago and is searching for an entry-level position in public relations. She describes herself as an all-American child who grew up in predominantly Anglo schools and neighborhoods. "A friend once told me that the only thing Hispanic 10 about me is my last name," she says. "In high school and college, I wanted to prove myself without quotas or empowerment. Now that I'm older, I see my friends, both Anglo and Hispanic, retreating back into ethnic pride. I think our generation is more embracing of cultural diversity. I was never into the 'movement' or anything, though. And the majority of my Hispanic peers in college were like me."

Many interviewees avoid using the "a" word—*assimilation*—it inspires images of selling out. The twentysomething generation has not divorced itself from Hispanic culture; they have redefined it. The image of a Hispanic is not one-dimensional for twentysomething Hispanics. They take pride in the diversity of their culture, but by no means will they be judged for or feel guilty about how Hispanic or mainstream they are. They will or will not speak Spanish. They will listen to R.E.M., Orquesta de la Luz, the Spin Doctors, Los Lobos, Public Enemy, Eddie Palmieri, Eric Clapton, The Doors, or the Texas Tornados. 11

Ruben Navarrette Jr., 26, writes for the *Los Angeles Times* and publishes *Hispanic Student,* a national magazine that helps prepare Hispanic high school students for college. He recently completed an account of his college experience, entitled *A Darker Shade of Crimson: Odyssey of a Harvard Chicano,* to be released by Bantam Books in October. Regarding the pressure older Hispanics place on younger generations to speak Spanish, he says, "It's motivated by fear that the older generation is getting left behind by their children. It's a foolish, stupid fear. I would rather have a Lena Cuerrero without Spanish than Michael Dukakis with Spanish. I speak Spanish, but I refuse to hold it up as a litmus test. I probably will teach my children to speak Spanish, but that's because we should know as many languages as we can, not to save my cultural soul." 12

That may be a difficult stretch for some older Hispanics. It means accepting that the Hispanic twentysomethings increasingly find no problems dating outside their ethnicity, having homosexual friends, supporting gender equality, discussing sexuality, and questioning and challenging their elders when they find their behavior absolutely appalling. Many already have crossed the lines of respect often drawn between Hispanic generations. 13

"We watched Nixon with Watergate. We saw the Iran *contra* hearings," Navarrette explains. "We know that older people are not perfect; they have flaws. My father was not similarly convinced. He saw his father as a saint, a god, a perfect being. We're not willing to follow our leaders off the proverbial cliff. We're not likely to say older means wiser. We're willing to try new things." 14

One father of a baby buster agrees. Rick Bela, president of the Hispanic Association on Corporate Responsibility (HACR), praises twentysomethings for their attitudes and talents. "I think they're the 15 products of a new technology. I'm very encouraged and excited about their ability to come up with solutions we've never had before. We haven't been that successful in solving old problems. They provide a new perspective unburdened by the prejudices of history that one generation often passes to the next."

The new agenda includes tolerance for people of different lifestyles, races, sexual orientations, ethnicity, religions, culture, and background. Twentysomethings see older Hispanics as a generation or two of people who complied with and pioneered the Civil Rights Movement in theory, but contradicted it in practice. 16

Aileen Torres, a 21-year-old senior at Columbia University majoring in Latin American and Iberian studies, considers her generation ahead of the civil rights game. "My father was not very accepting of others. He tried to instill his stereotypes of other cultures in me. I chose not to follow his advice. The older generation was less tolerant. The baby boomers didn't do much to put an end to ignorance. Because of them, this country was able to separate, especially people of color. They lied to us about race relations." 17

The lies lit up Los Angeles over a year ago, following the Rodney King verdict. Though most twentysomethings deny being shocked by any event short of nuclear annihilation, most of them cite the riots as an event they will remember like boomers recall the riots of the 1960s. 18

John Negrete, a 24-year-old student at DeVry Technical Institute, says he will never forget when the L.A. riots exploded. "I'm cruising down the freeway like I always do every day after school and see smoke rising everywhere. I turn on the radio and hear them [say], 'L.A.'s on fire. People are rioting,'" he recalls. "When I heard these guys were acquitted—they should have done what was right. They shouldn't have gotten off. My heart dropped. I got off the freeway and called my mom to let her know I was alright. It's going to stand out for the rest of my life. Afterwards, when it started to spread all over the United States, there was immediate hostility. But now people are more open because they see that everyone was getting a bad rap. Everyone wanted to get together with Clean Up L.A. I'd never done anything like that before, but I stood beside people like Edward James Olmos and people from all different backgrounds—Mexican, Korean, black, everyone." 19

These are the kinds of results twentysomethings respond to—collaboration, urgency, unity. If anybody had bothered to ask them—which nobody did—they could have told America the L.A. riots were bound to happen soon. 20

If America listens to the twentysomethings, it probably will find a group of adults with incredible political savvy and collaborative energy. They don't have time to waste. Saddled with the deterioration of 21 the environment, the economy, education, and race relations, they consider themselves cautious, careful, but direct.

Boomers hope to alleviate the burden heaped on the backs of the generation that inevitably will take their place, but twentysomethings don't expect them to make all the changes that need to be made. The boomers can play up a selfish hostility on the part of twentysomethings, but while no one is happy about their future incomes, job prospects, or opportunities to achieve financial prosperity, twentysomethings aren't complaining, emigrating, or planning social revolution. They're coping. 22

Grant Vitale, 27, an assistant to the national leadership coordinator for ASPIRA, a Washington, D.C.–based non-profit organization that serves Latino youth through leadership development and education, shrugs at the problems that cloud his generation's future. "I would definitely say I'm not hostile. As far as pay scales go, I expect them to be narrow. I take a personal approach. These are the cards I've been dealt, but I'm not bitter or angry about it." 23

Even for those busters who are furious about their situation, the focus is less concentrated on laying blame and hanging the culprits than solving the problems and moving on. 24

Hispanic twentysomethings are very similar to their mainstream counterparts. They worry about the state of their future; many anticipate a debt larger than their income. They find cultural diversity is one of their greatest assets. But they won't be caught waiting for a pat on the back. They're too busy for glorification. 25

They're often contradictory, but the differences of opinion are indicative of a generation that agrees to disagree on whether to use a vacuum or a broom—as long as the mess gets cleaned up and everyone lends a helping hand. And twentysomethings are willing to get down and dirty. "Our generation is a non-complacent, nonconformist generation. We're going to put an end to the crap behind politics. We don't want to see history repeated. We're tired of seeing negotiations get nowhere. We're willing to go to any extreme to get the results we want," says Torres. 26

Hispanic twentysomethings are not intimidated by the promise of a future that will be spent living from struggle to struggle. They are willing to sacrifice and contribute efficiently, quickly, and effectively to the changes America faces. The very influences upon which society bases its negative images of this generation are the motivating factors that the generation dubs its attributes. Independence, unity, collaboration, awareness, and service guarantee the survival of Hispanic twentysomethings as leaders of the future. They look forward to cooperating with any organization that refrains from overlooking, misleading, or misrepresenting them. Hispanic twentysomethings are not waiting for a green light or a pat on the back from their elders. They will see their ideals come to fruition. 27

THINKING ABOUT THE ESSAY

1. The first half of this essay offers a comparison and contrast between the way boomers perceive twentysomethings and the way twentysomethings perceive themselves. How does the author develop this comparison/contrast structure? Cite examples of paragraph structure, sentence structure, and the use of descriptive terms.
2. How does Aguilar make the transition from her rhetoric of comparison and contrast to her focus on twentysomethings as a separate entity? What paragraph marks this shift in focus? What other comparison and contrast between groups does she make other than between boomers and twentysomethings? Why is it important to her argument?
3. Have you ever been the target of blame for the shortcomings of your generation? If so, how did it make you feel? How did you respond to the situation? Was your response emotional, intellectual, or both? What was your opinion of the accusing person?
4. Explain the way Aguilar employs definition and illustration to support her thesis. Cite specific paragraphs to support your answer.

RESPONDING IN DISCUSSION

1. Sociologists sometimes refer to personalities as "affiliative" and "dominant." The most steadfast affiliative people identify very strongly with a group; the staunchest dominant people perceive themselves as independent from such identification. Where do you place yourself on this spectrum? What do you believe are the causes of your identification or lack of identification with a group?
2. Do some cultural, ethnic, or religious groups attempt to keep the individual within the fold, or are all groups more or less equal in their desire to maintain group solidarity? What other factors may contribute to this propensity—for example, class, geography, and technological change?
3. Media commentators suggest that media events such as the Rodney King beating and the O. J. Simpson trial and verdict served to divide the nation racially and ethnically. However, the author suggests that it may also have caused young people to line up against the older generation, which did its best to hide the undercurrent of racism in America. To what degree do you blame boomers for poor race relations in America? To what degree do you believe the twentysomething generation is able to bring such hidden issues out in the open?

4. One person interviewed in the essay states, "We know that older people are not perfect; they have flaws. My father was not similarly convinced. He saw his father as a saint, a god, a perfect being." Express your perception of your parents. Do they resemble the attitude of the father cited in the quotation? Why?

RESPONDING IN WRITING

1. Write a 500-word essay entitled "I'm Not Who You Think I Am," exploring some of the perceptions described in the first half of the essay you have just read.
2. Write an extended essay of at least 1,000 words comparing and contrasting yourself to a friend or acquaintance who does not share the same social, cultural, or ethnic roots as you do. Include such issues as respect for one's parents and society, outlook for the future, and trust in government.
3. John Lennon (a former member of the Beatles) once wrote in a song, "Father, you had me, I never had you." Using this title for an essay, explain whether this statement pertains to your own life or to the life of a close friend.
4. Argue for or against the proposition that any discrimination you have faced has come more from the older members of your own culture than from peers of different cultures.
5. Search for information on Latino\a youth on the Web. Try to find sufficient data to profile this generation in a 500–750-word essay.

Stone Soup

Barbara Kingsolver

Biologist, best-selling novelist, and essayist Barbara Kingsolver addresses the "brave new world" of the contemporary family in many of her writings. In "Stone Soup," published in the January 1995 issue of *Parenting,* she raises the interesting premise that the reconfiguration of the family into an amorphous shape of parents, step-parents, stepbrothers and -sisters, and half-brothers and -sisters is, in fact, a positive thing. According to the author, it more nearly resembles the old concept of the extended intergenerational family living in close proximity as was often the case in prior generations. It offers more resilience, latitude, and sense of perspective than the fictional "ideal" family. Kingsolver scoffs at those who claim that today divorce is too easy and that husbands and wives need to attempt to maintain their bonds at all costs. No divorce is a happy one, she claims, and only through the acceptance of a marriage that has "finished" (not failed) can the individual heal marital wounds and recover sufficiently to live a positive life. Kingsolver believes that those who look nostalgically on a past when family security, understanding, and safety were the norm simply don't know the facts about previous generations or are living in an elegiac state of mind based on a reality that never existed.

PREVIEWING THE ESSAY

Kingsolver has been hailed as an original thinker and an innovative, creative stylist. Her writing is replete with imagery, metaphor, allusion, and parable. It is probably a good idea to read this essay twice: first to glean her major argument; and second to consider the *way* she supports her argument through a mixture of personal observation, experience, and historical sources. Note how she weaves the thread of her argument by combining these methods. You may wish to ask, To what degree does her unique style "seduce" the reader into agreeing with her argument? Would her essay be as persuasive if she were a less original writer, or are her basic arguments strong (or weak) enough to stand (or fall) by themselves?

In the catalog of family values, where do we rank an occasion like this? 1
A curly-haired boy who wanted to run before he walked, age seven now, a soccer player scoring a winning goal. He turns to the bleachers with his fists in the air and a smile wide as a gap-toothed galaxy. His own cheering section of grown-ups and kids all leap to their feet and hug each other, delirious with love for this boy. He's Andy, my best friend's son. The cheering section includes his mother and her friends, his brother, his father and stepmother, a stepbrother and stepsister, and a grandparent. Lucky is the child with this many relatives on hand to hail a proud accomplishment. I'm there too, witnessing a family fortune. But in spite of myself, defensive words take shape in my head. I am thinking: I dare *anybody* to call this a broken home.

Families change, and remain the same. Why are our names for 2
home so slow to catch up to the truth of where we live?

When I was a child, I had two parents who loved me without cease. 3
One of them attended every excuse for attention I ever contrived, and the other made it to the ones with higher production values, like piano recitals and appendicitis. So I was a lucky child too. I played with a set of paper dolls called "The Family of Dolls," four in number, who came with the factory-assigned names of Dad, Mom, Sis, and Junior. I think you know what they looked like, at least before I loved them to death and their heads fell off.

Now I've replaced the dolls with a life. I knit my days around my 4
daughter's survival and happiness, and am proud to say her head is still on. But we aren't the Family of Dolls. Maybe you're not, either.

And if not, even though you are statistically no oddity, it's probably been suggested to you in a hundred ways that yours isn't exactly a real family, but an impostor family, a harbinger of cultural ruin, a slapdash substitute—something like counterfeit money. Here at the tail end of our century, most of us are up to our ears in the noisy business of trying to support and love a thing called family. But there's a current in the air with ferocious moral force that finds its way even into political campaigns, claiming there is only one right way to do it, the Way It Has Always Been.

In the face of a thriving, particolored world, this narrow view is so pickled and absurd I'm astonished that it gets airplay. And I'm astonished that it still stings. 5

Every parent has endured the arrogance of a child-unfriendly grump sitting in judgment, explaining what those kids of ours really need (for example, "a good licking"). If we're polite, we move our crew to another bench in the park. If we're forthright (as I am in my mind, only, for the rest of the day), we fix them with a sweet imperious stare and say, "Come back and let's talk about it after you've changed a thousand diapers." 6

But it's harder somehow to shrug off the Family-of-Dolls Family Values crew when they judge (from their safe distance) that divorced people, blended families, gay families, and single parents are failures. That our children are at risk, and the whole arrangement is messy and embarrassing. A marriage that ends is not called "finished," it's called *failed.* The children of this family may have been born to a happy union, but now they are called *the children of divorce.* 7

I had no idea how thoroughly these assumptions overlaid my culture until I went through divorce myself. I wrote to a friend: "This might be worse than being widowed. Overnight I've suffered the same losses—companionship, financial and practical support, my identity as a wife and partner, the future I'd taken for granted. I am lonely, grieving, and hard-pressed to take care of my household alone. But instead of bringing casseroles, people are acting like I had a fit and broke up the family china." 8

Once upon a time I held these beliefs about divorce: that everyone who does it could have chosen not to do it. That it's a lazy way out of marital problems. That it selfishly puts personal happiness ahead of family integrity. Now I tremble for my ignorance. It's easy, in fortunate times, to forget about the ambush that could leave your head reeling: serious mental or physical illness, death in the family, abandonment, financial calamity, humiliation, violence, despair. 9

I started out like any child, intent on being the Family of Dolls. I set upon young womanhood believing in most of the doctrines of my generation: I wore my skirts four inches above the knee. I had that Barbie with her zebra-striped swimsuit and a figure unlike anything 10 found in nature. And I understood the Prince Charming Theory of Marriage, a quest for Mr. Right that ends smack dab where you find him. I did not completely understand that another whole story *begins* there, and no fairy tale prepared me for the combination of bad luck and persistent hope that would interrupt my dream and lead me to other arrangements. Like a cancer diagnosis, a dying marriage is a thing to fight, to deny, and finally, when there's no choice left, to dig in and survive. Casseroles would help. Likewise, I imagine it must be a painful reckoning in adolescence (or later on) to realize one's own true love will never look like the soft-focus fragrance ads because Prince Charming (surprise!) is a princess. Or vice versa. Or has skin the color your parents didn't want you messing with, except in the Crayola box.

It's awfully easy to hold in contempt the straw broken home, and 11
that mythical category of persons who toss away nuclear family for the sheer fun of it. Even the legal terms we use have a suggestion of caprice. I resent the phrase "irreconcilable differences," which suggests a stubborn refusal to accept a spouse's little quirks. This is specious. Every happily married couple I know has loads of irreconcilable differences. Negotiating where to set the thermostat is not the point. A nonfunctioning marriage is a slow asphyxiation. It is waking up despised each morning, listening to the pulse of your own loneliness before the radio begins to blare its raucous gospel that you're nothing if you aren't loved. It is sharing your airless house with the threat of suicide or other kinds of violence, while the ghost that whispers, "Leave here and destroy your children," has passed over every door and nailed it shut. Disassembling a marriage in these circumstances is as much *fun* as amputating your own gangrenous leg. You do it, if you can, to save a life—or two, or more.

I know of no one who really went looking to hoe the harder row, 12
especially the daunting one of single parenthood. Yet it seems to be the most American of customs to blame the burdened for their destiny. We'd like so desperately to believe in freedom and justice for all, we can hardly name that rogue bad luck, even when he's a close enough snake to bite us. In the wake of my divorce, some friends (even a few close ones) chose to vanish, rather than linger within striking distance of misfortune.

But most stuck around, bless their hearts, and if I'm any the wiser 13
for my trials, it's from having learned the worth of steadfast friendship. And also, what not to say. The least helpful question is: "Did you want the divorce, or didn't you?" Did I want to keep that gangrenous leg, or not? How to explain, in a culture that venerates choice: two terrifying options are much worse than none at all. Give me any day the quick hand of cruel fate that will leave me scarred but blameless. As it was, I kept thinking of that wicked third-grade joke in which

some boy comes up behind you and grabs your ear, starts in with a prolonged tug, and asks, "Do you want this ear any longer?"

Still, the friend who holds your hand and says the wrong thing is made of dearer stuff than the one who stays away. And generally, through all of it, you live. My favorite fictional character, Kate Vaiden (in the novel by Reynolds Price), advises: "Strength just comes in one brand—you stand up at sunrise and meet what they send you and keep your hair combed." 14

Once you've weathered the straits, you get to cross the tricky juncture from casualty to survivor. If you're on your feet at the end of a year or two, and have begun putting together a happy new existence, those friends who were kind enough to feel sorry for you when you needed it must now accept you back to the ranks of the living. If you're truly blessed, they will dance at your second wedding. Everybody else, for heaven's sake, should stop throwing stones. 15

Arguing about whether nontraditional families deserve pity or tolerance is a little like the medieval debate about left-handedness as a mark of the devil. Divorce, remarriage, single parenthood, gay parents, and blended families simply are. They're facts of our time. Some of the reasons listed by sociologists for these family reconstructions are: the idea of marriage as a romantic partnership rather than a pragmatic one; a shift in women's expectations, from servility to self-respect and independence; and longevity (prior to antibiotics no marriage was expected to last many decades—in Colonial days the average couple lived to be married less than twelve years). Add to all this, our growing sense of entitlement to happiness and safety from abuse. Most would agree these are all good things. Yet their result—a culture in which serial monogamy and the consequent reshaping of families are the norm—gets diagnosed as "failing." 16

For many of us, once we have put ourselves Humpty-Dumpty–wise back together again, the main problem with our reorganized family is that other people think we have a problem. My daughter tells me the only time she's uncomfortable about being the child of divorced parents is when her friends say they feel sorry for her. It's a bizarre sympathy, given that half the kids in her school and nation are in the same boat, pursuing childish happiness with the same energy as their married-parent peers. When anyone asks how *she* feels about it, she spontaneously lists the benefits: our house is in the country and we have a dog, but she can go to her dad's neighborhood for the urban thrills of a pool and sidewalks for roller-skating. What's more, she has three sets of grandparents! 17

Why is it surprising that a child would revel in a widened family and the right to feel at home in more than one house? Isn't it the opposite that should worry us—a child with no home at all, or too few 18 resources to feel safe? The child at risk is the one whose parents are too immature themselves to guide wisely; too diminished by poverty to nurture; too far from opportunity to offer hope. The number of children in the U.S. living in poverty at this moment is almost unfathomably large: twenty percent. There are families among us that need help all right, and by no means are they new on the landscape. The rate at which teenage girls had babies in 1957 (ninety-six per thousand) was twice what it is now. That remarkable statistic is ignored by the religious right—probably because the teen birth rate was cut in half mainly by legalized abortion. In fact, the policy gatekeepers who coined the phrase "family values" have steadfastly ignored the desperation of too-small families, and since 1979 have steadily reduced the amount of financial support available to a single parent. But, this camp's most outspoken attacks seem aimed at the notion of families getting too complex, with add-ons and extras such as a gay parent's partner, or a remarried mother's new husband and his children.

To judge a family's value by its tidy symmetry is to purchase a book for its cover. There's no moral authority there. The famous family comprised by Dad, Mom, Sis, and Junior living as an isolated economic unit is not built on historical bedrock. In *The Way We Never Were,* Stephanie Coontz writes, "Whenever people propose that we go back to the traditional family, I always suggest that they pick a ballpark date for the family they have in mind." Colonial families were tidily disciplined, but their members (meaning everyone but infants) labored incessantly and died young. Then the Victorian family adopted a new division of labor, in which women's role was domestic and children were allowed time for study and play, but this was an upper-class construct supported by myriad slaves. Coontz writes, "For every nineteenth-century middle-class family that protected its wife and child within the family circle, there was an Irish or German girl scrubbing floors . . . A Welsh boy mining coal to keep the home-baked goodies warm, a black girl doing the family laundry, a black mother and child picking cotton to be made into clothes for the family, and a Jewish or an Italian daughter in a sweatshop making 'ladies' dresses or artificial flowers for the family to purchase." 19

The abolition of slavery brought slightly more democratic arrangements, in which extended families were harnessed together in cottage industries; at the turn of the century came a steep rise in child labor in mines and sweatshops. Twenty percent of American children lived in orphanages at the time; their parents were not necessarily dead, but couldn't afford to keep them. 20

During the Depression and up to the end of World War II, many millions of U.S. households were more multigenerational than nuclear. Women my grandmother's age were likely to live with a fluid assortment of elderly relatives, in-laws, siblings, and children. In 21 many cases they spent virtually every waking hour working in the company of other women—a companionable scenario in which it would be easier, I imagine, to tolerate an estranged or difficult spouse. I'm reluctant to idealize a life of so much hard work and so little spousal intimacy, but its advantage may have been resilience. A family so large and varied would not easily be brought down by a single blow: it could absorb a death, long illness, an abandonment here or there, and any number of irreconcilable differences.

The Family of Dolls came along midcentury as a great American experiment. A booming economy required a mobile labor force and demanded that women surrender jobs to returning soldiers. Families came to be defined by a single breadwinner. They struck out for single-family homes at an earlier age than ever before, and in unprecedented numbers they raised children in suburban isolation. The nuclear family was launched to sink or swim. 22

More than a few sank. Social historians corroborate that the suburban family of the postwar economic boom, which we have recently selected as our definition of "traditional," was no panacea. Twenty-five percent of Americans were poor in the mid-1950s, and as yet there were no food stamps. Sixty percent of the elderly lived on less than $1,000 a year, and most had no medical insurance. In the sequestered suburbs, alcoholism and sexual abuse of children were far more widespread than anyone imagined. 23

Expectations soared, and the economy sagged. It's hard to depend on one other adult for everything, come what may. In the last three decades, that amorphous, adaptable structure we call "family" has been reshaped once more by economic tides. Compared with fifties families, mothers are far more likely now to be employed. We are statistically more likely to divorce, and to live in blended families or other extranuclear arrangements. We are also more likely to plan and space our children, and to rate our marriages as "happy." We are less likely to suffer abuse without recourse, or to stare out at our lives through a glaze of prescription tranquilizers. Our aged parents are less likely to be destitute, and we're half as likely to have a teenage daughter turn up a mother herself. All in all, I would say that if "intact" in modern family-values jargon means living quietly desperate in the bell jar, then hip-hip-hooray for "broken." A neat family model constructed to service the Baby Boom economy seems to be returning gradually to a grand, lumpy shape that human families apparently have tended toward since they first took root in the Olduvai Gorge. We're social animals, deeply fond of companionship, and children love best to run in packs. If there is a *normal* for humans, at all, I expect it looks like two or three Families of Dolls, connected variously by kinship and passion, shuffled like cards and strewn over several shoeboxes. 24

The sooner we can let go the fairy tale of families functioning perfectly in isolation, the better we might embrace the relief of community. Even the admirable parents who've stayed married through thick and thin are very likely, at present, to incorporate other adults into their families—household help and baby-sitters if they can afford them or neighbors and grandparents if they can't. For single parents, this support is the rock-bottom definition of family. And most parents who have split apart, however painfully, still manage to maintain family continuity for their children, creating in many cases a boisterous phenomenon that Constance Ahrons in her book *The Good Divorce* calls the "binuclear family." Call it what you will—when ex-spouses beat swords into plowshares and jump up and down at a soccer game together, it makes for happy kids. 25

Cinderella, look, who needs her? All those evil stepsisters? That story always seemed like too much cotton-picking fuss over clothes. A childhood tale that fascinated me more was the one called "Stone Soup," and the gist of it is this: Once upon a time, a pair of beleaguered soldiers straggled home to a village empty-handed, in a land ruined by war. They were famished, but the villagers had so little they shouted evil words and slammed their doors. So the soldiers dragged out a big kettle, filled it with water, and put it on a fire to boil. They rolled a clean round stone into the pot, while the villagers peered through their curtains in amazement. 26

"What kind of soup is that?" they hooted. 27

"Stone soup," the soldiers replied. "Everybody can have some when it's done." 28

"Well, thanks," one matron grumbled, coming out with a shriveled carrot. "But it'd be better if you threw this in." 29

And so on, of course, a vegetable at a time, until the whole suspicious village managed to feed itself grandly. 30

Any family is a big empty pot, save for what gets thrown in. Each stew turns out different. Generosity, a resolve to turn bad luck into good, and respect for variety—these things will nourish a nation of children. Name-calling and suspicion will not. My soup contains a rock or two of hard times, and maybe yours does too. I expect it's a heck of a bouillabaise. 31

THINKING ABOUT THE ESSAY

1. Consider the structure of your own family. Does it resemble the one described in the cheering section of the soccer game that the author alludes to in the first paragraph? If so, why? If not, how is it different?

2. Kingsolver suggests that society cannot keep up with the changing social structures it contains. How does this idea resonate in your own life? What are the merits of being a member of a broad-based family that may exist owing to divorce? Consider your response either from personal experience or experience of your friends.
3. The famous psychologist Jerome Bruner claims we have two ways of thinking: the "paradigmatic" way (which means thinking by means of ordering, classifying, and abstracting) and the "narrative" way (which means thinking in terms of stories, characters, plots, and drama). In which of these two ways does the author construct her essay? Cite specific aspects of Kingsolver's essay to support your claim. Do you have a preference for either of these two methods of presenting ideas? If so, which? How does your preference affect your response to the essay?
4. Interpret the parable that the author provides at the end of the essay. What does it mean? What is its relevance to the overall theme of the essay?

RESPONDING IN DISCUSSION

1. The author suggests that there is far too much debate on the health of the middle-class family when the true victims of society (the poor, single-parent, at-risk families) are the ones we should be most concerned about. Discuss whether this is a fair way of dividing concerns about the health of American society. Should we address issues that affect our most vulnerable citizens first, or does each social class deserve equal attention?
2. The author claims that the idea that we live in a "fairy tale of families functioning perfectly in isolation" is a destructive one. Divide into groups of three or four and discuss whether this is indeed a fairy tale or a necessary evil in the light of the "dog-eat-dog" society we live in.
3. Discuss in small groups whether it is the configuration or contours of a family that distinguish its health or the personal issues of each family member that determine the psychological health of the family. Regardless of your view, however, discuss how the family as a group can assist the individual and how an individual family member can contribute toward the health of the group.
4. The author cites evidence that females in a family had time for leisure only when there was an exploited housekeeper to attend to the difficult chores of running a household. In groups of three or four, discuss whether there are any "unrecognized" household helpers who enable your family to lead a more culturally or socially enriched life. If your family lacks such an individual,

discuss how your lifestyle would be different with the addition of one.

5. Discuss your own family's attitude toward divorce. What cultural, social, ethnic, or other traditional values contribute to this attitude? Discuss whether you basically agree or disagree with the view of your family. Explain the relevance of generational differences to this issue.

RESPONDING IN WRITING

1. Write a journal entry describing an incident you viewed between a married couple (either your parents or another couple) that provided you with an insight into married life. First, describe as specifically as possible the event. Then relate how you translated that event into a generalization about the marriage institution.
2. Argue for or against the proposition that Kingsolver's essay has a major flaw because, while it discusses the merits of the new extended family, it fails to address the inner conflicts that lie within all members of a family, whether it is a traditional or nontraditional one. Be sure to support your arguments.
3. Interview a member of the D-Day generation as described in Noonan's essay in this section. Ask the respondent to compare and contrast the institution of marriage during the 1950s with that of today. Write a descriptive essay based on your interview.
4. Using a search engine, try inputting the word *family* and related words like *sister, stepfather, half-brother,* and similar combinations. What does the number of hits for each search tell you? Skim some of the sites the engine provides you. How open is cyberculture to nontraditional families? Write a report on your findings.

CONNECTIONS: FOR WRITING AND RESEARCH

1. Peggy Noonan describes the D-Day generation as a stoic one that expected little and respected institutions such as work and government. By contrast, Levine examines a different generation, one whose values are developed as a result of entirely different experience. To what do you ascribe the difference between the two generations?
2. Zill and Robinson claim that Generation X is becoming more community-minded, that is, rather than "saving the world" as their parents were bent on doing, they are more concerned with helping their locality. To what degree is this true for yourself and your friends?

3. Kingsolver discusses "intergenerational" families in her essay. Conduct a computer search on this subject, download relevant articles, and write an argumentative essay in which you support or reject the idea that intergenerational families are viable in American society today.
4. The essay by Zill and Robinson and the one by Aguilar focus on changing dynamics among twentysomethings of today compared to previous generations. Aguilar focuses on one ethnic group to which she belongs. Zill and Robinson, on the other hand, use data gleaned from polls that do not report on respondents' class, ethnicity, or race. How does this variable impact on the "accuracy" of each one's conclusions?
5. There are many ways of presenting arguments. Some authors tend to favor data and historical fact; others employ the "emotional touch" created via anecdote, personal experience, and description. Select two essays from this section: one that tends toward generalization and abstraction, and one that is more personal and emotional. Write a comparison-and-contrast essay explaining how the essays' authors use strategies to support their arguments.

2

CYBERNATION

Going on-line may become among the greatest social transformations in history. While the baby boomers were considered the first generation to grow up with television, Generation Xers may one day hold the distinction for being the first generation to be hooked into cyberspace. During the 1960s, social critic Marshall McLuhan claimed, "The medium is the message." That is, the form in which one communicates is more important than the content of what is communicated. So, for example, if it takes you five minutes to collect all the necessary source material for a research paper by going on-line rather than flipping through old-fashioned card catalogs, one could argue the time saved because of the new technology far outweighs the issue of whether you printed out your journal articles on a printer or read them from a weighty tome in the library stacks. But with change in technology comes change in society. And with the Cyber Age upon us, it even means learning a whole new vocabulary: FAQs, URLs, Web pages, Gophers, search engines, modems, and so forth. McLuhan also claimed that once a society becomes accustomed to its new technology, the technology becomes second nature so that we grow numb to its innovations. For example, how much awareness and effort do you put into turning on your TV remote control? In the essays that follow, we shall look at a few contours of this new "country."

The State in Cyberspace

Bill Gates

Bill Gates may be considered the guru of the computer industry, if not cyberspace itself. He is the richest man in the world and chief executive officer of the computer product company Microsoft. When Mr. Gates speaks, the ears of the computer industry listen. The following essay, first published in the spring 1995 edition of *New Perspectives Quarterly,* is a blend of political recommendations and business sense. It is meant to offer guidance for government and industry, as the inevitable growth of cyberspace continues.

PREVIEWING THE ESSAY

Do you know how a computer is connected to the information superhighway? How could less technologically advanced countries take advantage of the benefits of cyberspace with its ability to transmit multimedia information over long distances virtually instantaneously? For whom are such issues important?

Government has quite a few roles to play in cyberspace, particularly in setting a regulatory environment that encourages companies to invest in broadband information infrastructure—optic fiber cables and transfer technology capable of transmitting unprecedented amounts of data in two-way communication at rapid speed. 1

For most of the developed economies that doesn't involve substantial government money, but deregulation, for example, of the telephone and cable industries so that they can operate outside of their traditionally constricted realms in any way—voice, video and interactive communications—that services their consumers. 2

The approach will differ from country to country. In the United States today, broadcast television, cable and telephone systems are highly regulated. The central issue is thus unleashing the phone companies to provide other services, such as video, or unleashing companies on the video side to provide communications services. In Germany, all those services are within one government entity at this point. So, the approach they take will end up being different than in the US where there are multiple phone companies that want to invade each other's territory as well as a very strong and independent cable industry. 3

The approach is yet again different in a place like Singapore, where I just visited. They are not engaged in much debate about all this; there will be no referendum. They have just decided to do it. Their leaders fully understand that a broadband multimedia network 4 that will vastly multiply the possibilities of two-way, interactive communications is something a competitive future requires.

In many countries, the development of a digital infrastructure 5
gets tied into privatization efforts. Because private investors must have an incentive to invest in the future, governments must take a long-term approach to infrastructure. Particularly in countries that don't have much cable TV, there may well be a stronger role for government in infrastructure investment than elsewhere.

One thing that is worthwhile is pushing countries without exten- 6
sive cable networks to use ISDN (an enhancing technology that will enable digital transmission on phone lines—ed.) to connect up personal computers. If countries would take a high-volume/low-price approach to ISDN they would be moving toward interactive multimedia potential without having to lay optic fiber cable into every house.

Though the approaches will differ, all governments have to estab- 7
lish a reliable set of rules that opens things up and makes it clear that there will be tremendous business opportunities in developing infrastructure. That is probably the most important thing. As in many areas, what happens in the US will have a ripple effect; deregulation here will be a strong motivator for other countries to get moving quickly.

In addition to that, governments can lead the way in using inter- 8
active networks to reduce their own bureaucracy and paperwork. Governments can also help shape the way medical care and education are delivered through seeing to it that the fullest advantage is taken of new forms of electronic communications to disseminate knowledge as widely as possible.

Necessarily, governments have a key role, as with the already ex- 9
isting telephone systems, in ensuring the privacy and security of communication as well as universal service. Here, each society will have to make a political decision as to where to strike the balance between individual privacy and social order. Will the police, for example, be able to access and decode transactions? The consumer, the citizen and the business person need to know how much privacy they will be able to retain on these new information systems.

Finally, an important picture to get in one's mind is that the "so- 10
called information revolution" is not a big bang, but an evolutionary process. Every year there is going to be progress that will lead from on-line services to ISDN to broadband services. As the personal computer gets better, as productivity grows, as more information goes on line electronically, as the CD becomes a publishing platform for sales catalogues, for museums or for textbooks, we are learning how to present information electronically. All that experience carries over in the construction of a connected world as we reach higher and higher bandwidth at lower cost to the consumer.

THINKING ABOUT THE ESSAY

1. What is the thesis of the essay? Where in the essay is it most clearly stated or implied?
2. How many of the terms in the essay did you find unfamiliar or ambiguous? What strategies, if any, did you take in learning more about them?
3. Who is the intended audience of this essay? What elements in the essay led you to your conclusion?
4. According to Gates, what political and economic system or systems have the greatest ability to harness the power and benefits of cyberspace?
5. Describe in your own words the difference between the concepts of "revolution" and "evolution" as they are used in the essay.

RESPONDING IN DISCUSSION

1. Divide into groups of three and four, and create a simulation game whereby the group role-plays a government agency about to make recommendations on the introduction of a cyberspace environment in your country. Who will develop the infrastructure? Who will invest in it? Who will be its beneficiaries? What will be its functions? Write up your plan and discuss it with the rest of the class.
2. Discuss those elements of cyberspace that will one day be considered necessities, and those that will be considered luxuries or diversions.
3. Discuss the degree to which government should assist parents in developing means of censoring adult-oriented material in cyberspace.
4. Discuss whether providing loans to third world countries to develop their own cybersystems should be considered a form of foreign aid.

RESPONDING IN WRITING

1. Write an expository essay, discussing the ways cyberspace can help you communicate more effectively with representatives of the government.
2. Argue for or against the proposition that the United States should impose information sanctions on hostile countries as it imposes trade sanctions.
3. Argue for or against the proposition that commercial on-line services are analogous to commercial television, that is, they will

restrict "programming" and information to those elements they believe will attract the largest numbers of people.

4. Argue for or against the proposition that the government should provide subsidies to families too poor to afford their own hardware and software to wire their homes for cyberspace.
5. Connect to Microsoft Corporation's site on the Web. Download information on the company, and write a report on what you have found.
6. Enter the entire phrase "freedom of the press" into a search engine and explore some of the sites provided to you. Do you personally feel some of these sites need protection from government regulation? Write a brief essay defending your position.

The Web: Infotopia or Marketplace?

Peter McGrath

The following essay appeared in a long section of the January 27, 1997, issue of *Newsweek*. Entitled "America 2000," the section was devoted to a futuristic assessment of what the nation will look like at the turn of the century. In his article, Peter McGrath examines the connections between the Internet (which was conceived originally as an information system) and the World Wide Web's commercial implications. He considers the possibility that "commerce will soon drown information on the Internet," but also explains the subtle power of cyberspace to constantly reinvent itself. As he admits, we ultimately must accept the Internet "on trust."

PREVIEWING THE ESSAY

Do you believe, as McGrath does, that the Internet increasingly targets consumers instead of providing a free flow of information? Are the two functions necessarily incompatible? Explain your answer.

A current conceit says that Internet time must be reckoned in dog 1
years. The pace of change is so fast that one year on the Internet is like seven years in any other medium. By this scheme, it has been nearly a century since the Internet was born. It has been 14 years since the emergence of the World Wide Web as an electronic-publishing vehicle. And by the year 2000, the Internet will have undergone another two decades' worth of growth and development.

Every step has aroused great expectations. Some thought it would 2
usher in an era of cooperation, as both work and play became digitalized.

Others saw the "citizen-controlled" Internet as a radical challenge to establishment control of information outlets, or as a civic marketplace. In his book *Life After Television,* supply-side theorist George Gilder says the networked personal computer will transform capitalism into "a healing force in the present crisis of home and family, culture and community."

But today the Internet itself is being transformed—into something closer to a marketplace. Advertisements and sales brochures are proliferating among the Webzines and newsgroups and bulletin boards. "Cyberstores" offer everything from music CDs to certificates of deposit. The most interesting new technologies are those that foster transactions. As the vendors and the marketers crowd their way into the bitstream, is the Internet on the verge of becoming just one more mass commercial medium? Does anything remain of the original Infotopia? 3

It is almost a truism that no new communications medium turns out the way its inventors imagined. The developers of the Bell System conceived of the telephone as a business tool; they were both surprised and appalled when their customers diverted it to the "trivial" purpose of social conversation. The radio was meant to be a wireless telegraph, a medium of two-way messaging; none of its creators anticipated broadcasting and mass programming. Television began as radio with pictures; early programs were actually simulcasts, video transmissions of a radio program on a radio set with a radio audience. It took years for broadcasters to discover television as a medium with its own unique properties and powers. 4

So it is with the Internet. The original goal, in the 1960s, was a sharing of resources. The founders of network computing wanted researchers at Stanford to be able to use software on a machine at MIT, even where the two computers had incompatible operating systems. From there it was a short step to exchanges of messages and documents—the origin of e-mail. Soon the Internet became a reference medium, where research papers could be read by anyone on the network. It was the World Wide Web that brought the Internet into the consumer marketplace. Developed in 1990 as a system for delivering a graphics-rich, pagelike file over conventional telephone lines using Internet technology, the Web lured traditional news and entertainment companies into electronic-publishing ventures. The potential audience was vast: by the end of 1996, according to Jupiter Communications, a New York–based research-and-consulting firm, more than 15 million North American households had some form of online access. In the year 2000, the projection is that North America will have 38 million online households—more than one third of all households, most of them affluent. 5

But a funny thing happened on the way to Infotopia. The costs of electronic publication proved higher than expected, and the receipts 6 turned out to be negligible. The Web is awash in information, much of it created by small start-up companies, and the competition has made it difficult for traditional media companies to charge for access to their Web sites. Besides, many of the early Internet users were devout believers in the proposition that all information should be free, and that attitude still lingers. The result is that the Web is a marketplace of fierce price resistance. Last September *The Wall Street Journal,* for example, began charging a subscription fee of $49 a year for its online edition ($29 for subscribers to the printed newspaper) and saw a dramatic decline in its Web readership. Even *Slate,* Microsoft's political Webzine, abandoned its plans to sell subscriptions.

At the same time, advertising has failed to take up the slack. Despite the attractive demographics of online households, the Web is not yet a mass medium. Advertisers are suspicious of the Web, too, because its interactive qualities make it easy for consumers simply to bypass an ad. They are also uncomfortable with audience measurements in the new medium; the industry has yet no standard comparable to those used in print, radio and television. As reality sets in, many Web-site operators are scaling back expectations. Microsoft officials admitted recently that they expect to lose millions of dollars a year on MSNBC for at least the next four years. 7

But on another front, Web technology fosters commerce. The same interactive function that makes advertisers nervous leads to a new kind of marketing—the transactional advertisement. An example of this is a Web-based service called Auto-By-Tel, which allows prospective buyers to search for information about car models that match their preferences, then sends their names to the appropriate dealers near them. The dealers pay for the service and in return get qualified leads that would cost them far more to acquire through conventional means. In the case of small consumer goods that customers don't feel they need to inspect before purchase, the software can actually complete the sale for home delivery. The amazon.com Web site has created a successful market niche by selling books. The model is essentially mail-order retailing. 8

With the development of secure transmissions of credit information—Visa and MasterCard are jointly testing a system scheduled for introduction by early 1998—transactions will play an increasingly large part in Internet activity. The Web is particularly effective at selling services backed by research, such as discount stock trading, an area with several successful sites already, including e.Schwab and a Web-only company called E*Trade. Financial services generally lend themselves to Web marketing, as do travel services, because the transactions can be supported by extensive computer databases of useful information. And every month sees the introduction of new software to automate transactions. 9

The latest adaptation of Web technology is for business-to- 10
business marketing. This is done through "extranets," extensions of a company's private, internal network (or intranet) to corporate customers and suppliers. Extranets are a hot subject for companies like Netscape, the creator of the most widely used Web browser, and America Online, the country's largest commercial online service. An example of an apparently successful extranet is the one built by General Electric to sell machine and appliance parts to its customers; GE was expecting 1996 online sales of about $1 billion.

With such a flurry of activity, it's easy to imagine that commerce 11
will soon drown information on the Internet. That won't necessarily happen, but almost certainly the Web will contain a rising tide of information subsidized in some way by commercial activity. Advertising has always underwritten the largest share of most media companies' costs. The question is whether Web advertising will ever reach a volume that can support large investments in reporting news, building deep information databases and creating new entertainment. Many analysts believe the critical mass to be about 30 million households, which suggests that the Web will become a true mass medium about the year 2000. Nicholas Negroponte, founder of the cutting-edge MIT Media Lab and author of *Being Digital,* argues that the Web by its very nature may be too personalized ever to be a mass medium, but he believes that commerce may flourish there anyway, with advertising targeted to small market niches or even individual customers.

This blurring of the line between "editorial" content and advertis- 12
ing is precisely what worries most traditional publishers. The Web is already flooded with "information" sites that are centers of partisan pleading and crackpot theories masquerading as facts. In an environment without many of the traditional markers of high-quality content, how is the hapless consumer to tell the difference? The answer is, once again, a commercial one: brand names. As the Web expands and the number of "publishers" grows, brand names that are known and trusted will become progressively more important. Everything on the Web is ultimately about trust, says Negroponte. "We trust brands, rightly or wrongly. We trust friends . . . And we trust our own experience, which may be the most faulty of the lot. I have these same three choices in cyberspace."

In the dog years to come, cyberspace will continue its transforma- 13
tions. We can expect a rash of new "non-PC devices," such as Internet TVs and Internet telephones. The Internet TV in particular is a promising device, if only because it would benefit from the growing market in Web-based videogames—likely to be a hot area itself by the year 2000, as new video-compression techniques increase the realism of on line game-playing. Commerce, too, will continue to thrive, especially in the area of consumer purchases, which will benefit from the

development of electronic cash and "smart" cards that allow for "micropayments" of as little as 25 cents. We can also expect that commercial activities will enable further inroads into personal privacy, as customers willingly put more and more of their spending and consumption patterns into databases. Is that a troubling prospect? It depends on our confidence in new encryption techniques, and on Web sites' sincerity about deploying them. As Negroponte says, everything on the Web is ultimately about trust.

THINKING ABOUT THE ESSAY

1. What is the essay's thesis? Where is it stated?
2. How would you explain the style and tone of this essay? Do you find it difficult to follow? Why?
3. How does McGrath organize this essay? Where specifically does he employ comparison and contrast; analysis of process; analysis of causes and effects?
4. What is the "conceit" that links the introductory and concluding paragraphs? How effective is this strategy?

RESPONDING IN DISCUSSION

1. In small groups of classmates, review McGrath's essay and list all of the possible uses of the Internet that he mentions. Which of these applications seem most significant as you consider the technological future?
2. Which types of readers would respond most readily to this essay, and why? Are there groups or cultures for whom the essay would be largely irrelevant? Explain.
3. In paragraph 4 McGrath states, "It is almost a truism that no new communications medium turns out the way its inventors imagined." How can you imagine the use of the Internet in the 21st century?
4. McGrath argues in his essay that consumerism has penetrated Internet culture. What evidence does he provide? If buying things on the Internet can be done more easily and cheaply than in a store, is this not a practical use of "information"? Explain your position.

RESPONDING IN WRITING

1. Write an essay on the impact of advertising on Internet culture. Scan the World Wide Web, noting the types of advertising that

appear and their relative effectiveness. Incorporate this information in your essay.

2. Compare and contrast McGrath's tone in this essay and that of Bill Gates in his article at the beginning of the chapter.
3. If you disagree with McGrath's thesis or with a specific aspect of his essay, write a rebuttal, offering your own opinions. Provide evidence in support of your position.
4. Select a product—for instance, automobiles—and consider how it is advertised on television, in the newspapers, and on the Web. Write an essay on the similarities and differences in the presentations from medium to medium.

Life in Cyburbia

Randall Rothenberg

Going on-line is no longer an activity reserved for computer nerds, high tech aficionados, or computer scientists. In fact, Randall Rothenberg, in this essay first published in the February 1996 issue of *Esquire,* introduces us to a town where just about everyone is wired into the Internet. For the average citizen of Blacksburg, Virginia, going on-line is becoming as ordinary an activity as talking on the telephone. True, they had the incentive of being provided universal access by an experimental venture initiated by a nearby university, but many everyday citizens who one might think would be reticent about having this new-fangled gizmo placed in their homes have jumped at the chance. What will be the end result of this social experiment? After speaking to some of the locals who use the service and to some experts from various universities, the author offers some thoughts of his own.

PREVIEWING THE ESSAY

It has been written that the advent of air conditioning reduced public discourse in urban areas, for it ended the era of open windows that gave people direct access to their neighbors. Could the use of the Internet cause similar changes in our society? Has it altered the psychological dimension of your own communication habits?

Lions look pale and green under fluorescent light—especially when they're aging and Caucasian, as are most of the forty-one citizens gathered in the back room of the local Best Western for the bimonthly meeting of the Blacksburg, Virginia, Lions Club. Scientists and doctors abound—at my table alone sit three veterinarians—but 1 that doesn't alter the sacraments that open every such conclave. The Tail Twister, a stern gentleman answering to the name Lion Andy, stalks from table to table, levying loose-change fines on those who have neglected to wear club pins in their left lapels. After "My Country 'Tis of Thee" and the Pledge of Allegiance, eighty-three-year-old Lion Roy entreats the Lord to "help us be caring, loving, and serving in the Lionist tradition." Then, following the roast beef, potatoes au gratin, string beans, and peanut cake, Lion Matt, a dentist and the club's program chairman, introduces the guest speaker, a young woman whose message to the old men is as unsparing as it is enthusiastic: Get wired now.

"Forty percent of our town is connected to the Internet!" proclaims Susanne Huff, an administrator of the Blacksburg Electronic Village—the BEV, to its friends—a cyberspace equivalent of the physical municipality in which she and her audience reside. A grand experimental venture by the local government, Bell Atlantic, and Virginia Polytechnic Institute, the BEV is designed to "enhance the quality of people's lives by hooking them up with each other and with local businesses and with community groups," Susanne explains. She is as evangelistic as she is pert. "We started out with one hundred members. Now we have eleven thousand! We have doctors, lawyers, restaurants, grocery stores, on-line. People working at home and sending stuff in to their bosses. It's amazing what's going on! I can dial up a local call and pop over to France or Japan or anywhere I want to. Visit their libraries, download information. We're trying to enhance our lives. We're just using that line to connect all of us!" 2

Her breathless pitch concluded, she takes questions from the visibly excited crowd. Can you really order groceries on-line and have them delivered? Are there delays in accessing information from overseas? 3

Lion Matt is skeptical. "I don't know enough about what 'going on-line' means," he says. White-haired, hard-of-hearing Lion Roy does, and he is indignant. 4

"I'd like to know something," says Lion Roy, a former plant scientist. "After this talk of words like *excitement* and *enthusiasm,* I'm interested in Bible study, in business, and in investments. I'm not remotely interested in paying my bills in any way other than the way I do now. I don't want to buy anything I can't touch." He fairly spits his grievance. *"I can't for the life of me see what I can get out of this!"* 5

A murmur dashes from table to table. Finally, a Lion roars from across the room: "That's what they told Henry Ford, Roy!" 6

I have come to Blacksburg, Virginia, the most wired city in the United States, because, like old Lion Roy, I dangle uncomfortably between what the late British novelist C. P. Snow called "the two cultures," the intellectual and the scientific, whose lack of mutual 7 understanding is cleaving the country into warring factions. At issue is technology—the microchips that are invading us from every direction, forcing us to reshape our institutions, our lives, and our culture to accommodate them.

Don't get me wrong. I love computers and the Internet. In October, a typical month, I spent more than fifty hours on-line, sending E-mail, participating in conferences, and downloading poetry and pornography. But I can no longer ignore the ravages that seem to derive from the vaunted new technologies: the disappearing jobs, the social separation, the interpersonal malice, the growing preference among our political leaders and cultural avatars for virtual reality over, well, real reality. 8

To those who've fallen prey to the scientific culture's propaganda, these fears are irrational. The Wired Ones—my term for those who follow the you-ain't-hip-if-you-ain't-on-line credo of *Wired* magazine—tell us confidently that you cannot stop technology, should not question it, and will ultimately benefit from it. They claim support from history, economics, and common sense and consider those who resist computers to be at best curmudgeons, at worst Unabombers. Defy technology if you must, but prepare to be, as *Wired*'s executive editor, Kevin Kelly, avers, "noble but marginal." 9

Were their pronouncements empty blather, the Wired Ones themselves would be marginal. But time and money are being spent to further their vision. Computers sit in about twenty-three million homes in this country, a number that's expected to grow by about 24 percent a year during the next three years. Eleven out of every hundred adults in the U.S. and Canada found their way onto the Internet last summer and autumn, according to a Nielsen survey, spending an average of five and a half hours a week on-line. This vast potential market has lured the local telephone companies to commit up to $150 billion to wire the nation with fiber-optic cable that can deliver the Net to every living room in the nation. By late November, investors had plowed $75 billion of their own money into the top three publicly traded Internet companies, an amount greater than these fledgling enterprises were worth. 10

What *Newsweek* has dubbed "technomania" has flooded from the geeky margins of society into the very heart of our political, intellectual, and social life. *The New York Times* devotes a weekly section almost entirely to the Internet. Once the domain of the überhip, World Wide Web sites have become de rigueur for marketers as stodgy as Chemical Bank (http://www.spectra.net/mall/chemical) and Kellogg's cereals (http://www.kelloggs.com). A book by a dyslexic MIT professor who believes "the change from atoms to bits" is both "irrevocable and unstoppable" shoots to the top of the best-seller lists. And the House of Representatives has elected a Speaker who wants to cut 11

Medicare, Medicaid, and educational support but talks of the need for a "missionary spirit" that would tell "the poorest child in America, 'Internet's for you.'"

The opposition's pockets may not be so deep, but its voices are loud and influential. In books with titles like *The End of Work* and *The Cult of Information,* they tell us that technology is not empowering but diminishing us. It is no longer creating jobs, they say, but taking them away. Some, harking back to the nineteenth-century Yorkshiremen who smashed the new, mechanized mills that had taken their jobs, proudly call themselves neo-Luddites and, like their self-styled leader Kirkpatrick Sale, happily hammer computers into the kinds of bits you can see and appreciate. 12

The public is listening. About one quarter of all Americans say they have mixed feelings about computers, according to a recent opinion poll by Princeton Survey Research Associates. If employment and incomes continue to waste away, those numbers will certainly grow. The division of the workforce into the technologically adept and the uneducated and unemployable has become "the hottest unresolved topic in economics today," says Stanford University economist Gavin Wright. "You will find many economists, perhaps the majority, who would say it's technology that's eliminating the well-paying ordinary jobs and more or less putting people in minimum-wage or low-pay work, where most of the new jobs are available." 13

In Blacksburg, they have no such fears. 14

Bill Ellenbogen, a six-foot-five-inch, 260-pound leviathan who once knocked heads on the New York Giants' offensive line, seems an unlikely Virginia gentleman. 15

Back in the mid-seventies, he had a penchant for getting into fights, especially with the crosstown Jets. After playing for ten more teams—four NFL, two WFL, three Canadian, and one semipro—he returned to Blacksburg, where he'd been a standout for the Virginia Tech Hokies, earned a master's in education, tended bar, and, finally, bought a restaurant. He named it Bogen's. Thirteen years later, it's a pine-paneled local institution. 16

I ask him whether he keeps in touch with any of his old teammates. "Funny you should ask," he says, leaning against the barstool next to mine, talking above the crowd that's swarmed into the saloon to watch the World Series and quaff dollar-forty highballs. "A few months ago, *The Philadelphia Inquirer* did an article about the BEV, and it mentioned Bogen's and ran a picture of me. A day or two later, I got an E-mail message from Karl Chandler, who was on the offensive line with me. Hadn't heard from him in years." Reconnection: just one more in a long list of reasons that make the Internet, as far as Bill Ellenbogen's concerned, "akin to Gutenberg." 17

"I think it's the dawn of a new age," he tells me. Behind him, a pair of professional types hop back and forth to the computer terminal he has placed atop a pedestal between the pool tables and the dartboards. The men are settling a baseball bet by surfing their way to ESPN's site on the Web (http://espnet.sportszone.com)—exactly the kind of use Bill envisioned when he installed the Mac and began to advertise Bogen's as the "world's first cyberbar." 18

"Everyone's tapping into it," Bill says. "It's a sea change in the way information is going to be disseminated. The printed word will become less important. There's no reason for *The New York Times* to print that whole goddamn Sunday paper and fill our landfills when we can download it." 19

Bill Ellenbogen is a Wired One. In Blacksburg, of course, he is far from alone. The town, about nineteen square miles of university-dominated exurb nestled in the Blue Ridge mountains forty miles south of Roanoke, claims the highest per capita Internet and E-mail use in the world. The activity is largely private and invisible. Main Street up from Bogen's old colonial manse is what you'd expect in a sleepy, southern college community: a broad boulevard dotted here and there with a Mexican restaurant, a Baptist church, an ersatz British pub, and three barbershops cheek by jowl. There are few, if any, of the goateed and glassy-eyed cyberholics who haunt California's Silicon Valley and New York's Silicon Alley. 20

Yet imperceptibly, in houses and schools and stores, in apartment complexes wired for action, along lines made of copper or silicon, residents are surfing off the BEV's home page on the World Wide Web (http://www.bev.net) and checking out the new releases at the Moovies video store, posting apartment-for-rent notices on the "bburg.forsale" gopher, learning about the back-to-campus pizza-and-Coke special at VP Pie, studying which antibiotics can cause pseudomembranous colitis on Dr. Hendricks's searchable on-line database, investigating the availability of Jerry Pournelle sci-fi at the Tech library, and performing hundreds of other tasks each day. 21

Pioneering is nothing new to Blacksburg; the town was colonized by homesteaders who braved Shawnee raids to settle the territory. More than two centuries later—in 1987, to be exact—the settlement of Blacksburg's electronic village began when Virginia Tech invested $16 million to build a state-of-the-art digital telephone system that effectively placed a 19,200-baud modem on the desk of every student, staffer, and faculty member. At the time, the Internet was quite small, limited mostly to places like Bell Labs, Xerox Parc, a few universities, and some government agencies. The Hokies took to the technology, communicating via E-mail, downloading documents from the university mainframe, exploring the few public sites available. By the early 22

1990s, they were asking Tech's administrators why they couldn't go on-line at home. So the university struck a deal with the local phone company and the town government to wire Blacksburg with high-speed lines, establish community sites on the Internet, and provide residents with one of the least expensive Net-admission rates anywhere—$8.60 a month for unlimited access.

The goal is investigative—a team of Tech researchers is studying how and why people are using the network, making Blacksburg a sort of electronic Biosphere—but the project is far more passionate and purposeful than the typical scientific experiment. Week after week, BEV administrators and staffers descend on community groups like the Lions Club, proselytizing about the virtues of cyberspace. They see nothing less at stake than the survival of their own and similar communities in the nation's southern and midwestern backwaters, which were as savaged by the Industrial Revolution as eastern cities have been by the decay of manufacturing. Telecommuting, service industries, "knowledge work," can, they believe, restore them. 23

"The death of rural America—the network has the potential for turning that around," Andrew Cohill, the unofficial mayor of the Blacksburg Electronic Village, tells me. 24

Starting, perhaps, in places like the Bethel Elementary School in nearby Bethel, a rural, working-class community that—thanks to a commitment among the BEV's sponsors to wire one school in the poorer parts of surrounding Montgomery County for every school in affluent Blacksburg—has fifteen terminals with rapid access to the electro-byways. 25

One day not long ago, Melissa Matusevich, the district's social-studies coordinator, was approached by two fifth graders who wanted her to settle an argument—whether money was the same all over the world. She took them to a computer, did a Web search to find a currency-exchange-rate site, and rapidly developed an ad hoc curriculum incorporating both simple math and worldly investigations. Before long, the kids were receiving scanned-in pictures of foreign coins and paper money from E-mail correspondents around the world. "One of the most frustrating things for a teacher is to get a kid excited about a topic only to frustrate the kid when you can't find resources," Matusevich told me. "Those days are over!" 26

Big Bill Ellenbogen thinks it goes beyond resources. "It's like 1870, and a kid who could read versus a kid who couldn't," he says. "Computers are the reading of our era." 27

Couldn't that be a problem, I ask, especially for those poorer areas where, unlike Bethel, no patrons are available to provide for the have-nots? "It may be," says Bill, "but you can't stop it. You can try to stop the advance of technology, but it's not gonna happen." 28

We've been hearing that a lot lately, from none so loudly as Newt 29
Gingrich and his acolytes. Their credo belies the root meaning of the political doctrine—conservatism—to which they claim allegiance. Instead, they want what the Speaker calls "a revolution," driven by technology, that "will empower and enhance most people."

Newt has written glowingly of the time, a decade or so hence, 30
when "most Americans telecommute," when diagnostic chairs in our dens will allow doctors to examine us via cyberspace, when retraining for a new job will require us only to "enter the on-line learning system and describe what you need." But a purer version of his philosophy is proffered by a Washington organization with the unobjectionably nonpartisan name Progress & Freedom Foundation.

In another era—the 1950s, say—the PFF would have been called a 31
front group. Its president headed Gingrich's own political-action committee before establishing the foundation. Its chairman was President Reagan's science adviser and the proud papa of the discredited Star Wars missile-defense system. Its "fellows" include Gingrich disciple Arianna Huffington. And its message, as relayed in the preamble of its "Magna Carta for the Knowledge Age," is as radical as it is portentous: "The central event of the twentieth century is the overthrow of matter. In technology, economics, and the politics of nations, wealth—in the form of physical resources—has been losing value and significance."

What this means in practical terms is quite stark. The easy avail- 32
ability of information via the Internet "spells the death of the central institutional paradigm of modern life, the bureaucratic organization," the PFF says. Governments will crumble, and with them, such government functions as Social Security, which has been "left behind by information technology that empowers consumers" to choose their own retirement vehicles. Cities, too, will be unnecessary, because "advanced computing power" will "allow people to live farther away from crowded or dangerous urban areas."

"What digital technology—connected computing—allows us 33
to do," says Jeffrey Eisenach, the foundation's president, "is give the worker all the information and all the knowledge that the manager would have had and eliminate the knowledge priesthood, the bureaucracy."

I spend a morning in the Montgomery-Floyd Regional Library, a 34
ten-minute drive from Bogen's, where four terminals sit on a round table under a vine-covered canopy marked BLACKSBURG ELECTRONIC VILLAGE. A steady stream of men and women, most of them firmly middle-aged, enter, tap their way onto the BEV, knock about, sign off, and leave. Walter Zicko, the library's technology adviser, tells me that most people come in to send E-mail to friends, to post résumés, or just to surf for pleasure.

A weathered-looking older gentleman with dark, sparkling eyes and a thick black mustache seems so determined in his actions that I am moved to ask him what he is up to. I am surprised to get in response not a Virginia drawl but a dense New York accent. "I'm in a multiple-sclerosis newsgroup," says the man, Phil Kastin, a printing-plant superintendent who retired here from Manhattan. "I live on the outskirts of Blacksburg. I don't have a computer at home, so I come here. One of my daughters has MS. So I find information that people are putting up about injections, other treatments, reactions to medication. Some people post about medications they've been able to get in England and France that they can't get here. I E-mail this to my daughter in St. Louis so she can ask her doctor about it. 35

"In fact," says Phil, warming to the subject, "*I* found her doctor for her. My daughter liked her neurologist, but he wasn't an MS specialist. This other doctor in St. Louis was posting information about drugs that he was doing research on. I sent the information to her, and she switched. 36

"This," he adds, "has opened up a whole new world for me." 37

By rights, I should be with Phil Kastin and his fellow Wired Ones. Like many whose childhoods coincided with Telstar and the Salk vaccine, I was raised to believe that science and technology were my friends and our nation's salvation. I can still remember my father rousing me and my siblings to watch John Glenn blast into orbit, and even during the antitechnological fervor that emerged during Vietnam, I never could accept the counterculture's disdain for space flight, biotechnology, and the other wonders of this half century of achievement. 38

Naturally, when personal computers became available, I went into hock to buy one as quickly as I could. My Osborne I, at twenty-three pounds and 64 kilobytes of random-access memory the first "portable" computer, still sits in my brother's attic. I graduated to an Apple IIe (with twice the memory!), on which I ran an early, crude electronic bulletin board from my Hoboken, New Jersey, basement. 39

As a writer, I saw early the benefits that the Wired Ones today call "decentralizing" and "empowering." I dismissed a broker because I was able to download better information from the Dow Jones News Service. Hours spent at the library hunched over the *Readers' Guide to Periodical Literature* were reduced to minutes on Knowledge Index and Lexis/Nexis. When an illness kept me confined for two months, I telecommuted—editing stories at home and modeming them to the newspaper for which I worked. Now, the days begin with a review of E-mail on my Macintosh and a scan of my schedule on a Sharp Wizard and continue with shifts from Mac to PC to Thinkpad, from XyWrite to Word to Netscape, from 40

New York's ECHO on-line conferencing service to New York University's on-line library catalog. I am wired.

Wired and worried. For, more and more, I find myself communing with people I do not know, speaking in a language that has no sound, writing on pages that have no texture, engaging in chats that are deracinated versions of the physical and verbal interplay that, in the time before modems, made up my day. I wonder whether technology, while extending the reach of our words, is diminishing our opportunities for real, honest contact. 41

These concerns about technology are far from new. Philosopher John Dewey, writing decades before the Internet, prefigured its deleterious effect on human intercourse and democracy, positing that "ideas which are not communicated, shared, and reborn in expression are but soliloquy, and soliloquy is but broken and imperfect thought." 42

The Wired Ones deny that the new technologies have the power to atomize the public so completely. "I think that's a fantasy. It goes against everything we know about human nature," Eisenach says. "Will face-to-face communication always be important? Yes. Will telecommunications try to replace it? Yes. But this notion of an end point where the only way we interact is on a computer bulletin board is surreal and impossible." 43

Technology, though, does change culture, largely by altering the physical and social structures that support it. As Columbia University media scholar James W. Carey notes, the telegraph transformed finance, social relations, language, and thought by separating communication from transportation for the first time. It stamped out the florid writing that prevailed throughout the nineteenth century and replaced it with a lean style that took root in wire services and newspapers and blossomed on radio, on television, and, with writers like Hemingway, in literature. By giving buyers and sellers simultaneous access to commodity prices in different places, the telegraph created national markets and a national middle class. It even gave us time zones. 44

As much as the telegraph and successor technologies seemed to unite us, they have also served to separate us. Markets once were actual, central locations where merchants and townsfolk assembled to trade in food and notions. Today, they are psychographic constructs with no position in place or time. That the Internet will divide us even further, into small groups as disconnected from the common culture as a schizophrenic is from the world outside his head, seems indisputable. The very point of networking, as J. C. R. Licklider, one of the fathers of the Net, asserted a quarter century ago, is to isolate us from those who uncomfortably surround us. "Life will be happier for the on-line individual," he wrote, "because the people with whom 45 one interacts most strongly will be selected more by commonality of interests and goals than by accidents of proximity."

For MS sufferers and kids in rural communities—not to mention 46
stamp collectors and Pink Floyd fans—this is certainly a salutary development. But is it good for a society to be ripped into tens of thousands of little groups, each with its own agenda, its own mythology, and its own Web page? Before dismissing my concern as paranoia, just consider how computer bulletin boards, with their tales of black helicopters from the United Nations, have elevated the militia movement from a bunch of isolated kooks into a national force.

Indeed, networked communications, existing in a screen-based 47
parallel universe devoid of reality checks, are prone to the strident outbursts, abhorrent insults, and nervous fantasies that cause these little groups to form and thrive outside the mainstream. Blacksburg recently had its first experience with a political flame war when a Virginia Tech student posted four photos of nude women on a Web site for gay and bisexual men, Out and Proud (http://catalog.com/outproud), along with a message calling for homosexuals to "die a slow death." The student, whose name was withheld, was disciplined under a university statute that prohibits using the Internet to "harass, intimidate, or otherwise annoy another person."

Many Wired Ones are escaping the flame wars—and such atten- 48
dant cyberspace ordeals as adolescent sex talk and marketing scams—by opting out of America Online, the Usenet, and other mass-market networks in favor of closed, monitored conferencing systems like ECHO and the WELL. Soon, such recourse may be unnecessary. "Bozo filters"—software, like the antipornography program SurfWatch, that can sift through the Internet and discard unwanted information before it hits your eyes—are rapidly coming to market. "Within two years, we'll have very sophisticated news readers that will filter out all that dreck," says BEV mayor Cohill. "It'll search for words like 'great deal' and 'make money fast' and toss it in the trash."

In other words, our choice will be to live in the electronic equiva- 49
lent of gated communities—restricted to those who can pay and are willing to follow the rules—or to self-censor our world of offense. So much for the democratizing, empowering force of cyberspace.

None of this would be worth a worry if we didn't have a tendency 50
in this country to embrace what a University of Maine historian, Howard P. Segal, calls "technological utopianism." We not only grasp at every new technology as the nation's savior but conform ourselves socially and politically around its presumed power.

In the fifty years following the 1880s, a time when the United States 51
was undergoing the wrenching transition from an agricultural to an industrial economy, bookstores filled with idealistic paeans to electricity that extolled the same themes embedded in today's technomania. If the

Internet can create what Eisenach calls a "much more pastoral environment than we have today," so an earlier utopian, William Dean Howells, believed electricity would get "the good of the city and the country out of the one and into the other."

There are differences between past generations' utopians and our 52
own, to be sure. They saw the machine, its components acting in concert according to the will of a centralized authority, as a metaphor for society. That gave us planned communities, the Tennessee Valley Authority, even Marxism and the Great Society, under which social programs were, as one bureaucrat wrote at the time, "a machine to transform" a "raw material" called "people." The Wired Ones preferred metaphor is the Internet, its parts somehow self-organizing for the common good. Hence their desire to create a world without bosses or leaders, without cities or governments, and ultimately without moral or temporal authority beyond that of the financially—dare we use the word?—"empowered."

"Some who offer simplistic formulas that government's no longer 53
necessary in the age of information really have a different agenda in mind," Vice-President Al Gore, certainly one of the more wired public officials in America, says. "For some, it's survival of the fittest in drag, and any excuse will do."

I asked Jeff Eisenach how, in a world divided by technology, one 54
goes about affirming and inculcating core values. His answer gave little solace. "It's an issue of faith," he said. "I don't think it's resolvable by empiricism or analysis."

In Blacksburg, thankfully if a little naïvely, they do believe this is 55
a real dilemma, but one that can be solved. "That's the real can-of-worms question: Is technology a force for good or a force for evil?" says Cohill. "For me, the issue is this: Computers are here; how are we going to make them humane? My job is to make us masters of our destiny, not slaves."

At the Blacksburg Community Center, twenty senior citizens 56
gather for yet another pitch. This time, though, the authorities are preaching to the partially converted. All of these seniors are wired.

Bob Radspinner upgraded from a Commodore 64 and now 57
spends time trading E-mail with family in California and West Virginia. Nadine Newcomb, who works at Tech, is on a League of Women Voters Listserv—a closed, national discussion group. Earl Craven has his own home page (http://www.bev.net/users/homepages/ecraven), which features a current weather map of the U.S. and links to the 1996 Olympics site, the Social Security Administration, *The Roanoke Times,* and Babes on the Web. Not surprisingly, for a time it racked up more hits than any other home page on the BEV.

This group had its origins last December, after a BEV administra- 58
tor established a Listserv for senior citizens and started recruiting participants. Dennis Gentry signed up. He ran into Nadine on the tennis court and signed her up. Pretty soon, the kinds of technical questions you're likely to have if you've never used a computer moved them to organize once-a-month meetings. For most, it was the first time they'd laid eyes on one another.

"They say one of the worst things about growing old is getting lone- 59
some," Dennis, a thin, good-natured sixty-nine–year-old with a hearing aid, tells me. "You get on our Listserv, you'll never be lonesome."

Today, in fact, that is the subject of the gathering. After the sales 60
talk from a fellow selling an on-line service, Dennis introduces the issue to the group assembled in the game room. Something, he says, must be done to encourage people to use the group's Listserv.

"Frequently, questions are posted and I never see an answer," 61
agrees Harry Groot Jr., a Ross Perot look-alike who is running the meeting. "I wonder, are people going straight to the questioner on E-mail?"

"That does happen," answer Dennis. "It happens a lot." 62

So Harry provides a solution: Use the BEV's seniors' forum to get 63
discussions going. Don't fall off into private dialogue unless the subject is truly personal. "When you post an answer to a question, post it to the entire Listserv," he tells his friends. "I'm still gonna put chitchat up there. I run every day, and sometimes when I get back, I just wanna let people know what a beautiful day it is."

That leads Dorothy Bodell, a grandmotherly woman of sixty-four 64
who works part-time at the Tech library, to raise an issue that has been troubling her. "You know, that's something I want to know." She pauses, a bit uncomfortably. "I was having—I was having an eye problem the other day, and I wanted some support. Is that proper to put up?"

"Of course!" says Dennis. "Put it up!" 65

I am struck by a counterintuitive thought. This discussion has 66
nothing at all to do with technology. These senior citizens are debating a different subject of crucial importance to America, for which technology is only an excuse: how to revive the public square in a nation that's forgotten where it is. For them—for all of Blacksburg, in fact—the Internet is merely an excuse to bring people together, in real time, and in very real places, so that speech can flourish, hands can wave, and a wink can mean more than a ;-).

Far from diminishing the need for central institutions, the BEV is 67
creating new ones, like the seniors' group, and strengthening old ones, like the public library.

I mention this to Cohill over cappuccino at Mill Mountain, a cof- 68
fee joint across the street from Bogen's cyberbar. The BEV's mayor

surprises me by referring to Ernest Hemingway's classic memoir of Paris cafés in the 1920s. "I have a first edition of *A Moveable Feast,* and I've read it four or five times," Cohill tells me. "That's why I wanted you to meet me here. A café is a sensual experience. Being on the Net is a cerebral experience. Anyone who would substitute one for the other is either very wrong or very dysfunctional."

On my last night in Blacksburg, I wander over to Bogen's for 69
a final Pete's Wicked Ale and a grilled-chicken sandwich. I am startled to see Lion Matt, the program chairman of the Lions Club, sucking on an Amstel and surfing the Net. Somehow, he's managed to find his way onto the Web's Shakespeare Insult Server (http://www.cic.net/~mhyslop/Insult.html).

More than anything, he wants to be wired. "I figure about mid- 70
November," Lion Matt tells me, "I'm gonna have my own home page."

THINKING ABOUT THE ESSAY

1. To what degree does Blacksburg, Virginia, mirror the average suburban town in America? Explain by citing Rothenberg's descriptions of the locale and its people.
2. The essay shifts from an anecdotal, descriptive approach to a more analytic, philosophical one. Where does this shift occur? What are the reasons for using this rhetorical method?
3. What is Rothenberg's thesis? Where does he most succinctly present it?
4. Rothenberg states that the investigators of this experiment claim "they see nothing less at stake than the survival of their own and similar communities." According to the researchers, what, specifically, is threatening these communities?
5. How would you describe the attitude of the citizens of Blacksburg toward the "wiring" of their town? How does it compare with your own attitude toward the use of the Internet?

RESPONDING IN DISCUSSION

1. Divide into dyads (groups of two) and role-play a discussion between an advocate of the Internet and a resident of Blacksburg who is unfamiliar with this new technology. Make the goal of the advocate to convince his or her partner to subscribe to an in-home Internet service. Switch roles and repeat. Share your experience with the rest of the class.
2. Select a view presented by one of the "experts" cited in the essay (Casey, Dewey, Eisenach) and provide your own response to it.

3. The author states that he is "wired and worried." Explain the author's conflict in your own words.
4. Discuss the difference between some of the more pragmatic purposes to which the people of Blacksburg exploit the Internet and those that are solely recreational or frivolous.
5. Discuss the difference between what the mayor of Blacksburg terms a "cerebral" experience and a "sensual" one.

RESPONDING IN WRITING

1. Assuming the role of a resident of Blacksburg, write an essay explaining the effect the cyber-revolution has had on your town.
2. Argue for or against the proposition that providing Internet access to children in the inner cities can help them achieve educational parity with their more affluent counterparts elsewhere.
3. Argue for or against the proposition that the cyberspace revolution will only serve to further strengthen the power brokers in society
4. Write a descriptive essay of 500 to 600 words on the citizen whom Kevin Kelly, editor of *Wired* magazine, portrays as being "noble but marginal."
5. Think about one of your grandparents or any senior citizen you know well and search the Web for information of interest to him or her. Include hobbies, political concerns, financial concerns, and local events. Did you find sites that may inspire habitual visitation? Then write an essay analyzing the utility of the Web for older people.

Debugging Myself

Brian Hayes

Brian Hayes, former editor of the magazine *American Scientist,* writes in its September–October 1995 issue a meditation upon the relationship between himself and his computer. By doing so, he makes some general observations about the nature of computers as machines. Through this process, he helps the reader understand why computers make mistakes despite the best intentions of their users. He also demonstrates how old-fashioned human behaviors get in the way of acknowledging our unfounded presumptions that computers are totally reliable. In simple terms he poses and answers the question, Why can't a computer be more like a coffeepot?

PREVIEWING THE ESSAY

What are your expectations when you use a computer? What happens when those expectations are not borne out? Do you blame yourself, the computer, or the interaction that has transpired between you (the human) and it (the machine)?

A couple of years ago, I had one of those annoying moments of self-discovery. Sitting at my computer, I clicked on an icon to launch a program. The software obediently uncoiled itself from the storage disk and loaded into memory—then silently folded up again and went away. I clicked on the icon again, and the program went through the same futile pantomime. I clicked a third time, and watched the performance once more. The moment of self-discovery came just in time to save me from clicking yet again. What I discovered was that I must have a fairly peculiar mental model of how a computer works if I could believe that a fourth attempt might be any different from the first three. How long would I have gone on clicking? Did I think I might outlast the machine—prove that I'm more stubborn? If I kept clicking long enough, would I wear down its will to resist? Did I think of the computer as an animal that can be trained by repetition and discipline? Or perhaps I saw it as a dull child who will learn, eventually, if you keep drumming away at the same lesson? 1

Ever since that incident, I have been keeping a diary of computer bugs and my reactions to them. Whenever something goes wrong with one of my computers, I make a note of it: what happened, what I was doing when it happened, what I did about it. The bug logs now run to 25 pages. One reason for keeping these records is to learn something about the nature of computer malfunctions, but what interests me more is the human response to the machine and to the little surprises it holds in store for us. In other words, the aim is not so much to debug the computer as to debug myself. 2

SPHEXISHNESS

If I had been starting a car instead of a computer program, making two or three attempts in a row would not seem so foolish. You don't get out and call the tow truck when the engine fails to catch the first time you turn the key. And if it were a lawn mower I were trying to start, several pulls on the cord would be the norm; a mower that 3 roared to life on the first try might be disconcerting. Why should a computer be any different from these machines?

In point of fact, computers *are* rather different from lawn-mower 4
engines. From a theoretical point of view, a digital computer is a deterministic machine, whose actions can be predicted in complete detail. Specifically, a computer can be considered a deterministic finite-state automaton, or FSA. As the name suggests, a machine of this kind has only a finite number of possible states, or configurations, available to it. A snap-action light switch is an extremely simple FSA, with just two stable states—off and on. A pair of switches controlling a single lamp make up a slightly more elaborate FSA, with four states. The number of states in a digital computer is vastly larger: Roughly speaking, a computer that can store m bits of information has 2^m possible states. Values of m commonly exceed 100 million.

Ignoring some technicalities, a deterministic FSA works as fol- 5
lows. The machine starts out in some well-defined initial state; then, with each input received, it makes a transition to a new state, and possibly also produces some output. In the case of a computer, the initial state is the condition established when the power is first turned on; the inputs are events such as pressing a key or clicking the mouse; the outputs could include displaying information on a screen or sending it to a printer. At every instant the state of the machine is defined by the configuration of all the bits in memory as well as the bits in the registers of the central processing unit, and perhaps a few other bits also. (The bits stored on a magnetic disk may or may not be part of the machine state, depending on whether the disk is considered part of the computer or an auxiliary device.)

A finite-state automaton is deterministic if its next state and its 6
next output depend only on its current state and current input. Suppose in state q the machine receives input α, making a transition to state p and emitting output β. Then we know with absolute certainty that if the machine is ever again in state q, input α will evoke exactly the same response, so that we will again see state p and output β. There is no room for chance or variation. The sequence of events that brought the machine to state q does not matter. Events in the world outside the machine do not matter. Only the current state and current input matter.

Within this deterministic vision of computer operations, my at- 7
tempts to deal with a computer as if it were a balky lawn mower look fairly ludicrous. I was in state q and making input α; but each time I tried, the machine went through a cycle of operations that immediately returned it to state q. Input α would then inevitably begin the cycle all over again. The program was no more going to be started by continuing to click on its icon than a burned-out light bulb will be lit by continuing to flip the wall switch.

8 Douglas Hofstadter of Indiana University coined the word *sphexish* to describe behavior like mine. Wasps of the genus *Sphex* go through a brief ritual before burying a paralyzed cricket as nourishment for their offspring. If you move the cricket during the ritual, the wasp has to start all over again. Keep moving the cricket, and the wasp will keep repeating the same sequence of actions. A naturalist once played this trick 40 times in a row on a single wasp. As Hofstadter points out, the naturalist was being just as sphexish as the wasp. A metanaturalist from another planet would have had a hard time telling which species was being manipulated and which was doing the manipulating. Likewise in my contest with the computer, we both had to cooperate to keep up the dance of sphexishness.

MICROSTATES AND MACROSTATES

9 How embarrassing to be caught exhibiting the mental habits of an insect! (I really do need debugging.) But on reading through my diaries, I am led to wonder whether my behavior was really so sphexish after all. There is a fair body of evidence that just trying again sometimes *does* work. It's even possible that if I had gone ahead and clicked a fourth time, the program would have launched itself successfully.

10 At one point in my years of diary-keeping, I was having trouble with a communications program. I could start the software, but when I asked it to dial the telephone, the program died. This happened on three occasions, all within a month or so. In each case, I simply restarted the program—repeating exactly the same sequence of actions I had followed the first time—and it worked fine. I never discovered the cause of these sporadic failures.

11 Another time, the very program that provoked this long introspective debugging session—the program that put me in the sphexish loop described above—quit without warning. In this instance, however, when I clicked to restart it, all was well again. Another program failed to install correctly when I first loaded it onto a hard disk, but going through the same series of operations a second time cleared up the trouble. The diaries are full of other problems that just go away on their own or fix themselves overnight. Evidently, the balky-lawn-mower approach to computer operation is sometimes effective.

12 The bug diaries suggest that most of my problems are recurrent, but they are *not* reproducible on demand. For example, the complaint that turns up most frequently (nine instances) concerns a glitch in my word-processing software. On occasion the program would dump a jumble of unprintable characters into a document, like a digital inkblot. The error occurred following a specific sequence of actions,

but running through those actions would not reliably produce the error; it showed up only about one time out of 50.

The most infuriating bugs in my collection marred the operation 13
of a small utility program whose function was to provide a hierarchical display of menus and submenus. It was a handy tool—which now and then crashed the entire system. In particular, if I selected an item at some intermediate level in the nested structure of menus, the probability of a crash was about 0.1. Thus the crashes were just rare enough to tempt me to live dangerously.

How can these haphazard failures and fluky, random cures be rec- 14
onciled with the view of a computer as a totally deterministic machine? One answer is that a real, physical computer isn't truly deterministic. The finite-state machine of computer science is an abstraction, or idealization—something like the dimensionless point of geometry or the frictionless gears of elementary physics. A real computer has to be built out of imperfect parts. Because of hardware failures or design errors, the machine could conceivably get stuck between two discrete states. Quantum fluctuations could cause the system to shift spontaneously from one state to another. Certain possible inputs—such as a cosmic ray passing through a memory chip, or a lightning strike on the power line, or an irate user's sledge-hammer attack—could leave the machine in an indeterminate state. Any of these phenomena could disqualify the computer from the status of finite-state automaton.

A few events of this kind do show up in my bug diaries. Three 15
times, as I sat down at the computer in dry winter months, a spark zipped from my finger to the mouse, with interesting consequences. But it is extremely unlikely that outside disturbances or arbitrary changes of state can explain the hundreds of other incidents in the diaries. If the inkblot bug in my word processor was caused by cosmic-ray strikes, how did the rays find just the right bit to clobber on nine occasions, and in three different computers? The problem with such explanations is that they explain too much; they can explain *anything*.

With very rare exceptions, computers *do* function as determinis- 16
tic finite-state machines. If you put the machine in the same state and supply the same input, you will always get the same results. The catch is that putting the machine in the same state is no easy matter. A computer with $2^{100,000,000}$ possible states will necessarily have a great many states that superficially look alike but differ in their internal details.

In trying to reproduce a given state, you might run the same set 17
of programs and invoke the same commands on the same data. These visible aspects of the computer's configuration can be termed its *macrostate.* For every macrostate there are a multitude of possible *microstates,* corresponding to the underlying bit patterns. Although

the same programs are running in two macrostates, they may be loaded into different areas of memory, yielding very different microstates. Although the same commands are issued, they may be differently synchronized with the many unseen background processes that keep the computer going—processes for refreshing the display screen, blinking the cursor, reading the keyboard, and so on. Although a macrostate seems static, the microstate is changing with every cycle of the central processor chip, 10 or 50 or even 100 million times per second.

If the computer were making random transitions through its 18
$2^{100,000,000}$ microstates, the probability of its ever stumbling on the same state twice would be negligible. (At 100 million states per second it would take $10^{15,000,000}$ years on average.) Of course the transitions are not at all random, and their true pattern presumably makes repetition somewhat more likely. On the other hand, included in the state of most computers is the state of a built-in clock and calendar, which counts off the milliseconds over a period of some decades. The computer will not revisit a state until the calendar "rolls over."

Because of the one-to-many mapping between macrostates and 19
microstates, computers can remain rigidly deterministic in all their internal workings, but still seem wildly capricious to the poor sap at the keyboard. It's a nasty combination. It leaves me unsure whether the best approach to debugging is to correct the computer's logical errors or to heal its psychic wound.

THE PHASES OF THE MOON

A friend with experience of these matters once warned me: "Never let the 20
computer know you're in a hurry." The hazard, of course, is that the machine will sense your impending deadline and choose the most inconvenient moment to crash. The more intelligent computers even seem to know that Federal Express closes earlier on Saturday than on weekdays.

It is easy to mock such notions, which seem to require us to be- 21
lieve in a mischievous spirit inhabiting the silicon, always on the lookout for a chance to vex us. (Another friend advises me: "Don't anthropomorphize computers. They hate it.") But the idea of a computer reacting differently to a hurried user is not as implausible as it may seem. In the first place, urgency brings out a different spectrum of *human* bugs. I am capable of making mistakes either at leisure or in haste, but they tend to be different kinds of mistakes, and they probably expose different kinds of defects in the computer hardware and software.

Sometimes a speedy typist can create havoc even without mak- 22
ing an error. One of the most devastating of all computer bugs was

discovered about 10 years ago in the control software of a radiation-therapy machine called the Therac-25. The bug could lead to horrendous overdoses, and three patients died as a result. It turned out that one way of triggering the bug was to rapidly skip through a data-input screen, which allowed the radiation beam to be turned on before the computer had had time to adjust all the settings to their correct values. Typing the same sequence of keystrokes at a slower pace caused no trouble.

Bugs so erratic and mysterious that they seem to depend on the 23
phase of the moon are an old programmers' joke, but at least one such bug really did exist. (The story is told in Eric Raymond's *New Hacker's Dictionary.*) A program written by Guy L. Steele, Jr., who was then at MIT, rejected its own data files if they had been written during certain phases of the moon. The explanation was not in the least supernatural. The data files included a time stamp, and Steele had playfully added the lunar phase to the usual date and time information. At certain phases of the moon, the time stamp exceeded an 80-character limit on line lengths, with the result that the file became unreadable.

Prolonged exposure to subtle and elusive bugs like these can lead 24
people to approach the computer in an attitude of superstitious awe. They cling to whatever tricks or procedures worked the last time, without understanding the purpose of their own actions. They fear installing new versions of software, which might upset the delicate equilibrium of the entire system. The more severely afflicted practice cleansing rituals at the keyboard or offer sacrifices to propitiate the fickle gods of computation. I certainly don't endorse such behavior, which I see as another variety of sphexism. And yet I can't offer an alternative approach that can guarantee better results.

Every one of the malfunctions recorded in my diaries has a log- 25
ical, rational explanation. I'm utterly certain of that. The fact remains, however, that I have been able to track down the logical, rational cause in only a handful of cases. Those few diagnostic successes concern problems in software I wrote myself or programs for which I had the direct assistance of the developer. Without access to the source code (the original program text), there is little hope of truly understanding a software fault. In that circumstance, superstition is as good a tool as any other for dealing with the problem.

I should add that superstition has often enough been my own 26
refuge. Some years ago I instituted a campaign of "font hygiene" in the editorial offices of *American Scientist,* hoping to cure various murky computer ills. The problems were eventually dispelled, but I have no confidence that my elaborate precautions had anything to do with the remedy.

THE SPECTRUM OF BUGS

I have sorted the error reports in my diaries into five categories, according to severity. The worst kind of event is a crash (also known as a freeze or a bomb), in which the entire computer system comes to a standstill. Getting out of this predicament often requires a "reboot." The next class of malfunction is a total program failure, where a single program stops working entirely but the rest of the system keeps running. The three lesser categories I call major program faults, minor program faults and cosmetic flaws. 27

What is the spectrum of bugs in these categories? Before beginning the diaries, I would have guessed that the distribution would be similar to that of earthquakes and forest fires and other natural disasters: There would be lots of little ones and only a few big ones. [However], the actual distribution is just the opposite. Crashes are clearly the most common events, followed by total program failures, with the less severe problems trailing behind. 28

Reporting bias may have something to do with the shape of this spectrum. I was probably not as conscientious as I should have been about recording cosmetic flaws, and perhaps a fault that I consider major would be rated minor by more generous observers. But I think the main import of the spectrum can be trusted: When a computer fails, it usually fails big time. 29

The reason for this brittleness is no mystery. Most computer hardware and software cannot tolerate even the smallest malfunction. A single erroneous bit will derail an entire computation. In computers as in genetics—the analogy is a close one—most mutations are not merely harmful but lethal. Once a program gets onto the wrong track, there is almost no hope of recovery. Fragility is the price paid for the stabilizing effect of a digital architecture based on discrete states. The machine either functions perfectly or it does not function at all. 30

Cognoscenti will perceive that my statistics were gathered on microcomputers without a memory-protected multitasking operating system. On workstations and larger computers, system crashes are rare, because the operating system walls off each program in its own space; a program that runs amok can only destroy itself. The technology of memory protection will eventually reach smaller computers as well—it has been coming for 30 years now—with the result that many system crashes will be downgraded to program failures. That is an important gain. 31

Other oncoming developments are not so encouraging. As computers become more powerful, the size of both the microstate and the macrostate grows exponentially. This means there will be more pieces susceptible to failure, and quadratically more interactions among those pieces. The advent of parallel processing opens up a 32 whole new dimension of potential errors. And the new software architecture known as componentware or document-centered computing could also make things worse. If you have half-a-dozen components all working on the same document, what happens when one of those components does something the others don't like?

Coping with these problems is going to require better tools. Up to 33
now most tools for debugging have been intended for programmers and have been fully useful only with access to the source code. They present their information in terms of the microstate of the machine, which is difficult to relate to events in the user's world. What's needed is a tool that can diagnose faults in the macrostate, advising you, for example, that the system has crashed because two programs are locked in contention for the same hardware resource, or explaining that the program you have just tried to launch three times in a row needs more memory than is currently available. With information like that, computers might continue to be just as crazy, but people would be saner.

The best answer to the challenge of living on intimate terms with 34
fallible computers is to somehow create more robust hardware and software, which doesn't go to pieces at the first sign of trouble. Ultimately we might aspire to build computers that work as well as coffeepots or toasters or even lawn mowers—devices that tend to fail gradually and gracefully, and also rarely. But building a computer as good as a coffeepot looks like a daunting challenge. It is a task surprisingly similar in some respects to the better-known quest for a computer as good as a brain. Success will be a long time in coming.

BIBLIOGRAPHY

Hofstadter, Douglas R. 1979. *Gödel, Escher, Bach: An Eternal Golden Braid.* New York: Basic Books, pp. 360–361.

Leveson, Nancy G., and Clark S. Turner. 1993. An investigation of the Therac-25 accidents. *Computer,* July, pp. 18–41.

Raymond, Eric (ed.). 1991. *The New Hacker's Dictionary.* Cambridge, Mass.: The MIT Press, pp. 280–281.

THINKING ABOUT THE ESSAY

1. Do you demonstrate "sphexish" behavior when you use a computer? What about other times when you are confronted with a technological problem?
2. The author defines a computer from a theoretical point of view. Can you explain his definition in your own words? What terms in his definition, if any, gave you particular trouble?

3. The author divides the essay into four sections. How do their titles help to order and explain the structure of the essay?
4. What is the author's thesis? Where is it most clearly stated?
5. How would you describe the emotional tone of the essay? Is it ironic, playful, sardonic, or what? Provide examples from the writing to support your view.

RESPONDING IN DISCUSSION

1. Discuss the major purpose for the author's keeping his "bug diaries." Explain in your own words what he learned from them.
2. Discuss whether your knowledge of computers changed after reading the essay. If so, why? If not, why not?
3. Create your own metaphors for the concepts of "microstate" and "macrostate." Share them with the rest of the class.
4. Discuss whether the essay made you feel less intimidated by computers.

RESPONDING IN WRITING

1. Keep a diary for one week, recording your behavior and attitude toward the many interactions you have with the forms of technology you use (for example, computers, cars, telephones, toasters, microwaves). Share your reflections with the rest of the class.
2. Argue in an essay of 400 to 500 words for or against the proposition that Generation Xers are less likely to be guilty of "sphexishness" than older generations.
3. Describe an incident in your life where you encountered a serious problem while using a computer. What was the problem? How did you respond? What was the result?
4. Write an instructional manual for your fellow students entitled "How to Make Your Computer Your Friend."
5. Conduct a Web search of "computer bugs" or "computer malfunctions." Do you find serious literature on the subject, chat groups, sites to call, or anecdotal information? Write a report of 500 to 750 words on your findings.
6. Browse the FAQ (Frequently Asked Questions) or troubleshooting guides of homepages of software manufacturers like Microsoft, Netscape, etc. How many of the questions sound "sphexish" to you? If these questions are "frequently asked," does this support or undermine Hayes characterization of them as "sphexish"? Explain your position in a brief essay.

Gender Gap in Cyberspace

Deborah Tannen

Deborah Tannen received her Ph.D. in linguistics from the University of California at Berkeley. She has written both scholarly articles and best-selling books on language. Among the latter are *That's Not What I Meant* (1986), *You Just Don't Understand* (1990), and *Talking 9 to 5* (1994). In this brief article, first published in the May 16, 1994, edition of *Newsweek,* she lends her expertise to an analysis of the different ways men and women view computers and life on the Internet. She demonstrates that the same characteristics and behaviors that separate the genders in reality carry over to the world of virtual reality. This fact may give relief to those who believe technology will revamp our cognitive styles. But is it too early to tell?

PREVIEWING THE ESSAY

When you discuss computers with a member of the opposite gender, what differences (if any) do you find in your tone and attitude toward them? Do you believe the fact that you are a man or woman has some impact on the way you view these devices?

I was a computer pioneer, but I'm still something of a novice. That paradox is telling. 1

I was the second person on my block to get a computer. The first was my colleague Ralph. It was 1980. Ralph got a Radio Shack TRS-80; I got a used Apple II+. He helped me get started and went on to become a maven, reading computer magazines, hungering for the new technology he read about, and buying and mastering it as quickly as he could afford. I hung on to old equipment far too long because I dislike giving up what I'm used to, fear making the wrong decision about what to buy, and resent the time it takes to install and learn a new system. 2

My first Apple came with videogames; I gave them away. Playing games on the computer didn't interest me. If I had free time I'd spend it talking on the telephone to friends. 3

Ralph got hooked. His wife was often annoyed by the hours he spent at his computer and the money he spent upgrading it. My marriage had no such strains—until I discovered E-mail. Then I got hooked. E-mail draws me the same way the phone does: it's a souped-up conversation. 4

E-mail deepened my friendship with Ralph. Though his office was next to mine, we rarely had extended conversations because he is shy. Face to face he mumbled so, I could barely tell he was speaking. 5

But when we both got on E-mail, I started receiving long, self-revealing messages; we poured our hearts out to each other. A friend discovered that E-mail opened up that kind of communication with her father. He would never talk much on the phone (as her mother would), but they have become close since they both got on line.

Why, I wondered, would some men find it easier to open up on E-mail? It's a combination of the technology (which they enjoy) and the obliqueness of the written word, just as many men will reveal feelings in dribs and drabs while riding in the car or doing something, which they'd never talk about sitting face to face. It's too intense, too bearing-down on them, and once you start you have to keep going. With a computer in between, it's safer. 6

It was on E-mail, in fact, that I described to Ralph how boys in groups often struggle to get the upper hand whereas girls tend to maintain an appearance of cooperation. And he pointed out that this explained why boys are more likely to be captivated by computers than girls are. Boys are typically motivated by a social structure that says if you don't dominate you will be dominated. Computers, by their nature, balk; you type a perfectly appropriate command and it refuses to do what it should. Many boys and men are incited by this defiance: "I'm going to whip this into line and teach it who's boss! I'll get it to do what I say!" (and if they work hard enough, they always can). Girls and women are more likely to respond, "This thing won't cooperate. Get it away from me!" 7

Although no one wants to think of herself as "typical"—how much nicer to be *sui generis*—my relationship to my computer is—gulp—fairly typical for a woman. Most women (with plenty of exceptions) aren't excited by tinkering with the technology, grappling with the challenge of eliminating bugs or getting the biggest and best computer. These dynamics appeal to many men's interest in making sure they're on the top side of the inevitable who's-up–who's-down struggle that life is for them. E-mail appeals to my view of life as a contest for connections to others. When I see that I have fifteen messages, I feel loved. 8

I once posted a technical question on a computer network for linguists and was flooded with long dispositions, some pages long. I was staggered by the generosity and the expertise, but wondered where these guys found the time—and why all the answers I got were from men. 9

Like coed classrooms and meetings, discussions on E-mail networks tend to be dominated by male voices, unless they're specifically women-only, like single-sex schools. On line, women don't have to worry about getting the floor (you just send a message when you feel like it), but, according to linguists Susan Herrig and Laurel Sutton, who have studied this, they have the usual problems of having their messages ignored or attacked. The anonymity of public networks 10 frees a small number of men to send long, vituperative, sarcastic messages that many other men either can tolerate or actually enjoy, but that turn most women off.

The anonymity of networks leads to another sad part of the E-mail 11
story: there are men who deluge women with questions about their appearance and invitations to sex. On college campuses, as soon as women students log on, they are bombarded by references to sex, like going to work and finding pornographic posters adorning the walls.

Most women want one thing from a computer—to work. This is 12
significant counterevidence to the claim that men want to focus on information while women are interested in rapport. That claim I found was often true in casual conversation, in which there is no particular information to be conveyed. But with computers, it is often women who are more focused on information, because they don't respond to the challenge of getting equipment to submit.

Once I had learned the basics, my interest in computers waned. I 13
use it to write books (though I never mastered having it do bibliographies or tables of contents) and write checks (but not balance my checkbook). Much as I'd like to use it to do more, I begrudge the time it would take to learn.

Ralph's computer expertise costs him a lot of time. Chivalry re- 14
quires that he rescue novices in need, and he is called upon by damsel novices far more often than knaves. More men would rather study the instruction booklet than ask directions, as it were, from another person. "When I do help men," Ralph wrote (on E-mail, of course), "they want to be more involved. I once installed a hard drive for a guy, and he wanted to be there with me, wielding the screwdriver and giving his own advice where he could." Women, he finds, usually are not interested in what he's doing; they just want him to get the computer to the point where they can do what they want.

Which pretty much explains how I managed to be a pioneer with- 15
out becoming an expert.

THINKING ABOUT THE ESSAY

1. Do Tannen's descriptions of the different means men and women attend to their computers mirror your own experiences? Explain why or why not.
2. Is Tannen making any value judgments (that is, claiming one gender's relationship to computers is superior to the other's) or is she merely being descriptive? Explain your view.
3. Tannen published her essay in a news magazine designed for a broad popular audience. Point to certain stylistic and organizational strategies that reflect her appreciation of this audience's needs.

4. Tannen discusses many attributes unique to men and women. Does she suggest that these attributes are learned or innate, or is the issue beyond the domain of her concern? Explain.
5. Tannen states that "most women (with plenty of exceptions) aren't excited by tinkering with the technology." To what degree do these exceptions undermine her argument?

RESPONDING IN DISCUSSION

1. Divide into groups of three and four. Have each member of the group take a sheet of lined paper and draw a vertical line down the middle. On one side list those behaviors, atitudes, and functions regarding computer use and men; on the other, list the same domains regarding computer use and women. Discuss your findings with the rest of the class and compare them with the author's findings.
2. Discuss whether men's penchant for dominating their computers reflects the same types of attitudes found in male behavior as discussed in the article, "California's Dating Hell," which appears in a subsequent chapter.
3. Discuss how computer-literate women can join forces to help lessen some of the offensive male behavior over the Internet such as sexual harassment.
4. Set up a time and date to have an on-line class chat session to discuss the differences between men's and women's styles of communication. Report a summary of your findings in your next class. To make it more challenging, you may wish to disguise your gender to see if class members discern it through the style and content of your discourse.

RESPONDING IN WRITING

1. Write a female Internet users' "Bill of Rights."
2. For a creative writing exercise, write an imaginary biography of 400 to 500 words of the "Ralph" described in the essay.
3. Argue for or against the proposition that young women are much more savvy and less intimidated by the Internet than older women.
4. For a research project, download from a search engine articles about gender and cyberspace. Using at least three sources, in an essay of 1,000 to 1,500 words, support, refute, or modify Tannen's argument.

CONNECTIONS: FOR WRITING AND RESEARCH

1. Compare and contrast the essays by McGrath and Rothenberg. Are their visions of the United States as a cybernation incompatible?
2. Argue for or against the proposition that cyberspace will lead to a further gap between the affluent and the impoverished.
3. Read the essay by Pico Iyer in Chapter 9. Then write an essay of 400 to 500 words, arguing for or against the proposition that cyberspace growth will contribute to the global culture Iyer envisions.
4. Research how the Internet can provide greater access to information regarding job opportunities.
5. Discuss how a meticulous analysis of Hayes's personal use of computers (as described in his essay "Debugging Myself") could be transferred to the realms of television and music, so that viewers and listeners could gain more self-understanding of media effects.
6. Argue for or against the proposition that certain messages should be restricted from communication via the Internet. Include the nature of such messages and why they should be restricted.
7. Tannen speaks of a gender gap in cyberspace. Is there also a generation gap? Review the essays in Chapter 1 and then construct a response to this question.

3

PAY SCALES

For the D-Day generation (as Peggy Noonan calls the generation that grew up during the Depression and suffered through World War II), a high school diploma was considered a fair indication of a good basic education and the ticket to a job that paid a decent wage. As this chapter's essays suggest, the baby boomer generation extended the amount of education necessary for guaranteed entry-level jobs and careers that, despite ups and downs, would provide them with the necessities of life, some creature comforts, and enough left over for retirement. Now, however, a new generation has come along, the busters, and they find that even with a master's degree, getting that first job isn't so easy, and keeping it is sometimes a frustrating battle. This is because they face a number of obstacles that include boomers who jealously guard their seniority, a decrease in challenging jobs that match the skills obtained in college, and whole industries that seem to "turn over" from year to year, making last year's superstar corporation this year's has-been. And for those in the ever-growing underclass—those who lack education and even functional literacy—a job, any job, may seem to be a far-flung fantasy let alone job security. The following essays—dealing with job instability, inadequate salaries, changing family relationships, and the poor—portray America in a new economic light, where educated slackers in want of work are not so different from the homeless hungering for a good meal.

Why Can't I Find a Full-Time Job?

Barbara Anderman

Barbara Anderman, a 1992 graduate of the University of New Mexico, says she "survives on caffeine." You'd probably need a lot of java to keep going too if you held down four part-time jobs as she does. The following essay was first published in the July 1994 issue of *Glamour.* The author traces her story of a job hunt that shows that as the search for a full-time job would widen geographically, her hopes and expectations for good wages and benefits would diminish.

PREVIEWING THE ESSAY

What image comes to mind as you contemplate your first job after you graduate from college? If you intend to go on to graduate or professional school, what employment opportunities do you foresee lying ahead after another one or four or six years of education?

You go to college, you study hard, and at the end of four years, you get an entry-level job in the field of your choice. Right? I used to think so. 1

Despite the sob stories I heard from friends who'd graduated before me, I never believed finding a job would be a problem for *me.* As an undergraduate at the University of New Mexico, I worked at a laser-optics lab monitoring a $4 million budget. I had lots of responsibility and was well liked; I simply assumed the place would hire me after I graduated. But the lab, like other companies across the country, suffered cutbacks and imposed a hiring freeze. *Never mind,* I thought, *I'm more determined and more motivated than the competition. My drive to succeed will push me ahead of the pack.* I was wrong. 2

More and more college graduates are discovering that the real world is no longer catering to the American Dream. The statistics tell the story. According to Patrick Sheetz, Ph.D., director of the Collegiate Employment Research Institute at Michigan State University in East Lansing, there were 30 to 35 percent fewer jobs available for the class of 1992—my class—than there were for the class of 1990. The U.S. Bureau of Labor Statistics says that about 20 percent of college graduates today end up in non–college-level jobs. Temp jobs claim a larger share of the job market than at any time in U.S. history. 3

Call me a poster girl for the new economy. I started my job hunt in Albuquerque, and when nothing inspiring panned out, I took my 4 quest for employment on the road. From New Mexico to Seattle, job hunting was unrewarding, to say the least. I was a communications major in college, an avid reader, the friend classmates looked to for help with their term papers. I'd always hoped to work in the media (if I'd gotten the lab job, I would have made enough money to freelance in that field). But I soon learned to put aside my preferences, not to mention my financial expectations: a paycheck in the midtwenties, benefits, the ability to live alone, pay off my student loans and go out to dinner every so often without agonizing over it. Now it would be enough if I could share a modest apartment with roommates and still eat. So much for the lauded benefits of a college degree. I couldn't help but question exactly why it was I took out $10,000 in student loans. Let's not even talk about the credit card debt I ran up before graduation, when I still naively assumed my future employability was assured.

For two months, right after graduation, I sent out more than 5
150 résumés. I got little or no response. When I phoned to follow up on one job, there was only an answering-machine message: "We have received over 400 résumés. If it's been over two weeks since you sent us yours, please suffice it to say you are not being considered."

I switched to guerrilla tactics. I simply walked into a few offices 6
where I thought I might like to work. In Portland, Oregon, that resulted in my first coup: a position as the assistant at a small publishing company. A job in my field, yet! The catch: My new boss told me he could only afford to hire me part-time.

I took the job anyway, supplementing my income with assorted 7
other part-time jobs. I did freelance copyediting; I tutored for the local public schools; I signed on with a temp agency. I even did a stint as a nanny. These days I spend my mornings as an executive assistant at a biotechnology firm, my afternoons at the publishing house, and my weekends tutoring and copyediting.

It hasn't been easy making ends meet. I live with two roommates, 8
paying a rent that's reasonable by Portland standards but leaves little for my routine expenses. I can see a movie when the theater has its $3 discount night, but I can't afford the usual $7. I'm eating healthy these days, because fruit and vegetables are the cheapest buys in the supermarket. I have no health insurance, no vacation days, no employee savings plan.

Even with all this scrimping, it's been impossible to keep up with 9
my student-loan payments, which come to $130 a month. I've had to apply to the State of New Mexico for a one-year leniency period; for twelve months I'm required to pay only $5 a month, but interest keeps accruing on the loan. That means that when my year is up, my monthly bill will have risen to $150! But what can I do?

Despite my financial straits, I consider myself lucky. All of my jobs are interesting. I'm not flipping burgers or taking phone calls from strangers all day. I like the people I work with, and I'm actually getting to use my expensively acquired liberal-arts training. 10

My hunt to join the ranks of the securely employed continues. I just want a full-time job that offers health insurance, vacation days and a reasonable chance to learn and grow. 11

Should that really be so much for a college graduate to ask? 12

THINKING ABOUT THE ESSAY

1. Consider the last sentence of the essay, which is written in the form of a question. How would you answer it? How does the last question reinforce the question posed in the title of the essay?
2. Anderman relates that she was a communications major in college, a major usually considered within the area of the "liberal arts." Do you believe her major might be partly to blame for her failure to find a full-time job? Explain. Do you fear your job prospects will be similar to the author's when you graduate? Why or why not?
3. Describe the tone of the essay. Does the author appear angry, frustrated, confused, disappointed, desperate, or a combination of these? Explain your answer by citing excerpts from the text.
4. What is Anderman's thesis? Is it stated or implied? Explain.

RESPONDING IN DISCUSSION

1. Divide into groups of three or four and—as a committee—discuss what strategies the author should take to find more secure employment (for example, taking additional courses, attending graduate school, and networking). Share your plans for Barbara's future with the rest of the class.
2. At home or at your college computer center, go on-line and research the types of employment opportunities available through various Gophers, newsgroups, or Websites. Share your research with the class.
3. Compare and contrast the difference between planning one's career by researching what jobs will be in demand in the future or following your own career goals based on your deepest interests.
4. Discuss to what degree many college students become disappointed because their expectations for employment have been unfairly raised by idealistic parents, media portrayals, or enthusiastic but unrealistic friends.

RESPONDING IN WRITING

1. Using Anderman's techniques, write an essay explaining why you cannot find a job or why you did find a job.
2. Argue for or against the proposition that the best way not to become disillusioned when you enter the job market is to have no expectations.
3. Argue for or against the proposition that the reason so many college students and graduates are disappointed in their job hunt is that most Americans still live with the myth that America is the land of opportunity.
4. Discuss whether there is a correlation between your grades in college and your chances of finding satisfactory work in the job market.
5. Select a part of the country where you would like to work. Use the Web to research job opportunities there. Download information that you find useful and consolidate it in a survey of the local market that interests you.

Fitting the Poor into the Economy

Herbert J. Gans

Originally a refugee from the hostile political climate of pre–World War II Europe, Herbert Gans is current Robert S. Lynd professor of sociology at Columbia University. His many books and essays on social policy range from the individual's experience of everyday life to the influence of the media on society. First published in the October 1995 issue of *Technology Review,* this essay is based on ideas from his book, *The War against the Poor: The Underclass and Antipoverty Policy.* In it, the author takes a straightforward, unabashed look at what he believes are the implicit assumptions about the poor of our country as reflected in our social policies.

PREVIEWING THE ESSAY

What are your assumptions about "the poor"? That they are unlucky, lazy, or victims of poor choices or hidden conspiracies? Does your gut reaction to a homeless person equate him or her with a criminal element? What elements in your own experience contribute to your attitude? Do you think that the poor deserve public assistance? Justify your position.

The notion of the poor as too lazy or morally deficient to deserve assistance seems to be indestructible. Public policies limit poor people 1 to substandard services and incomes below the subsistence level, and Congress and state legislatures are tightening up even on these miserly allocations—holding those in the "underclass" responsible for their own sorry state. Indeed, labeling the poor as undeserving has lately become politically useful as a justification for the effort to eliminate much of the antipoverty safety net and permit tax cuts for the affluent people who do most of the voting.

Such misplaced blame offers mainstream society a convenient evasion of its own responsibility. Blaming poor men and women for not working, for example, takes the onus off both private enterprise and government for failing to supply employment. It is easier to charge poor unmarried mothers with lacking family values than to make sure that there are jobs for them and for the young men who are not marriageable because they are unable to support families. Indeed, the poor make excellent scapegoats for a range of social problems, such as street crime and drug and alcohol addiction. Never mind the reversal of cause and effect that underlies this point of view—for centuries crime, alcoholism, and single motherhood have risen whenever there has not been enough work and income to go around. 2

The undeserving underclass is also a useful notion for employers as the economy appears to be entering a period of long-term stagnation. Jobs are disappearing—some displaced by labor-saving technologies, others exported to newly industrializing, low-wage countries, others lost as companies "downsize" to face tougher global competition. Indeed, the true rate of unemployment—which includes involuntary part-time workers and long-term "discouraged" workers who have dropped out of the job market altogether—has remained in double digits for more than a generation and no longer seems to drop during times of economic strength. Labeling poor people as lacking the needed work ethic is a politically simple way of shedding them from a labor market that will most likely never need them again. 3

The most efficient antidote to poverty is not welfare but full employment. In the short run, therefore, today's war against the poor should be replaced with efforts to create jobs for now-surplus workers. New Deal–style programs of large-scale governmental employment, for example, can jump-start a slow economy. Besides being the fastest way to put people to work, a public-works program can improve the country's infrastructure, including highways, buildings, parks, and computer databases. 4

In addition, private enterprise and government should aim to stimulate the most promising labor-intensive economic activities and stop encouraging new technology that will further destroy jobs—reviving, for example, the practice of making cars and appliances partly by hand. A parallel policy would tax companies for their use of 5 labor-saving technology; the revenues from this tax would pay for alternative jobs for people in occupations that technology renders obsolete. This idea makes good business as well as social sense: human workers are needed as customers for the goods that machines now produce.

To distribute the jobs that do exist among more people, employers could shorten the work day, week, or year. Several large manufacturing companies in Western Europe already use worksharing to create a 35-hour week. Making significant inroads on U.S. joblessness may require reducing the work week to 30 hours. 6

FINDING SOLUTIONS, NOT SCAPEGOATS

A more generous welfare system would go a long way toward solving the problems of the remainder: those who cannot work or cannot find jobs. By persisting in the belief that poor people deserve their fate, society can easily justify a paltry and demeaning welfare system that pays recipients only about one-quarter of the median income. A system that paid closer to half the median income, by contrast, would enable those without work to remain full members of society and thus minimize the despair, anger, and various illnesses, as well as premature mortality, distinctive to the poor. 7

For such antipoverty policies to gain acceptance, mainstream America will have to unlearn the stereotype of poor people as immoral. Most of the poor are just as law-abiding as everyone else. (While a minority of poor people cheat on their welfare applications, an even larger minority of affluent people cheat on their tax returns—yet the notion of undeservingness is never applied to the middle or upper classes.) In admitting that the phenomena now explained as moral dereliction are actually traceable to poverty, Americans will force themselves to find solutions, not scapegoats, to the country's problems. 8

Most of the people assigned to today's undeserving underclass are the first victims of what is already being called the future "jobless economy." In the long run, if the cancer of joblessness spreads more widely among the population, large numbers of the present middle class will have to adapt to the reality that eventually most workers may no longer be employed full time. In that case, more drastic job-creation policies will be needed, including a ban on additional job-destroying technology and the establishment of permanent public employment modeled on the kind now associated with military spending. Worksharing would most likely be based on a 24-hour week. 9

At that point, everyone would in fact be working part time by today's standards, and new ways to maintain standards of living would have to be found. One approach, already being discussed in Europe, is a universal, subsistence-level income grant. This "demogrant," a 10 twenty-first-century version of the $1,000-per-person allotment that presidential candidate George McGovern proposed in 1972, would be taxed away from people still working full time. In any case, private and government agencies should begin now to study what policies might be needed to preserve the American way of life when the full-time job will no longer be around to pay for the American Dream.

It is possible, of course, that new sources of economic growth will suddenly develop to revive the full employment and prosperity of the post–World War II decades. And some labor-saving technologies may, in the long run, create more jobs than they destroy; that may well be the case for computers, which have spawned a large sector of the economy. Such happy outcomes cannot be counted on to materialize, however, and there remains the danger that the war on the poor will continue as the politically most convenient path. We will undoubtedly find that when the economy begins to threaten the descendants of today's middle and even affluent classes with becoming poor, and then "undeserving," policies that today seem utopian will be demanded, and quickly. 11

THINKING ABOUT THE ESSAY

1. The author states in his introduction, "The notion of the poor as too lazy or morally deficient to deserve assistance seems to be indestructible." Do you agree or disagree with the statement? Explain your view.
2. How does Gans structure his argument? Does he provide supporting points to back up his assertion that it is society that is responsible for the well-being of the poor? If so, where does he express them? If not, does it compromise his argument?
3. The author mentions the need for "New Deal–style programs." What was the New Deal? Why was it enacted? Why—according to the author—does our current economic situation warrant a new one?
4. The author claims that we should reduce the influence of new technology since it reduces the number of jobs. Is the author being antitechnology or prohuman? Explain your view.
5. The author claims the "poor make excellent scapegoats." Whether you agree with this statement or not, what factors exist that make them prime candidates for scapegoats?

RESPONDING IN DISCUSSION

1. Divide into groups of two (dyads). Have one person assume the role of a social security officer determining the status of an

individual applying for public assistance benefits. Have the other play the role of the seeker of such assistance. After 15 minutes of role playing, share your responses with the class.

2. Would it be fair to have a discussion about addressing the problems of the poor without having representatives from low-income families in your class? Discuss how a debate with more inclusive representation would change the tenor of your discussion.
3. Is Gans' plan to reduce the influence of new technologies fair to students who plan to enter careers in these fields? Discuss how Gans implicitly addresses this issue.
4. Discuss in small groups whether it is likely—as the author suggests—that poverty will trickle down to the middle and affluent classes.

RESPONDING IN WRITING

1. Write a personalized essay of 400 to 500 words entitled "My Encounter with Poverty" describing a situation, event, or condition in which either you or someone close to you experienced true poverty.
2. Write an article for your college newspaper entitled "Five Things Our Institution Can Do about Poverty."
3. Argue for or against the proposition that most Americans think the poor are lazy. Use personal experience, observation, personal accounts from those you know, and/or utterances by politicians.
4. Interview a student on your campus regarding her or his views on the "poor." Write a 500-word comparison-and-contrast essay comparing those views with those Gans claims are the predominant beliefs shared by most Americans.
5. Argue for or against Gans' opinion that the poor should receive benefits of up to 50 percent of society's median income so that they are able to live with "less despair, anger, and various illnesses."
6. Search the Net for information on Gans, who is a well-known sociologist. Then construct a profile of Gans, explaining how his attitudes and values are reflected in his essay that you just read.

Why Their World Might Crumble

Lester Thurow

A professor of economics at the Massachusetts Institute of Technology, Lester Thurow is the author of several books and numerous articles on the state of the national and international economy. In this essay, first published in the

November 19, 1995, edition of *The New York Times Magazine,* the author paints a grim portrait of the current economic condition of the United States. He reminds us that Americans are working longer for less money, and warns that social and fiscal mismanagement of a society can lead to its ruin, causing citizens to become disaffected with their government. The result may be lives that become both physically and psychically insular in an attempt to protect ourselves from the perceived threat of a hostile world—to use Thurow's analogy, much like the moats that protected medieval castles from foreign intruders. However, the difference, as the author points out, is that the Middle Ages never purported to be democratic, while we live with the "one person, one vote" concept of democracy that may be becoming more a myth than a reality.

PREVIEWING THE ESSAY

There is perhaps no greater cliché that issues from the mouths of politicians than the idea that we live in a democratic society—in other words, a society governed by the people. However, can a society based on huge inequalities of wealth and income ever be democratic? Explain.

1 The year 1968 was among the worst years this century for the United States—assassinations, riots, campus uprisings and the infamous Democratic National Convention in Chicago. But an event that attracted little or no attention at the time may ultimately prove to have the most lasting and destabilizing effects of all. Suddenly that year, like a surge in a long immobile glacier, economic inequality started to rise.

2 Among men and women working full time—the group most sharply affected—inequalities in earnings between the top 20 perce0nt of wage earners and the bottom 20 percent doubled in the next two and a half decades. By 1973, the median wage for all men working full time began to fall.

3 Over the next 20 years, men's earnings fell 11 percent, from $34,048 to $30,407, even though the earnings of the top 20 percent grew steadily and the real, per-capita gross domestic product (G.D.P.) rose 29 percent.

4 Within the family, American women came to the rescue of American men. Mostly by working many more hours per year, women kept median household incomes slowly rising until 1989. In 1989, however, median real wages for women working full time year-round also began to fall. Preliminary data for 1994 and early 1995 indicate that these wage declines are accelerating. As a result, since 1989 median household incomes have fallen more than 7 percent after correcting for inflation and family size, to $31,241 in 1993, from $33,582. Already working full time, women had no more extra hours of work effort to contribute to the family's income.

The same sharp rise in inequality has occurred in the distribution 5
of wealth. The share of total net worth of the top one-half of 1 percent of the population rose from 26 to 31 percent in just six years, between 1983 and 1989. By the early 1990's the share of wealth (more than 40 percent) held by the top 1 percent of the population was essentially double what it had been in the mid-1970's and back to where it was in the late 1920's, before the introduction of progressive taxation.

These are uncharted waters for American democracy. Since accu- 6
rate data have been kept, beginning in 1929, America has never experienced falling real wages for a majority of its work force while its per-capita G.D.P. was rising. In effect, we are conducting an enormous social and political experiment—something like putting a pressure cooker on the stove over a full flame and waiting to see how long it takes to explode.

Behind these changes lie technological shifts that demand a more 7
skilled work force, competition from lower-paid but well-educated workers in the rest of the world and two decades of Federal Reserve Board policies of creating unemployment to fight inflation. There has also been a big shift in the implicit contract between owners and workers.

After World War II, white-collar workers and managers came to 8
expect lifetime employment with rising wages, assuming their firms remained profitable. Blue-collar workers, who also expected and received real annual-wage increases, did face the prospect of occasional layoffs. But these were restricted mostly to younger workers, who could expect to be recalled in the next boom. This implicit contract has been smashed by companies with high and rising profits that are nevertheless reducing wages, eliminating fringe benefits and permanently laying off hundreds of thousands of workers from what had been society's best jobs.

The middle class is scared, and it should be. The supports for its 9
economic security are being kicked out from under it. The remedy must include a huge program of re-educating and retraining the bottom 60 percent of the work force, investments in research and high-tech infrastructure and a willingness to run the economy with tight labor markets so that labor shortages push wages upward. But it takes organization to do that, and it's not clear that America has the will to get organized to solve its problems.

Historically, some very successful societies have existed for mil- 10
lennia with enormous inequalities of wealth and income—ancient Egypt, imperial Rome, classical China, the Incas, the Aztecs. But all these societies had political and social ideologies that fit this economic reality. None believed in equality in any sense—not theoretically, not politically, not socially, not economically. Democracies have a problem with rising economic inequality precisely because they believe in political equality—"one person, one vote."

One solution to this divergent distribution of power is to drive out the 11
economically weak. A 19th-century economist, Herbert Spencer, introduced the idea of "survival of the fittest" capitalism, a phrase that Charles Darwin appropriated to explain evolution. Spencer believed that it was the duty of the economically strong to drive the economically weak into extinction; that drive was in fact the secret of capitalism's strength.

Until recently, Spencer's suggested solution was roundly rejected, 12
and democratic governments systematically worked to reduce earnings and wealth inequalities. A state-financed safety net protected the weak (the old, the sick, the unemployed, the poor) from economic extinction. Social investments in education, infrastructure and research and development helped raise the earning power of the middle class. The capitalist's power to exploit his work force was legally limited, and a combination of social and legal pressures insured that rising output was shared with the work force.

The Republicans' balanced-budget plan essentially offers a return 13
to Spencer's survival-of-the-fittest capitalism. It raises taxes on working Americans and lowers them for the wealthy. It shreds the safety net, apparently on the theory that individuals facing starvation will knuckle down and work. Fear will make them hold on so tightly to the economic trapeze that they won't fall off.

No one has ever tried survival-of-the-fittest capitalism for any ex- 14
tended period in a modern democracy, so we don't know how far rising inequality and falling real wages can go before something snaps. Social systems can certainly snap; the recent implosion of the Soviet Union is a good example. But to snap, there must be some alternative banner under which the population can quickly regroup. In the case of Communism, that alternative banner was capitalism. But if capitalism does not produce acceptable results, there simply isn't any alternative system under which the people can quickly regroup. As a result, a sudden social collapse is highly unlikely.

What is more likely is a vicious cycle of individual disaffection, 15
social disorganization, falling incomes and a slow downward spiral, something like the long slide from the peak of the Roman Empire to the bottom of the Middle Ages. There were those in the Middle Ages, for example, who knew everything the Romans knew about fertilizing crops. What later Europeans lost was the ability to get organized to fertilize. Without fertilization, crop yields fell so far that the best land yielded only three pieces of grain for each one that was planted. Put aside one seed to plant next year, subtract seeds eaten or spoiled by vermin and there is very little left to sustain life through the winter. There simply were not enough calories available to sustain vigorous activity, and the quality of life inevitably declined.

Today we are refusing to make the investments in the modern 16
equivalents of fertilization—education, infrastructure, research and

development. Public spending on infrastructure, as a percentage of G.D.P., has been cut in half in the last two decades and is scheduled to be reduced even further by Washington's budget cutters.

Rome's downward spiral did not begin with an external defeat. It began with a period of uncertainty and disorientation. Further military expansion no longer made sense, since Rome was at its natural geographic limits and facing empty deserts, steppes and forests. Our equivalent is the disorientation that came at the end of the cold war. The enemy was gone, yet defense budgets had to be maintained. 17

Rome was faced with huge numbers of immigrants who wanted to attain the higher standard of living they saw before them. But Rome had lost the ability to make them into Romans. Perhaps Proposition 187 in California means that America has also lost that ability. 18

Literacy, widespread in the Roman Empire, was restricted to a few cloistered monks in the depths of the Middle Ages. Today functional illiteracy is on the rise even amid a sharp escalation in the educational requirements for productive workers. 19

During the medieval era, banditry became widespread and was widely accepted (remember Robin Hood) as a populist revenge upon the defenders of the political and social order. Unwalled cities and free citizens were replaced by walled manor houses and serfs. Walled and gated communities are once again on the rise. Twenty-eight million Americans live in such communities, if one counts privately guarded apartment houses, and the number is expected to double in the next decade. 20

No one can know what will happen if inequality continues to rise and a large majority of our families experience falling real incomes. But if capitalism does not deliver rising real wages in a period when the total economic pie is expanding, its hold on the political allegiance of the population will be threatened. Similarly, if the democratic political process cannot reverse the trend to inequality, democracy will eventually be discredited. What we do know is that a large group of hostile voters who draw no benefits from the economic system and don't think the government cares is not a particularly promising recipe for economic or political success. 21

THINKING ABOUT THE ESSAY

1. How much control do you as an individual have over the economic decisions that are significant to your family, community, and society? If your family is a member of the middle class, is it scared as the author purports? Explain.
2. Examine the opening of Thurow's article. Do you find the use of facts and data effective? Why?

3. Thurow implies that we live in a hypocritical society, one that proposes democracy, but one that assures benefits only for the well-off. Do you agree? If so, is this hypocrisy intentional or accidental (for example, a result of poor planning or inertia)? If you do not agree, explain why democracy and growing inequality in wages can be rationalized.
4. Thurow uses historical comparison in his essay. Where and how does he apply it? What is his purpose?
5. What forms of evidence does Thurow present to support his thesis? Does he make good use of this evidence or is it selected in the way that politicians often bias statistics to help advance their agenda?

RESPONDING IN DISCUSSION

1. Divide into groups of three or four, and jot down the major complaints concerning society you hear from your family. Compare your list with other group members' lists. Which complaints seem to be universal? Which are singular? Share and discuss your results with the rest of the class.
2. The author raises an analogy regarding fertilization in Europe to drive home the point that America is not preparing itself for the future. Think up your own analogy and share it with the class. Discuss how relevant it is to the economic predicament advanced by the author.
3. Discuss psychological or social examples you have encountered in your life that exemplify working Americans' frustrations in response to the continued disparity in wages.
4. Is Spencer's idea of the survival of the fittest ultimately the most honest economic system given the self-preservation instincts of the individual? Explain your view.

RESPONDING IN WRITING

1. Write an imaginative essay, composed in the year 2015, from an armed fortress in which you live, describing daily life in a society that must protect itself from legions of dispossessed workers.
2. Write a 400-to-500-word descriptive essay concerning an incident you witnessed that graphically illustrated economic inequality between two workers.
3. Write a letter of 400 to 500 words to your local congressperson or senator, explaining why he or she should read Thurow's essay. Include a copy of the essay with your letter.

4. Argue for or against the proposition that Thurow overstates the issue of the American economic crisis since the United States still enjoys one of the highest standards of living in the world.
5. Write an essay discussing how the ideas advanced by Gans could help alleviate the economic crisis in America that Thurow describes.

Generational Tension in the Office

Suneel Ratan

Many baby boomers recall the line "Something is happening here, but you don't know what it is, do you, Mr. Jones?" from Bob Dylan's song "Ballad of a Thin Man." The Mr. Jones of the title has been interpreted as the man who avoided social change being wrought by the then-young baby boomers since he feared their lifestyles and sheer numbers were about to threaten his lifestyle. But nowadays, it is the aging baby boomers who are the Joneses, fearful that their younger counterparts in the workplace are threatening their security. In this essay, first published in the October 4, 1993, issue of the business-oriented magazine *Fortune,* Ratan provides his view of the great divide between twentysomethings and baby boomers, specifically its impact in the corporate workplace. What happens when an educated, underpaid generation weaned on computers must take orders from older bosses whose values, training, outlook, and philosophy are different from theirs? According to this author, the answer is intergenerational conflict of a special sort.

PREVIEWING THE ESSAY

Work, unlike school, has some very hard deadlines. You don't receive an incomplete grade for work not handed in by the end of the semester. Unsatisfactory work performance can lead to a dead-end job with little chance for advancement in salary or status. And the decision-making process is often left up to someone who is more concerned about his or her job than yours. How would you feel in such a situation? What would you feel toward the person in charge of making the decision? What would be your options if you were dissatisfied with the decision?

Hate to break this to you, boomers, but among twentysomethings gathering in bars, coffee houses, and Lollapalooza festivals across America, bashing you folks has become the new national pastime. Some of it is playful—surely we've *all* heard enough about the Sixties—but much of it is deadly serious. The beef is that boomers seemed to get the best of everything, from free love to careers, while today's young people get AIDS and McJobs. 1

If the sound of young people whining sounds annoyingly familiar, as from time immemorial, listen closer. This time it's different. Unlike their boomer siblings, Generation X, as the new crop have taken to calling themselves, from the title of a Douglas Coupland novel, aren't rebelling against the government or the culture. Instead, today's kids (whose numbers include the author of this story) are up in arms over economic and career prospects that look particularly bleak—with boomers as the targets of their resentments. That makes the workplace center-stage of the twentysomethings' rebellion, with younger people referring privately to their boomer bosses as "knotheads and control freaks," in the phrase of Jeffrey McManus, a 26-year-old computer instructor. 2

To hear twentysomethings tell it, boomers spend too much office time politicking and not enough time working. Boomer managers claim to be seeking younger employees' input when in reality they couldn't care less what Xers think. Worst of all, boomers seem threatened by young, cheap-to-employ hotshots who come in brimming with energy and—note well—superior technological savvy, and thus are doing everything in their power to keep the young'uns down. And while we're at it, with downsizing taking a wicked toll on support staff, can't you boomers do your own faxing? 3

Boomers are more than willing to take on twentysomethings in what's shaping up as a generational grudge match. Xers, fortysomethings say, are too cocky and aren't willing to pay their dues. That complaint is as old as humanity, but other knocks are more particular to the Xers. They aren't loyal or committed to work, detractors say, changing jobs more casually than sex partners and refusing to go that extra mile to do things right. Unlike workaholic boomers, twentysomethings like to play, and they even expect work to be fun. Irony of ironies, the boomer generation that came of age rejecting authority charges the next generation with—*sacré bleu!*—being unwilling to, uh, show appropriate deference to *their* authority. 4

Interviews with more than 60 Xers and boomers in the business world, as well as with sociologists and management consultants, reveal that a combination of clashing workplace values and the sour economic scene is creating lasting tensions that managers will have to deal with long after hiring has picked up. Faced with working for boomer bosses they find oppressive, many twentysomethings have abandoned corporate America, retreating into slackerdom or striking out on their own as entrepreneurs. The challenge for managers is to figure out ways to capture twentysomethings' enthusiasm to enliven existing companies—many of which certainly could use an infusion of youthful energy. 5

To chart the generational fault line, throw out textbook definitions that identify boomers as the 78 million Americans born between 6

1946 and 1964 and baby-busters as the 38 million born from 1965 to 1975. Bill Strauss and Neil Howe, authors of two books on generational issues, *Generations* and *13th Gen*, correctly point out that people born after 1960 have difficulty identifying with the coming-of-age experiences of older boomers. They call the generation born from 1961 to 1981 "13ers," denoting their status as the 13th generation since the founding of the republic. Says Strauss: "Our shorthand is that boomers are too young to remember Roosevelt dying, while 13ers are too young to remember Kennedy's assassination." Using Strauss and Howe's definition, 13ers—by subtracting from boomers' ranks the people born after 1960—*outnumber* boomers 79 million to 69 million. Of course, the still, small voice of the boomer skeptic intones, 32 million of the 13ers are under 21.

Just as the times in which they came of age are different, so too 7 are the factors that provoked boomers' and Xers' rebellions. Against a backdrop of unparalleled U.S. economic strength, boomers rose up not only against the Vietnam war but also against a culture and social system they thought repressive. Twentysomethings see themselves as the children of America's economic and social decline. They aren't angry at the Silent and World War II generations that have steered the economy onto the rocks and whose Social Security and Medicare payments threaten to bankrupt the government. To young people, those older generations paid their dues in the Depression, World War II, and Korea.

Instead, twentysomethings train their resentments on boomers, 8 whom the younger people see as having coasted through life—from their *Leave It to Beaver* childhoods in the 1950s to their current positions in management—without ever having built anything. Beyond that, twentysomethings identify boomers with the unraveling of American society that seemed to accompany the antiwar movement and the divorce wave that began sweeping across the country in the late 1960s.

For a taste of these sentiments, sit down on the banks of the Po- 9 tomac River in Washington, D.C., for a drink with Dana Neilsen, 25, an account executive with *AAA World* magazine. "We're the generation of divorced families and latchkey homes, and that's a big dose of realism," says Neilsen, the child of divorced parents and of a working mother. "The boomers had elementary schools built for them and then secondary schools and then colleges, and then as they entered the work force, companies made room for them. Now we come along and it seems as if all the resources have been used. Now they've moved into management levels, and they're not going anywhere. Where does that leave us?"

Some Xers, forced into joblessness or underemployment, are 10 downright bitter about the lousy cards they think they've been dealt.

Says a disgruntled Xer, a 28-year-old temp for a Fortune 500 company in San Francisco who has a master's degree: "The boomer manager I work for comes in and says, 'Wow, look at my shiny new, red convertible.' And I'm like, 'Look at my battle-ax '76 Nova.' I mean, I'm a 'burb kid. My parents weren't big spenders, but they gave me a comfortable upbringing, and that's something I feel I could never give my children, if I have any. Babyboomers drive themselves nutty talking about balancing work and family, but at least they have families."

Not all Xers blame the boomers entirely for their own frustrations; some instead cite their generation's inflated expectations. San Franciscan Paula Fujimoto, 24, says that paying $13,000 a year in tuition at Chicago's Northwestern University primed her to expect better than what she came to be in most of her first jobs: a glorified secretary. Even now, two years after graduation, she is settling for minimum wage—that's $4.25 an hour—trying to prove herself to a public relations firm. "I was frustrated because I grew up in a nice, upper-middle-class suburb, I studied hard, I did all the things you're supposed to do to get into a good school, and it was like people chose to ignore the fact I was intelligent," she says. Concludes Fujimoto, who still lives at her parents' home: "Our generation is way too cocky." Adds her friend 29-year-old My Tien Vo: "We've been significantly humbled." 11

Columnist Stanley Bing, the pseudonym of a 42-year-old executive too weak-kneed to let his real name be associated with his views, says Xers haven't been humbled nearly enough. "I didn't make more than $8,000 a year until I was 30," says Bing. "Instead of realizing that you eat dirt until you decide to get serious, you're whining. We didn't whine. We knew what it was to be young, poor, and striving." 12

The kids take remarks like these as emblematic of a smug boomer complacency about the difficulties young adults encounter today. Since 1968, when the Head Boomer, Bill Clinton, graduated from Georgetown, the annual cost of attending a four-year public university has risen 39% *after* inflation, to $6,500. Private university costs are up 94%, to $19,300. Despite the baby bust, universities are loosing 1.6 million newly minted bachelor's, professional, and doctoral degree recipients into the job market each year, 58% more than during the late 1960s. Yet employment in managerial and technical fields has grown only an average of 310,000 jobs annually over the past two years, compared with an average of 1.8 million jobs each year during the 1980s. Hiring may pick up again one day, but to people coming out of degree programs now, the outlook is bleak. Indeed, the Bureau of Labor Statistics forecasts that nearly one-third of college graduates from the classes of 1990 through 2005 will take jobs whose content doesn't really require a degree, up sharply from 19% in 1980. 13

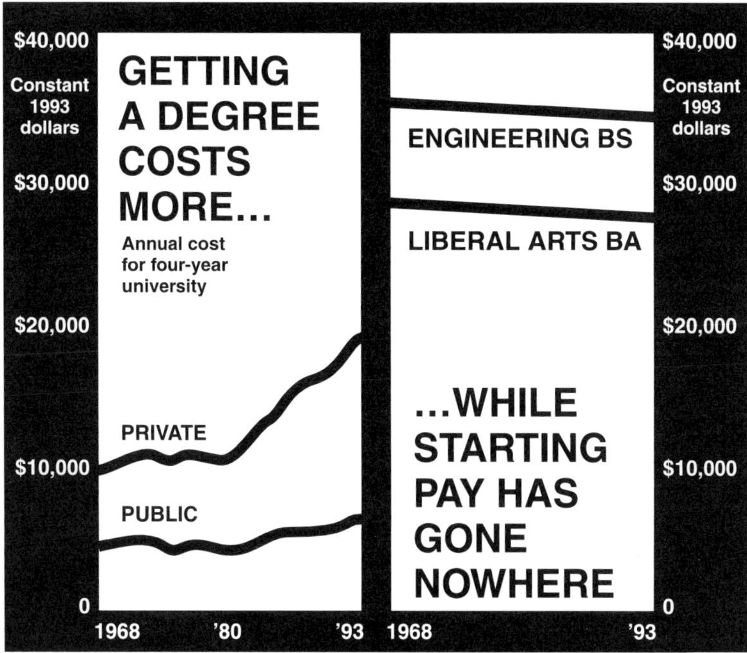

Fortune Chart/Sources: U.S. Dept. of Education; Northwestern University Lindquist-Endicott Report.

To hear twentysomethings tell it, boomer pinheadedness in the workplace runs far beyond lack of empathy to encompass a range of behaviors that can make working for people in their late 30s and 40s oppressive. To the over-50 set, some of the complaints will seem silly, such as boomer vs. twentysomething clashes over dress and appearance. But such conflicts are serious to Xers, who brand them a symptom of boomer control-freakishness. Recounts an Xer employee of a Midwestern consultancy: "Last year I had my hair shaved on the sides so you could see my scalp. My 42-year-old boss went to see the human resources manager about whether she could send me home until it grew back. This woman says she's a flower child. She still goes to see the Rolling Stones, even though now she pays a broker $400 for tickets. And she's worried about my haircut?" 14

Far worse is young workers' perception that many boomers seem more caught up in maneuvering for status in an organization than in working. Towers Perrin consultant Margaret Regan and David Cannon, a doctoral student at London Business School who has conducted extensive research on Generation X in the workplace, report independently that in focus group after focus group, twentysomethings' biggest complaint about their boomer managers is the politicking in which they engage. Says Cannon: "Younger people want to 15 make a contribution, and not a vague one, and they don't want to waste a lot of time. They see boomers, and not so much the senior people, as politicking and maneuvering and doing a lot of unnecessary make-work."

Xers *Fortune* interviewed aren't so naive as to think politics can be banished from the workplace. What amazes them is the degree to which scrapping for position and control can interfere with a company's work. A 29-year-old programmer for a Southern California software company described how a power struggle among the boomer managers overseeing development of a product delayed a planned 12-month project for a year. 16

The key villain, he says, was a middle-age vice president who insisted on making every decision—even if the staff had to wait weeks for her schedule to clear so she could weigh in. Says the programmer: "It's a bottom-line issue, but they ignore it and allow politics to drive decisions that could eventually cost them their jobs or their companies." That's what happened to the vice president, who was laid off when the company recently retrenched. 17

Twentysomethings see another aspect of their bosses' politicking in autocratic management that denies Xers a voice or the feeling that they have any ownership of their work. "For the young person, the attitude is 'Just tell me what you want to do and leave me alone,'" says consultant Regan. "Obviously the boss above them wants more direction and control." 18

What really grates on Xers is when bosses publicly avow participatory management but then cling to their old hierarchical ways. Says Megan Wheeler, 31, who has started her own software company in San Diego: "At the other places I worked they would tell you that you could have input into all these choices about hardware and software, but when it came down to the final decision, it didn't matter at all." 19

This leaves a thick residue of cynicism among Xers that kicks in when their bosses seem to find God in nostrums such as Total Quality Management. The young employee of the Midwestern consulting firm recalls, "A couple of weeks ago we rolled out a group vision and mission statement. Then the partner asked us what we thought. I mean, what did she expect us to say? I was sitting there thinking, You know, it's a miracle you're getting paid for this." 20

Put it all together and you can get some pretty disaffected people. "In the Eighties there was a lot of the same silliness, but at least you could earn a lot of money," says Deroy Murdock, 29, who in 1991 was laid off from ad agency Ogilvy & Mather in New York and has since prospered as an independent marketing and media consultant. "Today with wage stagnation the way it is, people's patience for nonsense has hit the floor." 21

What Xers don't see is that the same economic distress is often the source of what they perceive as doltish boomer behavior. Consultant Regan says that in a focus group of boomer managers, participants admitted that the advent of downsizing as the new corporate religion had made them so obsessed with keeping their jobs that career development for employees had gone out the window. "They weren't proud of it," Regan says. "From their perspective it has to do with the struggle for survival. They feel the pyramid was flattened and that they won't get the same opportunities as the people before them. At the same time, they don't feel the freedom that the twentysomethings have." 22

Margey Hillman, 44, director of multimedia programs for an educational software firm in San Diego, agrees that the fear among her boomer colleagues is palpable—and that much of it is focuses on their twentysomething employees. "Middle management is middle-aged, and we're scared," Hillman says. "A lot of us have been sitting on our asses for ten years. We don't know how to do whatever it is we did to get where we are in the first place, and we've let our skills wither. Now, along come these young people who not only know how to do what middle managers do and are current on the technology, they have no respect for middle managers and they won't tolerate us not doing it." 23

But don't give Xers credit for too much insight. Hillman says their complaints about politics and what seem to be arbitrary, control-freak decisions by boomer managers are based on what she calls "smart innocence"—a nice way of saying twentysomethings are naive. "Say you've been on the job for a year or two, and there's an argument over the kind of software package you're going to use for something," Hillman explains. "The younger worker doesn't know that the reason you're using a particular program is because the president of the company is sleeping with the president of another company. You're not going to explain this to them, so they say, 'This other package will help me work two to three times faster,' and I end up saying, 'We're going to use this other one because I picked it.' " 24

The boomers also give voice to the age-old complaint heard every time a new crop of youngsters enters the workplace: that those whippersnappers aren't patiently learning how the game is played—or waiting their turn. Either they come into a company and expect that, in short order, they should be running it, or they always seem to be looking for something better to come along and are thus disloyal. Says Barry Horowitz, 46, director of international transportation at Nike in Portland, Oregon: "You have to be prepared to start at the bottom. People coming out of college today think they don't have to start at the bottom and work their way through the system." 25

What's different this time is that it appears to Xers—and pretty much everyone else—that lifetime employment is a thing of the past. 26

Therefore, twentysomethings ask, where will loyalty and dues-paying get us?

Consider Jason James, 26, who has been temping for a year on a technical support desk at an IBM subsidiary in Raleigh, North Carolina. His father has spent his career at the computer giant, but James has no similar expectation. "There are career IBMers in my area being laid off, and they're shocked," says James, who graduated from the University of North Carolina. "They thought they had a job for life, and I don't get it. IBM only would give me a one-year job, so it's hard to be sympathetic. Maybe it's because I'm young—I'm able to adapt, I'm current on new technology, and I'm willing to work harder for less. They can get me for $13 an hour, while the full-time people make a lot more than that and get benefits, and some of them don't work as hard." 27

Faced with that lack of security and the prospect of working for bosses they can't stand, many twentysomethings figure it's simply better to take advantage of their youth and risk going it alone. Look at Megan Wheeler, the aforementioned programmer, and Aaron Singer, 25, who last year founded Ad Hoc Technologies, an educational software firm in La Jolla, California. With no capital beyond Singer's stripped-down Apple Macintosh SE, they got a consulting job and invested the proceeds in new equipment. They've taken in over $100,000 over the past year consulting for other companies while they work on their first product, an interactive CD-ROM–based game. 28

Singer hooked up with Wheeler, whom he knew from his childhood in Enid, Oklahoma, after poking around New York for two years looking for a job and doing stints as a computer consultant. Wheeler, an experienced software developer, started off her 20s as a professional ballet dancer in New York and Austin, Texas, then got into programming as her knees began to give out. Her previous job was as a $34,000-a-year programmer for another San Diego software developer. "Here it's not just a feeling that we're going to work," Singer says. "We're creating something that means a lot to us." 29

In a seedy neighborhood on the northwest side of Chicago, another young entrepreneur, Vincent Cobb, 27, works out of a converted loft that's also his apartment. Cobb's product is a foam-rubber, plastic-topped deskpad for the "mice" that are now standard equipment on most computers. His innovation is to cover them with art images such as Da Vinci's *Mona Lisa* or Van Gogh's *Starry Night.* After graduating from Miami University in Ohio, Cobb worked for a year selling computers at Nynex Business Centers and then for an outfit that makes scheduling software. 30

"If Michael Dell hadn't started his business out of his dorm room in college, he would have shortly after he had gone to work and gotten 31 a taste of what corporate life is like," says Cobb of Dell Computer's wunderkind 28-year-old CEO and founder, the ultimate icon for Xer entrepreneurs. "It's frustrating trying to launch a business, but it's better than working for a big company that's boring, dry, dull, and conservative, or for a small company that's stifling."

Smart managers will see that taking what Xers say seriously not 32
only will promote generational comity in the workplace but may also give companies a competitive edge. Consultant David Cannon says, "The fact is that Generation X is very well built for the organization of today. A company that gets into new products and does things differently is exhilarating to younger people."

One approach to harnessing twentysomethings' energy is to cre- 33
ate an entrepreneurial environment in which they can thrive. At Hewlett-Packard in Sunnyvale, California, 30-year-old marketer Laura Demmons is a lead member of a so-called garage team that's developing a communications product to be launched in early 1994. Under the garage concept H-P acts as a venture capitalist, in this case giving the team a $4 million budget—and virtually complete autonomy.

Demmons says her road hasn't been pot-hole–free. "The older 34
managers look at us as these young whippersnappers. I was frustrated. I felt like I could run circles around the managers, and I was doing it for less than half the money. I was going to leave for a startup when the vice president of the group called me in. I told him, 'I don't fit in here.' And he said, 'But you do fit in here,' and I was offered this garage opportunity." After extensive focus-group research, Demmons and her teammates formulated a business plan for "a really hot communications software product."

Still, Demmons ran into trouble when the manager to whom she 35
nominally reports, 38-year-old Kevin Schofield, tried to bring her back under his control. "Kevin was kind of struck in the old hierarchy. But I can just see him. It's like, I was this creature. I didn't want to be mean to him, but I just wanted a field to run in," says Demmons, who counts horseback riding among her hobbies. The situation was fixed by restoring her autonomy, and Demmons says Schofield "in hindsight, has been one of my biggest supporters." For his part, Schofield says, "To the extent there are frustrations, I understand them. That's why we're doing things that are different." Demmons's conclusion: "This product is so good. It's more than just the money that's important—it's the ownership question. It's like, please let me do this job. There are so many young people who are so good at what they do."

The bottom line with twentysomethings is that they'll respond if 36
boomer managers put meaning into the buzzwords they're prone to

mouthing—*empowerment, teamwork, communication.* "You have to have two-way communication to be successful," says Cathy Sigismonti, a 28-year-old marketing analyst at IVAC, a San Diego division of Eli Lilly that makes medical devices. "If you're asking me to do something and you tell me why you need it and what you're going to use it for, maybe I can figure out a way to do it faster," Sigismonti says. "And if I tell you that what you're asking is going to take 100 hours, then maybe you'll decide you don't need it after all."

Feedback and recognition are other no-brainers that Xers say their boomer managers too often overlook. Says Sigismonti, her finger tapping on a table for emphasis: "Tell me that I did a good job. Let me know." Adds John Doyle, a 31-year-old San Diego programmer: "We want recognition because when we were growing up the family unit wasn't very strong. It can be financial or something else. At a company event, it could be just pointing someone out and saying their name." 37

Xers bring a different set of values to the workplace, values that in many ways are a reaction to the workaholism they associate with their older boomer brethren. Says Margaret Regan: "In my employee surveys, the factors that predict job satisfaction among people in their 20s is that it be a fun place to work." The peril of an un-fun workplace is that Xer employees will consider their jobs no more than a paycheck and will clock out regularly at 5 o'clock, when the real fun begins for them. Says Scott Hess, a 27-year-old Chicago marketing writer: "The god we're worshipping is not the bottom line—it's quality of life." 38

The moral of this tale is that feeling threatened by Generation X and tightening up is the worst possible reaction for a boomer manager to have toward younger employees. Yes, we kids are impetuous, naive, and just a tad arrogant—and that's why we need smart but sensitive boomer managers who can smooth our rough edges while channeling our enthusiasm. Ally yourself with us while you can—or don't be surprised if, one day, you're asking one of *us* for work. 39

THINKING ABOUT THE ESSAY

1. What are the major differences in work attitude between baby boomers and Generation Xers? How does this difference contribute toward conflicts in the workplace? Would the author have found the same conflicts if he had selected for his analysis a field other than the business world (for example, health care, law, or education)? If so, why? If not, why not?
2. Explain the style of this essay. Are Ratan's language and sentence structure accessible or difficult? How does Ratan's style facilitate your reading of this relatively long essay?

3. Why, as the author states, have "twentysomethings . . . abandoned corporate America, retreating into slackerdom or striking out on their own as entrepreneurs"? Are his causal analysis and argument effective? Hasn't every generation of Americans experimented with finding alternatives to the corporate lifestyle? What difference, if any, exists between the current generation of job changers and earlier ones?
4. How does Ratan utilize interviews and case studies to structure his essay? Does he employ too many profiles or too few? Explain.
5. The author champions Xers who strike out on their own. Considering that most new businesses fail, is he providing false hope for frustrated corporate workers?

RESPONDING IN DISCUSSION

1. Divide into groups of three or four, and elect a chairperson who presides over a simulated business meeting concerning the introduction of a new product. Select the product, and role-play the meeting, keeping in mind that the boss has the final say in all matters. Afterwards, discuss with the class your feelings about the exercise.
2. Discuss how you felt toward a teacher when you received a grade on a test, term paper, or course that was lower than what you believed you deserved. Say what you did, if anything, to protest the grade.
3. Is the intergenerational conflict as described in the essay unique or just typical of all work environments in which there are younger and older workers? Explain.
4. The author cites a Generation Xer who claims that his generation is most concerned with "quality of life." Discuss what he means by that statement.
5. Find an Internet site full of corporate job listings. Test the validity of the author's claim of a technological generation gap by comparing job descriptions for managers and for staff employees. Using the "Find . . ." feature of your web browser, have the computer scan the site for the word "computer" or other more technical terms, and examine the listings that specify these subjects. Do computer skills appear equally prominently as requirements in candidates for positions at both levels?

RESPONDING IN WRITING

1. Write a comparative essay on the differences and similarities between younger and older workers that you have observed personally.

2. Describe your ideal job in 350 to 500 words.
3. Argue for or against the proposition that people at different stages in their lives have different needs so that there will inevitably be conflict in the workplace.
4. Utilizing one or more Web search engines, download information on "corporate downsizing." Who loses jobs when companies downsize: the young, the old, both? Present your findings in an essay of 750 to 1,000 words.

Married, with Househusband

Andrea Gabor

This essay explores the phenomenon of the househusband, a term that has been in use for decades. What makes this essay enlightening is its in-depth analysis of the phenomenon that includes statistical data and detailed interviews with subjects, so the term takes on more significance than a mere definition. First published in the November 1995 issue of *Working Woman* (a magazine that caters to the affluent, upscale female professional), it details a number of case studies that provide insights into the multilayered motives that have advanced the househusband movement and the varying lifestyles that exist in families with a househusband.

PREVIEWING THE ESSAY

Do you know a househusband? You may know men who do not work or men who work at home, but this is not what the author suggests by the term. A househusband is a man who intentionally stays home to take responsibility over the majority of household tasks such as childrearing, cleaning, and general maintenance of a home. It is also a role that is voluntary, and not the result of retirement, disability, unwanted unemployment, and the like. There is, however, a common thread that seems to run through all families that elect to have the man voluntarily stay at home or, at least, allow the woman to be the major breadwinner in the family. Although not stated directly, it is an essential part of the socioeconomic world described in the essay. Can you discern this common denominator?

As a foster child growing up in Brooklyn, Edith Nurbin always knew what she wanted: a house in the suburbs and a traditional life as a wife and mother. So when she married at 20, before finishing college, she picked Jay Weiner, who shared her ideal of family life and felt as 1 strongly as she did that children should be reared by their parents, not by a caretaker.

But life didn't turn out quite the way the Weiners planned it. Edie, already a star student at the City College of New York when she met Jay, never expected that her own intellectual ambitions would change her goals. While he became a public-school teacher, she joined a life-insurance trade association and helped develop a forecasting service that examines how long-term sociopolitical trends affect the industry. In 1977, she launched her own forecasting business, Weiner, Edrich, Brown, and when she became pregnant a year later, the couple realized that if anyone was going to quit work to raise their son, Jared, it was clearly going to be Jay. Not only would Edie soon be earning more, but as a city employee, Jay could take an extended leave of absence without jeopardizing his job. 2

Jay agreed to take three years off to raise Jared. With that decision, he joined the pioneers of a new male archetype: the househusband, who, for at least a few years, takes on the role traditionally filled by housewives, including the care and nurturing not only of a family but of a spouse's career as well. 3

These days, Edie and Jay Weiner have plenty of company. Men who give up working permanently to become homemakers are still in the vast minority, but as women's salaries and clout in the workplace increase, the number of families in which the wife's career takes precedence is growing rapidly. In 1993, 205,000 men between 25 and 59 were keeping house instead of holding paying jobs, a 49% increase since 1989, according to the Bureau of Labor Statistics. In 1994, close to half of the employed women in married couples provided "about half" or more of the family income, according to *Women: The New Providers,* a study published in May by the Families and Work Institute in New York and the Whirlpool Foundation in Benton Harbor, Mich. The number of women who outearn their husbands has also risen substantially, to close to one-quarter of dual-career couples, estimates Ellen Galinsky of the Families and Work Institute. That's up from 18% in 1987, according to a study by the Census Bureau. 4

The trend has a public face as well: Increasingly, the country's most powerful women are married to men who are willing to let their professional lives take a back seat (at least for a while) to their wives' careers. In some cases—usually when the couple has small children—the husband drops out of the work force entirely; in other cases, he calibrates his career to his wife's, much the way working women always have for their husbands. The example set by these high-profile couples is helping to legitimize the role of househusbands in less famous households. For example, Bill Good, the husband of the Commerce Department's undersecretary for technology administration, Mary Good, gave up his career as a chemist to follow his wife first to 5

Chicago, when she became an executive at Allied Signal, and then to Washington. Similarly, Laura D'Andrea Tyson, now national economic advisor, is married to screenwriter Erik Tarloff, who followed her to Washington, and who recalls with a mixture of humor and pique the question one acquaintance asked after her appointment: "What's the state of the old ego? What's it like to have a wife so much more important than yourself?" Another writer-husband, Benjamin Cheever, an avowed stay-at-home suburban husband married to *New York Times* movie critic Janet Maslin, frequently writes about the tribulations of being married to a prominent woman: "My last name is Cheever. My wife's last name is different," he wrote several years ago. "She writes for the *New York Times.* She has a byline. I've been called Mr. Byline. This I do not like."

Whether the woman is a Washington power broker or a little-known business executive, there is much more to these marriages than role reversal. They test the oldest, most fundamental emotional and practical assumptions about married life; along with reallocating household chores, they are redefining age-old gender roles and the balance of power within families. For the most successful, the experience is a personal adventure. "I wouldn't have missed this ride for the world," says Katherine Greenleaf, a mother of two whose husband, Peter, gave up his law practice in Maine for two years to follow her to Columbus, Ohio, where she was a vice president at the Limited until this spring. "I feel like I'm one of the first wave of professional women who haven't had to sacrifice having a husband and child." 6

In the best cases, families in which Mom brings home the bacon and Dad takes care of the kids can be more successful than the '50s ideal of the traditional family. "These relationships are experimental—they are *counter*traditional," says Pepper Schwartz, author of *Peer Marriage* and a sociologist at the University of Washington who studies the dynamics of marriage. In the absence of any clear guidelines, these couples have had to "make a very conscious choice" to create a new family model, says Schwartz. In making that choice, experts say, both husbands and wives are often happier and more satisfied with their roles—and their lives—than those who fall into traditional gender roles without fully evaluating their options. 7

MINOR TRIP-UPS, MAJOR PROBLEMS

As with more traditional unions, the adjustments to a role-reversal marriage are often trickiest when couples fall into it more by accident than by design. On the surface, Jay Weiner's decision to stay home and raise Jared for a few years while Edie supported the family seemed perfectly suited both to the family's needs and to his and 8

Edie's individual desires. It was the career issues they didn't anticipate that proved hardest to deal with. Jay, who loves to teach but became disillusioned with public-school politics early in his career, says he has "never sacrificed anything" for his marriage and revels in his role as full-time father. He became an expert diaper changer and a minor celebrity at local playgrounds. When the transit strike hit New York in 1980, he bought roller skates and could be seen zipping down Third Avenue behind a baby carriage, propelling Jared to his pediatrician's appointments.

Yet Jay, the son of a truck driver and homemaker, never com- 9
pletely shook his ideas about a woman's place in the home. He doesn't cook or clean, nor have the Weiner's hired a housekeeper. So even though her salary has climbed well into the six figures, Edie still does the housework and leaves the office in time to prepare a home-cooked meal two or three times a week.

These are concessions Edie, now 47, says she is happy to make, 10
however. "It's time and work, but housekeeping is the least of the issues" in their arrangement. Thornier problems involve limitations in building her business. Jay, 51, doesn't like her to go on overnight trips, so she has agreed never to be away for more than one night at a time. (No one in the Weiner family disputes that it is Edie who does most of the compromising.) Consequently, she cannot take on clients in Europe, the West Coast or the Far East, which automatically rules out at least 30% of the prospective clients who approach her. Recently, when CompUSA asked Edie to join its board, Jay objected to her taking the position because it involved attending six board meetings a year out of town. Although Edie stood firm this time, the arguments raged for weeks. And Jared, now 16, confesses that he sometimes wonders whether his parents will be able to put these disputes behind them; so far, he notes with visible relief, they always have.

In fact, role-reversal relationships usually work best in families 11
with young children, says Barbara Morrison, a couples and family therapist in New York, because there is a whole gamut of rules based on custom and cultural expectation. The responsibilities are so clear—and numerous—that the couple has to collaborate on a game plan. That's not the case for childless couples. The tensions of role reversal and the lack of structure can make these marriages "much more brittle," says Morrison.

Jared Weiner is the best testament to the choices his parents have 12
made. He has inherited his father's love of sports and his mother's peripatetic intelligence, and he attends one of the most competitive schools for gifted students in New York's public-school system. He tends to sympathize with his mother, though, when it comes to the restrictions Jay has placed on her business. "I know it's difficult for her," says Jared. Adds Edie, "He doesn't think I should have to turn down work."

TURNING TRADITION ON ITS EAR

The adjustments to role-reversal marriages are much easier for couples who are unfettered by traditional expectations. Even if they don't explicitly map out their future professional and family roles in advance, many men and women now enter marriage with an implicit understanding that, at the very least, the wife's career will play an important role in the relationship, says Morrison. They look to the example of couples like Supreme Court justice Sandra Day O'Connor and her husband, John: Although she followed his lead for the first several years of their marriage, it was "always understood" that she would work because the couple met at Stanford Law School. After their children were older, John adjusted gradually to her career, first as lawyer, then as state legislator and finally as Supreme Court justice. "Many women have an unconscious awareness of their need to find men who complement their professional goals, who will help them develop their potential," says Morrison. "If the man is at home, with his own anima—his inner femaleness—and if the couple has a good working relationship, those are the couples that can make this very powerful shift." 13

It was just such an understanding that led to the highly unconventional family life of Judith Kurland, 50, who became Boston's first female commissioner of health and hospitals in 1988, and her husband, Benny Lipchik. Like most in their generation, the two never discussed in advance how they would juggle their careers or raise their children. But when they married in 1974, it was understood by both that while Kurland was passionately devoted to her work, Lipchik worked as an accountant only for the paycheck. So when she became pregnant a month after their wedding, it seemed only natural for him to quit work if Kurland could keep her job as director of federal–state relations under Massachusetts governor Michael Dukakis. 14

While she logged 50- to 60-hour weeks establishing herself as a state public-policy leader, Lipchik took to homemaking and parenting as though he had been born to the job. When it came to finding things to do with the kids, "Benny had far more energy than I could ever have mustered," says Kurland. He spent hours playing ball with his son, and goodnaturedly submitted to his daughters when they tied ribbons in his hair and styled his mustache. The kids had so much fun "hanging out with Benny" that they refused to go to summer camp. Since Kurland spent most of her career in government jobs, where pay scales are much lower than in the private sector, the couple decided to do without a housekeeper. "He did everything—shop, cook, laundry, cleaning," says Kurland. He even insisted on washing the dinner dishes so she could relax with the kids. "Benny made it possible for me to be as close to guilt-free as a Jewish mother could be," she says. 15

For Lipchik, a South African emigrant whose father died when he was 8 and whose mother eked out a living as a seamstress, the biggest adjustment to his unusual marriage had less to do with his own expectations than with those of his peers. Although he was beloved by the neighborhood moms, who referred to themselves as "the park ladies and Ben," some men assumed that Lipchik was a "ne'er-do-well or that he couldn't hold down a job," Kurland recalls. At one party, a guest asked snidely whether Lipchik had come to the U.S. to "marry a rich American woman." Benny sanguinely replied that he had modeled himself on the lions of South Africa. "They're organized in prides—the women go out and do the hunting," he explained. The only difference in his pride, he added, is that "Judith insists that there be only one female." 16

Kurland learned just how indispensable Benny was in 1988, when she beat out several male candidates to become health commissioner. During the first few years in the job, she succeeded where her predecessors had failed; despite massive budget cuts, she rebuilt Boston's troubled City Hospital. And throughout the political battles, Benny and the kids remained her support and refuge. But in 1992, the couple's idyllic family life—and Judith's career trajectory—ended suddenly when Benny died of a massive heart attack at 46. Kurland decided not to seek a second term as health commissioner and began a less demanding career as a health-care consultant. "Without Benny, I knew I couldn't stay in a high-pressure political job and adequately care for the kids," she explains. 17

The Bonus for Men

As society becomes more accepting of the househusband phenomenon, men are increasingly finding that in helping to support the professional ambitions of their wives, they discover new opportunities of their own. In the *New Providers* study, 21% of the men surveyed said they would stay home to spend more time with their kids if money were no object—about twice the number in a similar study in 1981. (At the same time, the number of women who said they would want to spend more time with their children dropped to 31%, from 39% in the earlier study.) 18

Men are also finding that their wives' paychecks can help liberate them from unsatisfying jobs. It was the realization that his wife's work could help him plan a career change that helped lawyer Peter Greenleaf, 48, make the psychological leap from what his wife Kathy refers to as a "rigid male chauvinist" to househusband—at least for the time being. Peter has taken on traditional tasks such as planning meals and participating in school activities with the children. Kathy, on the other hand, learned that she must delegate tasks 19 she had always thought of as her own when she took an executive post at the Limited in Columbus.

20 The change in the Greenleaf's lives came incrementally with Kathy's increasing awareness of her own ambitions. While her children were small, she was "too busy juggling and too sleep-deprived," she says, to focus on career goals. It wasn't until 1993, 20 years after they married, that the couple decided it was time for Kathy, now 47, to make a major move, one that would put her career ahead of Peter's. When the Limited job came up, he agreed to give up his practice in Portland, Me., and shoulder the burdens of relocation. After their move last year, he got the kids settled in school and even took on some household duties, such as cooking, that he frankly doesn't enjoy. "I don't like being centered here [at home]. It's isolating," he says. "It's probably harder for men because they have no accepted role models outside the workplace."

21 Still, the payoff for Peter is clear: In recent years, Kathy's income has allowed him to suspend his law practice to take jobs with the Justice Department, which, though less lucrative than private practice, gave him a chance to learn new areas of the law. He saw the move to Ohio as an opportunity to build a new career in legal arbitration. "I've never been averse to risks," he says, "and Maine was beginning to feel small. We were ready for an adventure. Otherwise, mentally and emotionally, we might as well have retired."

22 After the big decisions were made, the Greenleafs found themselves navigating the more mundane challenges of role reversal. Coping with the kids has turned out to be the easy part: Peter enjoys attending their sporting events; he was even on a parents' field-hockey team, one of three dads among a scad of moms who played against his daughter's team. (His rambunctious performance on the field won him the Crazy Dad award, of which his daughter is particularly proud.)

23 More difficult were his efforts to pick up the slack at home. Probably the toughest negotiations involved decorating. The Greenleafs left most of their furniture at their house in Maine, which they planned to use as a vacation home. Furnishing their new house was difficult partly because Kathy found it hard to hand over a job she had always enjoyed—she second-guessed Peter even on relatively simple decisions. So they compromised: For the first several months in Ohio, they just "didn't have any furniture." In the end, they wound up picking a few pieces. In one shopping foray that says much about the couple's compatibility, Kathy found a dining room table; the following week, Peter went to the same store and, without knowing which table his wife had picked, selected the chairs that matched it.

24 Indeed, the Greenleafs agree that the Ohio Experiment—as they now refer to it—worked best when they were being "creative," not simply trying to reverse roles. In the end, however, they decided to

return to Maine. Kathy came to feel that the job simply wasn't worth the numerous sacrifices they had made to move to Ohio—chief among them having to leave their seven-acre ocean-front home. Although the fact that Peter never fully adjusted to life as a househusband played a role in the decision, Kathy insists that had she been totally committed to her job, he would have agreed to stay. Instead, the pull of the old family homestead, the relationships they had developed over the years and Kathy's own changing professional interests drew the Greenleaf family back to Maine. Now Peter is reestablishing his practice, and Kathy, who has had several job offers, is thinking of buying a business with friends.

Switching Roles by Design, Not Default

Being creative about their marriages is a challenge that younger cou- 25
ples are taking on with increasing deliberation. They are now much more likely to go into couples therapy *before* marriage, as a way to sort out the family roles they will play, especially when the wife has the bigger career, says Augustus Napier, a psychologist based in Atlanta and the author of *The Fragile Bond: In Search of an Intimate, Equal and Enduring Marriage.*

As professional women become more cognizant of their own am- 26
bitions, they are likelier to consciously choose mates who are willing to adapt to their careers. For example, Judith Giordan, 42, VP of research and development at the German chemical manufacturer Henkel, is in the vanguard of a new generation of women who have resolved to build their personal lives around their professional ones. While still in her 20s, Giordan concluded that motherhood was incompatible with her desire to succeed in the almost exclusively male bastion of industrial chemistry. By the time she was in her early 30s and a rising star at Polaroid, she despaired of ever finding a husband willing to accommodate her career. Sitting in a bar late one Saturday afternoon, Giordan complained to Larry Friedman, a fellow chemist and one of her closest friends at work, that most men were threatened by her professional goals. Friedman went to his car to fetch a Harvard alumni magazine so Giordan could look at the personal ads. Sipping rum toddies and composing an ad for Giordan, the two realized that perhaps *they* were meant for each other. Friedman, too, had once been intensely ambitious, but he was 15 years older and divorced, and his priorities had changed. He felt he had little in common with his first wife after a few years together, and was determined that if he ever remarried it would be to a woman who shared his interests.

In marrying Giordan, Friedman willingly played midwife to her 27
career—a meteoric professional odyssey he had once fantasized

about embarking on himself. Indeed, her financial success eclipsed his soon after they began living together in 1984; although he earned about 40% more than she did when they met, her salary today is three times his. Friedman has relocated twice and moved into a new field, as an academic administrator, in part because it offers him greater mobility. He's also made a point of encouraging Giordan to become active in professional organizations such as the American Chemical Society, of which he has long been a member, and he happily plays spouse at clubby scientific gatherings. Ever focused on her goal of becoming the chief of R&D for a major corporation—exhibiting a self-awareness that few women develop until relatively late in their professional lives—Giordan began planning last winter for the possibility of being asked to relocate yet again. Friedman, in response, added a final item to his Christmas wish list: German-language tapes that would prepare him for what could be Giordan's ultimate career move, from Philadelphia to Henkel headquarters in Düsseldorf.

Many of these couples started down the path toward role reversal 28 in the mid-1970s, and it has taken nearly two decades for the trend to gain even a modicum of official acceptability. When Felice Schwartz wrote the controversial 1989 *Harvard Business Review* article in which she exhorted corporations to accommodate working moms and establish what has become widely referred to as the mommy track, she decided not to mention dads in the piece. "At that time, I thought that corporate leaders were just becoming aware of the reality of women's need to take time off when they had babies," says Schwartz. "If I had gone into their offices and said, 'How about men?' they wouldn't have known what I was talking about. Interestingly, in just the last few years you can say it—not that it will be responded to positively, but it will be understood."

Of course, formidable hurdles remain even for those couples who 29 reverse roles gladly and consciously. Napier points out that many husbands who wind up married to high-powered, ambitious women come from families in which the father was often absent—a trend that is growing. On one hand, these men, whose mothers played a dominant role in the family, are often more supportive spouses and conscientious fathers than their more traditional counterparts. The downside, says Napier, is that they often wind up feeling insecure in relation to their accomplished wives. "The tension in these marriages is often exacerbated by the fact that the wife is overfunctioning," he says. "She's also coping with the kids, feeling burdened and pretty stressed." Ellen Galinsky of the Families and Work Institute has observed the same phenomenon. "Traditional roles die hard," she says. "Many of these women are angry at their husbands—angry that they are not [better] breadwinners." Often, adds Morrison, the wife's resentment and the husband's befuddlement go unaddressed for too long, building over time.

As with most marriages, the key to a successful role-reversed relationship is strongly tied to sex. "If, traditionally, the sexual role for maleness is about initiative and leading, while femaleness is about receptivity and yielding, then it can be a real psychological stretch if the gender roles and the sexual roles are incongruent," says Morrison. In other words, if you plan to bring home the bacon, it helps if you can also take the lead in bed, at least sometimes. 30

Sex aside, the best long-term hope for young couples may be what Pepper Schwartz refers to as "peer marriage," in which husband and wife trade career priorities back and forth, accommodating each other's personal and professional needs as well as those of their families, depending on what stage of family and work life each is in. Couples in peer marriages challenge not only traditional marriage and gender roles but also the linear career trajectory that most employers have always taken for granted, and that has long hobbled the careers of working moms. 31

Maintaining that balance—between nurturing careers, children and the relationship itself—is even harder, of course, than creating a life that allows switching roles in the first place. Sometimes, Schwartz says, it requires actually splitting responsibilities down the middle, which helps keep contributions from being divided into high- and low-prestige provinces. At other times, she says, the best approach is determining *equity,* in which each partner gives equally, but in a different coin—whatever it takes to keep the relationship collaborative, supportive and loving. Calculating when and how those contributions are made is often an inexact (and tiring) science. But for the couples who manage it, there's no question of their relationship's being a mere reversal of roles. They're writing a better script. 32

THINKING ABOUT THE ESSAY

1. To what social and economic classes do the families described in this essay belong? How does membership in these classes place them in a privileged position so that they can make economic choices unavailable to the majority of Americans?
2. What types of jobs do women with a househusband seem to hold? What is the relevance of their professions to their ability to have a nontraditional or countertraditional household?
3. When you evoke an image of a working woman (the title of the magazine from which this article is taken), what comes to mind? Does it conform to the image of the women as described in this

essay? Why? Why would Gabor's essay find a receptive audience in a magazine entitled *Working Woman?*

4. Does Gabor maintain a neutral, positive, or negative stance toward her subject? Is she a reporter or commentator? What evidence in the essay led you to your view?
5. How many parts comprise this essay? What is the relationship among these sections? Does Gabor advance her thesis effectively from section to section? Why?
6. Gabor waits until the essay is nearly finished before she makes the relevant and poignant remark, "As with most marriages, the key to a successful role-reversed relationship is strongly tied to sex." If this element is such a key, why did she wait until the end of the essay to bring it up. Is it a rhetorical device placed where it is for a purpose, or is it a supporting point that is misplaced in the context of the essay?

RESPONDING IN DISCUSSION

1. Gather in small groups with an equal mix of men and women, and discuss the level of acceptability each member has with the idea of living in a home with a househusband. Discuss your findings with the rest of the class.
2. Kingsolver suggests in her essay that affluent families usually have a "hidden member" such as a maid or maintenance person to assist in keeping up the home. Discuss whether homes with househusbands require this addition to the household.
3. The key issue that continuously arises in the essay regarding the family constellation and its relegation of duties is ambition. Discuss to what degree this essay is a reflection on the changing nature of ambition in American life rather than an exploration of changing family dynamics, or whether the essay is really a study of the relationship between the two.
4. Form groups of three or four, and review those parts of the text that address the shortcomings certain men feel about becoming househusbands. Discuss whether these concerns are culturally generated or based in economic reality.

RESPONDING IN WRITING

1. Interview a foreign student at your college regarding his or her attitude to the concept of the househusband. Write a 400-word profile of the student's response including his or her cultural, social, and family values.

2. Interview a member of your parents' generation who currently serves as a househusband. Write a summary of his attitudes concerning his role.
3. For a creative writing project, imagine that you are a male chief executive officer of a large corporation who has decided to become a househusband. In a 500-word essay, describe your first day at your new "job."
4. Argue for or against the proposition that alternating family roles during the course of a child's development will only prevent the child from developing a strong sense of identity.
5. Research the househusband phenomenon. Look into library resources—both traditional and computerized—and also conduct a search on the Web. Was there sufficient information? What does this tell you about the scope of the issue? Write a report summarizing your findings.

CONNECTIONS: FOR WRITING AND RESEARCH

1. Write a comparison-and-contrast essay exploring Anderman's experience in "Why Can't I Find a Full-Time Job?" and the portraits in "Generational Tension in the Office." Explain why their job situations are so divergent.
2. Write an essay that argues for or against the proposition that it is more "American" to concern oneself with the global ideas that Thurow advances than to address the issues explored in Ratan's "Generational Tension in the Office."
3. Write an essay of 400 to 500 words entitled "Student Jobs: The Ultimate Economic Exploitation."
4. For a research project, trace the history of changing attitudes by women toward work in America.
5. For a creative writing assignment, assume the persona of a member of the D-Day generation (as described in Noonan's essay) and write a letter entitled "Stop Your Whining" to a twentysomething employee.
6. Form an on-line discussion group with no more than four of your classmates. Arrange for a time and date, and discuss one of the essays in this section in a chat group. Present a group report on the results of your discussion.
7. Compare the apparently anarchistic family in Oates' "They All Just Went Away" (an essay that appears in Chapter 8) with the typical depiction of family life in "Married, with Househusband." What major economic, educational, social, and geographic factors distinguish them?

4

THE DATING GAME

Nearly all the essays in this chapter address the new concern about dating that has lately swept the pages of magazines, the broadcast airwaves, and the halls of academe: the issues of what constitutes consensual sex or date or acquaintance rape, and the precise roles of men and women, particularly regarding sexuality. At one time the definitions and contours of date and sex were securely in place, as were the roles of men and women regarding dating, courtship, and intimacy. Lately, however, the entire playing field has changed to the degree that even traditional terminology has become suspect. For example, what exactly is a date and what expectations does it connote? The current debate seems to reside between two opposing factions: those like Catherine MacKinnon (quoted in the article by Katie Roiphe) who see nearly all heterosexual sex as rape, and those like Roiphe herself, who as a "postfeminist" derides older radical feminists for portraying women as sexless, passive beings who can't make their own choices and are at the mercy of more powerful men. A more temperate view is expressed by Mary Gaitskill in her essay "On Not Being a Victim." She advances the thesis that solely portraying sexual behavior as extremes of female and male passivity or aggressivity helps no one find his or her own sense of self and personal understanding. One thing is clear, however. As Alan E. Guskin and Diana Trilling state in "Should Colleges Adopt Written Policies on Sex between Students," when legions of institutions of higher learning demonstrate interest in "official rules of engagement" regarding sexual encounters (such as the rules at Antioch College), the dating game isn't what it used to be.

California's "Dating Hell"

Susan Shirachi

Many women complain of dating hell, whether its cause is the lack of eligible men in large cities, the inability to find prospects in the bar scene, or the generally low level of mature men that can be found anywhere. What makes the observations in this essay—first published in the June 1994 issue of *Transpacific*—stand out from the usual litany of complaints is that the author's attribution of her dilemma resides in the difference in culture between men in Hawaii and Asian-Pacific men who live in California. Her ability to compare and contrast the attitudes, behaviors, and beliefs of these two groups provides an insight into the nature of American values, particularly as they pertain to American men's views of dating. While her conclusions may seem apparent, that mainland men are less compassionate and "lack a sense of their culture and a security in their male identity," her views are reached through true life experience and observation, and not via a poll or sound bite. Additionally, it affords readers the opportunity to garner a view of a particular cultural group to which few Americans have intimate access.

PREVIEWING THE ESSAY

For many of us, our culture is invisible. It is simply a composite of all our ways of interacting with the world. It is more likely that we learn about our cultural traits by having them pointed out by others than by knowing them through self-observation. What places the author of this essay in a privileged position that enables her to compare the traits among the groups she is describing? Are her observations colored by her disenchantment with her situation or do they seem fair appraisals of the life she experiences?

Forget the floods, the earthquakes, the riots and the fires. And don't even bother to mention the traffic and the smog. The toughest part about living in Southern California is the dearth of decent, single Pacific-Asian men. As a Hawaii native who came to California several years ago in search of adventure, excitement and marriageable men, I can testify to my severe disappointment with the dating scene in the Golden State. When I said "aloha" to the islands, I didn't know that I was bidding farewell to my chances of finding the perfect mate. 1

I remember dating in Hawaii as pure, clean fun. The men would invite you to the University of Hawaii football game at Aloha Stadium. Once there, you would have a tailgate party, throw back a few drinks and root for the Rainbows. And you could always count on your date 2 inviting you to a weekend picnic at Ala Moana Park or camping at Bellows Beach (famous for boogie-boarding and moonlight picnics). The feeling of familiarity, homogeneity and comfort is something that Hawaiians treasure, especially when dating. Pacific-Asian men in Hawaii are more monogamous than their California counterparts; they date their girlfriends for what seems like an eternity before marrying and wear their wedding band.

California men, on the other hand, bring new meaning to the 3
phrase "dating hell." Although I find California's Pacific-Asian men good-looking, they lack a spirit that seems unique to Hawaii and its people. I call it the "goodness of the soul." That translates into caring about a co-worker's emotional condition after the loss of a family member, choosing their wife and children over an extramarital affair, sharing the cost of a party with the host, not doing anything to intentionally hurt another person or animal and sincerely caring about their in-laws. Most California men seem to care only about their own needs, thinking secondarily about their parents, wives and family. In many ways, these California Pacific-Asians have become "too white." They lack a sense of their culture and a security in their male identity. They may look Asian, but they certainly do not act Asian or think Asian.

Island men who've relocated in California are only a little better. 4
They're easy to spot, with their casual gait (they never run) and Hawaiian pidgin talk. They use phrases like "Da ting," "Li dat" and "C'mon, no ack." Though I was raised in the islands, I sometimes have difficulty understanding their dialect. Like their California-born counterparts, however, they've also become too white. They would rather tailgate in front of their big-screen TVs than at a football game. And they're cheap, too. I was raised in an environment in which men paid for thc "privilege" of dating you. It was an unspoken code between dating couples. In California, these transplanted Hawaiians will sometimes grudgingly pay for dinner—and later make you wish they hadn't. They'll spend the rest of the evening complaining about the expense and how it would have been cheaper to go to a drive-in theater or have a zip pack at Zippy's [a local hangout in Hawaii].

At least with these transplanted island men, I'm reminded of hap- 5
pier days back in Hawaii. I can recall the gentle island breezes of a Sunday afternoon, the smell of rain on freshly cut grass and eating Spam musubis rolled in nori while watching the guys play basketball at Manoa Park.

My mother used to ask me, "What do you want to be when you 6
grow up?" I would tell her, "I want to be a veterinarian." My mother would beam with pride. That was a long time ago. If my mother should ask me, "What have you accomplished now that you've grown up?" I would probably answer her, "I'm a single Japanese American woman who is looking for a kind-hearted and employed husband and

would like some security with my job and marriage." Now, how's that for an answer?

Of course, you can just imagine the look on my mother's face. I'm sure that her comeback would be, "What, no children?" You just can't win with mothers. 7

THINKING ABOUT THE ESSAY

1. How does Shirachi construct her introduction? How does it prepare the reader for the body of the essay?
2. How does Shirachi compare the subtle differences between two groups of men?
3. Consider the tone of the essay. Is it ironic, whimsical, nostalgic, angry, or a combination of any of these? Is there any indication that the author is hiding any undercurrents of feeling? Refer to specific examples and consider, in particular, Shirachi's statement in the next to the last paragraph.
4. Has a cultural trait of yours ever been pointed out to you by a member of the opposite sex? What was the trait? How did you respond to the observation? Did you feel the observation was accurate? Did it have an impact on your behavior or attitude?
5. Are there any "pidgin" phrases or clichés that your male or female friends use that particularly annoy you, like "Wha's happenin?" or "Wha's up?" or "Don' even go there." If so, what is it about them that annoys you?

RESPONDING IN DISCUSSION

1. Divide into groups of four or five with representatives from each sex. List particularly annoying traits or habits that you find in the opposite sex. Which ones seem to be shared by the most number of people?
2. A major complaint of the author's seems to be that of being unappreciated. Discuss whether American culture seems to support this attitude that, in the words of the author, makes "men seem to care only about their own needs, thinking secondarily about their parents, wives and family."
3. In small groups, compare and contrast your own attitudes toward demonstrating appreciation on a date with your parents' generation's attitudes. Base your responses on discussions with your parents or their peers.
4. The author, in her attempt to demonstrate how important dating and finding a suitable mate arc to her, states, "Forget the floods,

the earthquakes, the riots and the fires. And don't even bother to mention the traffic and the smog." Discuss whether as a young man or woman, pursuing romantic relationships is currently at the top of your personal agenda.

RESPONDING IN WRITING

1. If you are keeping a diary or journal as part of your coursework, write an entry that describes in detail the communicative style of someone with whom you've had a date.
2. Interview a member of the D-Day generation (see the essay by Noonan), exploring his or her dating habits, attitudes, and behaviors. Reformulate your interview into an essay of approximately 500 words.
3. Watch a romantic comedy filmed during the 1940s and one filmed during the 1990s. Compare and contrast the way the characters established and maintained their relationships.
4. Compare and contrast two dates that you have had that suggest striking differences in the way that people behave.
5. Explore a dating chat group on the Web. Enter into it if you wish, or simply observe the nature of the discourse. Write an analytical essay in which you explore dating behavior on the Internet.

Pack Dating: For a Good Time, Call a Crowd

Trip Gabriel

In the 1950s a song titled "We Go Together" ("like two straws in a Coke") celebrated teenage love and a very traditional pattern of boy–girl dating. If dating in part is a cultural construct, then the ritual has changed significantly on today's college campuses, according to Trip Gabriel, a reporter for the Style section of *The New York Times.* This article (commissioned for a special January 5, 1997, *Education Life* supplement of the Sunday edition) asserts that college students today prefer to date or associate in packs. What we might term the "Friends" syndrome prevails on college campuses from Brown to Vassar to UCLA. Perhaps, as Gabriel suggests, the new forms and rituals shaping campus dating result from undergraduate lives that are far more problematic than those of previous generations. Utilizing numerous insights from students and authorities, Gabriel employs a lively style in offering readers a view of campus dating that might seem exotic but in reality is a response to the social and sexual realities of our times.

PREVIEWING THE ESSAY

The following essay confronts readers with views on dating and campus behavior that differ significantly from traditional values and attitudes. Why would young people prefer to date in groups rather than as couples? Is this phenomenon prevalent or atypical on your campus? Reviewing the essays in the first chapter, could you infer that pack dating is yet another piece of evidence indicating that a new generation actually exists and is not a media fabrication?

Rajib Chanda found the social scene at Brown University so grim that he formed HUGS, a computer-dating service to match students based on answers to a questionnaire. 1

The admittedly hokey notion of HUGS—it stands for Helping Undergraduates Socialize—drew an overwhelming response from campus sophisticates last Valentine's Day: nearly one-third of Brown's students, 1,500 in all, filled out questionnaires, including athletes and artists, fraternity brothers and rebels, heterosexuals and members of the gay and lesbian alliance. Mr. Chanda, a senior fraternity president, attributed the success of HUGS to a yearning for old-fashioned courtship, a way for students to dip a toe into the pool of intimacy and sex rather than plunge headfirst. 2

"In a normal Brown relationship, you meet, get drunk, hook up and then either avoid eye contact the next day or find yourself in a relationship," he told the campus newspaper. 3

At colleges across the country, students voice a similar lament: there is no real dating scene here. Instead of pairing off, undergraduates socialize in unpartnered packs. They go out to dinner in groups, attend movies in groups and at parties dance in a circle of five or six. The packs give students a sense of self-assurance and identity, but keep them from deeper, more committed relationships—which may be just the point. 4

None of this is to say that undergraduates of the mid-90's are chaste. To a generation grown jaded about warnings of AIDS and date rape, casual sex seems to be near an all-time high. Studies have documented a link between a boom in binge drinking on campuses and unplanned and unprotected sex. 5

Arthur Levine, the president of Teacher's College at Columbia University in New York, recently conducted a study of 9,100 students across the country, including focus groups on 30 campuses, and found that students prefer casual sexual liaisons to emotional intimacy and commitment. 6

"When students talked about relationships, the majority said they'd never seen a successful adult romantic relationship in their lives," said Dr. Levine, who is preparing a book-length study of 7 undergraduate life. "They're scared of relationships, of deep involvement, and that doesn't happen. Sex does happen. One way you overcome the fear of a relationship is you get loaded first, and after getting loaded, you go back to somebody's room and do it."

Dr. Levine collected slang terms used to describe sexual relations: 8 scamming, scrumping, mashing, shacking. "They're magnificent for their lack of romantic and emotional content," he said.

But the most popular term, in use almost everywhere for stu- 9 dent relationships circa 1997, is "hooking up." Depending on the context, a hook-up can mean anything from 20 minutes of strenuous kissing to spending the night together fully clothed to sexual intercourse.

"It's easy to go to a party on a Friday night and get a little loose 10 after drinking and find someone else who's a little loose and you casually hook up," said Patrick Saunders, a senior at Rice University in Houston. He described a friend who'd hooked up with the same woman once a week for five weeks, "but he won't call her."

Abigail Butler, who graduated from Vassar College in Poughkeep- 11 sie, N.Y., last year, said: "People who are interested in one another subtly arrange to be in the same place—the favorite campus pub, a friend's room—at the end of the night. They congregate there, hang out and disappear off into the night together. They may run into each other on the path the next day and not mention the previous night's activities at all.

"There's a lot of angst for a relationship—'Wouldn't it be nice if I 12 had a boyfriend'—but at the same time, people make fun of having one, like, 'She's married now.' "

There are exceptions. Students everywhere are able to point to 13 campus couples, often partners who met freshman year—maybe freshman week—and have been cocooned together ever since.

The norms of romance and sexuality also vary widely by campus. 14 At academically elite private schools, students say that long-term relationships may be rare because young people arrive on campus with atrophied social skills after studying hard in high school. Looking ahead to ambitious post-college careers, often not expecting to marry until age 30, they do not want to be tied down.

At big state schools, on the other hand, especially in the South 15 and Midwest, old-style courtship and early marriage live.

"There's a lot of casual dating that goes on just to get to know 16 people," said Edie Butler, a senior at the University of Kansas, Lawrence, who said three members of a rowing club she captains are already engaged. "A lot of people make plans to get married right after graduation."

The casual hook-up can also be standard practice at state schools. 17 A former sorority social director, who graduated from Indiana

University last year, said that a typical fraternity-row encounter consists of a one-night liaison after a party, followed by the "walk of shame" back across campus in the same clothes worn the night before.

"I was pretty bitter toward men my senior year," said the young woman, who spoke on condition of anonymity. "I didn't trust any of them." 18

No statistics are kept on the sexual practices of the nation's college students. Casual sex, a feature of campuses at least since the pill in the 1960's, may have once declined in the face of AIDS—but no longer. 19

"It hasn't cast a cool breeze at all," said Tirzah Brown, a sophomore at Lehigh University in Bethlehem, Pa., who as a peer health educator provides condoms and AIDS information to students. 20

Linell Juliet, a sexual health counselor at the University of Colorado, Boulder, said, "There was a lot less casual sex right around the mid-80's when AIDS first came out, but now it's back." 21

Only one-third of college women in a recent survey by the American Social Health Association said they used a condom for vaginal sex. AIDS educators say students' sense of abandon is fueled by a belief that successful, middle-class college populations are not at risk, and by fatigue with the safe-sex message, which has been drummed into them since junior high school. 22

H.I.V. infection rates are relatively low on campuses, about 1 in 500 students, according to the Centers for Disease Control and Prevention and the American College Health Association. But rates of other sexually transmitted diseases are soaring. Cases of venereal warts among 18- to 24-year-olds have risen 600 percent since 1968 and around 7 percent of college women have chlamydia (a gonorrhea-like venereal disease), which can lead to infertility and pregnancy complications. 23

"I think they're aware of what they're supposed to do, but they just don't do it," said Tori Bronaugh, a psychologist in the counseling department of Lehigh. "There's a denial that they are capable of death or of disease infecting them. Also, it takes place when they are drinking. They use the phrase, 'All of sudden I was in the bed and we were having sex.' " 24

A study two years ago by the Harvard School of Public Health focused wide attention on binge drinking on campuses. It found that nearly half of the nation's undergraduates—44 percent—binged at least once every two weeks (defined as consuming five drinks at a sitting for men and four for women). Among bingers, 20 percent engaged in unplanned sex, and 10 percent had unprotected sex. 25

Another study found that 60 percent of college women who have a sexually transmitted disease were drunk at the time of infection. 26

Some experts suggest that pack dating is partly an attempt to deal with the risk of disease: If sex partners are drawn from a small circle of friends, whose histories and habits are known to all members, the risk of exposure is theoretically lower. 27

At Rice University, a group of eight friends—half men and half women—regularly dines out together on weekends at a Tex-Mex or Vietnamese restaurant. Then they make the rounds of campus parties, where 10 kegs of beer might be flowing in adjacent dorm rooms. 28

In their years at college, most members of the group have had romantic flings with one another, but none have paired off exclusively for very long. "We go out to dinner and I'm struck—pretty much everyone else has hooked up with someone else in the group," said one of the men, who asked not to be identified. 29

Although group socializing has long been popular with young people, for evidence of its place in the *Zeitgeist* of this generation, look no further than the television show, "Friends," a big hit on campuses. The show is a testament to the propensity of young people to spend endless hours in coffee shops and one another's apartments, talking about practically nothing, while dancing around the possibility of romantic involvements. 30

"Intimacy is a big developmental task for this age group," said Kathy Reese, director of counseling and psychological services at Northwestern University in Evanston, Ill., who was perplexed that her 24-year-old daughter, a recent University of Chicago graduate, dated so little in college. 31

Dr. Bronaugh of Lehigh said that many students are cynical about the possibilities of lasting one-on-one relationships, based on family histories. 32

"A lot of these students come from families where parents have divorced, remarried, divorced again, and in their mind that's the norm— that there will be a risk should they get involved seriously with someone," Dr. Bronaugh said. 33

Still another explanation is that in the era of the $10,000 public-university tuition and board, when many students hold down jobs and double their course load to impress corporate recruiters, they simply don't have time for relationships. 34

"Our students are very stressed getting through school," said Darlene Mininni, director of sexual health education at the University of California, Los Angeles. In a poll of U.C.L.A. undergraduates she conducted, Ms. Mininni found, to her surprise, that 40 percent were virgins—higher than on other campuses, she said. "I hear people say, 'I've got to keep my G.P.A. high if I want to get to medical school,'" she said. "Students are really concerned about that and working like crazy. How do they have time for a life?" 35

Dr. Levine of Columbia, in his national survey of undergraduates, asked what students in the mid-90's did for fun. Twenty-one percent said "study." Eleven percent said "sleep." 36

THINKING ABOUT THE ESSAY

1. Is Gabriel's overall tone or attitude toward campus dating patterns negative or positive? How can you tell?
2. Do you agree with the author's main contention that "there is no real dating scene" on college campuses today, and that pack dating tends to "give students a sense of self-assurance and identity, but keep them from deeper, more committed relationships"? What evidence does Gabriel provide to substantiate this claim?
3. Imagine your parents as readers of this essay. What do you think their response would be? Why?
4. How effective is Gabriel's method of quoting and citing from interviews, studies, and reports? What types of material does the author quote or cite? Does the final result produce a reliable or convincing essay? Explain.

RESPONDING IN DISCUSSION

1. Organize the class into discussion groups consisting of four or five members. Then have each group member share his or her impressions of the campus dating scene. Next, determine as a group whether your campus conforms to Gabriel's basic thesis or is more traditional in its forms of social interaction.
2. Get together with another classmate and, based on your reading of Gabriel's essay, draw up a list of the various dating concerns of college students today. Do these concerns result in a composite sketch of the "new" college student? Explain your position in broader class discussion.
3. The early part of the essay extensively quotes Arthur Levine, president of Teachers College at Columbia University. (One of Levine's essays appears in Chapter 1.) Does the class agree or disagree with Levine's observations? Why?
4. As a group, re-read the essay's paragraphs dealing with AIDS. Are Gabriel's opinions well-informed? Discuss the impact of AIDS on dating patterns that you perceive in high school or college life.

RESPONDING IN WRITING

1. Research "college life" on the Web. Using a search engine, try inputting related words and phrases such as *campus dating, college sex,* and *college students and AIDS.* Download any useful material and, using it as a supplement to Gabriel's article, write an essay entitled "Dating and College Life Today."

2. Argue for or against the proposition that pack dating signifies fear of romance and intimacy by the current generation of college students.
3. Gabriel's observations might or might not reflect your own experience of dating. Explain the relevance of his essay to your own dating experience in high school or college. Analyze your various interactions and examine the various social contexts and cultural codes that have molded your experience.
4. Write a brief essay in which you connect Gabriel's essay to at least one additional essay in Chapter 1 ("Generations at the Crossroads"). Analyze the essays in relation to each other. Determine whether the essays are complementary or oppositional in their respective theses.

Should Colleges Adopt Written Policies on Sex between Students?

Alan E. Guskin and Diana Trilling

For generations there have been unwritten codes concerning permissible behavior involving sex and dating. Such codes may vary from culture to culture and from generation to generation, but it always has been assumed that by the time an individual reaches dating age, such "rules of engagement" are pretty much established so there is little chance of miscommunication. Recently however, some advocates claim we can no longer presume that such assumptions hold, particularly in the light of growing awareness of sexual abuse on campus on the part of men and the reluctance of colleges and universities to face up to this reality. These advocates claim that written policies are needed, particularly as a means of protecting women, for in nearly all cases, the male has a physical advantage over his counterpart in potentially sexual relationships. Opponents argue that this is merely a way of portraying men as "ruthless aggressors," and will only lead to hostility between the sexes rather than harmony. Guskin and Trilling examine the issue in this essay, which appeared in the November 4, 1994 issue of *CQ Researcher*.

PREVIEWING THE ESSAY

Consider your school's administration, faculty, and student body. Who sets the rules? Where would a student go if she or he had a complaint about sexual harassment? Who would be the person who sets the rules concerning such an issue? Would the policy be a "democratic" one (that is, voted on by representatives of all groups within the university) or would it be implemented autocratically by a single individual? Regardless of your position on the issue of written policies on sex between students, such concerns are at the heart of what constitutes the power of perception, opinion, and reasoned thought.

The growing avalanche of requests from other colleges and universities reinforces my sense that the Antioch policy is attracting attention because we may well be the first college that has found a path through the thicket of campus sexual abuses to a higher ground where we can educate people to deal with each other in healthy human relationships rather than attempt the hopeless task of policing student behavior. 1

Critics ask, how can Antioch, for so long the bastion of progressive thought, education innovation and student freedom from institutional regulation, create a policy that places restrictions on student sexual behavior? It seems as if the college, they say, has returned to an image of the helpless women of the 1950s. The policy, however, does not deal with the reimposition of constraints on freedom; it is not puritanical; it is not anti-romantic; it does not reimpose the perspectives of the 1950s. The Antioch College policy was developed by students' initiative and direct involvement to deal with the realities they face in the 1990s. 2

Antioch's sexual offense policy reflects the frustration and anger of students, particularly women, regarding the lack of responsiveness of colleges and universities to students who have experienced some form of sexual assault. The Antioch students did not push for this policy out of weakness but out of strength and their insistence that the college community acknowledge the depth of their concerns. They were not asking the institution to intervene on their behalf; rather, they were asserting their right to be treated fairly, with dignity and respect. . . . 3

The underlying philosophy asserts only one moral value: that each person has the right to have healthy human relationships and to define for himself or herself what that means. The goal is also rather simple but no less profound: that all students have a right to feel safe on the campus and to learn how to assert their interests in a sexual relationship. 4

A half-century ago, the gifted humorist James Thurber created a cartoon series—"The War between Men and Women"—in which he satirized the often-bizarre marital struggle between the sexes. We have only to compare Thurber's bloodless war with the death-dealing spirit which animates the sexual manual which was recently drafted by the students of Antioch College to recognize the dangerous distance we have traveled in the relation of men and women. 5

According to the Antioch rules, verbal permission must be requested and received before one's sexual partner may proceed from 6 one "level" (their word) to the next in sexual intimacy. Although the manual is at pains to address itself to men as well as women, it does a poor job of disguising its basic assumption that men are natural predators and that women are at one and the same time sacred vessels, shatterable at a touch, and the traffic managers of love.

This is scarcely a useful axiom to disseminate in our society, 7 but for several years now it has been establishing itself in our sexual culture, and it accounts, of course, for the increase in charges now being brought by women against men, the most recent and unpleasant of them the charge of sexual harassment brought by Paula Jones against President Clinton. A woman who doesn't flinch at alleging that the president of the United States attempted to seduce her by letting down his pants demands legal and financial recompense for the damage which this is supposed to have done to her delicate sensibility!

We live in a world which runs with the blood of hostility between 8 racial and religious groups, between ethnic and national groups. To these lamentable separations among people, we now add another division, a separatism of the sexes. Where it used to be that the act of love (as it was then called) was regarded as an aspect, and even a celebration, of our shared humanity, it now becomes a dehumanized exercise and a new arena for conflict. . . .

It is still possible for this trend to be reversed in our society if 9 feminism will take warning from all the other separatisms which now divide our world. Surely nothing is gained for society, nothing is gained for either men or women, by fostering the idea that men are ruthless aggressors against women and that women need to keep themselves in cautionary command of any relation which they have with men. Ours is not a moment in history in which to widen the divisions among people.

THINKING ABOUT THE ESSAY

1. To what degree does the Antioch College policy seem appropriate to you? Do you believe it is a good idea or a bad idea, or are there both positives and negatives to consider?
2. Is it Guskin and Trilling's purpose to explain or argue a position? Refer to the essay to support your viewpoint.
3. What are the authors' attitudes toward the Antioch policy? Do they see it as a positive step toward a reduction in campus sexual abuse or a necessary evil to be relied upon until a better solution presents itself?
4. Would you feel more secure or more intimidated if your campus had a policy like the one at Antioch?

5. In her essay in this chapter, Katie Roiphe claims that older feminists are dictating their own cultural and ideological biases concerning women's power to make their own decisions and defend themselves. Does the Antioch rule appear to treat women, in the words of Guskin and Trilling, as "sacred vessels, shatterable at a touch"?
6. How can the Antioch rule be enforced without a third-party witness? Is the rule largely symbolic or does it carry true legal and enforceable weight?

RESPONDING IN DISCUSSION

1. Divide into groups of three or four students. Draw up a list of the pros and cons of the Antioch written policies on sex between students. Share your list with the rest of the class, and see if any common threads arise among the responses.
2. Hold a mock trial wherein a student is accused of transgressing the Antioch policy. Have each student take on a role in the trial such as judge, prosecutor, defendant, or jury. Elect one student to serve as the court reporter. Afterwards discuss your personal responses to the mock trial and discuss any insights it provided in understanding the regulation's value or lack thereof.
3. What are your perceptions concerning a woman's ability to take care of herself in a potentially hostile dating situation? Are most women "fragile," "needy," or "dependent" so that they need an Antioch policy? Is the policy practical, at least, for those women who may not have the necessary skills to ward off unwanted advances?
4. Form groups of three or four students, and develop a guide that would be offered to all students to help them understand how to deal with ambiguous sexual situations. You may include such things as how to read nonverbal communication, developing assertiveness, and dating-site selection. Or, you may decide, after all, that the status quo is still the best guideline.

RESPONDING IN WRITING

1. Write a letter to the president of your college requesting or protesting the implementation of a written policy on sex between students.
2. Interview members of your parents' or grandparents' generation who attended college. Ask them about college life in general and whether it would have been a good idea to institute an Antioch-style policy when they were enrolled. Write a 400-word essay summarizing their responses.

3. For a research project, investigate on the Web the circumstances, individuals, events, and milieu within which the Antioch policy was created. Include the major players and a chronology of events from when the issue was first brought up until the policy was put into effect.
4. Argue for or against the proposition that the Antioch policy on sex between students has a subtext (that is, it subtly implies that men and women have certain attributes that can endanger themselves in private situations that only a law or policy can protect against).

Date Rape: State of Siege or State of Mind?

Katie Roiphe

This excerpt from Roiphe's book *The Morning After* was published in *Cosmopolitan* in January 1994. The book's popularity may be attributed to the fact that it was an extensive response to the 1960s women's movement, some of whose members she terms "rape-crisis feminists." In its thesis that some of traditional feminism is actually retrograde Victorianism, which sought to view women as helpless creatures, she offers the counter view that today's woman is more than capable of handling herself in social matters, including sexual ones. This has resonated positively among women of her own generation and raised the ire of some standard-bearers of the older generation. Since the book's publication, Roiphe has become somewhat of a gadfly among her elders, having written articles about such topics as the subservient role of male pornography actors in the X-rated movie industry.

PREVIEWING THE ESSAY

A major issue that Roiphe addresses here is what exactly constitutes consensual sex and what constitutes rape. As you read the essay, consider what conclusions the author makes. They may not necessarily be stated as straightforward assertions. But it is your job, as a careful reader, to infer from the information she offers, what her answer would be. How would you categorize her answer? Does it conform to yours? Did her arguments change your view on the topic?

ONE IN FOUR COLLEGE WOMEN HAS BEEN THE VICTIM OF RAPE OR ATTEMPTED RAPE. One in four. I remember standing outside the dining hall in college, looking at a purple poster with this statistic written in bold letters. It didn't seem right. If sexual assault 1 was really so pervasive, wasn't it strange that the intricate gossip networks hadn't picked up more than one or two shadowy instances of rape? If I was really standing in the middle of an "epidemic," a "crisis"—if 25 percent of my women friends were really being raped—wouldn't I know it?

These posters were not presenting facts. They were advertising a mood. Preoccupied with issues like date rape and sexual harassment, campus feminists produce endless images of women as victims—women offended by a professor's dirty joke, women pressured into sex by peers, women trying to say no but not managing to get it across. 2

This portrait of the delicate female bears a striking resemblance to that fifties ideal my mother and other women of her generation fought so hard to leave behind. They didn't like her passivity, her wide-eyed innocence. They didn't like that she was perpetually offended by sexual innuendo. They didn't like her excessive need for protection. She represented personal, social, and intellectual possibilities collapsed, and they worked and marched, shouted and wrote, to make her irrelevant for their daughters. But here she is again, with her pure intentions and her wide eyes. Only this time, it is the feminists themselves who are breathing new life into her. 3

Is there a rape crisis on campus? Measuring rape is not as straightforward as it might seem. Neil Gilbert, a professor of social welfare at the University of California at Berkeley, questions the validity of the one-in-four statistic. 4

Gilbert points out that in a 1985 survey undertaken by *Ms.* magazine and financed by the National Institute of Mental Health, 73 percent of the women categorized as rape victims did not initially define their experience as rape; it was Mary Koss, the psychologist conducting the study, who did so. 5

One of the questions used to define rape was: "Have you had sexual intercourse when you didn't want to because a man gave you alcohol or drugs?" The phrasing raises the issue of agency. Why aren't college women responsible for their own intake of alcohol and drugs? A man may give her drugs, but she herself decides to take them. If we assume that women are not all helpless and naive, then they should be held responsible for their choice to drink or take drugs. If a woman's judgment is "impaired" and she has sex, it isn't necessarily always the man's fault; it isn't necessarily always rape. 6

As Gilbert delves further into the numbers, he does not disprove the one-in-four statistic, but he does clarify what it means—the so-called rape epidemic on campuses is more a way of interpreting, a way of seeing, than an actual phenomenon. It is more about a change in sexual politics than a change in sexual behavior. Whether or not one in four college women has been raped, then, is a matter of opinion, not a matter of mathematical fact. 7

That rape is a fact in some women's lives is not in question. It's 8
hard to watch the solemn faces of young Bosnian girls, their words haltingly translated, as they tell of brutal rapes, or to read accounts of a suburban teenager raped and beaten while walking home from a shopping mall. We all agree that rape is a terrible thing, but we no longer agree on what rape is. Today's definition has stretched beyond bruises and knives, threats of death or violence, to include emotional pressure and the influence of alcohol. The lines between rape and sex begin to blur. The one-in-four statistic on those purple posters is measuring something elusive. It is measuring her word against his in a realm where words barely exist. There is a gray area in which one person's rape may be another's bad night. Definitions become entangled in passionate ideological battles. There hasn't been a remarkable change in the number of women being raped, just a change in how receptive the political climate is to those numbers.

"Acquaintance Rape: Is Dating Dangerous?" is a pamphlet com- 9
monly found at counseling centers. The cover title rises from the shards of a shattered photograph of a boy and girl dancing. Inside, the pamphlet offers a sample date-rape scenario. She thinks: He was really good-looking, and he had a great smile. . . . We talked and found we had a lot in common. I really liked him. When he asked me over to his place for a drink, I thought it would be okay. He was such a good listener and I wanted him to ask me out again.

She's just looking for a sensitive boy, a good listener with a nice 10
smile, but unfortunately, his intentions are not as pure as hers. Beneath that nice smile, he thinks: She looked really hot, wearing a sexy dress that showed off her great body. We started talking right away. I knew that she liked me by the way she kept smiling and touching my arm while she was speaking. She seemed pretty relaxed, so I asked her back to my place for a drink. . . . When she said yes, I knew that I was going to be lucky!

These cardboard stereotypes don't just educate freshmen about 11
rape. They also educate them about "dates" and about sexual desire. With titles like "Friends Raping Friends: Could It Happen to You?" date-rape pamphlets call into question all relationships between men and women. Beyond warning students about rape, the rape-crisis movement produces its own images of sexual behavior, in which men exert pressure and women resist. By defining the dangerous date in these terms—with this type of male and this type of female, and their different expectations—these pamphlets promote their own perspective on how men and women feel about sex: men are lascivious, women are innocent.

The sleek images of pressure and resistance projected in rape- 12
education movies, videotapes, pamphlets, and speeches create a model of acceptable sexual behavior. The don'ts imply their own set

of dos. The movement against rape, then, not only dictates the way sex shouldn't be but also the way it should be. Sex should be gentle, it should not be aggressive; it should be absolutely equal, it should not involve domination and submission; it should be tender, not ambivalent; it should communicate respect, it shouldn't communicate consuming desire.

In *Real Rape,* Susan Estrich, a professor of law at the University 13
of Southern California Law Center, slips her ideas about the nature of sexual encounters into her legal analysis of the problem of rape. She writes: "Many feminists would argue that so long as women are powerless relative to men, viewing a 'yes' as a sign of true consent is misguided. . . . Many women who say yes to men they know, whether on dates or on the job, would say no if they could. . . . Women's silence sometimes is the product not of passion and desire but of pressure and fear."

Like Estrich, most rape-crisis feminists claim they are not talking 14
about sex, they're talking about violence. But, like Estrich, they are also talking about sex. With their advice, their scenarios, their sample aggressive male, the message projects a clear comment on the nature of sexuality: Women are often unwilling participants. They say yes because they feel they have to, because they are intimidated by male power.

The idea of "consent" has been redefined beyond the simple asser- 15
tion that "no means no." Politically correct sex involves a yes, and a specific yes at that. According to the premise of "active consent," we can no longer afford ambiguity. We can no longer afford the dangers of unspoken consent. A former director of Columbia University's date-rape education program told *New York* magazine, "Stone silence throughout an entire physical encounter with someone is not explicit consent."

This apparently practical, apparently clinical proscription cloaks 16
retrograde assumptions about the way men and women experience sex. The idea that only an explicit yes means yes proposes that, like children, women have trouble communicating what they want. Beyond its dubious premise about the limits of female communication, the idea of active consent bolsters stereotypes of men just out to "get some" and women who don't really want any.

Rape-crisis feminists express nostalgia for the days of greater so- 17
cial control, when the university acted in loco parentis and women were protected from the insatiable force of male desire. The rhetoric of feminists and conservatives blurs and overlaps in this desire to keep our youth safe and pure.

By viewing rape as encompassing more than the use or threat of 18
physical violence to coerce someone into sex, rape-crisis feminists reinforce traditional views about the fragility of the female body and will. According to common definitions of date rape, even "verbal

coercion" or "manipulation" constitute rape. Verbal coercion is defined as "a women's consenting to unwanted sexual activity because of a man's verbal arguments not including verbal threats of force." The belief that verbal coercion is rape pervades workshops, counseling sessions, and student opinion pieces. The suggestion lurking beneath this definition of rape is that men are not just physically but also intellectually and emotionally more powerful than women.

Imagine men sitting around in a circle, talking about how she called him impotent and how she manipulated him into sex, how violated and dirty he felt afterward, how coercive she was, how she got him drunk first, how he hated his body and he couldn't eat for three weeks afterward. Imagine him calling this rape. Everyone feels the weight of emotional pressure at one time or another. The question is not whether people pressure each other but how our minds and our culture transform that pressure into full-blown assault. There would never be a rule or a law or even a pamphlet or peer counseling group for men who claimed to have been emotionally raped or verbally pressured into sex. And for the same reasons—assumption of basic competence, free will, and strength of character—there should be no such rules or groups or pamphlets about women. 19

In discussing rape, campus feminists often slip into an outdated sexist vocabulary. But we have to be careful about using rape as metaphor. The sheer physical fact of rape has always been loaded with cultural meaning. Throughout history, women's bodies have been seen as property, as chaste objects, as virtuous vessels to be "dishonored," "ruined," "defiled." Their purity or lack of purity has been a measure of value for the men to whom they belonged. 20

"Politically, I call it rape whenever a woman has sex and feels violated," writes Catharine MacKinnon, a law professor and feminist legal scholar best known for her crusade against pornography. The language of virtue and violation reinforces retrograde stereotypes. It backs women into old corners. Younger feminists share MacKinnon's vocabulary and the accompanying assumptions about women's bodies. In one student's account of date rape in the *Rag,* a feminist magazine at Harvard, she talks about the anguish of being "defiled." Another writes, "I long to be innocent again." With such anachronistic constructions of the female body, with all their assumptions about female purity, these young women frame their experience of rape in archaic, sexist terms. Of course, sophisticated modern-day feminists don't use words like *honor* or *virtue* anymore. They know better than to say date-rape victims have been "defiled." Instead, they call it "post-traumatic stress syndrome." They tell the victim she should not feel "shame," she should feel "traumatized." Within their overtly political psychology, forced penetration takes on a level of metaphysical significance: Date rape resonates through a woman's entire life. 21

Combating myths about rape is one of the central missions of the rape-crisis movement. They spend money and energy trying to break down myths like "She asked for it." But with all their noise about rape myths, rape-crisis feminists are generating their own. The plays, the poems, the pamphlets, the Take Back the Night speakouts, are propelled by the myth of innocence lost. 22

All the talk about empowering the voiceless dissolves into the image of the naive girl child who trusts the rakish man. This plot reaches back centuries. It propels Samuel Richardson's eighteenth-century epistolary novel, *Clarissa:* after hundreds of pages chronicling the minute details of her plight, her seduction and resistance, her break from her family, Clarissa is raped by the duplicitous Robert Lovelace. Afterward, she refuses to eat and fades toward a very virtuous, very religious death. Over a thousand pages are devoted to the story of her fall from innocence, a weighty event by eighteenth-century standards. But did these twentieth-century girls, raised on Madonna videos and the six o'clock news, really trust that people were good until they themselves were raped? Maybe. Were these girls, raised on horror movies and glossy Hollywood sex scenes, really as innocent as all that? Maybe. But maybe the myth of lost innocence is a trope—convenient, appealing, politically effective. 23

As long as we're taking back the night, we might as well take back our own purity. Sure, we were all kind of innocent, playing in the sandbox with bright red shovels—boys too. We can all look back through the tumultuous tunnel of adolescence on a honey-glazed childhood, with simple rules and early bedtimes. We don't have to look at parents fighting, at sibling struggles, at casting out one best friend for another in the Darwinian playground. This is not the innocence lost; this is the innocence we never had. 24

The idea of a fall from childhood grace, pinned on one particular moment, a moment over which we had no control, much lamented, gives our lives a compelling narrative structure. It's easy to see why the seventeen-year-old likes it; it's easy to see why the rape-crisis feminist likes it. It's a natural human impulse put to political purpose. But in generating and perpetuating such myths, we should keep in mind that myths about innocence have been used to keep women inside and behind veils. They have been used to keep them out of work and in labor. 25

It's not hard to imagine Clarissa, in jeans and a sweatshirt, transported into the twentieth century, at a Take Back the Night march. She would speak for a long time about her deception and rape, about verbal coercion and anorexia, about her ensuing post-traumatic stress syndrome. Latter-day Clarissas may worry more about their "self-esteem" than their virtue, but they are still attaching the same quasi-religious value to the physical act. 26

Calling It Rape, a play by Sonya Rasminsky, a recent Harvard graduate, is based on interviews with date-rape victims. The play, which has been performed at Harvard and may be taken into Boston-area high schools, begins with "To His Coy Mistress," by the seventeenth-century poet Andrew Marvell. Although generations of high school and college students have read this as a romantic poem, a poem about desire and the struggle against mortality, Rasminsky has reinterpreted it as a poem about rape. "Had we but world enough and time, this coyness, lady, were no crime." But what Andrew Marvell didn't know then and we know now is that the real crime is not her coyness but his verbal coercion. 27

A central idea of the rape-crisis movement is that sex has become our Tower of Babel. He doesn't know what she wants (not to have sex) and she doesn't know what he wants (to have sex)—until it's too late. He speaks boyspeak and she speaks girlspeak, and what comes out of all this verbal chaos is a lot of rapes. The theory of mixed signals and crossed stars has to do with more than gender politics. It comes in part from the much-discussed diversity that has so radically shifted the social composition of the college class since the fifties. 28

Take my own Harvard dorm: The Adams House dining hall is large, with high ceilings and dark paneling. It hasn't changed much for generations. As soon as the students start milling around, gathering salads, ice cream, and coffee onto green trays, there are signs of change. There are students in jeans, flannel shirts, short skirts, girls in jackets, boys in bracelets, two pierced noses, and lots of secondhand clothes. 29

Not so many years ago, this room was filled with boys in jackets and ties. Most of them were white, Christian, and what we now call privileged. Students came from the same social milieu with the same social rules, and it was assumed that everyone knew more or less how they were expected to behave with everyone else. Diversity and multiculturalism were unheard of, and if they had been, they would have been dirty words. With the shift in college environments, with the introduction of black kids, Asian kids, Jewish kids, kids from the wrong side of the tracks of nearly every railroad in the country, there was an accompanying anxiety about how people behave. When ivory tower meets melting pot, it causes tension, some confusion, some need for readjustment. In explaining the need for intensive "orientation" programs, including workshops on date rape, Columbia's assistant dean for freshmen stated in an interview in *The New York Times:* "You can't bring all these people together and say, 'Now be one big happy community,' without some sort of training. You can't just throw together somebody from a small town in Texas and someone from New York City and someone from a conservative fundamentalist home in the Midwest and say 'Now without any sort of conversation, be best friends and get along and respect one another.' " 30

Catherine Stimpson, a professor at Rutgers University and long-time advocate of women's studies programs, once pointed out that it's sometimes easier for people to talk about gender than to talk about class. *Miscommunication* is in some sense a word for the friction between the way we were and the way we are. 31

Just as the idea that we speak different languages is connected to gender—the arrival of women in classrooms, in dorms, and in offices—it is also connected to class. 32

When the Southern heiress goes out with the plumber's son from the Bronx, when the kid from rural Arkansas goes out with a boy from Exeter, the anxiety is that they have different expectations. The dangerous "miscommunication" that recurs through the literature on date rape is a code word for difference in background. The rhetoric surrounding date rape and sexual harassment is in part a response to cultural mixing. The idea that men don't know what women mean when women say no stems from something deeper and more complicated than feminist concerns with rape. People have asked me if I have ever been date-raped. And thinking back on complicated nights, on too many glasses of wine, on strange and familiar beds, I would have to say yes. With such a sweeping definition of rape, I wonder how many people there are, male or female, who haven't been date-raped at one point or another. People pressure and manipulate and cajole each other into all sorts of things all of the time. As Susan Sontag wrote, "Since Christianity upped the ante and concentrated on sexual behavior as the root of virtue, everything pertaining to sex has been a 'special case' in our culture, evoking peculiarly inconsistent attitudes." No human interactions are free from pressure, and the idea that sex is, or can be, makes it what Sontag calls a "special case," vulnerable to the inconsistent expectations of double standard. 33

With their expansive version of rape, rape-crisis feminists are inventing a kinder, gentler sexuality. Beneath the broad definition of rape, these feminists are endorsing their own utopian vision of sexual relations: sex without struggle, sex without power, sex without persuasion, sex without pursuit. If verbal coercion constitutes rape, then the word *rape* itself expands to include any kind of sex a woman experiences as negative. 34

When Martin Amis spoke at Princeton University, he included a controversial joke: "As far as I'm concerned, you can change your mind before, even during, but just not after sex." The reason this joke is funny, and the reason it's also too serious to be funny, is that in the current atmosphere you can change your mind afterward. Regret can signify rape. Since "verbal coercion" and "manipulation" are ambiguous, it's easy to decide afterward that he manipulated you. You can realize it weeks or even years later. This is a movement that deals in retrospective trauma. 35

Rape has become a catchall expression, a word used to define everything that is unpleasant and disturbing about relations between the sexes. Students say things like "I realize that sexual harassment is a kind of rape." If we refer to a whole range of behavior from emotional pressure to sexual harassment as "rape," then the idea gets diluted. It ceases to be powerful as either description or accusation. 36

Some feminists actually collapse the distinction between rape and sex. Catharine MacKinnon writes: "Compare victims' reports of rape with women's reports of sex. They look a lot alike. . . . In this light, the major distinction between intercourse (normal) and rape (abnormal) is that the normal happens so often that one cannot get anyone to see anything wrong with it." 37

There are a few feminists involved in rape education who object to the current expanding definitions of sexual assault. Gillian Greensite, founder of the rape-prevention education program at the University of California at Santa Cruz, writes that the seriousness of the crime "is being undermined by the growing tendency of some feminists to label all heterosexual miscommunication and insensitivity as acquaintance rape." From within the rape-crisis movement, Greensite's dissent makes an important point. If we are going to maintain an idea of rape, then we need to reserve it for instances of physical violence, or the threat of physical violence. 38

But some people want the melodrama. They want the absolute value placed on experience by absolute words. Words like *rape* and *verbal communication* channel the confusing now of experience into something easy to understand. The idea of date rape comes at us fast and coherent. It comes at us when we've just left home and haven't yet figured out where to put our new futons or how to organize our new social lives. The rhetoric about date rape defines the terms, gives names to nameless confusions and sorts through mixed feelings with a sort of insistent consistency. In the first rush of sexual experience, the fear of date rape offers a tangible framework to locate fears that are essentially abstract. 39

When my fifty-five-year-old mother was young, navigating her way through dates, there was a definite social compass. There were places not to let him put his hands. There were invisible lines. The Pill wasn't available. Abortion wasn't legal. And sex was just wrong. Her mother gave her "mad money" to take out on dates in case her date got drunk and she needed to escape. She had to go far enough to hold his interest but not far enough to endanger her reputation. 40

Now the rape-crisis feminists are offering new rules. They are giving a new political weight to the same old no. My mother's mother told her to drink sloe gin fizzes so she wouldn't drink too much and get too drunk and go too far. Now the date-rape pamphlets tell us: "Avoid excessive use of alcohol and drugs. Alcohol and 41 drugs interfere with clear thinking and effective communication." My mother's mother told her to stay away from empty rooms and dimly lighted streets. In *I Never Called It Rape,* Robin Warshaw writes, "Especially with recent acquaintances, women should insist on going only to public places such as restaurants and movie theaters."

There is a danger in these new rules. We shouldn't need to be reminded that the rigidly conformist fifties were not the heyday of women's power. Feminist Barbara Ehrenreich writes of "re-making love," but there is a danger in remaking love in its old image. The terms may have changed, but attitudes about sex and women's bodies have not. Rape-crisis feminists threaten the progress that's been made. They are chasing the same stereotypes our mothers spent so much energy escaping. 42

One day I was looking through my mother's bookshelves and I found her old battered copy of Germaine Greer's feminist classic, *The Female Eunuch.* The pages were dog-eared, and whole passages were marked with penciled notes. It was 1971 when Greer fanned the fires with *The Female Eunuch,* and it was 1971 when my mother read it, brand-new, explosive, a tough and sexy terrorism for the early stirring of the feminist movement. 43

Today's rape-crisis feminists threaten to create their own version of the desexualized woman Greer complained of twenty years ago. Her comments need to be recycled for present-day feminists. "It is often falsely assumed," Greer writes, "even by feminists, that sexuality is the enemy of the female who really wants to develop these aspects of her personality. . . . It was not the insistence upon her sex that weakened the American woman student's desire to make something of her education, but the insistence upon a passive sexual role. In fact, the chief instrument in the deflection and perversion of female energy is the denial of female sexuality for the substitution of femininity or sexlessness." 44

It is the passive sexual role that threatens us still, and it is the denial or female sexual agency that threatens to propel us backward. 45

THINKING ABOUT THE ESSAY

1. What is your image of the "typical" female college student? Does she need the education of "cardboard stereotypes" found in health pamphlets or is she a member of a new assertive generation that can think and act according to its own beliefs and impulses? Or, is it just too reductionist to paint a portrait of the "typical" student?
2. Does Roiphe intend this essay for one audience or several audiences? What internal evidence supports your response?

3. Try to reduce the logical structure of Roiphe's argument to a clearer set of major and minor propositions. Is her conclusion valid in light of her underlying reasons? Explain.
4. While traditionally there has been much written about the differences between men and women regarding responses to sex, Roiphe subtly points out some of the similarities. Where do these similarities appear, and do you agree with Roiphe's point of view?
5. Consider the last sentence of the essay. Select three or four examples from the text that Roiphe uses to reach this conclusion.
6. What assertion in the essay did you most agree with and why? What assertion in the essay did you most disagree with and why?

RESPONDING IN DISCUSSION

1. Attempt to develop definitions for some of the terms that the author includes in what she calls the "Tower of Babel" of the rape-crisis movement, terms such as *verbal coercion, manipulation, consent,* and *violation*. Share them with your class.
2. Divide into groups of three or four, and consider that Roiphe believes a good way to view rape is to "reserve it for instances of physical violence, or the threat of physical violence." Have each group member discuss his or her view of this explanation of rape. Then share your results with the rest of the class.
3. In Chapter 1 of this book, several commentators claimed that there is more intergenerational conflict within families than intragenerational conflict among members of different ethnic and racial groups. How does this argument bear on the subject matter of this essay? In other words, is there more conflict between the generations of women concerning the matter of appropriate demonstration of sexuality than there is between today's men and women of college age?
4. Discuss what the author means by the idea of rape becoming "diluted," and why she believes this is dangerous.

RESPONDING IN WRITING

1. Visit your college health clinic and select a pamphlet on sex education. Using Roiphe's view that women are treated as passive and fragile in such literature, describe whether the literature you have selected portrays women in this light.
2. Collect the various terms used in this essay that center on the issue of coercive sex. Interview four students—two men and

two women—and ask them to define each term. Write a comparison-and-contrast essay describing how the students perceived these terms.

3. Argue for or against the proposition that the open portrayal of sexuality in the media has created a culture in which there is a smaller division between the habits and mores of young men and women regarding sexual activity.
4. Conduct an analysis of sexual display on your campus. You may wish to include cautionary posters, announcements about seminars concerning sex, statements on T-shirts and buttons, and film and theater offerings. Write an essay of 500 to 600 words describing this selected "environment."
5. The author says that a poster she read stating ONE IN FOUR COLLEGE WOMEN HAS BEEN THE VICTIM OF RAPE OR ATTEMPTED RAPE is "not presenting facts," but "advertising a mood." Argue for or against the idea that Roiphe is merely advertising her own mood.
6. Search for rape avoidance advice on the Web. What kind of sites provide this advice? Are many of them college-affiliated? What does this tell you about the relative sensitivities on this issue in different cultural settings, especially in light of the essay?

On Not Being a Victim: Sex, Rape, and the Trouble with Following Rules

Mary Gaitskill

This article originally appeared as the cover story in the March 1994 issue of *Harper's Magazine*. Gaitskill combines personal experience, observation, reflections on her own readings, and an independent frame of mind to comment on a topic addressed by Roiphe and others, the "rape crisis." However, her view is quite different from most advocates on both sides of the woman-as-victim fence. Rather than placing human experience in neat cubbyholes of perception and response, she instead suggests that only through a certain amount of experimentation can we truly understand who we are. Only when we can separate our honest emotions about sex from what we are told we should feel can we begin to emerge as independent selves.

PREVIEWING THE ESSAY

Gaitskill disputes those who dismiss aspects of our popular culture out-of-hand. She criticizes writers who belittle 12-step programs, scoff at the concept of the inner child, and say that the troubles of the middle-class drown in insignificance when compared to the true tragedies in the world. Do you share this attitude about any of these so-called whiners? If so, where do you think you acquired this view?

In the early 1970s, I had an experience that could be described as acquaintance rape. Actually, I have had two or three such experiences, but this one most dramatically fits the profile. I was sixteen and staying in the apartment of a slightly older girl I'd just met in a seedy community center in Detroit. I'd been in her apartment for a few days when an older guy she knew came over and asked us if we wanted to drop some acid. In those years, doing acid with complete strangers was consistent with my idea of a possible good time, so I said yes. When I started peaking, my hostess decided she had to go see her boyfriend, and there I was, alone with this guy, who, suddenly, was in my face. 1

He seemed to be coming on to me, but I wasn't sure. My perception was quite loopy, and on top of that he was black and urban-poor, which meant that I, being very inexperienced and suburban-white, did not know how to read him the way I might have read another white kid. I tried to distract him with conversation, but it was hard, considering that I was having trouble with logical sentences, let alone repartee. During one long silence, I asked him what he was thinking. Avoiding my eyes, he answered, "That if I wasn't such a nice guy you could really be getting screwed." The remark sounded to me like a threat, albeit a low-key one. But instead of asking him to explain himself or to leave, I changed the subject. Some moments later, when he put his hand on my leg, I let myself be drawn into sex because I could not face the idea that if I said no, things might get ugly. I don't think he had any idea how unwilling I was—the cultural unfamiliarity cut both ways—and I suppose he may have thought that all white girls just kind of lie there and don't do or say much. My bad time was made worse by his extreme gentleness; he was obviously trying very hard to please me, which, for reasons I didn't understand, broke my heart. Even as inexperienced as I was, I sensed that in his own way he intended a romantic encounter. 2

For some time afterward I described this event as "the time I was raped." I knew when I said it that the statement wasn't quite accurate, that I hadn't, after all, said no. Yet it felt accurate to me. In spite of my ambiguous, even empathic feelings for my unchosen partner, unwanted sex on acid is a nightmare, and I did feel violated by the experience. At times I even flat-out lied about what had happened, grossly exaggerating the violence and the threat—not out of shame or guilt, but because the pumped-up version was more congruent with my feelings of violation than the confusing facts. Every now and then, in the middle of telling an exaggerated version of the story, I would 3 remember the actual man and internally pause, uncertain of how the memory squared with what I was saying or where my sense of violation was coming from—and then I would continue with my story. I am ashamed to admit this, both because it is embarrassing to me and because I am afraid the admission could be taken as evidence that women lie "to get revenge." I want to stress that I would not have lied that way in court or in any other context that might have had practical consequences; it didn't even occur to me to take my case to court. My lies were told not for revenge but in service of what I felt to be the metaphorical truth.

I remember my experience in Detroit, including its aftermath, every time I hear or read yet another discussion of what constitutes "date rape." I remember it when yet another critic castigates "victimism" and complains that everyone imagines himself or herself to be a victim and that no one accepts responsibility anymore. I could imagine telling my story as a verification that rape occurs by subtle threat as well as by overt force. I could also imagine telling it as if I were one of those crybabies who want to feel like victims. Both stories would be true and not true. The complete truth is more complicated than most of the intellectuals who have written scolding essays on victimism seem willing to accept. I didn't understand my own story fully until I described it to an older woman many years later, as a proof of the unreliability of feelings. "Oh, I think your feelings were reliable," she returned. "It sounds like you were raped. It sounds like you raped yourself." I immediately knew that what she said was true, that in failing even to try to speak up for myself, I had, in a sense, raped myself. 4

I don't say this in a tone of self-recrimination. I was in a difficult situation: I was very young, and he was aggressive. But my inability to speak for myself—to stand up for myself—had little to do with those facts. I was unable to stand up for myself because I had never been taught how. 5

When I was growing up in the 1960s, I was taught by the adult world that good girls never had sex and bad girls did. This rule had clarity going for it but little else; as it was presented to me, it allowed no room for what I actually might feel, what I might want or not want. Within the confines of this rule, I didn't count for much, and I quite vigorously rejected it. Then came the less clear "rules" of cultural trend and peer example that said that if you were cool you wanted to have sex as much as possible with as many people as possible. This message was never stated as a rule, but, considering how absolutely it was woven into the social etiquette of the day (at least in the circles I cared about), it may as well have been. It suited me better than the adults' rule—it allowed me my sexuality, at least—but again it didn't take into account what I might actually want or not want. 6

The encounter in Detroit, however, had nothing to do with being good or bad, cool or uncool. It was about someone wanting something I didn't want. Since I had been taught only how to follow rules that were somehow more important than I was, I didn't know what to do in a situation where no rules obtained and that required me to speak up on my own behalf. I had never been taught that my behalf mattered. And so I felt helpless, even victimized, without really knowing why. 7

My parents and my teachers believed that social rules existed to protect me and that adhering to these rules constituted social responsibility. Ironically, my parents did exactly what many commentators recommend as a remedy for victimism. They told me they loved me and that I mattered a lot, but this was not the message I got from the way they conducted themselves in relation to authority and social convention—which was not only that I didn't matter but that they didn't matter. In this, they were typical of other adults I knew as well as of the culture around them. When I began to have trouble in school, both socially and academically, a counselor exhorted me to "just play the game"—meaning to go along with everything from school policy to the adolescent pecking order—regardless of what I thought of "the game." My aunt, with whom I lived for a short while, actually burned my jeans and T-shirts because they violated what she understood to be the standards of decorum. A close friend of mine lived in a state of war with her father because of her hippie clothes and hair—which were, of course, de rigueur among her peers. Upon discovering that she was smoking pot, he had her institutionalized. 8

Many middle-class people—both men and women—were brought up, like I was, to equate responsibility with obeying external rules. And when the rules no longer work, they don't know what to do—much like the enraged, gun-wielding protagonist of the movie *Falling Down,* played by Michael Douglas, who ends his ridiculous trajectory by helplessly declaring: "I did everything they told me to." If I had been brought up to reach my own conclusions about which rules were congruent with my internal experience of the world, those rules would have had more meaning for me. Instead, I was usually given a series of static pronouncements. For example, when I was thirteen, I was told by my mother that I couldn't wear a short skirt because "nice girls don't wear skirts above the knee." I countered, of course, by saying that my friend Patty wore skirts above the knee. "Patty is not a nice girl," returned my mother. But Patty was nice. My mother is a very intelligent and sensitive person, but it didn't occur to her to define for me what she meant by "nice," what "nice" had to do with skirt length, and how the two definitions might relate to what I had observed to be nice or not nice—and then let me decide for myself. It's true that most thirteen-year-olds aren't interested in, or much 9 capable of, philosophical discourse, but that doesn't mean that adults can't explain themselves more completely to children. Part of becoming responsible is learning how to make a choice about where you stand in respect to the social code and then holding yourself accountable for your choice. In contrast, many children who grew up in my milieu were given abstract absolutes that were placed before us as if our thoughts, feelings, and observations were irrelevant.

Recently I heard a panel of feminists on talk radio advocating that 10
laws be passed prohibiting men from touching or making sexual comments to women on the street. Listeners called in to express reactions both pro and con, but the one I remember was a woman who said, "If a man touches me and I don't want it, I don't need a law. I'm gonna beat the hell out of him." The panelists were silent. Then one of them responded in an uncertain voice, "I guess I just never learned how to do that." I understood that the feminist might not want to get into a fistfight with a man likely to be a lot bigger than she, but if her self-respect was so easily shaken by an obscene comment made by some slob on the street, I wondered, how did she expect to get through life? She was exactly the kind of woman whom the cultural critics Camille Paglia and Katie Roiphe have derided as a "rape-crisis feminist"—puritans, sissies, closet-Victorian ladies who want to legislate the ambiguity out of sex. It was very easy for me to feel self-righteous, and I muttered sarcastically at my radio as the panel yammered about self-esteem.

I was conflicted, however. If there had been a time in my own life 11
when I couldn't stand up for myself, how could I expect other people to do it? It could be argued that the grown women on the panel should be more capable than a sixteen-year-old girl whacked out on acid. But such a notion presupposes that people develop at a predictable rate or react to circumstances by coming to universally agreed-upon conclusions. This is the crucial unspoken presumption at the center of the date-rape debate as well as of the larger discourse on victimism. It is a presumption that in a broad but potent sense reminds me of a rule.

Feminists who postulate that boys must obtain a spelled-out "yes" 12
before having sex are trying to establish rules, cut in stone, that will apply to any and every encounter and that every responsible person must obey. The new rule resembles the old good girl/bad girl rule not only because of its implicit suggestion that girls have to be protected but also because of its absolute nature, its iron-fisted denial of complexity and ambiguity. I bristle at such a rule and so do a lot of other people. But should we really be so puzzled and indignant that another rule has been presented? If people have been brought up believing that to be responsible is to obey certain rules, what are they going to do with a can of worms like "date rape" except try to make new rules that they see as more fair or useful than the old ones?

But the "rape-crisis feminists" are not the only absolutists here; their critics play the same game. Camille Paglia, author of *Sexual Personae,* has stated repeatedly that any girl who goes alone into a frat house and proceeds to tank up is cruising for a gang bang, and if she doesn't know that, well, then she's "an idiot." The remark is most striking not for its crude unkindness but for its reductive solipsism. It assumes that all college girls have had the same life experiences as Paglia, and have come to the same conclusions about them. By the time I got to college, I'd been living away from home for years and had been around the block several times. I never went to a frat house, but I got involved with men who lived in rowdy "boy houses" reeking of dirty socks and rock and roll. I would go over, drink, and spend the night with my lover of the moment; it never occurred to me that I was in danger of being gang-raped, and if I had been, I would have been shocked and badly hurt. My experience, though some of it had been bad, hadn't led me to conclude that boys plus alcohol equals gang bang, and I was not naive or idiotic. Katie Roiphe, author of *The Morning After: Fear, Sex, and Feminism on Campus,* criticizes girls who, in her view, create a myth of false innocence: "But did these twentieth-century girls, raised on Madonna videos and the six o'clock news, really trust that people were good until they themselves were raped? Maybe. Were these girls, raised on horror movies and glossy Hollywood sex scenes, really as innocent as all that?" I am sympathetic to Roiphe's annoyance, but I'm surprised that a smart chick like her apparently doesn't know that people process information and imagery (like Madonna videos and the news) with a complex subjectivity that doesn't in any predictable way alter their ideas about what they can expect from life. 13

Roiphe and Paglia are not exactly invoking rules, but their comments seem to derive from a belief that everyone except idiots interprets information and experience in the same way. In that sense, they are not so different in attitude from those ladies dedicated to establishing feminist-based rules and regulations for sex. Such rules, just like the old rules, assume a certain psychological uniformity of experience, a right way. 14

The accusatory and sometimes painfully emotional rhetoric conceals an attempt not only to make new rules but also to codify experience. The "rape-crisis feminists" obviously speak for many women and girls who have been raped or have felt raped in a wide variety of circumstances. They would not get so much play if they were not addressing a widespread and real experience of violation and hurt. By asking, "Were they really so innocent?" Roiphe doubts the veracity of the experience she presumes to address because it doesn't square with hers or with that of her friends. Having not felt violated herself—even though she says she has had an experience that many 15 would now call date rape—she cannot understand, or even quite believe, that anyone else would feel violated in similar circumstances. She therefore believes all the fuss to be a political ploy or, worse, a retrograde desire to return to crippling ideals of helpless femininity. In turn, Roiphe's detractors, who have not had her more sanguine "morning after" experience, believe her to be ignorant and callous, or a secret rape victim in deep denial. Both camps, believing their own experience to be the truth, seem unwilling to acknowledge the emotional truth on the other side.

It is at this point that the "date-rape debate" resembles the bigger debate about how and why Americans seem so eager to identify themselves and be identified by others as victims. Book after article has appeared, written in baffled yet hectoring language, deriding the P.C. goody-goodies who want to play victim and the spoiled, self-centered fools who attend twelve-step programs, meditate on their inner child, and study pious self-help books. The revisionist critics have all had a lot of fun with the recovery movement, getting into high dudgeon over those materially well-off people who describe their childhoods as "holocausts" and winding up with a fierce exhortation to return to rationality. Rarely do such critics make any but the most superficial attempt to understand why the population might behave thus. 16

In a fussing, fuming essay . . . that has almost become a prototype of the genre, David Rieff expressed his outrage and bewilderment that affluent people would feel hurt and disappointed by life. He angrily contrasted rich Americans obsessed with their inner children to third world parents concerned with feeding their actual children. On the most obvious level, the contrast is one that needs to be made, but I question Rieff's idea that suffering is one definable thing, that he knows what it is, and that since certain kinds of emotional pain don't fit this definition they can't really exist. This idea doesn't allow him to have much respect for other people's experience—or even to see it. It may be ridiculous and perversely self-aggrandizing for most people to describe whatever was bad about their childhood as a "holocaust," but I suspect that when people talk like that they are saying that as children they were not given enough of what they would later need in order to know who they are or to live truly responsible lives. Thus they find themselves in a state of bewildering loss that they can't articulate, except by wild exaggeration—much like I defined my inexplicable feelings after my Detroit episode. "Holocaust" may be a grossly inappropriate exaggeration. But to speak in exaggerated metaphors about psychic injury is not so much the act of a crybaby as it is a distorted attempt to explain one's own experience. I think the distortion comes from a desperate desire to make one's experience have consequence in the eyes of others, and that such desperation comes from a crushing doubt that one's own experience counts at all. 17

In her book *I'm Dysfunctional, You're Dysfunctional,* Wendy 18
Kaminer speaks harshly of women in some twelve-step programs who talk about being metaphorically raped. "It is an article of faith here that suffering is relative; no one says she'd rather be raped metaphorically than in fact," she writes, as if not even a crazy person would prefer a literal rape to a metaphorical one. But actually, I might. About two years after my "rape" in Detroit, I was raped for real. The experience was terrifying: my attacker repeatedly said he was going to kill me, and I thought he might. The terror was acute, but after it was over it actually affected me less than many other mundane instances of emotional brutality I've suffered or seen other people suffer. Frankly, I've been scarred more by experiences I had on the playground in elementary school. I realize that the observation may seem bizarre, but for me the rape was a clearly defined act, perpetrated upon me by a crazy ass-hole whom I didn't know or trust; it had nothing to do with me or who I was, and so, when it was over, it was relatively easy to dismiss. Emotional cruelty is more complicated. Its motives are often impossible to understand, and it is sometimes committed by people who say they like or even love you. Nearly always it's hard to know whether you played a role in what happened, and, if so, what the role was. The experience sticks to you. By the time I was raped, I had seen enough emotional cruelty to feel that the rape, although bad, was not especially traumatic.

My response may seem strange to some, but my point is that pain 19
can be an experience that defies codification. If thousands of Americans say that they are in psychic pain, I would not be so quick to write them off as self-indulgent fools. A metaphor like "the inner child" may be silly and schematic, but it has a fluid subjectivity, especially when projected out into the world by such a populist notion as "recovery." Ubiquitous recovery-movement phrases like "We're all victims" and "We're all co-dependent" may not seem to leave a lot of room for interpretation, but they are actually so vague that they beg for interpretation and projection. Such phrases may be fair game for ridicule, but it is shallow to judge them on their face value, as if they hold the same meaning for everyone. What is meant by an "inner child" depends on the person speaking, and not everyone will see it as a metaphor for helplessness. I suspect that most inner-child enthusiasts use the image of themselves as children not so that they can avoid being responsible but to learn responsibility by going back to the point in time when they should have been taught responsibility—the ability to think, choose, and stand up for themselves—and were not. As I understand it, the point of identifying an "inner child" is to locate the part of yourself that didn't develop into adulthood and then to develop it yourself.

Whether or not this works is an open question, but it is an at- 20
tempt to accept responsibility, not to flee it.

When I was in my late teens and early twenties, I could not bear to watch movies or read books that I considered demeaning to women in any way; I evaluated everything I saw or read in terms of whether it expressed a "positive image" of women. I was a very P.C. feminist before the term existed, and, by the measure of my current understanding, my critical rigidity followed from my inability to be responsible for my own feelings. In this context, being responsible would have meant that I let myself feel whatever discomfort, indignation, or disgust I experienced without allowing those feelings to determine my entire reaction to a given piece of work. In other words, it would have meant dealing with my feelings and what had caused them, rather than expecting the outside world to assuage them. I could have chosen not to see the world through the lens of my personal unhappiness and yet maintained a kind of respect for my unhappiness. For example, I could have decided to avoid certain films or books because of my feelings without blaming the film or book for making me feel the way I did. 21

My emotional irresponsibility did not spring from a need to feel victimized, although it may have looked that way to somebody else. I essentially was doing what I had seen most mainstream cultural critics do—it was from them that I learned to view works of art in terms of the message they imparted and, further, that the message could be judged on the basis of consensual ideas about what life is, and how it can and should be seen. My ideas, like most P.C. ideas, were extreme, but they were consistent with more mainstream thought—they just shifted the parameters of acceptability a bit. 22

Things haven't changed much: at least half the book and film reviews that I read praise or condemn a work on the basis of the likability of the characters (as if there is a standard idea of what is likable) or because the author's point of view is or is not "life-affirming"—or whatever the critic believes the correct attitude toward life to be. The lengthy and rather hysterical debate about the film *Thelma and Louise,* in which two ordinary women become outlaws after one of them shoots the other's rapist, was predicated on the idea that stories are supposed to function as instruction manuals, and that whether the film was good or bad depended on whether the instructions were correct. Such criticism assumes that viewers or readers need to see a certain type of moral universe reflected back at them or, empty vessels that they are, they might get confused or depressed or something. A respected mainstream essayist writing for *Time* faulted my novel *Two Girls, Fat and Thin* for its nasty male characters, which he took to be a moral statement about males generally. He ended his piece with the fervent wish that fiction not "diminish" men or women but rather seek to "raise our vision of" both—in other words, that it should present the "right" way to the reader, who is apparently not responsible enough to figure it out alone. 23

I have changed a lot from the P.C. teenager who walked out of movies that portrayed women in a demeaning light. As I've grown older, I've become more confident of myself and my ability to determine what happens to me, and, as a result, those images no longer have such a strong emotional charge. I don't believe they will affect my life in any practical sense unless I allow them to do so. I no longer feel that misogynistic stories are about me or even about women (whether they purport to be or not) but rather are about the kinds of experience the authors wish to render—and therefore are not my problem. I consider my current view more balanced, but that doesn't mean my earlier feelings were wrong. The reason I couldn't watch "disrespect to women" at that time was that such depictions were too close to my own experience (most of which was not unusual), and I found them painful. I was displaying a simplistic self-respect by not subjecting myself to something I was not ready to face. Being unable to separate my personal experience from what I saw on the screen, I was not dealing with my own particular experience—I think, paradoxically, because I hadn't yet learned to value it. It's hard to be responsible for something that isn't valuable. Someone criticizing me as dogmatic and narrow-minded would have had a point, but the point would have ignored the truth of my unacknowledged experience, and thus ignored me. 24

Many critics of the self-help culture argue against treating emotional or metaphoric reality as if it were equivalent to objective reality. I agree that they are not the same. But emotional truth is often bound up with truth of a more objective kind and must be taken into account. This is especially true of conundrums such as date rape and victimism, both of which often are discussed in terms of unspoken assumptions about emotional truth anyway. Sarah Crichton, in a cover story for *Newsweek* on "Sexual Correctness," described the "strange detour" taken by some feminists and suggested that "we're not creating a society of Angry Young Women. These are Scared Little Girls." The comment is both contemptuous and superficial; it shows no interest in why girls might be scared. By such logic, anger implicitly is deemed to be the more desirable emotional state because it appears more potent, and "scared" is used as a pejorative. It's possible to shame a person into hiding his or her fear, but if you don't address the cause of the fear, it won't go away. Crichton ends her piece by saying, "Those who are growing up in environments where they don't have to figure out what the rules should be, but need only follow what's been prescribed, are being robbed of the most important lesson there is to learn. And that's how to live." I couldn't agree more. But unless you've been taught how to think for yourself, you'll have a hard time figuring out your own rules, and you'll feel scared—especially when there is real danger of sexual assault. 25

One reason I had sex with strangers when I didn't really want to was that part of me wanted the adventure, and that tougher part ran roughshod over the part of me that was scared and uncertain. I'll bet the same thing happened to many of the boys with whom I had these experiences. All people have their tough, aggressive selves as well as their more delicate selves. If you haven't developed these characteristics in ways that are respectful of yourself and others, you will find it hard to be responsible for them. I don't think it's possible to develop yourself in such ways if you are attuned to following rules and codes that don't give your inner world enough importance. I was a strong-willed child with a lot of aggressive impulses, which, for various reasons, I was actively discouraged from developing. They stayed hidden under a surface of extreme passivity, and when they did appear it was often in a wildly irresponsible, almost crazy way. My early attraction to aggressive boys and men was in part a need to see somebody act out the distorted feelings I didn't know what to do with, whether it was destructive or not. I suspect that boys who treat girls with disrespectful aggression have failed to develop their more tender, sensitive side and futilely try to regain it by "possessing" a woman. Lists of instructions about what's nice and what isn't will not help people in such a muddled state, and it's my observation that many people are in such a state to a greater or lesser degree. 26

I am not idealistic enough to hope that we will ever live in a world without rape and other forms of sexual cruelty; I think men and women will always have to struggle to behave responsibly. But I think we could make the struggle less difficult by changing the way we teach responsibility and social conduct. To teach a boy that rape is "bad" is not as effective as making him see that rape is a violation of his own masculine dignity as well as a violation of the raped woman. It's true that children don't know big words and that teenage boys aren't all that interested in their own dignity. But these are things that children learn more easily by example than by words, and learning by example runs deep. 27

A few years ago I invited to dinner at my home a man I'd known casually for two years. We'd had dinner and comradely drinks a few times. I didn't have any intention of becoming sexual with him, but after dinner we slowly got drunk and were soon floundering on the couch. I was ambivalent not only because I was drunk but because I realized that although part of me was up for it, the rest of me was not. So I began to say no. He parried each "no" with charming banter and became more aggressive. I went along with it for a time because I was amused and even somewhat seduced by the sweet, junior-high spirit of his manner. But at some point I began to be alarmed, and then he did and said some things that turned my alarm into fright. I don't remember the exact sequence of words or events, but I do 28 remember taking one of his hands and both of mine, looking him in the eyes, and saying, "If this comes to a fight you would win, but it would be very ugly for both of us. Is that really what you want?" His expression changed and he dropped his eyes; afterward he left.

I consider that small decision to have been a responsible one because it was made by taking both my vulnerable feelings and my carnal impulses into account. When I spoke, my words came from my feeling of delicacy as well as from my capacity for aggression. And I respected my friend as well by addressing both sides of his nature. It is not hard for me to make such decisions now, but it took me a long time to get to this point. I only regret that it took so long, both for my young self and for the boys I was with, under circumstances that I now consider disrespectful to all concerned. 29

THINKING ABOUT THE ESSAY

1. How would you summarize Gaitskill's message or thesis? What is her purpose and how does she make her case? How does she appeal to her audience—through evidence, personal experience, general principles, or what? Cite specific passages to support your response.
2. Do you respond to the issue of victimization in an absolute way, that is, "the victim is always right" or "nobody has to be a victim if he or she doesn't want to be"? Or do you believe the issue has shades of gray? Explain your response.
3. Are there any situations in which you find it difficult to conform or understand expected rules of behavior? If so, what are they, and how do you feel in such situations?
4. Gaitskill states that although she was once raped, "it actually affected me less than many other mundane instances of emotional brutality." Judging from her reasoning of the incident, do you believe her or do you think she is repressing her true feelings?
5. Gaitskill criticizes two sets of social critics: the rape-crisis feminists and those who claim that victims aren't so innocent. What are her major arguments against each group?

RESPONDING IN DISCUSSION

1. Divide into groups of three or four and discuss whether the passivity the author seems to have displayed during earlier sexual encounters was a result of her generation. Consider whether today's generation of women are more assertive.

2. Discuss in class unwritten rules about behavior between men and women that seem to be less defined than they once were. Describe how they have affected you personally.
3. Discuss in class your definition of *feminist*. Where did you develop your definition? How does it compare to other students' definitions? Is there a general difference between the way thc women in your class respond to the term compared to the men. If so, what is the difference?
4. In groups of three or four, discuss your class background. This is perhaps best done by describing what your parents do for a living. Then tell how your background affects your behaviors in relating to the opposite sex.

RESPONDING IN WRITING

1. Describe a time in you life when you questioned or defied an unwritten rule about socializing at a party or other public event.
2. Interview three women: one in her twenties, one in her forties, and one in her sixties. Write an essay comparing and contrasting their sense of what psychologists call locus of control. That is, to what degree do they feel they can make independent decisions without concern with breaking convention or hurting other people's feelings?
3. Write a précis or summary of Gaitskill's essay. Be sure to include her major arguments and supporting points.
4. Argue for or against the view that all colleges and universities should require students to take a course on sexual responsibility and social conduct.
5. Conduct a Web search for Camille Paglia, an author whom Gaitskill refers to in her essay. Establish Paglia's position on the issues raised by Gaitskill and compare and contrast these viewpoints.

CONNECTIONS: FOR WRITING AND RESEARCH

1. Shirachi describes dating in Hawaii as being "pure, clean fun." Would the men she dated need a verbal consent policy? If not, to what degree did this policy arise from cultural practices in dating habits among mainland American men?
2. Write a letter to the Antioch College administration supporting or criticizing the institution's verbal consent policy.
3. Write an essay comparing Roiphe's and Gaitskill's views of victimization.

4. Select two of the four writers cited by Gaitskill, read their writings about sexual behavior, and provide a critique of their views about "women as victims."
5. To what degree does going away to college place attitudinal and behavioral demands on women that prior generations did not have to address?
6. How does Gabriel's essay relate to the other essays in this chapter? Is he addressing the same general topic or exploring an entirely different phenomenon?

5

COLLEGE SPORTS

At one time, there was a vast difference between college sports and professional sports, or at least there was a perception that the two were different. College sports were thought to be performed for the love of the game, rivalries were intense but ultimately benign, equipment was not up to the standards of professional gear, and players earned next to nothing for their efforts. College athletes were considered amateurs and not merely members of a training program preparing them for a move up to the professional leagues. Today, if you turn on your television at random to a sports channel, you are likely to see only minimal differences between college sporting events and their professional counterparts. The stakes have also changed profoundly. Walter Byers, writing in *The Sporting News,* claims college athletes should take advantage of their status to earn big bucks if offered them by commercial ventures. Meanwhile Tim Layden, writing in *Sports Illustrated,* demonstrates that with the widespread betting among college students, we no longer have enthusiastic fans, but rather nervous investors. Two other essays in this section address the issue of college sports for women—each touching on not only the idea of equality between the sexes, but also on what significance this equality has for the distribution of college sports funding. It is often said that nowadays sportswriters spend more time writing about player contracts and drug use among athletes than about athletic performance. You will find that the following recent essays primarily look at college sports from these and other nontraditional perspectives.

Under the Tarnished Dome

George Vecsey

First appearing as a column in the November 5, 1993, issue of the *National Catholic Reporter,* the following essay alludes to Don Yaeger and Douglas Looney's 1993 book *Under the Tarnished Dome,* a look at sports at the University of Notre Dame. The review was written by one of America's foremost sportswriters, George Vecsey, whose credentials make him a particularly salient choice as a reviewer for this work. First, he is a former religion writer turned sports columnist. Second, he was able to provide an insightful comparative perspective on Notre Dame's athletic policies since he had visited the school exactly 10 years before the book was written. As you will see, much changed during the decade from 1983 to 1993, so that Notre Dame sports of 1983 have little in common with their 1993 counterpart. While we expect change to occur in most of our institutions, Vecsey points out how even, as the reviewer puts it, "the home office of American Catholicism" can easily adopt the secular tactics of the culture at large.

PREVIEWING THE ESSAY

Most of us know that sports heroes like Babe Ruth or presidents like John F. Kennedy had personal flaws, but we usually still retain a certain respect for them that transcends their faults. Similarly, we may rationalize bingo games as fundraisers for churches as a harmless way to keep the local parish solvent. But what about long-standing, symbolic institutions that have a reputation for such abstract concepts as honesty, sacrifice, and fairness? Are such ideas relics of a naive past, held onto by a few idealists with little knowledge of the outside world, or is there a place for such values in our society? As you read the case of Notre Dame, you may wish to ask, "Is it enough to justify just about *anything* because you know everyone else is doing it?"

The last time I was on the Notre Dame campus was 1983 when I was invited to attend a conference of and about lay Catholics, presumably because I was a former religion writer rather than a current sports columnist or former Catholic. 1

It was midweek. The football presence on campus was not overwhelming, as it can be closer to game time. A business-suit kind of modern nun from the Deep South who, as I recall, was a practicing psychiatrist, was making her first visit to Notre Dame. She'd sent a message to Gerry Faust, coach of the Fighting Irish, that it was her lifelong ambition just to get to the stadium. 2

Faust sent a message back: Sister was welcome to watch practice. As long as she was in uniform. She had to rummage deep down in her suitcase and eagerly don her habit before she bustled over to the stadium. 3

Well, I thought, there you have it, the ultimate blending of reli- 4
gious faith and sporting fanaticism, the home office of American Catholicism and American football. Only it turns out that Faust relied too much on urgent sideline prayers and too little on recruiting the biggest, baddest boys in the land. Everybody loved Faust, but he was not a good coach, and Notre Dame fans were relieved when he was not rehired after the 1985 season. His record was 30 victories, 26 losses and one tie, which at Notre Dame is abysmal.

In his place, Notre Dame hired a wispy, lispy coach named Lou 5
Holtz, who proceeded to bring Notre Dame back to its rightful place. Never mind this Top 10 stuff. Notre Dame expects to be in the Top Five, if not the Top Three, or even the Top One.

But there was a price. Notre Dame has forfeited its right to brag 6
that its program is special. It has become like Oklahoma, Alabama, Colorado and even despised Miami, only with a mural of Touchdown Jesus raising his arms to signal six points at the end of the stadium.

Much of this material is familiar to anybody who writes for or 7
reads the sports pages. We all know how Notre Dame secretively cut its own television deal with NBC for $37.5 million from 1991–95, leaving its fellow universities in the lurch. We all know how Holtz brought the odor of scandal from his previous job at Minnesota. And football fans are aware that Holtz put a bear hug on an official who had made a call that displeased Holtz, which leads to the penultimate chapter called "Is Holtz Losing It?" and suggests he might be.

What he may not have realized is the depth of division and cyni- 8
cism among former Notre Dame players. This is the valuable contribution of Don Yaeger, who has written two other books on big-time college sports, and Douglas S. Looney, a senior writer for *Sports Illustrated.* They talked to more than 100 former Notre Dame players who described the culture shock from the sincere Gerry Faust to the wily Lou Holtz.

Former Holtz players describe the widespread use of illegal 9
steroids under Holtz. They claim the university had vastly under-reported the scope of the confidential positive tests for drugs. If a player was caught a time or two with naughty things floating about his system, Holtz would call him into his office and slap him on the wrist. Literally. Enough players tell this tale that I tend to believe it, although I cannot discount the possibility of mass hysteria in such a heightened atmosphere as Notre Dame.

But there was a worse sin than getting caught taking steroids. 10
That sin was getting injured. Players describe the state of limbo into which they fell because they made the mistake of having their knees crushed by some flying dock-walloper from another institution of higher learning. If they were hurt, Coach Holtz would stare right through them. They attained invisibility. Or if he did see them, Holtz would order them to hobble out there and win one for the Gipper.

Now I really don't believe the Gipper deathbed speech, do you? Remember, that was a Ronald Reagan movie. There's a movie going around about a practice player at Notre Dame who was allowed into one game as a senior, but apparently that movie gets all the subtleties wrong, and makes it sound like the players staged some kind of revolt to get their buddy in the game. Who needs more half-truths about Notre Dame? 11

But I think the book is real, as far as it goes. Its style is "gee whiz" in places, oral history in other places, official court documents in others. But I really believe the authors talked to these players and this is what they said, even if you factor in revenge, hatred, sadness, denial, fear, nostalgia, pain—all the feelings endemic to college football. 12

Of course a lot of them admit they were not exactly angels when they were at Notre Dame, so it's hard to know just how much they remember through the haze of drugs, alcohol, coaching terror, mass adulation and official looking-the-other-way. But the weight of their testimony is impressive. I wish only that the authors or publishers had seen fit to include an index so we could keep these people straight. 13

My problem is I'm not surprised at any of this. I've been covering college football too long to be surprised by anything. The players point out that some of them—it's usually somebody else—gained 40 pounds in one summer, and not from mom's home cooking, either. They felt used, hundreds of high school All-Americans being shoehorned into one electrically charged campus. 14

But the same thing happens at other places. That's football, son. It is the sport where sappy fans (like you) and sappy sportswriters (like me) gawk at the hippy-dippy guys running with the ball, and meanwhile burly clodhoppers are belting the whey out of each other at the line of scrimmage. Punching, holding, biting, gouging, spitting, kneeing. Whatever it takes. 15

"Mankind survives on bestial acts," Kurt Weil once wrote in a song. He was thinking of other things, but you could apply it to football. The thing was, Notre Dame used to have a claim on a certain type of young man: relatively high grades, relatively high muscle content, relatively high character. But Faust could not win with them. The decision to lower standards seems to have come from the top, after the worldly Fr. Theodore Hesburgh retired as president in 1987 and was replaced by Fr. Edward A. Malloy, a former Notre Dame basketball player. 16

"An axiom on college football is that speed on the football field and speed in the classroom are almost always in an inverse relationship," the authors write. 17

Holtz and his one-liners have provided us all with the same yuks, but the authors suggest that he wears out his welcomes. He always seems to be describing how his father listened to the games of the 18 university that now employs him. Apparently even the current regime at Notre Dame is tiring of his antics. Plus, he hasn't won a national championship since all the way back to January 1989. They might be happy to see him leave. Unless, of course, he were to win the national championship this year.

THINKING ABOUT THE ESSAY

1. Have you been in a campus situation in which you walked a thin line between honesty and dishonesty? If so, what was the situation, and how did you respond, and how did you explain your actions?
2. Vecsey enumerates some of the "sins" of the Notre Dame football culture—in particular, those that were encouraged or instigated by their new head coach, Lou Holtz. What is the author's view of these indiscretions? What is your view?
3. How would you describe the nature of Vecsey's review? Is it a critical review of a book, is it a description of a book, or is it a summary of events at Notre Dame, using the book as a reference?
4. Would winning the national championship justify all the questionable activities of Notre Dame football? How do you feel personally? What do you think the majority of Americans would think?
5. What is the overall thesis that Vecsey tries to convey in his review?

RESPONDING IN DISCUSSION

1. Divide into groups of three or four, and develop a group consensus on what personal qualities should go into an ideal college football coach. Share you conclusions with the rest of the class.
2. Conduct a secret ballot in class whereby students write on a piece of paper "approve" or "disapprove" to demonstrate their response to Holtz's actions. Have your instructor tally the responses. Then, based on the final vote, discuss what import the vote has on understanding the values of your class in particular and college students in general. Consider such issues as the type of institution you attend, such as private or public, religious or secular, large or small, or one with a strong or mild intercollegiate sports component.
3. Why is there so much focus on the state and stakes of college football rather than less valued college sports such as volleyball, baseball, and track and field? Is it because the colleges emphasize football's importance, so that interest trickles down to the students, or is there something inherent in the sport that makes it such a "hot commodity"?

4. Who should be held responsible for the flagrant use of steroids among student athletes: the coach who encourages it, or the administration who underreports it, or the fans who either ignore it or just take it for granted, or the students who take them?

RESPONDING IN WRITING

1. In a 400-word essay, describe a time in your life when an authority figure asked you to do something you felt was ethically questionable.
2. Describe a time in your life when you submitted to peer pressure. What was the outcome? What would have been the psychological and social results had you not succumbed?
3. Argue for or against the proposition that the overhaul of college football to reduce abusive acts must come at a national rather than local level.
4. Argue for or against the proposition that to end the abuse in college sports, you must end intercollegiate sports entirely.
5. For a research paper utilizing library and Web resources, investigate the illicit use of steroids in American life. Issues you might address include people's reasons for taking steroids illicitly. Where are they obtained? What are the penalties for their illegal sale and use? How do these penalties compare to those for other illicit drugs? Why are steroids tolerated by institutions such as colleges and universities whereas other illicit drugs are not?

A Sporting Chance?

Joannie M. Schrof

Writing in the large-circulation newsweekly *U.S. News & World Report* (April 11, 1994), Schrof begins her essay by calling 1994 "the year of the woman" owing to the popularity of the women's NCAA tournament. One might presume that women's sports have come a long way toward equity with their male counterparts. However, as you will read in the following essay, equality is quite a distance away. This catch-up game would be considered normal under most circumstances when historically one group has had a longstanding advantage over another. However, what makes the inequality between men's and women's sports particularly troubling to the author is that it defies a federal law, known as Title IX, guaranteeing equal sporting opportunities for male and female students. In effect, then, many colleges and universities are literally breaking the law but are going unpunished. Laws are created to protect the rights of individuals in spite of what the prevailing cultural and social climate might dictate. Schrof points out that the letter of the law is one thing; the attitude toward the law is another.

PREVIEWING THE ESSAY

Does Schrof effectively demonstrate that the sluggishness with which colleges and universities are conforming to the law regarding equal opportunities for women and men athletes is a result of inertia or of unimaginative, biased, or old-fashioned thinking? Or have truly "systemic" issues (such as lack of sufficient budgets and space for newly formed women's teams) resulted in this slowness?

This year's National Collegiate Athletic Association basketball tournament might have been dubbed "the year of the woman." Powerhouses of men's basketball, like returning champion North Carolina and Purdue University, ended up sending their men home early while their women advanced to the Final Four. In the championship competition last weekend, network television cameras captured battles waged by strong, skilled athletes in front of roaring, sellout crowds—testimony that women had finally arrived at the pinnacle of school sports. 1

But the cameras betray the truth. Indeed, such high-profile women's teams are noticeable precisely because they are so rare. Twenty-two years after the passage of the federal law known as Title IX—guaranteeing equal sporting opportunities for male and female students—women athletes are still second-class citizens in a man's world. Consider: 2

- There are nearly twice as many boys as girls playing high school sports, and more than twice as many college men as women. Colleges award twice as much money in athletic scholarships to men and spend more than five times as much to recruit male athletes. 3
- When the law passed, more than 90 percent of those coaching women's sports were themselves women; today, only about 48 percent of women's coaches are female. Likewise, women make up less than 3 percent of athletic directors at Division I colleges. 4
- Even in the more visible sports, such as basketball, coaches of women's teams earn only 59 percent of what coaches of men's teams make. 5
- Nearly every measure of parity, from equipment quality to promotion budgets, favors male athletes. When the NCAA recently polled 646 member colleges, it found that 645 of them weren't even close to meeting equity standards. 6

FITS AND STARTS

What began as a simple idea—boys and girls both can and should benefit from sports—quickly became embroiled in a political quagmire 7 that has kept true equity beyond reach for more than two decades. The passage of Title IX at first prompted a tremendous response, as campuses across the nation rushed to revamp their sports programs by the 1978 deadline. Within six years, the portion of school athletes who were female skyrocketed from 7 percent to about 33 percent. But a series of events have since stalled growth at that level. First, a 1984 Supreme Court decision overturned Title IX, causing the Education Department's Office of Civil Rights (OCR) to scrap all investigations. Four years later the law was restored, but it had become apparent that overburdened federal agencies lacked the resources to make inspections or enforce the law. The OCR has yet to withhold federal funds from a single offending school.

LITMUS TEST

Today, it is impossible to find an athletic director who does not pub- 8
licly proclaim support for the principle of gender equity in sports, but it is also nearly impossible to find a school that fully complies with the law. Title IX requires not only that the ratio of female and male athletes must match the makeup of the student body but also that everything from locker-room facilities to uniforms to promotion budgets be on par. In short, the test for genuine equity is that men would be happy to swap resources with women.

But they would be fools to trade. Susan True, of the National Fed- 9
eration of State High School Associations, reports that it is still commonplace at secondary schools for boys' teams, but not girls', to have assistant coaches; for boys to get new uniforms every year, while girls get them every three years; for boys to sleep two to a room on road trips, while girls sleep four to a room; for schools to offer boys, but not girls, junior varsity teams. The list goes on and on.

Resource distribution is even more lopsided at the college level, in 10
large part because high-visibility men's sports often make big money—a fact that has been used to justify existing inequities. But a team's earning capacity is irrelevant in the eyes of the law, which views athletics not as small businesses but as targets for equal educational opportunity. The opportunities are routinely unequal: Women athletes often don't even have locker rooms, they are routinely barred from weight-training facilities when men's teams want to use them and they operate within tiny budgets. Amie Stewart, a pitcher for the University of Nevada at Las Vegas softball team, speaks of the frustration she and her teammates feel when they have to travel 12 hours by bus, while the men's teams fly. And while the university built a new stadium with lights to promote the money-making potential of the men's team, the softball team plays during working hours on a field with a small set of

bleachers. "The team members always talk about writing letters to complain," says Stewart, "but what good would it do?" The university has plans to build a softball stadium when funds become available.

In fact, much of the gender equation comes down to money. Athletic directors say they're strapped for cash and that they must give priority to revenue-producing sports like men's basketball and football to keep generating the money to fund other athletic teams. But NCAA studies show that the majority of revenue-producing men's teams don't actually turn a profit; they eat up the money they make and often more. The seeming excesses of high-profile teams suggest that more money could be made available to equalize opportunities. It's a routine practice, for example, for an entire football squad to be roomed and fed at a local hotel the night before a home game. 11

Women's advocates say that sports officials are using money as an excuse to hide their basic contempt for women's sports. A plaintiff in a case against Colgate University testified before Congress that when women ice-hockey players addressed the school's Committee on Athletics to request funding closer to that of the men's team, one official kicked the meeting off with, "I'd better get comfortable. This one puts me to sleep." When an Alabama high school principal cut girls' basketball—the only girls' sport at the school, paid for largely by the players themselves—he cited as his reason the cost of paying referees. 12

In response to such incidents, women are turning in increasing numbers to the courts—and judges are listening. At least 35 lawsuits have been filed, and those that have been decided have nearly always favored female athletes and coaches. A 1992 Supreme Court ruling that women can sue for monetary damages opens up schools to the possibility of huge financial loss for noncompliance. A victorious class action suit against 19 schools of the California State University system last year suggests that suits against entire athletic conferences may be the next logical step in Title IX litigation. 13

The lawsuits show that change is possible. After Washington State University was sued in the 1980s, it revamped its sports program and is now considered a model of gender equity. "We learned that it is possible to achieve parity without killing big-time sports like football and basketball," says spokesman Rod Commons. "Our football team cut back on some amenities—the hotels we stay in aren't as nice—but it hasn't hurt us on the field. We've been to two bowl games since stepping up our gender-equity efforts." The school doubled its fund-raising income and upped its female athlete count by 67 by adding women's crew. 14

In the wake of the lawsuits, many athletic administrators are taking at least incremental steps toward more opportunities for women. But none promises to ensure nationwide equity. The NCAA approved gender-equity standards last year, but left it to the schools to monitor 15 compliance; next year, it will vote on a plan to make the awarding of scholarships more equitable. Fifty-nine colleges added women's soccer this year, a sport that can include about 30 players. The Gulf South, Southeastern and Big Ten conferences have passed rules that will increase participation for women in the near future. Rep. Cardiss Collins, an Illinois Democrat, hopes to speed reform with legislation that would require schools to disclose athletic budgets and report on progress toward equity. (An unexpected consequence of Title IX activism has been the elimination of some men's teams that, like most women's, don't make money or bring their school much prestige. Most women disapprove of achieving greater numerical equity by hurting male athletes rather than by truly creating new opportunities for women. But the courts have upheld schools' efforts to comply in this fashion.)

CULTURAL FERMENT

Widespread policy changes will come only with a broad shift in attitudes about girls and sports. Even today, illegal inequities are frequently justified by claims that women lack interest in athletics—a claim that is belied by the very active athletic-club system that college women support with dues and fees. Alternatively, critics hark back to turn-of-the-century views, dismissing women who do want to compete as unfeminine. When three students at Louisiana State University filed a lawsuit two weeks ago to upgrade their soccer team to varsity status, they were publicly derided as lesbians making unreasonable demands. 16

Even so, activists are optimistic that the cultural tide will turn irreversibly in favor of equality. "It's interesting to sit back and watch the dominoes of cultural change fall," says Donna Lopiano, director of the Women's Sports Foundation. "If you can stand the wait." Waiting is a luxury that female student-athletes can't afford. Samantha Clark, a plaintiff in the LSU case, will graduate in December, at the end of the next soccer season. "That's the end of the line for me in competitive sports," Clark says. "This is my very last chance." 17

THINKING ABOUT THE ESSAY

1. In a college environment, have you ever enjoyed material advantage because of your gender? Explain.
2. To what degree is a law necessary to ensure that women and men have equal access to college sports? What do you believe would occur if your college's administration alone determined how athletic funding was allocated?

3. Does the author effectively demonstrate that endowing women's sports with more funding is cost-effective? Is it important that she include this issue in her argument, or is conforming to the law (Title IX) a sufficient reason for enhancing sports for women in college?
4. The author states that "it is impossible to find an athletic director who does not publicly proclaim support for the principle of gender equity in sports." Why is it so important to take this public position?
5. Where in the text does the author discuss the solution to the inequality between men's and women's sports? What would you propose to reach this solution?

RESPONDING IN DISCUSSION

1. In groups of four or five, and with approximately equal distribution between genders, express your view as to the equality or inequality for sports opportunities for men and women on your campus. Share your views with the rest of the class.
2. Discuss the benefits of participating in competitive college sports for women. What are they? Do they build character and instill discipline as is traditionally thought? Or are these mere unfounded notions?
3. Jot down a list of prejudices or stereotypes concerning women that you believe may hinder their equal access to college sports. Rank-order them. Then discuss in class which you believe to be the most prevalent and which you believe to be the worst.
4. Schrof assumes that participation in intercollegiate sports is a positive thing. Yet many educators argue that there is too much emphasis on intercollegiate college sports, regardless of who is participating. Discuss whether focusing on expanding intercollegiate sports to accommodate women is actually counterproductive to the mission of a college or university.

RESPONDING IN WRITING

1. Interview a female member of an intercollegiate athletic team on your campus. Ask her to discuss her views on the state of college sports for women. In an essay of 500 words, describe her responses to issues such as the perceived equality with men's opportunities, her motives for playing, and the response she receives from others upon learning she is an athlete.
2. On your college campus visit the facilities of two commensurate teams distinguished only by the gender of the players (for

example, the women's basketball team and the men's basketball team). Write a 500-word descriptive essay comparing and contrasting their facilities.

3. Write a position paper for your college's athletic director. In it, articulate your views on equality of opportunity for men and women as they pertain to participation in college sports.
4. Argue for or against the proposition that the promotion of college sports for women is just an indirect attack on the importance of academics in college.
5. Conduct a search for men's college basketball websites and another for women's. What is the comparative outcome? Look for one school with a site for each. Do you find any noteworthy differences in the treatment of each topic? Pose a question to each sitekeeper and write a comparative essay evaluating responses.

Competing to Compete

Louis M. Guenin

The author is a member of the Division of Medical Ethics of Harvard Medical School. In the January–February 1996 issue of *Change,* he advances a unique means to provide "equal competitive access" for men and women in college sports. He attacks a federal law that applies "equal opportunity" in college sports by attempting to demonstrate that it addresses neither equality nor opportunity. In this regard, he is following the long tradition of Western rational thought that can be loosely referred to as induction. That is, he collects evidence and then demonstrates its implications. When reading the essay, pay particular care to the shades of meaning of many key words the author interrogates, abstract terms such as *nondiscrimination, equal opportunity, proportionality,* and *enrollment standards.* According to the author, it is in these subtle concepts that the difference between a fair system of college athletics and an impractical and unfair one reside. The author's process in illuminating the elusiveness of such terms demonstrates that authentic argumentation requires considerable foresight, planning, judgment, and reasoning, something many of us tend to forget in an age where everyone seems to have an opinion, and opinions are respected based on the popularity of the opinion-maker.

PREVIEWING THE ESSAY

Many societies still operate in a system whereby fairness and equality are not issues of concern. Birth into wealthy families, favors made to people in power, and even intimidation often determine one's ultimate access to "privilege." In

America today, we seem to have a movement of what some writers call "identity politics." In other words, nearly everyone is entitled to equal opportunity as a result of having been a member of a group that has suffered from less than full participation in the democratic process. As you read the following essay, you may wish to ask yourself several questions: To what degree am I concerned with the concepts of equality and justice in my life? To what degree should the government proactively dictate the redress of inequality? What complex issues arise in determining whether a group has legitimate grievances, and how can these grievances be addressed without taking rights away from others?

"Equal opportunity" was a compelling philosophical ideal before it became a legal one. As espoused by the French revolutionaries, the principle of *la carrière ouverte aux talents* ("careers open to talents") denied that birth may rightly bound a person's opportunities for life. For later egalitarians, the ideal of "equal opportunity" denies that social status of any kind should be permitted to bound opportunities. The more recent egalitarianism of the philosopher John Rawls includes a strong "principle of fair equality of opportunity," and it also includes a distributive principle whose effect is to offset even the constraining effect of lesser talents. 1

The question that all such accounts of "equal opportunity" must answer is "Opportunity to do what?" In recent times "equal opportunity" has been applied to intercollegiate athletics. There the concept has succumbed to a wooden interpretation, one made ominous because, at least for now, it enjoys the force of law. The interpretation to which I refer culminated last year in a ruling against Brown University. Ostensibly an exemplar of opportunities for women, Brown was found culpable of discrimination against women in athletics. According to the United States District Court for the District of Rhode Island, Brown has not been invidious about any accoutrement afforded men's vis-à-vis women's teams. Brown's offense is statistical. The proportion of its athletes who are women is less than the proportion of its undergraduate enrollment that is female. The court's ruling upheld the position of a federal agency that these two proportions must equate. If not reversed on appeal, such rule of equal proportions may compel colleges to distort resource allocations and thereby to overvalue intercollegiate athletics. Such fate, so I shall argue here, would avail a majority of neither sex. 2

THE INTERPRETATION OF NONDISCRIMINATION AS "EQUAL OPPORTUNITY"

Colleges and athletics now labor under the handicap of multilayered and confusing legal authorities following upon Title IX of the Education 3

Amendments of 1972. That statute forbids institutions that receive federal funds from discriminating "on the basis of sex." Congress stipulated in Title IX that it was not prohibiting quantitative "imbalances" in benefits that might from time to time be detected, but rather that it was prohibiting discriminatory practices. Thus it distinguished static statistical comparisons from acts and practices. In Title IX, Congress did not mention "equal opportunity" or athletics. Mention of athletics occurred in 1974 when the "Javits amendment" directed that implementing regulations should include provisions for intercollegiate athletics that reflect "the nature of particular sports." (This last phrase alluded to the effect of football's unusually large rosters on the arithmetic of opportunities.) The Department of Health, Education, and Welfare (HEW) then declared in a 1975 regulation that recipients of federal funds must provide "equal athletic opportunity" for the sexes. By the foregoing steps, nondiscrimination was translated to "equal opportunity."

4 Perhaps the most cohesive case for equality of opportunity is "justice as fairness," a comprehensive account of social justice presented by Rawls in *A Theory of Justice* (1971), a work likely to rank among the most influential in the history of moral and political philosophy. A revision of the theory appear in *Political Liberalism* (1993). Rawls's theory contrasts with the view of Burke and Hegel that society benefits from hierarchies. According to justice as fairness, a just society will provide fair equality of opportunity for all. It will do so by actively interdicting discriminatory barriers. Except for expenses of law enforcement, to interdict barriers is not to direct resource allocations. This we may see at once from our laws on equal opportunity in employment and housing. Such laws do not mandate jobs or buildings, they forbid invidious selection of employees and residents. That is not to say that justice as fairness as a whole neglects resource distributions. For Rawls, talents are merely "unearned outcomes of the natural lottery." Hence Rawls is not content to leave "careers open to talents." He introduces the "difference principle" in order to favor those less talented with fruits of the exercise by others of superior talents. The difference principle requires that goods be distributed equally unless an inequality operates to the greatest benefit of society's least advantaged. This is the offsetting mechanism to which I referred at the outset. For our present purposes it suffices to note that fair equality of opportunity is not a distributive principle. It remains a mandate of "pure procedural justice."

5 Since Rawls's theory extends only to large scale institutions like government, all of which together constitute "the basic structure" of society, the theory does not reach down as far as intrauniversity affairs. Moreover, his principle of fair equality of opportunity applies only to "positions of authority and offices of command." Thus "equal opportunity" in justice as fairness does not appear to embrace membership on

college teams. Is there then no philosophical justification for insisting on "equal opportunity" within an institution? To answer this, one might propose an extrapolation of justice as fairness, a local justice analogue of it, or some other egalitarian theory that does govern college policies about sports. If a college were deliberately to limit opportunity for some group, such a theory might direct that resources be deployed to redress the denied opportunity. To deny women membership on men's teams seems straightforwardly to be a denial of equal opportunity to enjoy that benefit. Within a local analogue of justice as fairness, such exclusion would render sex what Rawls calls a "relevant social position." Thereby the exclusion would become justifiable if and only if it somehow worked to the advantage of those disfavored by the inequality, namely, female varsity aspirants. Enhancement of their overall opportunity could occur, for example, if in contact sports when it appears contrary to women's best interests to join men's teams, a college fields separate women's teams. This is a different sense of enhancing opportunity than obtains in the implementation of policies like affirmative action in admissions. The latter ordinarily concerns no additional resource outlays. It concerns the allocation of places in an entering class of predetermined size. (Exceptions to such generality occur, as when a single-sex college first becomes coeducational.) Intercollegiate athletics for women does require additional outlays. It requires colleges to expand the size of their programs by the creation of separate women's teams.

6 After a career of describing freedom from discriminatory practices, if "equal opportunity" is to be mustered in the law as a principle directing the allocation of resources, it will require careful elaboration. Skipping over this point, the 1975 regulations declared that to provide "equal athletic opportunity," a college must "effectively accommodate the interests and abilities of both sexes." The implication of resource allocations here was apparent, but clarity was not. Then in a 1979 "policy interpretation" of "effective accommodation" by HEW's Office of Civil Rights (OCR), the train of clarity derailed. Confusing, inconsistent internally and with other pronouncements of OCR, prolix, and of disputed legal authority, this pronunciamento has held sway over colleges ever since.

7 At least one mandate of this policy can be simply put: colleges must match teams. For every men's team, if women may not join it, then so long as there are enough able women to play, a college must offer a women's team in the same sport. Then things get murky. To the obligation of matching teams, the 1979 policy appends what the court in *Brown* calls "a three-prong test" followed by a "two-part test" of "effective accommodation." (A useful maxim is that whenever a court or agency speaks of a "test" with "prongs," beware confusion. Here the "prongs" are not tests. They are merely a few among many

nonexclusive considerations, each beginning "whether.") One prong declares that a college will "effectively accommodate" student interests and abilities if it "continually" expands its women's program. This defense avails only the tardy—not Brown or any other commendably prompt respondent to Title IX that no longer expands its women's programs steadily. A second prong states that a college will pass muster if it meets the interests in intercollegiate athletics of every female student. Such a munificent outlay—even if financially feasible—would work conspicuous discrimination unless the interests of every male student were likewise met.

THE ENROLLMENT STANDARD

The only safe harbor, the remaining "prong," is for a college so to 8
contort things that "participation opportunities for male and female students are provided in numbers substantially proportionate to their respective enrollments." That is to say that the ratio of male:female positions on intercollegiate teams must equal the ratio of male:female undergraduates. (The latter proportion is known among men, and its inverse among women, as "*the* ratio.") The foregoing test of proportionality I shall hereafter call the "enrollment standard."

The significance of football under the enrollment standard has 9
been many times alluded to but rarely elucidated. Football's multiple platoons of 11 each, joined with the length of its season, the number of practices, and the effect of injuries, occasion large rosters. By dint of those large rosters and female disinterest in a matched women's football team, the enrollment standard directs a college to create many women's positions in other sports even if demand among women for those positions is low. In directing these results, the enrollment standard neglects, *inter alia,* the Javits amendment's call for regulations to heed "peculiarities." One notable peculiarity is the effect of injuries on the size of football rosters.

Colleges are accustomed to apportioning academic and athletic 10
offerings according to demand, but not according to undifferentiated enrollment. Hence most appear to fail the enrollment standard. Brown, for example, offers a robust array of 21 women's intercollegiate teams comprising approximately 400 athletes competing in every Division I women's sport except badminton, bowling, and equestrian events. Its purported failing is that during a recent year women were 51% of its enrollment while, by the court's count, only 38% of its intercollegiate athletes. Such comparison illustrates the banality of an arithmetic rendition of equal opportunity. It happens that the *Brown* court appears to have erred in its calculations. The court tallied players rather than roster openings even though

the enrollment standard clearly refers to "participation opportunities," not "participants." In a "clarification" issued in September, 1995 of its 1979 policy, OCR joins the court in contradicting its own enrollment standard: it will count, says OCR, "actual athletes participating." The *Brown* court also relied on preseason squad lists that proved inaccurate in comparison to the actual numbers of players who turned out; it considered data for only one academic year, despite fluctuations in the enrollment ratio and in other variables; and, contrary to OCR policy, it ignored intercollegiate club teams. Correcting for these errors, *Brown* asserts that 44% of the players on its 1994–95 intercollegiate teams were women and that positions available to women were 48% of positions available on the teams it funds. The latter proportion seems tolerably close to 51%, the proportion that women constituted of Brown's undergraduate enrollment at the time, especially since OCR in reviewing other institutions has allowed yet larger percentage discrepancies between the ratio of male:female athletes and male:female undergraduates.

REJECTING THE ENROLLMENT STANDARD

Logically prior to any such computations is the appropriateness of 11
the enrollment standard itself. The Big Ten Conference and some colleges have acquiesced in the enrollment standard. They are striving against great financial difficulty to attain it. Brown instead has challenged this interpretation of equal opportunity in an appeal that may reach the Supreme Court. Briefs in support of Brown have been filed as *amici curiae* by the American Council on Education, the Association of American Universities, the National Association of Independent Colleges and Universities, the National Association of State Universities and Land-Grant Colleges, seventeen colleges and universities, and a number of national coaches' associations.

I shall argue below that the enrollment standard is an inappropri- 12
ate interpretation of "equal opportunity." I shall propose another interpretation in its place. Before doing so, I should first like to suggest the detriment of overvaluing intercollegiate athletics.

Low Competitive Access: A Choice

The term "varsity" early came to describe a select team, a team cho- 13
sen to represent a college against other colleges. Long before Title IX, entreaties to create new varsity opportunities were routine. The requests came from club teams, and were frequently denied by athletic directors. Varsity or intercollegiate teams have thus always been elites. Men's varsities typically constitute a small portion of the

number of male undergraduates who would like to play, many of whom would appear willing to give their eye teeth for a spot on a varsity team. Equilibrium between inelastic supply and demand for men's varsity positions is reached as in any competitive market. Price is denominated in the currency of talent and dedication. At colleges operating major programs, few who are not recruited stand a chance of varsity membership.

We need not regard this as wrong. First, no sport is played by 14
more than eleven at a time. Each sport's rules fix the number of simultaneous participants and thereby bound the size of an efficient team. Debate continues whether to limit to 85 the number of grants-in-aid in football. But no one seriously contends that football rosters should exceed, say, 120 players. To add more players beyond an efficient roster size is to add them to the bench. Thus the roster sizes in a given sport of various colleges' teams will usually fall within a narrow range. What does vary among institutions and over time is *the ratio of the number of available intercollegiate roster positions to the number of undergraduates who desire one.* I shall hereafter call this ratio "competitive access."

Second, even if each sport were to call for twice the present num- 15
ber of simultaneous participants, it is not obvious that it would be good for more undergraduates to play intercollegiate athletics. Physical exercise, teamwork, discipline, and competition—these are all unquestionably valuable. Their benefits can be had in intramural play. If there were places for more students of either sex on intercollegiate teams, should more join? In their public posture, universities seek to describe the coupling of athletics and scholarship. It remains inescapable that a student's choice to compete in modern intercollegiate athletics ordinarily imposes a high academic cost, one that begins in high school. The exceptional scholar notwithstanding, most athletes confine themselves to a narrow subset of academic opportunities. They often shun demanding studies for which they will lack time or that appear difficult to handle after an afternoon of sprints and collisions. It is only a short distance to the cynics' portrayal of colleges as training grounds for professional teams. Some observers in fact recommend that colleges pay salaries to student athletes. Others applaud as liberation a player's "coming out" before graduation to join a professional team.

Contrary to the cynics, one may defend intercollegiate athletics. A 16
cogent defense may advert to character development, discipline, camaraderie and teamwork, institutional loyalties, and other goods that intercollegiate play fosters for players and colleges. That defense leans on an implicit premise, namely, that competitive access as above defined is *low.* Intercollegiate athletics is a delicately managed intrusion into academic values. If that implicit premise is unavailable, if more

students join intercollegiate teams, more students will slight education. Beyond some point, it will become difficult to defend the intrusion of an expanded athletic program as *de minimis.*

Current Competitive Access by Sex

Given the foregoing good reasons why competitive access should be 17
much less than one, we may scrutinize whether competitive access differs by sex. How does the ratio of men's intercollegiate positions to men desiring them compare to the ratio of women's intercollegiate positions to women desiring them? Brown has adduced substantial evidence that the interest of undergraduate women in intercollegiate athletics is markedly less than that of men. The evidence includes survey data and statistics (from studies by The University of Michigan Survey Research Center, The National Center of Health Statistics, and others) about high school students generally. For any such set, it is not uncommon to find women constituting as little as 35% of the subset containing those interested in intercollegiate athletics. One longitudinal study has shown a marked decline in female participation in athletics from junior to senior high school to college.

Under pressure from the enrollment standard, colleges have re- 18
cently created many new women's varsity positions despite how few may be the number of women desirous of them. Competitive access for women now appears to be significantly higher than that for men. This is manifest in the predicament of those women's teams that labor to attract an adequate turnout. Brown reports spots that have gone unclaimed on each of its women's intercollegiate teams, 65–80 spots in total, but none open on its men's teams. In basketball, perhaps the most well-developed women's intercollegiate competition, Brown has been prepared to carry 15 players, but last year only 12 joined. Many men's teams in major sports are virtually inaccessible to the unrecruited, and many male walkons join teams in minor sports despite little chance to play.

Objections to the Enrollment Standard

The enrollment standard ignores competitive access. It ignores the in- 19
terests of students altogether. Where women constitute half a hypothetical student body but only 35% of the subset desiring varsity membership, the remaining 65% of that interested subset must, according to the enrollment standard, compete for only half the college's varsity positions. Fixation on a male:female ratio resembles a hiring quota—one that neglects the fact that there may be relatively few members of the class it seeks to favor within the pool of suitable applicants. This contravenes Title IX's stipulation that numerical

imbalances are not per se discriminatory. Compelling supply without regard to demand, the enrollment standard imposes a stereotype. As in the inference that most Californians yearn for the beach, it treats the question of actual interests as trivial and the gross enrollment ratio of the sexes as sufficient to dictate the distribution of resources. This contradicts OCR's own requirement that colleges "effectively accommodate interests and abilities."

After more than 15 years of confusion under its 1979 policy, the in- 20
formal "clarification" recently circulated by OCR is remarkable. It does not repair or revise the enrollment standard. It signifies a reaffirmation of that standard and of the rest of the 1979 policy, including most especially the "prongs." To the confusion thus perpetuated it adds a few new ambiguities. Hypothetical examples are presented in an apparent attempt to illuminate policy, but the examples appear to assume unarticulated standards. According to one example, an institution need not engage in "fine tuning" if, after fluctuations in enrollment and athletic participation, there appears a discrepancy of 1% between the ratio of male:female athletes and the ratio of male:female undergraduates. Another example proceeds to excuse a discrepancy of 2%. Is 2% the maximum allowable discrepancy? What of a 5% discrepancy?

Strikingly, OCR's "clarification" unfolds as guidance on how OCR 21
views athletic programs. Assumed throughout is that whether an institution complies with Title IX is to be determined by the agency in its discretion. While colleges may be accustomed to lengthy desiderata constituting the eligibility conditions of accrediting agencies and funding sources, Title IX is a different matter entirely. It is a proscription of illegal acts. To leave what constitutes illegality within the discretion of an office that has propounded such confusingly formulated norms defies the need for clear, unambiguous notice of what acts are wrong—to say nothing of the desire that the norms be tenable.

A PROPOSED PRINCIPLE OF COMPETITIVE ACCESS

Only one desirous of a benefit would appear susceptible of suffering 22
discrimination with respect to it. Thus in describing the "relevant social position" whose welfare must be advanced in order to justify the exclusion of women from men's teams, I earlier referred not to all female undergraduates, but to those women who desire intercollegiate competition. What is denied that group by ineligibility for a men's team is not a guaranteed place on such a team, but rather it is whatever degree of competitive access to men's intercollegiate play then obtains for men within the institution. The most sensible redress to justify such exclusion is to provide the excluded group competitive access to the same extent as that foreclosed to it. This would come as

close as possible to Rawls's "general conception" of justice, which mandates equality of distribution unless inequality operates to the greatest benefit of the least advantaged.

Hence, in lieu of present policies, I suggest the following "princi- 23
ple of competitive access":

> ***Colleges and universities should attempt in good faith to arrange their athletic offerings so that competitive access for women shall approximately equal that of men.***

This principle expresses no compulsion to create or match any particular team. The choice of sports in which to field teams ought to be as much a function of relative demand as is the size of the teams fielded. The principle does embody recognition that one must compete to compete. It requires that the filters of competition for membership on intercollegiate teams be of approximately the same fineness.

Shortly below I suggest a refinement to the definition of "compet- 24
itive access." I shall first note that the above principle is to be regarded as a distributive one. It need not masquerade as a procedural principle. We have seen what confusion can arise between spending money and the virtually costfree task of prohibiting discriminatory acts. To mark this distinction, "access" is used here instead of "opportunity." This presents an interesting question for federal policy. Congress in Title IX prohibited discriminatory acts but did not attempt to instruct colleges on how to spend funds. Hence a regulation requiring a specific distributive policy may exceed statutory authority. That circumstance may merely reflect how intrainstitutional fairness is not an appropriate subject of federal fine tuning. Given that the enrollment standard is already a distributive policy, a clear distributive policy is at least superior to a confused one. In any case, the principle of competitive access is worthy of consideration by colleges and universities according to their own aspirations of local justice.

Arguments can be imagined that "revenue sports"—those such as 25
football and men's basketball that pay for themselves, and hence are better understood as "profitable sports," as I shall hereafter assume—should be excluded from the reckoning of competitive access. Sometimes it has been argued that revenue sports should be excluded categorically from any calculations under Title IX because they effectively finance entire athletic programs and therefore that nothing should be done to jeopardize them. This argument, broached in the Javits amendment, offered by alarmed men's coaches and athletic directors, and resented by some women, is but one indication of the discord sown by an untenable federal policy.

There is a more sophisticated version of the foregoing argument, 26
and in fact it leads us to recognize two forms of the principle of competitive access. This argument asserts that revenue sports do not

effect any net outlay of resources. Hence revenue sports should fall outside the discussion of what resources an institution should provide to any group. The discussion of fairness between the sexes should focus, according to the view I am describing, on the resources that an institution devotes to athletics for the respective sexes, not on the accident of who participates in sports for which the institution makes no net outlays. Consider an analogous situation. Suppose that a university operates a program to provide academic departments with extra funds to hire minority faculty and staff. Suppose further that neither its highly profitable continuing education center nor the university's development office, the latter operating on a portion of the funds it raises, receives any of those incentive funds, but that each of those units employs more minority faculty and staff, absolutely and proportionately, than the number employed by any academic department. We could not tenably charge the university with discrimination against academic departments in the allotment of those extra funds. For the self-sustaining units surpassing them in the attainment of a mutual goal have received none of the extra funds.

On the foregoing rationale, the strong form of the principle of 27
competitive access would incorporate the following definition:

> ***"Competitive access" is the ratio, computed separately by sex, of the number of available intercollegiate roster positions to the number of undergraduates who desire one, provided that the numerator shall exclude positions, and the denominator shall exclude desire for positions, on any financially self-sustaining team.***

A team would be recognized as "self-sustaining" if and only if, after charges for all direct and indirect costs, it was consistently profitable. The weak form of the principle or competitive access would employ the above definition without the proviso.

It should not be assumed which of the strong or weak forms of 28
the principle of competitive access would be more or less favorable to male or female aspirants. Assuming widespread interest in playing football and basketball, a large denominator might under the weak form produce a low value for male competitive access, resulting in fewer openings on women's teams than would result under the strong form applied in the same situation. On the other hand, in a college where male interest in football and basketball is not widespread, counting football players under the weak form might alone produce a higher value for male competitive access, and hence dictate more positions for women, than would the strong form. The actual results will depend entirely on student interests.

The strong form of the principle is the more realistic on other 29
grounds. It would treat women's sports *pari passu* with nonrevenue men's sports, often called "minor sports." Teams in minor sports share with women's teams in general the following characteristics:

consistent nonprofitability, small attendance, low ticket prices, no television revenue, modest equipment costs, and for outdoor sports, modest facilities costs. That is not to demean them, but only to accentuate that it is in supporting them that evenhandedness in net outlays is at stake.

The standard for equality of competitive access is stated as "good 30
faith." To require strict, contemporaneous equality of male and female competitive access would consign athletic directors each year—each season?—to the exercise of adjusting roster sizes in virtue of short-term fluctuations in interests. Such machinations would needlessly disappoint current players. One ought not subject teams to the spurious bijection implied by the beloved Yogi Berra when, at the opening of spring training, he directed his players to "pair off in threes."

Under either the strong or weak principle, the reckoning of com- 31
petitive access will pose statistical questions. Should one weigh expressions of interest according to the frequency or level at which a student has played a sport? How does one treat a single student's desire to play more than one intercollegiate sport? Institutions possess survey research capabilities with which to design the collection of data about interests and to infer insightful results. They collect similar data when they recruit applicants, plan facilities, and design curricula. And they already know the number of students who turn out for their teams. To suggest, as did the court to Brown, that a college's extant athletic program prejudices expressions of interest, and therefore that expressions of interest should be ignored, appears captious.

What the data on student interests may already indicate— 32
encouragingly, in my view—is that a greater proportion of women than men appreciate the academic cost of athletics. That cost appears such that no student with academic aspirations, male or female, need lament missing intercollegiate play. The principle of competitive access is neutral as to societal changes, for which some hope, as a result of which more young girls may begin athletics at an earlier age and enter college desirous of intercollegiate competition. Given the danger of overvaluing intercollegiate athletics, I claim that, for the welfare of young women and men, nothing stronger than such neutrality is warranted.

MONEYCHANGERS IN THE TEMPLE

What puts financial punch in the policies of OCR (now of the Depart- 33
ment of Education) is not only that additional teams must be established. Irrespective of the amount of revenue they may generate or consume, women's teams must be provided coaching, schedules, travel, housing, and recruiting resources "equivalent" to that provided

men's. A college must also award athletic grants-in-aid to substantially the same portion of its female athletes as the portion of male athletes to which it awards them. Absent retrenchments in men's programs, by virtue of the enrollment standard, a large part of a major athletic department's budget must approximately double.

To achieve such doubling, colleges seem prone to shocking com- 34
mercialization. While athletics has served as a facilitator in fundraising, the additional costs of women's programs now beckon fundraising for, rather than by, athletics. The pressures of operating approximately twice as many teams as previous revenues or subsidies could support have left colleges beholden to sponsors. These commercial entities have made remarkable inroads. Emblems of commercial entities appear on team uniforms. Advertising signs cover arenas and stadia. "Corporate" tents dot campus athletic facilities. To accommodate sponsors, colleges close parking lots during games to faculty, students, and alumni. Pregame and halftime performances by student bands are now curtailed so as to allow time for promotions. At some colleges, commercial announcements on behalf of sponsors are made during games between plays. In this contratemps, aesthetics and independence are overrun by marketing schemes. These commercial intrusions compound the delicately managed intrusion of athletics into the ambience of the academy.

Queried about commercialization, athletic administrators routinely 35
offer a succinct justification: "Title IX." Inflation and competition alone of course have effected substantial cost increases. But the dramatic financial effect of the enrollment standard and the concomitant embrace of marketing wizardry are unmistakable. Even the most financially secure of athletic departments, The University of Michigan's, incurred a deficit in current operations in a year in which it expanded its women's program. Successful athletic conferences have recently scrambled to expand. They disrupted their scheduling and defied geographical logic, all so that they might share gate receipts and television revenues of programs with large stadia and large viewing audiences. Thus does the Big Ten reprise Yogi Berra, explaining that it is now eleven.

Pari Passu or Punt

Meanwhile to relieve such budgetary pressures or to meet the enroll- 36
ment standard, or both, colleges have been terminating men's teams en masse. After producing numerous Olympic gold medalists, UCLA's men's swimming and diving teams are no more. Men's gymnastics, another source of Olympic glories, has virtually disappeared as a college sport. Colleges perforce are considering whether to refuse membership on men's track teams to walkons. After dropping eight men's teams in four years, Brown attempted to comply with the court's

finding of statistical discrimination by adopting a draconian plan. The plan mandated reductions in the size of men's rosters and mandated minimum sizes for women's rosters. Minimum women's rosters appear attainable only by the peculiar gambit of persuading women to fill erstwhile unwanted openings. The court ruled even that plan insufficient. When suits ensue that allege terminations of men's teams to be discriminatory, what justification can one give?

Were a college to erect dormitories to an extent beyond what student demand will sustain, empty rooms would be regarded as misallocated resources. A few athletic departments are self-supporting, but most are effectively subsidized. They consume genuinely institutional resources. When funds are used to create women's intercollegiate teams beyond the interests of women students, is that allocation fair to students—to women students—who desire better housing, more lab facilities, lower tuition, or easier access to courses? 37

If, with Rawls, we strive for reasoning on which all can agree, a consensus is attainable that a college receiving federal funds must treat women's interests in the activities that the college conducts no less favorably than it treats men's. The principle of competitive access may then be understood as an instance of a general principle requiring competitive access to a given benefit to be equal among "relevant social positions" unless some inequality would aid the disfavored. This principle commends evenhanded apportionment of the supply of all educational opportunities to demand. If that policy were allowed to relieve pressures that presently impinge, it could reintroduce a balanced perspective on the importance of intercollegiate competition. Such balance seems essential if we expect colleges and universities to reinforce the primacy of learning while continuing to provide the benefits of intramural and intercollegiate athletics. 38

THINKING ABOUT THE ESSAY

1. This is one of the more formally written essays in your textbook. What aspects of the writing distinguishes it from more conversational essays?
2. What is the "universe of discourse" this essay seems most appropriate for—a popular magazine, a professional magazine, a legal journal, or a courtroom presentation? Explain.
3. Why does the author call the application of equal opportunity to the world of college sports "a wooden interpretation"? What is the significance of this interpretation for the design and development of his argument?
4. The author provides both weak and strong forms of a definition of competitive access. Why are these definitions printed in bold

letters? What is the significance of these definitions to the author's argument? In what fields of human discourse are definitions regularly used?

5. Summarize the author's main argument against the current interpretations and practices regarding equal opportunities in college athletics. What modifications in the law does the author suggest? Do you personally believe these modifications are reasonable and achievable?

RESPONDING IN DISCUSSION

1. Divide into groups of three and four, and list those athletic teams at your college that have high recognition and those that have low recognition. Discuss whether the more "visible" sports should be given preference over the "minor" sports. Present your findings to the class.
2. Discuss whether there should be a disproportionate emphasis on recruiting in and championing of women's college sports since girls—from early childhood on—are latently discouraged from participating in competitive sports.
3. Is there competitive access for women at your college or university in the realm of intercollegiate sports? Discuss by providing anecdotes gleaned from your own experience.
4. The author claims that many women's sports teams go begging for women to fill openings, while the same does not obtain for men, and that it is wasteful to offer certain sports for which there is little demand. Discuss what might happen if the reverse were true (that is, if women's sports had far more applicants than openings, while major men's sports had few interested participants). Would the college simply reduce the level of funding for men's athletics, or would a different standard obtain?

RESPONDING IN WRITING

1. Describe a time in your life when you argued against a rule or regulation that you believed to be unfair. What issues were involved? What was your defense? What was the response?
2. Visit your library's audiovisual department, and borrow a videotape of a political debate or argument. Compare and contrast the views of each opposing party. Conclude with your own opinion as to which participant presented the better argument, being particularly careful not be "seduced" by the oratorical skills of the presenter.

3. Select an abstract principle such as "equality," "opportunity," "choice," or "consent." Provide your own extended definition of the term, attempting to be as precise as possible in your use of language.
4. Argue for or against the proposition that Guenin's two competitive access rules are the answer to equal opportunity in collegiate sports.

Hey, NCAA, Can You Spare a Dime?

Walter Byers

The author should know something about college sports. Byers was executive director of the National Collegiate Athletic Association for 35 years, from 1951 to 1986. In this essay taken from the November 13, 1995, issue of *The Sporting News,* he argues that colleges exploit their athletes, who make lots of money for their institutions but get none of the profits. At first glance it makes sense, but Byers is fighting the long-established notion that college athletes are amateurs. The author, on the other hand, claims that if a student earns a small salary working at the local Kmart, why not allow him or her to earn big bucks endorsing footwear or taking a share of the profits from television contracts? Byers claims that creating a free-market environment is the fair thing to do.

PREVIEWING THE ESSAY

How would you feel if a student sitting next to you in class earned hundreds of thousands of dollars for participating in an athletic shoe advertising campaign while you earned the minimum wage at the local fast-food operation? And to top it off, you are an A student while he or she is barely passing? Sure, it would be fair if the student made the money through his or her own initiative—but without being a member of a college team, he or she would never have such an opportunity. Consider this and other questions of ethics as you read the following essay. The author's ethical stance is a clear one and makes sense. Or does it?

The question as to whether college athletes should be paid, considering the big dollars in today's college sports entertainment business, certainly is a proper one—but it tends to distort the issue. The colleges already are paying their athletes in the form of one-year grants-in-aid, renewed or not subject to the respective coach's annual determination. 1

This specialized stipend is in the form of an industry-wide contract that sets a financial limit for all athletes. When an athlete signs the grant-in-aid contract, he forfeits his ability to determine how he'll make money, if the athlete wishes to retain eligibility at an NCAA member institute. 2

College athletes' basic rights have been taken away from them by a college cartel. The big-time schools are running a national, major league entertainment business without tax liability but with monopoly control of the compensation rate of the players. In essence, my book, *Unsportsmanlike Conduct,* is a major argument about individual freedom. I'm not asking the colleges to give back the millions of new dollars cascading into their bank accounts. Let's encourage them to be successful entrepreneurs. My argument is that the colleges should free athletes from the artificial rules that imprison them so that they can enter the marketplace and earn some of the rewards. The college supervisors and overseers who control the NCAA legislative and interpretive process have imprisoned today's athletes in a set of archaic rules dedicated to the nostalgic concept of amateurism, a modern-day code word for economic tyranny. 3

I argue that the NCAA colleges should abandon their industry-wide contract that sets a compensation cap on all athletes. The coach's control over grant-in-aid awards to athletes should be terminated. The colleges then should treat the athlete exactly the same as all other students in processing the scholarship and grant-in-aid awards for undergraduates. The same financial aid committee at each institution that handles awards for all students should determine the financial need and the extent of the financial aid extended to all athletes, male and female. Thereafter, the athlete should be entitled to the same freedoms as other students. The athlete should be able to access the marketplace just as other undergraduates and coaches. If athletes desire to write newspaper columns, conduct radio shows, become sports commentators, handle inventory at Kmart stores, work in clothing stores and sporting goods outlets, more power to them. 4

The experiences gained through these economic initiatives far outweigh any temporary advantages gained from excessive hours of viewing practice and game videotapes and pumping iron in the weight room. 5

The one-year grant-in-aid contract gives the coaches enormous control of the athlete. Placing the financial aid awards in the hands of the regular university financial-aid committee and curtailing the coaches' ability to effectively dictate offseason conditioning and practice regimens would contribute greatly to providing players with freedoms that they do not have now. 6

As an example: In signing his grant-in-aid contract the athlete does not donate his feet to his coach. If the college wants to permit 7 the athletics department or the coach to sell their athletes' feet to Nike or Reebok, so be it. But the players should have the freedom to endorse a shoe different than their coach, who may get paid some $300,000 as a result of the shoe contract. I argue that any player should have the right to endorse Reebok as opposed to his coach's deal with Nike, explaining that when the athlete learned to play the game he preferred Reebok and still feels that way.

Whenever deregulation is broached in an overly regulated industry, the conventional wisdom espoused by the main beneficiaries of the regulated monopoly is that all sorts of mad-cap activities will ensue. Various horror stories surface as to what might happen. Well, breaking up the AT&T and regional Bell monopoly took many years and dreadful results were predicted. But the results have been markedly beneficial. 8

My book sets forth a competitive opportunity plan which details new approaches to practice and game squads, enhanced recruiting opportunities for the also-ran colleges and greater freedom for athletes to transfer. With fixed limits on squad sizes and free transfer opportunities, the stockpiling of great players will be seriously limited. Athletes should be permitted to move freely like other students. 9

The present grant-in-aid system essentially was put in place in 1956. The thought was that if the colleges provided a free education to an athlete, it would eliminate the need for under-the-table payments. Secondly, if the colleges offered the same financial deals, it would enhance the competitive equality among the competing institutions. 10

Almost 40 years have passed and clearly the grant-in-aid contract has failed to achieve either objective. Violations of NCAA rules are at an all-time high. Side deals and extra money to players are reported in the media almost daily. Competitive equality among the colleges today is little more than a legal defense term for the industry-wide grant-in-aid contract. Among the 108 colleges that play Division I-A football, approximately 25 to 30 annually reap the main benefits from the television and bowl game appearances that winning seasons bring. Among the 305 Division I basketball teams, there are some 30 that annually dominate the polls and NCAA Tournament. 11

Before I retired, I played a part in implementing the NCAA Presidents Commission, which now has controlled the agenda of college athletics for almost 10 years. At that time, we approved projects costing well over $2 million designed to simplify and deregulate NCAA rules and make the athlete more a part of the student body. Unfortunately, the much-publicized presidential reform movement of the past 10 years has been little more than a public-relations venture. Presidents speak nationally of reform and student welfare, but then return to the campus to recruit new colleges for their major league conferences. They want more TV negotiating muscle and more of 12 their teams in bowl games and tournaments. At the national level, presidents gravely cut the number of grants-in-aid, then return to campus to generate more revenue for the campus supervisors and overseer.

The new Big 12 Conference has been taking bids for a football championship game. Thus far, six cities have filed bids ranging from offers of $6.88 to $8.21 million to host the event. One of the reform-minded presidents of the Big 12 told the *Kansas City Star* on October 1: "It all comes down to money. Whatever generates the most money is what we're interested in doing." 13

He should have explained that all money must go to the colleges and their staffs because NCAA rules preclude even one dollar from being added to the grant-in-aid compensation of the players. 14

THINKING ABOUT THE ESSAY

1. Byers probably has as much authority as anyone in America to discuss the topic of the economics of college sports. Do you believe this fact alone makes his views more credible than the average sports fan's? Explain.
2. What is Byers thesis? Where does he state it? What evidence does he provide to support his thesis?
3. Byers accepts the fact that some colleges are "running a national, major league entertainment business" and proceeds to provide a plan whereby it could be run more fairly. How does he present this formula? Does he question whether such a business is ethical? Why?
4. Byers refers to his book, *Unsportsmanlike Conduct: Exploiting College Athletes,* explaining that it sets forth a plan on how to create a fair and smoothly operating marketplace whereby all constituents in the college sports network will benefit. Does reading the essay make you curious about reading the book? Has Byers convinced you of his view in the essay, or would you feel more confident in rendering a decision after reading the book? Why?

RESPONDING IN DISCUSSION

1. Divide into groups of three and four. Jot down the various ways your college or university earns money (for example, through tuition, special fees, special events, grants, donations, and sports). Which of these seem appropriate to you? Are any of them questionable ways for an institution of higher learning to increase it resources? Share your answers with the class.

2. Discuss whether it is discriminatory to allow college athletes to earn large sums of money through product endorsements, since nearly all contracts would be "market-driven" so nearly all people who were able to take advantage of them would be men.
3. Divide into groups and discuss whether the most prudent thing to do to avoid scandals and illegal activities in college sports is to forbid all television contracts involving the broadcast of college sporting events.
4. Discuss whether decisions concerning intercollegiate sports at your school should be determined, at least in part, by members of the student body. Consider how such a mechanism could be put into place should such a rule go into effect.

RESPONDING IN WRITING

1. Write your school's sports director a letter offering your views on the ethics of allowing student athletes to profit from income derived from intercollegiate sporting events.
2. Argue for or against the proposition that all or a large percentage of profits from intercollegiate sporting events should go toward providing needy students with financial aid.
3. Argue for or against the proposition that if college students were given the opportunity to earn large sums of money, they would be exploited by lawyers, managers, and agents owing to their youth and inexperience.
4. Argue for or against the proposition that if college athletes profited from income derived from college sports, they would be more prone to taking illegal drugs to enhance their performance.
5. For a Web assignment, study the world of the NCAA. Present what you learn in an essay of 1,000 to 1,500 words.

Bettor Education

Tim Layden

Tim Layden's "Bettor Education" was first published in the April 3, 1995, issue of *Sports Illustrated.* It brings student sports betting out of the closet and displays it as a widespread activity that for many of its aficionados takes on more importance than standard college activities. One rule in betting is that "the house" ultimately wins, and many students who bet on sports end up with severe economic losses. But this is only the tip of the iceberg. The effects on the bettor's life may be overwhelming. Obsession with gambling can lead to failing grades, loss of contact with college life, and ultimately an addiction for life. Layden provides an array of statistics and anecdotes to demonstrate just how severe the problem is. But beneath these data and personal stories lies the social and cultural milieu of our society at large. The author suggests that the spread of legal casino gambling, lotteries, and bingo fundraisers at church leads to a society that appears to accept gambling. He also points out that many student gamblers are from affluent families who sometimes provide too much spending money to their children away at college.

PREVIEWING THE ESSAY

Is betting a pastime, a habit, or an addiction? If it is an addiction, to what exactly is the gambler addicted? Why does the author single out student bettors for his discussion? Is it one's status as a student that makes it onerous? Would a 20-year-old bettor not in college be more acceptable than his or her student counterpart?

The game was long over, but the action was just beginning. J. A. Davis, a 23-year-old Texas Tech senior, fought against the flow of departing fans as he weaved down the concrete aisles of Jones Stadium in Lubbock. He was in search of a better seat to catch the closing minutes of the Red Raiders' made-for-ESPN Thursday night football game against No. 1 Nebraska on Sept. 8. It didn't matter to Davis that Tech was already soundly beaten—it trailed 35–16 with barely two minutes to play—or that Nebraska had the ball. In his world, wins and losses are secondary to point spreads and over–unders, and on this day Davis had taken the Cornhuskers, giving 25-$\frac{1}{2}$ points. 1

"Two hundred bucks I had riding on that game," recalls Davis. "Lots of people had Nebraska, giving 27, 28 points—you never bet on Texas Tech—but I got in with my bookie at 25-$\frac{1}{2}$." Nebraska, with third-and-one on the Tech 30, the clock running. Davis, dying the slow, hopeless death of a gambler longing for points from a team that doesn't need any. "I'm thinking, This can't be happening," says Davis. "I'm going to lose 200 bucks, 220 with the juice [the vigorish, the bookie's 10% commission on losing bets], and be down going into the weekend." Then a bettor's miracle occurred: The Huskers scored a trash touchdown, running back Clinton Childs going 30 yards on a sweep. Kicker Tom Sieler's vital PAT pushed the margin to 26, covering the spread and turning Davis into a winner. 2

Davis celebrated with a friend who had $200 on the Cornhuskers, also spotting 25-½. "I had no right to win," Davis says, "but it gave me a jump on the weekend." College football: the color, the pageantry. 3

Meet the Juice Generation. For them, finance isn't a major, it's knowing how to spread $1,000 in wagers over 10 Saturday college 4 football games and stay alive for Sunday's and Monday's NFL bets with a zero balance in their checkbooks and their credit cards maxed out. Class participation is sitting in the back of a lecture hall with Vegas-style "spreadsheets" laid out, plotting a week's worth of plays on games from Seattle to Miami. Communication is a desperate call to some 1-900 tout service in search of this week's Lock of the Year. Road trip is a drive through the desert to Las Vegas or across Midwestern plains to Native American and riverboat casinos, both of which have proliferated like Home Depots.

There is nothing in the collegiate rite-of-passage handbook about 5
gambling. There are chapters on alcohol, drugs and sex laid out against a backdrop of winking acceptance. Kids. Society has hacked out a neutral zone of sorts and allowed undergraduates to briefly frolic in it. But gambling? Who knows from gambling—in particular sports gambling—on campus? It is the dirty little secret of college life in America, rampant and thriving. "It's ubiquitous, it's popular, it's pervasive," says psychologist Michael Frank of Richard Stockton College in Pomona, N.J., one of a scant few academicians who has studied the phenomenon. "Wherever you go in the country, you're going to find access to a bookmaker. It's true in casinos, it's true at the General Motors plant, and it's true on college campuses all over the country."

Not only true, but pandemic, according to William (B. J.) Jahoda, 6
52, who for nearly 10 years ran a $20 million a year illegal sports-betting operation for Chicago mob don Ernest Rocco Infelice. Upon being told that *SI* [*Sports Illustrated*] was doing a story on campus gambling, Jahoda said, "It's about time. What's taken you so long?" Jahoda, who is in the U.S. marshal's witness-protection program after testifying for the government against Infelice and mob enforcer Robert Salerno, said, "You see gambling on every campus. It is an epidemic. It really has been out of control."

This outbreak might seem inconsequential, considering that legal- 7
ized gambling is a growth industry in the U.S. However, most of the gambling that college students do is not legal. And just as we think of colleges as institutions of higher learning, so it is with gambling. "A kid finds a bookie on campus, he learns about gambling, he gets hooked," says Arnie Wexler, a leading consultant on problem gambling. For every college kid who derives nothing but entertainment from his betting, there is another who cons his parents to get money to cover his gambling losses, another who becomes so consumed with betting that he tosses away an education and another who plunges into gambling addiction. It is far from harmless recreation.

Hard information on campus gambling—on any gambling—is 8
scarce. There have been only two broad, national studies of gambling. The first, in 1974, found that 61% of the U.S. population gambled. The second, a Gallup poll in '89, raised that figure to 81% and concluded

that 31% of adults gambled weekly. "I'm sure that first number is at least 85% now; gambling is growing at a phenomenal rate in the United States," says Henry Lesieur, chair of the criminal justice department at Illinois State University and the acknowledged dean of American gambling researchers.

Lesieur headed a panel that in 1991 published the only wide- 9
spread study of gambling among college students. The study, with surveys at six schools in five states, concluded that 23% of the students gambled at least once a week.

That's it for numbers, because gambling, on campus and off, is 10
difficult to quantify. "It's hard to estimate illegal gambling," says sociologist Rachel Volberg, who has overseen several more narrowly focused studies of gambling. "We get a very low rate of responses to questions about sports betting with bookmakers. The numbers are affected by that difficulty."

Yet during two months of research, *SI* found that it was nearly im- 11
possible to visit a campus in search of organized gambling and not find either 1) sophisticated on- or off-campus bookmaking operations with a large student clientele or 2) legal casinos within a short distance of the schools, easily accessible to underage students—or both. Tom Decker, a retired FBI agent who investigated sports gambling, says, "You'd be shocked at how easy it is for kids to get involved in gambling and how many of them do. You and I could go into a bar in Athens, Georgia, right now, and within minutes we'd have the name of a bookie. Within minutes." (In fact you could bypass the bar and go straight to the University of Georgia campus, but we'll come back to that.)

"It's such a hidden thing on college campuses," says Wexler, a re- 12
covering compulsive gambler for 27 years. "But if you saw what happens when I go to a college campus and do a presentation and then ask the audience how many of them gamble, it would blow your mind. One hand goes up, and then another, then another. . . ."

Occasionally illegal college gambling operations will come to the 13
public's attention, usually when they've run afoul of the police. Since 1992 this has happened at Michigan State, Maine, Rhode Island and neighboring Bryant College, Texas, Arizona State and Northwestern. Sometimes college athletes are involved (Maine, Rhode Island, Bryant, Northwestern), which gives the incident a longer public shelf life. But college officials often dismiss the incidents as isolated and blame unsavory outside characters for corrupting their youth. The views of James Rund, interim associate vice president for student affairs at Arizona State, are typical. Of the busting of four students at his school in February 1994 for helping to run a bookmaking operation, Rund says, "To characterize it as a student gambling ring is an exaggeration and probably an inaccurate depiction of the circumstances." He says this despite the fact that names of members of 15 of Arizona State's 22 fraternities appeared in betting records seized by police.

Busting gambling rings is labor-intensive work for law-enforcement 14
agencies, and there's little chance that those apprehended and found guilty will receive heavy penalties since much of the public considers gambling a victimless crime. "The payoff is trivial," says Frank, meaning that perpetrators seldom receive long jail sentences (or any jail sentences at all). Interest fades.

Yet consider the evidence that gambling is a booming, nation- 15
wide campus industry:

The aforementioned ring busted in February 1994 by the Tempe 16
(Ariz.) police was operated by a 30-year-old former Tucson sportscaster, who was assisted by four Arizona State fraternity brothers. Of the 245 betting accounts uncovered, 140 belonged to fraternity members at the university. Police suspect at least 60 other Arizona State students were also book clients. An average of nearly $120,000 a month was wagered, mostly by students, through the book between August 1993 and February '94.

Andrew Stewart, a 24-year-old senior at Georgia, ran a basketball- 17
betting operation out of an apartment near campus until early March, when he quit because he and two partners were owed more than $10,000 by his clientele. The operation has been assumed by two other Georgia undergraduates. Stewart, who like all the other students in this story agreed to speak to *SI* only if he was identified by a fictitious name, says that the operation has 170 clients, "about a quarter" of whom bet nightly. Stewart's client list was culled from the 220 names in a friend's football book. How many of them are students? "All of them," says Stewart. "I know just about all of them." He and his two partners, both students, handled roughly $4,000 on a good night in basketball business, $10,000 on a busy Saturday, up to $75,000 a month.

Brian Cole, a 24-year-old marketing major at Clemson, ran a 18
$100,000-a-month betting operation during the 1993–94 school year, with a 54-student client list. Most of his clients carried other bettors on their accounts.

J. P. Browman, a 23-year-old senior at Florida, for the last four 19
years operated a book that catered exclusively to students at his university. J. P. has a wiretap detector on his home, a mnemonic phone number and, he says, $42,000 in profits. His only regret is that he can't put his bookmaking work on his resume.

Mike Tyler, a 21-year-old sophomore at Texas Tech, has con- 20
tacts with five different off-campus bookies in Lubbock and estimates that at least 200 other students have contacted bookies or made bets through him. This comes as no shock to Sgt. Tom McDonald of the Texas Department of Public Safety, who can name 58 illegal bookmakers in Lubbock County alone and says, "Nearly every bookmaker in this town got his start as a student at Texas Tech."

From the never-too-early-to-get-started department, on March 1 police in Nutley, N.J., busted a student-run sports gambling operation at Nutley High that took single bets as high as $1,000 and used threats of violence and kidnapping to get losers to pay up. One prosecutor said the operation was "sophisticated and exactly mirrors an adult-run organized crime bookmaking operation." This lends credence to assertions by many college gamblers that they started betting seriously in high school. 21

The conclusion is obvious: Gambling sells on campus like Green Day CDs. And the pervasiveness of campus gambling parallels the explosion in legal gambling in the U.S. (of which college students also partake). "How could a college kid think there's anything wrong with gambling?" asks Wexler, a tireless antigambling proselytizer. "There's legal gambling everywhere: lotteries, casinos, racetracks. Forget it." 22

But if you are remotely inclined to attach some higher standards to colleges and universities, if you would like to think of gambling as a opiate of the streetwise and uneducated, the trend is disarming. *SI* found no shortage of savvy 22-year-old bookmakers and rough-hewn 20-year-old bettors on campus. "Their behavior is the same as that of older gamblers," says Frank, the Richard Stockton College psychologist. "They lie, deceive, and they steal. They're just younger." 23

And if you're attached to the youthful enthusiasm that surrounds a college sporting event—the painted faces, the silly signs, the reckless support—there is reason to pause and wonder if perhaps some small corner of Cameron Indoor Stadium, just to name one arena, is Crazy because a few of the Crazies took Duke, minus 4, for $25. And to wonder, also, just how short the jump is from student to athlete and just how thin the line between pure competition and fixed games may be. Says Kentucky football coach Bill Curry, "There's an awful lot at stake when somebody asks you, 'How's [running back] Moe Williams's shoulder?' " 24

GAINESVILLE, FLA.: Lyle Ellington is a 21-year-old senior at Florida, a tall, athletic-looking fraternity kid. He has been betting since junior high, when he handicapped horse races at South Florida tracks. At Florida he became the biggest client for several prosperous campus bookies, including J. P. Browman. 25

"The most I ever bet on one game? Twenty-four grand. San Diego Chargers versus Miami Dolphins in 1991," says Ellington. "I took the Dolphins—I always take the Dolphins—and I was already up that week, like, 30 grand. Everyone's riding my coattails, so I decide to push it. I bet 24 G on Miami. Going into the fourth quarter the Dolphins are up by, like, 13. I'm staring $50,000 in the face. Then Rod Bernstine ripped out my heart. Scores three touchdowns in the fourth quarter. San Diego always kills me, though. I remember the Chargers were 26 playing the Los Angeles Raiders on a Sunday night a few years ago, and I took L.A., minus 6. The Raiders were up 9–7 with less than a minute left. Ronnie Lott intercepts the ball and falls to the ground. That's the way it ended. Cost me 12 grand. I was dying because I couldn't watch the game. I was pledging my fraternity. It was Hell Night.

"October 23. I have pro bookies, one up north and one in Miami, and that weekend I lost big-time, probably about $18,000. Add this up: I took 20 grand from the joint checking account I have with my mom. I owed, like, 35 grand to Allen, our neighbor, the internist, who had bailed me out before. I owed 20 grand to another guy—my mom still doesn't know about that—30 grand to another, although I've already paid him 17." 27

Campus gamblers seem old in much the same sense that college football players who weigh 280 pounds and bench-press sport-utility vehicles seem older than their classmates. The college bettor speaks the language of the trade—juice, vig, teaser, parlay, quarter ($25), dollar ($100), push—and sometimes deals in amounts that would buy sport-utility vehicles. It seems out of place in a youthful, academic setting. Gamblers come equipped with war stories of losing money and winning money, stories you expect to hear from older, harder men. They have the ability to make a campus hangout feel like a Keno lounge or a storefront off-track betting parlor. 28

In one sense the young men—and they are almost invariably men, not women—arrive on campus predisposed to becoming gamblers. "First of all, gambling gets you high, like drugs or alcohol," says Wexler. "Second, college kids are smart, and I've never met a dumb compulsive gambler. They think they can pick winners, and in the beginning they do. There's always an initial period of success." 29

The undergraduate environment is rich with enticements for the budding sports bettor—and full of opportunity for failure. There is no typical gambler: *SI* found students from wealthy and modest backgrounds alike who had thrown themselves into betting. But with the exception of the Southeast, where illegal wagering on college football is especially fierce, betting patterns across the country are similar. And bettors do tend to have some things in common: a degree of sports-obsessiveness (often an athletic past cut short in college by a lack of talent), a community in which to share their betting tales (usually a fraternity house) and a little resourcefulness. They are bright, if often naive. Put simply, lots of college sports bettors are clever frat-boy jocks who like to watch games with a crowd and get pumped by betting on them. And they are often clueless about the realm they have entered. 30

Jahoda, the former bookmaker for the mob, sees them as pigeons. "These kids are young and often affluent and always vulnerable," he says. "They are naive. They think they can do no wrong. They think 31 they're brilliant and they know what they're doing. When you're young, you're invincible. They're in an atmosphere where the games are important. Everyone tells them that gambling is healthy entertainment. They see the spreads on television. They think that it's healthy and legal and the thing to do."

Alex Andrews, a 24-year-old former student and admitted compulsive gambler from Bethesda, Md., who began betting illegally on sporting events in high school and continued through four years of fraternity life, recalls that college was for him a release from the parental controls that contained his teenage betting: "There are so many things going on in high school, things that are forced on you—you go to school, and you're expected to do well, you have to play sports, you have to do things socially—that even if you're gambling, it isn't the only thing in your life. I don't think you'll find many high school kids who, even if they gamble, sit around all day and do nothing else. But in college it becomes your choice. You're unsupervised. You can wake up at noon, blow off all your classes, call the bookie at four o'clock, watch all the games while you get drunk and then do the same thing all over again the next day." 32

On most campuses illegal sports gambling is seldom further than a conversation away. Somebody in the dorm knows a bookie. Somebody in the fraternity house knows a bookie. Somebody in the frat house is a bookie. "It's so easy," says Andy Gale, who finished St. Peter's College in Jersey City last year and is now in graduate school. "You can always find one person who knows somebody. If you want to get a bet down, it's no problem." 33

Often the process starts with football parlay cards, sucker sheets listing the line on an entire weekend's major college and pro football games. The bettor has to pick at least three games to win at 5-to-1 odds. The next step is making bets through a friend who knows a bookie. Eventually the bookie gives the student an account of his own and a number to use when he calls in his bets. Often the bookie is also a student, and it is common to hear college gamblers profess never to have placed a bet with a "professional bookie." Of course, a student taking bets is a professional bookie. 34

College kids are famously quick studies, and betting is a fascinating and tempting subject. A guy who in September of his freshman year wouldn't know an underdog from Underdog is by his junior year routinely parlaying Big Sky basketball with the NBA. Happens all the time, according to experts in gambling. 35

The sports-betting priorities of students mirror those of the adult public: NFL football is most popular, followed by college football, college basketball and the NBA. One exception to these rankings is the NCAA basketball tournament, which rivals the NFL in wagering frenzy. 36

The typical college plunger begins with $25 bets, frequently shared with friends, and graduates to $50 and $100 bets. Most of the bettors wager on far too many games, as many as 20 on a fall weekend. Given the bookie's built-in 10% edge on losing bets, this is fiscal suicide. 37

But no one gets into this with losing in mind. 38

CLEMSON, S.C.: B. J. Simpson is a 22-year-old senior at Clemson majoring in German and international trade. He sits in the living room of a friend's off-campus apartment, dressed in jeans and a baseball cap. In the background Virginia is playing Duke in basketball on ESPN. 39

"I started gambling in '93 when a fraternity brother was doing it," says Simpson. "Gambling just made the weekends fun. When I got back into it this past fall, I was normally doing just 25 or 50 bucks a game. There was a Thursday night game; the Cleveland Browns were playing the Houston Oilers, and I just went nuts. I had a $100 parlay on the Browns and the under, another $100 on the Browns straight and another $100 on the under. And I won everything. I was up like $420 on the night, and I was going out of my tree. I was downtown that night, going, 'I just won $420 by making a phone call.' But then I lost about $500 over the rest of the weekend. 40

"There was a week in late October that I just got killed on my picks. On Sunday my roommate and I went to this private club to drink until we blacked out. On Tuesday we bumped into each other at Sikes [a campus financial building]. I was walking out, he was walking in. We were both there to get a $200 emergency loan. 41

"I was dating a girl last semester and she knew pretty much not to talk to me on Sundays or Monday nights. After a game, if I won, we'd talk for a little bit. If I lost, I'd just be like, 'Look, it's not going to be a very good week for me. I'll get in touch with you when I have time.' If I won on a Monday night, I'd call her and say, 'Hey, we're going out to dinner tomorrow night.' If I lost, it was like, 'Well, I guess it's mac and cheese for the next four nights.' 42

"I work at a country club. All sorts were betting through me—waiters, cooks, golf pros. For some reason everybody on my ticket was just getting waxed on the bowl games. After the North Carolina–Texas Sun Bowl, my ticket, as a whole, was down $10,000. I didn't even call in $3,000 in bets on the Tennessee–Virginia Tech Gator Bowl. There were people I knew that for some reason were taking Virginia Tech, and there was a total of three grand on Virginia Tech. I didn't want to call it in because I was so worried Eddie [his bookie] wasn't going to take it in the first place. I was just like, Hell with that, I'm booking it myself. It ended up paying off, thank god. Leading up to that game, I honestly had a migraine headache. I'd heard 43 people talk about them, but I never realized what they were like. I had such a pain in my head for 24 hours a day. I couldn't sleep. My whole Christmas holiday was one constant migraine.

"After the Tennessee game I told myself I was done for good, but 44
if I can find a bookie next fall, I guarantee I'll gamble again. I'm sure it won't be a problem finding another bookie."

If you are 21 years old, you have been witness to the emergence of 45
USA Today, ESPN and all those other college football- and basketball-saturated networks, picture-in-picture television, widespread use of satellite dishes, published injury reports, ATMs, the Internet, Jeff Sagarin and Danny Sheridan. In the winter of 1968 it was a wondrous achievement that TVS was able to bring Lew Alcindor and Elvin Hayes into our homes. Now we get Iowa State and Fred (the Mayor) Hoiberg, plus 8, against Kansas at Allen Field House.

Sid Diamond, the 59-year-old director of the race and sports book 46
at the Excalibur Hotel and Casino in Las Vegas, stands behind the counter. (In Diamond's business, "the counter" is more than a slab of Formica, it's the invisible barrier that separates bettors from bookmakers.) To his right is a wall of glistening white boards listing the night's games, the scores of which will be constantly updated in grease pencil. To his left are the entry cards at a dozen racetracks. Television sets abound, playing a feast of games and races for an audience that sits in lounge chairs with armrests. On one side of Diamond, the Warriors and the Sixers. Behind him, Seton Hall and Pittsburgh. On the other side, the sixth at Golden Gate.

Diamond, a smallish, grandfatherly man has been on the house 47
side of the counter for 20 years. "Look over there," he says, pointing to the racing side of the room. "All older guys. Now look over here." He points to the seats facing the sports betting wall, even as the first-half scores on Ivy League basketball games—"Ivy League, who knows Ivy League?" asks Diamond—are being posted. "Young people," he says. Sure enough. To the left, Sansabelts and loafers. To the right, baggy shorts, T-shirts, and cool hiking boots.

"Fifteen years ago people knew Notre Dame played college foot- 48
ball," says Diamond. "Out here, maybe Southern Cal and UCLA. Now you can ask people and they can tell you all about Arizona State and Oregon State. These young people, they form opinions. Whether those opinions are correct or incorrect, that's not the point. They're not ignorant. They know what it means to lay 11-to-10 odds. They know the value of a point spread. You can't fool anybody anymore in this business. You can beat them, but with all these communications facilities out there, you can't fool them. Years ago you could."

Two miles up the Vegas strip from the Excalibur, Sonny Reizner 49
makes lines at the Desert Inn. He has been in this business for more than 20 years. "There's a young crowd in sports gambling now," says

Reizner. "And there's so much information out there about betting. These kids might not have the sophistication in terms of how to bet, but they follow the action."

Young gamblers embrace a lifestyle that revolves around, of all 50
things, CNN Headline News's sports ticker, the scoreboard that runs across the bottom of the screen beneath images of natural disasters, global politics and O. J. The routine is simple enough: Watch a game, channel-surf whenever possible to another game and, when commercials and timeouts clog the air, fire up CNN and cruise the ticker. "My god," says Clemson's B. J. Simpson, "I knew more national and international news than anyone else in my classes." Says Ted Moone, a sophomore at Georgia, "Why do you think they run that thing, anyway?"

For study materials there is a new generation of electronic and 51
print icons, and they're not exactly McNeil and Lehrer or the beat poets. They're anybody with a pick. Touts like the Gold Sheet and Leonard's Losers. *USA Today*'s Gordon Forbes. And more. "Nick Buoniconti's the man, [HBO's] Inside the NFL," Conrad White, a Georgia senior, says of the former NFL star who picks the pro games each week. ESPN's College GameDay is required Saturday-morning viewing, ditto that network's NFL GameDay on Sunday. Lee Corso. Ron Jaworski. Phil Simms. Anybody with a blazer and a guess. Or a laptop and a guess. J. A. Davis and his Texas Tech housemates, college guys with a modem, peruse an on-line service for betting information.

But much of what the student gamblers study is stale information, 52
already absorbed by the oddsmakers. "People watch ESPN and read a few newspapers and think they're informed to bet," says Wayne Allyn Root, a 33-year-old professional handicapper in Las Vegas. "It's old information, built into the point spread. You have to find something that the average person doesn't know about. I work 12 hours a day during football season, trying to get information, and I win between 57 and 62 percent of the time. How does somebody think he can win by watching SportsCenter? He's going to get slaughtered."

Moreover, with all of this potentially useless research, there is 53
precious little time for what the NCAA calls degree progress. "I'd say it's like another three-hour class with Sundays being the lab," says Jay Mitcher, a Clemson junior. "I sit around studying that stuff more than my schoolwork."

ATHENS, GA.: Sonny Martin is hunched over a wobbly wooden table in 54
the corner of a dumpy off-campus bar on Broad Street. He drinks from brown bottles of Anchor Steam and chain-smokes. Once a good high school baseball player, Martin is now a 21-year-old senior at Georgia. He has debt, a photographic memory of his betting history and a piker's vision of sports.

"I've always just liked sports a lot. Always been crazy about March 55
Madness. Always been crazy about the NFL," he says. "I started betting when I was a sophomore here, just to be more interested in the games. It's nice to have a team to root for. Me and my roommate heard that guys in the fraternity were betting on games. It turns out their bookie was living with one of the brothers. I got in touch with him, gave him my phone number, he gave me an account number. That's pretty much the procedure.

"The two of us started out pooling our money and betting about $25 56
a game, total. We started out with one game, USC–Arizona. We took Arizona; the line was Arizona by three. USC won outright, so we lost $27.50. The next day we put $50 on the Indianapolis Colts. They were playing New England, and Scott Zolak was the Patriot's quarterback. New England was horrible. Anyway, that ended up being New England's first win of the year, so we lost $55 more. So we put $100 on the Denver Broncos in the Sunday-night game, and they pulled through for us. The next night we took Miami, and Buffalo just killed 'em.

"That same year me and my roommate were down $600. He had 57
already taken out an IFC [Intra-Fraternity Council] loan for $300. We had $500 on the Rams against the Bucs on Sunday, $300 with one bookie, $200 with another bookie. Tampa Bay was up 27–3 at the half. We were pulling furniture into the middle of the room, trying to figure out how much we could get if we sold it. Then Jim Everett came back and had the game of his life, and the Rams pulled it out 31–27. It still wasn't enough to get us even.

"I was way up this fall. I turned everybody on to the Steelers. Bas- 58
ketball's been rough. Four of us together, we're down about $2,000. I'll tell you, if you're losing money, watching sports is the worst feeling in the world. You hate the game, you hate sports. You can't stand them."

This is what happens: The fan's appreciation of the game is eroded. 59
Whatever passion the bettor may have had as a fan dissolves into a flaming desperation tied to point spreads, over–unders and multigame wagers like parlays and teasers. We watch games in this country with blinders on anyway. We delude ourselves into believing that Dennis Rodman would rebound just as ferociously for free and that Steve Young wears denim shirts because he really doesn't care about the money he's paid. And that is absurd, because to the sports gambler the last Super Bowl wasn't Young's afternoon of deliverance. There was an 18-point spread on that game, and had the Chargers scored a garbage TD—as Nebraska did against Texas Tech—San Diego would have covered and to hell with Steve Young and the San Francisco 49ers. You lose.

It works no differently for the college student and his college 60
games. At first the game is the thing. A kid grows up an Oklahoma fan, watches all the games, wears crimson on Saturdays, the whole deal. He goes to college in Norman, starts betting on Sooner games.

Then Missouri games, Nebraska games and Texas games. The game is no longer the thing. The bet is the thing. Teams are like horses or numbers on a roulette wheel.

61 "I used to bet on Vanderbilt all the time in basketball," says Alex Andrews, the admitted compulsive gambler. "And I still don't know where Vanderbilt is. Where is Vanderbilt?"

62 There is a purity attached to college sports; despite the abuses of recruiting, under-the-table payments to players and the like, there remains a veneer of joy, shared by athletes and fans. That is less true in the pros. "When I was with the New York Knicks," says Kentucky basketball coach Rick Pitino, who coached in the NBA for two seasons, "I was always amazed at the people who stayed until the end of a game. Somebody finally told me why: the point spread. I believe our fans here stay because they love Kentucky basketball."

63 And many of them undoubtedly do. But this is what former mob bookie Jahoda means when he says of college students who gamble, "They are in an atmosphere where the games are important, . . ." The green campus bettor is given to wagering on his own school, and the gambling lines in college towns are skewed to reflect this audience. But once the college bettor becomes seasoned, games become cold propositions. Then it's not the Wisconsin Badgers, it's Wisconsin, minus 5.

64 Kevin Woods, a 20-year-old junior at UCLA, likes to bet against the Bruins in both football and basketball. "They're my moneymaker," he says. "They're always a hot pick, because it's easy to identify the games they won't cover." For a February road game at Southern Cal, UCLA was playing without point guard Tyus Edney and had lost four of five to the Trojans at the L.A. Sports Arena. Still, Woods got Southern Cal, plus 9-$\frac{1}{2}$—"A joke," he says—and bet $250. UCLA won 73–69, but the Trojans covered. Easy money.

65 A bettor turned bookie at Florida named Jerry (Slaw) Davidson says, "I went to every home game this season. I made about $400 when Auburn beat us that day, but I would have gladly traded it for a win." Be true to your school.

66 LUBBOCK, TEXAS: Mike Tyler, the Texas Tech sophomore, stands 6′1″, 192 pounds and has the easy presence of an athlete. In fact, he was a wrestler and a football player in high school. His fraternity pledge name is Gambler. He is standing on the porch of a warehouse-cum-cowboy nightclub, wearing a denim jacket and waxing cocksure.

67 "First of all," he says, "I can't tell you a lot of horror stories because I have very few. The reason is because I don't lose a whole lot of money. I'm what you call a successful bettor. I know what you're trying to get at here—some kind of pollution of innocence type story. Well, I win. I don't mean to glorify gambling, but I love it, and I don't think I'll ever be able to quit.

"My first season of gambling was in 10th grade, just small stuff. By the time I was a senior, I won $9,000 in one year. I've lost as much as $6,000 in one weekend, but I always look at that and think, Hell, I'll win it back. Last year, I won about $4,500, this year I'm up $2,000. On a Saturday during the fall, I'll bet, like, 12 college games. Tech games are an easy pick. In the winter, by the way, Lady Raiders basketball is an easy pick. The Lady Raiders always cover big. A college football game I feel strong about, I'll bet $500. If I'm just curious, maybe 50 or 60 bucks. On Sundays I want to bet every one. I'll put down a grand on a big game. You sit there with the remote control, greatest thing in the world. 68

"Everybody gambles around here. To say it's just in the Greek system, that would be wrong. It's everywhere. I mean, god, I've probably personally gotten lines with bookies or made bets on my account for 200 people. I've probably booked bet for 50 or 60 people. A lot of my friends call me to make a bet, honestly, I just book it myself. I guess I know I have to slow down someday, but I'll always have a bookie. That won't ever stop. I don't want it to stop. I came from no income at all, and now I can buy things. If it wasn't for gambling, I wouldn't have half the things I have. I live by the stroke of luck." 69

Luck is a tributary of the American Dream in the 1990s. Vast riches that can't be earned can surely be won, can they not? All You Need Is a Dollar and a Dream, as the folks at the New York State Lottery used to say. Gambling in one or more forms is legal in 48 states and Washington, D.C. This includes 37 state lotteries (plus Powerball, a multistate game, and a three-state lottery in New England), pari-mutuel wagering in 44 states, bingo in 47 states and a total of 545 casinos (Native American, riverboat and state licensed) in 22 states, with more opening all the time. Sports betting is legal in four states, although straight sports bookmaking is legit only in Nevada (and on a floating casino in international waters off the coast of Fort Lauderdale). 70

An upshot of this is a wide acceptance of gambling as an avocation, gambling as a hobby. "We're working with the first generation that has been raised when gambling has been seen as a positive thing," says Roger Svendsen, director of the Minnesota Compulsive Gambling Hotline, which serves a state where 17 casinos have been built on Native American reservations since 1988. "Instead of talking about gambling, we talk about gaming." 71

Says Lesieur, the gambling researcher, "What you have now, among college students, is a group of individuals who have no recollection of the time when gambling was outlawed. Gambling is simply around now. It's closer than ever before, and it's continuing to get closer." 72

This explosion has done more than predispose college gamblers to bet illegally; it has also given them a wide range of legal possibilities. Fraternities at California colleges have for years organized trips to Las Vegas; similar options have become available to students at 73 hundreds of colleges. Mystic Lake Casino in Prior Lake, Minn., for instance, is just a 40-minute drive from the University of Minnesota, and several smaller colleges are within an hour's ride.

Matt Carter, a 22-year-old from Prior Lake who attended St. John's University in Collegeville, Minn., recalls that Native American casino operators would encourage students to recruit friends for bus trips. "The casinos would find a kid wearing a college sweatshirt," he says. "They'd say, 'Hey, if you want to arrange trips, we can do that.' They'll send the bus all the way out to St. John's, a big old Greyhound. They'll put beer, pop, movies on it. You get paid by the person; they'd give you $150 or $200. A buddy of mine did it." 74

Riverboat casino "cruises"—in many cases, the boats never leave the pier—are available in five states from the heartland (Iowa) to the Mississippi Delta (Louisiana). Officials at Mississippi State and Ole Miss thought this was enough of a hazard to invite Wexler to their campus to speak on the evils of gambling, legal or otherwise. 75

The 1995 college student's parents and grandparents might have played bingo or bet on horse racing (at a racetrack, not at an OTB parlor or in the living room using a phone account). "Horse racing is much too slow for kids," says Diamond, the Vegas sports-book director. "Too much time between races, too little return for the investment." Casino games are lethally swift: A poor player can lose hundreds of dollars in 15 minutes at a $5-minimum blackjack table. A good—and lucky—player can win as much. The intoxication caused by such a pace is terrific. And then there are the women. "Video poker," says Wexler. "That's the game that started really bringing younger women into casinos." College women, too. Slots and video poker. No dealer. No other players. Nonjudgmental wagering. Vegas casinos increasingly attract young women in Champion sweatshirts, emblazoned with college names, who slam quarters and silver dollars into video poker machines and slots. 76

And college students' wagering can take bizarre forms. Last fall the Georgia campus was swept for 36 hours by a form of the old pyramid scheme. Eight people put up $100 each, and then each of them got eight more people to put up $100 apiece. When you reached the top of the pyramid, you "won" $800, a clear profit of $700. Essentially, you were betting $100 that the chain would last long enough for you to get your profit. It started one weekday at noon and was dead by the next night, leaving dozens of students $700 up and dozens of others $100 down. It is the nature of gambling that the simpler the bet, the more attractive. Why else would people play the lottery? 77

BLOOMINGTON, IND.: Steve (Lefty) McNeil, Bob Jacobs and Adam Grady are seniors and fraternity brothers at Indiana. One of them has a job for next year, one is looking for work, and the third hopes to attend law 78 school. They sit in jeans and sneakers, recalling their nearly two-year run with a local bookie and, in particular, the weekend last fall when they lost a combined $3,500, including $2,300 on the Dallas Cowboys, who failed to cover a 12-point spot against the Phoenix Cardinals.

"When it looked like we were going to lose," says McNeil, "we 79
drove to Lake Monroe [20 minutes away], and we wondered how the hell we were going to pay. It was the most sickening feeling I've ever had in my stomach. Eventually, you pay it off with creative financing."

"I started out so small," says Jacobs. "Everyone won with parlay 80
cards."

"The ridiculous becomes normal," says McNeil. "Two hundred 81
dollars easily becomes $500 without thinking about how much money that is. I would double my bets. My rationale became: I win, we're even. If I lose, there's no way I can pay what I owe either way."

"My mentality was that if I only bet $150 one night, I was mini- 82
mizing my losses," says Grady.

"I took out $500 on my parents' credit card to help pay my debt," 83
says McNeil, of how he paid his share of the $3,500 weekend loss—a bailout method he'd used before. "I would tell them that I had to buy some books or that I had a project that I needed money for. Or that there was a dance. Usually I told them it was a dance. They just thought I spent a lot of money."

To pay his third of the weekend loss, Jacobs cleaned out a savings 84
account started when he was in his early teens. Grady? "I have no idea," he says, "how I paid any of it."

A big part of the allure of sports betting for students is the avail- 85
ability of credit. For the college kid there's no pressure in making the first bet because bookies don't ask for cash up front. Everybody runs a tab, and the bookie establishes a limit at which he must pay off the bettor's winnings or the gambler must pay off his losses. Jimmy Vaccaro, director of the race and sports books at the Mirage Hotel in Las Vegas, stood in his establishment on a winter Friday and surmised, "You won't see a lot of college kids in here. Here, they've got to put up money to make a bet."

It's all just a paper game until the bettor reaches his maximum and 86
the bookie demands payment. "At first guys don't really think the bookie wants the money," says Timothy Mills, a Texas Tech senior who ran bets to his off-campus bookie for several fraternity brothers. "It hasn't hit them that what they're doing is real. Then the bookie says, 'Pay me, or you're not betting anymore.' That's when it hits them."

A compulsive gambler will tell you that he bets for the rush and not 87
for the money. The money is just the syringe that carries the adrenaline. Wexler, who hasn't placed a bet in nearly 27 years, once bet on hockey games for three months before he realized the game was played on ice. Yet, for the college bettor, money is a significant factor on two levels:

Many of the gamblers are fraternity kids with a plentiful initial 88
supply of their parents' funds. They are, in effect, playing with the house's money. Dad's house. It's not uncommon for a college bettor to get deep into his parents' pockets before he tells them that he's betting.

College students in general are cash poor. They see wagering as a 89
means to a sort of postadolescent wealth. "I'm gambling to make a profit," says Michael Smithson, a 21-year-old senior at Miami-Dade Community College and formerly a student at the University of Miami. "I see my friends going out and having a great lifestyle, and I want it too."

In either circumstance, the bettor ultimately needs money to pay 90
off his debts; A kid with moneyed parents will eventually have to look homeward to cover debts; a kid without resources will seek any means available to pay. "It is amazing what some people do," says Debbie Frapp, an addiction counselor at Texas Tech. "I've talked to students who have gambled away financial aid money, received emergency aid and gambled that away." It's common knowledge among campus bookies that the time to collect is at the start of the semester. "That's when people get money, from their parents, from the school," says Georgia student bookie Andrew Stewart.

Then again, college kids are a lousy credit risk. When Stewart 91
quit his book, he and his partners were more than $12,000 ahead, but they had been paid only about $2,500 cash.

College gamblers are also blind to the game's scripted outcome. 92
As Jahoda says, "They cannot do the math, and they have no aptitude." Sports gambling isn't an issue of teams and games, it's an issue of numbers and dollars. "We have people in Vegas whose entire job is to find a number," says Diamond. The number is a middle, the gambler's promised land between two different point spreads. Gambling syndicates hire runners to canvass sports books in search of a variance in the point spread. Philadelphia 76ers versus Houston Rockets. You get the Rockets minus 9 with one book and the Sixers plus 11 with another. If it's a 10-point game, you win both bets. Anything else, you lose only the vigorish. "These guys, they don't know a thing about the teams, and they don't care," says Diamond. "They're looking for numbers. Very smart guys."

Most college guys pick too many games, oblivious to the 93
bookie's edge. And they wander off into parlays and teasers, multiple-proposition sucker bets that are far more difficult to win than straight bets. They are guaranteed to lose. "They do not understand [sports betting] is a zero-sum game, intentionally designed for the house to get the sum and the player to get the zero," says Jahoda.

The bookie's ledger, of course, doesn't stop at zero. It starts there 94
and ends up with columns of numbers that add up to red ink and heartache for their clients.

THINKING ABOUT THE ESSAY

1. Consider what unwritten obligations you have as a student that would raise ethical issues if you were to gamble. Do you engage in gambling or other activities that would appear to contradict your role as a student? If so, how do you justify your activities?
2. How would you describe Layden's attitude toward the current world of student betting? How does he construct his argument? What is his overall ethical stance? Does it mirror your own? Explain.
3. How did you respond to the many anecdotes Layden presents concerning student betting? Do they make his presentation of the facts more powerful? Are you aware of similar stories at your own campus? If so, what is your attitude toward the students who engage in heavy betting? What, if any, public pronouncements has your college administration made concerning student betting?
4. Does Layden consider students the agents behind student betting or the victims of a society that condones betting and gambling, or is his stance somewhere in between? How does it compare to your own view concerning individual responsibility on the part of the student?
5. Layden's essay is one of the longer selections in this text. How does he organize it? Why would such a long essay appear in a popular magazine, *Sports Illustrated?* What demands does he place on the reader, and how does he sustain reader interest?

RESPONDING IN DISCUSSION

1. Have your class break up into groups of two students each. One student plays the role of a son or daughter who is using deception to get money from a parent to pay off a gambling debt; the other student plays the parent. After the encounter, discuss how you felt during the role playing.
2. Divide into groups of three or four, and list the various values in American society that encourage gambling. Rank-order them, and discuss how these same values could be channeled into "positive addictions."
3. Make a list of how the prevalence of gambling has influenced the way sports are played and the way spectators view sports. Discuss what evidence you have that gambling is the culprit in these situations.
4. There are ways that concerned groups have tried to reduce gambling such as gambling clinics, gamblers' anonymous groups, and public awareness campaigns. Discuss whether any of these could be used effectively to deter student gambling.

RESPONDING IN WRITING

1. Layden asserts that college betting is a widespread phenomenon. Write an essay supporting or disagreeing with his assessment.
2. Interview at least five women and five men on campus concerning their views on sports gambling. Write an essay summarizing the main differences between the attitudes of the men and those of the women. Conclude with your own theory about why the groups differ in their views.
3. Argue for or against the idea that if college athletes become businesspeople (as advocated by Byers in the previous essay), it will encourage student betting.
4. Argue for or against the proposition that if bookies or other illegal betting entrepreneurs are found to have large numbers of student customers, their punishment—in the event that they are caught—should be more severe.
5. Search the Net to see if you can locate any "betting" sites or bettor chat groups. Monitor these sites and report on your findings.

CONNECTIONS: FOR WRITING AND RESEARCH

1. Why is the idea of intercollegiate sports taken for granted as an integral part of college life? For a research project, trace the history of college sports in America, discussing the various social and cultural influences that have established it so strongly in our society.
2. How would you characterize the typical college sports fanatic? Does he or she have any qualities that distinguish him or her from the average student? If so, what are they? Can you infer anything about college sports fans from any of the essays in this part?
3. Write an essay explaining why the typical college student likes (or does not like) athletic coaches, regardless of their behavior, who create winning teams.
4. Write an expository essay of approximately 500 words explaining to what degree obsessive sports betting among college students demonstrates that traditional family values in America are at risk.
5. Compare and contrast the style of argumentation Guenin uses in "Competing to Compete" with Layden's style in "Bettor Education." What methods does each author use to advance his argument? How does each author structure his argument? How does the author's phrasing of the problem he is addressing help determine the method he uses in addressing it?

6

COMMON ADDICTIONS

Is it fair to lump smoking, drinking, prescription drugs, and crack cocaine in the same category as potentially addictive substances? The word *addiction* nearly always has a negative connotation in American culture, yet if you know someone (say, a diabetic) who must regularly take a life-saving drug to lead a normal life, you would be hard-pressed to make an ethical judgment against the individual. Are Americans' notions of unacceptable addictions more a factor of cultural bias than a response to true threats of society? Or is there legitimacy to placing restrictions on certain addictive products? Smoking is legal although it kills about 400,000 smokers each year, and anyone over age 21 with a couple of dollars can purchase cigarettes. Stimulants are used for children with attention deficit disorders, and only require a "note from the doctor" for purchase. Public health officials state that if someone would attempt to introduce alcoholic beverages on the market today, they would never pass the Food and Drug Administration guidelines. Yet possession of some drugs—like marijuana—can lead to years of jail time. These examples present just some of the conflicts over our nation's long obsession with addiction, whether it is addiction to illicit, prescription, or over-the-counter drugs, alcohol, or tobacco. To make matters worse, in the 1990s, we now have diagnoses such as work addiction, sexual addiction, gambling addiction, and spending addiction—and the list continues to rise. How should Americans as individuals and the United States as a society address this complex issue? While no solution is likely to be forthcoming anytime soon, the following essays offer a wide perspective on defining some of the personal, social, ethical, and legal boundaries.

A World Apart from a Liquor Legacy

Susan Cheever

Writing in the February 24, 1996, edition of the New York-based newspaper *Newsday,* Susan Cheever (novelist, essayist, and biographer) describes the intergenerational influence of alcohol use in her family. Her father, John Cheever, is considered by many to be one of the finest fiction writers of the post–World War II era, for his accurate, sardonic portrayals of the private life of affluent American families. Here, she writes about the private life of *her* family, who was often in the public eye among literary aficionados. She demonstrates that one need not be encouraged to turn to alcohol during social occasions or to relieve stress. One need only observe such uses in the family in order to model one's attitude and behavior toward its use.

PREVIEWING THE ESSAY

Cheever states that as a child she was "a little alarmed but also a little delighted by liquor's effect on my parents' friends." Must adults be cautious in exhibiting "adult" behavior around children? Does it take the spice out of life to always be concerned how one's children are interpreting your behavior? Is it enough to say to your child, "This is for when you get to be an adult"? Or, should parents spend time considering their behavior's effect on children even if it means altering their lifestyle and perhaps re-evaluating their public behaviors?

A couple of years ago, my daughter decided to do a survey of our local markets for a project at school; she wanted to find out how hard it was for a kid to buy beer. I gave her a 10-dollar bill and assured her that her quest was useless. Everyone knew that children shouldn't drink, I told her. She would be carded; everyone would ask for proof of age. 1

At three supermarkets within four blocks of our apartment my 11-year-old daughter bought liquor unquestioned. Only at our neighborhood delicatessen was she asked if she was buying it for her mother before she was allowed to pay for her six-pack. Alcohol is the drug of choice for many of my daughter's peers, and there's nothing to stop them from spending their allowances on beer and wine coolers long before high school. 2

I remember drinking as a teenager. I grew up in a world where drinking was the principal badge and privilege of adulthood. My parents' fixing themselves a drink was as sure an indicator of evening as the darkening of the sky. My father would pour my mother a Scotch on the rocks and then his own whiskey without ice—neat, he called it—and on festive occasions he would lovingly mix up a pitcher of iced martinis and strain the precious liquid into special glasses. 3

When my parents' friends came over, the fixing of the drinks became an elaborate ritual featuring the luminous ice bucket, silver tongs and swizzles and many bottles of different colors. They referred to this ceremony as the preprandial libation.

I was a little alarmed but also a little delighted by liquor's effect 4
on my parents' friends. I remember many men with smiling red faces leaning down to tell me jokes late at night, while their wives giggled in the other room at stories I didn't understand. Sometimes Mr. Warren or Mr. Boyer or even my Uncle Fred would come and sit on the edge of my bed and explain how much he loved his own children and what a good girl he knew I was.

I learned to respect my parents' moods. The morning was always 5
a bad time to make a mistake, and the evening was always the best time to ask for something. At 13—my daughter's age now—I was drinking diluted wine at grown-up cocktail parties and special occasions, but it wasn't until I was almost 20 that I understood its power.

It was a hot August day. A boyfriend had jilted me, or I had jilted 6
a boyfriend—I can't even remember which. I was feeling that kind of sharp post-adolescent despair that seems as if it will never end when my father mixed me a gin and tonic. I sat in my parents' dining room and drank, and I could feel the pain slipping away from me and being replaced by a great sense of well-being. The brook babbled past the mint beds outside the house. Sun slanted in through the summer air.

"I'm young," I thought as I sipped, "there will be many men in my 7
life." I was transported on the magic carpet of the drink from the painful details of the present to a greater world where everything had its place and everything was somehow for the best, a world where I had been vouchsafed the vision of cosmic order as long as I had a gin and tonic in my hand.

Of course, all this cheeriness eventually turned ugly, as it often 8
does. As an adult, it took a long, long time for me to learn that those soaring moments when I felt I could walk among the stars had their terrible price. These days I don't drink. My children are growing up in a household where there is no alcohol at all. I'm happy to be a mother who is in the same mood all day. They don't see me loosening up at evening time with a neat whiskey, and they don't have to deal with my hangovers when I take them to school.

I grew up in a world where everyone was drinking; my children 9
are growing up in a world where drinking and ice buckets and cocktail hour and friendly liquor store owners are only glimpsed in old black and white movies, artifacts as ancient and strange as the dinosaur skeletons at the Museum of Natural History. You can say I'm just doing the opposite of what my parents did, and in some ways you'd be right. You can say that I can't protect my children forever from the temptations of the outside world.

Nevertheless, I hope my daughter never uses the knowledge she gained in her survey of the neighborhood. I can be sure that our family doesn't march to the rhythms of a drinking life: the excruciating mornings, the expansive evenings and the dimly remembered nights, the endless personal dramas, the dozens of bitter breakups and dozens of passionate reconciliations. I can make sure they don't grow up to the clink of ice cubes and the crash of thrown crockery. I can hope my children don't have to spend all that time learning to be crazy and then learning to be sane. I can let them know that glamorous alcohol has an unglamorous side. 10

Maybe I can't protect them, but I can certainly inform them. At least they know the pleasures of living in a house where no one drinks, and where the moods are set by circumstances instead of substances. 11

THINKING ABOUT THE ESSAY

1. Were you surprised that the author's 11-year-old daughter was not carded by most of the liquor merchants in her neighborhood? Why? How easy has it been for you or any of your friends under legal age to obtain alcoholic beverages?
2. What role does liquor serve in your family's private or social life? To what degree does cultural acceptance or taboo affect this role?
3. What do you believe are the proper and improper uses of drinking alcohol? How did you acquire your beliefs? Do you uphold them or are they more theoretical than practical?
4. Why does the author live in an alcohol-free home? Is she being overcautious? Is it an extreme reaction to her experiences with alcohol and the culture of drinking in which she grew up? Explain.
5. Cheever's essay is an "op-ed" piece or a syndicated column. What are the guidelines governing such articles? How are they reflected in her essay?

RESPONDING IN DISCUSSION

1. Divide into groups of three and four. Discuss why drinking is such a popular pastime on many college campuses. Share your answers with the rest of the class.
2. Cut out a magazine commercial promoting a particular brand of liquor. Discuss the messages implicit in the ad by describing the appearance and demeanor of the models, their clothing and accessories, and the implied relationship between the drinker and the liquor as well as the relationships between and among drinkers.

3. Divide into groups of three and four and discuss the concept of responsible drinking. Is there such a thing? If so, what does it signify and how can it be taught or promoted? Share your responses with your classmates.
4. Review the description of drinking rituals in the author's household while she was growing up. What were its particular appeals? Why does she believe now that such rituals are not part of a healthy lifestyle?

RESPONDING IN WRITING

1. In a 500-word essay, describe a time in your life when you witnessed a friend or relative under the influence of alcohol. Was your attitude positive, negative, or a mixture of both? Explain.
2. Argue for or against the proposition that college students who drink tend to be conformists and be vulnerable to peer pressure, while their nondrinking counterparts are more independent-minded.
3. Argue for or against the proposition that peer influence is stronger than family influence in determining whether a young person begins drinking.
4. For a research project, study the function of drinking wine at dinner among European cultures. How does this practice differ from American social drinking or drinking rituals within the American family? Include at least four citations from different secondary reference sources.
5. Search for alcohol addiction advice on the Internet. Based on your findings, construct a list of sources and organizations people seeking help for alcohol problems can refer to.
6. Search the Internet for sites related to drinking, including but not limited to company homepages. Do you feel these pages glamorize drinking? Did you find any information echoing any of your own negative experiences with alcohol? Evaluate the results of your search in a 750–1,000 word essay.

Selling Smokes and Sex

Bob Herbert

Writing in the editorial pages of the January 1, 1996, *New York Times,* popular columnist Bob Herbert neatly sums up the history of cigarette advertising in the United States, demonstrating that there has always been a link between sexual innuendo and cigarettes ever since the 1870s, whether the targeted consumers have been men or women. Skyrocketing sales, increased market share, handsome profits—what business wouldn't want to find a way of enhancing these goals? Herbert doesn't doubt that advertising boosts cigarette sales. But he also suggests that promoting the sale of cigarettes—particularly among adolescents, the group most vulnerable to cigarette advertising—is an "obscenity."

PREVIEWING THE ESSAY

Psychologists often talk of "conscious" responses (that is, responses you are aware of) and "unconscious" responses (those that operate on a level that bypasses the rationale mind). What is the nature of your responses to cigarette advertising? Does your conscious mind say, "Just another company trying to trick me into giving them my money"? Do you think your "unconscious" is secretly operating, planting the idea that smoking is OK, fun, or fashionable? Spend a few moments considering your personal response to cigarette advertising prior to reading this essay.

For the cigarette makers, always on the alert for efficient ways to hook new smokers, especially young ones, it was a dandy idea. This was back in the 1870's and 80's, when it wasn't considered right for women to smoke, so the advertising was directed specifically at men and boys. 1

The idea, widely adopted and wildly successful, was to put a picture of a scantily dressed woman inside each pack of cigarettes. It drove adolescent boys into a frenzy. As a study by a team of cancer researchers in California put it: "The early use of 'soft pornography' as the basis for product promotion was reported to have had young boys scrambling after cigarette packs." 2

And, of course, they smoked the cigarettes. And like most people who light up those first few lethal sticks, they became addicted. 3

Naturally there was a backlash. Using "dirty pictures" to promote "nasty habits" among the very young drove a lot of adults into a frenzy. 4

"There was widespread consternation," the researchers said, "with what was perceived to be a powerful corrupting influence of the cigarette industry on young boys." 5

The first newspaper to denounce the practice editorially was *The New York Times,* in 1879. The protests led, eventually, to laws banning the sale of cigarettes to minors in many states. But nothing was ever able to stop the cigarette companies from targeting young people with their advertising. 6

When your product kills more than 400,000 of your customers each year (and that's just in the United States), you have to replace 7 them with somebody. And since there are few people over the age of 21 who are willing to take up smoking, the tobacco companies inevitably set their sights on the young.

The study by the cancer research team, from the University of California, San Diego, appeared in the *Journal of the National Cancer Institute* last October. It examined the links between adolescent smoking behavior and cigarette advertising. It found that adolescents were twice as likely to be influenced to smoke by advertising and cigarette promotions than by pressure from peers or relatives. 8

The study was extensive and showed the profound influence cigarette advertising has had over the past century. In 1913, for example, the R. J. Reynolds Tobacco Company was spending nearly $800,000 annually on advertising and promotion. That increased to $2.2 million by 1916 and $8.7 million by 1921. 9

From the company's perspective, it was money very well spent. R. J. Reynolds' market share rose from 0.2 percent in 1913, which represented the sale of 1.5 million Camel cigarettes, to 50 percent of all cigarette sales in 1921, when the company sold 1.83 *billion* Camels. 10

By the mid-1920's the cigarette companies felt much freer to target women with their advertising. Chesterfield came up with a campaign that used the slogan, "Blow some my way." And Lucky Strike hit the jackpot by urging women to "Reach for a Lucky instead of a sweet." In other words, smoking Lucky Strikes was a good way for women to avoid gaining weight. 11

According to the researchers, the Lucky Strike campaign resulted in "a rapid rise in sales, taking the brand from sales of 13.7 billion cigarettes in 1925 (third-ranked brand) to over 40 billion and market leadership by 1930." 12

But by the mid-1960's it was no longer possible to hide the disastrous health effects of cigarette smoking. The Surgeon General's report came out in 1964, initiating a public health campaign. As one study after another linked cigarettes to cancer and other diseases, fewer and fewer people were willing to heed the tobacco companies' insidious insistence that they start smoking. 13

But one group remained vulnerable—the group made up of members who think they are never going to die. 14

John Pierce, one of the authors of the study, said, "After 30 years of sustained public education about the health effects of smoking, adolescents are the only group that continues to take up smoking in significant numbers." 15

Tobacco merchants slipped soft-porn into cigarette packs more than 100 years ago because they knew there was a fortune to be made by hooking adolescents. Their slogan today might well be, "Now, more than ever." 16

THINKING ABOUT THE ESSAY

1. Have you known anyone who died of a disease linked to smoking? Are you aware of any celebrities who died from the effects of cigarette smoke? If so, how did you first respond to the news? Did it stir anger toward cigarette companies? Did you say to yourself that the person was responsible for his or her own behavior? Or was it a mixture of the two?
2. Herbert uses several rigorous studies to present "cause-effect" arguments in attempting to prove advertising increases the sales of cigarettes. Is this a good method of argumentation? Are there any flaws to this line of reasoning? Explain.
3. Follow the method of argumentation in the essay paragraph by paragraph. How does the author embed his essay with a thesis and supporting points while still keeping it readable and interesting? What tricks of the writing trade does he reveal in his style?

RESPONDING IN DISCUSSION

1. Divide into groups of three and four. Elect a group secretary or transcriber to draw three vertical columns down a piece of notebook paper. Label the first column "female," the second, "male," and the third, "male and female." Then have each member of the group volunteer the way cigarette advertisers use images, product promotions, special events, and other appeals to each of these three groups so as to encourage smoking. (For example, to whom do Virginia Slims–sponsored sporting events appeal?) Share your results with the rest of the class.
2. Bring to class a magazine ad that promotes smoking. Discuss the ad's various elements that attempt to suggest smoking is a positive activity.
3. Discuss whether cigarette advertising should enjoy the constitutional right of free speech.
4. Discuss whether there are effective ways of reducing cigarette smoking without banning advertising (for example, raising life insurance and disability premiums, increasing the tax on cigarettes, and taxing expenditures on cigarette advertising).

RESPONDING IN WRITING

1. Write a personal essay of approximately 400 words explaining why you do or don't smoke.
2. Some commentators have stated that since working-class people tend to smoke more than affluent people, a tax on cigarettes is an

unfair burden on those with moderate incomes. Argue for or against this proposition.

3. Argue for or against the proposition that employers have the right to do background checks on potential employees to determine if they are smokers, since smokers tend to be absent from work more than nonsmokers.
4. Some religions and sects forbid smoking. For a research project, investigate one such group, and in an essay of approximately 750 to 1,000 words, explain how the smoking prohibition is successfully upheld.
5. Locate a poster discussion of cigarette smoking on the Internet. What points of view do you find represented? Find an argument for or against smoking that you feel is provocative, and construct an argumentative essay in response to it.
6. Similar to your search for alcohol-related sites, find cigarette company homepages and evaluate their appeal to teens. Did you find any aspects that seem deliberately targeted to teens? Present your findings in a 500–750 word essay.

But It's Only Pot

Per Ola and Emily D'Aulaire

Serving as contributing writers for *Reader's Digest,* where the following essay appeared in this popular magazine's January 1997 issue, Per Ola and Emily D'Aulaire tackle the "pot" problem from a decidedly oppositional perspective. The authors intersperse sobering facts about the effects of marijuana with a dramatic case study of one young woman's experience with the substance. Their argument in opposition to marijuana usage thus combines selective data (provided by a consultant in pharmacology at Boston University School of Medicine) and a more personal and emotional account. As you read the essay, try to assess the reasons why the D'Aulaires object to the use of marijuana, and how effective their argument is.

PREVIEWING THE ESSAY

Do you consider marijuana to be a dangerous drug? Why or why not? Why do you think marijuana usage is increasing dramatically among youths aged 12–17?

When Heather Brooks entered high school in 1991, her guidance counselor pegged her as someone with high potential. In her first semester, she earned top grades. She participated in many extra- 1 curricular activities. A student of classical piano, Heather filled her family's suburban Chicago home with Chopin and Beethoven.

During her freshman year, 14-year-old Heather made friends with some older kids, and her life took a sudden turn. One evening while she was with them in a neighborhood park, a tall, good-looking junior named Justin handed her a marijuana cigarette. "Take a drag," he urged. "It'll mellow you out." 2

At first Heather held off. She'd always disapproved of drugs. But Justin reassured her. "It's not a drug," he said, "It's only pot." 3

Heather decided to give it a try. "Okay," she conceded. "Just one puff." 4

With instructions from her friends, she pulled the sweet-smelling smoke into her lungs and held it there until she thought she'd burst. Then came more puffs. As she blew out the wispy remnants of smoke, she felt dizzy—and euphoric. "Give me another drag," she begged, tugging on Justin's arm. 5

MARIJUANA contains around 60 compounds called cannabinoids. The most psychoactive of these is delta-9-tetrahydro-cannibinol (THC). Differences among plants cause the potency of marijuana to vary widely. But as a result of selective breeding, some of the marijuana smoked today can contain ten to 20 times more THC than there was in the pot smoked in the 1960s and early '70s. More than 400 other chemicals are also found in the plant. Many of their effects are still unknown. 6

When Heather pulled the smoke into her lungs that evening, the THC molecules slipped through tissue-paper-thin air sacs in her lungs and entered her bloodstream. Within minutes a hefty dose of THC was headed for Heather's brain. 7

A biological barrier in the brain admits the oxygen, nutrients, hormones and sugar it needs while blocking out unnecessary, sometimes harmful, compounds. Certain psychoactive drugs, however, can pierce this shield. Fat-soluble, the THC and other cannabinoids dissolve in the brain's cellular membranes, which are composed of fat molecules; then, like wet bars of soap, they slip through the barrier. 8

AFTER A FEW MORE DRAGS on the joint, Heather felt a deepening glow of contentment. Time slowed to a crawl. Colors and sounds seemed more intense. *Wow!* she thought. *This stuff is fantastic!* 9

Her high lasted four hours. 10

THE THC and other cannabinoids would remain in her body for weeks. The molecules dissolve not only in the brain but also in the liver, lungs, kidneys, testes and ovaries. 11

Unlike alcohol and other water-soluble drugs that are eliminated from the body fairly rapidly, cannabinoids slowly leach from the fat and re-enter the bloodstream before finally being purged via the urine. 12

HEATHER COULDN'T WAIT for the next invitation from her new friends. Because she'd taken the big step and smoked a joint, she felt a strong bond with them. She was confident someone would bring more pot to share. 13

She wasn't disappointed. The next weekend, when Justin offered her a joint, Heather took it eagerly. *Why do adults get so bent out of shape over a little pot?* she wondered. All she knew was that the more she smoked, the more outrageously fabulous she felt. 14

INSIDE THE BRAIN, each neuron (nerve cell) generates tiny electrical signals. Biochemicals called neurotransmitters shuttle between the neurons to pass along these signals until all the circuits needed to process and store a message—an image, sound, thought or sensation—have been completed. 15

Certain neurons, especially those that mediate balance, glucose craving and the perception of time, sound and color, have receptors that readily bind with THC. The THC molecules thus distort part of the brain's information-processing system, altering perception of time, while amplifying sounds and visual images. 16

AS HEATHER'S FRESHMAN YEAR—and her use of marijuana—progressed, pot was no longer just a social drug. First thing in the morning, she smoked a joint to get herself out of bed. She smoked in a friend's car on the way to school. Between classes she smoked in the bathroom. She was even stoned when she sang in a school choir concert. 17

To achieve a high, meanwhile, required ever increasing amounts of the substance. She graduated to using a bong, or water pipe, which concentrates the smoke inside a chamber so none is lost in the air. "The only thing wasted," a bong purveyor promised, "is you." 18

Heather didn't worry that she needed more and more of the stuff. To her, this was a sign of prowess. "Look how much I can smoke and not get loaded," she bragged. And she downplayed thoughts of addiction. Pot, her friends kept reminding her, wasn't any more habit-forming than milk. She was sure she could quit any time. 19

THE INTERACTION of THC with brain receptors triggers intracellular signals that produce the high experienced by marijuana users. Among chronic users, continued bombardment of the cells by THC may lead to a tolerance for the drug. When this happens, the user needs more and more pot to get high. 20

WHEN HEATHER'S PARENTS asked how school was going, she always flashed a big smile. "Everything's fine," she'd say. Because she'd 21 always been such a good daughter, Frank and Diana Brooks had every reason to believe her. Gradually, though, Heather had become a highly accomplished liar.

"I'll be at Amy's house after school," she said one morning, looking her mother squarely in the eye. Instead, Heather drove with her friends to a dead-end dirt road where they smoked pot until it was time to go home for dinner. 22

On Friday nights, Heather came home promptly at her eleven o'clock curfew and said good-night to her parents. After the sliver of light under their door went out, she waited ten minutes, then tiptoed downstairs and slipped out the door to go party. 23

When Heather's gang smoked pot, they also always drank—beer or tumblers of vodka and cranberry juice. The alcohol made Heather feel more mellow than ever. It also amazed her how much she could drink without ever getting sick. 24

THC AND ALCOHOL together have a greater effect than either by itself. While marijuana distorts information processing, alcohol enhances the effects of a neurotransmitter called GABA, which binds to neurons and slows their rate of firing, producing a sedative effect. 25

THC also can reduce nausea. Vomiting is the body's natural way of purging toxic substances. If the vomit message is suppressed, as it is during marijuana use, dangerous amounts of alcohol can remain, in rare cases causing alcohol poisoning, organ damage and even death. While Heather considered it a "perk" that she could down so much beer while smoking pot, her body was like a guitar string about to snap. 26

AT SCHOOL Heather's absences began to mount and her grades took a nose dive. Yet for a while she continued to fool her parents. When report cards were mailed, she intercepted them at home and, with skillful use of correction fluid and a photocopying machine, turned D's and F's to A's and B's. She even added some nice comments: "Heather is a pleasure to have in class," she wrote, imitating the handwriting of one of her teachers. 27

By the end of Heather's freshman year, her grade-point average had plummeted from 4.0 to 1.2, and she'd tallied up a staggering 39 absences. 28

Meanwhile, Heather dropped many of her extracurricular activities. When her parents asked why, she said she just needed some "space." Diana and Frank Brooks pinned this on normal teen-age turmoil. 29

By now, Heather no longer cared about anyone or anything—except her next high. Her drive and motivation were gone, replaced by total apathy. 30

Drugs had become her life. She couldn't stop. In her journal she wrote: "Pot is a motionless sea of destruction. I'm drowning." 31

Indeed, always in excellent health, Heather now felt sick much of the time. Her hands and feet were constantly cold. She woke up coughing and pushed her face deep into her pillow so her parents wouldn't hear her. She also noticed that her menstrual cycle had become irregular. 32

Heather's parent saw the changes in their daughter. But their questions turned up nothing, and they were worried. 33

SOME STUDIES SHOW that deep inside the brain, THC may depress the neuron of the hippocampus—where short-term memories are processed and sent to other brain areas for storage. As a result, the ability to learn and to remember recent events may be hampered. 34

Smoking marijuana can deliver three times more tar than smoking tobacco. Its irritating smoke dilates blood vessels; it also reddens the eyes and inflames delicate nasal tissues. Regular use can lead to chronic bronchitis. 35

Based on animal and in vitro studies using both human and animal material, it's possible that pot may impair the capacity of the white cells to fight invading infection. 36

Moreover, the drug tinkers with the appetite center in the brain stem, which causes bouts of the "munchies"—a craving for sugary food. 37

Marijuana's final insult is to the pituitary gland, which regulates sex hormones. In men, some studies show sperm production can drop. And in women, ovulation may be inhibited. 38

BY HER SOPHOMORE year, Heather knew all the tricks. To hide the smell of pot in her room, she stuffed an empty paper-towel roll with a sheet of fabric softener and exhaled into the tube. She carried eye drops to clear up bloodshot eyes. Before heading home, she gargled with mouthwash or chewed cinnamon-flavored gum. Often she brought a clean shirt to a party and left the smoke-saturated one behind. 39

As Heather's pot intake increased, she wanted even more. Encouraged by her friends, she experimented with a variety of mind-altering substances: LSD, mescaline, crack, codeine, cocaine and amphetamines. Through it all, however, marijuana remained her "drug of choice." It was what she started out with, and what she ended up with. 40

STUDIES SHOW that there are developmental stages in drug use, though one drug doesn't inevitably lead to the next stage of abuse. A marijuana user most likely started with alcohol and cigarettes. Researchers say few people experiment with other illicit drugs without having tried marijuana first. A 1994 analysis showed that adults who used pot as children are 17 times more likely to become regular cocaine users. 41

ONE WARM NIGHT toward the end of Heather's sophomore year, she attended what had become a typical party for her: the host's parents 42 were away, and there was plenty of liquor along with a variety of drugs. Heather wasn't supposed to be there. Through conferences with her guidance counselor, her parents had found out about her doctored grades and her frequent absences. They now suspected alcohol or drugs and grounded her. But that evening her parents had gone out. Heather figured she could slip away and be back before they returned.

Around 10 P.M., she hopped in the back seat of a car with four others for a ride home. Ryan, the driver, was both drunk and stoned. As he stomped on the accelerator on a straight stretch of highway, Heather saw the speedometer pass 100 m.p.h. 43

Moments later, the car slammed into a guardrail, rolled down an embankment and came to rest on its roof. Miraculously, everyone survived. Ryan's face was jammed onto the steering-wheel horn, which blared loudly. Others bled from their faces and dangled broken limbs. Numbed by alcohol, marijuana and cocaine, Heather was oblivious of her own injuries as she helped one of her friends from the tangled wreck. 44

When a person is suddenly injured, neurotransmitters called endorphins lock on to natural opiate receptors in the brain and temporarily block out pain. Marijuana is an analgesic, which provided another method for muting pain. 45

Heather had suffered severe injuries to her back and neck, and would need a year of physical therapy. 46

"I didn't know Ryan had been drinking," Heather lied to her parents. They wanted desperately to believe her. Relieved that she was alive, they forgave her "just this once" for sneaking out. From then on, they warned, they were tightening their watch. But while she recuperated at home, Heather smoked pot secretly. 47

Heather had been dating Charlie Evans. He was handsome, athletic and popular with the girls. He was also heavily into marijuana and cocaine. 48

One evening three months after her accident, Charlie appeared at the front door with an eight-ball of cocaine (about an eighth of an ounce). Her parents were out to dinner. Soon Heather and Charlie were sniffing the white powder through straws. 49

After several lines, her heart began to race, something that had never happened before. She smoked a few joints to "mellow out," but instead she became more jumpy. Looking down, she saw her shirt move with the heavy pounding of her heart. Terrified, she told Charlie to call for help. 50

He dialed 911. "Send someone quick," he yelled. He didn't wait around. "I've got to split before the cops get here," he said, going out the back door. 51

52 En route to the hospital, Heather's heart rate soared to 196 beats a minute. "Talk to us," a paramedic urged. "We don't want to lose you."

53 *Pot is a double-edged sword: it raises the heart's oxygen needs while lowering its supply. Just ten drags on a marijuana cigarette can overstimulate the heart muscle enough to push the heart rate from a normal 70 beats a minute to 100 beats and higher. The heart then needs more oxygen. Yet marijuana also elevates carbon monoxide levels in the blood, diminishing oxygen supply.*

54 *Cocaine, meanwhile, causes the heart to beat inefficiently and its vessels to narrow. With Heather, the combination of drugs made her heart dangerously out of control.*

55 Finding Heather in intensive care and learning that she'd overdosed on cocaine, Diana Brooks broke into anguished cries. This was the wakeup call that Heather had long needed—and her parents too. "You've hit rock bottom" Frank told his daughter later. "We're still your best friends—but we're going to be watching you every minute."

56 Each morning, Frank Brooks waited to leave for work until Heather was on her bus. When she returned, a parent was waiting for her. No more rides with friends. No more parties.

57 That summer, her parents took her to a La Jolla, Calif., beach house to get her away from her "friends." For four full weeks, Heather was shaky, nervous and sweaty as her body adjusted to a healthier lifestyle. She had so much difficulty adapting to any kind of schedule that she wasn't sure when to eat or sleep. Slowly, however, her numbed brain began to function. Frequently, she thought about the time she spent in the hospital: *I almost died, and none of my friends even came to visit.*

58 Returning to Chicago, Heather was as determined to turn her life around as she once seemed determined to destroy it. She doubled up on courses she had failed as a sophomore. The sounds of her piano once again filled the Brooks home.

59 As a senior, Heather traveled to Europe with the school choir. As she stood in an ancient cathedral, her soprano voice joining the others, she recalled the concert when she'd shown up stoned.

60 *Just three years ago,* she thought. *What a different person I am now.*

---

61 *Heather Brooks will always bear scars from her dance with the devil. She still has back pain from the accident, and occasionally she sees afterimages trailing behind moving objects, a legacy of her drug use.*

62 *But her hopes are as big as they once were. In 1995 she entered college, where she maintains high grades. She hopes to attend law school.*

63 *"It was a close call," she says today. "I almost let my dreams go up in a cloud of sweet-smelling smoke."*

THINKING ABOUT THE ESSAY

1. How familiar are you with *Reader's Digest?* From a careful reading of the essay, what can you surmise about the magazine's editorial viewpoint and about the audience it tries to address?
2. What is the main organizational pattern of this essay? Does it seem successful to you or not?
3. A sound argument requires the presentation of supporting ideas and evidence. Does the D'Aulaires' argument contain such reasoned support and evidence? Have they convinced or converted you? Explain.
4. In what style is the essay composed? What is the level of language used? How is the story of "Heather" presented?

RESPONDING IN DISCUSSION

1. Does the story of Heather distract you from the data presented in the italicized sections of the essay or reinforce the data's impact? Explain.
2. Working with classmates, conduct a poll of attitudes toward the D'Aulaires' essay. How many class members are in favor of the D'Aulaires' argument, and how many are opposed? Did the essay change anyone's opinion? Why or why not?
3. In groups of three or four, examine carefully the scientific information presented in this essay. What "process" or causal pattern emerges from the presentation of this data?
4. Examine the paragraphs dealing with the connection between alcohol and marijuana. Do you find this aspect of the argument effective? Explain.

RESPONDING IN WRITING

1. Recent studies indicate a dramatic increase in marijuana use by young people. Write an essay in which you analyze the possible causes for this rise.
2. Conduct a Web search or library search on the issue of marijuana legalization. Obtain useful articles and cite them in an argumentative essay that either advocates or opposes the legalization of pot.
3. Compare and contrast your understanding of marijuana with that of the D'Aulaires. Do you share their beliefs about the effects of marijuana on individuals? Draw your comparison carefully.

Prescriptions for Happiness?

Seymour Fisher, Ph.D., and Roger P. Greenberg, Ph.D.

In Aldous Huxley's novel *Brave New World,* society had legal access to a drug called soma that relieved stress, pain, and unhappiness. When the book first appeared over 50 years ago, few readers thought such a drug would become a reality. In the following essay, initially published in the September–October 1995 issue of *Psychology Today,* Fisher and Greenberg (respected clinicians at a major mental health center) suggest that is just how antidepressant drugs are being marketed today. In many cases, they claim, psychiatrists have decided the cure to inner conflict and problems with life can be had by simply taking a pill. However, the authors believe this form of treatment is not a cure, but only the simple masking of underlying problems. What is more radical, however, is that they claim that the purported benefits of these drugs may not even be a result of the drugs themselves, but merely a result of how the effects of these drugs were interpreted during the research phase of their development. If the authors are right, thousands of doctors are writing millions of prescriptions for drugs that may not have any inherent therapeutic properties. In our age of the U.S. government's Food and Drug Administration's rigorous rules concerning the introduction of drugs, this seems a bit far-fetched. Or is it?

PREVIEWING THE ESSAY

Do the authors present their arguments effectively, powerfully, and consistently? Is it hard for the layperson to argue with their claims? As you read what is apparently a long thought-out argument that challenges the medical establishment, ask yourself these questions: Does this aspect of their argument make sense? Are there other explanations to the situations the authors claim? If their arguments seem so logical, why hasn't anyone else figured out the weaknesses behind the research they analyze?

The air is filled with declarations and advertisements of the power of biological psychiatry to relieve people of their psychological distress. Some biological psychiatrists are so convinced of the superiority of their position that they are recommending young psychiatrists no longer be taught the essentials of doing psychotherapy. Feature stories in such magazines as *Newsweek* and *Time* have portrayed drugs like Prozac as possessing almost a mystical potency. The best-selling book *Listening to Prozac* by psychiatrist Peter Kramer, M.D., projects the idyllic possibility that psychotropic drugs may eventually be capable of correcting a spectrum of personality quirks and lacks. 1

As longtime faculty members of a number of psychiatry departments, we have personally witnessed the gradual but steadily accelerated 2 dedication to the idea that "mental illness" can be mastered with biologically based substances. Yet a careful sifting of the pertinent literature indicates that modesty and skepticism would be more appropriate responses to the research accumulated thus far. In 1989, we first raised radical questions about such biological claims in a book, *The Limits of Biological Treatments for Psychological Distress: Comparisons with Psychotherapy and Placebo* (Lawrence Erlbaum). Our approach has been to filter the studies that presumably anchor them through a series of logical and quantitative (meta-analytic) appraisals.

HOW EFFECTIVE ARE ANTIDEPRESSANT DRUGS?

Antidepressants, one of the major weapons in the biological thera- 3
peutic arsenal, illustrate well the largely unacknowledged uncertainty that exists in the biological approach to psychopathology. We suggest that, at present, no one actually knows how effective antidepressants are. Confident declarations about their potency go well beyond the existing evidence.

To get an understanding of the scientific status of antidepres- 4
sants, we analyzed how much more effective the antidepressants are than inert pills called "placebos." That is, if antidepressants are given to one depressed group and a placebo to another group, how much greater is the recovery of those taking the active drug as compared to those taking the inactive placebo? Generous claims that antidepressants usually produce improvement in about 60 to 70 percent of patients are not infrequent, whereas placebos are said to benefit 25 to 30 percent. If antidepressants were, indeed, so superior to placebos, this would be a persuasive advertisement for the biological approach.

We found 15 major reviews of the antidepressant literature. Surpris- 5
ingly, even the most positive reviews indicate that 30 to 40 percent of studies show no significant difference in response to drug versus placebo! The reviews indicate overall that one-third of patients do not improve with antidepressant treatment, one-third improve with placebos, and an additional third show a response to medication they would not have attained with placebos. In the most optimistic view of such findings, two-thirds of the cases (placebo responders and those who do not respond to anything) do as well with placebo as with active medication.

We also found two large-scale quantitative evaluations (meta- 6
analyses) integrating the outcomes of multiple studies of antidepressants. They clearly indicated, on the average, quite modest therapeutic power.

We were particularly impressed by the large variation in outcomes 7
of studies conducted at multiple clinical sites or centers. Consider a study that compared the effectiveness of an antidepressant among

patients at five different research centers. Although the pooled results demonstrate that the drug was generally more effective than placebo, the results from individual centers reveal much variation. After six weeks of treatment, every one of the six measures of effectiveness showed the antidepressant (imipramine) to be merely equivalent to placebo in two or more of the centers. In two of the settings, a difference favoring the medication was detected on only one of 12 outcome comparisons.

In other words, the pooled, apparently favorable, outcome data 8
conceal that dramatically different results could be obtained as a function of who conducted the study and the specific conditions at each locale. We can only conclude that a good deal of fragility characterized the apparent superiority of drug over placebo. The scientific literature is replete with analogous examples.

Incidentally, we also looked at whether modern studies, which are 9
presumably better protected against bias, use higher doses, and often involve longer treatment periods, show a greater superiority of the antidepressant than did earlier studies. The literature frequently asserts that failures to demonstrate antidepressant superiority are due to such methodological failures as not using high enough doses, and so forth.

We examined this issue in a pool of 16 studies assembled by psychi- 10
atrists John Kane and Jeffrey Lieberman in 1984. These studies all compare a standard drug, such as imipramine or amitriptyline, to a new drug and a placebo. They use clearer diagnostic definitions of depression than did the older studies and also adopt currently accepted standards for dosage levels and treatment duration. When we examined the data, we discovered that the advantage of drug over placebo was modest. Twenty-one percent more of the patients receiving a drug improved as compared to those on the placebo. Actually, most of the studies showed no difference in the percentage of patients significantly improved by drugs. There was no indication that these studies, using more careful methodology, achieved better outcomes than older studies.

Finally, it is crucial to recognize that several studies have established 11
that there is a high rate of relapse among those who have responded positively to an antidepressant but then are taken off treatment. The relapse rate may be 60 percent or more during the first year after treatment cessation. Many studies also show that any benefits of antidepressants wane in a few months, even while the drugs are still being taken. This highlights the complexity of evaluating antidepressants. They may be effective initially, but lose all value over a longer period.

ARE DRUG TRIALS BIASED?

As we burrowed deeper into the antidepressant literature, we learned 12
that there are also crucial problems in the methodology used to evaluate

psychotropic drugs. Most central is the question of whether this methodology properly shields drug trials from bias. Studies have shown that the more open to bias a drug trial is, the greater the apparent superiority of the drug over placebo. So questions about the trustworthiness of a given drug-testing procedure invite skepticism about the results.

The question of potential bias first came to our attention in studies comparing inactive placebos to active drugs. In the classic double-blind design, neither patient nor researcher knows who is receiving drug or placebo. We were struck by the fact that the presumed protection provided by the double-blind design was undermined by the use of placebos that simply do not arouse as many body sensations as do active drugs. Research shows that patients learn to discriminate between drug and placebo largely from body sensations and symptoms. 13

A substance like imipramine, one of the most frequently studied antidepressants, usually causes clearly defined sensations, such as dry mouth, tremor, sweating, constipation. Inactive placebos used in studies of antidepressants also apparently initiate some body sensations, but they are fewer, more inconsistent, and less intense as indicated by the fact that they are less often cited by patients as a source of discomfort causing them to drop out of treatment. 14

Vivid differences between the body sensations of drug and placebo groups could signal to patients as to whether they are receiving an active or an inactive agent. Further, they could supply discriminating cues to those responsible for the patient's day-to-day treatment. Nurses, for example, might adopt different attitudes toward patients they identify as being "on" versus "off" active treatment—and consequently communicate contrasting expectations. 15

THE BODY OF EVIDENCE

This is more than theoretical. Researchers have reported that in a double-blind study of imipramine, it was possible by means of side effects to identify a significant number of the patients taking the active drug. Those patients receiving a placebo have fewer signals (from self and others) indicating they are being actively treated and should be improving. By the same token, patients taking an active drug receive multiple signals that may well amplify potential placebo effects linked to the therapeutic context. Indeed, a doctor's strong belief in the power of the active drug enhances the apparent therapeutic power of the drug or placebo. 16

Is it possible that a large proportion of the difference in effectiveness often reported between antidepressants and placebos can be explained as a function of body sensation discrepancies? It is 17 conceivable, and fortunately there are research findings that shed light on the matter.

Consider an analysis by New Zealand psychologist Richard 18
Thomson. He reviewed double-blind, placebo-controlled studies of antidepressants completed between 1958 and 1972. Sixty-eight had employed an inert placebo and seven an active one (atropine) that produced a variety of body sensations. The antidepressant had a superior therapeutic effect in 59 percent of the studies using inert placebo—but in only one study (14 percent) using the active placebo. The active placebo eliminated any therapeutic advantage for the antidepressants, apparently because it convinced patients they were getting real medication.

HOW BLIND IS DOUBLE-BLIND?

Our concerns about the effects of inactive placebos on the double- 19
blind design led us to ask just how blind the double-blind really is. By the 1950s reports were already surfacing that for psychoactive drugs, the double-blind design is not as scientifically objective as originally assumed. In 1993 we searched the world literature and found 31 reports in which patients and researchers involved in studies were asked to guess who was receiving the active psychotropic drug and who the placebo. In 28 instances the guesses were significantly better than chance—and at times they were surprisingly accurate. In one double-blind study that called for administering either imipramine, phenelzine, or placebo to depressed patients, 78 percent of patients and 87 percent of psychiatrists correctly distinguished drug from placebo.

One particularly systematic report in the literature involved the 20
administration of alprazolam, imipramine, and placebo over an eight-week period to groups of patients who experienced panic attacks. Halfway through the treatment and also at the end, the physicians and the patients were asked to judge independently whether each patient was receiving an active drug or a placebo. If they thought an active drug was being administered, they had to decide whether it was alprazolam or imipramine. Both physicians (with an 88 percent success rate) and patients (83 percent) substantially exceeded chance in the correctness of their judgments. Furthermore, the physicians could distinguish alprazolam from imipramine significantly better than chance. The researchers concluded that "double-blind studies of these pharmacological treatments for panic disorder are not really 'blind.'"

Yet the vast majority of psychiatric drug efficacy studies have 21
simply *assumed* that the double-blind design is effective; they did not

test the blindness by determining whether patients and researchers were able to differentiate drug from placebo.

We take the somewhat radical view that this means most past studies of the efficacy of psychotropic drugs are, to unknown degrees, scientifically untrustworthy. At the least, we can no longer speak with confidence about the true differences in therapeutic power between active psychotropic drugs and placebos. We must suspend judgment until future studies are completed with more adequate controls for the defects of the double-blind paradigm. 22

Other bothersome questions arose as we scanned the cascade of studies focused on antidepressants. Of particular concern is how unrepresentative the patients are who end up in the clinical trials. There are the usual sampling problems having to do with which persons seek treatment for their discomfort, and, in addition, volunteer as subjects for a study. But there are others. Most prominent is the relatively high proportion of patients who "drop out" before the completion of their treatment programs. 23

Numerous dropouts occur in response to unpleasant side effects. In many published studies, 35 percent or more of patients fail to complete the research protocol. Various procedures have been developed to deal fairly with the question of how to classify the therapeutic outcomes of dropouts, but not can vitiate the simple fact that the final sample of fully treated patients has often been drastically reduced. 24

There are still other filters that increase sample selectivity. For example, studies often lose sizable segments of their samples by not including patients who are too depressed to speak, much less participate in a research protocol, or who are too disorganized to participate in formal psychological testing. We also found decisions not to permit particular racial or age groups to be represented in samples or to avoid using persons below a certain educational level. Additionally, researchers typically recruit patients whose depression is not accompanied by any other type of physical or mental disorder, a situation that does not hold for the depressed in the general population. 25

So we end up wondering about the final survivors in the average drug trial. To what degree do they typify the average individual in real life who seeks treatment? How much can be generalized from a sample made up of the "leftovers" from multiple depleting processes? Are we left with a relatively narrow band of those most willing to conform to the rather rigid demands of the research establishment? Are the survivors those most accepting of a dependent role? 26

The truth is that there are probably multiple kinds of survivors, depending upon the specific local conditions prevailing where the study was carried out. We would guess that some of the striking differences in results that appear in multicenter drug studies could be traced to specific forms of sampling bias. We do not know how 27 psychologically unique the persons are who get recruited into, and stick with, drug research enterprises. We are not the first to raise this question, but we are relatively more alarmed about the potential implications.

RESEARCHER MOTIVATION AND OUTCOME

We recently conducted an analysis that further demonstrates how 28
drug effectiveness diminishes as the opportunity for bias in research design wanes. This analysis seized on studies in which a newer antidepressant is compared (under double-blind conditions) with an older, standard antidepressant and a placebo. In such a context the efficacy of the newer drug (which the drug company hopes to introduce) is of central interest to the researcher, and the effectiveness of the older drug of peripheral import. Therefore if the double-blind is breached (as is likely), there would presumably be less bias to enhance the efficacy of the older drug than occurred in the original trials of that drug.

We predicted that the old drug would appear significantly less 29
powerful in the newer studies than it had in earlier designs, where it was of central interest to the researcher. To test this hypothesis, we located 22 double-blind studies in which newer antidepressants were compared with an older antidepressant drug (usually imipramine) and a placebo. Our meta-analysis revealed, as predicted, that the efficacy rates, based on clinicians' judgments of outcome, were quite modest for the older antidepressants. In fact, they were approximately one-half to one-quarter the average size of the effects reported in earlier studies when the older drug was the only agent appraised.

Let us be very clear as to what this signifies: When researchers 30
were evaluating the antidepressant in a context where they were no longer interested in proving its therapeutic power, there was a dramatic decrease in that apparent power, as compared to an earlier context when they were enthusiastically interested in demonstrating the drug's potency. A change in researcher motivation was enough to change outcome. Obviously this means too that the present double-blind design for testing drug efficacy is exquisitely vulnerable to bias.

Another matter of pertinence to the presumed biological rationale 31
for the efficacy of antidepressants is that no consistent links have been demonstrated between the concentration of drug in blood and its efficacy. Studies have found significant correlations for some drugs, but of low magnitude. Efforts to link plasma levels to therapeutic outcome have been disappointing.

Similarly, few data show a relationship between antidepressant 32
dosage levels and their therapeutic efficacy. That is, large doses of the

drug do not necessarily have greater effects than low doses. These inconsistencies are a bit jarring against the context of a biological explanatory framework.

We have led you through a detailed critique of the difficulties and problems that prevail in the body of research testing the power of the antidepressants. We conclude that it would be wise to be relatively modest in claims about their efficacy. Uncertainty and doubt are inescapable. 33

While we have chosen the research on the antidepressants to illustrate the uncertainties attached to biological treatments of psychological distress, reviews of other classes of psychotropic drugs yield similar findings. After a survey of anti-anxiety drugs, psychologist Ronald Lipman concluded there is little consistent evidence that they help patients with anxiety disorders: "Although it seems natural to assume that the anxiolytic medications would be the most effective psychotropic medications for the treatment of anxiety disorders, the evidence does not support this assumption." 34

BIOLOGICAL VERSUS PSYCHOLOGICAL?

The faith in the biological approach has been fueled by a great burst of research. Thousands of papers have appeared probing the efficacy of psychotropic drugs. A good deal of basic research has attacked fundamental issues related to the nature of brain functioning in those who display psychopathology. Researchers in these areas are dedicated and often do excellent work. However, in their zeal, in their commitment to the so-called biological, they are at times overcome by their expectations. Their hopes become rigidifying boundaries. Their vocabulary too easily becomes a jargon that camouflages oversimplified assumptions. 35

A good example of such oversimplification is the way in which the term *biological* is conceptualized. It is too often viewed as a realm distinctly different from the psychological. Those invested in the biological approach all too often practice the ancient Cartesian distinction between somatic-stuff and soul-stuff. In so doing they depreciate the scientific significance of the phenomena they exile to the soul-stuff category. 36

But paradoxically, they put a lot of interesting phenomena out of bounds to their prime methodology and restrict themselves to a narrowed domain. For example, if talk therapy is labeled as a "psychological" thing—not biological—this implies that biological research can only hover at the periphery of what psychotherapists do. A sizable block of behavior becomes off limits to the biologically dedicated. 37

In fact, if we adopt the view that the biological and psychological 38
are equivalent (biological monism), there is no convincing real-versus-unreal differentiation between the so-called psychological and biological. It *all* occurs in tissue and one is not more "real" than the other. A patient's attitude toward the therapist is just as biological in nature as a patient's response to an antidepressant. A response to a placebo is just as biological as a response to an antipsychotic drug. This may be an obvious point, but it has not yet been incorporated into the world views of either the biologically or psychologically oriented.

Take a look at a few examples in the research literature that high- 39
light the overlap or identity of what is so often split apart. In 1992, psychiatrist Lewis Baxter and colleagues showed that successful psychotherapy of obsessive-compulsive patients results in brain imagery changes equivalent to those produced by successful drug treatment. The brain apparently responds in equivalent ways to both the talk and drug approaches. Even more dramatic is a finding that instilling in the elderly the illusion of being in control of one's surroundings (by putting them in charge of some plants) significantly increased their life span compared to a control group. What could be a clearer demonstration of the biological nature of what is labeled as a psychological expectation than the postponement of death?

Why are we focusing on this historic Cartesian confusion? Be- 40
cause so many who pursue the so-called biological approach are by virtue of their tunnel vision motivated to overlook the psychosocial variables that mediate the administration of such agents as psychotropic drugs and electroconvulsive therapy. They do not permit themselves to seriously grasp that psychosocial variables are just as biological as a capsule containing an antidepressant. It is the failure to understand this that results in treating placebo effects as if they were extraneous or less of a biological reality than a chemical agent.

PLACEBO EFFECTS

Indeed, placebos have been shown to initiate certain effects usually 41
thought to be reserved for active drugs. For example, placebos clearly show dose-level effects. A larger dose of a placebo will have a greater impact than a lower dose. Placebos can also create addictions. Patients will poignantly declare that they cannot stop taking a particular placebo substance (which they assume is an active drug) because to do so causes them too much distress and discomfort.

Placebos can produce toxic effects such as rashes, apparent mem- 42
ory loss, fever, headaches, and more. These "toxic" effects may be painful and even overwhelming in their intensity. The placebo literature

is clear: Placebos are powerful body-altering substances, especially considering the wide range of body systems they can influence.

Actually, the power of the placebo complicates all efforts to test the 43
therapeutic efficacy of psychotropic drugs. When placebos alone can produce positive curative effects in the 40 to 50 percent range (occasionally even up to 70–80 percent), the active drug being tested is hard-pressed to demonstrate its superiority. Even if the active drug exceeds the placebo in potency, the question remains whether the advantage is at least partially due to the superior potential of the active drug itself to mobilize placebo effects because it is an active substance that stirs vivid body sensations. Because it is almost always an inactive substance (sugar pill) that arouses fewer genuine body sensations, the placebo is less convincingly perceived as having therapeutic prowess.

Drug researchers have tried, in vain, to rid themselves of placebo 44
effects, but these effects are forever present and frustrate efforts to demonstrate that psychoactive drugs have an independent "pure" biological impact. This state of affairs dramatically testifies that the labels "psychological" and "biological" refer largely to different perspectives on events that all occur in tissue. At present, it is somewhat illusory to separate the so-called biological and psychological effects of drugs used to treat emotional distress.

The literature is surprisingly full of instances of how social and 45
attitudinal factors modify the effects of active drugs. Antipsychotic medications are more effective if the patient likes rather than dislikes the physician administering them. An antipsychotic drug is less effective if patients are led to believe they are only taking an inactive placebo. Perhaps even more impressive, if a stimulant drug is administered with the deceptive instruction that it is a sedative, it can initiate a pattern of physiological response, such as decreased heart rate, that is sedative rather than arousing in nature. Such findings reaffirm how fine the line is between social and somatic domains.

What are the practical implications for distressed individuals and 46
their physicians? Administering a drug is not simply a medical (biological) act. It is, in addition, a complex social act whose effectiveness will be mediated by such factors as the patient's expectations of the drug and reactions to the body sensations created by that drug, and the physician's friendliness and degree of personal confidence in the drug's power. Practitioners who dispense psychotropic medications should become thoroughly acquainted with the psychological variables modifying the therapeutic impact of such drugs and tailor their own behavior accordingly. By the same token, distressed people seeking drug treatment should keep in mind that their probability of benefiting may depend in part on whether they choose a practitioner they truly like and respect. And remember this: You are the ultimate arbiter of a drug's efficacy.

How to go about mastering unhappiness, which ranges from "feeling blue" to despairing depression, puzzles everyone. Such popular quick fixes as alcohol, conversion to a new faith, and other splendid distractions have proven only partially helpful. When antidepressant drugs hit the shelves with their seeming scientific aura, they were easily seized upon. Apparently serious unhappiness (depression) could now be chemically neutralized in the way one banishes a toothache. 47

But the more we learn about the various states of unhappiness, the more we recognize that they are not simply "symptoms" awaiting removal. Depressed feelings have complex origins and functions. In numerous contexts—for example, chronic conflict with a spouse—depression may indicate a realistic appraisal of a troubling problem and motivate a serious effort to devise a solution. 48

While it is true that deep despair may interfere with sensible problem-solving, the fact is that, more and more, individuals are being instructed to take antidepressants at the earliest signs of depressive distress and this could interfere with the potentially constructive signaling value of such distress. Emotions are feelings full of information. Unhappiness is an emotion, and despite its negativity, should not be classified single-mindedly as a thing to tune out. This in no way implies that one should submit passively to the discomfort of feeling unhappy. Actually, we all learn to experiment with a variety of strategies for making ourselves feel better, but the ultimate aim is long-term effective action rather than a depersonalized "I feel fine." 49

THINKING ABOUT THE ESSAY

1. Universities often pay students to participate in all sorts of studies in return for a sum of money. Have you or any of your acquaintances ever participated in such a study? What is your attitude toward such studies and the researchers? Do you think you were being tricked by the researcher for the sake of proving a research question? Did you try to fool the researcher? Explain.
2. Fisher and Greenberg use vocabulary that pertains to the scientific and/or psychiatric professions. Look up any words unfamiliar to you such as *psychotropic, placebo, meta-analysis* and *double-blind* in a medical dictionary. Does a clearer understanding of the meaning of these terms make you feel more competent in understanding the intellectual universe of the essay? Explain.
3. Through the gradual cataloging of numerous research studies, Fisher and Greenberg build a long list of supporting evidence to advance their argument. Review the text and list the number of studies they critique, as well as the various types of confounding

factors they present to challenge the studies. Is their body of evidence sufficient to convince you of their argument? Do you see alternative views on interpreting their reasoning? Or do you feel you are not qualified to make an assessment? Explain.

4. What specific message are the authors sending concerning the nature of studies of antidepressant drugs? What general message might they be suggesting about observation and perception in general?

RESPONDING IN DISCUSSION

1. Divide into groups of three and four. Use personal experience in discussing how desired outcomes sometimes interfered with your accurate perception of an event or situation. Share your findings with the class.
2. Discuss in class what personal qualities or attributes you have that might make your observations and perceptions prone to distortion. Consider such things as your age, gender, and allegiance to a team, community, or country.
3. Are there any particular characteristics of scientific researchers that might make them prone to disregard certain evidence that a person with a different perspective might find relevant? Take for example a study attempting to determine the efficiency of an automobile. How might the conclusions of an engineer conducting research in a laboratory differ from the conclusions of a teenager test-driving the same vehicle?
4. The authors state in the final paragraph, "Emotions are feelings full of information." Based on your reading and your own experience, explain this sentence in your own words. How similar or different is your explanation from other responses in the class? To what do you attribute these differences?
5. Research the pros and cons of Prozac on the Web, as if you were a patient trying to protect yourself from the potential biases of your doctor. Treat the information in the Fisher/Greenberg article as if you had heard it from a concerned friend, and search the Web for enough substantiation to question your doctor.

RESPONDING IN WRITING

1. Describe a time in your life when you felt depressed. How did you respond? What did you or others do to make yourself feel better?
2. Assume the role of a researcher involved in one of the studies that the authors investigated. Defend your research and provide

an argument expressing your own view on why the authors' conclusions regarding your research are mistaken.

3. Arrange a meeting with three members from the student health staff or other branch of your school that deals with health issues. Have them read the article. Then, in a round table forum, discuss their responses to the article. Write a summary of their responses and conclusions.
4. Argue for or against the proposition that the Food and Drug Administration (FDA) should immediately sponsor new research into the efficacy of antidepressant drugs, using the authors' findings in this essay as a rationale.
5. Locate the Food and Drug Administration's website and scan it for information on antidepressant drugs. Condense your findings and write a report describing the FDA's policy on the subject.

Perceptions and Misperceptions of Race and Drug Use

Mindy Thompson Fullilove

Fullilove, in an editorial published in the February 24, 1993, issue of *The Journal of the American Medical Association* (*JAMA*), addresses the stereotypes many Americans have of the typical drug abuser, specifically those who take crack cocaine. Media images of this group, whether they are depicted on television news or popular police shows, often involve inner-city black adolescent abusers. But Fullilove claims that stereotyping such drug use may be considered "artifactual," in other words the result of a more deeply rooted correlation. In this case, the author argues, the correlation between crack cocaine use and one's neighborhood is a more appropriate and useful means of understanding and solving the problem. What is interesting about this sociologically oriented editorial is not so much its subject matter, but the fact that it was published in a magazine that is usually identified with medical science and research. This may be a sign that the concerns of doctors and other health professionals are widening beyond the limits of pure science.

PREVIEWING THE ESSAY

What are some of the "risk markers" that can identify whether someone is prone to using illicit substances? If one were to place a 75-year-old senior citizen female next to an 18-year-old adolescent male wearing an earring, whom do you believe would be the one most likely to use crack cocaine? Most

Americans would agree it would be the latter. Thus, the risk marker might be age, dress, and appearance. But this would not answer the question of why the latter was selected as the more likely candidate. Why does the author of this essay claim that in exploring correlations with crack cocaine use, it is more significant to consider the neighborhood, economics, and politics than it is to consider the easily available correlation of race? In other words, what is the significance of focusing on the *why* rather than the *who*?

In 1990 I coauthored an article entitled "Risk for Sexually Transmitted Diseases Among Black Adolescent Crack Users in Oakland and San Francisco, Calif."[1] We became interested in the connection between crack cocaine and sexually transmitted diseases because data from the Centers for Disease Control and Prevention, Atlanta, and from the San Francisco Department of Health indicated that gonorrhea rates among 15- to 19-year-old black women in the Bay Area had been increasing dramatically in neighborhoods that were also reporting high rates of crack cocaine–related arrests. We confined our survey to black adolescents because they were identified as being at greatest risk for both gonorrhea and involvement with crack cocaine sales and use in the Bay Area. One regrettable (but predictable) outcome of publishing this article, however, was that it contributed to an already pervasive belief that "crack is a black problem" or, worse, that crack use in the United States is confined to black, inner-city communities. 1

The study conducted by Lillie-Blanton and colleagues[2] that appears in this issue of *The Journal* takes significant steps to correct this perception. It offers strong evidence that race-specific explanations of crack use may, in fact, obscure the role that environmental and social characteristics play in the epidemiology of crack use. The authors' call for future studies of drug use that seek to include epidemiologic analyses of neighborhood-level social conditions is particularly important because, unlike race, many of these conditions are potentially modifiable through social, economic, and political interventions. 2

The United States remains a society where place of residence is highly correlated with race. It seems reasonable to suggest, therefore, that many studies describing a significant association between race and health status may in fact have described associations that are better explained by variables representing individual living conditions and/or characteristics of the social environment. 3

A 1981 study of gonorrhea infection in Colorado Springs, Colo., provides important support for this hypothesis. Potterat and 4

[1]Fullilove RE, Fullilove MT, Bowser BP, Gross SA. Risk of sexually transmitted disease among black adolescent crack users in Oakland and San Francisco, Calif. *JAMA*. 1990; 263: 851–855.

[2]Lillie-Blanton M, Anthony JC, Schuster CR. Probing the meaning of racial/ethnic group comparisons in crack cocaine smoking. *JAMA*. 1993; 269: 993–997.

colleagues[3] observed a significant association between risk for gonorrhea and age, membership in the military, and nonwhite race. To interpret these findings, the authors interviewed all infected cases and their partners and obtained information concerning where respondents lived and socialized, as well as how long they had known their partners prior to having sexual relations. The authors mapped responses and subsequently observed that one fifth of the community's census tracts contained four fifths of the gonorrhea cases, and that six of the community's 302 drinking establishments accounted for one half of the citations made by gonorrhea cases as places where they had recently socialized.

Potterat and colleagues' findings imply that race is the "epidemio- 5
logic clue" described by Lillie-Blanton and colleagues, viz., a proxy for important aspects of the cultural and social life of individuals. By going beyond surveillance data and examining the social milieu in which cases occurred, Potterat and colleagues are able to offer an important lesson: that there is more to understanding the risk factors for sexually transmitted diseases than is subsumed in the biology of race.

The observation that conditions such as drug abuse and sexually 6
transmitted diseases occur within social networks that have well-defined boundaries in communities and neighborhoods can also be inferred from other studies, for example, of the epidemiology of the acquired immunodeficiency syndrome in Belle Glade, Fla.,[4] or of the epidemiology of deaths from the acquired immunodeficiency syndrome in the South Bronx, N.Y.[5,6] In these studies there is a significant association between nonwhite race and disease status, but the geographic clustering of cases suggests that what we are really seeing is the manner in which residents of a particular community interact with each other.

Is it ever appropriate to use race as an explanatory variable in 7
biomedical or public health research in general or, more specifically, in studies that examine diseases associated with promiscuity or antisocial behavior? The answer, of course, is "yes." However, we must be precise about the research questions that we pose and the relationship race plays in the analyses we conduct. As suggested by Osborne and Feit[7] in a Commentary in *The Journal* devoted to this topic, "To

[3] Potterat JJ, Rothenberg RB, Woodhouse DE, Muth JB, Pratts CI, Fogle JS. Gonorrhea as a social disease. *Sex Transm Dis.* 1985; 12: 25–32.

[4] Castro KG, Lieb S, Jaffe HW, et al. Transmission of HIV in Belle Glade, Florida: lessons for other communities in the United States. *Science.* 1988; 239: 193–197.

[5] Wallace R, Fullilove MT, Widlace D. Family systems and deurbanization: implications for substance abuse. In: Lowinson JH, Ruiz P, Millman R, eds. *Substance Abuse: A Comprehensive Textbook.* 2nd ed. Baltimore, Md: Williams and Wilkins; 1992: 944–955.

[6] Wallace R. A synergism of plagues: 'planned shrinkage,' contagious housing destruction and AIDS in the Bronx. *Environ Res.* 1988; 47: 1–33.

[7] Osborne NG, Feit MD. The use of race in medical research. *JAMA.* 1992; 267: 275–279.

avoid erroneous conclusions, it is essential that authors define terms clearly, state the hypotheses on which the studies are based, and make a distinction between race as a risk factor and race as a risk marker." Lillie-Blanton and colleagues have pointed us in the appropriate direction by demonstrating that the frequently cited association between race and crack use does not signal the end of our investigations of this public health dilemma, but rather the beginning.

THINKING ABOUT THE ESSAY

1. Imagine a crack cocaine user. Who comes to mind? What is his or her race, age, gender, and dress? How do you suppose you developed this image?
2. What personal reasons did Fullilove have for writing this editorial? In terms of long-range policy, what were her motives for writing it?
3. What do we mean by the term *editorial?* What distinguishing features does it have from other forms of essay writing? How does this particular essay fit within the bounds of the editorial genre? How does it move beyond the standard editorial—for example, in the use of footnotes and documentation?
4. One sociologist defined her profession as finding the "cause of the cause" of human behavior. What does this mean? What significance does this definition have for the argument of this essay?

RESPONDING IN DISCUSSION

1. Divide into groups of three and four, and consider the title of the essay. Have each member explain his or her interpretation of it. If possible, come up with a shared explanation. Explain the group's response to the rest of the class.
2. The author states that "we must be precise about the research questions that we pose and the relationship race plays in the analyses we conduct." What does she mean by this statement?
3. The author attributes "neighborhood-level social conditions" as being important factors in one's use of crack cocaine, but she fails to discuss the "family-level condition". How important are a family's makeup, values, and behaviors in determining whether someone will use crack cocaine, regardless of one's neighborhood?
4. Sum up the message of this editorial in one sentence. Discuss your summary with the rest of the class. How similar or dissimilar is it to the responses of your classmates?

RESPONDING IN WRITING

1. Write a personal essay of approximately 400 words about a time in your life when you prejudged someone based upon their appearance only to find out later that you were off-base. Explain what factors in the person's appearance led to your stereotyping.
2. Write your own 250-word extended definition of the term *public health.*
3. Argue for or against the following proposition: Experience is the best teacher, so a member of a particular neighborhood is apt to give you more accurate information about illicit drug use in the neighborhood than an "imported" researcher can.
4. For a research paper that should include library and Web investigation, write an essay entitled "The Economics of Crack Cocaine," exploring it as a business. Consider such issues as supply and demand, organizational hierarchies, market research, and consumer identification.

CONNECTIONS: FOR WRITING AND RESEARCH

1. Write an essay comparing and contrasting the general deficiencies that Fisher and Greenberg point out in antidepressant research with the deficiencies Fullilove discusses concerning crack cocaine research. Pay particular attention to the concept of perception in researcher conclusions.
2. What are the risk factors Herbert points out of an individual's likelihood to start smoking? Would you include any that he has left out?
3. In her essay, Fullilove observes that drug abuse occurs "within social networks that have well-defined boundaries in communities and neighborhoods." Describe the type of community where Susan Cheever grew up. What elements of that community would contribute to her family's rituals and her own use of alcohol?
4. Select five magazine ads that promote drinking or five that promote smoking. Write an expository essay explaining how the use of models, imagery, props, color, and design are used to make each activity seem pleasurable in each ad. Attach the ads to the back of your essay so your instructor can use them as references.
5. Select from among the essays in this section the one that discusses the addiction you find most reprehensible. Write an argumentative essay explaining why you believe the drug you chose is the most potentially damaging to our society.
6. Argue for or against the proposition that there are such things as "positive addictions." Refer to at least two essays in this chapter to support your position.

7

POPULAR ENTERTAINMENT

With the proliferation of newer forms and modes of media—digital TV, video, interactive computers, on-line services, CD players, virtual reality machines—adding to the traditional ones such as film, radio, newspapers, magazines, and books, it may not be as profitable to ask "how much time do you spend with the media?" as it is to ask "how much time do you spend *apart* from the media?" Our reliance on the media for education, information, entertainment, aesthetic pleasure, and companionship has caused social critics to blame the media for determining the outcome of elections, increasing the crime rate, lowering the level of literacy, setting our family values, altering the quality of our personal relationships, and a host of other acts. As media monopolies rake in vast fortunes while social scientists and philosophers garner grants to study their influence, we, the users (or is it the used?) are bombarded by vast arrays, forms, and modes of information as rapidly as virtual bombs fall on an electronically imaged city in a video arcade game. Some of the loudest protests over the proliferation of media concern its effect on youth. Several of the essays in Chapter 7 address this issue. A radio talk show host has said, "I let my children watch television as much as they want. I just don't let them turn it on." But as you will see from the following essays, the appeal of "pop-acculturated" media may be too seductive and appealing for such a tactic to work.

Bimbo Watch

Judith Timson

Judith Timson, writing in the November 27, 1995, issue of the popular Canadian magazine *Maclean's*, attempts to debunk the idea that television and film are progressing in their efforts to reduce the display of women as sex objects. True, drama series offer a few female surgeons and attorneys who are meant to be admired for their brains and not their behinds, and a movie may portray a woman as a no-nonsense social reformer rather than a shapely form, but there is always a babe with her low-cut gown, bra-less T-shirt, and spandex shorts, or skimpy skirt waiting nearby, available by merely channel-surfing or changing screens at the local multiplex. Still, as most people know, in business it's the financial bottom line that counts, and the images that boost the profit margin the highest are bound to be the ones that proliferate.

PREVIEWING THE ESSAY

A male Generation X entrepreneur specializing in computer pornography recently attributed his newly found wealth to exploiting a combination of two phenomena that appeal to men: sex and technology. But his success may be due to merely "placing old wine in new bottles." Is the prevalence of exploiting women as sex objects in the visual media simply a matter of a producer taking advantage of basic instincts, or is he (or even she) promoting an image of women that is manipulative, being a sort of "visual drug dealer" who is secretly hooking viewers on a lifetime habit?

There is such a thing as the Official Breast, according to Naomi Wolf, 1
author of *The Beauty Myth*. The Official Breast is large, high, firm, perfectly proportioned and almost unattainable for most normal women. Pamela Anderson—or Pamela Lee, as she is now known—has the ultimate Official Breasts, and they appear regularly on "Baywatch," the California beach show in which even the sand castles look structurally enhanced.

With dialogue so banal ("There's been, like, no waves, all day") 2
that it makes "Melrose Place" look like *War and Peace*, "Baywatch" seems aimed primarily at the teenage market—which means that preteens would enjoy it. I discovered the show earlier this fall when an 11-year-old boy I know reported, mystified, that at his summer camp, several boys were jumping around the tent in ecstasy at the mention of Pamela Lee.

This is not uplifting news. Indeed, it's not even news, but simply 3
spandex-clad proof that more than three decades of feminism notwithstanding, nothing much has changed: bimbos, babes, breasts

and—a little further from "Baywatch"'s sunny shores—bitches still hold tremendous sway in popular culture.

I don't mean to do her wrong, but Lee's character, C. J. Parker—a 4
lifeguard with "a sunny Zen," as her newsclips would have it—is not taken seriously. The truth is, other blond beach girls make fun of her, accusing their love interests of flirting with her just because, as someone called Summer snippily put it in one episode, "she was probably running around in something skimpy."

When it comes to portrayals of women in the mass media these 5
days, we are all running around in something a little skimpy. You could call it giving real equality the short shrift, despite the surface nod to many tenets of modern feminism. Female news anchors abound, you can see amazingly feisty girl rock 'n' roll musicians on "MuchMusic," and in sitcom country, some mighty powerful women ride the range—Candice Bergen's wonderfully mouthy journalist, Murphy Brown, Ellen DeGeneres's gently subversive Ellen, and the deeply anarchistic, incomparable Roseanne. On the other hand, Marge Simpson, you're wanted in Remedial Feminism 101 . . . and take The Nanny, and Home Improvement's Tool Time Girl (who, coincidentally, used to be played by Lee) with you. But as for that big-haired, brain-dead wife and her equally inane daughter on "Married . . . with Children," don't bother, there should just be a permanent zap button on the channel changer to rid the screen of them forever.

Such outrage may be bracing, but it is not a simple matter these 6
days to assess how women are faring in popular culture. American author Susan J. Douglas, in her book *Where the Girls Are: Growing Up Female with the Mass Media,* an astute romp through the mass media's influence on girls and women from the Fifties to the present, puts it this way: "The war that has been raging in the media is not a simplistic war against women but a complex struggle between feminism and anti-feminism that has reflected, reinforced and exaggerated our culture's ambivalence about women's roles for over 35 years."

It's a mouthful, but what it means is, yes, on many prime-time 7
shows today you will see women portrayed as professionals—lawyers, judges and brain surgeons. But you don't need to be a brain surgeon to figure out that, as women become more powerful in real life, their clothes get tighter and shorter in the make-believe-it's-real world of television.

"Baywatch"—seemingly innocent of any more complex nuance 8
than "hey, why put on real clothes if we look this good in bathing suits?"—offers up endless variations on the scantily clad theme: women running on the beach half-naked, women playing handball half-naked, women doing their important paramedical duties half-naked, even giving mouth-to-mouth resuscitation (their revival rate is extraordinary).

Lest that not be enough evidence of babe-ism—i.e., not taking 9
women seriously by virtue of focusing primarily on their body parts—the show features most of these underdressed females (haven't they ever heard of coverups?) deferring, charmingly, to the male superhero as played by David Hasselhoff. That would be Mitch, head lifeguard. At least he rates a T-shirt, now and then.

While some of the plot lines, especially those featuring Mitch's 10
adorable son, Hobie, are sort of sweet and engaging, the values of "Baywatch"—now beamed worldwide to countries in which the kind of lifestyle the show celebrates might as well take place on Mars—are resolutely conservative. "I guess I don't believe in living together before marriage," muses the much more modestly endowed Stephanie, one of the few non-blonds on the show. Of course, Mitch smiles his approval.

Other television shows are more crafty. They talk a good game, 11
many of them showing snappy, independent young women going about their lives. But gender equality is simply not about ripping open a shower curtain to see a male character's "thing," as one of the bright young women on the smash hit sitcom "Friends" did last season, because he inadvertently saw her "boobies" while she was getting dressed. That's just majorly immature. And besides, didn't we already do this in the Seventies with that wacky Suzanne Somers in "Three's Company"?

I watched "Baywatch" with a savvy 13-year-old-girl. She enjoyed 12
the slo-mo of actor David Charvet bounding across the beach ("himbos" get great visual display here, too), but mostly she seemed bored. Moreover, she offered a coolly derisive "you've got to be kidding" when asked if she felt she had to live up to the beach bunny image in real life.

However, the teen magazines she and other girls buy today tell a 13
different story. They obsess, of course, about weight—"Want to ditch flab fast?"—but also about cleavage, about being a babe, albeit in a clever way: "Rule his world in a dress that glows." Some magazines feature prom dresses that would not look out of place on Oscar night, and one wonders how many teenage girls feel about having to fill out the top part of the dress.

Pop culture has become increasingly sexualized, and the result may 14
well be, despite the gains made by feminism, a bleak—and dangerous—time for young girls. But the sexualized culture cuts both ways: in a classroom of 13-year-old girls I recently sat in on, one said without a tad of embarrassment that she doesn't bother watching the crotches of her male friends "because they're so wimpy."

Which brings us back to the boys in the tent. Are they going to be 15
imprinted like hapless little ducks, jolted into hormonal action only by the likes of Pamela Lee? Probably not. Last year, I also sat in on a lively and poignant all-boy Grade 8 seminar at a Toronto alternative school, a school which stresses, above all, gender equality. While

some boys admitted that the first things they noticed about a girl were "her face," "her breasts" and possibly "her personality," one boy swooned over the Darlene character on "Roseanne"—not your basic bimbo. Moreover, several others seemed truly aghast about the pressure the girls they know feel to look a certain way (not quite seeing, however, their own connection to this pressure).

The search for a perfect body—on "Baywatch" there is no other— takes its toll on females of all ages. "Forget what 'Baywatch' does to young people, what about us?" wailed a 40-year-old woman. Those Grade 8 boys had a unique perspective on that: "My mom is always standing in front of the mirror complaining she's fat," said one of them. "I get tired of saying to her, 'Aw, Mom, you're not fat, now can I go out to play?'" 16

Just a little further down the road from the body brigade is the bitch bandwagon. Heather Locklear's venomous Amanda on "Melrose Place" (where, according to the show's ads, "the affairs are short and the skirts are shorter") may qualify to some critics and many viewers as mindless fun, but there is a nasty aftertaste. People who like women don't build entire television series around such a modern-day Cruella de Vil. 17

And for real, money-making misogyny, it is hard to top *True Lies,* the Arnold Schwarzenegger/Jamie Lee Curtis adventure-spy flick that was one of the top-grossing movies of 1994, a movie that older kids adore. From the famous opening sequence in which Arnold (aka Harry) is told to "ditch the bitch" (a cleavage-baring bad girl played by Tia Carrere), it does not go well for women. The bad girl gets smacked hard across the face, called a "stupid, undisciplined bitch" and ends up in a blouse-ripping cat fight with Curtis. Jamie Lee, playing the smart but ostensibly demure Helen, wife of Harry, is the object of the worst line in the movie. A creep named Simon gloats about her to Harry, not knowing she is his wife. "I got her pantin' like a dog. . . . She's got the most incredible body—a pair of titties that make you want to stand up and beg for buttermilk, an ass like a 10-year-old boy." 18

It is true that Harry subsequently beats up on Simon. But clearly, what he is really ticked off about is that this drooling, sexist slimeball is after his wife—oh, those property rights! Curiously, there were complaints from the American-Arab Anti-Discrimination Committee about the movie's treatment of Arabs, who are the story's main villains, but there was nary a peep from any quarter about its treatment of women. Is this, too, just mindless fun, and if so, what message does it send to male viewers of any age? 19

As for female viewers, we can take heart from author Douglas's opinion that among these persistent television and movie images of babes, bitches and bimbos, women were, and are, capable of "finding 20 feminist empowerment in the most unlikely places." From watching Joan Collins on "Dynasty," for instance, you could learn how to be assertive in your own life, says Douglas.

Perhaps this could mean taking away from "Baywatch" the resolution to be a stronger swimmer. But if you're really interested in sexual equality, you might be better off drawing your own line in the sand. Click! 21

THINKING ABOUT THE ESSAY

1. Have you watched any of the TV shows or films discussed in the essay or seen similarly styled shows? What was your personal response to seeing the blatant portrayal of women as sex objects?
2. To what degree has watching TV or films with alluring sexual characters determined the way you behave toward or view the opposite sex? To what degree has it influenced the way you dress?
3. Timson combines personal reflection and observation as supports in her essay without a statistic in sight. Is this an effective way of supporting her thesis? Explain.
4. What, specifically, does Timson view as the dangers of portraying women as sex objects in the media? Do you believe her views are well-founded or exaggerated? Why?

RESPONDING IN DISCUSSION

1. Have the class divide into groups of three or four. In group discussion, examine whether the portrayal of women as sex objects is a response to economic opportunity, the producers' true perspective of the nature of women, or a combination of both. Discuss your conclusions with the rest of the class.
2. Do TV and film producers gear their "product" to teens and preteens, adults, or both? Explain your view.
3. What other negative qualities (other than focusing solely on women's sexual attributes) do film and TV suggest about women when they are portrayed as babes?
4. Discuss with the class your own observations about the influence of watching programs that promote the "three B's" (bimbos, babes, and breasts) on your friends or acquaintances or society at large.
5. Discuss your view of the author's conclusion/solution. Is it practical? Is it naive? Is it simplistic? Explain your view.

RESPONDING IN WRITING

1. Write a letter of 400 to 500 words to the president of a major television network, voicing your opinion about programming that focuses on "bimbos, babes, breasts . . . and bitches."
2. Attend a movie or watch a television show that has—as one of its appeals—the portrayal of women as sex objects. Write an expository essay of 500 to 600 words, discussing how the director "uses" the women to ensure that audiences attend the movie.
3. Argue for or against the proposition that the portrayal of scantily clad women on such shows as "Baywatch" is merely harmless entertainment.
4. Argue for or against the proposition that condemning films and TV shows that show women in revealing clothing is just a revival of Victorianism, a form of the short-sighted mentality Katie Roiphe discusses in "Date Rape: State of Siege or State of Mind?"
5. Research on the Web the issue of sexual representation in the media. Identify at least 10 hits that are promising, and download or take notes on them. Write an essay summarizing and evaluating the information obtained.
6. Conduct separate Net searches for two TV actresses, one you admire and respect based on her role or roles, and one actress whom Timson might categorize as similar to the "Bimbo Watch" type. In exploring these sites, do you find the actresses are treated differently, or similarly? How do your findings affect your perception of Timson's argument?

Violent Reaction

Richard Lacayo

In this essay, chosen as the cover story of the June 12, 1995, edition of *Time*, Richard Lacayo demonstrates that several issues exist concerning violence in the media that are endemically American. In an autocratic regime, it is likely that if the head of state decreed media violence was bad, censorship would immediately follow. However, the "violence in media" argument discussed in this issue is "all-American." True, we are a country that purports to decry violence, but we are also believers in the free enterprise system and the rights guaranteed us in the First Amendment to the U.S. Constitution. This essay displays the various factions and frictions involved in the media violence debate. It shows how tricky it can be for politicians and businesspeople to steer a politically correct course (that is, condemning messages harmful to society as expressed in songs and films while defending the capitalist system and democracy that allow such media forms to flourish).

PREVIEWING THE ESSAY

Is it anybody's business what music you listen to or which movies you see? Suppose you read an account of someone committing a crime and claiming he was inspired to do so from listening to lyrics from your favorite CD. What issues would such an event raise in your mind? In the mind of society? How might politicians use the event to help advance their personal agendas?

Care to see the chief theater of operations in the culture wars? Just take a stroll through the Sherman Oaks Galleria, a twinkling mall in California's San Fernando Valley. This is where the great outpouring of pop culture comes to market, a market that caters to all the moods of the American disposition, from moonglow to bloodlust. At Sam Goody's, the chain record store, the CD bins are stuffed with amiable releases by Hootie and the Blowfish and Boyz II Men. But they also hold the gangsta rap of Bloods and Crips and Tupac Shakur. Nearby, at the Time Out video arcade, Jordan Trimas, 16, is playing Primal Rage, a game in which dinosaurs tear one another to pieces. "Sure, the violence influences kids," he shrugs. "But nobody can do anything about it." 1

At the Sherman Oaks multiplex, it's the same mixed bag. On the wide screens there's a face-off between the two top-grossing films of the week. *Casper (the Friendly Ghost)* offers his doe-eyed version of mortality against the merry bloodbath that is *Die Hard with a Vengeance*. But over at Taco Bell, 15-year-old Christopher Zahedi will tell you he prefers the rougher stuff. "I liked the part in *Pulp Fiction* where the guy points a gun and says a prayer from the Bible and then kills everybody," he offers. "You hear the gun go brrrr. It's cool." 2

In their worst nightmares a lot of parents can also hear that gun go brrrr. They aren't so sure it's cool, just as they aren't so sure it's cool when they come across the more stomach-turning specimens of pop music in their kids' CD collections. That's why, when Bob Dole went to Los Angeles last week to blast the entertainment industry, he touched a chord that transcended the party politics his remarks were shrewdly crafted to serve. Though popular culture has a long and proud history of offending the squares, during the current decade it has particularly kept its sharpest edges to the front. Whatever is scabrous and saw-toothed and in-your-face is probably brought to you by the major labels and the big studios. For parents, the pervasive electronic culture can start to look like some suspect 3 stranger who hangs around their kids too much, acting loutish, rude and drunk.

It was that anxiety Dole was speaking to when he accused the powers behind American movies, music and television of flooding the country with "nightmares of depravity." Warning that the more extreme products of pop culture threaten to undermine American kids, he called on the large media companies to swear off the hard stuff. "We must hold Hollywood and the entire entertainment industry accountable for putting profit ahead of common decency," Dole said, then raised the heat considerably by singling out one company, Time Warner, the media giant that includes the largest American music operation, the Warner film studio and a stable of magazines, including *Time.* One day after Dole's speech, William Bennett, the former Education Secretary and drug czar, sent letters to Time Warner board members asking the company to stop distributing rap with objectionable lyrics. 4

Later in the week, Dole's wife Libby announced that she would be selling more than $15,000 in Walt Disney stock after learning that Disney, through its subsidiary Miramax, is the distributor of *Priest.* The controversial film, which her husband had already denounced several weeks ago, depicts a gay clergyman and a sexually active straight one. And coming soon from Miramax is *Kids,* a raw depiction of a sex-obsessed, drug-bleary day in the life of some New York City teens. It's the sort of thing Mickey Mouse would have to peek at through trembling white-gloved fingers. 5

To be sure, Dole's remarks were an unmistakable pitch to the culturally conservative wing of the Republican Party, which will have a lot to say about who becomes the next G.O.P. presidential candidate. Dan Quayle, their favorite son, never entered the race. Pat Buchanan, their guilty pleasure, is probably too extreme to be elected. Even before it turned out that he once invested in an R-rated film, Phil Gramm of Texas had left them cold. Until recently, so had Dole, who never showed much interest in the politics of virtue before the Christian right emerged as a power bloc in the party. In an effort to gain their attention, he has been sniping for months at Hollywood. Last week's salvo was like a proposal of marriage. 6

But Dole's attacks resonate beyond the party faithful, in all senses of the word. In a *Time* poll conducted at the end of last week by Yankelovich Partners, Inc., 77% of those questioned said that they were very concerned or fairly concerned about violence in the media; 70% said the same about media representations of sex. With numbers like those, it's a safe bet that Campaign '96 will also be Murphy Brown II, a further chapter of the conservative assault on Hollywood that Quayle launched in 1992. 7

"What we need is a national debate over the relationship of liberty to virtue," says Gary Bauer, the former Reagan White House aide who is president of the Family Research Council. "If you expose children to uplifting and noble material, you're more likely to have noble citizens. If children are wallowing in sexual images and violence, that is bound to have an impact on those who are most vulnerable." 8

In Hollywood, whose denizens have already been ridiculed for getting too close to the Clinton White House, the outraged response to Dole has been quick and complete. The speech was "a '90s form of McCarthyism," said Oliver Stone, whose *Natural Born Killers* was on Dole's hit list of objectionable films. "I don't think the public is that stupid," said Clint Eastwood. TV producer Norman Lear said he was "turned off by the excesses in some films" but insisted that Hollywood these days is making more pictures like *The Lion King* and *A Little Princess.* 9

In his attack on purveyors of offensive pop culture, Dole took pains, at least for now, not to hit some prominent Republicans. When he cited a list of recent family films that were also sizable box-office hits, Dole included not only *The Lion King* and *Forrest Gump* but also *True Lies,* a movie that reduced a small army of bad guys to blood-splattered pieces. Then again, it starred Arnold Schwarzenegger, a G.O.P. muscleman. Another sometime Republican, Bruce Willis, is the star of *Die Hard with a Vengeance,* one of the many brutal-fun action pictures that escaped Dole's wrath. So did the gleefully smutty-minded Fox television network and its contributions to the history of crotch-grabbing, such as "Married . . . with Children." Fox is owned by Rupert Murdoch, a major contributor to conservative causes. 10

One day after the speech, which was written largely by Mari Maseng, wife of conservative columnist George Will, a Dole aide admitted that the Senator also had not seen most of the movies he talked about, nor had he heard most of the music. On Friday aboard his Gulfstream jet, Dole finally popped *Natural Born Killers* into the VCR. "Probably ought to take a look so I can say I've seen this thing," he joked to a *Time* reporter over the phone. "Then we can always throw it out the window." 11

Count on it to keep coming back. The violent and raunchy streak in civilization runs deep and long into the past. More teenage boys might be attracted to the classics if they knew about Homer's graphic descriptions of spear points ripping through flesh in *The Iliad* or the quarts of stage blood needed for any production of *Titus Andronicus.* As for sex, the lewd posturings in some paintings of Hieronymous Bosch would be rated NC-17 if they showed up at the multiplex. 12

But the rise of capitalism over the past two centuries has meant that all the resources of technology and free enterprise could at last be placed at the disposal of the enduring human fascination with 13 grunt and groan. By the early decades of the present century, there had emerged in the U.S. an entertainment industry that would eventually prove to be all-pervasive and ever more given to decking out our base impulses with sweaty and imaginative detail. It awaited only the youth culture that began stirring and shaking in the 1950s to take full advantage of the possibilities in rock, films and TV. The result was a pop culture more pointed and grown up, but also more shameless and adolescent; sometimes both at the same time. The great skirmishes against the blue-nosed guardians of culture—the Hays Office that policed movies in the '30s or the network censors who tormented the Smothers Brothers in the late '60s—became the stuff of baby-boomer folklore.

The complications set in during the '90s, when the boomers who were once pop culture's most dedicated consumers became the decision makers at media companies—but also the parents of the next generation. Pulled one way by their lifelong instinct for whatever is sensational, unsanitized or unofficial, they find themselves dragged in the other direction by their emerging second thoughts as citizens and parents. 14

Dole says he's not interested in government censorship, which in any event hasn't worked very well in the past. In the best tradition of Patrick Henry, Americans generally don't have much patience with government interference in First Amendment rights of expression, even when they may not much like what's being expressed. In the most highly publicized attempt in recent years to set the law on pop music, three members of 2 Live Crew were arrested in Florida in 1990 after a live performance. It took a local jury just two hours to acquit them on obscenity charges. 15

But the First Amendment applies only to attempts by government to restrain expression. It says nothing about decisions made by private media companies, and it does nothing to prevent them from choosing which songs or programs they will or will not promote. Five years ago, Simon & Schuster canceled plans to publish *American Psycho,* the sado-chic novel by Bret Easton Ellis, after advance complaints about passages detailing the sexual torture and mutilation of women. (It was subsequently published by Knopf, a division of Random House.) "It's our responsibility," says Martin Davis, then chairman of Simon & Schuster's corporate parent Paramount. "You have to stand for something." This is just the sort of thing that Dole says he has in mind: self-restraint on the part of producers and distributors. "I'm just saying sometimes you have to have corporate responsibility and remember the impact on children." 16

Some media execs claim there isn't much that companies can do to restrain artists once they have them on their rosters. "Artists make records, not record companies," says David Geffen, the film and 17 record producer who is now one-third of DreamWorks with Steven Spielberg and former Disney executive Jeffrey Katzenberg. "No record company tells them what to record."

But Geffen, whose label stopped distributing the Geto Boys in 1991 because he couldn't stomach their lyrics, also knows it's not so simple. Record companies routinely tell artists to remix their albums or record new tracks. Something like that happened two years ago at A&M records. Its president, Al Cafaro, heard a track intended for an album by the rap artist Intelligent Hoodlum. "Bullet in the Brain" was about killing a police officer. In the wake of the uproar over Ice-T's song "Cop Killer," record executives everywhere were thinking twice. "It was nothing that we could be party to," says Cafaro of the song. "I told him I couldn't release it." What did Intelligent Hoodlum do? "He took the song off the record." 18

Two weeks ago, in a conversation with *Time* editors and correspondents, House Speaker Newt Gingrich went one step further when he suggested that major radio advertisers band together to boycott stations that play "explicitly vicious" rap. "They could drive violent rap music off radio within weeks," he said. Talk like that makes record execs very nervous. They know their product can also be vulnerable to boycotts by record stores that are under pressure from consumer groups. "You can make waves, but you can't mess with retail," says Eric Brooks, president of Noo Trybe Records. "You need to have your album stocked in the store." 19

Though advertisers haven't banded together yet, some citizen groups are trying it. Dennis Walcott, president of the New York Urban League, organized a protest last week at radio station WQHT in New York to persuade the station to stop playing "Shimmy Shimmy Ya," a rap song that the protesters say encourages sex without condoms. "I'm not asking for censorship," says Walcott. "I'm asking for corporations who make money from these things to think about content and message." 20

The prominence of African-American organizations as critics of gangsta rap is a new element in this year's version of the culture wars. In his new campaign against Time Warner, Bill Bennett is allied with C. DeLores Tucker, head of the National Political Congress of Black Women. After a woman working at radio station WBLS in New York complained last year about the lyrics of one rap song, management established a committee to screen the playlist. For station head Pierre Sutton, who is black, it's simply a matter of "not in my house you don't." Says Sutton: "Artists have the right to say what they want to, and we have the right to decide with regard to the playing of same." When 1993 statistics showed that violent crime in Kansas City, Missouri, had risen 200% in one year, FM station KPRS decided no longer to broadcast violent, sexually explicit or misogynist rap. Under the new policy, KPRS rose from third to first place in the local ratings. 21

Though the cultural-pollution issue looks like an easy win for the Republicans, it's not a clean sweep. As the debate develops in weeks to come, the soft spots in their arguments are likely to become more apparent. For a party committed to free-market principles—and which also wants to defund public television and end government oversight of the airwaves—a problem is that pop culture represents the free market at its freest, meaning most able to make a profitable pitch to the grosser appetites. Some of the most violent American films, like the Stallone–Willis–Schwarzenegger action pictures, are also among the most successful American film exports because their bang-bang simplicities translate easily across cultural boundaries. Says Democratic Senator Bill Bradley of New Jersey: "The free market that the economic conservatives champion undermines the moral character that the social conservatives desire." 22

In the aftermath of the Oklahoma City bombing, the conservatives are also stuck with their own problem of violence in the media—and it's not just Schwarzenegger's body counts. "Jackbooted thugs," the description of federal law-enforcement agents in a fund-raising letter from the National Rifle Association, is a kind of cop-killer lyric in itself. So is "aim at the head"—radio talk-show host G. Gordon Liddy's suggestion for greeting federal law-enforcement agents at your door. 23

Republicans who talk about the real-life consequences of pop-culture vulgarity still scream at the suggestion of any link between talk-show belligerence and Oklahoma City. Americans aren't so sure. In the *Time* poll, 52% of those questioned said they believed that strong antigovernment rhetoric inspires people to violence. And a lot of Americans are already suspicious of any attempt to use the culture issue as a way to evade discussion of everything else that contributes to the fraying of American life, from threadbare schools to the flood of guns. In the *Time* poll, 55% of those questioned agreed that if candidates want to improve the nation's moral climate, there are more important issues to concentrate on than sex and violence in the entertainment industry. 24

With those weak points in mind, Bill Clinton took a swipe at Dole last week at a town meeting in Billings, Montana. Without mentioning the Senator by name, Clinton observed pointedly that "there are some public officials in our country who are only too happy to criticize the culture of violence being promoted by the media but are stone-cold silent when these other folks are talking and making violence seem O.K." 25

For Democrats, criticizing Hollywood amounts to biting the hand that feeds them. Media-company executives and major stars contributed heavily to Clinton's 1992 campaign and to Democratic coffers generally in last year's congressional elections. Even so, the Democrats appreciate the potential power of the cultural-pollution issue 26 and hope to position themselves prominently before Republicans get a lock on it.

They can point out, for example, that Tipper Gore was among the first crusaders against obscene rock lyrics. First Lady Hillary Clinton has made frequent, if muted, denunciations of media vulgarity, and now seems to be turning up the volume, most recently in her appearance on Oprah. And sandwiched into Bill Clinton's long State of the Union message in January was a plea to Hollywood "to assess the impact of your work and to understand the damage that comes from the incessant, repetitive, mindless violence and irresponsible conduct that permeates our media all the time." 27

In an interview with *Time* last week, Vice President Gore stepped up the rhetoric. "Some of the decisions made by executives in the entertainment industry, the advertising industry, the creative community, have been obscene and atrocious." It was fine with him, Gore added, to try to shame corporate executives into reining in their product, though he rejected the notion that "shaming alone is a magic solution." 28

It's also not as easy as it sounds. Some decisions by media companies may seem like no-brainers. How many rap songs about slicing women's throats does the world really need? But most other judgments of taste are more difficult calls. Both of the films that Dole deplored, *Natural Born Killers* and *True Romance,* happen to have been written by Quentin Tarantino. He's also the explosively gifted director of *Pulp Fiction,* the great cockeyed movie where that guy quotes from the Bible and the gun goes brrrr and some younger viewers think it's cool—lots of older viewers too. In the effort to achieve a kid-friendlier culture, do we want to end up with a sanitized one, free of the worst excesses of "death metal" but also purged of Tarantino? Or of sassy but not salacious rappers like Salt-N-Pepa? Or even, let it be said, deprived of the mixed bag of gifts and gas that is Oliver Stone? 29

The culture wars won't just be conducted in board rooms and at candidates' debates. For some time to come, they will surely be going on within our families and homes, and sometimes within ourselves as well. 30

THINKING ABOUT THE ESSAY

1. What is your gut reaction when you watch a film loaded with violence? How do you feel when you browse through a record store with loud rap music blasting through it? Is the effect temporary or long-term?
2. Is there a difference between "artistic violence" and "gratuitous violence" in the media? If so, what is it and how can it be determined?

3. Lacayo cites an antiviolence advocate stating, "I'm not asking for censorship. . . . I'm asking for corporations who make money from these things to think about content and message." What difference, if any, is there between the two concepts?
4. What is the major thesis of the essay? Does the author seem to have a personal view on the limits of media violence? Explain by citing the text.
5. The author structures his essay by exploring the views of the various "players" in the media violence debate. Who are these groups of individuals, what are their views, and what are their solutions to the problem as they perceive it?

RESPONDING IN DISCUSSION

1. Have a member of the class bring in an audiocassette or CD of a rap song with a violent message. Have the teacher play the song. Discuss with your classmates the emotions it evoked in you.
2. Select one student to bring to class the lyrics to a song, a segment of dialogue from a movie, or a short violent sequence from a movie. Read, listen to, or view it, and discuss what the message suggests.
3. Discuss whether opinion makers such as politicians and commentators who call for restrictions on media violence view the public as undiscerning individuals who are unable to make decisions for themselves.
4. Discuss why the author seems to absolve filmmaker Quentin Tarantino from the sins of portraying violence in his movies.

RESPONDING IN WRITING

1. Assume the role of a political candidate and write a speech of approximately 500 words outlining your views on violence in the media.
2. Argue for or against the proposition that people often criticize violence directed against a group they identify with and often celebrate violence directed at a group they detest.
3. In an expository essay of approximately 500 words explain how depicting violence in the media can be used to enlighten the public concerning important social issues.
4. Argue for or against the proposition that politicians use the media violence debate as a way of garnering support, and have little or no concern over its purported effects.

5. Go on-line and locate a violence-oriented newsgroup or chatroom. Write an essay of approximately 500 words describing the issues, orientations, and concerns of its members.

Parallel Worlds: The Surprising Similarities (and Differences) of Country-and-Western and Rap

Denise Noe

In this unusual comparison and contrast of two forms of popular culture, Denise Noe (who writes on a broad range of topics in various small presses) attempts to demonstrate that whether you attack the status quo in art is less significant than how you attack it. This raises significant issues about censorship, a subject previously addressed in Lacayo's "Violent Reaction." While rappers' messages have been condemned and attempts have been made to censor their music, Noe demonstrates that country-and-western, another type of music with subversive themes, remains unscathed in the eyes of the general public. This essay first appeared in the July–August 1995 issue of *The Humanist.*

PREVIEWING THE ESSAY

How does the tone of country-and-western music differ from that of rap? How do the two musical styles affect you emotionally? Do you have personal reasons for preferring one over the other?

In all of popular music today, there are probably no two genres that are more apparently dissimilar than country-and-western and rap: the one rural, white, and southern; the other urban, black, and identified with the two coasts ("New York style" versus "L.A. style"). Yet C&W and rap are surprisingly similar in many ways. In both C&W and rap, for example, lyrics are important. Both types of music tell stories, as do folk songs, and the story is much more than frosting for the rhythm and beat. 1

The ideologies espoused by these types of music are remarkably similar as well. We frequently stereotype country fans as simple-minded conservatives—"redneck," moralistic super-patriots à la Archie Bunker. But country music often speaks critically of mainstream American platitudes, especially in such highly charged areas as sexual morality, crime, and the Protestant work ethic. 2

The sexual ethos of C&W and rap are depressingly similar: the 3
men of both genres are champion chauvinists. Country singer Hank Williams, Jr., declares he's "Going Hunting Tonight," but he doesn't need a gun since he's hunting the "she-cats" in a singles bar. Male rappers such as Ice-T, Ice Cube, and Snoop Doggy Dogg are stridently misogynist, with "bitches" and "hos" their trademark terms for half of humanity; their enthusiastic depictions of women raped and murdered are terrifying. Indeed, the sexism of rap group NWA (Niggaz with Attitude) reached a real-life nadir when one member of the group beat up a woman he thought "dissed" them—and was praised for his brutality by the other members.

On a happier note, both rap and C&W feature strong female 4
voices as well. Women rappers are strong, confident, and raunchy: "I want a man, not a boy/to approach me/Your lame game really insults me. . . . I've got to sit on my feet to come down to your level," taunt lady rappers Entice and Barbie at Too Short in their duet/duel, "Don't Fight the Feeling." Likewise, Loretta Lynn rose to C&W fame with defiant songs like "Don't Come Home a-Drinkin' with Lovin' on Your Mind" and "Your Squaw Is on the Warpath Tonight."

Country Music can be bluntly honest about the realities of sex 5
and money—in sharp contrast to the "family values" rhetoric of the right. "Son of Hickory Hollow's Tramp" by Johnny Darrell salutes a mother who works as a prostitute to support her children. "Fancy" by Bobbie Gentry (and, more recently, Reba McEntire) describes a poverty-stricken woman's use of sex for survival and her rise to wealth on the ancient "gold mine." Both tunes are unapologetic about the pragmatic coping strategies of their heroines.

More startling than the resemblances in their male sexism and 6
"uppity" women are the parallels between C&W and rap in their treatment of criminality. Country-and-western music is very far from a rigid law-and-order mentality. The criminal's life is celebrated for its excitement and clear-cut rewards—a seemingly promising alternative to the dull grind of day-to-day labor.

"Ain't got no money/Ain't got no job/Let's find a place to rob," 7
sings a jaunty Ricky Van Shelton in "Crime of Passion." In "I Never Picked Cotton," Roy Clark is more subdued but still unrepentant when he says: "I never picked cotton/like my mother did and my sister did and my brother did/And I'll never die young/working in a coal mine like my daddy did." Waylon Jennings' "Good Ole Boys" boast gleefully of having "hot-wired a city truck/turned it over in the mayor's yard."

Similarly, rap songs like "Gangsta, Gangsta" and "Dopeman" by 8
NWA and "Drama" by Ice-T tell of the thrill and easy money offered by a life of crime. "Drama" records the dizzying high of the thief; "Gangsta, Gangsta," the rush of adrenaline experienced by a murderer

making a quick getaway. Of course, both C&W and rap songs do express the idea that in the long run crime doesn't pay. The sad narrator of Merle Haggard's "Mama Tried" "turned 21 in prison/doing life without parole," while the thief of Ice-T's "Drama" is forced to realize that "I wouldn't be here if I'd fed my brain/Got knowledge from schoolbooks/'stead of street crooks/Now all I get is penitentiary hard looks."

Though both C&W and rap narrators are often criminals, their attitudes toward law enforcement differ radically. The Irish Rovers' "Wasn't That a Party?" ("that little drag race down on Main Street/was just to see if the cops could run") pokes light-hearted fun at the police, while the Bobby Fuller Four's "I Fought the Law and the Law Won" expresses the most common C&W attitude: an acceptance that criminals must be caught, even if you are one. Neither song displays any anger toward the police, who are, after all, just doing their job. 9

To rappers, on the other hand, cops are the enemy. Two of the most notorious rap songs are Ice-T's "Cop Killer" and NWA's "Fuck tha Police" (which angrily asserts, "Some police think they have the authority to kill a minority"). Despite ample evidence of police brutality in the inner city, "Fuck tha Police" was almost certainly regarded by nonblack America as a paranoid shriek—until the world witnessed the infamous videotape of several of Los Angeles' finest brutally beating Rodney King while a dozen other "peace officers" nonchalantly looked on. 10

Interestingly, although the C&W view of law enforcement naturally sits better with the general public (certainly with the police themselves), the fact remains that country-and-western music contains a good deal of crime, violence, and casual sex. Yet it is easily accepted by white Americans while rap arouses alarm and calls for labeling. Why? 11

I believe there are three major reasons. The first, and simplest, is language. Rappers say "bitch," "ho," "fuck," and "motherfucker"; C&W artists don't. Country singers may say, "I'm in the mood to speak some French tonight" (Mary Chapin-Carpenter, "How Do") or "There's two kinds of cherries/and two kinds of fairies" (Merle Haggard, "My Own Kind of Hat"), but they avoid the bluntest Anglo-Saxon terms. 12

A second reason is race. African-Americans have a unique history of oppression in this country, and rap reflects the inner-city African-American experience. Then, too, whites expect angry, frightening messages from blacks and listen for them. Many blacks, on the other hand, hope for uplifting messages—and are dismayed when black artists seem to encourage or glorify the drug abuse and violence in their beleaguered communities. Thus, the focus on violence in rap—and the dismissal of same in C&W. 13

While the differing attitudes toward law enforcement are real enough, much of the difference between violence in country-and-western music and in rap lies not in the songs themselves but in the way they are heard. Thus, when Ice Cube says, "Let the suburbs see a nigga invasion/Point-blank, smoke the Caucasian," many whites interpret that as an incitement to violence. But when Johnny Cash's disgruntled factory worker in "Oney" crows, "Today's the day old Oney gets his," it's merely a joke. Likewise, when Ice Cube raps, "I've got a shotgun and here's the plot/Taking niggas out with the fire of buckshot" ("Gangsta, Gangsta"), he sends shudders through many African-Americans heartbroken by black-on-black violence; but when Johnny Cash sings of an equally nihilistic killing in "Folsom Prison Blues"—"Shot a man in Reno/just to watch him die"—the public taps its feet and hums along. . . . It's just a song, after all. 14

There is a third—and ironic—reason why rap is so widely attacked: Rap is actually closer to mainstream American economic ideology than country-and-western is. While C&W complains about the rough life of honest labor for poor and working-class people, rap ignores it almost entirely. "Work your fingers to the bone and what do you get?" asks Hoyt Axton in a satirical C&W song, then answers sardonically with its title: "Bony Fingers." Likewise, Johnny Paycheck's infamous "Take This Job and Shove It" is a blue-collar man's bitter protest against the rough and repetitive nature of his life's work. Work in C&W is hard and meaningless; it keeps one alive, but leaves the worker with little time or energy left to enjoy life. 15

Songs by female country singers reinforce this point in a different way; they insist that love (with sex) is more important than affluence. The heroine of Reba McEntire's "Little Rock" says she'll have to "slip [her wedding ring] off," feeling no loyalty to the workaholic husband who "sure likes his money" but neglects his wife's emotional and physical needs. Jeanne Pruett in "Back to Back" lampoons the trappings of wealth and proclaims, "I'd trade this mansion/for a run-down shack/and a man who don't believe in sleeping back to back." 16

Rap's protagonists, on the other hand, are shrewd, materialistic, and rabidly ambitious—although the means to their success are officially proscribed in our society. Not for them a "life that moves at a slower pace" (Alabama, "Down Home"); unlike the languorous hero of country-and-western, "catching these fish like they're going out of style" (Hank Williams, Jr., "Country State of Mind"), rap singers and rap characters alike are imbued with the great American determination to get ahead. 17

Rap's protagonists—drug dealers, burglars, armed robbers, and "gangstas"—live in a society where success is "a fistful of jewelry" (Eazy E, "No More ?s"), "Motorola phones, Sony color TVs" (Ice-T, "Drama"), where "without a BMW you're through" (NWA, "A Bitch Iz 18 a Bitch"). In NWA's "Dopeman," sometimes cited as an anti-drug song, the "Dopeman" is the archetypal American entrepreneur: clever, organized, ruthless, and not ruled by impulse—"To be a dopeman you must qualify/Don't get high off your own supply."

The proximity of rap to our success ethic arouses hostility because America is torn by a deep ideological contradiction: We proudly proclaim ourselves a moral (even religious) nation and tout our capitalist economic system. But the reality of a successful capitalist system is that it undermines conventional morality. A glance at the history books shows how our supposedly moral nation heaped rewards upon the aptly named "robber barons": the Rockefellers, Vanderbilts, Carnegies, and Morgans. The crack dealer is a contemporary version of the bootlegger—at least one of whom, Joe Kennedy, Sr., founded America's most famous political dynasty. (Indeed, I would not be surprised if history repeated itself and the son—or daughter—of a drug lord becomes this country's first African-American president.) 19

Capitalism is unparalleled in its ability to create goods and distribute services, but it is, like the hero of "Drama," "blind to what's wrong." The only real criterion of a person's worth becomes how much money she or he has—a successful crook is treated better than a poor, law-abiding failure. 20

In short, the laid-back anti-materialist of country-and-western can be dismissed with a shrug, but the rapper is attacked for that unforgivable sin: holding a mirror up to unpleasant truths. And one of them is that amoral ambition is as American as apple pie and the Saturday Night Special. 21

THINKING ABOUT THE ESSAY

1. How do you define the word *ideologies* as used by the author? How does it help to focus the thesis of the essay?
2. What implications does the author provide concerning the variable of race in distinguishing the public's views of country-and-western and of rap? How does your own identification with a particular race affect your response to these two forms of music?
3. What rhetorical techniques does the author use to provide evenhandedness and symmetry when comparing and contrasting the two forms of music?
4. What is the author's thesis? How does the introduction to the essay help to frame the thesis? Do you concur wholeheartedly with the supporting points used to defend the thesis or are there any with which you disagree? Explain.

RESPONDING IN DISCUSSION

1. Recruit students who own copies of the songs discussed in the essay. Have your teacher play them, and discuss how and to what degree you respond emotionally to the rap and country-and-western songs. Afterwards, analyze your emotional responses and share them with the class.
2. Discuss personal examples of racial "crossover" reactions to the two forms of music (for example, whites identifying with rap and African-Americans with country-and-western). Discuss how and why this crossover occurs.
3. In Pico Iyer's essay, "The Strange and Exciting Fruits of Global Culture," featured later in this textbook, the author claims that a cross-pollination of cultures is occurring because we are simultaneously exposed to such a diversity of cultural forms. Discuss whether this has had an impact on the two forms of music discussed in this essay.
4. Discuss whether either or both forms of music Noe discusses are healthy ways of expressing frustration and anger at the dominant culture, or are a danger to it.
5. In describing the relationship between rap's ideology and the robber barons, the author refers to "our supposedly moral nation." Talk about other citations by the author concerning American capitalism, and discuss what side of the ideological fence you place her in the light of her statements on the topic.

RESPONDING IN WRITING

1. Write a letter of 400 to 500 words encouraging or discouraging a radio station from providing ample air time to gangsta rap.
2. Analyze one contemporary country-and-western or rap song. Cover such details as class background, geographical origins, attitudes toward authority figures, drinking and smoking habits, language, sexual behavior, and so forth.
3. Select four CD jewel boxes or four promotional posters: two promoting a gangsta rap personality or group, the others promoting country-and-western artists. Write a comparison-and-contrast essay exploring the differences in presentational style between the two sets of artists. Include such details as facial demeanor, posture, dress, accessories such as jewelry, tattoos, musical instruments, hairstyles, and background to the picture. Conclude with your interpretation of the subliminal message implicit in the presentations of the artists.

4. Argue for or against the proposition that those who condemn the violent forms of rap music are denying the profound dissatisfaction that exists among urban youth and their need to express it.
5. Explore rap and country-and-western sites on the Internet. Write a comparative essay assessing your findings.

Dumb and Dumber: The Case against Hollywood

John H. Richardson

John H. Richardson, senior writer at *Premiere* magazine and novelist, makes his case against the "dumbing down" of the American cinema in his essay, which was originally published in the April 10, 1995, edition of *The New Republic*. Among the celluloid dreams that came out of Hollywood, many were and still are considered art on a par with work in such long-established art forms as painting, sculpture, music, and ballet. However, the idea of taste is a highly controversial one, and it requires someone with a broad background in his or her subject matter to be able to write intelligently on such a subjective issue. Luckily, Richardson demonstrates his knowledge of film history throughout the essay, so he is in a position to compare the films of yesterday and today. If your movie-viewing experience has been limited to the blockbuster hits whose titles checker the multiplex marquees, it may be difficult to defend or take exception with his views. Nevertheless, if nothing else, the essay should provide you with an insider's look at the film business today.

PREVIEWING THE ESSAY

How do you know if something is "good"? Do some people have the ability to make judgments more competently than others? If so, what characteristics would they necessarily possess? Knowledge? Insight? Intuition? Education?

I.

I just got back from Hollywood, where I had breakfast with Ricardo Mestres at the Bel Air Hotel. Mestres shot from Harvard to the head of Disney's Hollywood pictures, only to release a string of flops so unremittingly horrible that finally, after a deathwatch that seemed to go on for years, he lost his job. But there he was, with a spanking new title, dressed with casual confidence in khakis and a plaid shirt, 1 working on his second breakfast of the day. The head of Warner Brothers' film division sat across from us, the new chairman of Disney in the corner. A fire burned in the fireplace, a small rainforest flowered under a crystal chandelier. The room was as quiet as a handful of diamonds tumbling onto jeweler's felt.

Another night, I had dinner with Columbia executive Barry 2
Josephson. This time it was at Morton's, in its airy new space. Barry came in wearing the Hollywood executive uniform—Armani suit, Cartier watch, Italian loafers—and laughed good-naturedly while I examined the labels. Barry has gotten much more humble and charming since he became known as the executive most responsible for *The Last Action Hero.*

I also talked to a studio chairman who just escaped from a corpo- 3
rate meltdown, a producer of mediocre comedies, a screenwriter down on her luck, the wife of a famous hack action director and a lawyer who makes big studio deals. And this is what I can confidently report:

The tuna sashimi at Morton's (on a bed of avocado and mustard 4
greens) was as sweet and delicate as whipped cream, and the lemon pancakes at the Bel Air were delicious with a light raspberry syrup. Life in Hollywood is great—top actors are getting between $12 million and $20 million per picture, the U.S. box office hit almost $5.4 billion last year (the highest it's been since 1960), the telephone companies are jumping in, Ted Turner's New Line/Castle Rock/Turner Pictures empire seems to be emerging as the first new studio in decades. And when Steven Spielberg and Jeffrey Katzenberg and David Geffen announced some vague plans for another new studio, they snapped up a couple of billion dollars just like that. "It's getting more corporate and it's harder to get a decision," the lawyer told me, "but the money is unbelievable."

There's one little problem: that odor in the room . . . the stink of 5
the movies. Probably you've wondered about this and then pushed it out of your mind, telling yourself that we only remember the handful of good movies from the old days and not the thousands of lame ones, that the past always seems more glorious, that even the ancient Greeks thought they were the puny descendants of a race of giants, that maybe you just missed all the really good ones. But as the time approaches to watch *Forrest Gump* scoop up all those Oscars, that argument fades, and the inner voice gets louder: these movies suck.

Listen to that inner voice. Hollywood movies are in terrible 6
shape. Our greatest living filmmakers, such as Martin Scorsese, Woody Allen and Francis Ford Coppola, are in slumps of varying lengths. The important social movie like *The Grapes of Wrath* or *On the Waterfront* is all but dead, replaced at best by sincere and unremarkable issue movies like *When A Man Loves A Woman* and

Philadelphia. The only big-canvas filmmaker of stature we have today is Oliver Stone, God help us.

Just look at our top Oscar contenders. *Gump* was well-made and had a certain sweetness, if you like that sort of thing, but it's still a lot closer to *Beaches* than *The Bridge on the River Kwai. Pulp Fiction* was lively and clever, but at bottom it's just an MTV version of old Hollywood themes, with all the boring parts left out. *Quiz Show* and *Nobody's Fool* get points for trying, but they don't exactly rank with *The Third Man* or *Annie Hall* or *The Godfather.* They're closer to good efforts than good movies. 7

After that, the bottom drops off dramatically: the dreary sameness of all the erotic thrillers and buddy-o-matic action epics, the dispiritingly endless stream of sequels and remakes and Disney comedies. So many movies feel cobbled-together these days—action films like *True Lies* and *Patriot Games* are so distended by their set-piece action sequences that the rest of the movie feels like filler, and comedies from *Wayne's World* to *The Addams Family* are so perfunctory about their stories that they make the Bob Hope and Bing Crosby road movies seem downright sophisticated. 8

Even the best Hollywood movies of the past decade seem to prove this point. My personal list of favorites includes *Who Framed Roger Rabbit? Edward Scissorhands, Reversal of Fortune, Blue Velvet, Dead Ringers, GoodFellas* and a few exceptional genre films like *T2* and *Die Hard.* These are ambitious, intelligent movies, with the architectural coherence of art. *Edward Scissorhands* and *Roger Rabbit* create their own magical worlds, setting up internal rules and elaborating them with brilliance. *Reversal of Fortune* is smart on the level of literature, where motives and morals are complex. *T2* and *Die Hard* have the brio of great pop, as *Psycho* did in its time. But, alas, none of these movies felt important. And none came out in the past three years. Like Edward Scissorhands himself, the artists who made them seem so disengaged from the culture at large that they prefer working in their backyards, on topiary gardens. 9

It's almost a given that the only interesting movies today are coming out of the fringes, from first-time and independent directors enjoying a brief flurry of creative independence before the studios put them to work making Cheez Whiz. But if you actually go and see these movies, you find that most are depressingly short of their hype. From *Slacker* to *Clerks,* they have some fresh and funny moments, but masterpieces of cinema they are not. 10

Foreign filmmaking isn't much better. A steady trickle of smart imports still arrives—*In The Name of the Father, The Piano, Heavenly Creatures* and that brief bright stretch of Pedro Almodovar delights in the '80s—but nothing to match the standards of Truffaut, Fellini and Buñuel. Foreign filmmakers seem almost as hobbled by the celluloid 11 past as Americans: *Shallow Grave* is fun filmmaking, but, like *Pulp Fiction* and *Reservoir Dogs,* it's just a splashy version of a very familiar tale.

12 This isn't just my opinion. Even in Hollywood, it is the consensus. A screenwriter friend told me it was the times: "Music is over, art is over, movies are over." A studio chairman blamed it on the culture at large, comparing our lite movies to our lite president. A movie publicist told me that, when he went out to sell his wares, he felt like "the emperor's new dry cleaner"—a *publicist.* All of which made Mestres and Josephson perfect sources, the representative men of their time. They had personally launched some of the worst movies of the past five years. Why did they do it? Why Jim Belushi in *Taking Care of Business?* Why Patrick Dempsey in *Run?* What's wrong with Hollywood?

13 The natural first suspicion is that people like Josephson and Mestres are just overpaid fools. But this assumption is both glib and wrong. Ricardo is like Ozzie and Harriet's smarter son, incredibly well-scrubbed, exuding all-American decency and so disciplined that if he tips the scales an extra pound that morning he'll cut his Chinese chicken salad in half. Barry, too, is a smart, likable, hard working guy.

14 So we move to assumption No. 2: maybe they were just trying to give the public the junk they thought it wanted. Absolutely not, they both insist. "Obviously there's this assumption that we've become jaded and just grind out product," Ricardo said. "But we never set out to make a bad movie." They seemed sincere, and I believed them. My jaded publicist friend said the same thing. "Everybody wakes up in the morning and says, 'I want to make a movie that's successful critically and also makes money,'" he told me. "I believe that." (Though he added the last sentence in an almost wistful voice.) I remembered that both Ricardo and Barry have a few good efforts to their (partial) credit: Ricardo with *Swing Kids* and *Bound by Honor* and Barry with *In the Line of Fire.* So how did these smart guys wind up making such horrible movies? Ricardo talked about the culture of Disney, about being trapped by the high-concept, low-budget approach to comedy that worked so well for them early in the 1980s, about not having money for stars. And it all made sense, sort of.

15 Then I remembered a scene from *Taking Care of Business.* Jim Belushi and a Japanese businessman are at a lunch meeting with an obnoxious career woman. Finally Belushi puts the career woman in her place by walking out on this exit line: "Nice titties." Then the Japanese businessman walks out in solidarity, repeating the line. I think the joke is that he doesn't really know what he's saying, being Japanese. When I first saw this scene I had to rewind my VCR twice to make sure that I'd really seen it, and ever since I have tried to picture Ricardo and his hypersmart then-boss, Jeffrey Katzenberg, sitting in a screening room watching it. What did they say to each other? What did they think? Did their wives see this movie?

Ricardo explained it this way: they knew the picture wasn't working, but they couldn't stop it. "You hire the director, and the director owns the set." The director of *Taking Care of Business* was Arthur Hiller, who had just directed *Outrageous Fortune.* Which made him considerably hotter than most of the people Disney hired in those days, when they were avatars of the faster-cheaper-better school of filmmaking. So what were they going to do? Fire him and hire somebody who *hadn't* just directed a hit? 16

And what was Barry going to do? Having worked as a manager and producer, he'd just gotten his first job as a studio executive when he found the script then called *Extremely Violent.* It seemed pretty funny, with a hooky high-concept about a comic book movie hero coming into the real world. Then Arnold Schwarzenegger committed to it, and Barry roped in director John McTiernan (*Die Hard*) and hired Shane Black (*Lethal Weapon*) to fix the script. From the standpoint of an executive, Barry was doing great. He had assembled a big star, a hot screenwriter, a hot director. And if he did start to worry about the script not quite coming together, what was he going to do? With a big hole in the summer schedule to fill, and the production clock ticking away, was he going to say *The Last Action Hero* wasn't ready to go? *Not* make his first picture with the hottest star in Hollywood? 17

II.

So they are not fools, and they are not just cynically making junk. The answer, as always, is that the machine makes what it is set up to make. Contemporary Hollywood has evolved a peculiar culture that is set up to make junk, and there are a lot of very specific reasons for this—calibrations, as it were, on the machine. Here is a partial list: 18

1. *The deal is more important than the movie.* 19

Hollywood isn't really geared to make movies anymore, as it was during the studio system, when actors were chattel on long-term contract. Now the town is geared to make deals, to sign actors and directors to projects, and the movie is just the by-product of the deal. When Barry started *The Last Action Hero,* he made a great deal. As an executive, that was really almost all he could do. It was up to the other guys to make the movie. Same with *Baby's Day Out.* When John Hughes went to Fox's Joe Roth and said he'd like to follow up *Home Alone* with a movie about a baby loose in New York City, was Roth going to say no? Would you? Would you have said no to a package of Arnold Schwarzenegger, Ivan Reitman and Danny DeVito, even if the idea of Schwarzenegger pregnant made you a little nervous? It works the other way, too; despite its stream of horrible movies, Disney gave up a chance to sign Tim Burton to a long-term contract because Burton 20 didn't want to give up all the merchandising rights (theme parks, toys, etc.) to his characters—so Disney lost the chance to work with a brilliant director because of greed over a deal point.

2. *The rise of the executive.* 21

The last great period of American movies was during the early 1970s, when the baffled older generation of Hollywood let the kids take over and unleashed such directors as Scorsese, Coppola, Bob Rafelson and Peter Bogdanovich. Then Michael Cimino brought all that to a halt with *Heaven's Gate,* spending so much money that he bankrupted United Artists—a studio that often boasted of its executive-free policy of letting the filmmakers make their movies without interference (and which gave us *Some Like It Hot, The Apartment, West Side Story, In The Heat of the Night, Annie Hall, Rocky* and *One Flew Over the Cuckoo's Nest*). After that, the executives took over. Suddenly they were everywhere. On the lower levels, they micromanaged script development as never before. On the higher levels, they second-guessed the executives on the lower levels. They loved nothing more than to make movies of off pitches, because then they were the stars (a trend that has slowed, thankfully). All of which led to movies like *The Rocketeer* or *Alien,*[3] so tortured by executives in the production process that they ended up almost lifeless. Contrast those with films that rose out of total production chaos, like *Casablanca, Apocalypse Now* and even (on a much lesser level) *The Fugitive.* 22

3. *The rise of everybody but writers and directors.* 23

Once I heard John Huston tell a joke. It was late in his life, and he was carrying an oxygen bottle everywhere he went, taking a suck on a tube whenever the air in the real world got too thin. "These two producers were lost in the desert," Huston began, in his scratchy wised-up voice. "They're dying of thirst, crawling along, when"—suuuck— "they come upon an oasis. What a beautiful sight! They're saved! They fall to their knees, and one of them scoops the delicious sweet water to his face when"—suuuuccck—"the other producer stops him. 'Wait,' he shouts. 'Let me piss in it first.'" Since Huston's day, with the growing power of agents, executives, actors, even lawyers, that's been the rule. Ask the artists, if you're in the mood to hear a bitter diatribe. Director Tim Hunter told me once that he had made *River's Edge* from the first draft, because even though it might have been a little better rewritten, he was afraid the development process would leach out the peculiar moments that made the movie so fresh, like Dennis Hopper toting around an inflatable love doll. Hunter was perfectly happy to extend his experience to a categorical imperative: "I think the movies would be better if people just shot first drafts," he said. I'll go even further: in the theater, the writer is king and directors know their place, and that's the way it should be. Hollywood got this backward because film evolved from scriptless spectacle to silent film to talkie. By the time it became a fully literary activity, the director already had hegemony. And just 24 when it seemed impossible, things are getting worse—with the general decline in reverence for non-airport books, Hollywood's necessary-evil feeling about writers has gotten out of control. Whenever possible they find writers who don't seem like real writers, guys working as lifeguards or ex-Navy Seals. "Get me rewrite" has gone from joke to fad, with as many as thirty writers teaming up on a single script, as with *The Flintstones*. This makes the executives and producers feel more creative, since they are guiding the process, but it doesn't make for great scenarios. Almost without exception, individuals write the best movies, from Preston Sturges to James Agee to Paul Schrader.

25 4. *The rise of screenwriting programs.*

26 The 1980s also saw a tremendous increase in screenwriting programs. On an assignment for a magazine, I took one of these courses, and learned that a movie should introduce two buddies, build their relationship to a crisis, separate the buddies so that they can learn some lessons on their own and then bring them back together. This is the model of movies as different as *Rain Man* and *E.T.* The reason I didn't emerge from the course with a million-dollar screenplay is because taking the course doesn't teach you how to create characters like the rain man or E.T. All it does is give you a glib way to talk about your plot and an artificial way to look at structure. The damage would be limited to a few thousand hapless screenplays except for one thing: executives take these classes.

27 "Every executive I know has taken them," one told me. They go on their own, the better to learn "structure." Pity the poor screenwriter, faced with dozens of pages of notes asking: What is the inciting incident? Who is the antagonist? And this may get even worse with the rise of computer screenwriting programs. At dinner with my screenwriter friend in L.A. (at Woo Lae Oak, Hollywood's Korean restaurant, where the tuna sashimi rivals Morton's), she told me excitedly about a brand new computer program that takes any given premise and spits out all the possible story developments. I have a sinking feeling we have just found out whether movies can get even worse.

28 5. *Jeffrey Abrams.*

29 More than anyone else, Abrams was the writer who exemplified the high-concept, Robert McKee's Story Structure™ approach to screenwriting: yuppie loses his filofax, escaped con finds it and takes over his life while yuppie goes through morally uplifting poverty. Yuppie gets shot in the head (how's that for an inciting incident?) and becomes as a child again. Abrams did not come up with Vegas-lounge-lizard-becomes-king-of-England, but I am holding him spiritually responsible. The real problem is that executives love this kind of story, partly because they're easy to sell on a poster and partly because they're easy to defend—it's not like we were doing complex family drama, boss—we were doing yuppie-shot-in-the-head. We

were doing crook-finds-filofax. Once in a while these movies do work—a mermaid in Manhattan? Talk about yer fish out of water!—but most of the time they turn out to be as thin as the ideas they are based on. Remember cop-gives-waitress-two-million-dollar-tip? How about hooker-with-heart-of-gold-pretends-to-be-guy's-girlfriend? Or guy-offers-one-million-dollars-to-sleep-with-your-wife?

6. *The hit-driven film economy.* 30

Increasingly, Hollywood films are divided into hits or misses, 31
strikeouts or home runs. Budgets continue to rise. (The average studio film cost $34 million last year.) It is also more and more expensive to promote big movies—a "prints and ads" budget of $30 million is not uncommon. This inflation puts even more pressure on the big movies to perform, giving more power to the actors who might open them. This year Kevin Costner got script approval and his choice of director for *Waterworld,* two decisions that helped drive the budget upward of $170 million even before promotional expenses (and the storm that sunk the set). These economic realities make it less likely for studios to take any risks at all, on big or small pictures. There are also some arcane reasons driving studios to the blockbuster mentality, such as the "terms" clause in distribution contracts that gives a studio its biggest cut in a movie's first weeks of release—generally the terms (after exhibitor expenses) are 90 to 10 favoring the studio, which means that a movie that builds on word of mouth makes the studio much less money than a movie that opens to 30 million and drops quickly. This structure makes a smash more profitable than a sleeper that grosses more. Terms can be renegotiated, but it's not easy. This shift began with the antitrust breakup of the studio theater chains in 1948 and went into high gear after *Jaws,* when studios shifted from platform releases to wide releases, and the mark of success shifted from "play-dates" (how many theaters a movie was playing in) to grosses.

7. *Everybody knows that nobody knows everything.* 32

Over the last decade, William Goldman's famous phrase explain- 33
ing Hollywood—"nobody knows anything"—has become so popular it is practically a mantra. This has had a subtle demoralizing effect, encouraging executives like Barry and Ricardo to ignore their own judgment. As Ricardo put it: "You never know. Plenty of movies you think are trash turn out unbelievable, and vice versa." That much is true, but beyond that, Goldman is dead wrong. Hitchcock knew something about making thrillers. Scorsese knows something about obsession. And William Goldman knows something about writing scripts.

8. *General pervasive corporate cowardice.* 34

Hollywood screenwriters tell this joke: A screenwriter turns in his 35
script, and the next day he calls his executive to ask what he thought. "I don't know," says the executive. "I'm the only one who read it."

Like Ricardo, today's Hollywood is almost universally well-scrubbed and hardworking. They alternate fat-free meals with Met-Rx shakes and never drink more than one cocktail. They also live in constant fear of losing their vastly overpaid jobs, so their primary purpose is to make sure nothing goes wrong. That means that their real secret jobs are to say no—if they say yes, they might get stuck with some wild-man with a vision. Every now and then these nervous suits try to get more control by eliminating the producer and making the movies themselves. What they don't understand is that most people who make great movies are out of control, from Von Stroheim with his amazing eleven-hour mogul-maddening *Greed* to, yes, Michael Cimino. (Have you actually seen *Heaven's Gate?* It's darn close to being a brilliant movie.) The simple truth is that corporations don't make great movies, mavericks do, and mavericks are almost by definition erratic, free-spending, frequently intoxicated and generally unmanageable. It's no accident that one of the few brilliant studio records in recent history—the mid-'70s run at Paramount that gave us *The Godfather* and *Chinatown*—was supervised by a bunch of maverick executives with cocaine straws surgically attached to their nostrils. But that logic will never move the suits; better to make cookie-cutter high-concept films, the kind of movie a corporation can understand.

9. *There is too much money.* 36

Hollywood is a homogeneous place. Almost everyone likes rock 37 and took drugs in the '60s and tries to stay true to the hippie spirit (even though you have to manage your money wisely) and pays at least lip service to feminism. Everyone likes pleasure and welcomes new ideas and loves art deco and keeps up with the new bands. And they're all white. The problem here isn't their politics—only a Philistine judges art exclusively (or even primarily) by its politics—but the insularity of their lives. They've been everywhere, but they spend a lot of time at the hotel.

10. *Body-snatching foreign directors.* 38

To combat their insularity, Hollywood quickly hires any foreign 39 director whose films show any potential for slickness. But then it puts them through the Hollywood mind-meld. One Hollywood wife of my acquaintance, married to a man who went from foreign art films to Hollywood action epics, calls this the "invasion of the pod people." They become obsessed with box office, success, the taste of the audience. The examples are many and depressing: Peter Weir going from *The Last Wave* to *Green Card,* Kenneth Branagh from *Henry V* to *Frankenstein,* Michael Caton-Jones from *Scandal* to *Doc Hollywood,* Fred Schepsi from *Devil's Playground* and *The Chant of Jimmy Blacksmith* to—does someone have a handkerchief?—*Mr. Baseball.*

40 11. *General pervasive corporate cowardice II: movie stars as job insurance.*

41 Stars are paid huge salaries on the theory that they can open movies. Most of the time they don't, though. The list of movies that hit without stars goes on almost forever: *E.T., Star Wars, Dirty Dancing, 2001: A Space Odyssey, 48 Hrs., Blazing Saddles, Easy Rider* . . . and so on. Again we have to ask if people in Hollywood are just total morons or if there is some systemic cause. Again, the answer is the less satisfying one. Movie stars are insurance. Maybe they'll open the picture, maybe not, but at least they will give you some bragging rights about working with a big star. (Remember that bragging rights are a medium of exchange in Hollywood, making an executive or producer "hot" and bringing in more opportunities.) Stars also attract material, and directors, so it's good to be friendly with them. And stars are also represented by agents, and if you have no friends among agents, you'll get last pick of everything—witness the drought of decent material Disney's Jeffrey Katzenberg experienced when he went to war with superagent Mike Ovitz.

42 12. *Everyone is creative.*

43 The most obnoxious phrase in Hollywood is "I'm good with story." Anyone who says this is wrong. What real artists know is that every story is specific, growing out of character and place, and that it has certain organic requirements, and that often a story's peculiarities and mistakes are part of what make it unique. That's why they're so nervous every time they start a new one. In the rush to mark scripts with their scent, creative executives and actors and directors and producers forget that you can add a lot of great colors together, but unless you really know what you're doing you end up with brown.

44 13. *Corporate mentality trickle-down effect.*

45 Everyone goes to Hollywood with dreams of making great movies. But the town is hard to crack, very hard, and people adapt to every system by doing the things the system rewards. So after a few years of failure they settle for making successful ones. Then they suppress the memory of their early ideals and begin to develop a fetish for telling everyone their grosses. And that's the best-case scenario. I know a smart woman who went to Hollywood to write screenplays and made a quick sale, but after a while she started to feel her own ideas were too esoteric. Perhaps they were, but instead of getting out of Hollywood, she became obsessed with learning "the formula." I actually heard her use the phrase, "That's not the formula." The moral of the story is that writing for an audience, though often invigorating, tends to corrupt the artistic soul . . . and writing for an audience that you feel is beneath you really corrupts your soul. And Hollywood today is a deeply corrupt place.

III.

Those are the small reasons, some of them. But the biggest reason for Hollywood's current malaise is the same thing that has always been its strength. By its nature, Hollywood is the most democratic of art forms, tuned to the public like Liberace's piano. And when Hollywood meets the public's highest and most passionate needs, the result can be glorious—as the Depression gave us *Sullivan's Travels* and Vietnam gave us *The Deer Hunter*. 46

But today we are mired deep in the slough of postmodernism. Arthur C. Danto says art ended a few decades ago, and Francis Fukuyama says history itself has ended. It seems as if all that's left for us to do is to root among the shells and rinds of old forms, rearranging them (or in the case of certain Republican politicians, resurrecting them). While it's likely that these guys are suffering a bad case of what William Safire once called "anomie-too-ism," there's no doubt that as a nation we've got a major case of the blahs. We suffer from what literary critic Harold Bloom calls "belatedness." Even our bands are stuck, redoing punk, redoing thrash, redoing country, redoing rap ad nauseum. They don't sing to warn us about the hard rain gonna fall, they sing, "I want to be Bob Dylan." So we sit in front of our T.V.s channel-surfing, waiting for the next big thing. Maybe it'll be the Internet, maybe virtual reality. . . . 47

The movies reflect this malaise. They flop around, desperately trying to please us, but the one thing they dare not do is try to challenge us—because we don't want them to. As candy drives out vegetables, wish-fulfillment has driven out all attempt at realism. Movies have always told lies, given us *Top Hat* in the middle of the Depression, but now that's all they tell us. A movie like *The Best Years of Our Lives* is inconceivable today. Happy-ending-itis marred one of this year's few decent movies, *The Shawshank Redemption*—any gritty prison movie that ends up with two ex-cons embracing on a beach has gone grievously offtrack. Filmmakers justify their lies with paeans to the power of the imagination (remember *Radio Flyer?*), to the "true lies" of art, like sweaty rapists insisting on their innocence. The smartest figure out a fresh way to give us the same old lie, and we reward them lavishly. What is *Forrest Gump* but the story of a new superhero, Stupidman, who flies through all the traumas of our time without a single scratch, and gets rich, too. 48

There are signs of hope. Some of the very movies I've been attacking here also hint that Hollywood is getting restless. Consider this unexpected similarity between *Pulp Fiction* and *Forrest Gump:* as *Pulp Fiction* breaks tradition with its trochal form, so *Gump* breaks the 49 contemporary rules, taking the Seinfeld-like approach of telling a story about a guy sitting on a bench, with hardly any sex, little violence, no plot, no antagonist. These may be incremental changes, but they are real, and the vast popularity of *Pulp* and *Gump* show that the audience is ready for a change, too. There are also movies out there doing their best to finish off their tired genres once and for all, as *Natural Born Killers* tried to kill off the lovers-on-the-lam movie, and *The Last Action Hero* tried to explode the action movie. Even the Philistine foreign market made a giant hit—$198 million!—out of the steroid-free *Four Weddings and a Funeral.*

Who knows, maybe even Ricardo Mestres and Barry Josephson 50
will be part of a brighter future. Ricardo has landed Robin Williams to star in a script called *Jack,* with Francis Ford Coppola directing, and Barry was promoted to president of production at Columbia, where there's a buzz on his upcoming releases, *Bad Boys* and *Money Train.* I hope all three movies are great, I really do. It's true that *Jack* is another inner-child story about a kid who grows so fast that he looks 40 when he's still just 10, and *Bad Boys* and *Money Train* sound like your basic action fair, but there's always hope, and the trailers are always bright with promise. So maybe if we just keep wishing on our movie stars (and click our heels together three times) there will be a happy ending for us all. In the meantime, you'll find me sitting in some overpriced restaurant, picking at another plate of tuna sashimi and drinking a vodka martini—straight up with an olive. And make it a double, please. I'm on my way to the Multiplex, and I need all the help I can get.

THINKING ABOUT THE ESSAY

1. The author begins his essay with anecdotes citing a couple of meetings he's had with movie executives. What function does this serve in structuring his thesis? What function does it serve in gaining the reader's attention?
2. Richardson compares and contrasts older films with newer ones, demonstrating a broad knowledge of films and film history. To what degree does this give his argument authority? To what degree does his knowledge affect your own confidence in intelligently responding to the essay?
3. In describing contemporary filmmaking, the author uses terms such as "cobbled-together," "making Cheez Whiz," "well-made," bland films that contrast with the few films "with the architectural coherence of art." What comparative points does he make between good and bad movies?

4. What implicit analogies is the author making between current filmmaking and our society at large? What other elements of our culture seem to fit the current Hollywood paradigm?
5. How does the manipulation of television shows by their producers as described in the essay "Bimbo Watch" affect the public similarly to the "dumb and dumber" tendencies in Hollywood filmmaking?

RESPONDING IN DISCUSSION

1. Divide into groups of three and four. Select two or three movies that everyone in the group has seen. Discuss the quality of the movies, using some of the criteria proposed by the author, and share your findings with the rest of the class.
2. Prior to class, devise a concept for a movie you believe has aesthetic appeal. In class, pair off with a classmate, and role-play the pitching of your concept to your partner, who will role-play the producer. Reverse roles and repeat. Discuss your responses to the exercise with your class.
3. Discuss your position on movies. Are they art or entertainment? Explain your view.
4. Select a film from any of those discussed in the essay, and explain why you take a contrary position to the one held by the author. For example, explain why you thought *Forrest Gump* was a great film or why you thought *Blue Velvet* was awful.
5. Discuss what you believe to be the effects on society of films that always end happily, even a "gritty prison movie" like *The Shawshank Redemption,* a film cited by the author.

RESPONDING IN WRITING

1. Write an expository essay of 500 words describing the minimum requirements of a "good" film.
2. Write an essay comparing and contrasting a film you thought was good with a film you thought was bad.
3. For a research project, select one of the enumerated reasons listed by the author to explain why current Hollywood films have become so mediocre. Go to your library, and using Magazine Index Plus or a similar research vehicle, enter a keyword that will provide you with four or five articles on your topic. Read the articles and use the information you garner to further explore the point you have researched. Write an essay of 750 to 1,000 words on your topic using at least four bibliographic citations.

4. Argue for or against the proposition that the homogenization of Hollywood films is just one example of the many being controlled by the few.

Spike Lee: Fast Forward

Sharon Fitzgerald

Freelance writer Sharon Fitzgerald profiles a fellow New Yorker who (unlike most of his film director contemporaries) lives apart from the glamour of the West Coast or the upscale New York City environs of the Upper East Side or Tribeca, favoring instead his Brooklyn neighborhood as homebase of operations. Writing in the October–November 1995 edition of *American Visions,* the author gets "up close and personal" with Spike Lee, one of the most famous independent film director-writer-producers in America. What distinguishes Mr. Lee from other successful contemporaries is his race. The author vividly portrays how his identification as an African-American influences his movies, his lifestyle, and his mission.

PREVIEWING THE ESSAY

Have you ever seen a Spike Lee movie? What was your reaction to it? Do you consider the filmmaker simply as a well-known member of the film industry or does his race enter into any consideration or appraisal of his life and work? After all, you probably don't leave a Tom Hanks or Tom Cruise movie saying, "I just saw a film featuring a white actor."

The walls of 40 Acres and a Mule Filmworks fairly shout how far Shelton "Spike" Lee has traveled, and how quickly. Mounted, framed and hanging opposite the front door are three courtside tickets to the NBA championships, a leisure status symbol of modern moviemakers. At $550 a pop, the VIP value of seat 9, row AA, court 28 at Madison Square Garden is indisputable. Extended alongside last season's tickets are front-page clippings confirming that this spectator is a headliner. 1

New York City's leading tabloids are all represented here. *Newsday* quotes "Spike Lee on Reggie Miller: I Thought the Brother Had More Class." The *Post* exclaims: "Spiked!" The *Daily News* retorts, "Thanks a Lot, Spike." All three refer to Lee's trash talk with the Indiana Pacer—court-to-curb action that spurred Miller on to a fourth-quarter, 25-point miracle in last year's NBA Eastern Conference playoff games against the Knicks. 2

Between 40 Acres' second-floor office and third-floor conference 3
room, assorted posters present more of Lee's tastes and accomplishments. In gilded frames are the signs of 1970s film fare, such as *Hit Man, Mandingo, The Education of Sonny Carson* and *Cornbread, Earl and Me.* A *Jurassic Park* poster is inscribed, "For Spike—Roarrr," and signed by Steven Spielberg; the one from *Taxi Driver* is autographed by Robert De Niro. Although the hometown advantage is maintained by posters from such Spike Lee joints as *Malcolm X, Mo' Better Blues* and *Do the Right Thing,* there is also an array of retro images promoting French translations of American films.

The large, well-lit office is a multipurpose expanse without walls 4
to separate the staff's wood desks or to interrupt their nonstop activities. Topics of conversation—the sizes of promotional T-shirts, phone calls to be made or answered, schedules and guests for movie screenings, the quality of that day's cord of edited film—continually shift. On a front burner bubbles *Girl 6,* which opens next year; the story of baseball legend Jackie Robinson simmers in prepreproduction. Not surprisingly, the background music is the 40 Acres and a Mule Musicworks soundtrack of *Clockers,* Lee's current movie release.

On the room's horizon, upon a slightly elevated platform, is the 5
desk of the 38-year-old mastermind. Lee's is a panoramic view of the creative kingdom—a director's view. Separate but not inaccessible, he can work the phones, review the paperwork, and make eye contact with everyone who enters. On first take, he appears relaxed with his roles both in and out of the spotlight.

It helps that he has chosen a low-key demeanor and raised it to an 6
art form, an expertise revealed when he is the focus of a camera. To start with, he does very little blinking. This is a rather tricky fact to observe behind those dark-frame eyeglasses that ID him as clearly as the goatee, baseball cap and diamond stud in his left earlobe. When they do move, his heavy eyelids fall and rise on a low shutter speed.

Second, Lee's fashion choices, at least on this day, appear to be 7
influenced by the what-you-see-is-what-you-get school of design: wrinkled T-shirt, denim shorts, tube socks and sneakers. It is a cool inner tempo that keeps him on point, his arms folded behind him, while a makeup artists dabs, a photo assistant adjusts, and a photographer begins clicking away.

After taking several sphinxlike shots, the photographer tries liven- 8
ing things up. "Hey, Spike," he says, "you can be animated if you like." Lee's right eyebrow arches slightly as he considers the invitation. He shifts one pound of body weight from his right to his left foot. A smile starts—and stops—at the left corner of his mouth. "That's as animated as it gets," he says.

It has been 10 years since the summer of 1985, when this stealth 9
bomber surprised Hollywood body counters with *She's Gotta Have It.*

The exploits of Nola Darling, a homegirl with sexual attitude, rocked and tantalized audiences. However, the lion's share of attention was paid to the film's director-producer-writer-co-star, a hefty hyphenate, even by Hollywood standards. Lee's pithy Brooklynese invited comparisons to fellow Knicks fan Woody Allen, but the folklore embellishing his against-the-odds achievement was more akin to the spin that propelled Sylvester Stallone. Not since *Rocky* had American filmgoers been as stunned by the arrival of a heavyweight.

Still, for young black filmmakers, Spike Lee represented more 10
than a bankable name; he was a torchbearer, a homey who brought some to get some. He seemed to open the door for a league of independent directors: John Singleton, Robert Townsend, the brothers Hudlin and Hughes.

With characteristic aplomb—outspoken yet soft-spoken—Lee sep- 11
arates fact from fiction. "In every interview I do," he says, "this whole thing comes up about a black renaissance. The way I see it is this: I'm not the first African-American filmmaker. Those who torched this path for me were people like Oscar Micheaux, Gordon Parks, Michael Schultz, Melvin Van Peebles, Ossie Davis. I just picked it up.

"Filmmaking is what I love. I love doing it, and I am very grateful 12
and blessed that I have been able to really go from film to film to film, which is something that not too many African-American film directors have been able to do."

With *Clockers,* Lee will have gone "from film to film to film" 13
eight times since the debut of *She's Gotta Have It.* True to its lineage, *Clockers* will undoubtedly provoke controversy and push button after button.

On its surface, *Clockers*—co-produced by Lee, Martin Scorcese 14
and Jon Kilik and based on the best-selling novel by Richard Price—offers an intimate and violent look at the inner-city drug trade. The turmoil is revealed through Strike (Mekhi Phifer), a 19-year-old around-the-clock crack dealer who—after the brutal murder of a rival and the arrest of his hardworking older brother—is forced to rethink the dangerous circumstances of his life.

Strike remains the pursued in the film's multilayered game of cat- 15
and-mouse. Rocco Klein (Harvey Keitel), a homicide detective, prods him for the truth. Rodney Little (Delroy Lindo), the elder drug dealer, demands his undying allegiance. Andre the Giant (Keith David), a housing policeman and local figurehead, warns him to end his corrupt influence on the project's community.

In Price's novel, the experiences of Strike and Rocco command 16
center stage; in his initial screenplay, contracted by Universal for director Scorcese and actor Robert De Niro, the focus was on Rocco's police investigation. When Scorcese and De Niro opted for the movie *Casino* and Universal asked Lee to take over *Clockers,* he agreed, but

shifted the emphasis. The new screenplay, co-written by Price and Lee, makes Strike the epicenter of the dramatic quakes, and the bonds connecting black men underscore the tragedies.

"I really wasn't as much into that cop stuff as I was in the relationship between the two brothers," Lee says. "One is clocking and the other is on the up-and-up. How is it that two brothers that are brought up in the same household—where everything they are exposed to is the same—why is it that one brother goes left and the other goes right? 17

"But another interesting thing was the whole struggle, this battle between Rodney, played by Delroy Lindo, and Andre the Giant, played by Keith David. You have these two strong black male figures in a community in which there are not a lot of men in the households. You have all of these generations of young black kids that are longing for father figures, and these two guys are out there. 18

"Unfortunately, most of these kids are going to want to choose Rodney because he has the cash and the flash, and they don't see Andre driving a fancy car or throwing money around. They see him going to work as a housing authority cop, and they definitely don't want to be a cop. In close-up, you see they are fighting for Strike, essentially for Strike's soul." 19

His affinity to the urban parable still intact, Lee has sallied onto the gritty terrain usually the province of gangsta films, a genre he has been inclined to avoid. "That was really one of my main concerns when Universal called me to do *Clockers,*" he says. "I did not want to further contribute to the genre. It is not the total expression of our experience in this country, and it has been beat to death. I'm tired of it. 20

"It is still my hope that we black filmmakers as a collective group will put that genre to rest, to bed, and try to tell all the other great stories that are out there. In doing *Clockers,* we hoped that we would execute what we wanted to say so well that it would be like the final nail in the coffin." 21

However, if Lee has learned anything over the past years, it is that his work rarely goes down quietly. "I'm not surprised anymore," he says. "In doing *Do the Right Thing,* I never expected people to say that I was trying to start an uprising among black folks and burn this country down. In *Mo' Better Blues,* I never expected the *New York Times* to label me anti-Semitic because of the portrayals of Mo and Josh Flatbush. All I want to do is tell the story. When I write a script, I'm not saying, 'Uh-oh. I'd better leave that out because I might get into trouble.' I really don't operate like that." 22

The aftermath, he admits, can be exhausting. "When *Do the Right Thing* came out, I had to go on '*Nightline,*'" he says. "People were saying it was an irresponsible film; therefore, that was going to have a direct effect on the box office, which it did. At the beginning, I used 23 to spend a lot of time defending my work, but as I got older and I did more films, I just resigned myself to letting the films speak for themselves. At a point, if you don't stop, you can kill yourself from always defending your work.

"As far as critics go—and this might be true for audiences, too—I 24
sometimes think that they let the persona of Spike Lee get in the way of enjoying or really understanding the films that I make. I mean, it shouldn't be about whether you like the Knicks or not, or that you don't like my commercials or that you don't like Spike. I hope they don't let that color things. Just go and see the film."

In short, he wants to be treated like any other serious artist. "The 25
first movie Woody Allen made after that thing with what's-her-name got great reviews," he says. "The fact that he might be labeled a child molester never came up. They separated that part of his life from Woody Allen the filmmaker. I think that sometimes they don't do the same for me."

Could it be because his work is so controversial? "I don't know," 26
he says. "One thing it has to do with is the fact that some of the media has portrayed me as being a racist or prejudiced. One of the worst things that has happened was that *Esquire* magazine cover which was titled 'Spike Lee Hates Your Cracker Ass.' People thought that was a quote out of my mouth. If I was white and I saw Spike Lee's face on the cover of this magazine and it says, 'Spike Hates Your Cracker Ass,' why would I want to see his films?"

In an industry that devours talent—both the dark and the light 27
meat—the bottom line is survival. From the beginning, Lee sprinkled his sound bites with the word on black powerlessness in Hollywood. He also fought this exclusion head-on—demanding creative control, hiring interns to cut their teeth behind the scenes, launching 40 Acres and a Mule Musicworks to produce his films' soundtracks, opening T-shirt emporiums in Brooklyn and Hollywood, and following up film releases with books describing how he got the job done.

His marketing and entrepreneurial savvy is almost legendary, and 28
so is his support of black artists. "The checks have never bounced," says composer Raymond Jones, who wrote the opening music for *Clockers* and has contributed to Lee's films since *School Daze.* "Spike ups the ante every time. He sets his expectations very high, and you want to meet them. Plus, he's insightful; he hears things from a combination of perspectives."

Early on, Lee challenged other power brokers, including Eddie 29
Murphy and Whoopi Goldberg, to use their clout to help open doors for African Americans. In the past year, he has backed up rising filmmakers as the executive producer on the movies *Drop Squad, New Jersey Drive* and *Tales From the Hood.* In his estimation, the reluctance of African-American artists to form strong economic alliances is the

result of a divisive historical experience, which must be overcome by any means necessary.

30 "It all really has to do with slavery," he says. "We have been taught over hundreds of years not to trust each other, and that is still with us today. Spielberg, [David] Geffen and [Jeffrey] Katzenberg have all gotten a lot of money, and they said, 'We'll get more if we pool our resources and work together.' We as a people have not really found out how to do that yet, but we will.

31 "The only reason that Warner Brothers gave in and started to fund *Malcolm X* again was then Tracy Chapman, The Artist Formerly Known as Prince, Michael Jordan, Magic [Johnson], Oprah [Winfrey], Bill Cosby, Janet Jackson and Peggy Cooper Cafritz down in D.C. came together on a joint venture the same way that Katzenberg, Geffen and Spielberg came together on DreamWorks.

32 "That's some heavyweights, and that's what it took, because otherwise that film was not getting made. Warner Brothers understood exactly what it was to have these people writing checks for me to continue. Two days later, they started funding us. That is power.

33 "But I will acknowledge—and I think that everyone knows, this is not a revelation—that Hollywood is just like any other place in America, and the playing field is not level. So if you're an African American, you know that you have more hurdles thrown in your way, more obstacles. And you can bitch and moan about it, or you can try to jump those hurdles and smash those obstacles. And it's not fair, and that's the way it is."

34 Not content to rely on the rewards of the film industry, Lee has carved a position for himself in the culture's commercial landscape. Mars Blackmon may not have nabbed Nola, but he was nobody's passing fancy, and neither are those Nike ads, nor those "X" caps and other 40 Acres promotobilia. "I've always felt that if opportunities came to me, I should take advantage of them," says Lee. "I was not going to limit myself by saying that I would not do anything outside the movies."

35 Thus, in extraordinary fashion, Lee is achieving what few artists—black or white—have been able to master: He speaks his mind and maintains a popular persona. All the while, the hype factor is not lost on him. He seems acutely aware of the dangers that accompany his high profile. He is also quick to admit that there are African-American artists among his detractors.

36 "I've never really thought of myself as a spokesperson for 35 million African Americans," he says, "and I've never tried to present myself that way. All my views have been solely my views, and I think that there are African-American people who agree with me, but we also have African Americans who don't agree. I think this a good time to state that it is a fallacy that all of my critics are white,

because that is not the case either. I have a lot of black critics, people like Stanley 'Crotch.'"

He evenly recalls how his role as director of *Malcolm X* brought 37
him under fire, most notably from Amiri Baraka. "His whole criticism centered around the idea that I was bourgeois and all these other things, too middle-class," says Lee. "I had to be a card-carrying member of the Socialist Party.

"I just look at it like a lot of people had their own agendas, and I 38
think with Baraka, a lot had to do with jealousy. He considered himself the father of the black arts movement, and he's been given his due. But, you know, black artists now are able to make a whole lot more money, and I think we are in a lot more control of our art than they were back then. We get a lot more publicity, too. So I think that might have something to do with it."

Lee's ninth film, *Girl 6,* scheduled to open in several months, will 39
be of particular interest to those who have questioned his presentation of female characters. ("bell hooks thinks that I am a man hater, I mean a woman hater," he says.) The movie chronicles the endeavors of a struggling actress, intent on achieving success because of her talent and not her appearance, who takes a job as a phone sex operator to earn the money to make that big move West.

Word-of-mouth describes the film as a funny, lighthearted look at 40
sex and what women have to put up with to get ahead. The movie's fantasy sequences will feature cameo appearances by the likes of Madonna, Halle Berry and Quentin Tarantino.

"I know that you have Julie Dash and Leslie Harris," Lee says, 41
"but I feel that the only way that African-American women will be fully satisfied with the portrayal of African-American women in cinema is when African-American women write the screenplays that African-American women are directing. Then I think that women will probably get a portrayal closer to the one they like. As long as men are doing it, even if they are black men, I don't think that women are going to be satisfied. I have acknowledged in several interviews that that is something that I have to work on—not just the portrayals, but to try to really give women characters as much depth as the male ones.

"But don't you think that there is a male world and a female 42
world and then a place where we intersect? I think that we are really different and that there are a lot of misunderstandings, particularly between black men and black women. That's something that needs to be addressed also. I don't think that you do that by calling black women hos or bitches or skeezers; that's for sure."

With *Girl 6,* Lee apparently decided to begin by reforming the 43
basics. "There were mostly women in the cast and crew," says Ina Mayhew, the artistic director of both *Girl 6* and *Clockers.* "It must

have been very interesting for Spike to work with so many women, when he's used to being around men most of the time."

One cannot help wondering about the impact of Lee-the-filmmaker on his old neighborhood of Fort Greene, Brooklyn. Even with the boutique Spike's Joint down the block, DeKalb Avenue doesn't look any different from other New York thoroughfares. There's a takeout Chinese joint, a grocery, a fruit stand, the usual day-to-day, hand-to-mouth institutions. It may be a few more years before the artist emerges who admits that he was influenced by the comings and goings of his homeboy Spike Lee. But one only has to ask to discover what remaining on his turf has meant to the filmmaker. 44

"It keeps me grounded," he says. "I grew up here, and I think it makes me a better filmmaker. Living where I live, I'm not out of touch. I mean, Fort Greene is not like Brooklyn Heights. You have people here who have money; you've also got people here on welfare. Across the street on Myrtle Avenue are the Fort Greene projects. So you have this vast spectrum—people making it, people struggling to make it, people in between. 45

"I'm very observant. For the most part, I don't even talk; I just watch and listen to people. I think if Spike Lee moved to Hollywood—if I had a house in Beverly Hills or Bel Air or Malibu—sooner or later you would see that reflected in my films. It would have to be." 46

THINKING ABOUT THE ESSAY

1. What aspects of Spike Lee's life does the author depict, other than his role as a filmmaker? What rhetorical methods does she use to depict them?
2. Does the author provide you with a comprehensive portrait of Spike Lee's personality and style? Where and how does she do so?
3. To what degree would you consider Lee an "independent filmmaker," using the criteria provided by Richardson in the previous essay? Explain your view.
4. What has made Spike Lee's films controversial? Does Lee consider the controversy surrounding his films implicit in their portrayals and messages or merely a result of media hype? What is your personal view of the degree to which his films are controversial or even inflammatory? Explain.
5. Thousands of film students each year dream of achieving the status of Spike Lee. Does the essay suggest a recipe for success in Hollywood, or does it suggest that it is the filmmaker's individual abilities and talents that have brought him renown? Explain.

RESPONDING IN DISCUSSION

1. Divide into groups of three and four and discuss those qualities needed to achieve Spike Lee's independence and success as a filmmaker. For example, how significant are single-minded pursuit of a goal, attending the best film schools, connections and networking, and a vision or mission? Share your conclusions with the rest of the class.
2. Discuss whether the essay is more a portrait of a contemporary artist than a portrait of a contemporary filmmaker. Cite examples in the essay to support your view.
3. Is Spike Lee's films' success due to his subject matter rather than any inherent aesthetic abilities (such as screenwriting, directorial mastery, and ability to work with actors) that are usually discussed in a portrait of a filmmaker? Or is it a combination of both?
4. How does Spike Lee rate as a creative filmmaker, using the criteria set out by Richardson in his essay that discusses what makes a "good film" and enumerates the elements that have diminished the quality of Hollywood movies? From the portrait provided in this essay, does Lee seem to have protected himself from Hollywood's current bottom-line culture?
5. To what degree has identification with your own race determined your response to questions 3 and 4 in this section?

RESPONDING IN WRITING

1. Write an expository essay of 400 to 500 words, explaining how Spike Lee has influenced African-Americans via activities other than his filmmaking.
2. Conduct an on-line search of film reviews of any of Spike Lee's recent movies. Read the complete texts of at least four of them, and write an essay of 750 to 1,000 words comparing and contrasting the degree to which the reviewers focus their attention on an analysis of racial depictions and conflict instead of considering aesthetic elements (such as the production values and quality of the directing, acting, and story structure).
3. Argue for or against the proposition that if Spike Lee were a white film director, attention to his work would be much less pronounced.
4. In her essay, "Planet of the White Guys," included in this anthology, Barbara Ehrenreich states that most white people are implicitly racist. Defend or reject her thesis by discussing race relations as depicted in *Do the Right Thing, Mo' Better Blues, Malcolm X,* or *Clockers* after viewing one of these films on videotape.

CONNECTIONS: FOR WRITING AND RESEARCH

1. View a Spike Lee film in class. Write a 400-to-500–word evaluation of its message. Select a partner in class, discuss the differences between your evaluations, and share them with the rest of the class.
2. Write an extended essay arguing for or against the proposition that Rebecca Walker, in her essay "Changing the Face of Feminism," which appears in the next chapter, is doing a disservice to the basic tenets of that movement because portrayals of women—as discussed in the essay "Bimbo Watch"—demonstrate that little has changed in depicting and regarding women as chiefly sex objects.
3. Argue for or against the proposition that the deterioration in quality of Hollywood films is not due to anything intrinsic about the film business, but rather results from the general deterioration of the quality of American life in such areas as the environment, professionalism in the job place, media in general, and sports.
4. For a research project, study the history of ratings in media, and write a research paper of 1,000 to 1,500 words discussing how measuring audience response has altered the type of "product" that the media provides.
5. Discuss how the Generation X population is having an impact on film, music, and television.
6. Write a step-by-step process analysis essay entitled "How to Create a Dumb Movie."

8

GENDER ISSUES

Probably no society in history has reevaluated the roles of men and women as has the United States since the end of World War II. The deluge of pronouncements, laws, writing, and debates on gender issues has probably created more, rather than less, confusion, misunderstanding, and misperception between and among both sexes. Take, for example, the word *feminism.* What does it mean? Ask a dozen people, and you may get as many definitions. As the essays in this section demonstrate, there is no longer clear agreement (if ever there was) that men dominate all aspects of our culture. And some of these opinions come from women who have deeply and broadly studied the gender wars. Or take the concept of "victim." While early feminism portrayed women as seeking equality because they were the victims of society's favoritism toward men, many women today believe the identification with victimization prevents women from achieving equal status. Even among women scholars the idea is growing that men are going through such a profound identity crisis that they are mired in issues that take them further away from the true issues at hand. Regardless of the current issues, however, it is fairly certain that in an open society such as the United States, gender roles will not revert to what they once were. Social, economic, and political changes are just too profound to reinstate the status quo. While the following essays cannot possibly solve these complex issues, they do raise points that more superficial assertions fail to recognize.

Changing the Face of Feminism

Rebecca Walker

This young African-American author and editor of *To Be Real: Telling the Truth and Changing the Face of Feminism* is the daughter of well-known contemporary writer Alice Walker, whose works include *The Color Purple.* Writing in the January 1996 issue of *Essence,* a magazine geared toward African-American women, Rebecca Walker explores the evolution she underwent from her version of a "card-carrying" feminist of her mother's generation to an independent thinker, who struggled successfully to understand and accept her own views on gender issues, views that issued from the heart rather than the headlines. In this short essay, she demonstrates how "while honoring my complexities, I have found common ground with feminism."

PREVIEWING THE ESSAY

Where did Walker develop her initial ideas about gender relations? Why were they so strongly embedded in her belief system? What elements of her generation dissuaded her from following lockstep with the previous one?

A year ago my life was like a feminist ghetto. Every decision I made had to be filtered through my image of what was politically correct for female empowerment. Everything had a gendered explanation, and whatever didn't fit into my concept of feminism was "bad, patriarchal and problematic." 1

I couldn't be intimate with a male friend who once called someone a pussy. I couldn't live with a partner because I would never be able to maintain my independence. I couldn't utter thoughts of dislike or jealousy toward another woman because that would mean I was unfeminist. 2

My existence was an ongoing state of saying no to many elements of the universe. The parts of me that didn't mesh with my ideals made me feel insecure and confused about my values and my identity. Curiosity about pornography and sadomasochism, an attraction to the stable domestic partnership, feelings of competitiveness with other women—not to mention a desire to start a business and a love for people who challenged and sometimes flatly opposed my feminist beliefs—represented contradictions to my sense of how to make feminist revolution that I had no idea how to reconcile. 3

The ever-shifting ideals of feminism have left many young women and men struggling with the reality of who we are. As one woman said to me at a small midwestern college where I was giving a lecture, "I feel I can't be a feminist because I am not strong enough, not good 4 enough, not disciplined enough." Depending on which feminist mythology she was exposed to, she believed that to be a feminist one must (1) live in poverty, (2) critique constantly, (3) never marry, (4) censor pornography and/or (5) worship the goddess.

5 Today, too many people believe that a feminist must never compromise herself. She can never make concessions for love or money, and she must always be devoted to elevating her gender. Many young women fear that if they want to own a BMW or want to be treated "like a lady" or listen to misogynist hip-hop or occasionally prioritize racial oppression over gender oppression, then they will not be allowed to consider themselves part of a history of societal transformation on behalf of women.

6 From my experience talking with young women, it has become clear to me that we are struggling with more than the media's distorted characterizations of feminism. For many of us, embracing feminism suggests an identity and a way of life that does not allow for individuality or complexity. We fear that the identity will dictate and regulate our lives, that it will force us to choose inflexible and unchanging sides: female against male, Black against White, oppressed against oppressor, good against bad.

7 This way of ordering the world is especially difficult for a generation that has grown up transgender, bisexual and interracial. Many of us were raised by knowing and loving people who are racist, sexist and otherwise afflicted. For us, the lines between "us" and "them" are often blurred. As a result, we find ourselves seeking to create identities that include more than they exclude, or that explore rather than define.

8 Luckily, many young women and men are determined to bring their bright minds and conscious commitment to feminism as an ongoing movement for social change. They are looking beyond the boundaries of what is "correct" and "incorrect" and broadening the notions of who and what constitute a feminist community.

9 I, for one, am continuing to build upon a legacy that challenges the patriarchy yet encourages the confidence it takes to theorize one's own life. While honoring my complexities, I have found common ground with feminism.

THINKING ABOUT THE ESSAY

1. Walker claims that her existence "was an ongoing state of saying no to many elements of the universe." What were these elements? Are you now or have you previously been in a similar situation? Explain.
2. Walker compares her "political correctness" to "life . . . in a feminist ghetto." What does she mean? Are there aspects of your

thinking and responses to life that you suspect may not derive from your authentic responses, but arise from some preconceived notion of how you should think?

3. Is Walker's experience typical of a female Generation Xer? How many of the five rules of being a feminist have you ever considered as fact? Have you grown up, as she seems to have, in a generation that is "transgender, bisexual and interracial"?
4. What is Walker's personal opinion concerning "compromise" in weaving her own views and experience with the legacy of feminism? How do they compare to your own?
5. Does the essay have a thesis? If so, what is it?

RESPONDING IN DISCUSSION

1. Divide into groups of three and four. As a group, list qualities you believe to be implicit in the term *feminism.* Compare your list to those of the rest of the class.
2. What are two elements of feminism you believe to be valuable and sensible? What are two that you believe are whimsical or irrational? Consider that Walker claims traditional feminists believed it was necessary to "live in poverty."
3. What is the implied audience of this essay? All women? Educated women? American women? Women with concerns about feminism? Young women contemplating gender issues? What clues does the author provide that led you to your conclusion?
4. Describe the attributes needed for the personality of a woman who would follow Walker's pursuit of "honoring my complexities."
5. Visit www.feminist.com and explore the information about "The Third Wave" which Walker cofounded. In what ways does the material you find at this site affect your perception of Walker as an authoritative speaker?

RESPONDING IN WRITING

1. In a descriptive/narrative essay of 400 words, discuss a time in your life when you interacted with a member of the opposite gender based upon the way you *thought* was the proper way to behave rather than your "authentic" feelings about the person.
2. Argue for or against the proposition that the "feminist stereotype" that Walker evokes in her essay is a contrivance, and not based on the true attributes of even the most vehement feminist.

3. Compare and contrast the idea of a "static feminism" versus an "exploratory feminism."
4. Select one of the essays from the section "Generations at the Crossroads" and demonstrate how the values expressed by Walker are consistent with those of Generation X in general.
5. Visit a website devoted to Rebecca Walker's famous mother Alice Walker. Scan information on Alice Walker, conduct additional research if necessary, and then write a comparative essay on the two women that stresses their common concerns.

Feminism and Nomenclature

Richard Grenier

Writing in the July 3, 1995, issue of *Insight on the News,* Grenier takes a humorous look at our obsession for finding the "politically correct" method of naming. He suggests that women who decided to keep their maiden names or demanded to be referred to as Ms., or worked hard at dispensing with sexist language did not consider the historical evidence that changing naming conventions has repercussions beyond merely getting used to or easily altering the perceived power structure of a culture. Grenier claims the effort "often backfires or goes off in a crazy direction." Is the author merely presenting in satirical fashion what happens when a social idea becomes an obsession, or does he demonstrate that changes in language use—regardless of their intention—should be carefully thought out regarding their motivation, intention, and effect?

PREVIEWING THE ESSAY

Is a woman's decision to keep her maiden name once she marries more symbolic than effective in promoting the idea of equality? Ask a married woman who had to choose between keeping her original name and adopting her husband's. What variables went into her decision?

To think if all had gone well and feminists had their way about everything, maybe some day I'd have been able to assume my wife's maiden name, Baker, and never have to tell anyone how to spell or pronounce my name again. 1

But the feminists are losing ground. Rats! I knew it was too good to last. Names are a more complicated business than you'd think. If I were a Hungarian, my name would be Grenier Richard. Then again, if I were a Spaniard, my name would be Richard Grenier Zelaznik, 2 which would give me a saucy flavor, I think. People could say that that darn Grenier Zelaznik is a no-good son-of-a-gun. Naturally, Zelaznik was my mother's maiden name, a piece of Poland she was only too glad to leave behind when she married my father.

In our own time the most interesting shifts in the morphology of 3
name and title have been produced by social revolution. After the Bolsheviks took power, *gospadin* (mister) was banned in favor of *tovarich* (comrade). In this the Bolsheviks were imitating the French Revolution, which banned *monsieur* in favor of *citoyen* (citizen), prompting an English wit to reprove them for undue ceremoniousness. Why *citizen?* Why not *biped?* Biped Danton. Biped Robespierre. With the Restoration, *monsieur* (literally "my sire") came back with a bang, and was extended to masses of people who'd never had any title of courtesy at all. Instead of the aristocracy being pushed down, the masses were pushed up.

For that's the way it goes with word engineering. It often back- 4
fires or goes off in a crazy direction. Not only *monsieur* is back, but so is *gospadin.* When our fearless feminists entered into mortal combat to alter our male-dominated language—introducing such lilting locutions as "he/she" and "he or eventually she" (hesitating only before "person-eating tiger" and the command, "Person the guns!")—they faced weighty historical obstacles.

In launching their belligerent campaign to have married women 5
keep their maiden names, they were taking on, in fact, the history of the human race.

For every society known to history, prehistory, anthropology or 6
geology has been dominated by men; sorry about that. So when the great age of family names dawned for the common people, it seemed reasonable for the woman to take her husband's name.

But this discouraged sexual equality, sexual freedom, illegitimate 7
birth and women's lacrosse teams. And our feminists had to put a stop to that.

But now the tide has turned and we're surging ahead into a virile, 8
male-dominated future. Ten years ago, nearly half the women whose marriage announcements were carried in *The New York Times* (that sort) kept their maiden name. But now they've gone and split into three approximately equal groups: those who keep their maiden name, those who take their husband's name and those who can't make up their mind. Even hard-liners are often prepared to take their husbands' names when they have children.

We must remember that the more strident forms of feminism 9
have always been the preserve of educated women—America's educated classes in general being notorious worldwide for their sedulous conformity to whatever norm comes into fashion. According to a study last year for *American Demographics:* Of women with high school diplomas, maiden names were kept by 5 percent, college

degrees 15 percent and graduate degrees 20 percent. But now educated young ladies are jumping off the bandwagon.

The whole thing is reminiscent of the Quakers' vehement efforts in the 18th century to level everybody down to "thou." Before the Quakers, English was like most other European languages in preserving so-called "formal" and "intimate" forms for the second person singular: "you" and "thou." In fact, use was determined by rank and social position. Shakespeare's Hamlet calls his mother and other noblemen "you." Queen Gertrude, with never a slip, calls Hamlet, children, servants and other social inferiors "thou." 10

The Quakers hated this differentiation by rank and wanted to bring noblemen down to "thou." But the whole thing backfired and everybody was elevated to "you." 11

On the other hand, modish publications today are again depriving us of all courtesy titles (Mr., Mrs. and Miss), pushing us back down to where we were over 200 years ago. So the way this zany world works, I'm trying desperately to find a way of turning this antifeminist reaction to my advantage. Is male oppression back? Can I oppress women again? Actually I never did oppress women that I can remember. But I told a woman the other night that I never got really drunk, and she said, "How would you know?" So perhaps I've been oppressing women all along without realizing it. But it's okay again now, I gather. I think I'll try it for a while and find out. 12

THINKING ABOUT THE ESSAY

1. Is Grenier making light of a serious topic? Does he have the authority—as a man—to make pronouncements on the significance or insignificance of attempting to render language less sexist?
2. What options does a woman have if she doesn't want to adopt her husband's last name? After all, her original name is her father's. What about the idea of selecting any name she wishes?
3. The author claims that it is generally the educated classes that take on the latest "fashion." What other reason or reasons might there be for educated women to favor keeping their own names after marriage?
4. What is the author's main argument? What specific supporting points does he use to advance it?

RESPONDING IN DISCUSSION

1. Divide into groups of three and four, and discuss your personal opinion about language and its contribution toward maintaining a sexist society. Rate your opinion as "no contribution," "some

contribution," or "strong contribution." Then discuss your view and ranking with the class.

2. Is the author doing a disservice to the serious subject of sexist language by making comparisons with other language issues that bear no relevance to it, or are his analogies apt?
3. What is your response to some recently outdated modes of identifying couples, such as the absence of the woman's name (as in Mr. and Mrs. Robert Jones) or the prominence of the man (as in Dr. and Mrs. Robert Jones)? Why was such nomenclature considered appropriate at one time? What response would a title such as Dr. and Mr. Roberta Jones have elicited 30 years ago? What about today?
4. To whom is the author referring when he mentions the third of women who "can't make up their mind" regarding a change of their maiden name to their husband's name? What does this group ultimately do?

RESPONDING IN WRITING

1. If you are a single woman, write a personal essay on why you would keep or change your last name should you marry. If you are a single man, write a personal essay explaining what your position would be regarding your wife's choice of naming. If you are married, explain how the decision was made concerning changing a family name.
2. Argue for or against the idea that courtesy titles should be maintained in the workplace, regardless of one's stature or gender.
3. Write an essay discussing the relationship between the trend toward more eclectic extended families as discussed in "Stone Soup" by Kingsolver, and the relaxation of concerns about naming.
4. Argue for or against the proposition that the tone and content of this essay is entirely unsuitable for a topic as serious as sexism and language.
5. Research "sexist language" on the Web. How factual or emotional are the items listed? Write an evaluative report on your findings.

Silly Men, Banal Men

Ellen Frankel Paul

Ellen Frankel Paul is deputy director of the Social Philosophy and Policy Center and professor of political science and philosophy at Bowling Green

State University in Ohio. She has written numerous scholarly articles, and is the author or editor of many books, among them *Moral Revolution and Economic Science, Property Rights and Eminent Domain,* and *Equity and Gender: The Comparable Worth Debate*. In this essay, first published in the September–October 1993 issue of *Society,* she shares her observations on two so-called men's movements' origins, missions, and effects. While the two movements she describes purportedly work to reevaluate and heal male–female relationships, mainly by allowing men to delve more deeply into their "hidden selves," the author is highly skeptical about whether they are successful in their goal.

PREVIEWING THE ESSAY

The origin of the joke, "I'd never want to join a club that would accept me as a member," is attributed to several comics. However, its implied message is clear as a humorous self-effacement of the speaker. But the jest has serious implications in analyzing Paul's message for she implies that one's joining a men's movement suggests the individual feels something is not right with himself. Otherwise, why join? Have you ever joined or contemplated joining a club, religious sect or cult, society, gang, or organization because you felt it would help you solve a problem with living? What influenced your decision? What were the perceived benefits? What were the actual benefits?

We live in an age of endlessly proliferating movements. It seems as 1 though the members of no readily identifiable group can truly feel "empowered" unless their most zealous partisans trumpet their "oppression," that they are the victims of a callous society indifferent to their plight. Feminists denounce "patriarchy"; gays castigate "homophobic" straights; African-Americans rebuke white Americans as unreconstructed "racists"; Hispanics admonish "Anglos"; the "differently abled" denounce the "abled"; Native Americans rebuke the European invaders. All demand legal protection from anti-discrimination laws so that they might vindicate their "rights" in courts of law.

Whether one is temporarily a member of a disaffected group (as 2 are pregnant women) or permanently a member of a group to which we will all be privy someday (the "aged," over-forty set) victimhood has become something of a reverse status symbol. In the waning days of the twentieth century, no one seems satisfied until he or she can claim the mantle of victim. Rather than yearning to be free, Americans now yearn to be oppressed, to have their grievances and disappointments with life exorcised on the national stage. A fin-de-siècle funk has seized the nation: no one is content with his lot, and we all want to blame our malaise upon someone else. That someone else, in nearly all accounts of the victim mongers, is white, middle-class men. Thus, it was inevitable that sooner or later a men's movement should emerge not to expiate this Hydra of guilt, not to confess and repent, not to rise in righteous indignation, but to claim its own mantle of victimhood.

The men's movement—or more precisely, the men's movements, for there are two major trends that are widely divergent—is largely a reaction to a quarter-century of flagellation of men by radical feminists. The bill of indictment is so familiar that it needs no elaborate rehearsal here. Merely stating the main charges will suffice: women are the victims of a patriarchal society dominated by men who oppress and exploit women; women earn a mere 70 percent of men's wages; even when women appear successful in the male-dominated business world they face discrimination in advancement and salaries and an unbridgeable "glass ceiling"; women's bodies are exploited by men who use them as mere sex objects, whether as prostitutes or wives, and fantasize about them through lurid, pornographic depictions; men beat their wives, "date rape" their girlfriends, sexually harass their female co-workers, and wantonly rape women in their homes and on the streets. 3

Movements of all sorts tend to be dominated by their most extreme fringe, and the women's movement is no exception. Media attention hones in on the sensational, and such concerns of liberal feminists as equal opportunity and equality of rights are simply too colorless to capture the public spotlight. The men's movement, at least the variant of it that is portrayed in venues such as the news magazines *Time* and *Newsweek* and television shows like "20/20" and the daytime talk shows, is likewise dominated by its kookiest element. It is only the wild-man, mythopoetic branch of the movement —with its wilderness outings, myths, rituals, ancient chants, initiation rites, and beating of drums—that has pierced the public consciousness, attaining notoriety precisely because of its zaniness. 4

There is, however, another version of the movement that shares little in common with the hairy-man crowd. This sect dwells in the universities, the natural home of all things outré and radical, yet stultifying and pedestrian. This academic men's movement or AMM for short (academics are incapable of writing without acronyms) is, as one would anticipate, no fun at all. It is the stillborn offspring of radical feminism, itself a creature of the universities. NOMAS—the National Organization of Men against Sexism—is its flagship fraternity. Need one say much more? 5

HAIRY, SILLY MEN

Hairy-man men's movement (HMMM) types, *Iron John*'s Robert Bly or *Fire in the Belly*'s Sam Keen, reacted to the feminists' onslaught on the 6 male ego neither by accepting their bill of indictment, as did their AMM rivals, nor by defending the macho man, strong silent-type stereotype of masculinity popular a generation ago. HMMM's engage instead in overwrought lamentations over the wounds inflicted on men by the Industrial Revolution. Men too, they declaim, are intensely miserable, alienated from their true heritage, deprived of initiation into the mysteries of maleness. The Industrial Revolution removed fathers from their sons and left the lads to be ruled by the world of "WOMAN."

Robert Bly wants a wild man who can shout and be fierce, yet not 7
dominate women, demand "land and empire," or embrace the model of machismo. This wild man is not a savage, rather he "resembles a Zen priest, a shaman, or a woodsman," a man who has examined his "wound," recovered the Dionysian element in his nature, found the key under his mother's pillow, and confronted the Iron John of Grimm's fairy tales. Sam Keen urges men to abandon "motherland," plummet the depths of their "disease" and alienation, and undertake a quest for the "grail." He champions a new vision of man "with fire in his belly and passion in his heart." He urges men to pursue the "ancient way of the hero's journey," to depart from "everyday normality" to descend "into the strange land of disease, demons, dreadful powers, treasures, and maidens guarded by dragons. . . ."

Keen urges men to form groups in which they can discuss their 8
feelings and problems, with the likeliest candidates for membership being men in crisis from failed marriages, troubled careers, or drug addiction. Discuss your initiation into manhood, your conquests and battles, your power relationships; examine your values and your work, your sexual history and your conflicts with women; construct a chart of your emotional landscape, and practice "expressing rather than repressing your feelings"; read feminist literature with an open mind, and listen to women without interrupting; create rituals for the group and engage in social, "virile" action.

From these and other writings of like-minded gurus of the hairy- 9
man persuasion, has emerged a self-help industry of New Warrior Training Adventure Weekends, a First International Men's Conference described as "A Journey Toward Conscious Manhood," and Robert Bly's own weekend retreats which have attracted over 50,000 paying customers. White, middle-aged professionals rehearse their grief, engage in communal bonding through incantations, drum beating, and chants, and wallow in public confessions of the most intimate sort. Accompanying them on these weekend flings of self-discovery are numerous journalists, some of whom delight in lampooning the movement in the pages of *Esquire, GQ,* and *The American Spectator,* while others like PBS's Bill Moyers and "20/20"'s Hugh Downs are smitten.

It is as though the consciousness-raising sessions of the 10
early 1970s—the ones that prompted more than a few middle-aged

housewives to desert their husbands and children and worship the she-goddess—have returned with a macabre vengeance to entice men not only to become as self-absorbed, whining, petulant, and resentful as their ex-mates, but to appear utterly asinine in the process. Do women really want men who wail about their lost fathers and their overbearing mommies, while cavorting in Indian feathers, chanting "Ho"? Is this what feminism has wrought? Far from recovering the virile, hairy man, the HMMM is fathering snively, adolescent wimps. I cannot claim to speak for the silent majority of my gender (and certainly not for the politically correct woman), but I do not think I would be out on a wobbly limb if I hazarded a guess that most women would prefer Clark Gable to Robert Bly, Clint Eastwood to Sam Keen. There is something to be said for the strong silent type, the dependable, aloof, take-charge hero, if the alternative is the more than faintly ridiculous wild man.

FEMINISM'S BANAL SONS

Radical feminists have nothing but enmity for the mythopoetic, hairy-man men's movement. They resent being blamed for men's discontents, and not being possessed of a sense of irony, they fail to see how their own metaphorical drumbeat of male-bashing may have called forth the real-life drumbeating. It is, apparently, permissible to blame all of women's problems on men, but tit-for-tat is considered iniquitous. 11

But what would a men's movement tailored to the concerns of the radical feminists look like? It would be a movement that rids men of Freud's Oedipus complex and "Jungian-style archetypes that still idealize 'heroic' male violence," writes author Riane Eisler. It is this "dominator male psyche," she continues, "that today threatens all life on this planet." Theology professor Rosemary Radford Ruether opines that we all need a men's movement "in the sense of men who have come to understand the evils of patriarchy, the injustice that that [sic] has [sic] done to women, and the way that distorted all social relations." 12

Such a men's movement would explore men's feminine side and their "androgynous potential as whole human beings," offers Gloria Steinem. Acceptable male groupings would have the following characteristics, according to Steinem: they would forswear "hierarchial" language and use only language that breaks down barriers between the sexes; they would nurture children, engage in social activism, and make women feel safe; they would "cross boundaries of homophobia, racism, class, and distance from women." 13

The academically based men's movement approaches these feminist ideals, for it is consciously grounded in the teachings of the women's movement. Its practitioners accept the radical feminists' bill of indictment, and their writings exhibit much angst about the disruptive, exploitative, oppressive, and often violent role men have played in history, especially toward women. As eco-feminist Margo Adair would likely say, it is the antithesis of the "hierarchial/militarist thinking" exemplified by Iron John. It is her "real men's movement," the one that is "profeminist, gay affirmative, and enhancing to men's lives." It is not the wild-man backlash, but the movement of the feminist, domesticated male. 14

Rethinking Masculinity: Philosophical Explorations in Light of Feminism, a collection of essays edited by philosophers Larry May and Robert Strikwetda, is emblematic of this academically based men's movement. The concerns of the essayists mirror the feminists' appeal for a more touchy-feely, sensitized, non-aggressive male. Men too need more intimate friendships in their lives, as women have with other women; fathers need to nurture their children or they will continue to be distant apparitions to their offspring; pornography supports patriarchy and the subordination of women; men must work on their relationships with other men and with women. The gay lifestyle too is much on the mind of several essayists. One focuses on the stereotypical male image and how it plays out in the guise of gay male athletes. Another bemoans the rampant homophobia in society that makes men fearful of intimacy with other men. 15

Hugh LaFollette, a professor of philosophy at East Tennessee State University, expresses the essayists' overarching distress about "relationships" when he writes: "My concern [is] . . . to ask how real men, men who reject stereotypical male–female roles—men who are sensitive to the insights of feminism—should relate with women." What makes intimate, romantic relationships between members of the opposite sex so difficult, he thinks, is that we are products of a "pervasively sexist culture." 16

Through sexist stereotypes promulgated by television, movies, books, and music, children absorb gender roles that shape their minds and make "informed, unbiased choice difficult if not impossible." Men have been inculcated with the belief that they should never appear weak or vulnerable, and thus it is difficult for men to bring trust to a relationship. 17

LaFollette ponders two hypothetical scenarios that bedevil even relatively liberal men and their relationships with their wives. Even men who think themselves free of stereotypical male notions may find such notions reasserting themselves in situations when the man wants to relocate while his wife is content with her current employment. The couple might discuss how to balance financial security, fairness, the 18 amenities of the two communities, neighborhoods conducive to child rearing, climate, or quality of the public schools, yet attitudes formed by "the sexist culture" likely will intrude: the male asserting that his interests are superior; and the female acquiescing as a dutiful spouse should.

This "internal gender police" may also intrude on decisions about child care. Should they decide on breastfeeding, much of the initial infant care will fall to the mother, and this pattern will probably persist. LaFollette proceeds to examine another tense point in modern, two-career marriages. Who does the housework? Is the man "helping" the woman? How do rights, justice, and equity play themselves out on this battlefield? Rights seem more appropriate for exchanges between strangers, while couples who focus on justice and equity may already be experiencing the crumbling of a relationship. He suggests that couples concentrate on "mutual care" instead, that is, on promoting each other's interests. 19

LaFollette's musings on male/female romantic interactions and his preferred solution of jettisoning rights and equality language and substituting "caring," echoes the branch of feminism that argues that women really are different from men. Women are more sensitive, caring, pacific creatures whom men should emulate. Yet, one wonders, is the aggressive, invulnerable, take-control male just a social stereotype foisted upon us by society? 20

Societies that have run on "female" attributes have throughout history been scant, marginal, and short-lived. Is human nature so malleable that men can readily jettison their leading historical role in politics, warfare, culture, business, and nearly every other social function that drives human civilization? This is the grand experiment that radical feminism demands. It is the theoretical underpinning of the tumultuous public debate now roiling our society over the admission of homosexuals to the military and women to combat. 21

There has been a revolution in male/female relationships across the board over the last quarter-century from the mailroom to the executive suite, and perhaps more significantly, from the kitchen to the commode (the one with the green gunk germinating in it). As women have entered the workplace in record numbers, invaded the formerly male-dominated turf of operating rooms and loading docks, men have lost their moorings on how women ought to be regarded. Not surprisingly, charges of sexual harassment have proliferated. Men are uneasy during the workday, and no less perplexed when they return home. This is especially true of professional men married to ambitious women on the fast track. It is no wonder that many of these men find themselves cavorting in the forest, attired in 22 feathers, pounding out their frustrations on large, booming drums, while their cousins of the academy ruminate on how they can find a place in a world in which radical feminists set the ideological agenda.

The pace of social change has been so fast that it is, indeed, accurate to describe it as revolutionary rather then evolutionary. The socially acceptable model of the family is no longer the breadwinner dad, the stay-at-home mom, and the two or more kids, the model that set the standard for the early post–Second World War years. Now there is no one model, as no-fault divorce left in its wake single mothers raising children, blended families, and single dads, as decades of inflation forced families into the two-paycheck cauldron, and as the taboo against illegitimacy succumbed to the mores of the late-1960s sexual revolution. 23

Radical feminism is a reflection of these broader social trends, rather than their cause, and the men's movements derive from both those social forces and feminism's reaction to them. Regardless of how one appraises these assorted movements, they reflect the panoply of human responses to social turmoil, the pain and anguish felt by millions of Americans as the world of their childhood slips away. 24

Yet, there is definitely an upside to all of this social upheaval and personal anxiety. The revolution has been accomplished in the workplace and in the graduate and professional schools with alacrity and relative harmony. If men were indeed the patriarchal oppressors of the radical feminists' nightmares, this revolution would not have been so bloodless. Change in the interpersonal realm has not gone nearly as smoothly, and as in any revolution there are victims aplenty, particularly the children of poor, never-married women, and the children of divorce. 25

Other victims are the raped and murdered women, the beaten wives, and the abused children. Sometimes one wonders whether all of social history can be turned on its head by human will alone. Is the proliferation of sex crimes against women and the kidnapping and slaughter of helpless young children an unintended result of unchaining men from their traditional role since the cave of providing for and protecting women and children? Are men becoming extraneous when women can bear and raise children without them and many women bring home just as much (or more) bacon as their mates? 26

Perhaps in the next quarter-century a new modus vivendi will be struck between the sexes. Then our era will be seen as a tumultuous transition period that caused suffering, but brought about much-needed social change that made life for most Americans more fulfilling . . . but somehow I doubt it. 27

THINKING ABOUT THE ESSAY

1. Paul's credentials as an academic scholar and thinker are impressive. Is this essay geared to a highly intellectual audience or a more general one? How did you arrive at your conclusion?
2. Paul refers to the "wild-man" men's group as "silly" and calls the academic men's movement "banal." What basic attributes of each group provide her with these descriptors?
3. How is the essay structured? Where does the introduction begin and end? Where does its body begin and end? Where, in the text, do you find the author's conclusion? What markers helped you to pinpoint these divisions?
4. Paul states that "media attention hones in on the sensational." Is the author guilty of this same offense, that is, focusing on "fringe groups" rather on the way the typical man attempts to cope with his role in society? Does the essay make a valuable contribution to understanding American social life, or does it more resemble a journalistic example of daytime TV talk show? Explain your answer.
5. Is there a specific profile of the typical man who might join one of the men's movements? Does the author identify the type in her essay? What is your personal impression of the type?

RESPONDING IN DISCUSSION

1. Divide into groups of three and four, and write down the various reasons why a man might join one of the two men's movements that are discussed by the author. Compare your notes with those in the other groups.
2. View a videotape of a men's movement session. What was the role of the group leader? What inspired the men to join in the activity? What was your response to it? Do you feel the men benefited from the experience?
3. Divide into groups of three and four, and analyze the author's statement that movements "reflect the panoply of human responses to social turmoil, the pain and anguish felt by millions of Americans as the world of their childhood slips away." As a group, write a half-page explanation of this statement. Have a member of the group read it aloud, and follow with a class discussion.
4. The author suggests that "the pace of social change has been so fast . . . it is revolutionary rather than evolutionary." In small groups discuss alternative methods for men to deal with social change other than the formation of and participation in men's groups.

5. Consider "child visitation" as a sub-issue of a "men's movement" and use these two phrases as required terms at three or four different search engines (try www.1st.com for easy access to multiple engines). Do you feel this is an issue where men would be concerned about how they are perceived as a group?

RESPONDING IN WRITING

1. Assume the role of a husband participating in a "wild-man" weekend. Write home to your wife, relating your experiences and feelings.
2. Argue for or against the proposition that a wild-man retreat is harmless recreation and should not be taken as a serious social statement.
3. Argue for or against the proposition that a male member of Generation X would never become a member of either of the two men's movements described in the essay.
4. Argue for or against the proposition that men's movement activities should also include women so that the men can get feedback from the perspective of the opposite gender.
5. For an Internet research project, compare and contrast the views expressed in several items written by advocates and opponents of the "hairy-man men's movement."

Stillborn

Maribeth Fischer

In an essay published in the Fall 1994 issue of *The Iowa Review,* Maribeth Fischer presents a moving, first-person account of a family tragedy that even today is not widely accepted as a social norm: a married women with children leaving her family for another man. However, the skeleton outline of this story does nothing to reveal the profound emotional turmoil suffered by all the parties involved. In a story that delves into the sensitive issues of love, guilt, commitment, fear, betrayal, and sorrow, Fischer allows us unique insights into her own struggle with a family tragedy in an attempt to make some sense of a dark side of life few people in committed relationships allow themselves to consider. In her search for meaning regarding her mother's act, she considers the view of one author who claims "that ultimately our most painful decisions are borne *not* of grief or fear, love or regret or joy but, instead, of a terrible selfishness which lies beneath the surface of our lives like a cancer." Nearly the entire essay is devoted to Fischer's attempt to understand and accept her mother's action by considering it within the context of their lives and personal histories. This is a difficult process, for there are no external signs of abuse, neglect, or personal hardship in her mother's life. The issues addressed here are far more subtle than those in your typical Hollywood melodrama. For this reason, the essay deserves a close and careful reading so as to discern the motives behind the mother's action and her daughter's attempt at coming to terms with it.

PREVIEWING THE ESSAY

As you read this essay, consider what subtle conflicts determine the mother's major choice to leave her family. How have specific events from the past coalesced into helping her to choose her course of action? On the other hand, consider the daughter's anguish over feeling rejected by her mother. Into what aspects of her mother's life does she delve in an attempt to reconcile herself to her mother's action, even to understand and sympathize with it?

> *"Nothing hurts as bad as they say it does," she told me later. "And clear, pure memory doesn't hurt at all. What hurts is forgetting."*
>
> —Josephine Humphreys, *Rich in Love*

A few Sundays ago my mother phoned as I was eating dinner in front of the TV, her voice startling me because it wasn't her usual time to call. The minute I picked up the receiver, she said, "I don't want to talk, but I just had to phone you, Beth." 1

"What's wrong?" 2

"Nothing, nothing at all," she told me. "It's just that I found another book—" She paused. "It's about a mother who leaves." 3

She didn't need to say anything else. I scribbled the title and the author's name on the back of a mail-order catalogue and hung up after promising to buy the book as soon as I finished with classes the following afternoon. "It's hardback," she cautioned just before I got off the phone. "I'll send you the money if you need it." 4

After hanging up, I sat still for a moment, listening numbly to the voices on the TV and remembering that summer five years before when my mother first left our family to be with a man who was nothing more to me than a name and a photograph from her 1959 high school yearbook. I was twenty-two at the time, newly married and living in Iowa. It was a summer of drought, of endless bone-white skies and acres of dying cornfields. I could hardly imagine then, as the sun brutalized the landscape, that grief wasn't simply something to get through, like a bad season or a dry spell. 5

I stared down at the new title in my hand. Ever since my mother left, I've been reading novels and short stories about women who 6 leave their families. I know, of course, that the books won't give me the answers, but that's not what I want anymore. I am simply trying to find in fiction what I can not find in real life—understanding.

When I read Richard Ford's short story "Great Falls," my mother 7
had only been gone for three months. It was September and I still believed that she'd be home in time for Christmas. The story was told from the perspective of an eleven-year-old boy named Joe, who made me think of my younger brother Mark, only a year older. Home in New Jersey, Mark would have started school already and I tried to picture him in the mornings, waking up, realizing—as I did every day—she's gone and, worse, *she left*.

"And my mother herself—why would she do what she did?" Joe 8
asks at the end of the story. I have never known the answer to these questions, have never asked anyone their answers. Though possibly it—the answer—is simple: it is just low-life, some coldness in us all, some helplessness that causes us to misunderstand life when it is pure and plain, makes our existence seem like the border between two nothings, and makes us no more or less than animals who meet on the road—watchful, unforgiving, without patience or desire.

I read that quote ten, fifteen times, the words "low-life" and "cold- 9
ness" echoing in my head long after I'd put the book away. How I hated what those words suggested; how I still do: that ultimately our most painful decisions are borne *not* of grief or fear, love or regret or joy but, instead, of a terrible selfishness which lies beneath the surface of our lives like a cancer. I hated the implication that it was that simple, that arbitrary, that just as anyone could be struck with illness—so could any of us be struck by this "coldness," this numbing inability to distinguish right from wrong.

There were other books. In one, the mother who left had dark 10
permed hair and long blood-red fingernails. She drank too much whiskey and talked too loudly about the men—and the women—she had loved. In another, the mother was sick, abusing her daughter sexually. And in the novel my mother phoned to tell me about a few Sundays ago—*Father Melancholy's Daughter* by Gail Godwin—the mother who left her family dies before she has a chance to come home, before her daughter can understand.

Last week I read the novel *Rich in Love* by Josephine Humphreys. 11
In this story, the mother leaves so abruptly that when her daughter comes home from school the door of her mother's car is hanging open and her macramé purse, along with a bag of groceries, is still sitting on the front seat, where a container of butter pecan ice cream has melted. Two hundred pages later, the mother returns, her leaving "like a television serial that had gotten so complicated the plot could only be resolved by calling itself a dream, backing up and starting all over again."

I realized, then, that for most people, most women, what my mother did five years ago truly is unimaginable. And yet I, her oldest daughter, not only have to imagine it, I have to understand it. 12

Recently I listened to a friend of mine, an artist, talk about how she wants to go to an artist's colony to work on some paintings. But she can't bear to leave her children—in ten years she has never been away from them for more than a few days. As she talks of leaving, something happens in her face, to her eyes. Although the children—a boy, ten, a girl, six—are not here with us in this restaurant, they are present in the tightening of my friend's jaw, in the way she nervously grips the stem of her wine glass. She is suddenly so anxious that her husband reaches to cover her hand with his own. Susan has heard my mother's story; she hasn't judged it, and wouldn't judge it, yet I know that she cannot imagine ever doing what my mother has done. I also know, however, that until the day she left, my mother herself could not have imagined it either. 13

I wish I could explain to Susan how it happened so quickly. *Nobody* thinks she can do it. Maybe that's why, of all the books I've read, the only insight that rings true for me is the detail about the ice cream melting all over the front seat of the car. I know it really does happen this way, as you are carrying groceries into the house or ironing your son's favorite soccer shirt or standing in front of your closet wondering what to wear. I know the unimaginable becomes imaginable in a moment just that ordinary. 14

Until the day my mother walked out, I naively thought that it was only a certain kind of woman who would do such a thing; a woman who shouldn't have had children or never really wanted them in the first place; a woman whose daughters spoke of her with contempt and shame. And if she was a good woman and she just happened to have made a mistake, well then, she'd come back, wouldn't she? Just like Meryl Streep in *Kramer vs. Kramer.* She'd come back full of regrets and promises never to leave her son again. 15

Two weeks before my mother left and flew to Montana with Nick, her former high school sweetheart, my husband and I came home from Iowa to visit. It was then, my first morning back, that my mother confessed to me her longing to leave. Dan, my stepfather, had left for work over an hour before; my younger brother was at school; my husband was asleep in my childhood bed. My mother and I were sitting in the kitchen, picking at a plate of hot blueberry muffins. Rain clattered against the bay windows, which were steamed from the heat of the oven. 16

"I think I'm in love with someone else," my mother said quietly, staring down at her hands. She spoke the words so quickly that I couldn't understand them at first. They sounded like pig Latin, *mai nai ovelay ithway omeonesay.* I remember feeling frustrated, wanting 17 to shout at her. What are you talking about? Even now I'm not sure if she repeated what she'd said or if the words themselves unscrambled. All I know is that I heard them as an echo, blurred and distorted, as if she'd shouted them across a distance. *I'm in love with someone else.*

Outside everything looked very shiny and very green: Bottle- 18
green, Apple-green, Sea-green. Olive-green—as if my sister and I were still kids and had just gone down a row of Crayolas and scribbled long streaks of that color over and over across the window. Nick, my mother called him, this man she apparently loved. *Nick.* The name was familiar and I recognized the way she said it, the same way that I could identify songs I hadn't heard in years. Vaguely, I remembered kneeling on the living room floor with my mother when I was still young enough not to be in school. It was raining then too, a slow-silent drizzle like lines of static across an old black and white movie. Twenty-eight years old, already divorced from my father, she was showing me her scrapbook and high school yearbook, pointing to a photograph of a thin, dark-eyed boy I didn't recognize. I wondered if this was when I first heard my mother say Nick's name. "This is the boy I dated before I married your father," she might have confessed. Five or six years old, I would have looked at her in amazement, shocked to think of her dating or going to parties, incredulous to realize that once my mother had been young—as young as the high school girls who lived across the street from us.

Whenever I asked my mother why she and my father had di- 19
vorced, a divorce they had always described as "amicable," she would turn away and answer quietly, "Your dad and I are good friends now, Beth. That's all that matters." Or, "Our marriage was pretty painful," she would say, "I really don't want to talk about it." The minute I heard about Nick, though, I questioned that "painful marriage." I wondered if he was the real reason I couldn't remember my father ever living with us.

Sitting in my mother's kitchen two weeks before she left with 20
Nick, I heard her say that she had practically been engaged to him when she was twenty and that her parents had convinced her to break it off. "They never gave him a chance," she said. She sounded distant as she spoke of it, a cadence of sorrow in her voice that I'd never heard before. I thought of how, when my older brother and I were kids, we used to tie rubber bands around empty shoe boxes and pluck them as if they were guitars. But we could never control their deformed, squeaking twang; we could never make real music. My mother's voice had that same wire-tweaked quiver. I wanted to lay a steady palm against the shuddering cords of her throat.

"I don't mean to make this sound like a soap opera," she said. "It 21
wasn't. It was just the fifties. But we wanted different things then, Beth. I wanted a nice house and good clothes for myself and my

children—I don't think there's anything wrong with that either—and my mother kept telling me that I'd never have that with Nick, that Nick would never amount to anything, that if I married him it would be the biggest mistake of my life." She shook her head, brushing the memory away like a strand of hair fallen in front of her eyes. "When I look back, I don't understand it," she whispered. "I was twenty years old then. Why didn't I stand up to my parents?" She spoke so softly that I could barely hear her: "I was afraid." Her face was lacquered with tears; I felt as if I was staring at her through a window. Without looking at me, she continued: "So, I ended it. I sent Nick a Christmas card and told him I'd decided to marry your dad. I wanted to write a letter, I wanted to explain, but didn't know how, I didn't know what to say. . . ." She shrugged and tried to smile, as if to show me that she understood how ridiculous this all was, but her face crumpled and she began to cry. Outside the rain had stopped. The sky, a flat yellow-brown, was the color of water stains on old love letters. "What I did to Nick was the cruelest thing I have ever done to another person," my mother said. "And I've never gotten over it."

It was then that she told me that Nick had phoned her one after- 22
noon a few weeks before. It was the first time she had heard from him in over twenty-eight years. He was at his sister's, he said. Her name had come up, and he got to wondering how her life had turned out.

"What did you tell him?" I didn't look at her when I asked, afraid 23
of the truth I might see in her eyes.

Gently, she touched my arm. "I told him I was happy," she said. 24
"And I meant it. I was."

"Then what—" 25

But she held up her hand to stop me. "Nick told me he had busi- 26
ness in Philadelphia, and he wanted to know if I could meet him for lunch—" She glanced at me hesitantly. "I told Dan about it, Maribeth. I honestly didn't think it would be a big deal and certainly I had nothing to hide." She started crying again. "It's not what you might be thinking. The entire lunch Nick and I talked about our kids and afterwards we didn't even hug goodbye. I figured I'd never see him again."

"So *what* happened?" 27

"I don't know. Dan brought me home and then went back to the 28
office for a few hours and I—" She drew in her breath, seemed to hold it in her throat for a moment and then blew the words out like smoke. "I phoned Nick, Maribeth. I told him I'd never stopped loving him."

"You did?" I asked incredulously. "You?" 29

She left abruptly on a Monday morning. For the first time in her life 30
she rode in a taxi alone, then boarded an airplane without her husband or children. She went to Milwaukee, the city where she and Nick had grown up, where they had met and fallen in love. The following

morning they flew to Montana, a place my mother had never been. Later, try as I might, I couldn't picture her in such barren, open surroundings, in "a landscape dominated only by sky" and "punctuated," as she would eventually write, "not by sounds but by stillness." Earlier that spring, however, Nick, a roofing consultant, had been contracted to fix the leaking stone walls of a small church near the town of Hardin, Montana. Stone by stone his crew would take the building apart that summer and then slowly rebuild it. My mother would spend her afternoons in a tiny café, drinking iced tea and trying to concentrate enough to read. Most days, she would tell me, she couldn't get through more than a page.

In Iowa the drought continued. For weeks at a time it seemed this was all anyone talked about. In the afternoons the local pancake house where I waitressed was filled with farmers drinking cup after cup of coffee. There was nothing to do except pray for rain, and hope. Often, driving west along Route 30 towards the next town, I would see women standing on their porches, staring out at the flat expanse of yellow-blue sky, waiting. In July there was talk of bussing in a tribe of Sioux Indians from South Dakota to perform a rain dance. 31

I too spent the summer waiting, first for letters, then for the sound of her voice over the phone. At night I would sit for hours, watching as the sun set and the Iowa sky darkened, tightening like skin around a wound. I tried to picture her in Montana, tried to imagine her sitting at a dinner table with him, laughing softly as she took a sip of wine. I wondered what he looked like and what about him was special enough that my mother would abandon her life to be with him. Each time I thought of him, though, all I could see was the vague image of that dark-eyed boy from the yearbook; and all I could hear was the echo of my mother's voice: "I never stopped loving him." 32

By the autumn my mother and Nick had returned to Milwaukee and were living in a small two-bedroom apartment just off the interstate. Alone, with no friends, no one she could talk to in the long afternoons when Nick was at work, my mother often phoned me. She told me of the different recipes she was trying; she described the books she was reading—Jane Smiley's *The Age of Grief;* Mona Simpson's *Anywhere but Here;* she tried to laugh at herself for feeling such exhilaration the day she passed the Wisconsin driver's test. "I did it," she said, her voice ebullient. "Can you believe it, Beth?" 33

Quietly, I congratulated her. I knew it didn't matter that my mother had been driving all her life. It was as if she were seventeen, as if she had gotten her license for the first time. 34

When she phoned me on September fourteenth, however, I knew the minute I heard her voice that everything had changed. "It's me," she whispered when I picked up the phone. She sounded scared. 35

"Are you all right?" I said. 36

"I don't know. I was okay when I woke up. I was going to do some reading and I'd taken some spaghetti sauce out of the freezer for dinner—" She began to weep. "All of a sudden the pain just started washing over me, Beth, and I couldn't stop it. I realized it was Dan's birthday yesterday and our anniversary tomorrow and I didn't understand what I was doing here anymore. *Why* am I taking spaghetti sauce out of this freezer, *why* am I not home in my own kitchen?" She was sobbing now. "And that's not all." 37

She was waiting for me to remember and, of course, I did: on this day fourteen years ago she had given birth to a stillborn, a seven-pound boy named and baptized Daniel Joseph. In all the years since it had happened, she had spoken of it to me only once before. 38

"There's been so much loss," she said. "And it's too much, Beth. It's just too much." 39

I remember feeling frightened for her. There was such unrestrained sorrow in her voice that I thought of water, black ocean water on a moonless night—and how afraid I was to enter it, to wade deeper than my calves. 40

Outside it was a bright autumn day. A breeze riffled the papers spread out on my coffee table. I heard a bus pull away from the stop outside my apartment. I thought of the other September fourteenth, of the day the baby had been born. 41

It had been a rainy Friday. My sister, brother and I had come home from school to an empty house and a neighbor waving at us from under a dark umbrella across the street. "Over here, kids!" she called. "Your parents aren't home." The three of us raced across the street, kicking up arcs of rain behind us. My older brother won as always, beating my sister and me to the neighbor's porch. "She's having the baby, isn't she?" His delighted squeal seemed to skip over the puddles like a stone flung sideways across the surface of a pond. My sister and I were also shouting by now: "Is she having the baby?" 42

The neighbor offered a tenuous smile. "I think I'll let Dan tell you all about that when he gets here," she said. 43

A few hours later, my stepfather picked us up and took us home. "Your mother had a boy," he told us as he tried to get us to come sit with him on the couch. But we were jumping and screaming in celebration. My brother was yelling to the tune of "Old McDonald"—"B-B-B-O-Y, B-B-B-O-Y, B-B-B-O-Y, Yes I have a Bro-ther!"—until finally my stepfather blurted it out—that the baby was dead. 44

On the phone now, fourteen years later, I asked, "Is it the baby, Mom? Is that why you're so upset?" I was upset myself. "Should I call Dan?" 45

"There's really no point," she whispered. "I've hurt him too much already." 46

"It's not irreparable," I said. "You can still go home." 47

For a moment she didn't say anything. I felt how the echo of that 48
word—*home*—hung between us, static in the line so that it seemed we were losing our connection.

"I can't," she said finally. She sounded surprised, as if this wasn't 49
what she had planned on saying. Again she repeated it, testing the words the way I had once tested a snowflake on the tip of my tongue. "I can't." Her voice was choked with something I couldn't name—panic or resignation perhaps, or maybe simple grief. After she hung up, I remember standing for what seemed a long time with the phone against my ear, coiling the cord around and around my fingers as if, somehow, I could reel my mother closer.

She is driving home from the food store one morning in late Septem- 50
ber. It is early, only a little past seven, but she has been unable to sleep lately and decided she would get the shopping out of the way. It is cold out. When she came out of the apartment this morning she noticed the windshields of the cars were covered with a layer of frost as thin as parchment paper. Already she wears a winter coat and, as she is setting the grocery bags into the back seat of her car, she sees her breath dissipate into the cold morning sky. In New Jersey it would still be warm, she thinks, she would be having coffee on the side porch, twelve-year-old Mark would be getting dressed for school in the clothes she bought him last spring.

She is almost at the turn-off to her apartment complex when she 51
sees the children waiting at the bus stop, sees the group of women, their mothers, standing in a huddle around them, trying to shield the children from the wind blowing off Lake Michigan. Suddenly she feels ill. She thinks of Mark, of how each morning, after he was dressed and his bookbag was packed, he'd come to her room and wake her by laying a warm washcloth on her face, the same way Dan had woken him. She thinks of his face in the window of the school bus, remembers that he was so scared on his first day of kindergarten that he threw up. She is afraid she herself will be sick and pulls the car onto the shoulder of the road. Later she will call me. She will tell me this story.

Still, she will fly home to see Mark twice that autumn and, twice, 52
despite the obvious pain she is feeling, she will return to Milwaukee. I picture her that autumn in the various gift shops near her apartment, where she spends afternoons hoping to find in some pre-printed Hallmark card words which might somehow neutralize her family's anger. Too dressed up in the clothes she has no other place to wear, she lingers at the racks of specialty cards: "To A Special Daughter"; "To A Wonderful Son"; "Have I told you I love you lately?"; "How much I miss you, let me count the days." I wonder if she notices the blue and white posters one aisle over advertising Yom Kippur cards.

Does she know this means "Day of Atonement"? Does she know that all she has to do to be forgiven is come home?

My mother and Nick returned to Montana for Thanksgiving, hop- 53
ing, I imagined, to find again the brief happiness my mother must have felt there earlier that summer. I was convinced, however, that waking to the silence of a hotel, eating Thanksgiving dinner in a restaurant—being without her children on a holiday—would only remind her of all that she had lost. Consequently, I allowed myself to hope: as I stood alone in my own kitchen on Thanksgiving morning, making stuffing the way she had taught me and baking the traditional pies she had always made, I promised that soon she would come home. She had to, I thought. How could we get through the holidays without her? And how could she get through them without us?

I pictured her in Montana, lying alone in the queen-sized bed of 54
the Western Inn where they were staying, waiting for Nick to return from the dining room with the pot of coffee and the freshly baked brioche which the concierge set out each morning. I could see her growing impatient and hungry, wondering what was taking so long, could see her wrapping herself in the thin chenille bedspread and walking to the high latticed windows, which reminded her more of Europe, she wrote, than of the "Wild West."

In Iowa, as I set out the china and silver we'd received as wedding 55
gifts, as I served turkey to the friends my husband and I had invited to dinner, as I wrapped leftovers for them to take home, as later that night I sat in the dark eating piece after piece of French silk pie, I pictured my mother standing at this window, her head against the glass, the sunlight falling over her like a white slip. Perhaps this is when she would feel the heaviness in her body, the stillness. Perhaps this is when she would realize that the new life she had wanted so much with Nick had quietly died inside of her. I could see her crying now, could see her moving slowly across the room towards the phone. . . .

I replayed this scene in my mind until it became spliced into all 56
our other home movies: my older brother and I as toddlers fighting over a tricycle; my younger sister's first birthday party; the endless reels of my mother and stepfather's trip to Arizona the month before Nick phoned—minutes and minutes of blurred purple and red canyon walls like the insides of the huge heart we had walked through as kids at the Franklin Institute in downtown Philadelphia. And then I pictured my mother standing at the window in that hotel room, her pain so focused it became its own landscape.

The Thanksgiving weekend passed, however, and nothing hap- 57
pened. When I talked to my mother a week later, she admitted that the holiday had been horrible. But it no longer mattered, because whatever "horrible" meant, my mother hadn't called us; she hadn't come home.

"Was her life that bad?" I sobbed to my husband. "Was it so awful that she'd rather be in pain than come back to us?" 58

When I recall those weeks between Thanksgiving and Christmas, weeks which a poet once referred to as "the unimaginable present," I remember only the confusion and disbelief: she wasn't coming home. Maybe this was why I watched the documentary about stillborns that was on TV that November. I was willing to look anywhere for a clue—some hint—which would help me to understand: *Why?* 59

I learned that in Australian hospitals, unlike many in the U.S., doctors allow a woman who has had a stillborn to hold her baby after delivery. A nurse will take pictures of the child, sometimes let the mother dress the baby in something special to be buried in. Psychologists say that the greatest regret of the mothers of stillborns is that they never held their child, never got a chance to say goodbye. Their sons and daughters were simply whisked out of sight as if they had never existed. 60

I hadn't expected the show to upset me. But as I clicked the TV off and watched the screen fade from green to grey to black, I felt as if something was blackening inside of me too. I couldn't stop thinking about the dark-haired woman on TV who had given birth to three stillborns. For each she had a photo album filled with pictures of her dead child and of herself as she underwent labor. As she was being interviewed, she had almost frantically flipped through the pages of these albums, ordering the cameraman to focus in on the pictures. At one point she had stopped him, pointing to a favorite photograph and trying to explain why she liked it. She tried not to cry when she spoke, but her voice cracked and she had to turn away. I had been horrified. 61

Later, however, I realized that this horror was unjustified. Those photographs were all she had, the only proof of the life she had borne, a life which *had* existed, despite what everyone told her. And it struck me that perhaps what was truly horrible was *not* that a woman would save a photo album full of pictures of her dead child, but that she wouldn't; that instead, afraid of being called crazy or morbid, she would do what everyone said she should—she would forget. 62

I remembered the afternoon before my mother's stillborn was delivered. By then he hadn't kicked in almost two days. Already she must have known that he was dead. My sister and I had no idea that anything was wrong, however, and so we spent the afternoon coloring pictures for the baby's room. 63

My mother lay flat in the four-poster double bed, a heating pad rolled like a washcloth beneath her breasts. Each time we finished a drawing we brought it to show her. As we stood hesitantly near her bed, she would smile, momentarily looking away from my stepfather who sat at the desk near the window, absently rolling a pencil over 64 the wood in harsh, jerking movements. "Thanks, guys," she'd say, holding the picture in front of her face and studying it before she set it carefully on the night stand with all the others. There must have been twenty or thirty of them. My sister and I would have colored all night, I think, if it hadn't been for my stepfather.

Entering the room once again with another drawing, my sister behind me, I saw my mother softly punching her clenched fist against her distended stomach. She froze when she saw us peering in the doorway, our pictures held in front of us like invitations for admittance. She cupped her hand slowly, protectively, to her stomach then. In that split second before my stepfather turned away from us, I thought I noticed tears on his face. But he snapped his dark eyes away from me before I could be sure. All I could see was his back, a grey shape outlined by a too-bright September sun, which seemed to lie to us about the season. 65

"It's okay," my mother said, staring not at us but at my stepfather. And then turning her strange quivering smile on my sister and me, she gestured with both arms. "Come here. Let me see what you colored this time," and we scrambled into the room, hopping knees first onto the bed. I remembered her softness, the damp sweaty smell of her thin velour robe, and then the surprisingly sharp grip of my stepfather's fingers clamped tight around my wrist as he jerked me from my mother. 66

"That's enough," he said. He tried to hold his voice rigid with control but it came out shaky and painfully frazzled. 67

My mother said, "It's okay, Dan, really." 68

In their odd watery stares, I saw an entire conversation that I didn't understand. 69

My stepfather shook his head and then more gently pulled my sister and me from the bed. "No, it's not okay." Then, "God damn it, Laura, you don't need to do this right now." 70

She started to cry. "Yes, I do, this is exactly what I need." 71

"How can it be?" he snapped. "You're not all right." 72

"I will be if you'd just let it alone," she said, her voice growing louder. 73

But my stepfather pulled us away. "I'm sorry, girls, I don't mean to make you feel bad, but your mom needs to rest for a while." 74

My sister and I went back to our room. We began to clean up and, without talking, arrange the crayons into systematic rows of colors. Midnight-blue, navy, ultramarine, cornflower, skyblue. Darkest to lightest. And then another color. 75

Fourteen years later, the November after my mother had left, it wasn't so easy to find a means of ordering the world. As I paced about my apartment in Iowa, pictures of the Australian woman in my mind, I sensed for the first time that my mother probably wouldn't come home—not because of Nick, not because of the baby who had 76 died, but because somehow, in all the years of forgetting, some part of my mother had died. How dramatic this sounded and yet as I got up from the couch I couldn't help but recall a conversation I'd had with my mother earlier that autumn. She had been seeing a psychologist in an effort to understand how a woman like herself, a woman who had always prided herself on being a good mother, a good wife, could so suddenly leave. The psychologist, she told me, had written under diagnosis "prolonged grief." My mother had laughed at this. "What do you mean?" she had asked. "What do you think I'm grieving for? I was happy."

"So happy that you left," he reminded her quietly. 77

Absently, I flicked on the stereo. Anne Murray, one of my 78 mother's favorites, was singing "Daydream Believer": "Cheer up, sleepy Jean/Oh, what can it mean. . . ." Through all those conversations when I had asked her to come home, when she had whispered, "I can't, Beth. Please try to understand," she must have known, as I did now, that if she returned we would pretend once again. We would pretend that her leaving had been a whim; we would pretend that she was happy. We would forget—just as we had after the baby died.

She had talked to my sister and me about the stillborn only once, 79 years after the fact. I don't know how the conversation came up or why we were discussing it. I simply remembered her describing how her friends pretended nothing had happened, how they acted as if the baby hadn't been real.

"He would have been so sick," they had told her. 80

"It's better this way. . . ." 81

"At least you didn't bring him home and start loving him. . . ." 82

She told us, too, that when my stepfather reached out to hold the 83 baby in the delivery room, the nurse had stepped back and abruptly pulled him away. "It's better if you don't," the nurse apologized. "There's really no point."

"Dan said he had black hair," my mother had told us. "That's all I 84 know." She had turned to stare outside the window, something she did often when she was upset, as if looking at another landscape was all it took to distance herself from the one she was in.

After a moment, she said, "Nobody understood that the baby was 85 already real to me, that he had a personality even in the womb. At the end of the pregnancy, he used to wake up every night at four in the morning—right on the nose. I'd go into the room Dan had fixed up and sit in the rocking chair and sing to him and rub my belly until he settled down." She had laughed quizzically, the way people do at jokes they don't understand. "I mean, I knew even before he was born that he wasn't going to let me sleep through the night the way you guys did—" She had shaken her head in wonderment. "To think that I hadn't already started loving him," she'd said.

I put a pot of water on for tea and went to sit at the table, waiting for it to boil. When I began to cry, my sounds seemingly enormous and out of place in the quiet and darkness, I thought it was for the Australian woman with three dead children, but then it occurred to me that I was crying for my mother, for all that I had never understood. I realized too that I was crying for my own loss. Because all through childhood and adolescence, when I thought I was getting to know my mother, and later, after I was married, when the two of us would sit at the kitchen table for hours, talking and drinking tea—all that time, she had been so distant to me, as unknown to me, as that dark-haired woman on the other side of the world, that woman who, unlike my mother, had understood what it means to grieve. 86

It's not the stillborn baby I think of so much anymore when September fourteenth interrupts my life like a cold, leaving me achy and tired. It's my mother's wobbly but bright smile as she fixed our lunches before school the morning before the baby was born, knowing that he hadn't kicked or moved for more than two days. It is her making sure we each had a quarter to buy a soft pretzel at recess; it's her going to the hospital without the diaper bag packed full of pastel-colored baby clothes. It is my mother carrying a dead baby inside of her and never letting go of that pink crescent of a smile, which, when I think of it now, seems almost separate from her face. As if that smile had nothing to do with my mother at all. 87

THINKING ABOUT THE ESSAY

1. Did your attitude toward the mother's actions change during the course of the essay? If so, what particular moments caused these changes? What thesis emerges from Fischer's essay by the end of her narrative?
2. The author describes in detail the moment in which her mother told her she was going to leave the family. Have you ever experienced this form of "heightened reality" owing to a tragic situation? If not, have you ever witnessed someone else go through this experience? How would you characterize it?
3. The author places great significance on the event of her stillborn brother. Besides the immediate tragedy implicit in this event, does it have any symbolic resonance within the larger context of the mother's life and choices? It may be helpful to consider a simple definition of *symbol* as something that represents something else.
4. Listen to Anne Murray's recording of "Daydream Believer," cited in the text as being one of the mother's favorites. Is there anything in the song's lyrics or tone that seems to resonate with the mother's inner life or external circumstances? If so, describe it.

5. Consider the use of description in the text, such as depiction of the day when the author's mother left the family: "It was a summer of drought, of endless bone-white skies and acres of dying cornfields." Where else in the text does the physical environment seem to mirror the inner life of the family?

RESPONDING IN DISCUSSION

1. Divide into groups of three or four and analyze the epigraph by Josephine Humphreys at the beginning of the essay. Summarize its meaning in two ways: first, as it pertains to life in general; and second, as it pertains to the essay. Share your interpretation with the rest of the class.
2. Would the story have had the same impact if the father were the one who abandoned the family? Would there have been a story if the father had been the one to leave? Is there anything in the story that makes it a "women's story," particularly in the light of the reasons for abandonment and the response of the mother once she has severed her ties with the family?
3. Although authors have regularly written about a wife and mother leaving her family (for example, Ibsen's play *A Doll's House* from the 1870s), society still seems shocked by such incidents. Why?
4. Relate this story to Kingsolver's discussion of the "new family dynamic." Does the emotional pain in this story demonstrate that Kingsolver's claim that the problem is simply that society has not caught up with the new trends and definitions of marriage? Does it refute her suggestions that flexibility in marriage is a positive phenomenon, or does it demand that we look at each "failed" or "finished" marriage independently?

RESPONDING IN WRITING

1. Explain the circumstances under which you would leave your family, presenting the reasons for your action.
2. Considering the various motives that led the mother to leave her family (for example, the realization that she had rejected her true love owing to her mother's influence, that the pain of the stillborn child maintains an invisible presence in the house, that she is not happy with her present husband, and that she sees Nick as a conduit for her salvation), write an essay either defending or rejecting the mother's choice.

3. Argue for or against the proposition that it is worse for a man to leave his family because it will almost certainly be for superficial reasons—money, sex, boredom—than for a woman, who will only make the choice after serious and anguished deliberation.
4. Argue for or against the proposition that many marriages that are in jeopardy contain issues that are far too complex for marriage counselors to successfully address.
5. If your class members are "wired," enter a chat group and discuss Fischer's essay. Based on the exchange of ideas, write an essay analyzing the causes and effects of the mother's decision to leave her family.

They All Just Went Away

Where a House Has Been Abandoned, You Can Be Sure There Has Been a Sad Story

Joyce Carol Oates

Prolific novelist, literary critic, and essayist Joyce Carol Oates has been an observer and critic of the American scene for over 30 years. In "They All Just Went Away" (first published in the highly regarded *The New Yorker* in 1995), she interweaves the theme of abandonment and flight—a vital part of the American myth of freedom and wanderlust—with the mysteries and secrets of a troubled household. Even the essay's title—which refers to a family's dissolution—connotes a certain irrationality that cannot be explained by purported experts such as psychologists, social workers, and other social service providers. The first section of the essay describes a particular American landscape where whole communities just seem to vanish, their homes reverting to a mixture of human relics and growing vegetation. The second section provides a "case study" of one such home, describing the mysterious Weidel family whose home life is viewed by the community as a mixture of known abuse and dysfunction, and rumor. Most of us like to think of the family unit as an intact, knowable entity. It lends harmony and stability to our lives, and gives us the impression that families around us share this coherence so that we may live in relative peace in our communities. This essay shatters this myth, demonstrating how even the "family next door" may be embroiled in relationships and divisions that mere observation can only scratch the surface. As you read, you may wish to consider the function of presenting a "self" to the world, both as an individual and as a member of your family.

PREVIEWING THE ESSAY

The subtitle to this essay reads, "Where a house has been abandoned, you can be sure there has been a sad story." Although Oates describes an abandoned wooden structure in rural New York State, one formerly inhabited by a single family, her statement could be applied to almost any home, apartment, or other dwelling. Consider some of the abandoned structures in your hometown or current neighborhood. What visible or invisible traces have been left behind to indicate why certain dwelling places have been abandoned?

I must have been a lonely child. Until the age of twelve or thirteen, my most intense, happiest hours were spent tramping desolate fields, woods, and creek banks near my family's farmhouse in Millersport, New York. No one knew where I went. My father, working most of the day at Harrison's, a division of General Motors in Lockport, and at other times preoccupied, would not have asked; if my mother asked, I might have answered in a way that would deflect curiosity. I was an articulate, verbal child. Yet I could not explain what drew me to the abandoned houses, barns, silos, corncribs. A hike of miles through fields of spiky grass, across outcroppings of shale as steeply angled as stairs, was a lark if the reward was an empty house. 1

Some of these houses had been inhabited as "homes" fairly recently —they had not yet reverted to the wild. Others, abandoned during the Depression, had long since begun to rot and collapse, engulfed by vegetation (trumpet vine, wisteria, rose of Sharon, willow) that elsewhere, on our property, for instance, were kept neatly trimmed. I was drawn to both kinds of houses, though the more recently inhabited were more forbidding and therefore more inviting. 2

To push open a door into such silence: the absolute emptiness of a house whose occupants have departed. Often, the crack of broken glass underfoot. A startled buzzing of flies, hornets. The slithering, ticklish sensation of a garter snake crawling across floorboards. 3

Left behind, as if in haste, were remnants of a lost household. A broken toy on the floor, a baby's bottle. A rain-soaked sofa, looking as if it had been gutted with a hunter's skilled knife. Strips of wallpaper like shredded skin. Smashed crockery, piles of tin cans; soda, beer, whiskey bottles. An icebox, its door yawning open. Once, on a counter, a dirt-stiffened rag that, unfolded like precious cloth, revealed itself to be a woman's cheaply glamorous "see-through" blouse, threaded with glitter-strips of gold. 4

This was a long time ago, yet it is more vivid to me than anything now. 5

This was when I was too young to think the house is the mother's body; you have been expelled and are forbidden now to reenter. 6

Always, I was prepared to see a face at a high, empty window. A woman's hand uplifted in greeting, or in warning. *Hello! Come in! Stay away! Run! Who are you?* A movement in the corner of my eye: the blurred motion of a person passing through a doorway, or glimpsed through a window. There might be a single shriek of laughter from a barn—piercing as a bird's cry. Murmurous, teasing voices confused with wind rippling through tall, coarse, gone-to-seed grass. Voices that, when you pause to listen, fade immediately and are gone. 7

The sky in such places of abandonment was always of the hue and brightness of tin, as if the melancholy rural poverty of tin roofs reflected upward. 8

A house: a structural arrangement of space, geometrically laid out to provide what are called rooms, these divided from one another by verticals and horizontals called walls, ceilings, floors. The house contains the home but is not identical with it. The house anticipates the home and will very likely survive it, reverting again simply to house when home (that is, life) departs. For only where there is life can there be home. 9

I have never found the visual equivalent of these abandoned farmhouses of upstate New York, of northern Erie County, in the area of the long, meandering Tonawanda Creek and the Barge Canal. You think most immediately of the canvases of Edward Hopper: those dreamily stylized visions of a lost America, houses never depicted as homes, and human beings, if you look closer, never depicted as other than mannequins. For Hopper is not a realist but a surrealist. His dreams are of the ordinary, as if, even in imagination, the artist were trapped in an unyielding daylight consciousness. There seems almost a kind of rage, a revenge against such restraints, in Hopper's studied, endlessly repeated *simplicity*. By contrast, Charles Burchfield, with his numerous oils and watercolors—frequently of upstate New York landscapes, houses, and farms—rendered the real as visionary and luminous, suffused with a Blakean rapture and a kind of radical simplicity, too. Then there are the shimmering New England barns, fields, and skies of our contemporary Wolf Kahn—images evoked by memory, almost on the verge of dissolution. But the "real"—what assaults the eye before the eye begins its work of selection—is never on the verge of dissolution, still less of appropriation. The real is raw, jarring, unexpected, sometimes trashy, sometimes luminous. Above all, the real is arbitrary. For to be a realist (in art or in life) is to acknowledge that all things might be other than they are. That there is no design, no intention, no aesthetic or moral or teleological imprimatur but, rather, the equivalent of Darwin's great vision of a blind, purposeless, ceaseless evolutionary process that yields no "products"—only temporary strategies against extinction. 10

Yet, being human, we think, To what purpose these broken-off things, if not to be gathered up, at last, in a single ecstatic vision? 11

There is a strange and profound and unknowable reality to these abandoned houses where jealously guarded, even prized possessions have become mere trash: windowpanes long ago smashed, and the spaces where they had been festooned with cobwebs, and cobwebs brushing against your face, catching in your hair like caresses. The peculiar, dank smell of wood rot and mildew, in one of the houses I most recall that had partly burned down, the smell of smoke and scorch, in early summer pervading even the lyric smell of honeysuckle—these haunting smells, never, at the time of experiencing, given specific sources, names. 12

Where a house has been abandoned—unworthy of being sold to new tenants, very likely seized by the county for default on taxes and the property held in escrow—you can be sure there has been a sad story. There have been devastated lives. Lives to be spoken of pityingly. How they went wrong. Why did she marry him, why did she stay with him? Just desperate people. Ignorant. Poor white trash. Runs in the family. A wrong turn. 13

Shall I say for the record that ours was a happy, close-knit, and unextraordinary family for our time, place, and economic status? Yet what was vividly real in the solid-built old farmhouse that contained my home (my family consisted of my father, mother, younger brother, grandfather, and grandmother, who owned the property—a slow-failing farm whose principal crop had become Bartlett pears by the time I was a girl) was of far less significance to me than what was real elsewhere. A gone-to-seed landscape had an authority that seemed to me incontestable: the powerful authority of silence in houses from which the human voice had vanished. For the abandoned house contained the future of any house—the lilac tree pushing through the rotted veranda, hornets' nests beneath eaves, windows smashed by vandals, human excrement left to dry on a parlor floor once scrubbed on hands and knees. 14

The abandoned, the devastated, was the profound experience, whereas involvement in family life—the fever, the bliss, the abrasions, the infinite distractions of human love—was so clearly temporary. Like a television screen upon which antic images (at this time, in the fifties, minimally varying gradations of gray) appear fleetingly and are gone. 15

I have seemed to suggest that the abandoned houses were all distant from our house, but in fact the one that had been partly gutted by fire—which I will call the Weidel house—was perhaps a half mile away. If you drove, turning right off Transit Road, which was our road, onto the old Creek Road, it would have been a distance of a 16 mile or more, but if you crossed through our back potato field and through the marshy woods which no one seemed to own, it was a quick walk.

The Weidels' dog, Slossie, a mixed breed with a stumpy, energetic tail and a sweet disposition, sand-colored, rheumy-eyed, as hungry for affection as for the scraps we sometimes fed her, trotted over frequently to play with my brother and me. Though, strictly speaking, Slossie was not wanted at our house. None of the Weidels were wanted. 17

The "Weidel house," it would be called for years. The "Weidel property." As if the very land—which the family had not owned in any case, but only rented, partly with county-welfare support—were somehow imprinted with that name, a man's identity. Or infamy. 18

For tales were told of the father who drank, beat and terrorized his family, "did things to" his daughters, and finally set the house on fire and fled and was arrested, disappearing forever from the proper, decent life of our community. There was no romance in Mr. Weidel, whom my father knew only slightly and despised as a drinker, and as a wife- and child-beater. Mr. Weidel was a railway worker in Lockport, or perhaps an ex-railway worker, for he seemed to work only sporadically, though he always wore a railwayman's cap. He and his elder sons were hunters, owning a shotgun among them, and one or two deer rifles. His face was broad, fair, vein-swollen, with a look of flushed, alcoholic reproach. He was tall and heavyset, with graying black whiskers that sprouted like quills. His eyes had a way of swerving in their sockets, seeking you out when you could not slip away quickly enough. *H'lo there, little Joyce! Joycie! Joycie Oates, h'lo!* He wore rubber boots that flapped, unbuckled, about his feet. 19

Mrs. Weidel was a faded-pretty, apologetic woman with a body that seemed to have become bloated, as with a perpetual pregnancy. Her bosom had sunk to her waist. Her legs were encased, sausagelike, in flesh-colored support hose. *How can that woman live with him? That pig.* There was disdain, disgust, in this frequent refrain. *Why doesn't she leave him? Did you see that black eye? Did you hear them the other night? Take the girls away, at least.* It was thought that she could, for Mrs. Weidel was the only one in the family who seemed to work at all regularly. She was hired for seasonal canning in a tomato factory in lower Lockport and may have done housecleaning in the city. 20

A shifting household of relatives and rumored "boarders" lived in the Weidel house. There were six Weidel children, four sons and two daughters. Ruth was a year older than I, and Dorothy two years younger. There was an older brother of Mr. Weidel's, who walked with a cane and was said to be an ex-convict, from Attica. The eldest Weidel son, Roy, owned a motorcycle, and friends of his often visited, fellow-bikers. There were loud parties, frequent disputes, and tales of Mr. Weidel's chasing his wife with a butcher knife, a claw hammer, 21 the shotgun, threatening to "blow her head off." Mrs. Weidel and the younger children fled outdoors in terror and hid in the hayloft. Sheriff's deputies drove out to the house, but no charges were ever pressed against Mr. Weidel. Until the fire, which was so public that it couldn't be denied.

There was the summer day—I was eleven years old—that 22
Mr. Weidel shot Slossie. We heard the poor creature yelping and whimpering for what seemed like hours. When my father came home from work, he went to speak to Mr. Weidel, though my mother begged him not to. By this time, the dog had dragged herself beneath the Weidels' house to die. Mr. Weidel was furious at the intrusion, drunk, defensive—Slossie was his goddam dog, he said, she'd been getting in the way, she was "old." But my father convinced him to put the poor dog out of her misery. So Mr. Weidel made one of his sons drag Slossie out from beneath the house, and he straddled her and shot her a second time, and a third, at close range. My father, who'd never hunted, who'd never owned a gun, backed off, a hand over his eyes.

Afterward, my father would say of that day that walking away 23
from that drunken son of a bitch with a rifle in his hands was about the hardest thing he'd ever done. He'd expected a shot between his shoulders.

The fire was the following year, around Thanksgiving. 24

After the Weidels were gone from Millersport and the house stood 25
empty, I discovered Slossie's grave. I'm sure it was Slossie's grave. It was beyond the dog hutch, in the weedy back yard, a sunken patch of earth measuring about three feet by four with one of Mrs. Weidel's big whitewashed rocks at the head.

Morning glories grew in clusters on the posts of the front porch. 26
Mrs. Weidel had planted hollyhocks, sunflowers, and trumpet vine in the yard. Tough, weedlike flowers that would survive for years.

It had been said of Ruth and her sister Dorothy that they were 27
"slow." Yet Ruth was never slow to fly into a rage when she was teased by neighborhood boys or by her older brothers. She waved her fists and stammered obscenities, words that stung like hail. Her face darkened with blood, and her full, thick lips quivered with a strange sort of pleasure. How you loved to see Ruth Weidel fly into one of her rages; it was like holding a lighted match to flammable material.

The Weidel house was like any other run-down wood-frame house, 28
said by my grandfather to have been "thrown up" in the nineteen-twenties. It had no cellar, only a concrete-block foundation—an emptiness that gradually filled with debris. It had an upstairs with several small bedrooms. There was no attic. No insulation. Steep, almost vertical stairs. The previous tenant had started to construct a front porch of raw planks, never completed or painted. (Though Mrs. Weidel added "touches" to the porch—chairs, a woven-rush rug,

geraniums in flowerpots.) The roof of the house was made of sheets of tin, scarred and scabbed like skin, and the front was covered in simulated-brick asphalt siding pieced together with lumberyard scraps. All year round, a number of the windows were covered in transparent duct tape and never opened. From a distance, the house was the fading dun color of a deer's winter coat.

Our house had an attic and a cellar and a deep well and a solid ce- 29
ment foundation. My father did all the carpentry on our house, most of the shingling, the painting, the masonry. I would not know until I was an adult that he'd come from what's called a "broken home" himself—what an image, luridly visual, of a house literally broken, split in two, its secrets spilled out onto the ground for all to see, like entrails.

My mother, unlike Mrs. Weidel, had time to houseclean. It was a 30
continuous task, a mother's responsibility. My mother planted vegetables, strawberries, beds of flowers. Petunias and pansies and zinnias. Crimson peonies that flowered for my birthday, in mid-June.

I remember the night of the fire vividly, as if it had been a festive af- 31
fair to which I'd been invited.

There was the sound of a siren on the Creek Road. There were 32
shouts, and an astonishing burst of flame in the night, in the direction of the Weidel house. The air was moist, and reflected and magnified the fire, surrounding it like a nimbus. My grandparents would claim there had never been such excitement in Millersport, and perhaps that was true. My father dressed hurriedly and went to help the firefighters, and my mother and the rest of us watched from upstairs windows. The fire began at about 1 A.M., and it would be past 4 A.M. before my seven-year-old brother and I got back to bed.

Yet what was so exciting an event was, in fact, an ending, with 33
nothing to follow. Immediately afterward, the Weidels disappeared from Millersport and from our lives. It was said that Mr. Weidel fled "as a fugitive" but was captured and arrested the next day, in Buffalo. The family was broken up, scattered, the younger children placed in foster homes. That quickly, the Weidels were gone.

For a long time, the smell of wood smoke, scorch, pervaded the 34
air of Millersport, the fresh, damp smell of earth sullied by its presence. Neighbors complained that the Weidel house should be razed at the county's expense, bulldozed over, and the property sold. But nothing was done, for years. Who knows why? When I went away to college, the old falling-down house was still there.

How swiftly, in a single season, a human habitation can turn 35
wild. The bumpy cinder driveway over which the eldest Weidel son had ridden his motorcycle was soon stippled with tall weeds.

What had happened to Roy Weidel? It was said he'd joined the 36
Navy. No, he had a police record and could not have joined the Navy.

He'd disappeared. Asked by the police to give a sworn statement about the night of his father's "arson," he'd panicked and fled.

Signs were posted—"No TRESPASSING," "THIS PROPERTY CONDEMNED BY ERIE CO."—and they, too, over a period of months, became shabby and faded. My parents warned me never to wander onto the Weidel property. There was a well with a loose-fitting cover, among other dangers. As if *I* would fall into a well! I smiled to think how little my parents knew me. How little anyone knew me. 37

Have I said that my father never struck his children, as Mr. Weidel struck his? And did worse things to them, to the girls sometimes, it was whispered. Yes, and Mrs. Weidel, who seemed so soft and apologetic and sad, she, too, had beaten the younger children when she'd been drinking. County social workers came around to question neighbors, and spread the story of what they learned along the way. 38

In fact, I may have been disciplined, spanked, a few times. Like most children, I don't remember. I remember Mr. Weidel spanking his children until they screamed (though I wasn't a witness, was I?), but I don't remember being spanked by my parents, and in any case, if I was, it was no more than I deserved. 39

I'd seen Mr. Weidel urinating once at the roadside. The loose-flying skein of the kerosene he'd flung around the house before setting the fire must have resembled the stream of his urine, transparent and glittering. But they laughed, saying Mr. Weidel had been too drunk, or too careless, to have done an adequate job of sprinkling kerosene through the downstairs of the house. Wasn't it like him, such a slovenly job. Only part of the house has burned, a wall of the kitchen and an adjoining woodshed. 40

Had Mr. Weidel wanted to burn his family alive in their beds? Mrs. Weidel testified no, they'd all been awake, they'd run out into the yard before the fire began. They'd never been in any danger, she swore. But Mr. Weidel was indicted on several counts of attempted murder, along with other charges. 41

For so many years the Weidel house remained standing. There was something defiant about it, like someone who has been mortally wounded but will not die. In the weedy front yard, Mrs. Weidel's display of whitewashed rocks and plaster-of-Paris gnomes and the clay pedestal with the shiny blue glass ball disappeared from view within a year or so. Brambles grew everywhere. I forced myself to taste a small bitter red berry but spat it out, it made my mouth pucker so. 42

What did it mean that Erie County had "condemned" the Weidel property? The downstairs windows were carelessly boarded over, and both the front and rear doors were unlocked, collapsing on their hinges. Broken glass underfoot and a sickish stench of burn, mildew, decay. Yet there were "touches"—on what remained of a kitchen wall, a Holstein calendar from a local feed store, a child's crayon drawing. 43

Upstairs, children's clothes, socks and old shoes heaped on the floor. I recognized with a thrill of repugnance an old red sweater of Ruth's, angora-fuzzy. There were broken Christmas-tree ornaments, a naked pink plastic doll. Toppled bedsprings, filthy mattresses streaked with yellow and rust-colored stains. The mattresses looked as if they'd been gutted, their stuffing strewn about. The most terrible punishment, I thought, would be to be forced to lie down on such a mattress.

I thought of Mrs. Weidel, her swollen, blackened eyes, her bruised face. Shouts and sirens in the night, the sheriff's patrol car. But no charges filed. The social worker told my mother how Mrs. Weidel had screamed at the county people, insisting her husband hadn't done anything wrong and shouldn't go to jail. The names she'd called them! Unrepeatable. 44

She was the wife of that man, they'd had babies together. The law had no right to interfere. The law had nothing to do with them. 45

As a woman and as a writer, I have long wondered at the wellsprings of female masochism. Or what, in despair of a more subtle, less reductive phrase, we can call the congeries of predilections toward self-hurt, self-erasure, self-repudiation in women. These predilections are presumably "learned"—"acquired"—but perhaps also imprinted in our genes, of biological necessity, neurophysiological fate, predilections that predate culture. Indeed, may shape culture. Do not say, "Yes, but these are isolated, peripheral examples. They are marginal Americans, uneducated. They tell us nothing about ourselves." They tell us everything about ourselves, and even the telling, the exposure, is a kind of cutting, an inscription in the flesh. 46

Yet what could possibly be the evolutionary advantage of self-hurt in the female? Abnegation in the face of another's cruelty? Acquiescence to another's will? This loathsome secret that women do not care to speak of, or even acknowledge. 47

Two or three years later, in high school, twelve miles away in a consolidated district school to which, as a sophomore, I went by school bus, Ruth Weidel appeared. She was living now with relatives in Lockport. She looked, at sixteen, like a woman in her twenties; big-breasted, with full, strong thighs and burnished-brown hair inexpertly bleached. Ruth's homeroom was "special education," but she took some classes with the rest of us. If she recognized me, in our home-economics class, she was careful to give no sign. 48

There was a tacit understanding that "something had happened" to Ruth Weidel, and her teachers treated her guardedly. Ruth was special, the way a handicapped person is special. She was withdrawn, quiet; if still prone to violent outbursts of rage, she might have been on medication to control it. Her eyes, like her father's, seemed always about to swerve in their sockets. Her face was round, fleshy, like a pudding, her 49 nose oily-pored. Yet she wore lipstick, she was "glamorous"—almost. In gym class, Ruth's large breasts straining against her T-shirt and the shining rippled muscles and fatty flesh of her thighs were amazing to us; we were so much thinner and less female, so much younger.

I believed that I should protect Ruth Weidel, so I told none of the 50
other students about her family. Even to Ruth, for a long time I pretended not to know who she was. I can't explain how Ruth could have possibly believed me, yet this seems to have been so. Quite purposefully, I befriended Ruth. I thought her face would lose its sallow hardness if she could be made to smile, and so it became a kind of challenge to me to induce Ruth Weidel to smile. She was lonely and miserable at school, and flattered by my attention. For so few "normal" girls sought out "specialed" girls. At first she may have been suspicious, but by degrees she became trusting. I thought of Slossie: trust shows in the eyes.

I sat with Ruth at lunch in the school cafeteria and eventually I 51
asked her about the house on the old Creek Road, and she lied bluntly, to my face, insisting that an uncle of hers had owned that house. She'd only visited a few times. She and her family. I asked, "How did the fire start?" and Ruth said, slowly, each word sucked like a pebble in the mouth, "Lightning. Lightning hit it. One night in a storm." I asked, "Are you living with your mother now, Ruth?" and Ruth shrugged, and made a face, and said, "She's O.K. I see her sometimes." I asked about Dorothy. I asked where Mrs. Weidel was. I said that my mother had always liked her mother, and missed her when she went away. But Ruth seemed not to hear. Her gaze had drifted. I said, "Why did you all move away?" Ruth did not reply, though I could hear her breathing hard. "Why did you abandon your house? It could have been fixed. It's still there. Your mom's hollyhocks are still there. You should come out and see it sometime. You could visit me." Ruth shrugged, and laughed. She gave me a sidelong glance, almost flirtatiously. It was startling to see how good-looking she could be, how sullen-sexy; to know how men would stare at her who would never so much as glance at a girl like me. Ruth said slowly, as if she'd come to a final, adamant conclusion to the problem that had long vexed her, "They all just went away."

Another time, after lunch with Ruth, I left a plastic change purse 52
with a few coins in it on the ledge in one of the girls' lavatories, where Ruth was washing her hands. I don't recall whether I left it on purpose or not. But when I returned, after waiting for Ruth to leave the lavatory, the change purse was gone.

Once or twice, I invited Ruth Weidel to come home with me on 53
the school bus some afternoon, to Millersport, to have supper with my family and stay the night. I must not have truly believed she might accept, for my mother would have been horrified and would have forced me to rescind the invitation. Ruth had hesitated, as if she

wanted to say yes, wanted very badly to say yes, but finally she said, "No. I guess I better not."

THINKING ABOUT THE ESSAY

1. The author begins her essay by describing her environment from the perspective of a girl in puberty. Why do views of our neighborhoods or dwellings change over time even if the actual physical structures remain relatively the same? What is it about early memories of houses that provide us with such poignant images years later? Do you have similar responses to a certain neighborhood you knew when you were 12 or 13 as the author does?
2. The author retains a very strong and dramatic eye for detail, describing specific household items, vegetation, and people. She also compares her memories to the work of certain American painters whose subject matter included many of the same landscapes things she describes. To what do you attribute this unique way of looking and remembering? To the special talents and education of the author? To her sensitivity to her surroundings? Can these abilities be learned or are they endowed from birth?
3. The author states, "There was a strange and profound and unknowable reality to these abandoned houses." Do you agree with the author, or do you believe this "unknowable reality" is simply a matter of not digging deep enough to understand the causes behind their abandonment? Is there something about family life that is ultimately unknowable to the outsider? If so, what function does this privacy serve?
4. Toward the end of the text, the author shifts gears and enters into a polemic about the nature of gender in the role of masochism. She even suggests that women may be genetically disposed to masochism. Examine her rationale behind her conjecture. Do you believe this is an example of pure sexism or does the author have a valid point? How does her raising of this issue pertain to the story of the Weidel family in general?

RESPONDING IN DISCUSSION

1. Oates is relating a story of a dysfunctional family that occurred at least 30 years ago. Divide into groups of three or four, and discuss whether such a family system is as likely to occur today as in the previous generation. Also, discuss whether the profound problems in the family would have gone unaddressed for so long today as they did at the time they occurred.

2. Oates invokes an imaginary sad story of a house that has been abandoned: "There have been devastated lives. Lives to be spoken of pityingly. How they went wrong. Why did she marry him, why did she stay with him? Just desperate people. Ignorant. Poor white trash. Runs in the family. A wrong turn." Discuss to what degree such depictions are stereotypes. Is it true that "families gone wrong" come from particular social and economic classes? If not, what is a common denominator among them?
3. Divide into groups of three and four. Through the process of brainstorming, have your group create a list of at least 10 behaviors, attitudes, and beliefs that can contribute to a severely dysfunctional family. Then rank-order the list with the most serious offense ranked 1 and the least serious ranked 10.
4. The Weidel family's dissolution seems to be partly due to the fact that they were isolated and sequestered from the rest of society, so that no one outside was able to observe and attempt to intervene, negotiate, or arbitrate any of the family problems. Using Kingsolver's idea of the new extended family, discuss how broader interaction with other family members might have reduced the profound problems in the Weidel family.
5. Discuss how contemporary social service agencies such as child welfare boards, juvenile justice courts, and new laws regarding domestic violence might or might not have successfully addressed some problems in the Weidel household.

RESPONDING IN WRITING

1. Oates is a noted novelist and short story writer. What notable elements do you find in this essay that confirm her stature as a writer of fiction? Write an essay exploring this subject.
2. Write an essay explaining the relationship between family issues and gender issues as presented in Oates' essay.
3. Argue for or against the proposition that law enforcement agents should have less restricted powers in cases where spousal abuse is reported or even suspected. Be sure to include at least three supporting points to back up your thesis.
4. For a research project, investigate the cultural values among family units in two cultures, focusing on how such values impact on the laws concerning the definition of and sanctions against spousal abuse.
5. Conduct both library and Web searches for information on Oates. Focus on her preoccupation with the lives of women. Then, using "They All Just Went Away" as a foundation, write an evaluation of the author's interest in gender roles, incorporating

information that you have located from your library and Web sources.

CONNECTIONS: FOR WRITING AND RESEARCH

1. Write an essay of 750 to 1,000 words, comparing and contrasting the perspectives in Paul's essay "Silly Men, Banal Men" and Grenier's "Feminism and Nomenclature."
2. Compare and contrast Roiphe's views on the liberated woman in Chapter 4 ("The Dating Game") with those of any writer here in Chapter 8. Consider what and whose concerns the authors address and why.
3. There is a wide range of styles in the five essays in this chapter. Contrast the personal, firsthand, experiential approach of Joyce Carol Oates and Maribeth Fischer with the more abstract, didactic approach of the other writers in this chapter. Do you prefer one approach over the other? Which do you believe has a greater impact on the reader? Is each approach a matter of personal style or does it signify something greater (for example, the way a writer views the world)?
4. Write a letter to Rebecca Walker praising or criticizing her evolution from a "party-line feminist" to an independent thinker.
5. Write a 400-word descriptive essay portraying a man whom you know who fits into either of the categories characterized by Paul as "silly men" and "banal men."
6. Discuss how feminism will have altered relationships between men and women by the year 2020 in such domains as the workplace, home, child rearing, public policy, and politics.

9

THE DIVERSITY DEBATE

The current diversity debate that has permeated the American conscious and conscience comes in many nomenclatures and subdivisions. Among them are multiculturalism, cultural diversity, identity politics, racial politics, and ethnic self-determination. Reading the pages of today's magazines and newspapers, and watching issues-oriented television programming, one could probably find as many catchphrases and buzzwords as the society will tolerate. Are these terms meaningful concepts or helpful explanatory principles to help us understand where we come from, realize to which groups we belong, or get a clearer idea of our social standing? Or are they empty signifiers used as tools by whatever interest group happens to be pushing its particular agenda onto the American scene? Regardless of your view, it is evident that the diversity issue permeates American life and thought. As a simple reality check to see if this holds true, just look through the current edition of any good-quality newspaper or magazine in your library's periodicals section. At least one article or column will surely be devoted to the subject in any publication you pick up. The following essays have been gleaned from among the most challenging of these writings. All grapple with some of the significant issues that are presumably a result of our heterogeneous society and our checkered past that has included racism, discrimination, and privilege owing to social, ethnic, and racial differences.

The Street Where I Live

June Jordan

June Jordan, award-winning poet, essayist, political activist, and professor of African-American studies at the University of California–Berkeley, has written for decades on issues centering on American life from her perspective as a black woman. Her essay, "The Street Where I Live," was first published in the December 1995 issue of *The Progressive*. In it she takes on the subjects of diversity, race, and the perception of race's significance in American life. In presenting her ideas from a personal rather than ideological viewpoint, she implies that all Americans could use a bit more common sense when it comes to judging the significance of events puffed up by the media—"pseudo-events" as dubbed by famous historian Daniel Boorstein.

PREVIEWING THE ESSAY

Do you think of yourself first and foremost as a member of a group or as an independent being? Perhaps the answer to this question depends on the context within which you find yourself. For example, if you receive straight A's during a semester, would you attribute your grades to your actions as a member of a group or as an individual? What if you were expected to identify with a racial, ethnic, or social group? Would your response be solely a gut reaction, or might you be persuaded by the logic of the proselytizer?

This is one big country. And if people in North Dakota spoke one language, while folks in South Dakota, or New Mexico, spoke another, a different language, that would seem reasonable to me, even appropriate. And, so, I dispute all the various "nationwide" analyses and projections, each one colder than cold. "Nationwide" is too wide, too broad, to mean anything. 1

On the block where I live, there are black families, white families, Southeast Asian Americans, Chinese Americans, "interracial" students, elderly folks, newlyweds, Jews, and Christians. This is a short little street of great good calm. And I defy anybody to identify more than two or three things that I may have in common with the household next door. They're black. I'm black. They live on this street. So do I. But what does race or residence in this city mean to them? I have no idea. And beyond that? Personally, I would not assume anything about them or anybody else on my block except that they're likely to be friendly in a California ("If you ever need anything . . .") way. 2

So when I started to read and hear about "the great racial divide," a week ago, I thought, "Sure. Is that something like Continental Drift? Or what?" And when I started to read and hear about race as 3 the only and the biggest deal on the table, I thought, "Sure. Is that something like regular black man Rodney King and multimillionaire O. J. Simpson equally symbolize what, exactly? And the fact that, for example, I'm female is, suddenly and forever, beside the point?"

And, so, when some newspaper guy called from L.A. for a comment about the Million Man March, I said, "First of all, I was not invited. Secondly, I have one thing to say to and about anything or anybody wants to sunder me from the black man who is my son: 'You can go to hell!'" 4

And when a colleague (of sorts) of mine went off about domestic violence "versus" Mark Fuhrman and the L.A.P.D., I said, "How come you can't see that Mark Fuhrman and the L.A.P.D. and racism, per se, suck Mack trucks, absolutely, yes, and, also, anybody busts up his wife is totally reprehensible, and I don't forgive or forget anything or anybody who's just plain ugly and wrong: Mark Fuhrman and O. J. Simpson." 5

And when Minister Farrakhan proclaimed himself "God's Messenger" with not so much as a momentary twinkle of quasi-uneasiness, and when Minister Farrakhan went lyrical about the number nine symbolizing a pregnant woman with "a male child" inside her, and so on and so forth, I thought, "Well, there it is: CNN-TV gives this guy two-and-a-half hours of uninterrupted international television time—way more than the Pope, President Clinton, Nelson Mandela—and then what?" More "nationwide" pseudo-analysis and projection about "the significance" of the importance that CNN-TV, and most of the American mass media, invest Farrakhan with. 6

And then I read and I heard about who supported and who opposed the Million Man March, for a couple of days, but then, happily, happily, I realized that my local, real life preempts all of these national constructions and destructions. 7

On Thursday, October 12, 1995, 5,000 Americans of every description rallied at U.C. Berkeley. There were "Queers for Affirmative Action," "Jews for Affirmative Action," "Asians for Affirmative Action." and Native American dances for affirmative action. Everybody was invited to the rally, and everybody showed up. As a matter of fact, the leadership for this fantastic success was a new U.C. Berkeley student organization called Diversity in Action. As the name suggests, the members of this incredibly effective task force include African-American young men with dreads or shaved heads and Irish-American young men with blond ponytails and Chicana young women and Vietnamese-American young men and women, and like that, on and on. 8

This ecstatic, mighty throng gathered together to demand restoration of affirmative action throughout the University of California system, and to assert our intelligent resistance to demagogic, racialized, un-American manipulations that would deny American history, deplore American diversity, and destroy our manifest, principled unity. 9

When I spoke, I pointed to the very recent (September 12) finding by the 1995 National Research Council report on the quality of Ph.D. education in the United States: with the most heterogeneous student population in the world, U.C. Berkeley is the leading, the top, university in America, or, as *The New York Times* reported, "No other university even comes close." Our main speaker for this great day was the Reverend Jesse Jackson, and we greeted him with an endless tumult of genuine cheers and excitement. He came through with a rousing argument in favor of "real world" politics and policies and, therefore, affirmative action. He implored us to "turn to" each other and "not turn on" each other. He inveighed against the list of odious visions out here: racism, sexism, anti-Semitism, homophobia. And he implored us to get angry and vote Gingrich and company out of power in 1996. 10

On Tuesday, October 17, 1995, our U.C. faculty senate voted 124 to 2 to rescind the U.C. Regents' ruling against affirmative action. This vote does not mean the Regents will have to reverse themselves, but it does mean that the faculty stands with the students who stand with the chancellors, united in opposition to the Regents, and united in passionate support of affirmative action. 11

The "nationwide" assault on affirmative action began right here, in Northern California. And it looks to me like we may bury that particular outrage right here, where it was born. For sure, the fight is on, and it does seem far from hopeless. 12

So, yes, this is one big country. I happen to live on the Pacific Rim, which, for better or for worse, harbors the demographic and economic forecast for all of the U.S.A. in the Twenty-First Century. 13

And I trust what I can see and what I can hear and what I can do on my block, and around the corner, and on the campus where I teach. 14

And, just now, I am awfully glad to live nowhere else but here: right here. 15

THINKING ABOUT THE ESSAY

1. How would you characterize the personality of the author based on the style of this essay and on her responses to public issues? Does she show a healthy independence of spirit? Is she disrespectful of the opinions of others? Explain.
2. Many writers claim the public responds to racial matters with emotion rather than reason. How did you respond to specific events such as the O. J. Simpson verdict, the testimony of Mark Fuhrman (the racist police officer), the Million Man March, and the Rodney King incident? Was it emotionally, rationally, or a mixture of both?

3. Jordan describes where she lives as an environment with a rich and varied population. Consider the immediate neighborhood where you grew up. To what degree did its racial, ethnic, and cultural makeup affect the way you view others who are not members of your own race or culture? To what extent did it make you perceive that such variables were even factors in identifying people?
4. What is the author's thesis? Is it stated directly or indirectly? Where, in the essay, is it most specifically articulated?
5. Does the author believe diversity is good, bad, or irrelevant? Explain your view.

RESPONDING IN DISCUSSION

1. Divide into groups of three and four and have each student draw up a list with the following words written vertically down the page: *race, age, gender, personality, political beliefs, religion, marital status,* and *income.* Have each member of the group rank-order each characteristic in terms of how important it is as a means of identifying with that person. Tabulate the results, and present your findings to the class. Discuss variations between your group and others.
2. Discuss with your class whether you have ever taken a particular side on a racial issue out of a sense of peer pressure rather than from a clear consideration of the facts.
3. Discuss whether college students have a special privilege in trying out different group affiliations, since the college and university life is a process for exploration and experimentation in personal identity and personal growth.
4. Regarding her generation, Rebecca Walker in her essay "Changing the Face of Feminism" states, "we find ourselves seeking to create identities that include more than they exclude, or that explore rather than define." Does Jordan seem to implicitly champion this way of looking at the world? If so, why? If not, why not?
5. Jordan refers to some "odious visions out here." What are her personal and public reasons for considering them odious? Does this demonstrate her strength of character and understanding or does it show that even she is not as tolerant as she would like us to think?

RESPONDING IN WRITING

1. In a personal essay of 400 to 500 words, describe a time in your life when you held an opinion concerning an issue of race that eventually evolved as you became more mature or knowledgeable.

2. Describe a time when you conformed to a particular view of a national event because you didn't want to alienate yourself from your friends.
3. If you've ever seen a dog playing with its owner, it is evident that the dog harbors no ill will based on race, culture, or ethnicity. Write a humorous essay of approximately 500 words entitled, "Why Can't a Human Be More Like a Dog (or Cat)?"
4. Argue for or against the proposition that members of different races who are members of similar economic classes are more comfortable with one another than members of the same race whose economic statuses radically differ.
5. Select one of the people or events that Jordan alludes to in her essay, and scan the World Wide Web for information on the subject. Review the information that you locate, and then write an essay relating the subject to the diversity debate in America today.

Planet of the White Guys

Barbara Ehrenreich

Author Barbara Ehrenreich's several books on contemporary American life range from gender issues to politics to economics. In this essay published in the March 13, 1995, issue of *Time,* she presents her case against what she perceives as white males' backlash against the idea and practice of affirmative action. While acknowledging that no one should be discriminated against, including white males, she argues—using supporting points such as poll data and personal observation—that affirmative action needs to stay in place until we all are truly "color blind" and until white males admit that for centuries they have had their own implicit "affirmative action" policy that provided them preferences in job hiring based solely on the color of their skin.

PREVIEWING THE ESSAY

Do you have implicit assumptions about strangers solely because of their race? Would it matter how they dressed (for example, in a business suit, in sneakers and a sweatshirt, in overalls, or in a tennis outfit)? If so, is it wrong to have such assumptions if they are not judgmental, but rather purely descriptive? After all, isn't the propensity to classify part of human nature? Or is any type of stereotyping or assumption about a person you don't know the wrong thing to do simply because you are not perceiving that person as an individual but as part of a group, and intentionally or unintentionally reducing that person's humanity?

On the planet inhabited by the anti-affirmative action activists, the only form of discrimination left is the kind that operates against white males. There, in the name of redressing ancient wrongs, white men are routinely shoved aside to make room for less qualified women and minorities. These favored ones have no problems at all—except for that niggling worry that their colleagues see them as underqualified "affirmative-action babies." Maybe there was once an evil called racism in this charmed place—30 or 300 years ago, that is—but it's been replaced by affirmative action. 1

Now I agree that discrimination is an ugly thing no matter who's at the receiving end, and that it may be worth reviewing affirmative action, as President Clinton has proposed, to see whether it's been fairly applied. People should not be made to suffer for the wicked things perpetrated by their ancestors or by those who merely looked like them. Competent white men should be hired over less competent women and minorities, otherwise, sooner or later, the trains won't run on time and the planes will fall down from the sky. 2

But it would be a shame if Clinton's "review" sidesteps the undeniable persistence of racism in the workplace and just about everywhere else. Consider the recent lesson from Rutgers University. Here we have a perfectly nice liberal fellow, a college president with a record of responsiveness to minority concerns. He opens his mouth to talk about minority test scores, and then—like a Tourette's syndrome victim in the grip of a seizure—he comes out with the words "genetic hereditary background." Translated from the academese: minorities are dumb, and they're dumb because they're born that way. 3

Can we be honest here? I've been around white folks most of my life—from left-wingers to right-wingers, from crude-mouthed louts to prissy-minded elitists—and I've heard enough to know that *The Bell Curve* is just a long-winded version of what an awful lot of white people actually believe. Take a look, for example, at a survey reported by the National Opinion Research Center in 1991, which found a majority of whites asserting that minorities are lazier, more violence-prone and less intelligent than whites. Even among the politically correct, the standard praise word for a minority person is "articulate," as if to say, "Isn't it amazing how well he can speak!" 4

Prejudice of the quiet, subliminal kind doesn't flow from the same place as hate. All you have to do to be infected is look around: at the top of the power hierarchy—filling more than 90% of top corporate-leadership slots and a grossly disproportionate share of managerial and professional positions—you see white men. Meanwhile, you tend to find minorities clustered in the kind of menial roles—busing dishes, unloading trucks—that our parents warned were waiting for us too if we didn't get our homework done. 5

So what is the brain to make of this data? It does what brains are designed to do: it simplifies and serves up the quickie generalizations that are meant to guide us through a complex world. Thus when we see a black colleague, who may be an engineer or a judge, the brain, in its innocence, announces helpfully, "Janitor-type approaching, wearing a suit." 6

Maybe it's easier for a woman to acknowledge this because subliminal prejudice hurts women too. Studies have shown, for example, that people are more likely to find an article convincing if it is signed by "Bob Someone" instead of, say, "Barbara Someone." It's just the brain's little habit of parceling reality into tidy equations, such as female = probable fluffhead. The truth is that each of us carries around an image of competence in our mind, and its face is neither female nor black. Hence our readiness to believe, whenever we hear of a white male losing out to a minority or a woman, that the white guy was actually more qualified. In Jesse Helms' winning 1990 campaign commercial, a white man crumples up a rejection letter, while the voice-over reminds him that he was "the best-qualified." But was he? Is he always? And why don't we ever hear a white guy worry out loud that his colleagues suspect he got the job—as white men have for centuries—in part because he's male and white? 7

It's a measure of the ambient racism that we find it so hard to believe that affirmative action may actually be doing something right: ensuring that the best guy gets the job, regardless of that guy's race or sex. Eventually, when the occupational hierarchy is so thoroughly integrated that it no longer makes sense for the subconscious minds to invest the notion of competence with a particular skin color or type of genitalia, affirmative action can indeed be cast aside like training wheels. 8

Meanwhile, aggrieved white men can console themselves with the gains their wives have made. Numerically speaking, white women are the biggest beneficiaries of affirmative action, and because white women tend to marry white men, it follows that white men are, numerically speaking, among the top beneficiaries too. On this planet, Bob Dole and Pat Buchanan may not have been able to figure that out yet, but most white guys, I like to think, are plenty smart enough. 9

THINKING ABOUT THE ESSAY

1. The author states that "it may be worth reviewing affirmative action." Does the use of the word *may* demonstrate ambiguity or uncertainty in the author's views? Explain.
2. The authors states, "when we see a black colleague, . . . the brain, . . . announces helpfully, 'Janitor-type approaching, wearing a

suit.'" How does she know that is what people think? Is she referring to all people?

3. What does the author mean by "prejudice of the quiet, subliminal kind" and "ambient racism"?
4. What is the author's thesis? Is it stated explicitly or suggested implicitly?
5. The author cites specific examples to advance her arguments, citing the remarks of the president of Rutgers University and the ad campaign of Jesse Helms. Is it fair to use a few examples to generalize about the society at large? Does the author balance these examples with general observations? Why or why not?

RESPONDING IN DISCUSSION

1. Divide into groups of three and four. Discuss whether—as the author suggests—women are more sensitive to negative stereotyping than men since they are more often its victims. Share your conclusions with your class.
2. Divide into pairs, and, without asking questions, size up your partner by listing your assumptions of his or her preferences regarding music, academic major, politics, heroes, movies, work habits, and so on. After completing the exercise, show your partner your conclusions and discuss how you arrived at your answers. Share your responses with the rest of the class. How much of your perception was based on stereotyping? How much was based on personal observation?
3. Divide into small groups, and discuss the author's statement that "affirmative action may actually be doing something right: ensuring that the best guy gets the job, regardless of that guy's race or sex." How many in the group agree with the statement? Discuss your findings with the rest of the class.
4. Are there situations where affirmative action can be unfair to a person even if it is applied as fairly as possible?

RESPONDING IN WRITING

1. In a 400-word essay, describe a time in your life when you were either given preference owing to your race or discriminated against on account of it.
2. Write a proposal to the president of your college or university, outlining a course that would teach students to overcome subconscious racism, and suggesting yourself as the instructor.

3. Argue for or against the proposition that affirmative action is unfair because it does not consider one's economic background, education level of one's family, home life, and neighborhood of origin in determining discrimination.
4. Argue for or against the proposition that affirmative action is unfair to Generation Xers since it is their parents' generation who harbored the racial prejudice that led to its legislation.
5. Contrast Ehrenreich's beliefs about people's assumptions toward members of different races with June Jordan's assumptions. (Jordan states, "I defy anybody to identify more than two or three things that I may have in common with the household next door. They're black. I'm black. They live on this street. So do I. But what does race or residence in this city mean to them? I have no idea. . . . Personally, I would not assume anything about them or anybody else on my block.") Is Jordan an exception to the rule or does Ehrenreich overgeneralize and overstate her case?
6. Ehrenreich alludes to a recent book entitled *The Bell Curve* by Richard Herrnstein and Charles Murray. Conduct a Web search for this book and its author. Then write a report on the controversy surrounding it.

The Strange and Exciting Fruits of Global Culture

Pico Iyer

Pico Iyer's writing career started with "Let's Go" guides for college students embarking on low-cost trips to Europe. He moved on to more in-depth travel reportage that has been published in two books: *Video Nights in Kathmandu* and *Falling off the Map*. In this essay, first published in the January–February 1996 issue of the *Utne Reader,* he describes a new culture of diversity that not only is in the world around us, but has changed us from the inside as we synthesize influences from cultures all around the world, making us closer to what some writers have called the "universal citizen."

PREVIEWING THE ESSAY

How many different cultures do you encounter in the course of a week? Do you eat out in a Chinese restaurant? Do you listen to music influenced by Jamaican reggae or African drumming? Do you wear any clothing inspired by images you have seen on MTV? If so, are these activities done for convenience, style, and variety, or do they give you a broader personal perspective on the way you look at the world?

I was born in England to a family from India, and when I was very young we moved to California. By the time I was 7 I was an American resident, an English subject, and an Indian native. Nowadays, I go back and forth between my family's apartments in California and my girlfriend's flat in Japan. More and more, I am an unaffiliated soul for whom everywhere is home, and nowhere. 1

When I was young I used to think that this was a relatively unusual state of affairs. But this is becoming the norm; more and more of us are like global villagers. We have a hundred different cultures clashing and singing and conspiring within us. And every time a Californian goes to Thailand and marries a young woman from Bangkok and every time a Thai family decides to move to Hollywood and start a new life there, the products of those unions are almost unprecedented international cultures with a voice and an accent and an angle on the world we've never seen before. 2

In England the Booker Prize is given to the finest novel of the year, and in recent years the prize has almost always gone to writers from India, Canada, New Zealand, Australia—that is, from the ex-colonies. The Empire is striking back, as they say. 3

If you go to a small town like Da Lat in Vietnam you will find local bands who speak no English playing note-perfect versions of "Hotel California" by the Eagles. Conversely, one of the most accomplished singers of Vietnamese music in the world is a young blond woman from Muncie, Indiana, who doesn't speak a word of Vietnamese, but reproduces the sounds melodiously. What this suggests to me is not only that culture can begin to heal the wounds politics creates, but also that all of us in the age of world music are willy-nilly citizens of the world. In a postnational order, none of us need find Mali any more alien than Manhattan. 4

With all these changes happening at the speed of light, it's not hard to see the prospects for darkness beginning to gather in the shadows. I suspect that all of us feel very acutely the danger of Madonna CDs in Tibet or Kentucky Fried Chicken parlors in Beijing. But homogeneity is not one of those dangers. The Kentucky Fried Chicken outlet in Tiananmen Square is as Chinese in its way as the Mao Zedong mausoleum around the corner, but, emblematic of new China, is more open and more hospitable to outside influences. 5

All of us are heir to opportunities, openings, and possibilities that were scarcely imaginable to our grandparents. Ours is the first generation that can jump on a plane today and more or less be in Tibet tomorrow. Ours is the first generation that can walk down the street and meet Tibetans in our midst. And so, if ours is the first generation that can corrupt Tibet with our videos and our images and our ideas, it's also the first, really, that can begin to share with Tibet the benefits of our progress. And—best of all from our point of view—can learn from Tibet. 6

Thoreau famously said that the deepest source of the Nile and the truest Orient are the ones within us. Why go all around the world, he said, to count the cats in Zanzibar? Nowadays we can go around the world without ever leaving our homes. We can visit Zanzibar or the Orient just by walking down the street. The great challenge, beauty, and promise of our age is the way in which it allows us to become fluent in the languages of a hundred cultures while never really forgetting that the true Himalayas and the true Patagonia are the ones that lie within us all. 7

THINKING ABOUT THE ESSAY

1. Is the author's background more diverse than the average American student's? If so, do you believe it has a bearing on the author's perspective concerning cultural diversity? Why?
2. Does Iyer seem to enjoy being a person with an identity that includes a mixture of cultures? If so, where in the text does he suggest this?
3. Do you live in or have you spent time in a community with a broad range of cultural diversity? How did it make you feel? Uncomfortable, threatened, guarded, enchanted, confused, curious? A combination of any of these?
4. What is the significance of the author paraphrasing the 19th-century writer Thoreau?
5. What is Iyer's thesis? Is it expressed explicitly in one sentence or does he imply it? If the latter, how does he imply it? How does he employ comparison and contrast, illustration, and appeal to authority to support his thesis?

RESPONDING IN DISCUSSION

1. Divide into groups of three or four, and discuss what elements in American culture have been influenced by cultures from abroad. Consider such aspects as music, clothes, hair styles, and given names. After you have listed these elements, discuss whether they are weak or superficial influences that may be accounted for by current style, or whether they are now well rooted in our society. Share and compare your findings with the rest of the class.
2. Discuss a cultural trait of a person from another country that at first made you feel uncomfortable, but which you eventually grew to understand and accept, and perhaps even now do yourself.

3. The author states, "We have a hundred different cultures clashing and singing and conspiring within us." Relate this observation to your own life.
4. Discuss the aspects of your behavior, thinking, and beliefs that you consider American.
5. Discuss your observations of a family that is culturally diverse through marriage that transcended cultural or geographic boundaries.

RESPONDING IN WRITING

1. In a descriptive essay of 400 to 500 words, discuss a time in your life when you were with a culturally diverse group of people that made you aware that you were American, or, if you are a visiting student from another country, that made you aware of your culture of origin.
2. Argue for or against the proposition that the author makes poor use of supporting points to advance his thesis because he has purposely selected unusual cultural configurations (for example, a young blond woman from Indiana who sings in Vietnamese).
3. Argue for or against the proposition that the author is merely reflecting the diversity of his own cultural background rather than describing the experience of most Americans.
4. Compare and contrast Iyer's views on the synthesizing of cultures with June Jordan's description of the people who live on her block.
5. According to Iyer, we inhabit an increasingly global world. To test his thesis, select any topic of interest to you and try to find a site or bulletin board on the Internet that addresses your subject. Determine if you are dealing with messages or information from around the world. Then write an essay on your findings, using the Internet as an example supporting Iyer's thesis.

How Liberals Lost Their Virtue over Race

Shelby Steele

Shelby Steele, a well-known black author, writes against the grain of many intellectuals in the affirmative action debate in this essay, which was first published in the January 9, 1995, issue of *Newsweek.* The author of the landmark book *The Content of Our Character* (whose title echoes a line from a speech by

Dr. Martin Luther King, Jr.), Steele claims that affirmative action has hurt those whom it was intended to help. He also feels that it was implemented merely to alleviate the guilt of the "oppressors" rather than out of concern for the oppressed. He does not, however, let mean-spirited opponents of affirmative action off the hook. Rather, he calls for a new perspective on how to tend to racial injustice that has plagued America for generations.

PREVIEWING THE ESSAY

What is your own definition of affirmative action? Do you automatically respond negatively or positively to the term, or do you view it ambivalently, as something with both good and bad elements?

When asked what the Republican landslide might mean for the problems of race and poverty in America, I remembered a meeting I had a few months ago with a California state legislator. He is a Democrat and a liberal of legendary reputation who believes he has been on the proper side of racial issues for more than 30 years. He was fierce in his support of affirmative action, and in his condemnation of those who opposed it. And yet he did not know whether it was succeeding or failing on campuses or in workplaces across the state. He could not say what its side effects were, whom it helped, whom it hurt or how much it cost. Here was a pristine ignorance about a social policy he claimed to uphold so fiercely that he would "leave the state" if it was abolished—a possibility, if the California initiative banning affirmative action gets onto the ballot in '96. 1

I think this legislator represents a common American corruption that contributed greatly to the left-liberal-Democratic denouement of Nov. 8: the use of social policy on race and poverty more to display virtue than to solve social problems. 2

Since the late '60s the left—which has generated most of America's policies on race and poverty—has followed a simple paradigm. First it offered a structural explanation for the problems of minorities and the poor. They were seen as victims of institutional racism, corporate greed and bad educational systems, and the left created a social policy that tried to atone for their victimization with compassion. This policy of compensatory deference was driven more by the needs of those who devised it than by those it was supposed to help. It did not train or educate the poor, or end the discrimination that minorities faced. It simply showed deference to them in compensation for their suffering—a maneuver that made deference synonymous with social virtue. Thus countless Americans—like the legislator—could be utterly ignorant about affirmative action, yet still support it. Once deference is socially virtuous in itself, affirmative action is virtuous by definition. 3

Social reform was reduced to a series of expedient devices—group preferences, quotas, set-asides, redistricting, race and gender norming. After these devices came a vernacular of social virtue—diversity, multiculturalism, pluralism, role models, self-esteem and the endless stream of euphemisms associated with political correctness. It is a deferential language that enables us to signal our social virtue through talk alone. Compensatory deference is what defines political correctness, just as its absence defines incorrectness. 4

But a group preference is not a virtue, and a word like *diversity* is so vacuous that in some places it connotes integration, and in others (many college campuses) it justifies segregation. We don't know whether multiculturalism blends or separates cultures. The American left doesn't know either, doesn't understand its own jerry-built nomenclatures or its imprecise ideas. 5

On Nov. 8 Americans voted, not against social virtue, but against the peculiar idea of virtue that emerged from the 1960s. This idea formed in reaction to a little-acknowledged yet extremely powerful effect of the civil-rights movement: the shame that marked America as it finally came to terms with its racial history. No nation can openly admit to three centuries of dehumanizing racial oppression without going through an era of crippling shame. 6

This sense of national disgrace—quickly compounded in the '60s by a misguided war, a women's movement, a youth rebellion and even an environmental movement—sank the nation into a conundrum. Shame put America in great need of social redemption, but it also robbed the country of the moral authority to pursue that redemption in a principled way. How could a society that had been living by white entitlements suddenly seek redemptive social justice by asking its former victims to pursue difficult democratic principles—advancement by merit and equal and colorblind opportunity? 7

Social policymaking over the last 30 years was made by people and institutions lacking in moral authority to make principled decisions. Policy was made *defensively* to protect institutions from shame and the threat of legal action. Institutions that had discriminated now offered minorities the same group entitlements whites had long enjoyed. Racial quotas came in during the Nixon administration, not because Republicans believed in them, but because they lacked the moral authority to resist them. 8

American liberalism had a chance back in, say, 1968 to help the nation reclaim an honest sense of social virtue. Suppose liberals had rolled up their sleeves and insisted that minorities achieve academically at the same level as others, and then helped them to do so? Suppose they had said to those who had been oppressed that now—through a commitment to rigor and principle—you will develop an excellence that makes your equality manifest? What if liberalism had 9 made minority schools as academically rigorous as the best suburban schools? And suppose it was an article of the liberal faith that making excuses for minority underachievement only extended their oppression? Instead, liberalism gave short shrift to achievement among minority students until they were 18, and then gave them a preferential admission to college—a tactic that makes universities seem virtuous but leaves blacks with a college dropout rate of more than 72 percent.

10 Today America appears to be emerging from its era of shame and to be searching for a new and more pragmatic idea of virtue. Although it is not yet apparent whether American conservatism (of the populist, downsizing, tax-cutting and decentralizing variety) offers such an idea, it clearly has been much enhanced by the nation's exhaustion with virtue-driven social engineering. With the recent elections, there was the feeling that we were witnessing the rejection of old ideas as much as embracing new ones, so it is hard to say whether a new notion of virtue has emerged. And certainly conservatism comes to power with a stunning lack of moral authority over the issues of poverty and race. Conservatives can pick apart liberals for their tiresome excesses, but there is no denying that conservatives had to be dragged into an acceptance of racial tolerance. What's more, free-market conservatism seems inherently to "blame the victim," to see a failure to thrive as a failure of character. Against this image, a reference to "orphanages" (an idea worth considering under a different name) plays as a sneer, a bullying remark by those who would be cruel to the poor.

ULTIMATE TEST

11 But I think there is an honesty in conservatism about how people actually get ahead in society that can be extremely helpful to minorities and the poor. Why should the underprivileged be encouraged to depend on American idealism rather than to participate in its pragmatism? Under liberalism, little was asked of minorities and the poor except that they linger in an identity of victimization and grievance. Today's conservatives—Democrat or Republican—can win converts among these groups if they compassionately teach the values that the vast majority of Americans endorse: hard work, entrepreneurialism, strong education and family stability. Whether there is an effort to teach and bring people along will be the ultimate test of whether the election represented a shift to conservative meanness or a return to Jeffersonian democracy and the classic liberalism of individual freedom and responsibility. My hope is that today's conservative will turn out to be a classic liberal.

THINKING ABOUT THE ESSAY

1. Do you know someone whose life was directly influenced by an affirmative action policy? What was it? How do you know affirmative action was a variable in the event?
2. Steele lists and dismisses many terms that have come to be associated with affirmative action. What about the term *affirmative action* itself? Is it an adequate descriptive term for what it represents? Can you think of an alternative term?
3. Steele places a large emphasis on the general idea of social virtue versus the specific concept of social virtue as it came to be used in defending and rationalizing affirmative action. What are the differences between the general and specific uses of the term?
4. Steel claims that "countless Americans . . . could be utterly ignorant about affirmative action, yet still support it." Who are these Americans? Do you know any? Explain their personal view on the subject?
5. What is Steele's thesis? Is it stated or implied? Explain. How does Steele employ comparison and contrast, definition, and causal analysis to support his thesis? Cite specific examples from the text.

RESPONDING IN DISCUSSION

1. Divide into groups of between three and five, and create a simulation game whereby you assume the role of a college committee whose task is to determine whether to continue an affirmative action policy at your school. After discussion, take a vote on the subject and report your findings to the class.
2. How much of the nation's argument over affirmative action is a result of emotion and how much of reasoned debate? Under which of these domains does the author's writing fall? Explain.
3. Discuss your concept of liberalism. How does it compare to the "classic liberalism" the author refers to in the essay or to "1960s liberalism"? What import do these two forms of liberalism have for the way inequality as a result of race is addressed?
4. How much of the essay's assertions are based on empirical fact and how much are unsubstantiated opinion?

RESPONDING IN WRITING

1. In approximately 500 to 750 words, write an extended definition of the term *social virtue* as used by the author in describing proponents of affirmative action.

2. Argue for or against the proposition that, by suggesting minority students did not receive equality in education below the age of 18, the author is contradicting his own position by inadvertently suggesting that affirmative action should be extended to include early school years as well as college.
3. Argue for or against the proposition that since most racism is unconscious (as Ehrenreich argues), affirmative action is needed until we not only have equality of ability but "equality of perception."
4. Argue for or against the proposition that the author's remedies are "pie in the sky" notions so long as there is economic inequality in America.
5. If your college has a website, scan it for information on its affirmative action policy. You may also want to see if the college's affirmative action or personnel officer has an e-mail address at which you can request information. Once you have obtained this information, offer a report in which you discuss the college's approach to the issue.

Racism Has Its Privileges

The Case for Affirmative Action

Roger Wilkins

Writing in the March 27, 1995, issue of *The Nation,* Wilkins, who is an editorial board member of that same magazine and professor of history at George Mason University in Virginia, provides a broad perspective concerning the case for affirmative action in the United States. He discusses issues of the moment (such as statements by our current political leaders that downplay the history of racism in America) as well as racist attitudes lodged in the foundations of our country's origins. The result is an argument that attempts to demonstrate that the previous 375 years of discrimination, racist perceptions, beliefs, and practice in the United States have not been alleviated in the 30 years since affirmative action has been in effect. He also includes in his essay a discussion that many other writers on the topic seem to circumvent, that is, what exactly affirmative action is and how it is meant to operate.

PREVIEWING THE ESSAY

To what degree are you aware of today's purported angry white male backlash against affirmative action policies? Has anyone personally voiced his or her opinion on the subject to you? If so, what was the person's argument? What was his or her remedy?

The storm that has been gathering over affirmative action for the past few years has burst. Two conservative California professors are leading a drive to place an initiative on the state ballot in 1996 that will ask Californians to vote affirmative action up or down. Since the state is beloved in political circles for its electoral votes, advance talk of the initiative has put the issue high on the national agenda. Three Republican presidential contenders—Bob Dole, Phil Gramm and Lamar Alexander—have already begun taking shots at various equal opportunity programs. Congressional review of the Clinton Administration's enforcement of these programs has begun. The President has started his own review, promising adherence to principles of nondiscrimination and full opportunity while asserting the need to prune those programs that are unfair or malfunctioning. 1

It is almost an article of political faith that one of the major influences in last November's election was the backlash against affirmative action among "angry white men," who are convinced it has stacked the deck against them. Their attitudes are shaped and their anger heightened by unquestioned and virtually uncheckable anecdotes about victimized whites flooding the culture. For example, *Washington Post* columnist Richard Cohen recently began what purported to be a serious analysis and attack on affirmative action by recounting that he had once missed out on a job someplace because they "needed a woman." 2

Well, I have an anecdote too, and it, together with Cohen's, offers some important insights about the debate that has flared recently around the issues of race, gender and justice. Some years ago, after watching me teach as a visiting professor for two semesters, members of the history department at George Mason University invited me to compete for a full professorship and endowed chair. Mason, like other institutions in Virginia's higher education system, was under a court order to desegregate. I went through the appropriate application and review process and, in due course, was appointed. A few years later, not long after I had been honored as one of the university's distinguished professors, I was shown an article by a white historian asserting that he had been a candidate for that chair but that at the last moment the job had been whisked away and handed to an unqualified black. I checked the story and discovered that this fellow had, in fact, applied but had not even passed the first threshold. But his "reverse discrimination" story is out there polluting the atmosphere in which this debate is taking place. 3

Affirmative action, as I understand it, was not designed to punish anyone; it was, rather—as a result of a clear-eyed look at how America actually works—an attempt to enlarge opportunity for *everybody*. As 4 amply documented in the 1968 Kerner Commission report on racial disorders, when left to their own devices, American institutions in such areas as college admissions, hiring decisions and loan approvals had been making choices that discriminated against blacks. That discrimination, which flowed from doing what came naturally, hurt more than blacks: It hurt the entire nation, as the riots of the late 1960s demonstrated. Though the Kerner report focused on blacks, similar findings could have been made about other minorities and women.

Affirmative action required institutions to develop plans enabling them to go beyond business as usual and search for qualified people in places where they did not ordinarily conduct their searches or their business. Affirmative action programs generally require some proof that there has been a good-faith effort to follow the plan and numerical guidelines against which to judge the sincerity and the success of the effort. The idea of affirmative action is *not* to force people into positions for which they are unqualified but to encourage institutions to develop realistic criteria for the enterprise at hand and then to find a reasonably diverse mix of people qualified to be engaged in it. Without the requirements calling for plans, good-faith efforts and the setting of broad numerical goals, many institutions would do what they had always done: assert that they had looked but "couldn't find anyone qualified," and then go out and hire the white man they wanted to hire in the first place. 5

Affirmative action has done wonderful things for the United States by enlarging opportunity and developing and utilizing a far broader array of the skills available in the American population than in the past. It has not outlived its usefulness. It was never designed to be a program to eliminate poverty. It has not always been used wisely, and some of its permutations do have to be reconsidered, refined or, in some cases, abandoned. It is not a quota program, and those cases where rigid numbers are used (except under a court or administrative order after a specific finding of discrimination) are a bastardization of an otherwise highly beneficial set of public policies. 6

President Clinton is right to review what is being done under present laws and to express a willingness to eliminate activities that either don't work or are unfair. Any program that has been in place for thirty years should be reviewed. Getting rid of what doesn't work is both good government and good politics. Gross abuses of affirmative action provide ammunition for its opponents and undercut the moral authority of the entire effort. But the President should retain—and strengthen where required—those programs necessary to enlarge social justice. 7

What makes the affirmative action issue so difficult is that it engages blacks and whites exactly at those points where they differ the most. There are some areas, such as rooting for the local football team, where their experiences and views are virtually identical. There 8 are others—sometimes including work and school—where their experiences and views both overlap and diverge. And finally, there are areas such as affirmative action and inextricably related notions about the presence of racism in society where the divergences draw out almost all the points of difference between the races.

THIS LAND IS MY LAND

Blacks and whites experience America very differently. Though we often inhabit the same space, we operate in very disparate psychic spheres. 9

Whites have an easy sense of ownership of the country; they feel they are entitled to receive all that is best in it. Many of them believe that their country—though it may have some faults—is superior to all others and that, as Americans, they are superior as well. Many of them think of this as a white country and some of them even experience it that way. They think of it as a land of opportunity—a good place with a lot of good people in it. Some suspect (others *know*) that the presence of blacks messes everything up. 10

To blacks there's nothing very easy about life in America, and any sense of ownership comes hard because we encounter so much resistance in making our way through the ordinary occurrences of life. And I'm not even talking here about overt acts of discrimination but simply about the way whites intrude on and disturb our psychic space without even thinking about it. 11

A telling example of this was given to me by a black college student in Oklahoma. He said whites give him looks that say: "What are *you* doing here?" 12

"When do they give you that look?" I asked. 13

"Every time I walk in a door," he replied. 14

When he said that, every black person in the room nodded and smiled in a way that indicated recognition based on thousands of such moments in their own lives. 15

For most blacks, America is either a land of denied opportunity or one in which the opportunities are still grudgingly extended and extremely limited. For some—that one-third who are mired in poverty, many of them isolated in dangerous ghettos—America is a land of desperadoes and desperation. In places where whites see a lot of idealism, blacks see, at best, idealism mixed heavily with hypocrisy. Blacks accept America's greatness, but are unable to ignore ugly warts that many whites seem to need not to see. I am reminded here of James Baldwin's searing observation from *The Fire Next Time:* 16

> The American Negro has the great advantage of having never believed that collection of myths to which white Americans cling: that

> their ancestors were all freedom-loving heroes, that they were born in the greatest country the world has ever seen, or that Americans are invincible in battle and wise in peace, that Americans have always dealt honorably with Mexicans and Indians and all other neighbors or inferiors, that American men are the world's most direct and virile, that American women are pure.

It goes without saying, then, that blacks and whites remember America differently. The past is hugely important since we argue a lot about who we are on the basis of who we think we have been, and we derive much of our sense of the future from how we think we've done in the past. In a nation in which few people know much history these are perilous arguments, because in such a vacuum, people tend to weave historical fables tailored to their political or psychic needs. 17

Blacks are still recovering the story of their role in America, which so many white historians simply ignored or told in ways that made black people ashamed. But in a culture that batters us, learning the real history is vital in helping blacks feel fully human. It also helps us understand just how deeply American we are, how richly we have given, how much has been taken from us and how much has yet to be restored. Supporters of affirmative action believe that broad and deep damage has been done to American culture by racism and sexism over the whole course of American history and that they are still powerful forces today. We believe that minorities and women are still disadvantaged in our highly competitive society and that affirmative action is absolutely necessary to level the playing field. 18

Not all white Americans oppose this view and not all black Americans support it. There are a substantial number of whites in this country who have been able to escape our racist and sexist past and to enter fully into the quest for equal justice. There are other white Americans who are not racists but who more or less passively accept the powerful suggestions coming at them from all points in the culture that whites are entitled to privilege and to freedom from competition with blacks. And then there are racists who just don't like blacks or who actively despise us. There are still others who may or may not feel deep antipathy, but who know how to manipulate racism and white anxiety for their own ends. Virtually all the people in the last category oppose affirmative action and some of them make a practice of preying upon those in the second category who are not paying attention or who, like the *Post*'s Richard Cohen, are simply confused. 19

THE POLITICS OF DENIAL

One of these political predators is Senate majority leader Bob Dole. In his offhandedly lethal way, Dole delivered a benediction of "let me 20 now forgive us" on *Meet the Press* recently. After crediting affirmative action for the 62 percent of the white male vote garnered by the Republicans, he remarked that slavery was "before we were born" and wondered whether future generations ought to have to continue "paying a price" for those ancient wrongs.

Such a view holds that whatever racial problems we once may have had have been solved over the course of the past thirty years and that most of our current racial friction is caused by racial and gender preferences that almost invariably work to displace some "qualified" white male. Words and phrases like *punish* or *preference* or *reverse discrimination* or *quota* are dropped into the discourse to buttress this view, as are those anecdotes about injustice to whites. Proponents of affirmative action see these arguments as disingenuous but ingenious because they reduce serious and complex social, political, economic, historical and psychological issues to bumper-sticker slogans designed to elicit Pavlovian responses. 21

The fact is that the successful public relations assault on affirmative action flows on a river of racism that is as broad, powerful and American as the Mississippi. And, like the Mississippi, racism can be violent and deadly and is a permanent feature of American life. But while nobody who is sane denies the reality of the Mississippi, millions of Americans who are deemed sane—some of whom are powerful and some even thought wise—deny, wholly or in part, that racism exists. 22

It is critical to understand the workings of denial in this debate because it is used to obliterate the facts that created the need for the remedy in the first place. One of the best examples of denial was provided recently by the nation's most famous former history professor, House Speaker Newt Gingrich. According to *The Washington Post,* "Gingrich dismissed the argument that the beneficiaries of affirmative action, commonly African Americans, have been subjected to discrimination over a period of centuries. 'That is true of virtually every American,' Gingrich said, noting that the Irish were discriminated against by the English, for example." 23

That is breathtaking stuff coming from somebody who should know that blacks have been on this North American continent for 375 years and that for 245 the country permitted slavery. Gingrich should also know that for the next hundred years we had legalized subordination of blacks, under a suffocating blanket of condescension and frequently enforced by nightriding terrorists. We've had only thirty years of something else. 24

That something else is a nation trying to lift its ideals out of a thick, often impenetrable slough of racism. Racism is a hard word for what over the centuries became second nature in America—preferences across the board for white men and, following in their wake, white women. Many of these men seem to feel that it is un-American to 25 ask them to share anything with blacks—particularly their work, their neighborhoods or "their" women. To protect these things—apparently essential to their identity—they engage in all forms of denial. For a historian to assert that "virtually every American" shares the history I have just outlined comes very close to lying.

Denial of racism is much like the denials that accompany addictions to alcohol, drugs or gambling. It is probably not stretching the analogy too much to suggest that many racist whites are so addicted to their unwanted privileges and so threatened by the prospect of losing them that all kinds of defenses become acceptable, including insistent distortions of reality in the form of hypocrisy, lying or the most outrageous political demagogy. 26

"THOSE PEOPLE" DON'T DESERVE HELP

The demagogues have reverted to a new version of quite an old trick. 27 Before the 1950s, whites who were busy denying that the nation was unfair to blacks would simply assert that we didn't deserve equal treatment because we were *inferior*. These days it is not permissible in most public circles to say that blacks are inferior, but it is perfectly acceptable to target the *behavior* of blacks, specifically poor blacks. The argument then follows a fairly predictable line: The behavior of poor blacks requires a severe rethinking of national social policy, it is said. Advantaged blacks really don't need affirmative action anymore, and when they are the objects of such programs, some qualified white person (unqualified white people don't show up in these arguments) is (as Dole might put it) "punished." While it is possible that color-blind affirmative action programs benefiting all disadvantaged Americans are needed, those (i.e., blacks) whose behavior is so distressing must be punished by restricting welfare, shriveling the safety net and expanding the prison opportunity. All of that would presumably give us, in William Bennett's words, "what we want—a color-blind society," for which the white American psyche is presumably fully prepared.

There are at least three layers of unreality in these precepts. The 28 first is that the United States is not now and probably never will be a color-blind society. It is the most color-conscious society on earth. Over the course of 375 years, whites have given blacks absolutely no reason to believe that they can behave in a color-blind manner. In many areas of our lives—particularly in employment, housing and education—affirmative action is required to counter deeply ingrained racist patterns of behavior.

Second, while I don't hold the view that all blacks who behave 29 badly are blameless victims of a brutal system, I do believe that many poor blacks have, indeed, been brutalized by our culture, and I know of *no* blacks, rich or poor, who haven't been hurt in some measure by the racism in this country. The current mood (and, in some cases like the Speaker's, the cultivated ignorance) completely ignores the fact that some blacks never escaped the straight line of oppression that ran from slavery through the semislavery of sharecropping to the late mid-century migration from Southern farms into isolated pockets of urban poverty. Their families have always been excluded, poor and without skills, and so they were utterly defenseless when the enormous American economic dislocations that began in the mid-1970s slammed into their communities, followed closely by deadly waves of crack cocaine. One would think that the double-digit unemployment suffered consistently over the past two decades by blacks who were *looking for work* would be a permanent feature of the discussions about race, responsibility, welfare and rights.

But a discussion of the huge numbers of black workers who are 30
becoming economically redundant would raise difficult questions about the efficiency of the economy at a time when millions of white men feel insecure. Any honest appraisal of unemployment would reveal that millions of low-skilled white men were being severely damaged by corporate and Federal Reserve decisions; it might also refocus the anger of those whites in the middle ranks whose careers have been shattered by the corporate downsizing fad.

But people's attention is kept trained on the behavior of some 31
poor blacks by politicians and television news shows, reinforcing the stereotypes of blacks as dangerous, as threats, as unqualified. Frightened whites direct their rage at pushy blacks rather than at the corporations that export manufacturing operations to low-wage countries, or at the Federal Reserve, which imposes interest rate hikes that slow down the economy.

WHO BENEFITS? WE ALL DO

There is one final denial that blankets all the rest. It is that only soci- 32
ety's "victims"—blacks, other minorities and women (who should, for God's sake, renounce their victimological outlooks)—have been injured by white male supremacy. Viewed in this light, affirmative action remedies are a kind of zero-sum game in which only the "victims" benefit. But racist and sexist whites who are not able to accept the full humanity of other people are themselves badly damaged—morally stunted—people. The principal product of a racist and sexist society is damaged people and institutions—victims and victimizers alike. Journalism and education, two enterprises with which I am familiar, provide two good examples.

Journalistic institutions often view the nation through a lens that bends reality to support white privilege. A recent issue of *U.S. News & World Report* introduced a package of articles on these issues with a question on its cover: "Does affirmative action mean NO WHITE MEN NEED APPLY?" The words "No white men need apply" were printed in red against a white background and were at least four times larger than the other words in the question. Inside, the lead story was illustrated by a painting that carries out the cover theme, with a wan white man separated from the opportunity ladders eagerly being scaled by women and dark men. And the story yielded up the following sentence: "Affirmative action poses a conflict between two cherished American principles: the belief that all Americans deserve equal opportunities and the idea that hard work and merit, not race or religion or gender or birthright, should determine who prospers and who does not." 33

Whoever wrote that sentence was in the thrall of one of the myths that Baldwin was talking about. The sentence suggests—as many people do when talking about affirmative action—that America is a meritocratic society. But what kind of meritocracy excludes women and blacks and other minorities from all meaningful competition? And even in the competition among white men, money, family and connections often count for much more than merit, test results (for whatever they're worth) and hard work. 34

The *U.S. News* story perpetuates and strengthens the view that many of my white students absorb from their parents: that white men now have few chances in this society. The fact is that white men still control virtually everything in America except the wealth held by widows. According to the Urban Institute, 53 percent of black men aged 25–34 are either unemployed or earn too little to lift a family of four from poverty. 35

Educational institutions that don't teach accurately about why America looks the way it does and why the distribution of winners and losers is as it is also injure our society. Here is another anecdote. 36

A warm, brilliant young white male student of mine came in just before he was to graduate and said that my course in race, law and culture, which he had just finished, had been the most valuable and the most disturbing he had ever taken. I asked how it had been disturbing. 37

"I learned that my two heroes are racists," he said. 38

"Who are your heroes and how are they racists?" I asked. 39

"My mom and dad," he said. "After thinking about what I was learning, I understood that they had spent all my life making me into the same kind of racists they were." 40

Affirmative action had brought me together with him when he was 22. Affirmative action puts people together in ways that make that kind of revelation possible. Nobody is a loser when that happens. The country gains. 41

And that, in the end, is the case for affirmative action. The arguments supporting it should be made on the basis of its broad contributions to the entire American community. It is insufficient to vilify white males and to skewer them as the whiners that journalism of the kind practiced by *U.S. News* invites us to do. These are people who, from the beginning of the Republic, have been taught that skin color is destiny and that whiteness is to be revered. Listen to Jefferson, writing in the year the Constitution was drafted: 42

> The first difference that strikes us is that of colour. . . . And is the difference of no importance? Is it not the foundation of a greater or less share of beauty in the two races? Are not the fine mixtures of red and white . . . in the one, preferable to that eternal monotony, which reigns in the countenances, that immoveable veil of black which covers all the emotions of the other race? Add to these, flowing hair, a more elegant symmetry of form, their own judgment in favor of the whites, declared by their preference for them, as uniformly as is the preference of the Oran-ootan for the black women over those of his own species. The circumstance of superior beauty, is thought worthy attention in the propagation of our horses, dogs, and other domestic animals; why not in that of man?

In a society so conceived and so dedicated, it is understandable that white males would take their preferences as a matter of natural right and consider any alteration of that a primal offense. But a nation that operates in that way abandons its soul and its economic strength, and will remain mired in ugliness and moral squalor because so many people are excluded from the possibility of decent lives and from forming any sense of community with the rest of society.

Seen only as a corrective for ancient wrongs, affirmative action 43
may be dismissed by the likes of Gingrich, Gramm and Dole, just as attempts to federalize decent treatment of the freed slaves were dismissed after Reconstruction more than a century ago. Then, striking down the Civil Rights Act of 1875, Justice Joseph Bradley wrote of blacks that "there must be some stage in the progress of his elevation when he takes the rank of a mere citizen, and ceases to be the special favorite of the laws, and when his rights, as a citizen or a man, are to be protected in the ordinary modes by which other men's rights are protected."

But white skin has made some citizens—particularly white 44
males—*the special favorites of the culture.* It may be that we will need affirmative action until most white males are really ready for a colorblind society—that is, when they are ready to assume "the rank of a mere citizen." As a nation we took a hard look at that special favoritism thirty years ago. Though the centuries of cultural preference enjoyed by white males still overwhelmingly skew power and wealth

their way, we have in fact achieved a more meritocratic society as a result of affirmative action than we have ever previously enjoyed in this country.

If we want to continue making things better in this society, we'd 45
better figure out ways to protect and defend affirmative action against the confused, the frightened, the manipulators and, yes, the liars in politics, journalism, education and wherever else they may be found. In the name of longstanding American prejudice and myths and in the service of their own narrow interests, power-lusts or blindness, they are truly victimizing the rest of us, perverting the ideals they claim to stand for and destroying the nation they pretend to serve.

THINKING ABOUT THE ESSAY

1. Wilkins refers to "uncheckable anecdotes about victimized whites." Do you believe these anecdotes are sufficient for an argument against affirmative action? Or would you require stronger forms of proof, such as substantiated case histories and statistics? Explain.
2. Wilkins asserts that part of affirmative action is "to find a reasonably diverse mix of people qualified to be engaged in" a workplace. But he claims it is easy to give mere lip service to this practice, and just hire a white man anyway. Could the reverse practice be true—that is, pretending to seek a diversity of candidates and intentionally hiring a minority? If so, why has Wilkins not mentioned this possibility? Do you consider both scenarios equally egregious? Explain.
3. Wilkins devotes a good deal of his essay to demonstrating the difference between the "psychic spheres" of blacks and whites. How do these spheres differ? How do they provide a rationale for affirmative action? How does Wilkins know such spheres exist?
4. Wilkins' essay uses the method of elimination of supporting points in the section that begins, "There are at least three layers of unreality in these precepts." How effective is this rhetorical device in presenting his argument in favor of affirmative action? How has he structured it to maximize its rhetorical power?
5. Can you explain the thesis of this essay? Refer to the text, and be as specific as possible to avoid making such general statements such as "Affirmative action is good." How does Wilkins develop his thesis throughout the five major sections of the essay? What is the subject of each section, and how does it advance his thesis?

RESPONDING IN DISCUSSION

1. Divide into groups of three and four and list those elements of our society that, according to Wilkins, have made white males "the special favorites of the culture." If you disagree with the statement, list those elements demonstrating that they are not the favorites. Discuss your conclusions with the rest of the class.
2. Divide into small groups and prepare a presentation to the class that compares and contrasts the views of Steele with those of Wilkins. Present your efforts in a forum, and allow for a question-and-answer period to follow that allows fellow students to address your presentation.
3. For a homework assignment, visit your library's periodical section, and find four or five issues of general news magazines published within the past two years whose covers reflect a perspective on affirmative action. Bring copies or reproductions of the cover pages to class, and discuss the implicit messages contained in their design and text.
4. Discuss the similarities between the author's concept of "psychic spheres" and Ehrenreich's concept of "prejudice of the quiet, subliminal kind."
5. Extract from the text all empirical evidence demonstrating that blacks in general have a tougher time of aspiring to basic tenets of American values. Is this evidence sufficient to make the case for affirmative action? If so, why? If not, why not?

RESPONDING IN WRITING

1. Write an essay in response to Roger Wilkins' article, explaining your generation's views of race relations, perceptions, and attitudes.
2. In an essay of 400 to 500 words, describe an acquaintance who denies racism in a way that, as the author puts it, "is much like the denials that accompany addictions to alcohol and drugs."
3. Argue for or against the proposition that Wilkins unfairly uses reports and anecdotes to advance his view by (1) using such tactics as citing the 1968 Kerner Commission report (which is now about 30 years old) that discrimination occurs in American institutions, and (2) relying on one misguided anecdote by a professor who believed he was discriminated against on account of race.
4. Argue for or against the idea that if, as the author claims, racism has not been erased after 375 years of oppression in America, it never will be.

5. Write a comparative essay treating the approaches of Steele and Wilkins to affirmative action. State your own position on the controversy.
6. Conduct an Internet search for information on Roger Wilkins. Then in an evaluative essay, explain how his article reflects the biography of the man.

CONNECTIONS: FOR WRITING AND RESEARCH

1. Using your own experience and observation, write a 500-word essay comparing and contrasting one aspect of seeming external harmony as it exists between the races in the United States and the true unspoken attitudes.
2. Compare and contrast Ehrenreich's view of "unconscious racism" among whites with Steele's views concerning "social virtue."
3. Argue for or against the proposition that it is easy to critique the issues of diversity and racism as do the authors in this section, but far more difficult to resolve them.
4. Argue for or against the proposition that it is not conflict between the races that is endangering our society, but rather the opposing interests of the "haves" and the "have-nots." Refer to at least three essays in this textbook to amplify your remarks.
5. Argue for or against the proposition that anyone who benefits from affirmative action ends up feeling the stigma that he or she has been selected based on a policy decision rather than on ability and personal accomplishment.
6. In an essay of 750 to 1,000 words, discuss the similarities in purpose and method of "Silly Men, Banal Men" (addressing men attempting to remedy gender conflict) with the efforts of liberals whose social policies have attempted to remedy the problem of racism.
7. Argue for or against the proposition that the best way to understand people is through direct personal observation and independent thinking as Jordan demonstrates in her essay, rather than placing individuals into restricted categories of race, or identifying oneself as a member of a race.

10

ARMED AND DANGEROUS

America's fetish for guns is perhaps an outgrowth of the myth of the Wild West, the importance we place on personal safety and individualism, the fear that our police cannot protect us, the power weapons place in the hands of the powerless or the dispossessed, issues of Constitutional interpretation, paranoia, fear of the State—the list goes on and on. One thing is certain. Arguments over gun laws, ownership, use, and misuse are perhaps nowhere as greatly in evidence as in the United States, whether they are mounted by politicians soliciting votes, interest groups such as the National Rifle Association, or members of minority clergy who have seen the havoc guns wreck upon their communities. There may be no other area of the law where such diverse ordinances exist based upon local governments' views on whether guns are a means of protection for the average citizen or a scourge destroying our youth. For example, the Sullivan Law in New York City—perhaps one of the strictest gun control laws of all—makes it an arduous task to purchase a gun legally. Yet homicide by means of guns is rampant there. Meanwhile, in other states a potent firearm can be purchased legally with a driver's license and a signature. Some claim that it is in the best interests of law-abiding citizens to have easy access to weapons, and they say that they have the statistics to prove it. In the following essays, you will read a cross-section of reports from the frontlines of the firearms controversy: from Fromer's vivid description of a teenage boy lying in a morgue (the sort of depiction that Ernest Hemingway in his war correspondence called "the natural history of death") to dour predictions of the outcomes of new laws purportedly meant to diminish violent crime (as in Tucker's "Three Strikes and You're Dead").

A Trip to the Morgue

A Boy Becomes a Body

Margot Joan Fromer

Margot Fromer is a Washington-based writer whose most recent book is *Surviving Childhood.* She first published this essay in the March 31, 1996, issue of *The Washington Post.* Much of her essay focuses on her witness to and response to the corpse of a young man lying on a District of Columbia autopsy table. Along the way, she reflects on the stream of images that come to mind as she considers his lifeless body: She attempts to resuscitate his existence through imagining his life and thoughts; she fantasizes revenge upon his killer; she considers appropriate ways of using his death as a deterrent to other would-be young killers, and as an educational tool to show his peers the results of violence. Welsh poet Dylan Thomas once wrote, "After the first death, there is no other." However, Fromer concludes that unfortunately, despite a golden opportunity to give this young man's death meaning, there is no doubt that many others will follow.

PREVIEWING THE ESSAY

Have you ever seen a deceased young person—a victim of disease, accident, homicide, or suicide? If so, what ran through your mind? Surely you have seen a depiction of one in a movie or on television. What was your response to the mediated image? Did you consider his or her background, life, goals, beliefs, wants, likes, and dislikes? Consider the difference between the Hollywood version and the real-life version that the author presents to her audience in this essay.

The boy, 16 years old, lay on his back, staring blankly at the ceiling of the morgue. He wore black shorts—those big loose baggy ones that look as if they're going to fall off any minute. Kids like them, maybe because it's easy to hide a gun in them, especially when their oversized T-shirt hangs down around their butts. 1

But this boy wore a tank top—it had been terribly hot out—and black high-top sneakers with no socks. He had on purple underpants. They were some shiny polyester material, but he probably thought they were silk. I'm sure he believed they were sexy (cool, he would say—not sexy), bought to impress a girl. 2

The air conditioning was broken, and the big floor fan just pushed the fetid air around, whiffling the boy's shirt and shorts and blowing hot smells my way. I moved my head so I wouldn't catch it full in the face. 3

Just 16 years old. The boy's face in repose had a sweetness in it that I haven't seen on a teenager for ages. Even rich suburban kids wear sullen, petulant expressions these days, and this fellow was a long, long way from there. I wanted to stroke his cheek. 4

His body was long and lean, his face and legs almost hairless. The muscles just under the skin were firm. He may have been a budding athlete, maybe a basketball player or a long-distance runner. He was a beautiful boy, really, no longer a child and not yet a man—in perfect physical shape. 5

But he was dead. 6

A single .22 caliber bullet had entered the middle of his lower back, nicked the pulmonary artery and lodged in his shoulder. 7

His 15-year-old buddy had shot him. 8

That's all I know. I don't know who he was, why he died or what happened to his killer. And I don't want to know. I was there only to see an autopsy and perhaps to write about it. 9

The morgue at the D.C. Medical Examiners Office is huge. I tried not to inhale too deeply of the stench that swirled around me every time someone opened the big refrigerator. Paperwork lay on the counter beside the boy. An X-ray clipped to the viewing box on the wall showed the dark black of the bullet standing out starkly against the lighter grey of his shoulder blade and spine. A morgue technician took Polaroid photos and cut away the boy's clothes. 10

I thought about the purple underpants. They seemed a frivolous item for a boy who lived in one of the grimmest neighborhoods in the District. What did he feel when he bought them? Did his girlfriend buy them for him, the two of them giggling while the shopkeeper kept an eye on them, positive he was going to be ripped off yet again? Were they a source of derision among his friends? Did his killer know what he wore under those baggy pants? 11

The answers seemed overwhelmingly important. Perhaps I made them so because of the other feelings that threatened to swamp me: I wanted to storm the D.C. Jail, grab the boy's murderer by the scruff and drag him down into this stinking chamber. When he turned away in revulsion from the body on the morgue table with the running water tinged red with his victim's blood, I wanted to slap him across the face and force him to watch. 12

I wanted to push his nose into it the way you push a puppy's nose close to the pile of feces to teach it not to make in the house. I wanted to scream at him: "Look what you did!" 13

I wanted to see his face tighten in horror, as I'm sure mine did when I saw the technician scoop blood out of the body cavity with a white plastic foam cup, the same kind of mundane, ubiquitous cups from which every one of us has drunk gallons of coffee. I wanted that 14

15-year-old to dream about oceans of blood pouring out of them for the rest of his life.

15 I wanted to hear him gasp when the technician cut a crescent-shaped slice into the boy's scalp and then, as if he were preparing a navel orange, peeled the scalp up over the cranium to hang loose on the face. I wanted the killer to watch while the technician neatly opened the skull so the pathologist could remove the brain. I wanted the smell of human sawdust to remain in his nostrils forever.

16 I wanted him to imagine himself on that death table.

17 I wanted that for the killer then, and I want it now for other young people while they still have a chance. In 1995 there were 360 murders in the District—almost one a day. This year the bodies continue to stream to the morgue.

18 I want young people to get a close look at the carnage they create. I want them to go on high school field trips to the morgue. And not just to an empty autopsy room, horrifying enough with its steel tables and plastic tubing and small hanging scales—very much like the ones in the produce section at the supermarket. I want them to see a body on the table, and a brain on the scale. I want them to see what happens when you pull a gun out of those baggy pants and squeeze back on the trigger. I want them to see what happens when you lose your temper and blow someone away.

19 I want them to know where "away" is—to see what happens between the time the plastic body bag is loaded into the Medical Examiner's van and the time the body finally lies neatly dressed in Sunday clothes, waiting for the preacher to say what a good boy he was.

20 Parents who are up in arms over teaching sex education and evolution would probably have apoplexy at the merest suggestion that their kids be required to witness the end result of violent death. The National Rifle Association would be all over their pet congressmen to squelch such a shocking idea (while at the same time pouring more money into placing more guns into children's hands through "family firearm training").

21 But why not? Some gangs require murder as the initiation fee for full-fledged membership. Why not let all these over-anxious gang wannabes see what happens if they are chosen as the admission ticket. And the ones who never leave the house without heavy artillery, the ones who will kill if you insult their girlfriend—a trip to the morgue would illustrate nicely that old saw about sticks and stones.

22 At least they'd begin to see what it means to be dead at the morgue. It means arriving in clothes stained with feces and urine that escaped as your life blood leaked out onto the pavement. It means impassive strangers heaving you onto a steel table and photographing

your naked body, your wounds. It means someone slitting you open from throat to pelvis and poking through your innards.

When one kid says to another, "You're dead meat, man," I want them to see what they're saying. 23

I want them to be forced to do this, but of course it won't happen. I won't be able to drag that 15-year-old murderer off the streets (where he surely is, not on death row where he surely belongs) and stand behind him as he vomits over the results of his quick draw with a .22. He will not have the morgue stench in his nostrils for days, and in his mind for years. 24

And he will never, not once, see in his mind's eye a pair of purple underpants on an adolescent who died with his own gun snugged deep in a pocket of those cool pants. 25

THINKING ABOUT THE ESSAY

1. What inferences did you draw about the dead boy from the opening two paragraphs? What was his race? His economic status? His family life? His neighborhood? What led you to your conclusions?
2. Fromer describes the boy's physical appearance, attire, and physique. Then she states that she doesn't want to "know who he was, why he died or what happened to his killer." Why not? Is it true that she doesn't "know who he was"? Explain.
3. Why does Fromer seem so obsessed about understanding the implication of his wearing purple underpants? Do they have further implications beyond his attire? If so, what are they?
4. As Fromer describes the autopsy process in graphic detail, she claims she wants his killer to witness it. Why? Are there other people she implies she'd like to have witness the autopsy? If so, who are they and why does she want them there?
5. What is the implied relationship between the author and the reader? What is the essay's intended effect upon the reader? Fromer writes, "I was there only to see an autopsy and perhaps to write about it." Does this provide you with her motivation? Explain.

RESPONDING IN DISCUSSION

1. Divide into groups of three and four. Enumerate the various ways the author believes the boy's death could have meaning to others. Discuss whether the intended effects she wishes these strategies to have would indeed be successful. Discuss your conclusions with the rest of the class.

2. Discuss whether you would like to be in the morgue with the author when several orderlies march in with the boy's killer and force him to witness the autopsy, as she envisions. Would you feel some form of justice exacted? Explain your response to your class.
3. Discuss whether your response to the essay would be different had it described the murder and autopsy of a middle-aged adult.
4. Discuss whether depictions of widespread shooting and carnage in the movies and television sanitize, desensitize, or trivialize the image of killing among youth who have a proclivity toward violence.
5. Discuss the age at which a person should be treated as an adult in crimes involving murder. Consider that the boy who murdered the victim in the essay was 15 years old.

RESPONDING IN WRITING

1. Argue for or against the proposition that all high school classes should be required to take field trips to the local morgue to witness an autopsy performed on a murder victim (preferably a young one).
2. Analyze the techniques that Fromer employs in her essay to sharply register her viewpoint with the reader.
3. For a creative writing assignment, write a first-person narrative of 400 to 500 words from the point of view of the killer, explaining why he shot the victim.
4. Argue for or against the proposition that parents of minors who commit violent crime should be punished. Include a sufficient number of supporting points and specific methods of punishment.
5. Research gun violence among young people, using the Net to generate information on the subject. Then write an essay analyzing the causes and effects of gun violence, incorporating data that you have obtained via the Net.

Cease Fire

Can Our Trigger-Happy Country Protect Its Children?

Isabel Wilkerson, Randi Rose, and Deborah Prothrow-Stith

Wilkerson, Rose, and Prothrow-Stith, writing in *Family Circle* (the majority of whose subscribers are women and mothers), have targeted their audience well for this article that first appeared in the magazine's March 16, 1994, issue. It provides a combination of anecdotes and statistics that demonstrate guns and child safety is not just an issue of the inner cities but rather a national epidemic that transcends class, race, and geography. The essay contains a rather efficient argument against the thesis that "guns don't kill people, people kill people" or, as one sardonic writer has put it, "guns don't kill people, bullets kill people." The authors portray several deaths of minors by guns—either intentionally or by accident—that could have been avoided by preventive measures. However, the essay also demonstrates that in some instances, prevention is not a significant option.

PREVIEWING THE ESSAY

Common sense would dictate that parents would do everything in their power to keep their own firearms out of the hands of their own children. Why, then, do we hear of so many incidents of children who die from accidental shootings that result from getting hold of their family's gun? Do many gun owners just not care, are they just not careful, or what?

It was late in the school year, on a clear May morning, when Jason Smith, a high school sophomore in Red Hill, Pennsylvania, decided to settle the score with the 6′5″ classmate who had bullied him for months. In another time and place, Jason might have challenged him to a fight in the school year or, worst case, pulled a switchblade after class. But this is the 90s. It is as easy to find a pistol as a book. That would show him. 1

Jason, 15, knew he would see his tormentor, 16-year-old Michael Swann, first thing that Monday morning. They took biology together, first period, at Upper Perkiomen High School. Jason got a 9-millimeter Ruger, a semiautomatic pistol that belonged to his mother's boyfriend, out of a locked gun cabinet and fired a shot in his bedroom to make sure it worked. Satisfied, he stuffed it in his book bag and headed off to school. 2

He was late that day by half an hour. He handed his pass to the biology teacher, Barbara Ryan, and walked over to his desk. The class was in the middle of a lesson on pig anatomy. There were lifeless fetal pigs on the laboratory tables, and the students were about to dissect them. Jason set his bag on his desk and pulled out his books and a pencil. 3

Michael, the boy who had punched and shoved the 5′4″ Jason at his locker for much of the year and had pulled Jason's seat out from under him the Thursday before, was sitting two desks behind him. Jason pulled the pistol out of the bag, walked over to Michael's desk, stood over his nemesis—taller than Michael for once—and shot him in the head. 4

5 "Laugh at this," Jason said, cursing Michael. Then he shot him again.

6 At first their 22 classmates thought some test tubes had been dropped, or that there had been an explosion in the chemistry lab across the hall. When they realized what had happened, they ran and hid behind laboratory tables or crouched behind the teacher's desk. Mrs. Ryan slumped to the floor. Some students were in shock, others were in tears. Some wanted to stop Jason and talk to him, but they knew they couldn't. Jason walked out calmly and sat under a tree, where the police found him minutes later.

7 There were thousands of Michael Swanns in 1993—children 19 and under who, because they got on someone's bad side or were playing with a gun or simply gave up on life or were in the wrong place at the wrong time, died by gunfire. In Denver, Carl Banks, 18, was shot while taking his brothers and sisters trick-or-treating. In Boston, Louis Brown, 16, was shot walking to school. In El Cajon, California, Jessica Reuhl, 9, was shot by a sniper who then killed himself. In Chicago, Steven Wright, 5, shot himself in the mouth with a .44 Magnum he found under his mother's mattress. In Seattle, Loetta Coston, 9, was shot riding in her family's car after her mother had honked the horn at another driver.

8 Every day 14 children die in gun accidents, suicides and homicides. Hundreds more are wounded, many crippled for life. What makes this rising wave of killing so heart-breaking is that the deaths were often preventable; many children might still be alive if a gun had not been at hand. But there are more than 200 million guns for an estimated 259 million people in this country, with women and young people forming a growing new market. More than half the 2,508 students polled in a study for the Harvard School of Public Health last year said they could get a gun if they wanted one. More than 20 percent of them said they could get one "within an hour."

9 Guns now seem to be the problem solver of preference, a final solution aimed increasingly at child targets. The country that overcame polio—a killer of children of generations past—seems unable to protect its young from gunfire. "We are raising a generation of children in a culture of violence," says James Garbarino, Ph.D., a child psychologist who is president of the Erikson Institute for Advanced Study in Child Development in Chicago. "They are soaking up the gun culture like little sponges."

10 In greater numbers than ever, murder—a crime formerly associated with mob figures and drug dealers—is claiming the nation's children. In 1987 the number of children murdered with guns was 1,270; in 1992 (the latest year that figures are available from the FBI) it more than doubled—to 2,804. Even when victims survive, they often

go on to lives of pain and paralysis. It is a fate that has made some inner-city neighborhoods resemble hospital grounds, as young people in wheelchairs—victims of drive-by shootings—roll across mean streets: war veterans before they are of fighting age. An estimated $4 billion a year, much of the cost borne by taxpayers, is spent on hospitalization for firearm injuries.

Almost as disturbing as the violence itself are the lengths to which people just go to avoid it. The duck-and-cover drill of the '50s has returned to schools, not because people fear a nuclear attack but because children in the '90s must know how to dodge a bullet. Across the country, schools have removed lockers from their halls for fear of students' storing weapons with their books and gym shorts. Many high schools, with security guards who check pockets and book bags, seem more like airports on watch for terrorists. In 1988 only 2 percent of the nation's 50 largest school districts used metal detectors to screen out weapons. By 1993, 50 percent of them did. 11

As the death toll rises, lawmakers and citizens and a determined gun lobby continue to struggle over new gun-control measures. Nineteen states have enacted laws making it illegal for a minor to possess a gun. In 11 states gun owners are liable for gun accidents involving children. Nationwide, more and more gun-amnesty programs are encouraging owners to trade their weapons for toys, food and other items. Still, the gun remains a tough opponent, one that President Clinton has taken on, calling for new health-care initiatives, increased police protection and the licensing of gun-owners nationwide. But even supporters concede that the Brady Law, the toughest gun-control legislation passed by Congress in more than 20 years, is no match for a country with nearly as many guns as people. A new handgun is produced every 20 seconds. 12

Red Hill, Pennsylvania, the hometown of Jason Smith and Michael Swann, is the last place that people might expect gun violence. It is a quiet rural town of about 1,800 people, with machine shops and chocolate factories, surrounded by dairy and hog farms. In this old community, about 35 miles northwest of Philadelphia, some families have lived for generations, and neighbors figure that if the Smiths and Swanns traced their roots back far enough, they might find that Jason and Michael were related. On warm summer nights after the shooting, parents and teenagers alike would gather on street corners and in people's front yards to talk about what happened, as if talking about it would help it make sense. "People don't know what to believe," says Roxie Kulp, a lifelong resident and a neighbor of the Smiths. "Jason felt trapped, and we don't know why." 13

The town is now bitter and divided, with some people feeling anguish for the Swanns and others rallying behind Jason, saying Michael had it coming. Both boys were handsome; their smiling, dimpled faces in family and school photos give no hint of the tragedy 14 to come. Townspeople say that Michael, a farm boy big for his age, had a history of bullying kids. The morning he died, Roxie Kulp says, Michael was seen burning holes in somebody's boat tarp with cigarettes. They say he carried a switchblade, and they considered him fast because he hung out in Philadelphia.

15 Jason, on the other hand, was quiet and never bothered anybody, friends say. Until May 24, the day he killed Michael. He pleaded guilty and is now serving 12½ to 25 years in state prison after a plea bargain with prosecutors.

16 Rafael Saldana was a lively child who liked to sit up front in class and help the teacher erase the blackboard or collect papers, who dreamed about cars and sports, sang in the school choir and liked to run up and hug people. He was 10 years old, chubby and bright faced, and he lived in a rented house in Houston with his mother, stepfather and 14-year-old brother. It was there that he died from a single gunshot wound—on Mother's Day.

17 Rafael and his brother, who has not been named by the authorities because of his age, had been playing with their stepfather's 10-millimeter semiautomatic pistol. The boys were pretending to shoot each other. The gun was unloaded on that hot, muggy morning, and each time they pulled the trigger, the "victim" played dead, just like in the TV cartoons. Later that evening in the living room, the brothers picked up the gun again while their mother and stepfather were in another room. This time the gun was loaded, but the boys didn't know it. The older brother fired as he always had, the gun aimed point-blank at Rafael's head. Every day a child dies in a handgun-shooting accident.

18 The next morning, Karen Holt, the principal at South Houston Elementary School, had to break the news to classmates that the fourth grader everybody called Ralph was dead. "It was one of the most difficult things I have ever had to do as a principal," she recalls. At first the 10-year-olds just sat there quietly, too numb to speak. Can this be true? Then they started crying, and all the questions came. "What does this mean? Will he be back after summer vacation? How could this be? Why did this have to happen to Ralph?"

19 With the proliferation of guns, particularly the newer, more sophisticated handguns that many people keep on hand for protection, the number of children killed in their own homes has risen steadily in recent years. An estimated 700 children 19 and under died in shooting accidents in 1992, up from 567 in 1989. About 350 of those accidents occurred in the home, according to the National Safety Council. A 1988 analysis of 266 accidental handgun shooting deaths of children found that in almost a third of the cases, the shooter and victim were related.

So it was with Rafael and his brother. Their stepfather, Juan Castillo Cedeno, was charged with violating a recently enacted Houston gun-safety ordinance that seeks to prosecute parents who do not properly secure their guns. It is a misdemeanor charge punishable by a fine of up to $500 and six months in jail. Cedeno's trial, the first under the new law, was scheduled to begin this month in Houston municipal court. Rafael's brother was released to his mother's custody. 20

After Rafael died, his classmates decorated his desk with a wreath made out of construction paper, and planted a baby plum tree in his memory at a special ceremony. The whole school turned out. His mother and grandparents came as well. Everyone held hands as the principal said a prayer, thanking God for the brief time they knew Rafael. Some classmates wrote a poem to him and were going to read it at his funeral, but there was a mix-up and his aunt read it, which was OK with them. The children took up a collection and bought a book that they placed in the library in his memory. They wrote letters to him and put them in a box that they buried in front of the school near the hole they dug for the tree. It was a way for them to mourn their friend Ralph, who they now understood would not be returning from summer vacation after all. 21

On a brisk March afternoon, at the end of spring break last year, Charity Metz, a 17-year-old senior at Jasper High School in Harrison County, Indiana, left her father at a friend's house and told him she would see him back at the farm. He never saw her alive again. She drove home, walked out to the barn, knelt down on a blanket and shot herself with a .22-caliber revolver she got from her father's truck. 22

Two months earlier, Kurt Witte, a 15-year-old sophomore at Jasper High who liked hunting rabbit and worked part-time on a farm, took his father's pistol and shot himself in the woods behind his family's house. The previous August, Scott Schneider, quarterback of the high school football team and a member of the student council, shot himself in his bedroom two days before school started. 23

Of all the ways a child can die, suicide may be the most perplexing. Every six hours, someone under 19 commits suicide with a firearm. Jasper has certainly had more than its share in the past two years. The sorrowful trilogy of suicides has torn at this rural town of German Catholics, where everybody knows everyone and people work hard and are devoutly religious. Deer and squirrel hunting are seasonal rituals there, and guns were something you always just took for granted. There is no evidence that three suicides in a row were anything but coincidence, but people here are questioning whether they may have been too hard on their children, whether they expected 24 too much or pressed too hard for good grades and perfection, and whether the pressures of a world with AIDS and drugs and violence were just too much to bear.

25 It got to the point that Jeff Jessee, assistant principal at Jasper High School, began dreading any more news. "I'm a little jumpy when my phone rings in the morning," he says. "I don't know if it's a teacher calling in sick or another call telling me a student has committed suicide."

26 To those who knew Charity Metz, she was a cheerful, down-to-earth teenager. She let her light brown hair hang down around a pretty face that was rarely made up. She talked of becoming a nurse or an anesthesiologist. "She was just the greatest person I ever knew," said Rachel Wessel, her best friend. Charity liked romance novels, historical ones. She liked fishing at the little pond, where it was peaceful, and running, and listening to Reba McEntyre. "Poison" was her favorite perfume. She worked part time at the Jasper Cinema's box office. "I usually put people in the box office who've got a friendly face," says the theater manager, Debbie Sattler. "She always had a smile on her face."

27 What the smile concealed—and what even her closest friend did not know—was that Charity was pregnant. She wore baggy pants and tops, the style for a lot of teenagers, and nobody realized her condition or could have imagined how far along she was. The baby, which was apparently due any day, did not survive. It was a boy. He was buried in her arms.

28 Charity left questions that will never be answered and snatches of conversation clues, some believe that her friends will be deciphering for years. Rachel cannot stop thinking about the day Charity asked her what she would do if she ever got pregnant. "I'd probably kill myself," Rachel said. She never imagined how seriously her words might be taken. "So would I," Charity responded.

29 In 1990, the most recent year for which statistics are available, 1,474 people aged 10 to 19 killed themselves with guns. The odds that suicidal adolescents will kill themselves double when a gun is kept in the home, according to the Centers for Disease Control.

30 For more than a year now, there has been a suicide watch in Jasper. Some families have gotten rid of their guns. Parents are looking for signs of depression—loss of appetite, sleeping problems, lethargy—and listening for talk of death. There were counseling sessions at the school, where all the problems and fears came out. "Some of the kids feel, 'Where did my childhood go?'" Jessee says. "It's kind of like opening the side door of a volcano."

31 Charity's friend Rachel still has a hard time understanding what went wrong. "At times when I really need her, I get angry because she's not here."

Launice Smith did not live long enough to learn to write her name or go to kindergarten or plant pumpkin seeds at Halloween with the other children in her preschool. She was alive for only four years—the length of time between Olympic Games or presidential elections.

She lived in Fort Dupont Dwellings, a weary housing project in a battle-scarred section of Washington, D.C. Last September, she went with her mother, Angelia, to a pickup football game at the abandoned grade school near their housing complex. It was hot out, and neighbors welcomed a break. Her mother propped Launice up to see the neighborhood boys try to score their touchdowns. Suddenly, the pop-pop-pop of gunfire rang out, and bullets flew into the crowd. Launice was hit in the head. She died four days later. 32

The bullets were apparently intended for Kervin Brown, a 26-year-old man who died the day of the shooting from gunshot wounds to the chest, neck and back. Launice was caught in the middle. Two young men from the neighborhood, Steven Chadwick, 19, and Anthony Dawkins, 22, have been charged in the shooting. 33

Launice had just started at Plummer Elementary School that week. She had big bright eyes and wore her hair in pigtails with little barrettes at the ends. She would cry and cry when her mother left her at school. Then she would settle down to finger painting like the rest of the children. 34

Launice's teacher, Jacqueline Pogue, worries that she may show up to work one day and another small student will be missing. "I would be able to understand if it were just a fluke," Pogue says, "if it were just Launice. But I could come in here tomorrow and hear it was another one of my kids. You can't promise them safety." 35

In 1985, 862 black children under 19 were killed by gunfire. By 1990, the number had more than doubled to 2,057. Firearm homicide is the leading cause of death for young black men, according to the National Center for Health Statistics. The FBI says that although blacks made up 12 percent of the U.S. population in 1992, they were nearly half of those murdered that year. 36

More than most homicides, Launice's death attracted a deep soul-searching in a city worn down by gun violence. Launice became a kind of poster child for campaigns against killing. She was buried in a tiny white casket in the "babyland" section of a Washington cemetery. Dignitaries turned out to pay their respects. The Rev. Jesse Jackson spoke at her funeral. He called her "an angel" sent to wake up the country. A group of mothers whose children had been killed sat in a row up front. President Clinton sent condolences. 37

Launice's short life left little to eulogize. The words on her funeral program were sadly brief and innocent. "She was a spirited and beautiful child," it read. "She had an extreme love for music and dancing. She also had an extreme fondness for Barney the dinosaur 38 and loved her doll baby very much. She was quick to smile and learn from everyone. She was extremely close to her mother. We will miss her very much."

At Launice's preschool class, the other 4-year-olds do not know exactly what happened, but they have an idea. Still, at playtime, when they finish finger painting and listening to the stories about Spot going to school, they go to their play area and make guns from their Legos and building blocks. 39

THINKING ABOUT THE ESSAY

1. Did reading the various anecdotes about killing and accidental deaths by guns make you feel that they were isolated instances or part of a trend? Explain.
2. Many young people are picked on by bullies. However, few shoot their tormentors. Are there understandable reasons why certain individuals, like Jason Smith, act on their murderous impulses while the vast majority do not? Or are such occurrences beyond our grasp to understand?
3. The rhetoric of the essay moves from anecdote to statistical data. What purpose may the authors have had in structuring their essay this way? Did you find it personally effective in presenting the information? Why?
4. Who is the audience for this essay? How might the magazine that the essay appeared in influence the style?
5. Compare your emotional responses to this essay and the preceding one. How did they differ? Which essay involved you more? Which left you with a stronger impression? Explain.

RESPONDING IN DISCUSSION

1. Divide into groups of three and four. Discuss what the punishment should be for owning a handgun in a home with children but not locking it up. Discuss whether such a law would reduce handgun accidents among children. Discuss how it would be enforced.
2. Discuss whether anyone convicted of killing a minor—whether it be homicide or manslaughter—should receive more severe sentencing than someone convicted of a commensurate crime against an adult.
3. Discuss whether there is a correlation between gun ownership and teenage suicide.

4. Discuss whether simply shooting a handgun in public other than at licensed target ranges should be met with a harsh penalty.
5. Conduct two quick searches on the Internet, one for depression and one for gun sales. Is it easier to find counseling or a handgun? Does this affect your perception of gun control?

RESPONDING IN WRITING

1. In a 500-word essay, argue for or against the proposition that anyone purchasing a gun must receive extensive training in gun accident prevention, or be refused insurance.
2. In a 750-to-1,000–word essay, offer a plan for a nationwide gun safety campaign—along the lines of tobacco and drug abuse prevention—that could be instituted for gun owners.
3. Argue for or against the proposition that the best audience to address in order to effect safer gun ownership is mothers of young children.
4. Compare and contrast this essay with "A Trip to the Morgue."
5. Using an Internet search engine, try to locate information on any of the following groups: School Crime Stoppers, National Crime Prevention Council, KIDSNET, and Ad Hoc Group against Crime. Based on information retrieved, write a report on what groups are doing to confront gun crimes involving children.

Gunslinging in America

Fred Guterl

Gun control is an issue that tends to polarize public opinion. The following essay's author, who is a senior editor for *Discover* magazine, attempts to separate emotion from "scientific" fact in his approach to the controversy. Despite the ominous title of the essay, which appeared in the May 1996 issue of *Discover,* Guterl attempts a balanced presentation of the data deriving from recent studies that examine whether gun ownership increases or decreases one's chances of violent death. In his attempt to clarify the debate, Guterl employs a subtle line of reasoning that takes readers through familiar territory before leaving them with a decision that only they can formulate.

PREVIEWING THE ESSAY

Is it possible to be completely objective about an issue as controversial as gun control? In fact, what is the value of objectivity or the relevance of science in attempting to formulate an opinion or viewpoint on a debatable topic?

Sam Walker was not your average American gun owner. For one thing, he had no interest whatsoever in hunting. And whereas the average gun owner owns at least three guns, Walker owned only one, a .38-caliber revolver, which friends persuaded him to buy for the sole purpose of protecting himself and his family in their suburban Houston home. Walker didn't even particularly like guns. He still hadn't gotten around to acquainting himself with his new weapon when his burglar alarm went off one weekday morning last December. Notified by his security company of the intrusion, Walker rushed home from work, quietly entered the house, took the gun out from the spot where he had left it for safekeeping, and, hearing a noise, moved stealthily up the stairs and opened a closet door. He saw a movement, a figure, and in a split second fired. The smoothly oiled gun worked perfectly, and Walker's aim was true. A body fell to the floor. It was his 16-year-old daughter. She had cut school that day and had hidden in the closet to avoid her father. It wound up costing her her life. 1

If Walker's tragic story argues against the benefits to be gained by gun ownership, consider an incident that happened a month later, across the country in New York City. One weekday morning in January, in front of a Brooklyn government building, Eric Immesberger stopped to give a man directions. Suddenly a second man came out from behind a pillar and knocked Immesberger to the ground. The two men then demanded his wallet and started beating him. Now, it just so happens that Immesberger is an investigator for the Brooklyn district attorney, and, more to the point, he was armed with a 9-millimeter semiautomatic handgun. He managed to pull his weapon and shoot one of the robbers in the chest. The other fled. Immesberger was later treated at a hospital for a broken nose. 2

Which case better represents the reality of owning a gun? It depends, of course, on whom you ask. But one point is indisputable: murder is committed more frequently in the United States than just about anywhere else in the developed world, and guns are its chief instrument. For African American males between the ages of 14 and 25, guns are the leading cause of death. And despite the recent downward blip in the numbers, crimes in the United States are far more likely to lead to death than they are in any other developed country. Every two and a half years, guns kill as many Americans as died in the Vietnam War. The litany of statistics is as deadening as it is depressing. Although few people would argue that cleansing the population of all 3 guns wouldn't go a long way to trimming the firearms fatality rate, the country's 230 million guns, shielded by the Second Amendment, seem likely to remain in circulation for a long time.

Lacking a consensus on gun control, lawmakers have in recent years at least tried to put fewer guns in the hands of criminals and more in the hands of law-abiding citizens. The Brady Bill, for instance, seeks to curtail the proliferation of handguns, the weapons of choice for both crime and self-defense, by imposing background checks and a waiting period on new purchases. At the same time, the states are passing laws making it easy for residents to carry concealed handguns. But is arming the citizenry a good way to offset the risk of crime? 4

In the last decade researchers have focused unprecedented attention on the problem, and authors of some of the more dramatic studies have managed to amass impressively large stacks of press clippings. But science has not been especially helpful here. So far, nobody has been able to marshal convincing evidence for either side of the debate. "The first point that's obvious in any scientific reading of the field is the extreme paucity of data," says Franklin Zimring, a professor of law at the University of California at Berkeley. "What we have is critically flawed—on both sides." Indeed, the scientific literature on the subject seems to teach very little, except for the tedious fact that it is difficult to say anything rigorously scientific about human behavior—particularly aggression. 5

What's obvious by now to most scientists is that assessing the risk of owning a gun is nothing like assessing the risk of smoking cigarettes was 30 or 40 years ago. Back then medical researchers convinced themselves quickly of the cause-and-effect relationship between cigarettes and cancer. Although they had no direct, mechanistic proof, the epidemiological evidence proved the case far beyond any reasonable doubt. With guns, such a link has proved elusive, to say the least. Researchers think that about half of American households possess guns, they're fairly sure that about two-thirds of these households have handguns, and they believe the proportion of handguns, within the total number of guns of all types, is rising. Their reasoning rests partly on the assumption that most guns bought these days are intended for self-defense; because of their small size, handguns are the overwhelming choice for this purpose. They also assume that the relative number of handguns owned will be reflected in the relative number of firearms deaths caused by handguns—about 60 percent. 6

Given the magnitude of the violence and the prevalence of the weapons, it is surprising that science has come to the issue of risk only recently. Criminologists have spent several decades exploring the impact of guns on crime and the behavior of criminals, but they have 7 neglected the question of individual risk. When the medical profession got interested in guns in the early 1980s, it made them a public health issue, looking at the risk to the public at large. Emergency room doctors see the associated hazards every day, in the children who die or are wounded by playing with guns, in the successful and unsuccessful teenage suicides, and in countless other gun-related accidents claiming victims of all ages. The doctors concerned themselves not only with unintended firings but also with accidents such as Walker's, in which the gun itself functions properly in only a narrow mechanical sense and the risk is more clearly seen in retrospect. And this public health perspective spurred renewed interest in studies that test to what degree the presence of guns increases the likelihood of death to their owners. But this approach, of course, focused on gun ownership as a societal issue; it did not assume the point of view of the individual. Doing so would have treated a gun as a consumer product, like a power drill or a lawn mower or a food processor, that carries with it a certain risk of accidental injury or death that must be weighed against its benefits.

8 Many of these public health studies attracted a great deal of publicity because they seemed to settle the question of risk once and for all. Arthur Kellermann, an emergency room doctor, is perhaps the most prolific and visible of the medical researchers who have tried to quantify the risk of owning a gun. Although he is a southerner who was raised with guns and who likes target shooting, he has nonetheless become a major source of bumper-sticker statistics for gun-control advocates. He insists that he has proved not only that a gun is a poor deterrent to residential crime but that having one actually increases the chance that somebody in your home will be shot and killed. In particular, his studies conclude that gun-owning households, when compared with gunless ones, are almost three times as likely to be the scene of a homicide and almost five times as likely to be the scene of a suicide. "If having a gun in the home was a good deterrent," Kellermann says, "then we should have seen few guns in the homes of murder victims. But we found the opposite."

9 Kellermann's work has drawn fire from researchers who suspect that his passion for the issue has blinded him to ambiguities in his data. "Kellermann has decided that guns are bad, and he's out to prove it," says Yale sociologist Albert Reiss. Although in general criminologists don't object to Kellermann's research methods, they part company in their interpretation of his results. His evidence, say critics, is so riddled with uncertainties as to preclude any definitive interpretation.

10 Upon close inspection, Kellermann's results are much more modest than his dramatic conclusions would indicate. He chose to study guns in the home not only because lots of people buy them for self-defense

and keep them in a drawer beside their beds but also because *home* is a well-defined place that simplifies the task of collecting data. Police homicide records specifically include the location of each incident and the weapon used, and it was a straightforward matter for Kellermann to follow up each case by interviewing surviving family members and friends. The problem was in coming up with a suitable control group against which to draw comparisons. Ideally, you want to pair each victim with a control that differs from the victim only in that one was shot and the other wasn't. Kellermann devised a clever methodology for doing so. For each victim, he randomly selected one neighbor after another until he found someone who was the same age, sex, and race. Eventually he assembled "matched pairs" for 388 homicide victims.

When he compared the victims with the control group, however, he found that many more factors differentiated the two groups than their victim status. It turned out that the households in which homicides took place were more likely to contain a family member who abused alcohol or drugs and had a history of domestic violence—these factors contributed to the likelihood of homicide independent of the existence of guns. Kellermann took pains to compensate for these other factors using standard statistical techniques of epidemiology. In essence, he tried to estimate how much each factor, such as alcohol abuse, might have influenced the homicide rate among victims in his study, and then he adjusted his figures accordingly. 11

What neither Kellermann nor his critics can know for certain is whether this statistical juggling actually uncovers any underlying trends or whether something else is going on that Kellermann himself hasn't accounted for. Kellerman himself admits the possibility of some kind of "psychological confounding"—that some intangible factor such as aggression, rather than merely the presence of guns, is influencing the results. Critics also point out that the victims in Kellermann's study may have gotten guns because they felt themselves to be threatened in some way, which means they might have suffered higher homicide rates even if they hadn't bothered to arm themselves. "Kellermann has shown that homicide victims are more likely to keep a gun at home, but criminologists have known that for years," says Gary Kleck, of Florida State University in Tallahassee. 12

Kellermann's even more dramatic figures on suicide in the home are especially problematic, mainly because Kellermann relies on the numbers without offering an explanation. "There's no theory to account for his conclusion," says Zimring. Suicide is also thought to be prone to substitution—that is, although guns are the preferred instrument of suicide in the United States, a person bent on suicide can easily find a substitute if need be. Since Kellermann's study focuses on suicides in the home, it doesn't account for the victim who, lacking a gun, decides instead to jump off a bridge. 13

Regardless of their personal feelings on guns, criminologists, who tend to look at violence through the lens of police statistics and surveys, are usually more open than doctors to the possibility that a gun can now and then deter a crime. Trouble is, social scientists are poorly equipped to measure events that do not occur—crimes that are averted because the would-be victim had a gun. As a result, criminologists have resorted to surveys to get at this phenomenon. Most recently, Kleck conducted a survey to find out how often gun owners actually use their guns in self-defense. His controversial results depict the country's gun owners as holding back a tidal wave of violence and crime. He estimates that 2.5 million times each year, somebody somewhere in America uses a gun in self-defense. This figure has become a mantra of the National Rifle Association (with whom Kleck has no affiliation). 14

Most other criminologists are critical of Kleck's methods, and almost all of them are incredulous at the results. A big complaint is that he leaves it to his survey respondents to define a "defensive gun use," so he may have captured incidents that most people would consider trivial. "An awful lot of what some people would call self-defense is, like, somebody asks you for a quarter and you tell them to get lost, but as you walk away you keep your hand on your gun," says Philip Cook, a Duke University economist. In addition, many incidents that people report as self-defense may in fact be assaults, in which the respondent takes a more active role than he admits. "In many instances, we may only be talking to one side of an argument," says Zimring. 15

What this criticism comes down to is that Kleck, like Kellermann and all the other researchers in this field, is guilty of failing to explain what happens when people carry guns, and how possessing one affects their interactions with criminals. As Reiss puts it, "We know very little about how motivation enters into an action." Zimring likens efforts to understand the deterrent effect of guns to "dancing with clouds." Kleck himself admits that "the better the research, the more it tends to support the null hypothesis—that gun ownership and control laws have no net effect on violence." 16

Even when a seemingly perfect opportunity for a real-life experiment presents itself, as it did recently to criminologist David McDowall, the null hypothesis is often all that a criminologist is left with. Several years ago, Florida, Mississippi, and Oregon adopted "shall issue" laws requiring the states to issue a license to almost anybody who wants to carry a concealed handgun. McDowall saw that the effect of these laws would give him a laboratory in which to test the arms-race hypothesis: he could find out whether criminals, knowing their victims are more likely to be armed with handguns, are more likely to use guns themselves. He could also find out whether citizens, when armed, can deter crime. 17

After the new laws were passed, permits to carry concealed handguns rose enormously—in Florida the number of licenses soared from 17,000 before the law was passed in 1987 to 141,000 seven years later. After studying five cities, McDowall found that the rate of firearms homicides increased overall by 26 percent. Although this would seem to support the arms-race hypothesis, the results were inconsistent. Whereas McDowall had expected the effects of the liberalized laws to be greatest in Miami, the biggest city in the study and the one with the highest crime rate, the rise in homicides there was too small to be statistically significant. However, McDowall believes his evidence is strong enough to show that armed citizens do not decrease the number of firearms-related deaths. 18

Despite the frustrating lack of clarity, researchers are universally optimistic that, with time and the accretion of data, insight into the mechanism of violence will come, and with it, a greater consensus on the real risks of guns. For the time being, however, there will remain very little one researcher can say about risk that another researcher cannot refute. Most favor restricting the availability of guns by mandating background checks and waiting periods, which serve to some degree to keep guns out of the hands of "hotheads" and criminals. There is also a consensus that higher homicide rates have everything to do with the preponderance of guns—an obvious inference when considering, say, crime statistics of London and New York. These two cities have similar crime rates, but the homicide rate from burglaries and robberies in gun-rich New York is vastly higher—54 times higher in 1992, according to Zimring. "America doesn't have a crime problem," he says, "it has a lethal violence problem. It's that thin layer of lethal crime that Americans are afraid of." 19

Given that purging guns from the population is problematic, would the world be safer if each law-abiding citizen carried a gun? Alessandro Veralli hesitates before answering this question. For most of his adult life, he has carried a concealed handgun almost everywhere he goes, whether it's out to the movies with his wife or to the local hardware store on a Saturday afternoon. Yet Veralli, a Master Firearms Instructor for the New York City Police Department and an NRA life member, admits that as a civilian he has had very little opportunity to use his gun. If he ever found himself a customer at a liquor store that was being held up, in most cases his training and common sense would tell him to lie low rather than start a shoot-out. If he was out with his wife and a thief demanded his wallet, he would probably hand it over. "In a robbery, there's not much you can do except maybe shoot at the guy as he's walking away," he says. "But what if he shoots back? I'd be putting my wife in danger, and for what?" He carries a gun for the hypothetical extreme case when having it might 20 mean the difference between life and death. "Personally I'd hate to get into a bad situation and think that I might have been able to do something if I had had a gun," he says.

But should other citizens carry guns? "I'm tempted to say yes," he says, but then he demurs. "Maybe it makes sense in other parts of the country where they have more space. New York, though, is too crowded. There's something about all these people being confined in a small space. People can fly off the handle over little things. I don't think I'd want to see each and every one of them carrying a gun." 21

THINKING ABOUT THE ESSAY

1. Guterl cites several experts and reports on gun violence. How does he present these findings? What is his overall purpose? What does he assume about his audience?
2. Explain the effect of the first two paragraphs. How do they connect to the third paragraph and to the body of the essay?
3. There are four major sections in this essay. What is the logical development from section to section?
4. This essay utilizes several comparative strategies to develop its thesis. Identify these comparative devices and explain their significance.
5. Is there a thesis in this essay? Explain.

RESPONDING IN DISCUSSION

1. Divide into dyads (groups of two). Have one person list all data from the essay supporting gun ownership. Have the other person identify all opposing data. Share your findings with the rest of the class.
2. Discuss whether Guterl ever stakes out his own position on gun control and gun violence or merely retreats behind a facade of scientific objectivity. Do class members approve of his overall purpose or find it objectionable?
3. Form small groups of four or five individuals and then discuss the ways in which the group would conduct a "scientific" experiment on the impact of guns in households. Use Guterl's presentation of Kellermann's research methodology and findings as guidelines.
4. As a group, discuss the case studies of Sam Walker and Eric Immesberger—presented by Guterl at the start of the essay—and the focus on Alessandro Veralli at the end. What do their stories add to the article? What final point does Guterl want to make?

RESPONDING IN WRITING

1. Argue for or against the proposition that "science" can ultimately provide us with useful data on the relationship of violence to the prevalence of weapons.
2. Write a 750-to-1,000–word essay in which you try to fairly present both sides of the debate on gun control. Construct a thesis that reflects this attempt at objectivity.
3. Guterl states that "one point is indisputable: murder is committed more frequently in the United States than just about anywhere else in the developed world, and guns are its chief instrument" (paragraph 3). Write an analytical essay in which you attempt to explain the underlying causes behind this "indisputable" fact.
4. Utilizing the Web, conduct a search for scientific data on guns and violence. Download this information and incorporate it in an essay analyzing the data and suggesting a conclusion or argumentative position on the subject.

Three Strikes and You're Dead

William Tucker

The debate surrounding capital punishment is given a new twist in this article first published in the March 1994 issue of *The American Spectator*. Tucker, who is the New York correspondent for the magazine, attempts to separate rational and appropriate sentencing of criminals from legislation that is advanced for political motives, which nowadays usually may be reduced to the idea of "getting tough on crime." Is the "three-strikes-and-you're-out" movement (which would sentence to life without parole anyone who commits three violent felonies) a way to reduce crime, or is it merely a means to reduce the public's fear of crime, thereby benefiting only the politicians who advocate it? The author attempts to use logic in finding the right solution to sentencing policy. In this regard, he abstains from the hysterical rhetoric that is often fueled by fear and anger. Whether you agree with him is a matter only your values and judgment can help you determine.

PREVIEWING THE ESSAY

When you consider appropriate sentencing guidelines for violent criminals, is your response based on emotion, reason, or a combination of both? How should lawmakers entrusted with making these policies approach the subject?

Should they go with their gut feeling or should they place emotion aside and consider the issues as they would any other type of legal decision?

> *5 Young Robbers Took the Cash, Then Killed Anyway, Police Say*
> —*New York Times* headline, February 3, 1994

Imagine that five years from now you're walking down a dark street and somebody points a gun in your face, announcing a stick-up. Unknown to you, the possessor of the gun is a "two-time loser"—a career criminal who already has two violent felony convictions on his record. 1

As you fumble for your wallet, you have a sudden realization. The man with the gun is someone you saw on a bus just a few days ago. You even remember the stop where he got off. You try to keep this recognition out of your face, but suddenly the man senses it. He remembers, too. He knows your face, you know his face. It's going to be a simple matter for you to identify him to the police. 2

Under the "three-strikes-and-you're-out" reform recently adopted by the state legislature, the man with the gun now has the following options: (1) he can take your money and run, knowing your testimony to the police will bring him life in prison; or (2) he can blow your head off and eliminate the principal witness to his crime. The penalty for that: also life in prison. 3

How much do you think your life would be worth at that moment? 4

"Three strikes and you're out" is the latest fad in the anti-crime debate. Get three violent crimes on your record, and you go to jail for life, with no chance of parole. The idea grows out of the basic perception that about 70 percent of all violent crime is committed by only a handful of "hard-core" criminals. Lock these people up—so the theory goes—and throw away the key, and the streets will be safe again. 5

The state of Washington adopted such a law by public referendum in 1990. Both New York's Governor Mario Cuomo and California's Governor Pete Wilson have hopped on board. In a cover story, *Time* reported that 81 percent of the public wants the reform. The *Wall Street Journal* has written favorable editorials. President Clinton received the loudest ovation from both sides of the aisle for proposing it during his State of the Union Address. In a field which, like public education, is beginning to be dominated by fads, "three strikes" is the idea of the year. 6

Unfortunately, it isn't going to work. In fact, the predictable result will be that more and more violent crimes will escalate into murders. That's because Americans, liberal and conservative alike, haven't yet grasped what it means to live without the ultimate punishment itself: the death penalty. 7

Until 1960, capital punishment was practiced routinely in the United States. Anyone who killed someone lived with the reasonable 8 expectation that he might forfeit his own life in return. Phrases such as "hanging for it" and "going to the chair" were part of the language. In retrospect, the era is remembered as a period of wanton slaughter. In truth, between 1930 to 1950, the number of executions per year ranged between 117 and 199—about three or four for each state. Since murders numbered between 5,000 and 7,000 per year, the likelihood of execution for murder was about 1 in 25. (With 24,000 murders in 1992 and 38 executions, the expectation is now 1 in 625.)

Equally important in that era was the swiftness and certainty of capital punishment. The spectacle of the condemned killer mocking the state year after year with legal chicanery did not exist. On February 15, 1933, Giuseppe Zangara, an anarchist, attempted to assassinate President-elect Franklin Roosevelt and fatally shot the mayor of Chicago instead. Zangara had been tried and executed before Roosevelt took the oath of office on March 21. (By contrast, James Earl Ray tied up Congress with his protestations of innocence fifteen years after the assassination of Martin Luther King, and Sirhan Sirhan comes up for parole in California every two years.) 9

During the 1950s, the rate of execution did taper off. The number fell below 100 in 1950, below 50 in 1958. Ideological opposition mounted and, under the Warren Court, appeals became vastly more complicated. Charles Starkweather, who killed thirteen people, was executed in Nebraska in 1959. Richard Speck, who killed eight nursing students in 1966, died in jail. In 1964, the number of executions dwindled to fifteen, and after 1966 they stopped altogether. The Supreme Court outlawed all remaining capital-punishment laws in *Furman* v. *Georgia* (1972). 10

What happened to murder rates after executions all but ended in the early 1960s? Although records are incomplete (the FBI's Uniform Crime Reports didn't become uniform until 1958), what evidence exists suggests that murder rates dropped steadily from 1935 to 1960. The incidence of decline held for blacks, too—despite a vast migration from the rural South to the cities, where crime rates are always higher. America was becoming less violent. Anyone peering into the future in 1963 would have predicted that peace and prosperity were making us into a far more civilized society. 11

Instead, in 1964, the trend abruptly reversed. From a low of 4.6 per 100,000 in 1963, the murder rate climbed 10 percent per year in 1966 and 1967, eventually peaking at 10.2 per 100,000 in 1980. The early 1980s saw some tapering off, but rates rose again after 1987, reaching 9.8 per 100,000 in 1991. 12

To the naked eye, it would seem as if the loss of the death penalty had something (if not everything) to do with this historic reversal. The public is certainly convinced that it did. From the historical low 13 point of 1966—the only year in which a plurality of respondents to the Gallup Poll opposed the death penalty—support has risen steadily to 76 percent in 1993 (down from a peak of 79 percent in 1988).

As a result, thirty-seven states have now adopted capital punishment for at least some type of murder. Generally, statutes impose the death penalty for the following crimes: (1) premeditated murder, (2) felony murder (murder committed during the course of another crime), (3) murder-for-hire, (4) murder with torture, (5) multiple murder, or (6) terrorist murder. (Some states also specify murder of a policeman or prison guard.) 14

Such explicit definitions represent an enormous improvement over the old haphazard system in which—as the Supreme Court rightly observed in *Furman* (1972)—the chances of receiving the death penalty in the U.S. were as arbitrary as "being struck by lightning." As late as the 1950s, Louisiana and Mississippi had mobile electric chairs that rumbled from one county jail to the next, executing people for who-knows-what. At the time of *Furman,* North Carolina was still executing people for burglary. Furman himself was to be executed for rape. Another problem was that in many states the death penalty for certain crimes was mandatory. This led to guessing games between a jury and the prosecutor, in which a jury would acquit someone it believed to be guilty because the members didn't believe the death penalty was justified. 15

These confusions have now been resolved in a legislative effort that has made the procedures surrounding the death penalty as reasonable and fair as can be expected. In every state, the jury first returns its verdict of guilt or innocence. Only after guilt has been established does the proceeding enter the "penalty phase." At this point, either the judge or the jury decides whether capital punishment should be imposed, usually after hearing testimony from both the defendant and members of the victim's family. 16

Yet even this procedure does not pass muster with the judicial and law-school elites that oppose the death penalty on purely ideological grounds. (One-third of the opponents of the death penalty say they wouldn't support it even if it could be shown to deter murder.) Litigation groups drag appeals on endlessly—often at public expense. Opponents delay and delay, hoping that one day the Supreme Court will tire of the whole process and once again declare it "cruel and unusual" that 2,600 convicts have been kept waiting so long on Death Row. 17

The possibilities for sophistry are endless. Between 1979 and 1987, the California Supreme Court under Chief Justice Rose Bird overturned thirty-seven out of forty death sentences on purely technical grounds. In one case, where an armed robber had shot and killed a Brink's guard, the court said the verdict was improper because the 18 jury had failed to consider whether the robber was only shooting the guard to "immobilize" him. In another case, an ex-convict sought out and killed three people in a grocery store, one of whom was the principal witness in a prison friend's robbery conviction. The ex-con, who had received a hundred dollar payment from the prison friend's son, killed his victims execution-style. Even so, the Bird Court found no "intent to kill." Voters threw out the Bird Court en masse in a 1987 election and installed a new majority that is not ideologically opposed to capital punishment. Yet California still has carried out only one execution among its 328 murderers on Death Row.

Other states are in the same bind. With 24,000 murders each year nationwide, the justice system still can't seem to find anybody who is guilty of anything. There are other ramifications, however, that are equally damaging. The justice system is what you might call an "ecology." In any such complex systems—as the environmentalists love to tell us—it is impossible to change one thing without altering everything else as well. 19

One of the oldest truisms of justice is that the punishment should fit the crime. Penalties must be neither too harsh nor too soft. But it is equally important that clear and recognizable differentials be maintained in the penalties for qualitatively different levels of crime. If burglarizing a house carries a penalty of three years in jail, then burglarizing and burning the house down to destroy the evidence must carry a considerably stricter penalty. Otherwise, there will be an incentive for burglars to up the ante to improve their chances of escape. 20

Murder is generally considered the ultimate crime. Other violent crimes may leave a person scarred for life, but murder ends life. For that reason, it is necessary to have a qualitatively different form of punishment available. For most of history, this has been the death penalty. 21

Once the death penalty is abandoned, however, everything else must change. Because the top charge has been lowered, the punishment for all other crimes must be lowered as well. When first-degree murder (killing with a motive) was punishable by death, it was possible to mete out 20-years-to-life sentences for second-degree ("impulsive") killings. Robbery and rape could be punished by 10-to-15-year sentences, burglary and assault by 5 years, and so on. Now all that is different. If a planned, premeditated murder is only worth 25-years-to-life, then unplanned murders can only be worth 10-to-15. Rape and robbery must be lowered to 5-to-7, burglaries to 1-to-2 years, and so on down the line. 22

Today, as everyone knows, sentencing in the American justice system is an elaborate ruse to fool the public into the impression that long 23 terms are being handed out, while in fact actual prison time is relatively short. Right now, the average convicted murderer in the U.S. serves eleven years in prison. Rape gets five years, robbery less than four, assault or burglary two, drug trafficking less than two, and auto theft is free.

Weak as these sentences may be, it still might be argued that they retain something of a differential between rape and robbery, on the one hand, and murder on the other. If you rape a woman, you get five years. If you slit her throat to keep her from talking, you double your jail time. Not much to discourage a hardened criminal, perhaps, but enough to give a first-time offender pause. What is going to happen, though, when we decide to "get tough" and start raising sentences for *non*-murders? The only outcome will be to blur, once again, the distinction between "violent crime" and homicide. 24

Women's groups, for example, have argued in recent years that rape is in many ways worse than death—a crime that leaves a woman scarred for life. Armed with these perceptions, they have pushed legislation to raise the penalty for rape to as high as twenty years. But the statutory penalty for murder in nearly every state is also twenty years—and in reality is only half that. What does that say to a rapist? "Kill your victim. She is the principal witness to the crime. If she identifies you, you will get twenty years in jail. If you kill her, you get the same twenty years. What's the difference? Dead women tell no tales." 25

The same logic will be even more compelling under "three strikes and you're out." As a criminal's violent record grows, he will be less and less amenable to the idea of getting caught. Facing life in jail for a third felony, he will be ready to kill anybody and anything in order to avoid apprehension. Granted, the police often faced this dilemma in trying to apprehend a murderer facing a certain death sentence. In the old days, many a killer vowed he would "never be taken alive." But the police, at least, are *prepared* for such confrontations. (As a result, killers often surrendered at newspaper offices in order to avoid shoot-outs.) Under "three strikes and you're out," however, these risks will be imposed upon the general public. 26

There is a terrifying, inexorable logic to all this—one that criminals themselves often do not recognize until it is too late. Last January, for example, a 22-year-old black pre-med student from the Bronx allegedly drove to a shopping mall in suburban Rockland County and hijacked a jeep from two local teenagers. Holding them at gunpoint, he assured the two youths over and over, "I'm not going to hurt you." In fact, he probably didn't *mean* to hurt them. But once the crime begins, a fearful logic is set in motion. "These people know me," the criminal says to himself. "They've seen my face. Unless I do something, they'll go to the police and identify me." 27

So instead, the pre-med student tied up the two youths and drove them to a secluded woods. But even that wasn't good enough. Eventually, they would get away and describe him to the police. How do you wipe a face from someone's memory? 28

So the student put his gun to their heads and shot both. One youth died instantly. The other jerked his head and suffered a nonfatal wound. Left for dead, he quickly made it to a nearby house and called the police. The pre-med student was nabbed a half-hour later on the Bronx River Parkway. The youth who survived the shooting will be the principal witness at his trial. 29

Did this 22-year-old novice *want* to kill his victims? Almost certainly not. But without the specter of a death penalty, there is nothing to stand between apprehension and impulse. Would an experienced criminal have done things differently? He would have shot the kid a second time just to make sure. The cops would probably still be looking for him. 30

John Coughlin, a retired detective with the New York City Police Department, remembers a time when things were different. As a rookie patrolman in the 1950s, he and his partners spent day after day protecting store owners along Brooklyn's Flatbush Avenue. "At the time, we were allowed to stop and frisk anyone whom the store owner believed was 'casing' the place," says Coughlin. "These searches often turned up guns—which meant an immediate arrest under the old Sullivan Law." 31

What surprises Coughlin—in retrospect—is how often the guns turned out to be unloaded. "At least a third of the time, there were no bullets in the gun, or the firing pin was missing, or the gun had been disabled. These guys wanted the *fear* the gun would bring, but they didn't want even the *chance* that someone might *accidentally* get killed during the stick-up. They knew a robbery meant jail, while a murder meant the electric chair." 32

Today the calculus is reversed. Many robbers deliberately kill their victims, knowing that they are reducing their chances of being caught. In some circles, it has become a matter of proving you "have heart" to eliminate the victims of your crime. Particularly in gang crimes, the peer pressure to prove your manhood by pulling the trigger may be overwhelming. 33

The need to maintain a differential between crimes of violence and murder has long been recognized as one of the greatest responsibilities of the justice system. In *The Spirit of the Laws* (1748), Montesquieu, after surveying the criminal justice systems of the whole world, criticized his own countrymen of the risks of failing to make this distinction: 34

> It is a great abuse amongst us [the French] to condemn to the same punishment a person that only robs on the highway and another

who robs and murders. Surely, for the public security, some difference should be made in the punishment.

In China, those who add murder to robbery are cut in pieces: but not so for those who only rob; to this difference it is owing that though they rob in that country they never murder.

In Russia, where the punishment of robbery and murder is the same, they always murder. The dead, they say, tell no tales.

Where there is no difference in the penalty, there should be some expectation of pardon. In England they never murder on the highway, because robbers have some hopes of transportation [exile], which is not the case in respect to those that commit murder.

Montesquieu, of course, was criticizing the overuse of the death penalty, and the same criticism could have been made in the U.S. as late as 1972. But the logic also applies to its underuse: without a significant differentiation between violence and homicide, there is nothing to inhibit the rapist/robber from killing his victim. 35

The change in the *kind* of murder committed over the past thirty years makes it clear that this is happening. When liberals argued against the death penalty in the 1960s, they inevitably pointed out that 90 percent of all murders were "crimes of passion"—unplanned, impulsive killings among families and friends. "The death penalty isn't going to deter these crimes," they argued—and they were probably correct. 36

Since then, however, "crimes of passion" have declined to less than 70 percent of all murders. The remainder are "stranger murders"—crimes committed at random or in the act of committing other crimes. *These are the murders that were being deterred by the death penalty.* 37

There is no way around this logic. Basically, we have two choices: (1) we can go on living with the mayhem that surrounds us; or (2) we can restore capital punishment for first-degree murder. What we cannot do, though, is start raising the penalties for other crimes. Three-strikes-you're-out will only turn more victims of violent crime into murder victims. Dead men tell no tales. 38

THINKING ABOUT THE ESSAY

1. Examine the introduction that Tucker presents in paragraphs 1 through 4. How does the "logic" of the imaginary incident condition the logic of Tucker's argument?
2. What is Tucker's view about the extended appeals process? What rationale does he provide for his view?
3. What is the thesis of the essay? Where is it most succinctly stated?
4. Where, if any place in the essay, does Tucker prove that capital punishment is a deterrent to crime? How significant is his consideration of this factor to the import of his thesis?

5. Tucker discusses several examples of sophistry (clever but faulty reasoning) in the way "killers" literally "get away with murder." Is it fair to condemn the judicial process of sentencing by providing three egregious examples? Explain.

RESPONDING IN DISCUSSION

1. Divide into groups of three and four and discuss your views on the death penalty. Are you in favor of it and, if so, for what crimes should it be administered? Share your answers with the rest of the class. Also, mention whether your views were modified during your group discussion.
2. Tucker states that "once the death penalty is abandoned, however, everything else must change." Discuss whether life without parole as the standard sentence for murder allows severe sentencing for other crimes, or, in the author's words, presents "clear and recognizable differentials." Explain your view.
3. Discuss whether the personality profiles of young killers portrayed in "A Trip to the Morgue" and "Cease Fire" make Tucker's solution to violent crime merely wishful thinking.
4. Considering that so many prisoners claim they prefer death to life without parole, discuss which of the two alternatives might be the better deterrent to violent crime.

RESPONDING IN WRITING

1. Assume the role of a person wrongfully condemned for murder. Write a letter to your governor the night before your execution, pleading your innocence and condemning your punishment.
2. Argue for or against the proposition that if Tucker proposes restoring capital punishment for first-degree murder, he should first witness an autopsy of an executed murderer or the execution itself.
3. Argue for or against the proposition that even if capital punishment does not deter murder, it still should be mandated for convicted murderers.
4. Argue for or against the proposition that religious and moral factors should override logical argument in determining issues such as capital punishment.
5. Go on-line and read messages of some professional newsgroups whose members are in the criminal justice field. Select several messages regarding capital punishment, and write a report on your findings.

Don't Leave Home without It

R. Daniel Foster

The title of this essay is borrowed from an old American Express advertisement, but its message perhaps demonstrates a sign of the times. While many people nowadays walk around with a credit card, the author of this essay demonstrates that—owing to growing violence in our society—carrying a "piece" for physical security may become as acceptable as carrying "plastic" for financial security. Writing in the April 1994 edition of *Los Angeles Magazine,* the author takes the reader on a field trip through the universe of gun shops, target ranges, and gun advocates that are a significant if hidden part of the Southern California landscape. Rather than finding mountain men or survivalists, however, he finds that gun owners, even those who stretch the "gun carry" regulations, are likely to be affluent citizens with the same values and concerns as any moderate American.

PREVIEWING THE ESSAY

A Supreme Court justice once said the only things certain were death and taxes. In America, perhaps we could add guns. What is your view of gun ownership for law-abiding citizens? Perhaps more important, where and how did you cultivate your view?

The killing threshold. As a resident of Los Angeles, you've undoubtedly run up against it. It's that critical juncture of dismay reached when your pregnant neighbor is stabbed at the local ATM. When you open the "Metro" section to read yet another "Man Killed in Carjacking Attempt" or "Family of Five Slain by Intruder" headline. Following each surge of intolerance, round after round of gun legislation is served up: Institute waiting periods and pass the Brady bill. Ban automatic weapons. Ban Black Talon bullets. Virtually every major newspaper, from the *Los Angeles Times* to the *Boston Globe,* posts a righteous editorial hailing the virtues of restricting access to guns. 1

My assignment was to discover if perhaps that thinking is backward, to postulate on the theory that gun-control laws may in fact spawn more violence than they curb. To theorize about the city's high level of fear, the lack of police support and the idea that legitimate citizens are rendered helpless when their access to guns is restricted. 2

I also considered the possibility that criminals, whose only waiting period consists of the 15 minutes it takes to score a $50 shotgun on Crenshaw, are indeed the greatest proponents of strict gun-control measures. 3

My first revelation in this month-long slog through the conun- 4
drum called gun control was that citizens are arming themselves in unprecedented numbers. According to the Bureau of Alcohol, Tobacco and Firearms, there are about 211 million guns currently in circulation. Indeed, one out of every two U.S. households harbors guns. Closer to home, weapons purchases in California have jumped 20 percent since last year, according to the California Department of Justice. (Some 658,720 gun permits were issued in the state in 1993.)

But my first revelation was soon followed by another, perhaps 5
more profound, one: Many of the same people who are buying weapons are also carrying them—in everything from glove compartments to purses and fanny packs—despite the fact that in Los Angeles County, it is illegal to do so without a permit (obtainable only in rare circumstances). Gun experts in the city place the number of those in the county who pack pieces illegally at about 400,000. "Statewide," says Paxton Quigley, author of *Armed & Female,* a book about how women can—and should—arm themselves, "I would say about a million people carry guns illegally."

Quigley, who conducts self-defense and shooting seminars for 6
women, says modern gun owners are not only concealing weapons, they're discovering inventive ways to do so. At her seminars, she sells a line of cases that conceal guns, including a waist pack and a briefcase with a special compartment that can harbor a .357 Magnum.

Indeed, concealing guns has become a growing business. For ex- 7
ample, at Mr. Polish, an auto restoration and detailing shop in West L.A., owner Chick Cowdin installs up to three compartments that can conceal weapons in cars each day.

"A lot of people," says Cowdin, "keep their guns loaded or keep 8
the ammunition clip in the same compartment. [California law states that handguns must be kept in a locked trunk or locked container other than the glove compartment; ammunition must be stored separately.] They know they're doing something illegal, but they're scared out of their wits."

In fact, gun-shop owners across the city say hundreds of thou- 9
sands breathed easier in January, when the state legislature decided to keep it a misdemeanor to carry a concealed firearm instead of quadrupling the sentence.

Simply put, people want to level the playing field. They want 10
something other than Mace, pepper spray or a personal-attack alarm when faced with the armed thug lurking in their closets or yanking them from their cars. And we're not just talking about the people one might expect, the jewelers and pawnshop owners or rednecks who sport bumper stickers on their four-wheel-drives that read I'LL GIVE UP MY GUN WHEN THEY PRY IT FROM MY COLD, DEAD FINGERS. No, these are ordinary citizens who faithfully read the *New York Times Book Review*

and raise African violets in their solariums: surgeons, lawyers, Encino home makers, nurses, the guy who tunes your piano and the woman who teaches your five-year-old how to finger paint.

"You would be surprised to know the people who are getting trained," says Beverly Hills Gun Club owner Arthur Kassel. "They're extremely liberal people. In fact, many are celebrities who speak out about the problems guns cause, but then come here for target practice. There's a late-night talk-show host who comes here who would really surprise you." 11

Attendance at the club has shot up 40 percent since last year. The six area locations of Target Range and Gun World report a "substantial increase" in membership. Meanwhile, the Warner Center Gun Club, replete with sprawling leather couches and plush burgundy carpet, opened nine months ago in the heart of the west Valley—an enclave that dreads the encroachment of urban crime like none other—and it already has 10,000 members, 3,000 of whom have been trained at the facility. There's also Armed and Literate, a group of some 40 local writers that formed three years ago to talk about gun legislation and go on shooting outings. 12

"These are highly intelligent people who are not only concerned about their safety but see gun ownership as a political issue in terms of the Second Amendment," says Quigley, who's a member. "They run the gamut in terms of political affiliation." 13

Half of the dozens of gun owners I talked to admitted carrying their weapons. One man says he's an expert at spotting gun carriers in malls: "It's their body language, the way they touch their waist packs or shoulder bags. I spot them all the time." 14

"I carry mine in the car," says Jeanne Pontius, a financial consultant from the Valley. "I'm a single woman, living alone, and I have to travel, sometimes to not the best of neighborhoods. We all need to be responsible for ourselves." 15

Quigley says Pontius represents a new breed of gun owner in Los Angeles. "When I began my seminars, about one-third of the students had been raped or sexually abused," she says. "Most of the people who come now haven't had that experience. And they come for training to make sure it stays that way." 16

No matter their gender, professional status or ideology, there is one theme heard consistently among gun owners when discussing why they arm themselves: We can no longer rely on our police force for protection. They point to the fact that the police department is woefully understaffed: "There are only 800 officers on the streets at any given time—if you're lucky," says Scott Reitz, lead firearms and tactics instructor for the LAPD's Metropolitan Division. 17

What's more, many of the officers themselves feel their effectiveness has been diminished by restrictions on the use of force, especially 18 in the wake of the Rodney King beating. "We just feel defeated," says one Metro Division officer.

And adding to the anxiety is a widely held belief among many Angelenos that the police force is on a slowdown, because of the King verdicts and unresolved labor issues. 19

Perhaps most unsettling is the argument that police are apparently not well trained to protect citizens when a crisis calls for gunfire. "Less than 20 percent of the rounds fired by policemen in the United States actually strike their intended targets," says Reitz. "Nationwide, lots of officers have little or no training in shooting whatsoever." He adds, however, that specialized divisions, like Metro Division, boast an 80 percent target-hit rate. 20

And if the police seem ineffective, gun control has proved woefully inadequate. We have a dazzling array of 20,000 local, state and federal gun-control laws, but guess what? Guns are now as ubiquitous as cars. Criminals don't obey gun-control laws, goes the argument—that's why they are called criminals. 21

They are also cowards, according to a National Institute of Justice study, which found that felons surveyed in 10 state correctional facilities believed an armed victim to be an obviously unattractive victim. Seventy-four percent said they avoided entering houses at night for fear a homeowner would be armed. 22

"What nobody ever looks at is how many crimes are stopped by the mere presence of a firearm, without anyone ever firing a shot," says Reitz. [According to Florida State University criminologist Gary Kleck, citizens shoot their assailants in only 2 percent of cases.] 23

What's more, gun advocates argue, while more people are carrying illegally, they're apparently doing so responsibly, since, according to studies published in the *American Journal of Public Health,* domestic homicide rates fall, not rise, in relation to increasing gun ownership. 24

In fact, during the past three years, as the number of handguns increased, crime rates in L.A. fell in nearly every category: homicide, rape, robbery, burglary and aggravated assault. 25

Reason, then, they say, tells us to keep guns away from criminals and instead put them in the hands of upstanding citizens. The question is how? Even if a plan like Rhode Island senator John Chafee's worked—the Republican proposes to "turn off the spigot" and ban the manufacture, sale and possession of hand-guns—crooks would steal guns, smuggle them in from other countries or simply make them, argue Quigley and others. 26

Many gun advocates offer that instead of cutting off the supply or even implementing waiting periods, like California's 15-day law, there should be a mandatory instantaneous computer check implemented whenever a firearm is purchased. Records should be scanned to spot criminal activity, mental instability, drug use, medical problems or 27 anything else that would preclude the ability to use a weapon correctly. The cost of the check, they say, could be tied to licensing fees.

Many gun advocates also insist that those who possess guns should be properly trained. Until now, anyone could purchase a gun in California without a lick of training in safety or shooting. But a note of sanity was recently introduced by the California Department of Justice: As of April 1, all handgun purchasers must obtain a firearms-safety certificate prior to buying a gun. Some, however, believe the requirement—the certificates can be had by simply passing a written test or watching a two-hour video—falls far short of what's needed. Reitz and others advocate renewing licenses to possess or carry guns every two years so that safety and proficiency in handling weapons can be refreshed. And safety rules must also be reviewed to guard the 1.2 million school-age latchkey children who have access to guns in their homes. 28

The whole issue of guns and control, of course, is a dicey one, and, not wanting to approach the subject from ignorance, I decided to get weapons training from Reitz, a graduate of the FBI's sniper school and a decade-long member of the LAPD's SWAT team. Reitz operates his Pistolcraft seminars out of the Angeles National Forest outdoor shooting range. 29

As the son of Minnesota hunters, I'm no stranger to guns. I hadn't shot one in 18 years, but after the initial fear, I recalled the pleasure of holding a gun, the distinctive kick as it went off. I think that satisfaction is partly at the core of the gun-control debate. How can one hold and shoot a weapon capable of instantly killing a fellow human and have it feel good? 30

The other students and I were all, in fact, enjoying ourselves immensely as we blasted apart cardboard that approximated our species' hearts and brains. I was later encouraged by the instructor to take more training, buy a gun and use it as a martial-arts weapon. I declined. 31

Guns unquestionably cause pain. Curiously, they also deliver pleasure, probably because humans want to understand power, harness it and ultimately aim it at something. And what could be more powerful than a gun? 32

I also learned that gun owners consider their weapons tools, not inherently good or evil. "Guns are like cars," says Reitz. "If we have more automobiles, there will be more accidents. Many responsible drivers don't drink and don't get in accidents, but do we take all the cars away? That's legitimizing the criminal's position—allowing them to dictate what we can and cannot have, because they're the ones wrongly using the guns." 33

I'm not certain his argument is analogous. It's similar to a comparison related by a manager of a gun range: "The idea that guns 34 cause violence is like believing trailer parks attract hurricanes." Cars and trailer parks have ancillary uses, whereas guns are limited in their scope to cause destruction and, so the argument goes, should be more tightly regulated.

Most people do, however, tend to stereotype anyone who happens 35
to own a gun. Reitz says many are typecast as "para-military commandos." During the training, I met a screenwriter who, with his wife, owns two 45-caliber pistols with seven-round magazines, one police rifle with a four-shot magazine, a defensive shotgun with a six-shot magazine and a sniper rifle, the kind used by police in hostage situations. I was astounded that one could own such an arsenal and claim that guns helped promote "a sense of quietude."

"Possessing a gun comes with the responsibility of not being an 36
asshole," he countered. "I don't run around telling people I have them in my house. You don't see guns on my walls or gun magazines lying around, because I don't want people to be frightened and think I'm a military nut. Having guns doesn't make me feel strong, powerful or more like a man. I realize that ego and emotional reactions, when paired with guns, are a volatile mix. Rather, the responsibility of having guns is extreme. I hope they're something I will never have to use."

In the game of warfare, whether it be during cold wars or in the 37
streets of Los Angeles, weapons are always safeguards to be held in reserve. The problem, of course, is how to handle those who don't play by the rules.

When I began research on this article, my opinions on gun con- 38
trol were much the same as they are now. It's a basic viewpoint held by many: Those who can prove (and continue to prove through relicensing) they can shoulder the responsibility of owning guns should be allowed to have them. Everyone else is out of luck. The debate, however, grows heated when we grapple over what are acceptable, effective restrictions.

Achieving that goal by passing reactive, spotty legislation in at- 39
tempts to lull people into a false sense of security is not working. Guns, of course, are only the surface issue in crime—underlying that are drugs, a shallow social structure and other root causes. But instead of a patchwork of gun-control laws, perhaps a comprehensive system of training in both safety and shooting, along with stringent background checks, could at least keep guns in the proper hands. The alternative is that we collectively continue to shoot ourselves in the foot.

THINKING ABOUT THE ESSAY

1. Foster cites a report that "domestic homicide rates fall, not rise, in relation to increasing gun ownership." How does this statistic

square with statistics discussed in the essay by Wilkerson, Rose, and Prothrow-Stith regarding unintentional deaths due to gun ownership? Explain how you view the trade-off.

2. Foster claims to feel pressure and power when using a handgun. To what degree—if any—would these sensations encourage shootings, particularly among young people? Consider Wilkerson, Rose, and Prothrow-Stith's case involving the death of a bully.
3. The author acknowledges that many gun owners are carrying guns illegally. Should these otherwise law-abiding citizens be penalized if caught? If so, what should be the punishment? Or, should we remove all laws that forbid carrying them as some local jurisdictions have done?
4. What is Foster's thesis? How does he employ personal experience, observation, interviews, and data to support his thesis? Cite specific examples.

RESPONDING IN DISCUSSION

1. Divide into groups of three and four and, as a group, discuss your attitudes regarding legal gun ownership and the influence, if any, the essay had on your view. Share the results of your discussion with the rest of the class.
2. Tucker, in the previous essay, calls for severe punishment for capital crimes. Discuss what effect enacting severe sentencing for illegal gun ownership would have on crime and violence.
3. Gun ownership—like capital punishment—is a distinctly American issue. (No other Western country has the death penalty and there is virtually no private handgun ownership in these same countries.) What makes these issues so prominent in American culture?
4. Discuss whether increased gun ownership will have any deterrent effect on violent crime in the future.
5. Conduct a search for the phrase "where to shoot in California" and find a listing of gun clubs in the L.A. area. Considering the expenses of membership in such a club, what can you conclude about some California gun owners? Does this information affect your perception of gun control issues?

RESPONDING IN WRITING

1. Write an essay explaining why you would or would not purchase a handgun.

2. Do you think that gun controls will reduce violence? Answer this question in a 500-to-750–word essay.
3. Argue for or against the proposition that the nonchalant manner in which guns are displayed and used in the media discourages responsible gun ownership.
4. Argue for or against the proposition that until we examine and address the root causes of violence in our society, raising such issues as gun ownership are merely attempts to make the best of a bad social condition.
5. Download information on the National Rifle Association (NRA). How would you characterize its information on gun ownership? Write a 750-to-1,000–word report on your findings.

CONNECTIONS: FOR WRITING AND RESEARCH

1. Argue for or against the proposition that adults who have children under age 10 should not be allowed to own handguns. Incorporate Guterl's findings into your essay.
2. Argue for or against the proposition that gangsta rap music—as described in Noe's "Parallel Worlds: The Surprising Similarities (and Differences) of Country-and-Western and Rap"—encourages the use of guns in the commission of crimes.
3. Compare and contrast the values expressed in gangsta rap and the behaviors of the people described in Foster's essay.
4. Compare and contrast the methods of deterring violent crime discussed by Fromer in "A Trip to the Morgue" and Tucker in "Three Strikes and You're Dead."
5. For a research project, search the Web for material that compares and contrasts public opinion on capital punishment in the United States and that in another Western country. Present your findings in a 750-to-1,000–word essay.
6. For a research project, write a historical analysis of the introduction and establishment of the Brady Bill.
7. Examine the ways in which the authors in Chapter 10 employ data to substantiate their main points. Which writer do you think is most successful in employing data to convince you of his or her (or in one case their) position?

11

NEW AMERICANS

At one time, the expression that the United States is "a nation of immigrants" was basically a descriptive term used to denote the composition of our population. However, today, that term is a threatening one to many who perceive immigrants as an ominous group ready to challenge, if not destroy, the "American way of life." Some native-born Americans (ignoring the fact that their ancestors were immigrants too) see the new tide of people coming to our shores or landing at our airports as a potential menace to the stability of our jobs, neighborhoods, language, and customs. The result has often been downright hostility, leading to acts of violence against members of the new immigrant groups (Indians, Vietnamese, Mexicans, among others) and the introduction of legislation to limit immigration through quotas or to deny basic benefits to the children of immigrants (as in California's Proposition 187). But to what degree are such responses mere uninformed emotional reactions rather than judicial analyses of the issues? Reading the following essays, you will find that many social observers and researchers who spend years studying the subject believe immigrants contribute far more to the economy and society than they take from it. Regardless of where your views fall on the issue of mass immigration, knowledge rather than hearsay will certainly place you in a better position to understand the subject, and perhaps assist you in regarding the immigrant as an individual with the same human needs and desires as anyone, and place a "human face" on the nebulous image so often presented in the media or even the individual who may sit next to you in the classroom.

American Dreamer

Bharati Mukherjee

The "idea" of America and what it means to be an American is a topic that has preoccupied writers since the founding of the nation. In "American Dreamer," the well-known novelist, short story writer, and essayist Bharati Mukherjee offers a personal account of her passage from India to the United States, her life and education on two continents, and her understanding of the American Dream. Mukherjee is the author of *Jasmine* (1989) and *The Middleman and Other Stories,* which won the 1988 National Book Critic's Circle Award for fiction. Here she does not simplify the immigrant's experience or present it in one-dimensional form. Among other things, she refuses to be "hyphenated," insisting on being treated as an American, not an Asian-American. Combining the narrative flair of a novelist and the analytical powers of a perceptive essayist, Mukherjee explores the subtle contours of identity for Americans as we near the turn of the century. This essay first appeared in the January–February 1997 issue of *Mother Jones.*

PREVIEWING THE ESSAY

Mukherjee asks, "Why is it that hyphenation is imposed only on nonwhite Americans?" How would you answer her?

The United States exists as a sovereign nation. "America," in contrast, exists as a myth of democracy and equal opportunity to live by, or as an ideal goal to reach. 1

I am a naturalized U.S. citizen, which means that, unlike native-born citizens, I had to prove to the U.S. government that I merited citizenship. What I didn't have to disclose was that I desired "America," which to me is the stage for the drama of self-transformation. 2

I was born in Calcutta and first came to the United States—to Iowa City, to be precise—on a summer evening in 1961. I flew into a small airport surrounded by cornfields and pastures, ready to carry out the two commands my father had written out for me the night before I left Calcutta: Spend two years studying creative writing at the Iowa Writers' Workshop, then come back home and marry the bridegroom he selected for me from our caste and class. 3

In traditional Hindu families like ours, men provided and women were provided for. My father was a patriarch and I a pliant daughter. The neighborhood I'd grown up in was homogeneously Hindu, Bengali-speaking, and middle-class. I didn't expect myself to ever 4 disobey or disappoint my father by setting my own goals and taking charge of my future.

When I landed in Iowa 35 years ago, I found myself in a society 5
in which almost everyone was Christian, white, and moderately well-off. In the women's dormitory I lived in my first year, apart from six international graduate students (all of us were from Asia and considered "exotic"), the only non-Christian was Jewish, and the only nonwhite an African-American from Georgia. I didn't anticipate then, that over the next 35 years, the Iowa population would become so diverse that it would have 6,931 children from non-English-speaking homes registered as students in its schools, nor that Iowans would be in the grip of a cultural crisis in which resentment against immigrants, particularly refugees from Vietnam, Sudan, and Bosnia, as well as unskilled Spanish-speaking workers, would become politicized enough to cause the Immigration and Naturalization Service to open an "enforcement" office in Cedar Rapids in October for the tracking and deporting of undocumented aliens.

In Calcutta in the '50s, I heard no talk of "identity crisis"— 6
communal or individual. The concept itself—of a person not knowing who he or she is—was unimaginable in our hierarchical, classification-obsessed society. One's identity was fixed, derived from religion, caste, patrimony, and mother tongue. A Hindu Indian's last name announced his or her forefathers' caste and place of origin. A Mukherjee could *only* be a Brahmin from Bengal. Hindu tradition forbade intercaste, interlanguage, interethnic marriages. Bengali tradition even discouraged emigration: To remove oneself from Bengal was to dilute true culture.

Until the age of 8, I lived in a house crowded with 40 or 50 rela- 7
tives. My identity was viscerally connected with ancestral soil and genealogy. I was who I was because I was Dr. Sudhir Lal Mukherjee's daughter, because I was a Hindu Brahmin, because I was Bengali-speaking, and because my *desh*—the Bengali word for homeland—was an East Bengal village called Faridpur.

The University of Iowa classroom was my first experience of coeduca- 8
tion. And after not too long, I fell in love with a fellow student named Clark Blaise, an American of Canadian origin, and impulsively married him during a lunch break in a lawyer's office above a coffee shop.

That act cut me off forever from the rules and ways of upper- 9
middle-class life in Bengal, and hurled me into a New World life of scary improvisations and heady explorations. Until my lunch-break wedding, I had seen myself as an Indian foreign student who intended to return to India to live. The five-minute ceremony in the

lawyer's office suddenly changed me into a transient with conflicting loyalties to two very different cultures.

The first 10 years into marriage, years spent mostly in my husband's native Canada, I thought of myself as an expatriate Bengali permanently stranded in North America because of destiny or desire. My first novel, *The Tiger's Daughter,* embodies the loneliness I felt but could not acknowledge, even to myself, as I negotiated the no man's land between the country of my past and the continent of my present. Shaped by memory, textured with nostalgia for a class and culture I had abandoned, this novel quite naturally became an expression of the expatriate consciousness. 10

It took me a decade of painful introspection to put nostalgia in perspective and to make the transition from expatriate to immigrant. After a 14-year stay in Canada, I forced my husband and our two sons to relocate to the United States. But the transition from foreign student to U.S. citizen, from detached onlooker to committed immigrant, has not been easy. 11

The years in Canada were particularly harsh. Canada is a country that officially, and proudly, resists cultural fusion. For all its rhetoric about a cultural "mosaic," Canada refuses to renovate its national self-image to include its changing complexion. It is a New World country with Old World concepts of a fixed, exclusivist national identity. Canadian official rhetoric designated me as one of the "visible minority" who, even though I spoke the Canadian languages of English and French, was straining "the absorptive capacity" of Canada. Canadians of color were routinely treated as "not real" Canadians. One example: In 1985 a terrorist bomb, planted in an Air-India jet on Canadian soil, blew up after leaving Montreal, killing 329 passengers, most of whom were Canadians of Indian origin. The prime minister of Canada at the time, Brian Mulroney, phoned the prime minister of India to offer Canada's condolences for India's loss. 12

Those years of race-related harassments in Canada politicized me and deepened my love of the ideals embedded in the American Bill of Rights. I don't forget that the architects of the Constitution and the Bill of Rights were white males and slaveholders. But through their declaration, they provided us with the enthusiasm for human rights, and the initial framework from which other empowerments could be conceived and enfranchised communities expanded. 13

I am a naturalized U.S. citizen and I take my American citizenship very seriously. I am not an economic refugee, nor am I a seeker of political asylum. I am a voluntary immigrant. I became a citizen by choice, not by simple accident of birth. 14

Yet these days, questions such as who is an American and what is American culture are being posed with belligerence, and being answered with violence. Scapegoating of immigrants has once again 15 become the politicians' easy remedy for all that ails the nation. Hate speeches fill auditoriums for demagogues willing to profit from stirring up racial animosity. An April Gallup poll indicated that half of Americans would like to bar almost all legal immigration for the next five years.

The United States, like every sovereign nation, has a right to formulate its immigration policies. But in this decade of continual, large-scale diasporas, it is imperative that we come to some agreement about who "we" are, and what our goals are for the nation, now that our community includes people of many races, ethnicities, languages, and religions. 16

The debate about American culture and American identity has to date been monopolized largely by Eurocentrists and ethnocentrists whose rhetoric has been flamboyantly divisive, pitting a phantom "us" against a demonized "them." 17

All countries view themselves by their ideals. Indians idealize the cultural continuum, the inherent value system of India, and are properly incensed when foreigners see nothing but poverty, intolerance, strife, and injustice. Americans see themselves as the embodiments of liberty, openness, and individualism, even as the world judges them for drugs, crime, violence, bigotry, militarism, and homelessness. I was in Singapore in 1994 when the American teenager Michael Fay was sentenced to caning for having spraypainted some cars. While I saw Fay's actions as those of an individual, and his sentence as too harsh, the overwhelming local sentiment was that vandalism was an "American" crime, and that flogging Fay would deter Singapore youths from becoming "Americanized." 18

Conversely, in 1994, in Tavares, Florida, the Lake County School Board announced its policy (since overturned) requiring middle school teachers to instruct their students that American culture, by which the board meant European-American culture, is inherently "superior to other foreign or historic cultures." The policy's misguided implication was that culture in the United States has not been affected by the American Indian, African-American, Latin-American, and Asian-American segments of the population. The sinister implication was that our national identity is so fragile that it can absorb diverse and immigrant cultures only by recontextualizing them as deficient. 19

Our nation is unique in human history in that the founding idea of "America" was in opposition to the tenet that a nation is a collection of like-looking, like-speaking, like-worshipping people. The primary criterion for nationhood in Europe is homogeneity of culture, race, and religion—which has contributed to blood-soaked balkanization in the former Yugoslavia and the former Soviet Union. 20

America's pioneering European ancestors gave up the easy homogeneity of their native countries for a new version of Utopia. Now, in the 1990s, we have the exciting chance to follow that tradition and assist in the making of a new American culture that differs from both the enforced assimilation of a "melting pot" and the Canadian model of a multicultural "mosaic." 21

The multicultural mosaic implies a contiguity of fixed, self-sufficient, utterly distinct cultures. Multiculturalism, as it has been practiced in the United States in the past 10 years, implies the existence of a central culture, ringed by peripheral cultures. The fallout of official multiculturalism is the establishment of one culture as the norm and the rest as aberrations. At the same time, the multiculturalist emphasis on race- and ethnicity-based group identity leads to a lack of respect for individual differences within each group, and to vilification of those individuals who place the good of the nation above the interests of their particular racial or ethnic communities. 22

We must be alert to the dangers of an "us" vs. "them" mentality. In California, this mentality is manifesting itself as increased violence between minority, ethnic communities. The attack on Korean-American merchants in South Central Los Angeles in the wake of the Rodney King beating trial is only one recent example of the tragic side effects of this mentality. On the national level, the politicization of ethnic identities has encouraged the scapegoating of legal immigrants, who are blamed for economic and social problems brought about by flawed domestic and foreign policies. 23

We need to discourage the retention of cultural memory if the aim of that retention is cultural balkanization. We must think of American culture and nationhood as a constantly reforming, transmogrifying "we." 24

In this age of diasporas, one's biological identity may not be one's only identity. Erosions and accretions come with the act of emigration. The experience of cutting myself off from a biological homeland and settling in an adopted homeland that is not always welcoming to its dark-complexioned citizens has tested me as a person, and made me the writer I am today. 25

I choose to describe myself on my own terms, as an American, rather than as an Asian-American. Why is it that hyphenation is imposed only on nonwhite Americans? Rejecting hyphenation is my refusal to categorize the cultural landscape into a center and its peripheries; it is to demand that the American nation deliver the promises of its dream and its Constitution to all its citizens equally. 26

My rejection of hyphenation has been misrepresented as race treachery by some India-born academics on U.S. campuses who have appointed themselves guardians of the "purity" of ethnic cultures. 27

Many of them, though they reside permanently in the United States and participate in its economy, consistently denounce American ideals and institutions. They direct their rage at me because, by becoming a U.S. citizen and exercising my voting rights, I have invested in the present and not the past; because I have committed myself to help shape the future of my adopted homeland; and because I celebrate racial and cultural mongrelization.

What excites me is that as a nation we have not only the chance to retain those values we treasure from our original cultures but also the chance to acknowledge that the outer forms of those values are likely to change. Among Indian immigrants, I see a great deal of guilt about the inability to hang on to what they commonly term "pure culture." Parents express rage or despair at their U.S.-born children's forgetting of, or indifference to, some aspects of Indian culture. Of those parents I would ask: What is it we have lost if our children are acculturating into the culture in which we are living? Is it so terrible that our children are discovering or are inventing homelands for themselves? 28

Some first-generation Indo-Americans, embittered by racism and by unofficial "glass ceilings," construct a phantom identity, more-Indian-than-Indians-in-India, as a defense against marginalization. I ask: Why don't you get actively involved in fighting discrimination? Make your voice heard. Choose the forum most appropriate for you. If you are a citizen, let your vote count. Reinvest your energy and resources into revitalizing your city's disadvantaged residents and neighborhoods. Know your constitutional rights, and when they are violated, use the agencies of redress the Constitution makes available to you. Expect change, and when it comes, deal with it! 29

As a writer, my literary agenda begins by acknowledging that America has transformed me. It does not end until I show that I (along with the hundreds of thousands of immigrants like me) am minute by minute transforming America. The transformation is a two-way process: It affects both the individual and the national-cultural identity. 30

Others who write stories of migration often talk of arrival at a new place as a loss, the loss of communal memory and the erosion of an original culture. I want to talk of arrival as a gain. 31

THINKING ABOUT THE ESSAY

1. Mukherjee organizes her essay in three major parts. What is the substance of each section and the purpose of this three-part approach?

2. What explicit or implicit reasons does Mukherjee give for writing this essay? Is her purpose to tell a story, to explain, or to argue?
3. This essay appeared in a magazine known for a liberal or progressive editorial policy. Would you characterize the tone of the essay in these terms or does the "liberal" label do a disservice to Mukherjee's thesis? Explain.
4. How does Mukherjee employ comparison and contrast and definition to structure the essay and amplify her ideas?

RESPONDING IN DISCUSSION

1. In groups of three or four, discuss your view of current immigration to the United States and how Mukherjee's essay has reinforced, challenged, or changed your position.
2. Mukherjee alludes to Eurocentrists and ethnocentrists. Discuss with your class the meanings of these words and your attitude toward them.
3. Divide into small groups and discuss one of Mukherjee's key assertions that America transforms immigrants even as immigrants transform America. Provide evidence of this two-way process of transformation to the rest of the class.
4. Mukherjee speaks of the need to "negotiate" culture. Discuss with your class a time when you helped an immigrant to negotiate or feel more at ease with American culture. By contrast, discuss a time when you visited or traveled through a neighborhood composed largely of immigrant groups of which you were not a member. How did the experience affect your sense of security and identity?

RESPONDING IN WRITING

1. Write a 300-word precis or abstract of Mukherjee's essay, capturing as many of her most important ideas as possible.
2. Write a brief essay in response to Mukherjee's observation, "We must be alert to the dangers of an 'us' vs. 'them' mentality." Relate your comments specifically to ethnic and immigrant groups.
3. Interview an immigrant. To prepare for this assignment, develop a list of questions designed to elicit responses such as the need for friends, civic societies, family, community, economic stability, communication, and so forth as a means of easing him or her into the lifestyle and culture of a new country. Based on your interview, write a 750-to-1,000–word profile of your subject.

4. Download from a search engine all information that you can find on Bharati Mukherjee. Using this information and the information provided in her essay, compose a 500-to-1,000–word biographical sketch of the author, highlighting her accomplishments and her importance as a "new" American writer.

Go North, Young Man

Richard Rodriguez

Richard Rodriguez gained national fame during the 1980s with a series of books and articles about the immigrant experiences of biculturalism, education, and language. His best-known book is autobiographical *Hunger of Memory: The Education of Richard Rodriguez* published in 1982. Gainsaying the party line of many Americans of Latino descent, he does not endorse bilingual education or affirmative action. In personal interviews he has called himself a citizen of the world. This essay was first published in the July–August 1995 issue of *Mother Jones*. Writing in his usual unique literary style on topical issues, Rodriguez attempts to demonstrate that the new immigrants have not only altered policy, politics, and society in America, but have changed the entire worldview of what constitutes the so-called West as America was conceived during the 19th century when an earlier generation of immigrants came here.

PREVIEWING THE ESSAY

Quick! Where did you get your notion about the part of the country where you live? If you live in a western state, why is it considered western? If you live in the New York area, why are you considered to be from the East? After all, if you live in Florida, you might consider Washington, D.C., to be "up north" while if you live in Boston you might consider it south. We may take for granted the way we define ourselves, but what historical, social, and political forces determined our views, and to what degree do such identifications control the way we perceive our world?

Traditionally, America has been an east–west country. We have read our history, right to left across the page. We were oblivious of Canada. We barely noticed Mexico, except when Mexico got in the way of our westward migration, which we interpreted as the will of God, "manifest destiny." 1

In a Protestant country that believed in rebirth (the Easter promise), land became our metaphor for possibility. As long as there 2 was land ahead of us—Ohio, Illinois, Nebraska—we could believe in change; we could abandon our in-laws, leave disappointments behind, to start anew further west. California symbolized ultimate possibility, future-time, the end of the line, where loonies and prophets lived, where America's fads necessarily began.

Nineteenth century real estate developers and 20th-century Hollywood moguls may have advertised the futuristic myth of California to the rest of America. But the myth was one Americans were predisposed to believe. The idea of California was invented by Americans many miles away. Only a few early voices from California ever warned against optimism. Two decades after California became American territory, the conservationist John Muir stood at the edge of California and realized that America is a finite idea: We need to preserve the land, if the dream of America is to survive. Word of Muir's discovery slowly traveled backward in time, from the barely populated West (the future) to the crowded brick cities of the East Coast (the past). 3

I grew up in California of the 1950s, when the state was filling with people from New York and Oklahoma. Everyone was busy losing weight and changing hair color and becoming someone new. There was, then, still plenty of cheap land for tract houses, under the cloudless sky. 4

The 1950s, the 1960s—those years were our golden age. Edmund G. "Pat" Brown was governor of optimism. He created the University of California system, a decade before the children of the suburbs rebelled, portraying themselves as the "counterculture." Brown constructed freeways that permitted Californians to move farther and farther away from anything resembling an urban center. He even made the water run up the side of a mountain. 5

By the 1970s, optimism was running out of space. Los Angeles needed to reinvent itself as Orange County. Then Orange County got too crowded and had to reinvent itself as North County San Diego. Then Californians started moving into the foothills or out to the desert, complaining all the while of the traffic and of the soiled air. And the immigrants! 6

Suddenly, foreign immigrants were everywhere—Iranians were buying into Beverly Hills; the Vietnamese were moving into San Jose; the Chinese were taking all the spaces in the biochemistry courses at UCLA. And Mexicans, poor Mexicans, were making hotel beds, picking peaches in the Central Valley, changing diapers, even impersonating Italian chefs at Santa Monica restaurants. 7

The Mexicans and the Chinese had long inhabited California. But they never resided within the golden myth of the state. Nineteenth-century California restricted the Chinese to Chinatowns or to a city's outskirts. Mexicans were neither here nor there. They 8 were imported by California to perform cheap labor, then deported in bad economic times.

The East Coast had incorporated Ellis Island in its myth. The West Coast regarded the non-European immigrant as doubly foreign. Though Spaniards may have colonized the place and though Mexico briefly claimed it, California took its meaning from "internal immigrants" —Americans from Minnesota or Brooklyn who came West to remake their parents' version of America. 9

But sometime in the 1970s, it became clear to many Californians that the famous blond myth of the state was in jeopardy. ("We are sorry to intrude, senor, we are only looking for work.") Was L.A. "becoming" Mexican? 10

Latin Americans arrived, describing California as "el norte." The "West Coast" was a finite idea; *el norte* in the Latin American lexicon means wide-open. Whose compass was right? 11

Meanwhile, with the lifting of anti-Asian immigration restrictions, jumbo jets were arriving at LAX from Bangkok and Seoul. People getting off the planes said about California, "This is where the United States begins." Californians objected, "No, no. California is where the United States comes to an end—we don't have enough room for you." Whose compass was truer? 12

It has taken two more decades for the East Coast to get the point. Magazines and television stories from New York today describe the golden state as "tarnished." The more interesting possibility is that California has become the intersection between comedy and tragedy. Foreign immigrants are replanting optimism on California soil; the native-born know the wisdom of finitude. Each side has a knowledge to give the other. 13

Already, everywhere in California, there is evidence of miscegenation—Keanu Reeves, sushi tacos, blond Buddhists, Salvadoran Pentecostals. But the forces that could lead to marriage also create gridlock on the Santa Monica freeway. The native-born Californian sits disgruntled in traffic going nowhere. The flatbed truck in front of him is filled with Mexicans; in the Mercedes next to him is a Japanese businessman using a car phone. 14

There are signs of backlash. Pete Wilson has become the last east–west governor of California. In a state founded by people seeking a softer winter and famous internationally for being "laid back," Californians vote for Proposition 187, hoping that illegal immigrants will stay away if there are no welfare dollars. 15

But immigrants are most disconcerting to California because they are everywhere working, transforming the ethos of the state from leisure to labor. Los Angeles is becoming a vast working city, on the order of Hong Kong or Mexico City. Chinese kids are raising 16 the admission standards to the University of California. Mexican immigrant kids are undercutting union wages, raising rents in once-black neighborhoods.

Californians used to resist any metaphor drawn from their state's perennial earthquakes and floods and fires. Now Californians take their meaning from natural calamity. People turn away from the sea, imagine the future as existing backward in time. 17

"I'm leaving California, I'm going to Colorado."

"I'm headed for Arizona."

After hitting the coastline like flies against glass, we look in new directions. Did Southern California's urban sprawl invent NAFTA? For the first time, Californians now talk of the North and the South—new points on our national compass. 18

"I've just bought a condo in Baja."

"I'm leaving California for Seattle."

"I'm moving to Vancouver. I want someplace cleaner."

"Go North, young man."

Puerto Ricans, Mexicans: early in this century we were immigrants. Or not immigrants exactly. Puerto Ricans had awakened one day to discover that they suddenly lived on U.S. territory. Mexicans had seen Mexico's northern territory annexed and renamed the southwestern United States.

We were people from the South in an east–west country. We were people of mixed blood in a black and white nation. We were Catholics in a Protestant land. Many millions of us were Indians in an east–west country that imagined the Indian to be dead. 19

Today, Los Angeles is the largest Indian city in the United States, though Hollywood filmmakers persist in making movies about the dead Indian. (For seven bucks, you can see cowboys slaughter Indians in the Kevin Costner movie—and regret it from your comfortable chair.) On any day along Sunset Boulevard you can see Toltecs and Aztecs and Mayans. 20

Puerto Ricans, Mexicans—we are the earliest Latin American immigrants to the United States. We have turned into fools. We argue among ourselves, criticize one another for becoming too much the gringo or maybe not gringo enough. We criticize each other for speaking too much Spanish or not enough Spanish. We demand that politicians provide us with bilingual voting ballots, but we do not trouble to vote. 21

Octavio Paz, the Mexican writer, has observed that the Mexican-American is caught between cultures, thus a victim of history— 22 unwilling to become a Mexican again, unable to belong to the United States. Michael Novak, the United States writer, has observed that what unites people throughout the Americas is that we all have said goodbye to our motherland. To Europe. To Africa. To Asia. Farewell!

The only trouble is: *Adios* was never part of the Mexican-American or Puerto Rican vocabulary. There was no need to turn one's back on the past. Many have traveled back and forth, between rivals, between past and future, commuters between the Third World and First. After a few months in New York or Los Angeles, it would be time to head "home." After a few months back in Mexico or Puerto Rico, it would be time to head "home" to the United States. 23

We were nothing like the famous Ellis Island immigrants who arrived in America with no expectation of return to the "old country." In a nation that believed in the future, we were a puzzle. 24

We were also a scandal to Puerto Rico and Mexico. Our Spanish turned bad. Our values were changing—though no one could say why or how exactly. *Abuelita* (grandmother) complained that we were growing more guarded. Alone. 25

There is a name that Mexico uses for children who have forgotten their true address: *pocho*. The *pocho* is the child who wanders away, ends up in the United States, among the gringos, where he forgets his true home. 26

The Americas began with a confusion about maps and a joke about our father's mistake. Columbus imagined himself in a part of the world where there were Indians. 27

We smile because our 15th-century *papi* thought hc was in India. I'm not certain, however, that even today we know where in the world we live. We are only beginning to look at the map. We are only beginning to wonder what the map of the hemisphere might mean. 28

Latin Americans have long complained that the gringo, with characteristic arrogance, hijacked the word *American* and gave it all to himself—"the way he stole the land." I remember, years ago, my aunt in Mexico City scolding me when I told her I came from "America." *Pocho!* Didn't I realize that the entire hemisphere is America? "Listen," my Mexican aunt told me, "people who live in the United States are *norteamericanos*." 29

Well, I think to myself—my aunt is now dead, God rest her soul—I wonder what she would have thought a couple of years ago when the great leaders—the president of Mexico, the president of the United States, the Canadian prime minister—gathered to sign the North American Free Trade Agreement. Mexico signed a document acknowledging that she is a North American. 30

I predict that Mexico will suffer a nervous breakdown in the next 10 years. She will have to check into the Betty Ford Clinic for a long 31 rest. She will need to determine just what exactly it means that she is, with the dread gringo, a *norteamericana.*

Canada, meanwhile, worries about the impact of the Nashville music channel on its cable TV; Pat Buchanan imagines a vast wall along our southern flank; and Mexican nationalists fear a Clinton bailout of the lowly peso. 32

We all speak of North America. But has anyone ever actually met a North American? Oh, there are Mexicans. And there are Canadians. And there are so-called Americans. But a North American? 33

I know one. 34

Let me tell you about him—this North American. He is a Mixteco Indian who comes from the Mexican state of Oaxaca. He is trilingual. His primary language is the language of his tribe. His second language is Spanish, the language of Cortes. Also, he has a working knowledge of U.S. English, because, for several months of the year, he works near Stockton, Calif. 35

He commutes over thousands of miles of dirt roads and freeways, knows several centuries, two currencies, two sets of hypocrisy. He is a criminal in one country and an embarrassment to the other. He is pursued as an "illegal" by the U.S. border patrol. He is preyed upon by Mexican officers who want to shake him down because he has hidden U.S. dollars in his shoes. 36

In Oaxaca, he lives in a 16th-century village, where his wife watches blond Venezuelan soap operas. A picture of la Virgen de Guadalupe rests over his bed. In Stockton, there is no Virgin Mary, only the other Madonna—the material girl. 37

He is the first North American. 38

A journalist once asked Chou En-lai, the Chinese premier under Mao Zedong, what he thought of the French Revolution. Chou En-lai gave a wonderful Chinese reply: "It's too early to tell." 39

I think it may even be too early to tell what the story of Columbus means. The latest chapter of the Columbus saga may be taking place right now, as Latin American teenagers with Indian faces violate the U.S. border. The Mexican kids standing on the line tonight between Tijuana and San Diego—if you ask them why they are coming to the United States of America, they will not say anything about Thomas Jefferson or The Federalist Papers. They have only heard that there is a job in a Glendale dry cleaner's or that some farmer is hiring near Fresno. 40

They insist: They will be returning to Mexico in a few months. They are only going to the United States for the dollars. They certainly don't intend to become gringos. They don't want anything to do with the United States, except the dollars. 41

But the months will pass, and the teenagers will be changed in the United States. When they go back to their Mexican village, they 42 will no longer be easy. They will expect an independence and an authority that the village cannot give them. Much to their surprise, they will have been Americanized by the job in Glendale.

For work in the United States is our primary source of identity. 43
There is no more telling question we Americans ask one another than "What do you do?" We do not ask about family or village or religion. We ask about work.

The Mexican teenagers will return to Glendale. 44

Mexicans, Puerto Ricans—most of us end up in the United States, liv- 45
ing in the city. Peasants end up in the middle of a vast modern metropolis, having known only the village, with its three blocks of familiar facades.

The arriving generation is always the bravest. New immigrants 46
often change religion with their move to the city. They need to make their peace with isolation, so far from relatives. They learn subway and bus routes that take them far from every day. Long before they can read English, they learn how to recognize danger and opportunity. Their lives are defined by change.

Their children or their grandchildren become, often, very differ- 47
ent. The best and the brightest, perhaps, will go off to college—become the first in their family—but they talk about "keeping" their culture. They start speaking Spanish, as a way of not changing; they eat in the cafeteria only with others who look like themselves. They talk incessantly about "culture" as though it were some little thing that can be preserved and kept in a box.

The unluckiest children of immigrants drop out of high school. 48
They speak neither good English nor Spanish. Some end up in gangs—family, man—"blood." They shoot other kids who look exactly like themselves. If they try to leave their gang, the gang will come after them for their act of betrayal. If they venture to some other part of the city, they might get shot or they might merely be unable to decipher the freeway exits that speed by.

They retreat to their "turf"—three blocks, just like in their grand- 49
mother's village, where the journey began.

One of the things that Mexico had never acknowledged about my 50
father—I insist that you at least entertain this idea—is the possibility that my father and others like him were the great revolutionaries of Mexico. *Pocho* pioneers. They, not Pancho Villa, not Zapata, were heralds of the modern age in Mexico. They left for the United States and then they came back to Mexico. And they changed Mexico forever.

A childhood friend of my father's—he worked in Chicago in the 51
1920s, then returned one night to his village in Michoacan with appliances for *mamasita* and crisp dollars. The village gathered round

him—this is a true story—and asked, "What is it like up there in Chicago?"

The man said, "It's OK." 52

That rumor of "OK" spread across Michoacan, down to Jalisco, all the way down to Oaxaca, from village to village to village. 53

Futurists and diplomats talk about a "new moment in the Americas." The Latin American elite have condos in Miami and send their children to Ivy League schools. U.S. and Canadian businessmen project the future on a north–south graph. But for many decades before any of this, Latin American peasants have been traveling back and forth, north and south. 54

Today, there are remote villages in Latin America that are among the most international places on earth. Tiny Peruvian villages know when farmers are picking pears in the Yakima valley in Washington state. 55

I am the son of a prophet. I am a fool. I am a victim of history. I am confused. I do not know whether I am coming or going. I speak bad Spanish. And yet I tell Latin America this: Because I grew up Hispanic in California, I know more Guatemalans then I would if I had grown up in Mexico, more Brazilians than if I lived in Peru. Because I live in California, it is routine for me to know Nicaraguans and Salvadorans and Cubans. As routine as knowing Chinese or Vietnamese. 56

My fellow Californians complain loudly about the uncouth southern invasion. I say this to California: Immigration is always illegal. It is a rude act, the leaving of home. Immigration begins as a violation of custom, a youthful act of defiance, an insult to the village. I know a man from El Salvador who has not spoken to his father since the day he left his father's village. Immigrants horrify the grandmothers they leave behind. 57

Illegal immigrants trouble U.S. environmentalists and Mexican nationalists. Illegal immigrants must trouble anyone, on either side of the line, who imagines that the poor are under control. 58

But they have also been our civilization's prophets. They, long before the rest of us, saw the hemisphere whole. 59

THINKING ABOUT THE ESSAY

1. How did your family develop roots in the community in which you live? To what degree did economic, social, and geographic factors influence the movement of your family to a certain place?
2. Rodriguez suggests that "myth" has a great deal to do with immigration trends. What are the myths he exposes, and how did they influence the people who acted upon them?

3. What image of the immigrant does the author project? Opportunist? Hero? Victim? Manipulator? Knowledgeable person? Ignorant person? Or is he or she a combination of these? Explain by citing specific references in the text.
4. What is the main thesis of the essay? Where is it most clearly expressed?
5. Based upon your analysis of the tone of the essay, what emotion best sums up the author's attitude toward the "new immigrants" specifically and all immigrants in general?

RESPONDING IN DISCUSSION

1. Divide the class into small groups. On paper, draw a "psychological map" of your "universe." For example, you may wish to include figures that indicate your home, your room, your college, your state, your route to school, your place of employment, and so forth. Discuss how your "world" differs from those of other members in your class. Share with your class the degree to which you define yourself according to the map you've created.
2. Discuss with your class how your identification with your family, culture, language, religion, and age group helps to determine "where you're from." Discuss how this identification serves to exclude others from your daily life.
3. Discuss the degree to which immigrants have contributed to the style of life that Pico Iyer refers to as "global culture" in his essay "The Strange and Exciting Fruits of Global Culture."
4. Discuss to what degree the author's unique style and voice make his argument appear more seductive. Select specific sentences in the essay that demonstrate the author's unique voice and ability to use language in original and interesting ways. Discuss whether these same sentences appeal to you as a reader and, depending on your response, why or why not.

RESPONDING IN WRITING

1. Assuming the role of a young person seeking work in the United States, write a 400-to-500–word letter to your family, explaining why you chose to leave, what your goals are, and what your current experience is in the destination of your choice.
2. Write an essay of 750-to-1,000–words comparing and contrasting the experience of Latinos as described in Aguilar's "Boom or Bust?" with those in Rodriguez's essay.

3. Argue for or against the proposition that the migratory patterns and practices of the immigrants as described by Rodriguez ultimately doom conservative and nationalistic individuals' and groups' desire to keep "America for Americans."
4. For a research project, study the concept of "paradigm" in a reference book and then write an expository essay explaining how the new immigrants are changing the paradigm of what is considered to be a North American.
5. Determine a date and time for an on-line computer chat with four to five members of your class. Adopt a temporary screen name that suggests a person of a particular immigrant group, and role-play that person during your chat time. Report on your experience with your classmates in a brief essay.

Making Americans: Immigration and Tolerance

William J. Bennett

A leader in the American Conservative movement, William J. Bennett served in the Reagan and Bush administrations as director of the National Endowment for the Arts, Secretary of Education, and "drug czar." His most famous publication, *The Book of Virtues,* was a best-seller for many months. While many hard-line conservatives demand an end to all immigration, Bennett is not one of them. Instead, he calls for a policy that would create a method whereby immigrants would be acculturated into American values and society, so that they could more readily contribute to it. Bennett has been criticized by some of his fellow conservatives regarding this position. This essay originally appeared in the February 1995 issue of *Current.* You may be the judge as to whether it is true, as the author claims, that his ideas are in keeping with the conservative values of America.

PREVIEWING THE ESSAY

When you encounter an individual who is most likely an immigrant with a low economic status (signs may include his or her manner of dress, accent, physical features, skin color, and body language different from your friends), what is your immediate reaction? Hostility? Curiosity? Suspicion? Caution? Explain. If you yourself are a recent immigrant, how do you respond to a native-born citizen who gives you the "once over"? Anger? Frustration? Humor? Where do these responses originate? From stereotypes? What you've been taught? Or is it solely a matter of feeling uncomfortable with difference?

Proposition 187, California's ballot initiative which deprives illegal aliens of such publicly funded services as education and health care, won an overwhelming victory last month. A handful of states have expressed interest in putting similar measures on the ballot. Legislation may be introduced in the 104th Congress that would reduce legal immigrant quotas by as much as 50 percent. And some prominent conservatives are now arguing for a moratorium on legal immigration. 1

Just a few years ago, immigration issues went virtually unmentioned; soon they will be near the top of the national political agenda. For the first time in decades, the GOP will decide immigration policy—and at a time when Republicans are engaged in a vigorous debate about what direction to go. The new majority party now has an opportunity to craft legislation that is responsible, effective and consonant with the best aspects of the American character. 2

The most contentious part of the entire immigration debate is illegal immigration. When Jack Kemp and I came out in opposition to Proposition 187, we knew we were going against strong and deep political currents. But I believed then and I believe now that the proposition is meretricious, shortsighted (i.e., throwing 300,000 children out of school and onto the streets) and employs means that are profoundly anti-conservative and pernicious (to wit: charging private citizens with the duty of identifying people they "suspect" to be illegal and requiring them to turn the names over to state and federal authorities). It is worth noting that there are already reports from California that Proposition 187 is creating fear among legal immigrants and massive confusion in courts and schools, and among doctors, police officers and social service providers. 3

Illegal immigration is a very serious problem, and all Americans, especially Californians, are right to be upset and angry. Every sovereign nation has the right and the duty to control its borders. We need to put into place policies that will curb illegal immigration and assist the states in their efforts to do the same. These measures should include beefing up border patrols and deploying them more intelligently; expediting the deportation process, particularly for illegal immigrants convicted of a crime; cracking down on fraudulent immigration documents; overhauling the Immigration and Naturalization Service; changing some of the requirements for immigration sponsorship; and reducing the number of employment eligibility documents. A number of these proposals have been recommended by the House Republican Task Force on Illegal Immigration and the new Republican majority will, I hope, act on them. 4

There is also this obvious but often overlooked point to be made. Politicians need to legislate with an eye toward predictable consequences. As Proposition 187 demonstrates, this is no small matter. One of the reasons California has a much more serious illegal immi- 5 gration problem than border states such as Arizona and Texas is that in the 1980s some California politicians supported policies that induced illegal immigration into their state.

In 1985, for example, one of the people who pushed hardest to include a "guest worker" provision in the immigration reform bill (which enjoyed strong support from California agricultural interests) was then-Sen. Pete Wilson. He eventually supported a scaled-back version of his original amendment, which allowed 350,000 "guest workers" into the country temporarily so that crops could be harvested at cheap rates. In 1986 Sen. Wilson, along with others, held up passage of the Immigration Reform and Control Act until that provision was added. The legislative compromise that resulted and which Wilson supported legalized more than 1 million illegal immigrants. Having put in place a job magnet and having essentially laid out a welcome mat for illegal immigrants in the 1980s, Gov. Wilson should not be surprised that he now has an illegal immigration problem. 6

But the larger and more important issue before Congress and the country is legal immigration. While there are some minor reforms worth examining, my views on legal immigration are guided by an explicit underlying conviction: Legal immigrants are a net plus for America and hence current policy is essentially viable. In this, the distinction between legal and illegal is fundamental. And making this distinction is critical to policy. 7

Studies show that legal immigrants are often self-selected on the basis of industry, hard-work, self-reliance and a respect for time-honored American principles. They hold strong family values and deeply rooted religious faith. And immigrants are making important contributions to America in the fields of science, engineering, biotechnology, computer hardware and software, to mention just a few. 8

EMPIRICAL EVIDENCE

The Manhattan Institute and the Urban Institute have provided important empirical evidence about immigration. In 1993, the United States admitted just over 900,000 legal immigrants. While recent decades have seen large numbers of immigrants arrive in this country, their numbers are half what they were during the last wave of immigration. Eight percent of our population is foreign-born, compared with double that figure at the turn of the century. Contrary to popular opinion, immigration does not cause higher unemployment rates for U.S. workers (in part because of the jobs immigrants create with new businesses they start). Except for refugees, immigrants who arrived in the past decade receive welfare payments at lower rates than native-born Americans. They are a huge net contributor to Social Security, 9 and annual taxes paid by immigrants more than offset their costs to society, generating a net annual surplus of $25 billion to $30 billion.

In one of the most comprehensive studies ever done on the link 10
between crime and legal immigration, economists Kristin Butcher and Anne Morrison Piehl find "no evidence that immigrants are more likely to engage in criminal activity than natives. In the individual data, in fact, whether or not one controls for other demographic characteristics, immigrants are significantly less likely to commit crime. . . . [We] find no evidence that areas with high levels of immigration have experienced disproportionate growth in criminal activity over the last decade."

Historians have noted that during the 19th century there were 11
real questions about whether the Irish, Italians, Chinese and Polish immigrants were capable of being assimilated. The Irish were despised "for their ignorance, poverty and superstition." German immigrants were considered an affront to American culture, in part because they wanted to preserve their traditions and language. In the early part of this century, Jewish immigrants were among the least skilled of all immigrant groups that arrived.

There are two important historical facts to keep in mind. The first 12
is that during times of economic uncertainty and social despair, immigrants are always among the first (and easiest) targets of public antipathy. The second is that virtually every group that has come to America's shores has been spurned upon its arrival, and anti-immigration sentiments have run through public opinion polls for as long as we have had reliable information. Yet these groups have not only assimilated, they have become welcome and valuable members of American society. (Recent public opinion surveys show that the once-despised Irish now consistently rate as the nationality which most benefits this nation.)

CULTURAL ARENA

The immigration issue evokes the strongest passions in the cultural, 13
and not the economic, arena. Indeed, immigration cannot be fully understood outside a larger cultural context. There is an alarming reluctance in our schools and universities to affirm, advance and transmit our common American culture. And while it has profound implications for immigration, I believe contemporary American society's most serious problems are more fundamental than, and different from, immigration. Our problem does not have to do with legal immigration but with assimilation—and assimilation not just for people born in foreign lands but for the people born in this nation.

Cultural anthropologist David Murray has referred to new-born children as the "ultimate undocumented aliens." By that he means that children are not born with any culture or society; they must be helped to become citizens every bit as urgently as, say, refugees from Southeast Asia. If we fail the American-born children, they will be the aliens who overwhelm us. And this is precisely what we are seeing happen today. 14

Because of American diffidence and neglect, many children are not being acculturated and socialized. The repayment for that neglect is now being played out on our urban streets, in hospital emergency rooms, in our courts and our classrooms. In too many places, republican virtues are not being inculcated. 15

The advocates for ending immigration argue that immigrants pose a cultural threat to America and that our society is no longer capable of assimilating them. But pinning the blame on immigrants for America's social decay is a dodge and a distraction. And it happens to be exactly wrong. One can make a strong argument that many new immigrants have been corrupted by those same degraded aspects of American culture that trouble so many American parents. 16

It's time we get on with the real work that needs to be done: Revivify our character-forming institutions and put an end to misguided government-sponsored politics that foster social fragmentation, resegregation and racial tension. The argument for dismantling the current welfare state and stopping its corrupting dependency has received an extensive public hearing. But there are three other areas that bear on this issue. 17

- *Bilingualism:* Mastery of English is a key to individual opportunity in America. Teaching English to those whose native language is not English is a continuation of the struggle to provide for all Americans the opportunity to participate fully in our political, economic and social life. Having a common language is an essential condition of a unified nation. We should not be bashful about proclaiming fluency in this language as a critical education goal, and we should not be timid in reforming our policies so as to secure it. 18
- *Multiculturalism:* One of the arguments that the anti-immigration advocates rely on is that immigrants promote ethnic separatism and their foreign culture will contaminate our culture. In fact, radical multiculturalism has its origins in America and finds its intellectual home in America's elite universities. Francis Fukuyama has pointed out that "the ideological assault on traditional family values . . . was not the creation of recently arrived Chicano agricultural workers or Haitian boat people, much less of Chinese or Korean immigrants." Rather, he says, it "originated right in the heart of America's well-established white, Anglo Saxon community." 19

- *Counting by Race:* Quotas, race norming, racial gerrymandering and set-asides undercut the rounding American principle of equality under the law. These policies judge individuals on the color of their skin, not on the "content of their character," and they have the effect of prying Americans apart. We need to reestablish a principle that many of us thought we settled three decades ago: the moral case for putting a *de jure* end to racial discrimination and preferences. A good place to advance the cause is in California, where right now a group is undertaking an effort to place a civil rights initiative on the primary election ballot in 1996. Called the California Civil Rights Initiative, it is a constitutional amendment prohibiting the state and its "subdivisions" (colleges, agencies, or local governments) from "us[ing] race, color, ethnicity, national origin, sex or religion as a criterion for either discriminating against, or granting preferential treatment to, any individual group in the operation of the state's system of public employment, public education or public contracting." 20

"The first step in liquidating a people is to erase its memory," the historian Milan Hubl says in Milan Kundera's *The Book of Laughter and Forgetting*. "Destroy its books, its culture, its history. Then have somebody write new books, manufacture a new culture, invent a new history. Before long the nation will begin to forget what it is and what it was." 21

Our collective cultural task is to remember what we were and what we still are. If we once again get that right, then immigrants will fit in and flourish, as they always have. If we keep getting it wrong, then it won't really matter where the people come from. For whatever their place of origin, they will be citizens without a culture, and they will bear children without a future. 22

THINKING ABOUT THE ESSAY

1. Did you respond favorably or negatively to the first paragraph of the essay (which discusses the nature and result of Proposition 187) before reading the entire piece? Did Bennett's arguments change your views after reading through the essay? Explain.
2. Have immigration laws affected you either directly or indirectly? If so, which laws? Remember that policies may affect an individual in subtle ways so you may have to dig deeply into your experience to answer the question.
3. Is the author more concerned about legal immigration or illegal immigration? Why?

4. Where in the essay does the author place the blame for America's failure to harness the benefits of legal immigrants? What, precisely, is his argument concerning the origins of this failure?
5. The author cites another writer who comments that in America there is an "ideological assault on traditional family values." Where, if at all, does the author discuss who is making this assault and what is the nature of this assault? How does the answer to this question help to strengthen or weaken Bennett's argument?

RESPONDING IN DISCUSSION

1. Divide into five roughly equal groups, and discuss your view of Proposition 187. Share your conclusions with the rest of the class.
2. Reread Jordan's essay "The Street Where I Live" and compare her implicit view of "collective culture" with Bennett's.
3. Bennett's approval of legal immigration hinges on the idea that this policy contributes positively to American society. Discuss the beliefs suggesting that legal immigration is harmful to American society.
4. Discuss an event in your life that made you confront your own conception about immigration in general or a particular immigrant.

RESPONDING IN WRITING

1. Write a descriptive portrait of 400-to-500 words of a recent immigrant with whom you are acquainted. Include his or her attitudes, values, outlook, habits, and customs.
2. Write a "cookbook-style" expository essay of 500-to-600 words, explaining how an immigrant can become a full-fledged American. Your tone may be serious or humorous.
3. Argue for or against the proposition that the chief reason immigrants come to America is to earn money, and that they become socialized only to the extent that it will help them in this pursuit.
4. Argue for or against the proposition that the America Bennett holds as being the ideal one is a romantic, outdated notion. Use any of the articles in Chapter 1 ("Generations at the Crossroads") or other parts of this textbook to advance your view.
5. When asked publicly, people often hesitate to share their true feelings about immigrants. Have your class form an on-line chat group, select a time and date to discuss the issue, and, using "screen names," anonymously discuss your views on immigration. Report on your on-line chat in an essay of 500-to-750 words.

What to Do about Immigration

Linda Chavez

Linda Chavez is the author of *Out of the Barrio* (Basic Books, 1991) and a member of the Center for Equal Opportunity (a Washington, D.C., think tank). Here she does a macro-analysis of the immigration issue, gainsaying the easy slogans and superficial observations to which many Americans—both typical citizens and so-called experts—subscribe. Her quantitative and qualitative analysis tries to distinguish between constructive and destructive policies with the goal that America will arrive at a commonsense approach to the question. "What to Do about Immigration" first appeared in the March 1995 issue of *Commentary*.

PREVIEWING THE ESSAY

Exactly what facts do you actually know about immigration? For example, how many illegal and legal immigrants live in America today? How many enter each year? How much money does our government spend on entitlements for them? Do they contribute more to the economy than they take from it? Do they have a higher incidence of crime than native-born Americans? If you are not familiar with the hard facts, is it fair to draw a conclusion about the subject?

Despite overwhelming opposition from the media, from leaders of the religious and civil-rights communities, from the education establishment, and even from prominent conservatives like Jack Kemp and William J. Bennett, California voters last fall enthusiastically adopted Proposition 187, which bars illegal aliens from receiving welfare, education, or health benefits except for emergency medical treatment. 1

The anger toward illegal immigrants had grown steadily among Californians in recent years, fueled both by the huge number of illegal aliens living in the state—nearly two million, or about half of the country's entire illegal population—and by the state's lingering economic recession. And the resentment had deepened as the apparent costs of providing benefits to illegal aliens rose; for the fiscal year 1994–95, that figure is estimated to stand at $2.35 billion. California, moreover, had gone far beyond what was required by federal law in granting benefits to illegal aliens, including in-state tuition in the Cal-State University system and free prenatal care. 2

As if all this were not tinder enough, in mid-October 70,000 mostly Latin demonstrators marched through downtown Los Angeles waving Mexican and Guatemalan flags and shouting *"Viva la Raza."* 3

Tracking polls, which had shown Proposition 187 ahead by only 5 points just prior to the demonstration, registered a fourfold jump in the three days immediately following.

Proposition 187's success has inspired activists in several other states to consider similar measures, but their plans may be derailed if the law is declared unconstitutional. (A federal court has enjoined California from enforcing Proposition 187, pending the outcome of a suit.) Nonetheless, the proposal's popularity has launched a long-overdue national debate on immigration—legal as well as illegal. 4

Like so much American social policy, immigration policy is a monument to the law of unintended consequences. Although assurances to the contrary were offered by the legislators responsible for the last major overhaul of the nation's immigration law, the 1965 Immigration and Nationality Act, that law profoundly altered both the makeup and the size of the immigrant flow. Until 1965, most immigrants came from Europe; today, some 80 percent of those legally admitted are from Asia or Latin America. The new law also significantly increased the pool of eligible applicants by giving preference to family members of immigrants already here. 5

But these changes might not have had such striking effects had they not coincided with dramatic developments in civil-rights law and with the expansion of the welfare state. As it is, immigration now intersects with two of the most troubling issues of our time: race and entitlements. 6

In 1993 (the last year for which figures are available), over 800,000 legal immigrants were admitted to the United States and an estimated 300,000 illegal aliens settled here, more or less permanently. Over the last decade, as many as ten million legal and illegal immigrants established permanent residence—a number higher than at any period in our history, including the peak immigration decade of 1900–10. 7

To be sure, these numbers are somewhat misleading: because our population is so much larger now than it was at the beginning of the century, the rate of immigration is much lower, barely one-third of what it was then. And while the proportion of persons living in the U.S. who are foreign-born is high by recent standards—about 8 percent in the last census—it is still lower than it was for every decade between 1850 and 1950. 8

The numbers alone, however, do not fully describe the dimensions of the immigration issue. Americans are not just concerned about the size of the immigrant population; they are worried about the kind of people who are coming, how they got here, and whether they are likely to become a benefit or a burden to our society. There is deep suspicion that today's immigrants are fundamentally different from earlier waves. In recent polls, 59 percent of Americans say that 9 immigration was good for the country in the past, but only 29 percent think it is a good thing now. Former Colorado Governor Richard Lamm, who favors restricting immigration, summed up this national ambivalence: "I know that earlier large waves of immigrants didn't 'overturn' America, but there are . . . reasons to believe that today's migration is different from earlier flows."

Immigration enthusiasts (among whom I count myself, albeit 10
with some important reservations) like to point out that Americans have never been eager to accept new arrivals, for all our rhetoric about being an "immigrant nation." As Rita Simon of the American University law school noted recently, "We view immigrants with rose-colored glasses, turned backward." Perhaps, then, there is nothing much new in the worries so many people express about whether this generation of immigrants will indeed assimilate to American norms. But comforting as the thought may be that today's Mexicans, Vietnamese, Pakistanis, and Filipinos are the equivalent of yesterday's Italians, Jews, Poles, and Irish, it fails to take into account the tremendous transformation America itself has undergone in the last half-century.

The America to which Europeans immigrated—first northern Eu- 11
ropeans in the 19th century and then southern and eastern Europeans in the first quarter of the 20th—was a self-confident, culturally homogeneous nation. There was never any question that immigrants would be expected to learn English and to conform to the laws, customs, and traditions of their new country (although even then, some immigration restrictionists questioned whether certain groups were capable of such conformity). And immigrants themselves—especially their children—eagerly wanted to adapt. Public schools taught newcomers not only a new language, but new dress, manners, history, myths, and even hygiene to transform them into Americans who sounded, looked, acted, thought, and smelled the part.

In those days there were no advocates insisting that America 12
must accommodate itself to the immigrants; the burden of change rested solely with the new arrivals. To be sure, by their sheer numbers they managed subtly to alter certain features of their new country. Because of them, the U.S. is less Protestant than it would otherwise have been; no doubt American cuisine and art are richer; and the pantheon of American heroes from Christopher Columbus to Joe DiMaggio to Albert Einstein is more diverse. Still, until fairly recently, Americans—native-stock or of later lineage—understood what it meant to be American, and it meant roughly the same thing regardless of where one's ancestors came from.

We are from less sure what it means to be American today. Thus 13
the question, "What to do about immigration?" is inextricably wound up with how we define our national identity.

Some critics of immigration—most notably John O'Sullivan, the editor of *National Review,* and Peter Brimelow, author of the forthcoming *Alien Nation*—believe that national identity must be defined in explicitly racial and ethnic terms and that the current high levels of nonwhite immigration will drastically alter that identity. O'Sullivan argues: 14

> A nation is an ethno-cultural unit—a body that begins its life as a cultural in-gathering but, by dint of common history, habits, tastes, shared experiences, tales, songs, memories, and, above all, intermarriage, becomes progressively more like an extended family—that is, more ethnic—over time.

As long as America's core remained overwhelmingly WASP, so this argument goes, it was possible for Italian Catholics or Russian Jews or Japanese Buddhists to become American. Both O'Sullivan and Brimelow fear, however, that the large numbers of nonwhites who are now coming in will undermine the assimilative capacity of the nation; they both cite Census Bureau projections that the majority of the U.S. population will become nonwhite (or more accurately, non-Hispanic white) by the year 2050; and they both blame current immigration policy for this portentous outcome. 15

But is race or ethnicity really the issue? If so, O'Sullivan and Brimelow can relax. Yes, the majority of immigrants admitted to the U.S. in the last twenty years have been relatively dark-skinned Mexicans, Filipinos, Vietnamese, Chinese, Koreans, etc. Yet by the year 2050, their great grandchildren are unlikely to look much like them. Intermarriage rates in the U.S. have never been higher; nor have mixed-race births. The Population Reference Bureau (PRB) recently touted this development in its monthly newsletter in a front-page article, "Interracial Baby Boomlet in Progress?" Births to mixed Japanese/white couples now exceed those to all-Japanese couples. There are now so many ethnically-mixed persons in the U.S. that the Census Bureau is debating whether to create a special classification for them. (Perhaps it should consider calling the category "American.") Not even groups with strong traditions or religious prohibitions against intermarriage seem exempt from the trend. About half of all American Jews, for example, marry non-Jews. 16

Nor is the inclination to intermarry diminishing among more recent immigrant groups. One-third of young, U.S.-born Hispanics marry non-Hispanics; and perhaps more significantly, nearly half of all Hispanics consider themselves white. Peter Brimelow dismisses this phenomenon, noting that those of Mexican origin, who make up nearly two-thirds of the entire group, are predominantly Indian. But he misses the point. By defining themselves as white, Hispanics are identifying with the majority. In a recent survey, a majority of 17

Hispanics said the group with which they felt they had most in common was whites, and so did Asians.

In short, the problem of national identity is not primarily connected with heredity or ethnicity. It is, rather, a function of culture. But on this score, the evidence is decidedly less reassuring. 18

From the White House to Madison Avenue to Main Street, the idea has taken hold that the United States is a multicultural society. Many doubt that such a thing as American culture even exists. When I recently told a university audience that American blacks, Hispanics, Asians, and whites have more in common with one another than they do with their contemporaries in any of their ancestral homelands, the students literally gasped in disbelief. "I don't know what you mean by 'American culture,'" one young Puerto Rican woman told me. "I have a right to my own culture and language." She said this, however, in perfect English, leaving me wondering just what culture and language she might be referring to. 19

But if the irony of her situation escaped this particular student—whose coloring and features suggested predominantly Spanish ancestry—her political statement was clear. A European-looking, English-speaking Hispanic who chooses to reject American culture, she represents the flip side of the large number of brown-skinned Hispanics who see themselves as white. It is hard to know how many such persons there are, but their numbers are surely growing as ethnicity becomes increasingly politicized. 20

Into this confusing mix come immigrants who, unlike these ersatz ethnics, truly are culturally different from those around them. And such are the misgivings of the rest of us that we no longer seem able or willing to help these newcomers become Americans. Public schools, which worked to acculturate previous immigrant groups, now see it as their mission to preserve immigrant languages and culture. The Los Angeles school system, which educates more Latino immigrant children than any in the nation, prides itself on teaching these youngsters primarily in Spanish for three years or more. Denver public-school officials recently ordered one local high school to stop teaching 450 Hispanic youngsters in English, and transferred out 51 Asian students so that the school could concentrate on its Spanish bilingual program. The demand for Spanish-speaking teachers is so great that districts from Los Angeles to Chicago have begun importing instructors from Mexico, Spain, and Puerto Rico; in 1993, Mexico signed an agreement with California, to provide both teachers and 40,000 textbooks for the state's Spanish-language classrooms. 21

Yet bilingual education did not originally grow out of the pressures of immigration. It started as a small, federally funded program to help Mexican-American children (largely native-born) in the Southwest, and it was already in place years before the large influx of 22

Spanish-speaking immigrants in the 1970s and 80s. Its chief sponsor, former Senator Ralph Yarborough (D-Tex), declared that the purpose of his bilingual-education bill was not "to create pockets of different languages throughout the country . . . but just to try to make [Mexican-American] children fully literate in English." By 1975, however, civil-rights enforcement agencies in Washington were insisting (on the basis of a Supreme Court ruling involving the Civil Rights Act of 1964) that school districts teach "language-minority" youngsters, mostly Mexican-Americans and Puerto Ricans, in Spanish or face a cut-off of all federal funds.

In the early stage of the program, the overwhelming majority of students in bilingual classes were U.S.-born; today, nearly 60 percent still are. What is more, many of these children are more fluent in English than Spanish—no one knows exactly how many, because most states use an arbitrary cut-off score (usually the 30th or 40th percentile) on a standardized English test to place Hispanic youngsters in Spanish-language programs, rather than testing to see whether they are more fluent in English or in Spanish. 23

Bilingual voting ballots, which are now mandated by the federal government, were also an outgrowth not of immigration but of civil-rights legislation—in this case, the 1975 Amendments to the Voting Rights Act of 1965—and they too were aimed at a U.S.-born population: namely, Mexican-Americans living in the Southwest. The main impetus behind the amendments was to give Washington the same power to oversee federal elections in areas where Hispanics lived as the original Act gave it over the Deep South, where egregious efforts were being made to prevent blacks from voting. 24

Since few Spanish-speaking immigrants naturalize and since few can therefore vote, the 1975 amendments have had little effect on them. But thanks to additional amendments adopted in 1982, and a series of court decisions, the Voting Rights Act is now used mainly to create districts which pack in as many Hispanics (or blacks) as feasible in order to assure the election of minority candidates. This practice has received widespread publicity because of the often bizarrely gerrymandered districts that result, but what is less well-known is that immigrants—including illegal aliens—often make up the majority of persons entitled to representation in these new Hispanic districts. 25

So far, at least, the act has not been invoked to create safe districts for Asians, although in principle they qualify under the same "language-minority" designation as Hispanics. The law already requires federal ballots to be printed in Chinese, Vietnamese, and Korean, among other languages; and the huge increase in the Asian immigrant population in California probably means that the courts will before long use their presence to justify the need for safe seats for Asians. Since Asians are too widely dispersed for simple ethnic 26 gerrymandering to suffice, we may expect the courts to order new remedies such as cumulative voting. This technique, which allows voters to cast multiple ballots for a single candidate in a multi-member, at-large race, would, for example, enable Asians comprising only 14 percent of the electorate in a given city to elect one representative on a six-member city council even if no whites voted for the Asian candidate.

The manipulation of both the Bilingual Education Act and the Voting Rights Act points to a central problem of our present immigration policy: the current confluence of ethnic-based entitlements and the large influx of newcomers eligible to receive them creates an ever-growing demand for such programs. 27

One solution, favored by those who want to restrict immigration for other reasons, is to cut off the flow of immigrants. Yet while this might diminish the clientele for ethnic entitlements, the programs would continue to serve the native-born populations for whom they were originally created. For it is not immigrants who clamor for these programs. Asian immigrants, for one, have largely eschewed bilingual education in favor of English-immersion programs. Even some Latino immigrant parents have staged protests in California, New York, and New Jersey upon discovering that their children were being taught in Spanish; others simply withdraw their children, sending them to parochial schools that teach all students in English. 28

The other solution to the problem of ethnic entitlements, of course, would be simply to end them for everyone. There are many good reasons for doing this, even if immigration were to cease altogether. Race- and ethnic-based entitlements have been a bane of American social policy for the last quarter-century. They have divided Americans, increased group hostility, and perverted the whole notion of color-blind justice. Furthermore, they are the foundation on which the entire edifice of multiculturalism is built. Without the enticement of racial and ethnic preferences in education, employment, voting, and elsewhere, group identity, instead of intensifying in recent years, might have diminished. 29

Multicultural education has become the main instrument to help preserve group identity. But multicultural education is no more a byproduct of increased Latin and Asian immigration than are bilingual education and ballots, ethnic voting districts, and affirmative action. In fact, multicultural education first came into being largely to address the demands of blacks for proportional representation in the curriculum—though by now it has spread (some would say, metastasized) to the point where all students are encouraged to think of themselves primarily as members of groups rather than as Americans. 30

Thus, when California recently adopted a new textbook series for kindergarten through eighth grade, ethnic protestors turned out at school-board hearings in San Francisco, Los Angeles, San Diego, Oakland, and other cities, insisting upon changes not only in the treatment of blacks but also in the way the series dealt with Indians, Hispanics, Jews, Muslims, and even conservative Christians. 31

Critics of immigration like O'Sullivan and Brimelow believe that multiculturalism would, in O'Sullivan's words, "be easier to dismantle if immigration were reduced." But the California story suggests that, if anything, it is ethnic diversity itself that might actually hasten the demise of multiculturalism. Like a house of cards that has grown too unwieldy, multicultural education may collapse of its own weight if it is required to include the distinct stories of each of the hundreds of different groups now in the schools. 32

But the unraveling of multicultural education, salutary a prospect as it may be, is hardly a good reason for maintaining our current immigration policy. Clearly, that policy needs changing in ways that are consistent with our national interests and values. I would argue, indeed, that our immigration policy should reinforce our national identity —which is not necessarily the same thing as our racial or ethnic composition. 33

What, then, should we do? Let me deal with legal immigration first. 34

- Change the system to one that favors skills. The basis of the current system is the principle of family reunification, adopted in 1965 with the expectation that this would maintain the ethnic balance of the U.S. population as it existed at the time. Of course things have not worked out that way. But questions of ethnic balance aside, there is nothing sacrosanct about family reunification as a guiding principle of immigration policy, and we should not be deterred from changing it out of fear that such a move might be interpreted as racist. 35

  In any case, the problem with the current immigrant pool is not that there are too many Latinos and Asians per se, but that too many of the people we now admit are low-skilled. Mexicans come with only about seven years of schooling on average, and less than a quarter have obtained high-school diplomas. Such newcomers face a much more difficult period of adjustment and bring fewer benefits to the U.S. economy than would more highly skilled immigrants. 36

  It is true that under current criteria, which include only 140,000 slots for skills-based admissions, immigrants are twice as likely to hold Ph.D.'s as are U.S.-born persons. But they are also more likely to be high-school drop-outs. We ought to admit more 37 of the former and fewer of the latter, and regardless of their country of origin. As it turns out, immigrants from Africa and Asia have among the highest average levels of education. Nearly 90 percent of all African immigrants are high-school graduates—a figure 15 percent higher than that for Canadian immigrants. And Indians, Taiwanese, and Iranians have among the highest proportions of college or graduate degrees.

- Encourage immigrants to assimilate. Immigration policy entails more than laws regulating who gets admitted and under what criteria. It also involves—or at least should involve—how we incorporate immigrants into our society. On that score, we are doing much more poorly now than we did in the past, in part because we have given up on the notion that we have an obligation to assimilate immigrants. Regardless of what other changes we make in immigration policy, we must reverse course on this issue. If immigration to the U.S. ceased tomorrow, we would still have twenty million foreign-born persons living here, plus their children. Assimilation is essential for them, as well as for the rest of us, if we are to stop the further fragmenting of our society. 38

First and foremost, this means encouraging immigrants and their children to learn English, which in practical terms means abolishing bilingual education in favor of English-immersion programs in the public schools. By now we have nearly thirty years of experience demonstrating that bilingual education helps children neither to learn English nor to do better in school. Latino immigrants in particular have been badly served by bilingual education—and by their putative leaders, usually U.S.-born, who are the main lobby behind this expensive, ineffective, and wasteful program. 39

But bilingual education is not the only culprit. With so many services available in their native language, immigrants have fewer incentives today to learn English than they did in the past. Private services—native-language newspapers, advertising, etc.—fall outside the scope of public policy. But government services ought to be provided only in English. A common language has been critical to our success in forging a sense of national identity. Our public policies should preserve and protect that heritage. If the courts continue to obstruct local and state efforts to make English the official language of government, we should pass a federal constitutional amendment to ensure it. 40

- Limit welfare benefits. Although immigrants as a whole are somewhat more likely than natives to receive welfare, the opposite is true of those of working age (15–64). In addition, immigrants have higher labor-force–participation rates than natives, with 41

Hispanic men having among the highest—83.4 percent compared with 75 percent for non-Hispanic whites. If we modify our admission criteria to favor more highly skilled immigrants, welfare among working-age immigrants should drop below even the current rate of about 3 percent, alleviating much of the concern about immigrants and welfare.

The problem is high dependency rates among refugees and elderly immigrants. Among the former, this is a direct result of U.S. policy, which guarantees cash and medical assistance to all persons admitted under the refugee-resettlement program. Having been admitted, they are then attracted to states with relatively high benefits, and this tends to encourage long-term dependency. Thus, in California, some two-thirds of Laotian and Cambodian refugees and more than one-third of Vietnamese refugees remain on welfare after more than five years in the U.S. 42

While dealing comprehensively with this situation entails the much larger issue of welfare reform, it is possible to make a dent in it by redesigning programs to limit the number of months refugees can receive assistance. One of the most promising possibilities would be to turn over responsibility for such assistance to private agencies, such as Catholic Charities, Lutheran Immigration and Refugee Service, and the Council of Jewish Federations, which have proved more successful at moving refugees off welfare. In Chicago, 74 percent of refugees in an experimental private resettlement project found work within six months of arrival, and only 2 percent remained on welfare after thirteen months, compared with more than 40 percent in the state-administered program. 43

The problem of elderly immigrants is more complicated. In 1990, 55 percent of elderly Chinese immigrants in California who had arrived between 1980 and 1987 were on welfare, as were 21 percent of elderly Mexican immigrants. Because they have worked too few years or at insufficient wages to qualify for adequate Social Security benefits, most such recipients obtain Supplemental Security Income (SSI). 44

But many of these immigrants are the parents of resident aliens who brought them here under family-reunification provisions. Anyone who sponsors an immigrant must guarantee that he will not become a public burden, and is required to accept full financial responsibility for up to five years. Simply enforcing these provisions would greatly alleviate the problem of welfare dependency among elderly immigrants. (Among recipients in California that should not pose a problem, since 50 percent of their children's households in 1990 had incomes over $50,000, and 11 percent over $100,000.) We might also consider lengthening the number of years sponsors are required to 45 ovide support to family members; Canada currently requires a ten-year commitment.

All these reforms are addressed to the policies governing legal immigration. What about illegal immigration? 46

Like welfare dependency among immigrants, illegal immigration is not so big a problem as many people imagine (in one recent poll, two-thirds said they thought most immigrants are illegal aliens). Estimates of overall numbers vary widely, with some commentators hysterically claiming more than ten million illegal aliens. But the more reliable Census Bureau estimates about four million, with (as noted earlier) another 300,000 or so added each year. 47

In theory, no amount of illegal immigration is acceptable, since the phenomenon represents our failure to maintain secure borders, a prerequisite of national sovereignty. In practice, however, it is unlikely that we will ever completely eradicate illegal immigration: our borders are too long and porous and our society too free and prosperous. But there are steps we can take that would significantly reduce the current flow. 48

- Stop illegal aliens at the border. There is no mainstream support for mass round-ups and deportations of the type used in the 1930s and 50s to roust illegal aliens; nor could such a program withstand legal challenge. Therefore, the only way to reduce the flow is to contain it at the border. The frontier between Mexico and the U.S. is 2,000 miles long, but only about 250 miles of it are traversable. Most illegal aliens enter in a handful of places near metropolitan areas—about 65 percent around San Diego and El Paso. 49

  We know that it is possible to reduce the flow significantly with more Immigration and Naturalization Service (INS) personnel and better equipment and technology. A recent two-month, $25-million experiment in beefed-up border control near San Diego halved the number of illegal crossings; similar experiments in El Paso produced comparable results. While the most determined may seek alternative routes of entry, for the large majority rough terrain will limit the opportunity. 50
- Deport alien criminals. Apprehending and deporting illegal aliens who have successfully gotten past the border requires more resources and more draconian enforcement measures than most Americans would be willing to endorse; but there is overwhelming support for deporting those arrested for criminal acts in the U.S. In order to do this, however, local law-enforcement officials must be able to ascertain the status of persons in their custody, which they cannot now do easily. A pilot program in Phoenix, which allows police officers 24-hour access to INS records, might 51

prove an effective model for enhancing local police efforts and making more deportations feasible.

- Outlaw sanctuaries. Several cities, including San Francisco, Sacramento, and Chicago, have enacted ordinances banning city employees from contacting the INS if they know someone is in the country illegally. These ordinances are an outrage and show utter disregard for the rule of law. Any city that chooses to obstruct immigration enforcement should lose all federal funds. 52
- Deny welfare benefits to illegal aliens. This is what California voters thought they were enacting with Proposition 187. In fact, in most states illegal aliens are already prohibited from receiving welfare and any but emergency medical treatment, but the authorities lack adequate means to verify the legal status of recipients. Consequently, a pilot program instituted in the early 1980s, the Alien Status Verification Index, should be expanded and upgraded with access to on-line INS data bases so that the status of welfare recipients can be checked. 53

  A potentially more intractable problem is that U.S.-born children of illegal aliens are eligible, as citizens, for AFDC and other welfare benefits. Indeed, one out of four new AFDC recipients in California is a child of illegal-alien parents. The only way to prevent them from receiving benefits is to deny them citizenship in the first place, which would probably require a constitutional amendment. I would not suggest that we travel this route, at least not until we have exhausted all other means of keeping illegal aliens out. But neither should we consider the mere discussion of the issue taboo, as it is in most public-policy circles today. Especially now, when U.S. citizenship entails many more rights and benefits than responsibilities, it should not be beyond the pale to reconsider what entitles a person to obtain it. 54
- Repeal employer sanctions. While we are looking at ways to prevent illegal immigration, we ought to acknowledge that the linchpin of our current policy—punishing the employers of illegal aliens—has been a miserable failure. The Immigration Reform and Control act of 1986, which established such sanctions, did virtually nothing to reduce the flow into the country. If anything, it probably contributed to the problem of welfare dependency among the four million illegal aliens already here, by making it more difficult for them to support themselves. 55

  In typical fashion, those who falsely promised that employer sanctions would fix the illegal-alien problem now think they can tinker with the existing provisions to make it work. Senator Alan Simpson proposes a national identity care; the U.S. Commission on Immigration Reform thinks a national computerized work registry will do the trick. 56

But the purpose of both would be to enable employers to become better policemen for the immigration system, when they should never have been put in that position in the first place. Nor should the rest of us have to put up with more regulations and infringements on our privacy. It is simply wrong to burden the 98.5 percent of persons who are legally in the country with cumbersome and probably ineffective new requirements in order to try to punish the 1.5 percent of persons who have no right to be here. 57

- These recommendations probably will not satisfy the most ardent foes of immigration, like the Federation for American Immigration Reform (FAIR), the most influential restrictionist organization now operating. But many restrictionists are confused or just plain wrong about the nature of the immigration problem. 58

FAIR, for example, focuses almost exclusively on two issues: the size of current immigration, and its economic consequences. But neither of these is the heart of the matter. 59

FAIR's roots are in the population-control and environmentalist movements: this explains its preoccupation with numbers. Its founder, John Tanton, is a past president of Zero Population Growth and chairman of the National Sierra Club Population Committee. FAIR's two most prominent demographer-gurus are Garrett Hardin and Leon Bouvier, both of whom have been actively involved with population-control groups. Their primary concern is that immigrants—no matter where they are from or what their social and economic characteristics—add to the size of the population. (Bouvier has actually said that he believes the ideal U.S. population would be 150 million persons, though he has not clearly spelled out what he would do with the other 100 million of us who are already here.) 60

It is true that immigrants account for about half of current population growth in the U.S. Nonetheless, U.S. population growth as a whole is relatively modest, at 1 percent per year. Even with immigrants, including the more fecund Latins, we are in no danger of a Malthusian population explosion. 61

FAIR's other chief concern, the economic impact of immigration, probably has more resonance in the general debate; but here, too, confusion reigns. For years economists have discussed the consequences of immigration—legal and illegal—without coming to a definitive consensus. On one side are those like Julian Simon of the University of Maryland, who argue that immigration is a big plus for the economy, actually improving the standard of living of the native-born. At the other end of the spectrum are those like Donald Huddle of Rice University, the author of an influential 1993 study for the Carrying Capacity Network, a population-control group in Washington. Huddle estimates that immigrants (legal and illegal) cost more than 62

$42.5 billion a year in net public assistance and displace more than two million American workers, incurring $12 billion a year in additional public-assistance costs for those displaced.

Huddle's figures have been widely disputed, including most recently in a General Accounting Office study. Even George Borjas of the University of California, San Diego, easily the most influential academic critic of current policy, estimates that immigration brings economic benefits to the U.S. in the range of $6 to $20 billion annually —small, but still a net positive gain. More importantly, Borjas acknowledges that these benefits could be increased significantly if we changed our policy to attract more skilled immigrants. 63

No economic model, however, can adequately capture the more subtle benefits that Americans have clearly derived from immigration, and not just from the flows that brought many of our grandparents and great-grandparents here. As Francis Fukuyama* and others have argued, most immigrants still seem to personify the very traits we think of as typically American: optimism, ambition, perseverance —the qualities that have made this country great. The ranks of successful immigrant entrepreneurs are legion; in Silicon Valley alone, recent immigrants have built many of the major technology companies, including Sun Microsystems, AST, and Borland International. 64

Immigrants have also transformed urban America over the last decade, from Korean grocers in New York to Salvadoran busboys and janitors in Washington, Mexican babysitters and construction workers in Los Angeles, Cambodian doughnut-shop owners in Long Beach, Haitian cooks in Miami, Russian taxi drivers in Philadelphia, and Filipino nurses and Indian doctors in public hospitals practically everywhere. As they always have done, immigrants still take the difficult, often dirty, low-paying, thankless jobs that other Americans shun. When they open their own businesses, these are frequently located in blighted, crime-ridden neighborhoods long since abandoned by American enterprise. And their children often outperform those who have been here for generations. This year, as in the last several, more than one-third of the finalists in the Westinghouse high-school science competition bore names like Chen, Yu, Dasgupta, Khazanov, Bunyavanich, and Hattangadi. 65

The contrast between the immigrant poor and the American underclass is especially striking. As the sociologist William Julius Wilson and others have observed, Mexican immigrants in Chicago, despite their relative poverty and much lower levels of education, show few of the dysfunctional characteristics of unemployment, crime, welfare dependency, and drug use common among the city's black and Puerto Rican underclass. In cities like Los Angeles and Washington, where 66

*"Immigrants and Family Values," *Commentary,* May 1993.

American blacks and Latino immigrants inhabit the same poor neighborhoods, the despair of the former seems all the more intense by contrast to the striving of the latter—as if one group had given up on America even as the other was proving the continued existence of opportunity.

For all our anxiety about immigrants, then, in the end it is Americans of all classes who are caught in the middle of a national identity crisis. It is still possible to turn immigrants into what St. John de Crevecoeur called "a new race of men," provided the rest of us still want to do this. But if we, the affluent no less than the poor among us, cease to believe that being an American has any worth or meaning, we should not blame immigrants, most of whom entertain no such doubts. 67

THINKING ABOUT THE ESSAY

1. How many of the facts and figures that Chavez cites were familiar to you? Has the simple task of learning them influenced your view on immigration? Explain.
2. To what degree does the author's seeming knowledge of the subject contribute to her authority? To what degree does it contribute toward your respecting her views?
3. Chavez seems to believe that U.S. policies actually undermine the value that immigrants can contribute to our society. What are some of these policies? What are her solutions?
4. In this detailed analysis of the immigration issue, the author confronts many issues. What is her thesis? Does she make her thesis clear? Where in the essay is her thesis most clearly stated?
5. The author's name suggests that her family has been immigrants. Do you feel her family's non-native heritage may have impacted her beliefs about immigrants? Explain.

RESPONDING IN DISCUSSION

1. Divide your class into groups of four or six. Have two or three students role-play members of FAIR, the group discussed by Chavez as being vehemently anti-immigration. Have two or three remaining members of your group role-play immigration advocates. Conduct a mini-debate within your group, and discuss the outcome with your class.
2. Compare the issue of immigrant assimilation as discussed by Bennett and Chavez. Do they concur on the degree to which immigrants want to assimilate? Discuss by citing relevant passages in both essays.

3. Chavez calls for stopping illegal aliens at the border, yet nearly half arrive via air through our airports. Does this demonstrate a poorly thought out solution? Explain why or why not. Discuss shortcomings in any of her other solutions you discover.
4. Chavez cites another author who advocates turning immigrants into "a new race of men." In the essay, "The Strange and Exciting Fruits of Global Culture," Pico Iyer also suggests the formation of such a group. Discuss how the groups would differ in their basic nature and composition.
5. Discuss what Chavez means by the idea that the "city's black and Puerto Rican underclass" have "given up on America." According to the author, what distinguishes these groups from the new immigrant groups?
6. Visit us-immigration.com and judge the accessibility of information on how to legally immigrate to the United States.

RESPONDING IN WRITING

1. Write a letter to your local congressperson, asking him or her to either support or reject Proposition 187.
2. Argue for or against the proposition that Chavez's idea of allowing more highly educated immigrants into the United States is unfair, discriminatory, and even anti-American.
3. Argue for or against the proposition that the native-born American poor could solve their financial and social dilemmas by simply imitating the behaviors of recent immigrants.
4. For a research project, do a computer search of articles related to one of the reforms that Chavez proposes in her essay (for example, stopping illegal aliens at the border, outlawing sanctuaries, or deporting alien criminals). After you have gathered five or six articles on your subject, write a paper of 1,000-to-1,500 words describing current policies and activities currently underway in the United States to address the reform.

Nationalism and Anti-Immigrant Movements

Ivan Light

Ivan Light is a professor of sociology at the University of California at Los Angeles (UCLA) and the author of *Race, Ethnicity, and Entrepreneurship in Urban America.* He has also co-edited the volume *Immigration and Entrepreneurship.* In the following essay, the author takes the reader on a brief cross-cultural and historical tour of nationalist movements as he explains the social and political climates that give rise to the concept and creation of nationalism. These issues are particularly pertinent today as we witness the potentially egregious effects of nationalism in Africa and the Balkans, while seeing its negative effects on a smaller scale closer to home. What spurs nationalist movements? How do governments manipulate the masses? Why do countries welcome immigration one decade, and seethe against it the next? Is it mere chance or is there method to this madness? Light provides the reader with an insight on the subtle but significant geopolitical issues that contribute toward the subject. With respect to nationalism, he attempts to demonstrate that it is not a particular people or nation that is necessarily the culprit, but the situation that a nation or people finds itself in. In this regard, he provides examples of how even the United States is not immune to its effects. This essay was first published in the January–February 1996 issue of *Society*.

PREVIEWING THE ESSAY

Do you determine your allegiance to your country, do social and political factors manipulate you into adopting this allegiance, or is it a give and take and take between the self and the nation-state? The last time you felt pride in your nation's accomplishments, what was the source of that pride? How did it come to be lodged in your consciousness?

Before we can ask whether the public rhetoric of nationalism has created a renewed emphasis on national character, national phenotypes, and national culture, we must first define nationalism. After all, if nationalism already means fervent phenotypic and cultural loyalty and identification, then this question contains its own answer. If, however, we mean by nationalism the self-interest of the nation-state both as policy and principle, then we have asked a much shrewder question, one that does not resolve itself into tautology. That second question really asks whether the nation-state must be numbered among the causes of popular racism and ethno-religious chauvinism. This question can be answered yes very simply if we propose that prior and spontaneous popular racism and ethno-chauvinism frame the ideology and actions of ultranationalist states, which then feed back to the public the same chauvinism and racism the public required, fanning the flame that created the state in the first place. 1

This case is not very challenging. Much more challenging is to ask whether the mere existence of nation-states in a world of nation-states tends to promote fervent phenotypic and cultural loyalty and identification in publics at home and abroad. If this were so, then the coming into existence of nation-states where none previously existed, as in Eastern Europe and Yugoslavia, would tend of itself to inflame ethnophenotypic awareness and, on the fringe, racism and xenophobia. A case for this proposition might run as follows. When proclaimed as a 2 principle, nationalism is the nation-state's self-interest. The nation-state derives its legitimacy from the nation it serves. Since many historical nations represent an ethno-cultural tradition and a phenotypic stock, the nation-state, on this neo-Hitlerian interpretation, exists to benefit that ethno-culturally and phenotypically defined people. Serbia exists to benefit the Serbs; Russia to benefit the Russians; Germany, the Germans, and so on. Nation-states also use nationalism to promote internal acceptance of their nation-strengthening policies, bombarding the public with ethno-phenotypic awareness in the process. In short, the legitimacy of the nation-state ultimately derives from the service of the nation, and the practical work of statecraft tends continually to arouse and inflame the ethno-phenotypic awareness and even chauvinism of the nation while reactively arousing the same feelings in their nation-state's neighbors, who turn to their own nation-state for protection.

3 If this theory were correct, every nation would ultimately become quite racist and chauvinist, thus fulfilling its essence. Since all states do not, in fact, turn into local versions of Hitler's Germany, which was quite extreme, there must be some flaw in the theory. In the discussion that follows, I propose that this neo-Hitlerian, neo-Hobbesian theory, while not wholly wrong, drastically overstates the actual encouragement that nation-state nationalism affords popular ethnocultural and phenotypic loyalty and identification. In essence, this superficially plausible theory overlooks recurrent instances in which the self-interest of the nation-state requires it to ignore, dampen, or even to suppress popular ethno-chauvinism and racism rather than to intensify them. In these cases, states actively discourage what, according to the neo-Hitlerian theory, their very existence and claims to legitimacy compel them to encourage. Moreover, when nation-states do so, they act legitimately in the interest of the nation they represent because, in point of fact, the self-interest of neither nation nor nation-state is invariably served by encouraging or catering to the intense and passionate attachment of citizens to the dominant phenotype or traditional ethno-religious culture of their nation. Sometimes this is the case, but sometimes, and this is important, it is not.

4 To illustrate this point, I turn to a comparative analysis of anti-immigrant movements in Europe and North America. A social movement is anti-immigrant when it seeks the reduction of immigration, the speedy end of immigration, the rapid and entire cultural assimilation of immigrants, or the expulsion of at least some of the existing immigrant population from the host society. Anti-immigrant movements stress ethno-cultural and phenotypical continuity of the host nation. Indeed, this continuity is the heart of the resistance to immigration that is the raison d'etre of anti-immigrant movements. And there is some justification for these movements. In

actuality, immigrants may threaten the ethno-cultural continuity of the host nation. For example, Muslim immigrants threaten the underlying Christian identity of European and North American nations. As matters stand, there are already more Muslims than Episcopalians in the United States, and, when the Muslims have overtaken the Catholics too, the United States will have become a predominantly Muslim nation. If permitted to intermarry with native people, immigrants also threaten the phenotypical continuity of the nation. For example, if Asian immigrants intermarry with white Americans, their native-born offspring will be Eurasians, not Caucasians. Americans will no longer look like white people from Europe.

Anti-immigrant movements resist changes in the dominant phe- 5
notype of their nation and in its ethnocultural character out of intense loyalty to that dominant phenotype and ethno-religious cultural tradition. In this sense, anti-immigrant movements are conservative because they cling to an existing phenotype and traditional ethnic culture. Anti-immigrant movements also epitomize that intense popular loyalty to and identification with dominant phenotype and culture that the neo-Hitlerian theory attributes to the very existence of the nation-state itself.

Anti-immigrant movements have existed in the past and exist now 6
in both North America and Europe. The Le Pen movement in France, the Republikaner Party in Germany, the Proposition 187 campaign in California, and the Official English movement in the United States all illustrate contemporary anti-immigrant movements that have undertaken political action. At the cultural level, signs of popular opposition to immigration are present in all the immigrant-receiving countries. In Canada, Sikhs were refused permission to wear turbans during school athletic periods. The wearing of turbans in public school undermines the cultural continuity of Anglo-Canadian society based upon Christianity. Even if the boys play rugby, a traditional sport, players in turbans represent unwelcome cultural change in Canada. In France, Muslim girls have been denied permission to wear veils to school for the same reason. In Germany, skinheads attacked immigrants on the street, and, in some well publicized incidents, burned their homes. In the United States, "patriot militias" and "Christian identity" churches mix violence, racism, religious chauvinism, and anti-immigrant fervor in a common ideological pot. In California, Light Up the Border sends citizen-members to illuminate the U.S.–Mexican border at their own expense, in hope of compelling more vigilant enforcement of border controls.

Anti-immigrant movements are self-proclaimedly nationalistic. 7
That is, they declare that the interest of the nation is the touchstone of their policy, and they define the interest of the nation as phenotypical and ethno-cultural continuity. "This is a Christian

nation, and it should remain one" epitomizes their demand. Although rarely challenged directly, both claims are quite wrong. One cannot assume that phenotypic and ethno-religious loyalty and identification are synonymous with the interest either of the nation-state or of the nation itself. In reality, the self-interest of both the nation and the nation-state often requires immigration, even at the risk of cultural and phenotypical change. A nation's welfare may justify either accepting or excluding immigrants, depending partially upon circumstances and partially upon who determines what the nation's true interests are. Thus, Adolf Hitler and Helmut Kohl express quite different policy conceptions of what Germany's national interest is. National self-interest is rarely unambiguous. For the most part, in pursuing its self-interest, a nation has to make trade-offs between different and often conflicting components of its interests, only one of which is the continuity of its ethno-cultural and phenotypical stock. A nation, as well as its nation-state, has many interests, and the service of one may undermine another, creating awkward and difficult policy choices.

Just for starters, nations and nation-states both have economic 8
and political interests that sometimes conflict with one another. For example, a nation's self-interest may require foreign policies that undermine its economic interest, or vice versa. Thus, writing in the context of the post-NAFTA debate over Mexico's $40 billion loan guarantee, Henry Kissinger declared that the national security interests of the United States required a stable and prosperous Mexico. In Kissinger's opinion, despite its economic risks, the loan guarantee was justified by its political advantages. Experts have long made comparable arguments about the foreign policy advantages of Mexican immigration to the United States. Because immigration from Mexico to California strengthened consumer demand in Mexico, stabilized Mexico's internal politics, and reduced its unemployment, thus giving Mexico time to reform and democratize and to stabilize its population growth, immigration from Mexico arguably benefited the United States and the U.S. nation. Weighed against these overriding international stakes, localized and transitory economic discomfort from Mexican immigration was inconsequential. Compared to this big issue, who cares whether illegal aliens abuse welfare? Certainly, the experts claimed, the complaints of the Southwestern and Pacific regions about illegal aliens should not endanger the overriding national interest that the United States has in propping up Mexico. Whether one agrees with this line or not, the line is simultaneously nationalistic and pro-immigration.

If we acknowledge that nations and nation-states can have or, at 9
least, think that they have racial and cultural interests in addition to economic and political interests, we set the stage for yet more complex

trade-offs. A nation's racial interest means here its preference for the continuity of a racial stock and its dominant phenotypes. A nation's cultural interest means its strong preference for cultural continuity, implying, at a minimum, an assimilationist demand upon any immigrants present and, at the maximum, the fearful exclusion of any and all immigrants who might, were they admitted, change the ethno-cultural character of the nation. These are conservative interests, because they seek to safeguard the ethno-cultural and phenotypic status quo. We can imagine a nation that requires immigration for economic or political purposes but that rejects immigration for cultural and racial reasons, or vice versa. In such a case, a nation does not have a simple national self-interest. Rather, it has to make a tough policy choice among alternative values. It cannot have everything. Therefore, its policy determination of what is national self-interest must evolve from a balance of conflicting internal interests, giving preeminence to whichever interests most need attention at any given time. These are tough and controversial decisions that cannot count upon internal consensus.

For example, when debating the racially motivated exclusion of 10
Asian immigrants in 1912, the U.S. Congress had to decide whether California's loudly proclaimed racial and cultural interest in Japanese exclusion was worth antagonizing the Japanese Empire. California was a white man's society, and it wanted to stay that way. President Taft did not think that California's racial purity was compensation enough for antagonizing the Japanese, so he vetoed the bill. Undeterred, and under pressure from racist voters in California, Congress passed a more exclusionary immigration bill in 1916, but President Wilson vetoed it for the same foreign policy reason as had President Taft. However, Congress overrode Wilson's veto in 1917, writing into law the Immigration Act of February 5, 1917, which first created an Asian "barred zone" from which immigration to the United States was prohibited. In effect, the five years of deliberations that preceded this legislation determined that ethno-cultural and phenotypical continuity in California were more important to national interest than were affronts to the Japanese Empire. As expected, the racist immigration legislation enraged the Japanese. This rage embittered U.S.–Japanese relations for decades and surfaced again in Japanese plans to bomb Pearl Harbor, partially an act of racial revenge. Indeed, the Japanese still nurse this anger. To the extent that the racist immigration bill of 1917 damaged U.S. relations with Japan and helped to bring on U.S. involvement in World War II in 1941, the racial exclusion of Japanese from the United States, however ardently demanded in California, was not really in the self-interest of the United States in 1917. In hindsight, we now see that the policy definition of national self-interest ought to have paid more attention

to the long-term diplomatic and military implications of immigration policy and less attention to the racial and cultural complaints of California. However, the United States had to choose which dimension of its self-interest was most important, and it chose badly.

Nations differ in the prominence they award their political, economic, cultural, and racial interests. In Germany, the law virtually excludes fully acculturated, German-born Turks from citizenship, but the same law expedites the naturalization of just-arrived non-German-speaking *volksdeutsch* from Russia or Poland. This contrast suggests that German nationalism sets high priority upon the continuity of Germany's ethnoracial stock and its dominant phenotypes. Culture does not matter nearly as much as does phenotype in Germany. In Israel, in contrast, defending dominant phenotype counts for nothing in national immigration policy. Instead, Israeli nationalism seeks maximum immigration, but religion (not phenotype) determines the fitness of immigrants for citizenship: Only Jewish immigrants are acceptable, and all Jewish immigrants are awarded immediate citizenship. However, Israel expects total and swift Hebraization of all immigrants, a tough policy of total cultural assimilation. Discouraging immigration, France nonetheless permits the naturalization of fully assimilated aliens; however, it rejects cultural pluralism among new citizens. All citizens must become wholly and exclusively French. French means having cultural continuity with the past, so one cannot be French who does not speak French as his or her native tongue. This demand is compatible with France's long-standing "mission to civilize," a cultural interest of the French nation. Thus, both Israel and France impose cultural tests of fitness for naturalization, and these tests suggest that cultural interests outrank phenotypical ones in these states. 11

The United States and, especially, Canada have long conceived of immigration as an economic resource and have promptly admitted to full citizenship unacculturated individuals, who, moreover, because of policies of multiculturalism, are released from any obligation to learn English. Additionally, the United States and Canada currently have immigration policies that are virtually color-blind. These are liberal policies, in the sense that they ignore the conservative interest in cultural and phenotypical continuity of the nation. Do these liberal policies mean that North American states crafted immigration policies without regard to perceived national self-interest? Such is the usual claim of anti-immigrant critics. However, the legislative history of immigration debates puts that idea to rest. When one examines the actual congressional debates that accompanied U.S. immigration legislation, one finds that hard-headed and often naked self-interest is and always has been the supreme arbiter of immigration policy. In effect, the behavior of these North American states simply shows that on this continent, policy makers have ranked the nation's and the 12 nation-state's economic and political interests ahead of any cultural and racial interests.

When the United States abandoned the national origins quota 13
system in 1965, thus opening the door to immigration from Latin America and Asia, a liberal action, several nationalistic reasons obtained. First, and arguably most important, the United States was then wading into an unpopular war against North Vietnam, an Asian adversary. In the context of the domestic Civil Rights movement, a domestic policy crisis of that decade, the U.S. State Department concluded that liberalization of immigration policy was a top-priority foreign policy issue. Competing with the communists for world leadership, the United States simply had to clean up its racist international image. For political reasons, the United States could not accept the opprobrium of a racist immigration law in the context of world condemnation of its segregationist civil society. Secretary of State Dean Rusk bluntly told Congress that foreign policy required a color-blind immigration law, and Congress gave him that law. Second, labor force projections showed that catastrophic shortages of engineering and medical personnel would materialize unless the United States opened its doors to foreign engineers, doctors, and nurses. These projections were well founded. Currently, about a third of our medical personnel and engineers are foreign born. Were it not for these immigrants, many of them non-white and non-Christian, the economy and health care systems of the United States would be in much worse shape than they are, bad as that current situation is. In this sense, a liberal immigration policy was arguably in the national self-interest of the United States and of the American nation.

One can legitimately object that "this is now, that was then." 14
True, whatever national purposes immigration laws may once have served or been intended to serve, a critic can always claim that they outlived that purpose and now undermine the nation's interest. Such claims give rise to anti-immigrant social movements. Anti-immigrant movements arise when citizens sense that immigration no longer serves national self-interest and has become a bad deal for the recipient country. This turn of events is nowhere clearer than in Germany, which welcomed guest workers to participate in building its postwar economic miracle. No one complained about too many foreigners in 1955. However, with the miracle completed and the country facing slower growth, ordinary Germans began to feel that the economic benefits of guest workers no longer outweighed the cost to the nation's ethno-cultural and phenotypical continuity. Indeed, many declared that immigration's economic impact, once a benefit, had become adverse because guest workers took jobs from Germans instead of making it possible for Germans to obtain better jobs, as had originally been the case. When in 1989 reunification dumped cheap

East German labor on already saturated West German job markets, it became harder than ever to make a case for the continuing economic benefit provided by non-German workers, who appeared, indeed, to have the better of the immigration bargain. Under these circumstances, Germany's anti-immigrant movement and the rightwing parties affiliated with it threatened to take control of the government away from the mainstream parties on this issue.

When immigration policies are reversed, the final judgment de- 15
pends upon what motivates voters and policy makers, who often hold different conceptions of national self-interest. If voters are wholly indifferent to phenotypic or cultural continuity in their society—a rare state of affairs—they will evaluate immigration laws strictly on economic, political, military, and even humanitarian grounds. Even conservative voters become pro-immigration when they perceive overriding economic and political benefits of immigration that compensate the perceived racial and cultural costs of immigration. Conservatives can make a trade-off. In conservative countries, liberal immigration laws arise when enough conservatives agree that the nation's interest demands immigration even at some inconvenience to the phenotypical and cultural continuity of the population. In a society like Germany, whose population stresses racial and cultural continuity, many voters are conservative in this sense. Only very substantial economic and political benefits will induce German voters to open the doors to foreigners and immigration. And, should those benefits diminish in perceived value, the nation's doors slam shut quickly. Conversely, in societies like Canada and the United States, whose voters are by European standards unusually materialistic, slight economic and political benefits will justify pro-immigration policies.

Even in North America, one must from time to time ask whether 16
immigration laws still make nationalist sense under current conditions, or whether they have outlived their utility. The answer depends in part upon our evaluation of what have been the economic and political costs of this immigration. For decades, there was no sign of any such cost. In the 1980s, social science research in the United States began for the first time to turn up some evidence of limited and sector-specific job competition between immigrant workers and native blacks and Latinos. Additionally, as Governor Pete Wilson's reelection campaign in California made very clear to everyone in the United States, research has universally concluded that illegal immigrants take slightly more in state-supported medical and educational services than they contribute to California in taxes. True, the immigrants provide a useful and ubiquitous low-wage labor force in farm, factory, and home. Were they excluded in the interest of cultural and racial continuity, California would pay an economic price. Nonetheless, these recent reports suggest that immigration's domestic economic effects

are not completely positive anymore. There is some basis for claiming that the economic effects only became negative in the 1980s. These changes certainly weaken the electorate's conviction that current immigration is in the national self-interest of the United States. Under the circumstance, the baseline conservatives find fewer compensations for the perceived racial and cultural costs of immigration.

Even with these damaging changes, there still remains some case for existing U.S. immigration laws. First, the United States still needs Asian engineers and health professionals for the very reasons anticipated in the 1965 legislation. The United States still does not produce enough of these personnel to fill critical domestic needs. Second, as assassinations and peso devaluation make clear, Mexico is teetering on the verge of political and economic collapse. To restrict Mexican immigration now would increase the political turbulence within Mexico, increasing the likelihood of civil war and Guatemala-style repression on the southern border of the United States. Mexicans are also quite sensitive to the racist implications of California's Proposition 187 and of anti-immigrant talk elsewhere in the United States. A new Mexican government, arising from the chaos of PRI collapse, might well be anti-U.S. in spirit. Arguably, immigrant competition in the jobs and housing market is a sacrifice California must make to reduce that political risk to the United States. 17

If we now ask who sees which side of this debate, an important fact comes to light. Whether in Europe or North America, policy makers have superior access to the international picture. That is, balancing indignant conservative voters, who worry about ethnocultural and phenotypical continuity, and economic and foreign policy issues, they look for the supreme national interest, restrained by domestic politics, at least they think about what it might be. This international perspective permits policy makers to sacrifice pawns when necessary, obtaining the greater national interest by surrendering the lesser. Conversely, voters generalize the national interest from their own perceived cultural, racial, economic, or political interest. They think that immigration harms the country just because it harms them, their religion, or their race or diminishes their culture's dominance. In a way, immigrant-bashing citizens must take this perspective because they are otherwise open to the objection that their parochial interest should be sacrificed in the greater national interest. Of course, nations must sacrifice pawns, but no one wants to be that pawn. 18

We again and again encounter the spectacle of nationalistic politicians trying to hold anti-immigrant movements at bay. From the politicians' point of view, the anti-immigrant movement often reverses national priorities, sacrificing long-term national interests to the transitory, partial interest of some ethno-racial group or region. For example, a senator might plausibly believe that having enough engineers and doctors is worth some decline in cultural and 19 phenotypical continuity. Conversely, at the grass roots, people see their personal, their ethno-racial, and their regional interests most clearly and can hardly be induced to contemplate the political and economic interests of the whole nation. If an immigrant has taken Smith's job, or the jobs of people like Smith, Smith's probable political response is anti-immigrant protest, even if that protest undermines the stability of a friendly government or jeopardizes his nation's access to foreign-trained engineers. One Smith makes no difference. However, if enough Smiths come forward, politicians must redefine national self-interest to Smith's shortsighted advantage—or be replaced by others who will.

THINKING ABOUT THE ESSAY

1. What emotional response does the word *nationalism* invoke in your mind? Something positive or negative? Or does your response depend upon the context in which you hear or read the word? Explain.
2. Does the author implicitly or explicitly distinguish between healthy and unhealthy nationalism? Or is nationalism a phenomenon that is always promoted merely to favor the stability of the nation-state that encourages it?
3. The author says in his introduction that before discussing nationalism, we must define it. What method does the author use in defining nationalism? Is it a dictionary-style definition or an extended one? Which paragraphs, in particular, provide his definition of nationalism?
4. In discussing this politically charged topic, the author uses many terms that are unique to his subject matter. Among these are *xenophobia, ethno-phenotypic, ethno-chauvinism, ethno-religious, neo-Hobbesian* and *neo-Hitlerian.* What assumptions is he making about the intended readership of this essay? To what degree do you feel that you are a member of that readership?
5. The author claims that nationalism and immigration policies serve different functions in different countries. What specific functions do they serve in the United States? Where in the essay does the author provide this comparative information?

RESPONDING IN DISCUSSION

1. Divide into groups of three and four and discuss under what circumstances the United States would necessarily promote nationalism. Share your conclusions with the rest of the class.

2. Discuss what tools exist today that would make it easier for a nation to promote nationalism than, say, 100 years ago.
3. Discuss some of the more arcane terms used in this essay, and explain their meanings in your own words.
4. Discuss the current climate and degree of nationalism in the United States as it relates to Americans' attitudes toward immigration.
5. Discuss whether in the light of the fact that conservative opinion leaders like Bennett and Chavez support immigration, it is unlikely that nationalism in the United States will ever surface in a hateful or destructive manner as it has in other parts of the world.

RESPONDING IN WRITING

1. Summarize in outline form this rather complex essay by listing the major causes and functions of the various forms of nationalism.
2. Using the ideas in Thurow's essay, "Why Their World Might Crumble," argue for or against the proposition that a moderate amount of nationalism among Generation X employees may be a good thing.
3. Argue for or against the view that nationalism is a largely outmoded form of ideology since the world is controlled by a small group of economic investors whose reach transcends governmental, political, and geographic boundaries.
4. For a research project, scan the Internet for recent relationships between the United States and Mexico. Then write an essay on the pros and cons of an open-border policy between the two countries.

CONNECTIONS: FOR WRITING AND RESEARCH

1. Argue for or against the proposition that it is the children of earlier immigrants who have created the conditions that Bennett decries as leading to cultural decay, thus undermining his contention that immigrants are not responsible for the destruction of "family values."
2. Compare and contrast the concept of the "first North American" as described by Rodriguez with the world citizens Iyer describes as the "fruits of global culture."
3. Discuss why the attitudes, emotions, values, and outlook of the young Hispanics discussed in Aguilar's "Boom or Bust?" resemble (or do not resemble) the immigrants portrayed in Rodriguez's essay.

4. For a research project, report on the history of California's Proposition 187 from its beginnings to its current status.
5. For a creative writing project, write home to your family, describing your college or university as though it were a foreign country to which you have recently emigrated.
6. For a research project, go on-line and join a newsgroup that focuses on immigration issues. Keep a daily log of messages and discussions for a period of seven or eight hours of on-line time. Write a report describing the concerns and views of the newsgroup members.
7. Two essays in this part—those by Mukherjee and Rodriguez—appeared in the same magazine, *Mother Jones*. Conduct research on this publication, and then assess its editorial policy, referring to the essays that you have read to substantiate your analysis.

INDEX